D0922905

THE TIMES ATLAS OF THE WORLD

COMPACT EDITION

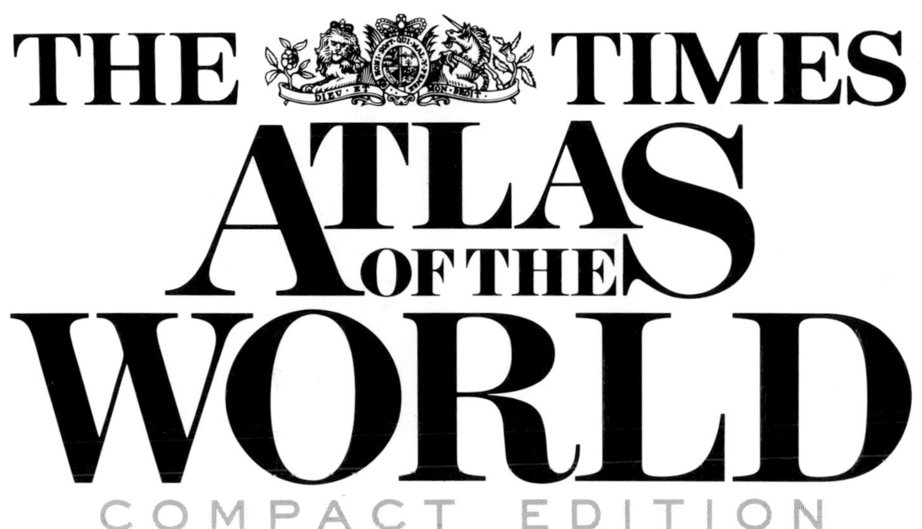

THE TIMES ATLAS OF THE WORLD

COMPACT EDITION

TIMES BOOKS

A Division of HarperCollins*Publishers*

This edition published 1994 by Times Books
A Division of HarperCollins Publishers
77-85 Fulham Palace Road, London W6 8JB

© Times Books and Bartholomew 1994

First Published by Bartholomew 1991
Revised 1992, 1993

ISBN 0 7230 0668 7

Printed in Hong Kong

All rights reserved. No part of this publication may be reproduced, stored in a
retrieval system, or transmitted, in any form or by any means, electronic,
mechanical, photocopying, recording or otherwise without the prior
permission of the publishers.

Details included in this atlas are subject to change without notice. Whilst
every effort is made to keep information up to date the publishers will not be
responsible for any loss, damage or inconvenience caused by inaccuracies in
this atlas. The publishers are always pleased to acknowledge any corrections
brought to their notice, and record their appreciation of the valuable services
rendered in the past by map users in assisting to maintain the accuracy of
their publications

GH 7349

CONTENTS

World Physical **viii-ix**
World Political **x-xi**
World Time Zones **xii-xiii**
World Environment **xiv-xv**
Key to Symbols **xvi**

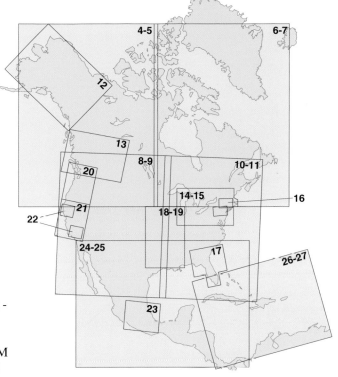

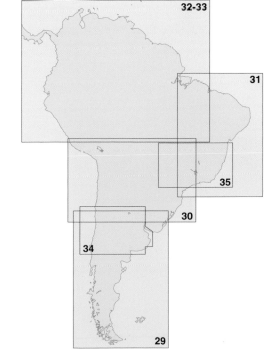

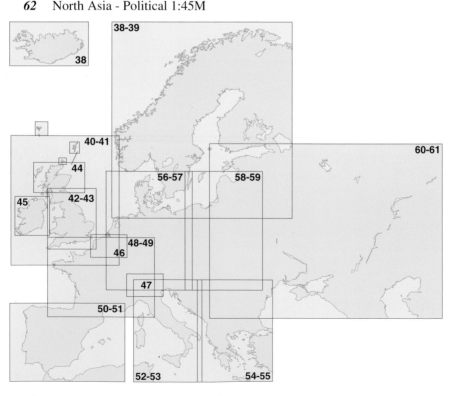

96-97
95
98-99
101
100-101

106-107
108-109
110-111

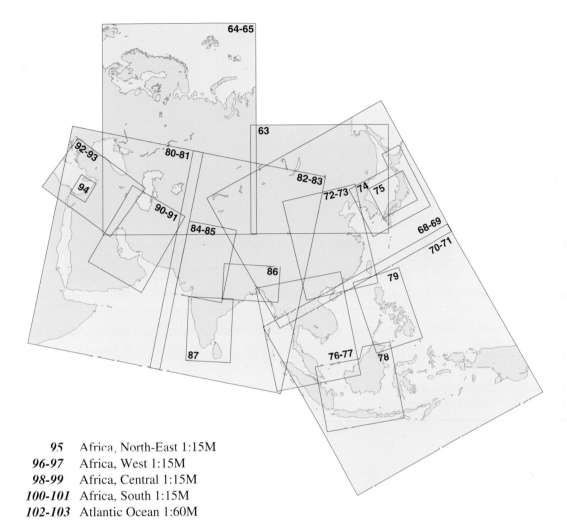

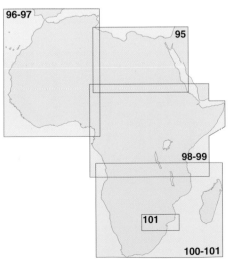

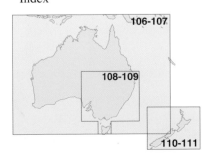

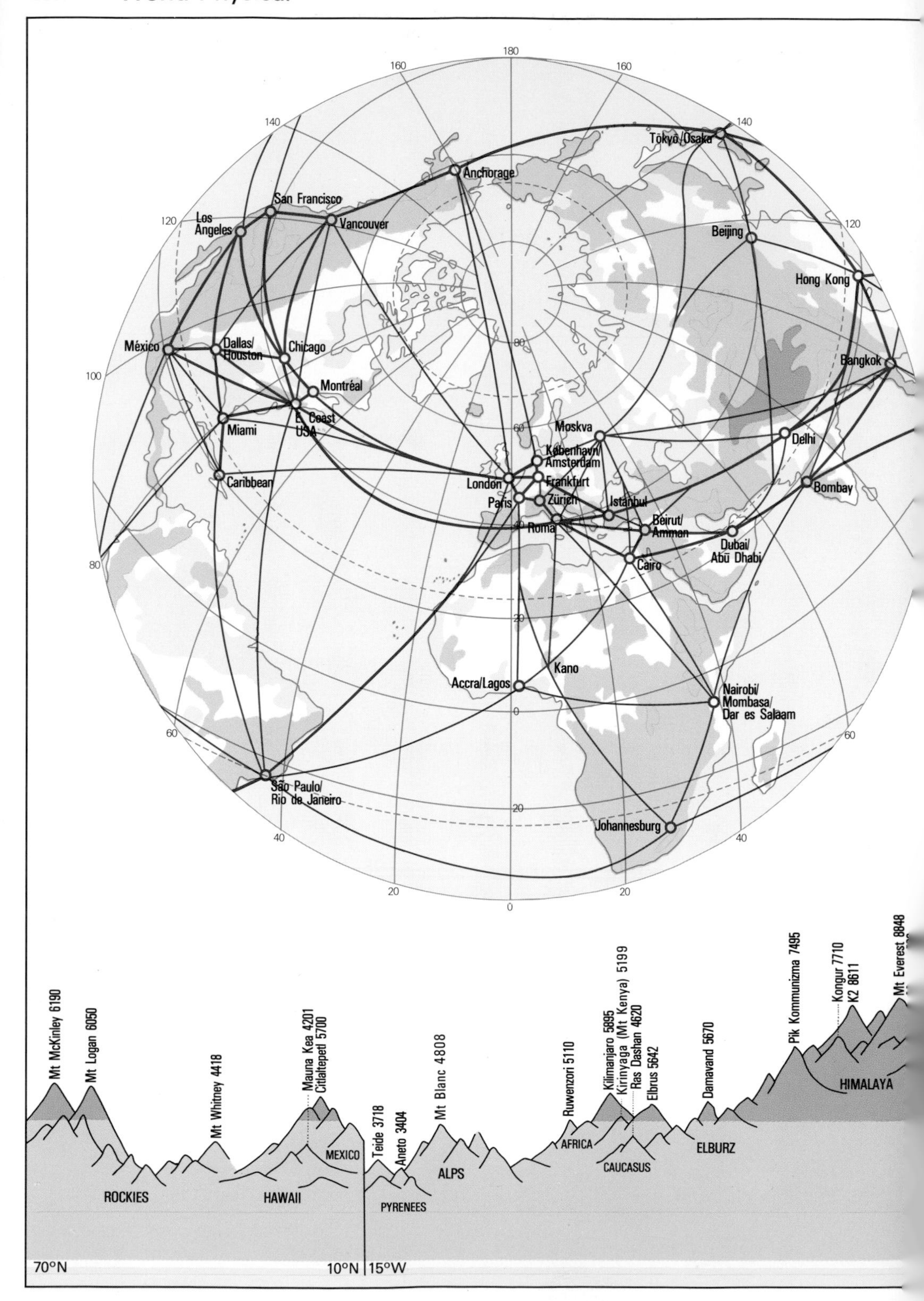

Tōkyō/Osaka
Anchorage
San Francisco
Los Angeles
Vancouver
Beijing
Hong Kong
Bangkok
México
Dallas/Houston
Chicago
Montréal
E Coast USA
Miami
Caribbean
Delhi
Bombay
Moskva
København/Amsterdam
London
Paris
Frankfurt
Zürich
Istanbul
Beirut/Amman
Roma
Dubai/Abū Dhabi
Cairo
Kano
Accra/Lagos
Nairobi/Mombasa/Dar es Salaam
São Paulo/Rio de Janeiro
Johannesburg

Mt McKinley 6190
Mt Logan 6050
Mt Whitney 4418
Mauna Kea 4201
Citlaltepetl 5700
MEXICO
Teide 3718
Aneto 3404
Mt Blanc 4808
ALPS
PYRENEES
Ruwenzori 5110
Kilimanjaro 5895
Kirinyaga (Mt Kenya) 5199
Ras Dashan 4620
Elbrus 5642
AFRICA
CAUCASUS
Damavand 5670
ELBURZ
Pik Kommunizma 7495
Kongur 7710
K2 8611
Mt Everest 8848
HIMALAYA

ROCKIES
HAWAII

70°N
10°N 15°W

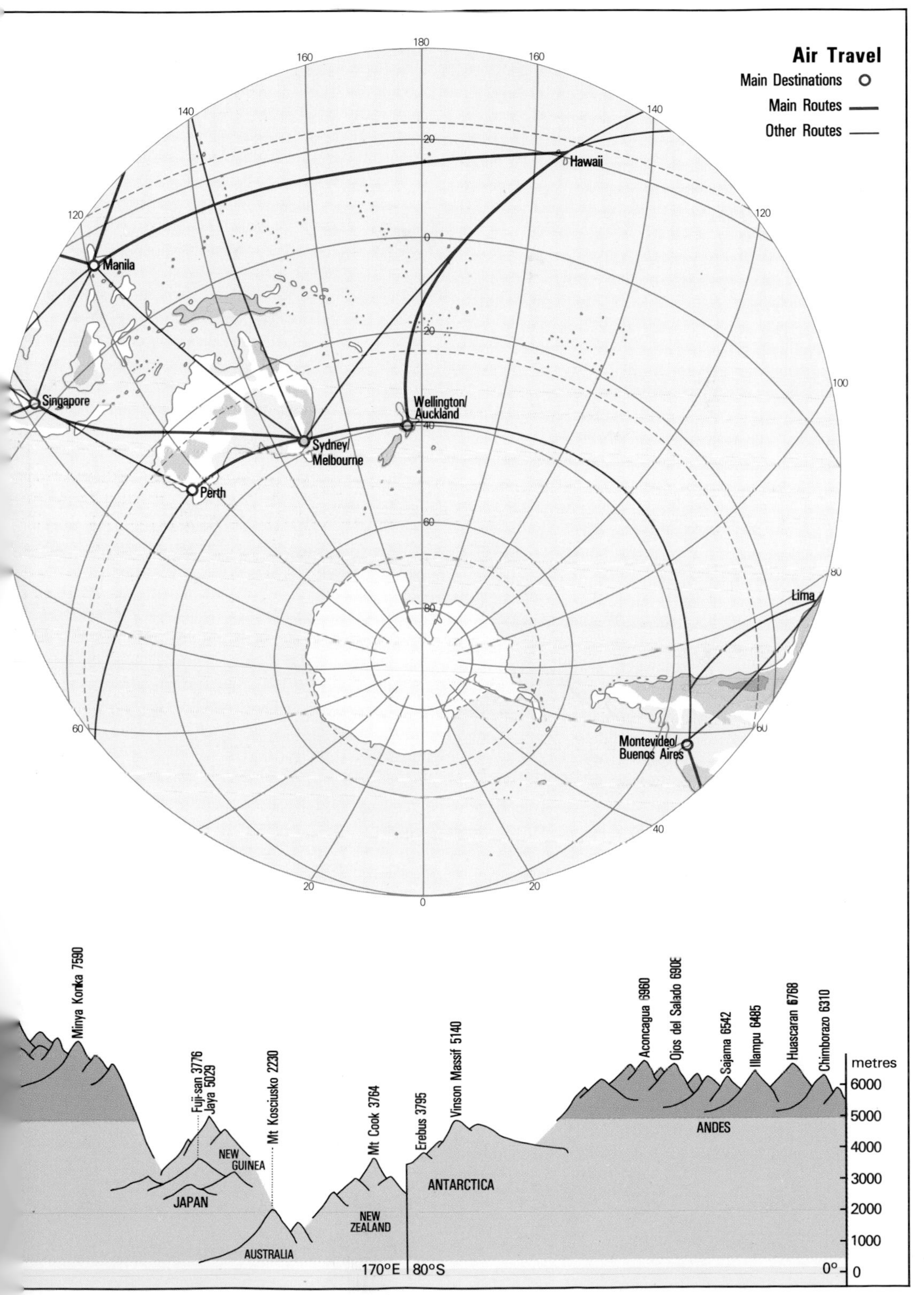

Air Travel
Main Destinations ○
Main Routes ▬
Other Routes ▬

Hawaii

Manila

Singapore

Perth

Sydney/
Melbourne

Wellington/
Auckland

Lima

Montevideo/
Buenos Aires

ANTARCTICA

Minya Konka 7590

Fuji-san 3776
Jaya 5029

Mt Koscuisko 2230

Mt Cook 3764

Erebus 3795

Vinson Massif 5140

Aconcagua 9960

Ojos del Salado 6908

Sajama 6542

Illampu 6485

Huascaran 6768

Chimborazo 6310

metres
6000
5000
4000
3000
2000
1000
0

ANDES

NEW
GUINEA

JAPAN

AUSTRALIA

NEW
ZEALAND

170°E   80°S

0°

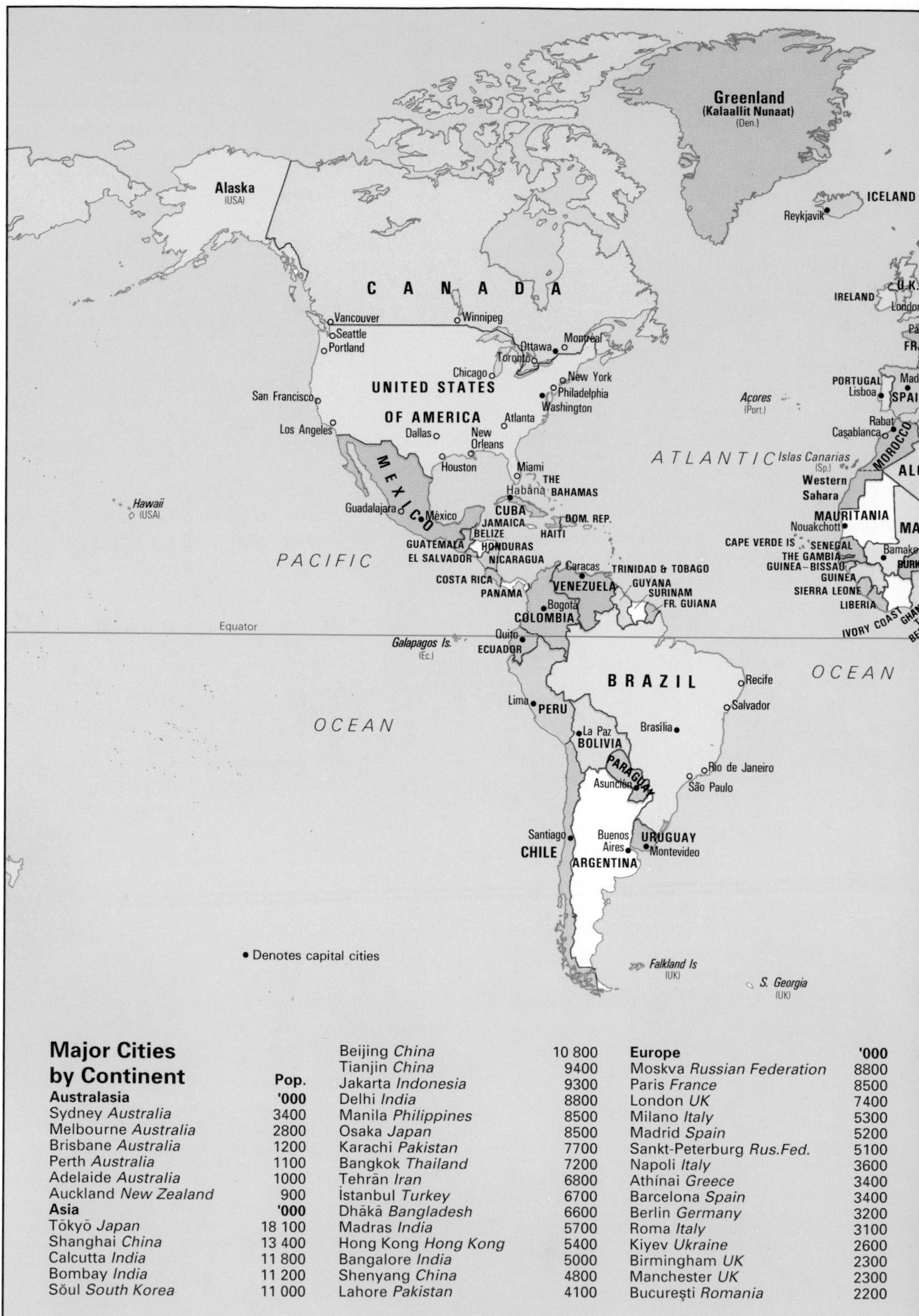

• Denotes capital cities

Major Cities by Continent

	Pop.
Australasia	**'000**
Sydney *Australia*	3400
Melbourne *Australia*	2800
Brisbane *Australia*	1200
Perth *Australia*	1100
Adelaide *Australia*	1000
Auckland *New Zealand*	900
Asia	**'000**
Tōkyō *Japan*	18 100
Shanghai *China*	13 400
Calcutta *India*	11 800
Bombay *India*	11 200
Sŏul *South Korea*	11 000

Beijing *China*	10 800
Tianjin *China*	9400
Jakarta *Indonesia*	9300
Delhi *India*	8800
Manila *Philippines*	8500
Osaka *Japan*	8500
Karachi *Pakistan*	7700
Bangkok *Thailand*	7200
Tehrān *Iran*	6800
İstanbul *Turkey*	6700
Dhākā *Bangladesh*	6600
Madras *India*	5700
Hong Kong *Hong Kong*	5400
Bangalore *India*	5000
Shenyang *China*	4800
Lahore *Pakistan*	4100

Europe	**'000**
Moskva *Russian Federation*	8800
Paris *France*	8500
London *UK*	7400
Milano *Italy*	5300
Madrid *Spain*	5200
Sankt-Peterburg *Rus.Fed.*	5100
Napoli *Italy*	3600
Athínai *Greece*	3400
Barcelona *Spain*	3400
Berlin *Germany*	3200
Roma *Italy*	3100
Kiyev *Ukraine*	2600
Birmingham *UK*	2300
Manchester *UK*	2300
Bucureşti *Romania*	2200

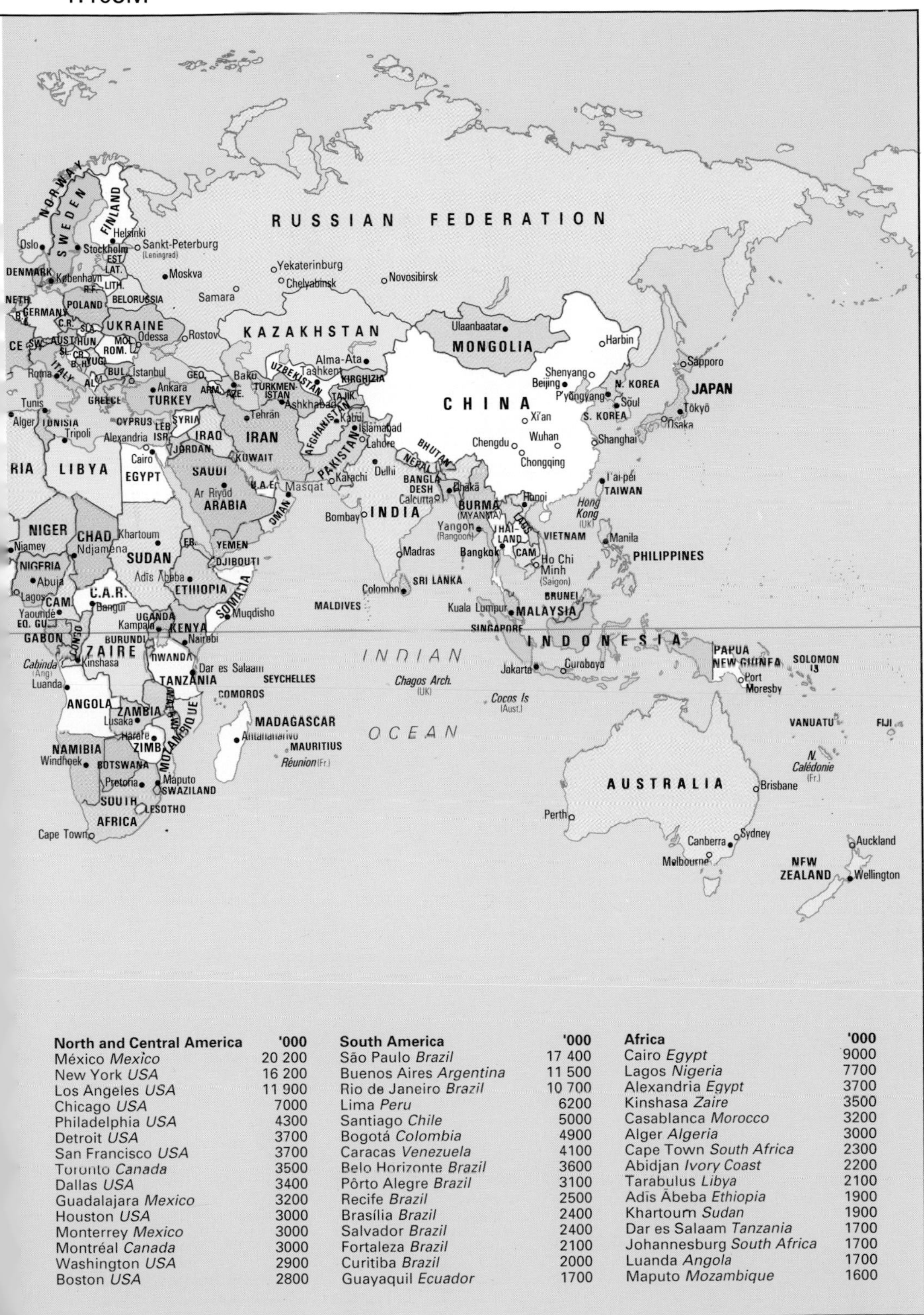

North and Central America	'000	South America	'000	Africa	'000
México *Mexico*	20 200	São Paulo *Brazil*	17 400	Cairo *Egypt*	9000
New York *USA*	16 200	Buenos Aires *Argentina*	11 500	Lagos *Nigeria*	7700
Los Angeles *USA*	11 900	Rio de Janeiro *Brazil*	10 700	Alexandria *Egypt*	3700
Chicago *USA*	7000	Lima *Peru*	6200	Kinshasa *Zaire*	3500
Philadelphia *USA*	4300	Santiago *Chile*	5000	Casablanca *Morocco*	3200
Detroit *USA*	3700	Bogotá *Colombia*	4900	Alger *Algeria*	3000
San Francisco *USA*	3700	Caracas *Venezuela*	4100	Cape Town *South Africa*	2300
Toronto *Canada*	3500	Belo Horizonte *Brazil*	3600	Abidjan *Ivory Coast*	2200
Dallas *USA*	3400	Pôrto Alegre *Brazil*	3100	Tarabulus *Libya*	2100
Guadalajara *Mexico*	3200	Recife *Brazil*	2500	Adis Ābeba *Ethiopia*	1900
Houston *USA*	3000	Brasília *Brazil*	2400	Khartoum *Sudan*	1900
Monterrey *Mexico*	3000	Salvador *Brazil*	2400	Dar es Salaam *Tanzania*	1700
Montréal *Canada*	3000	Fortaleza *Brazil*	2100	Johannesburg *South Africa*	1700
Washington *USA*	2900	Curitiba *Brazil*	2000	Luanda *Angola*	1700
Boston *USA*	2800	Guayaquil *Ecuador*	1700	Maputo *Mozambique*	1600

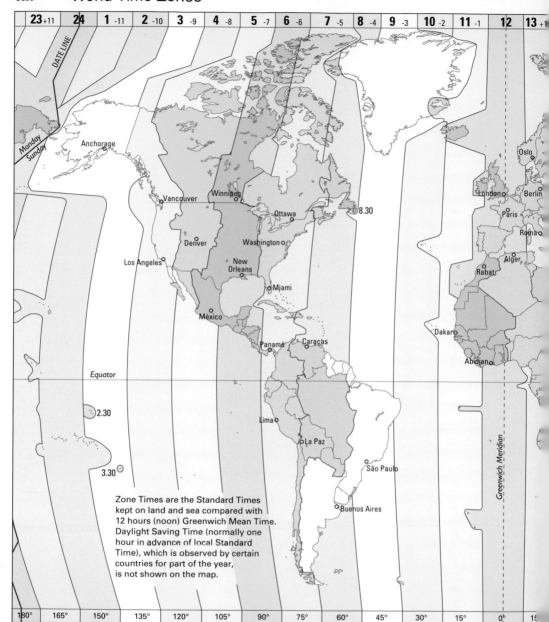

| 23 +11 | 24 | 1 -11 | 2 -10 | 3 -9 | 4 -8 | 5 -7 | 6 -6 | 7 -5 | 8 -4 | 9 -3 | 10 -2 | 11 -1 | 12 | 13 + |

DATE LINE

Monday
Sunday

Anchorage

Oslo

Vancouver
Winnipeg
Ottawa
London
Berlin
8.30
Paris

Denver
Washington
Roma

Los Angeles
New
Orleans
Alger
Rabat

México
Miami

Dakar

Panamá
Caracas
Abidjan

Equator

2.30

Lima

3.30

La Paz

São Paulo

Zone Times are the Standard Times
kept on land and sea compared with
12 hours (noon) Greenwich Mean Time.
Daylight Saving Time (normally one
hour in advance of local Standard
Time), which is observed by certain
countries for part of the year,
is not shown on the map.

Buenos Aires

Greenwich Meridian

| 180° | 165° | 150° | 135° | 120° | 105° | 90° | 75° | 60° | 45° | 30° | 15° | 0° | 1 |

Journey Times

Sail
(via Cape)
164 days

Steam
(via Cape)
43 days

Steam
(via Suez)
30 days

Supertanker
(via Cape)
28 days

Singapore ←

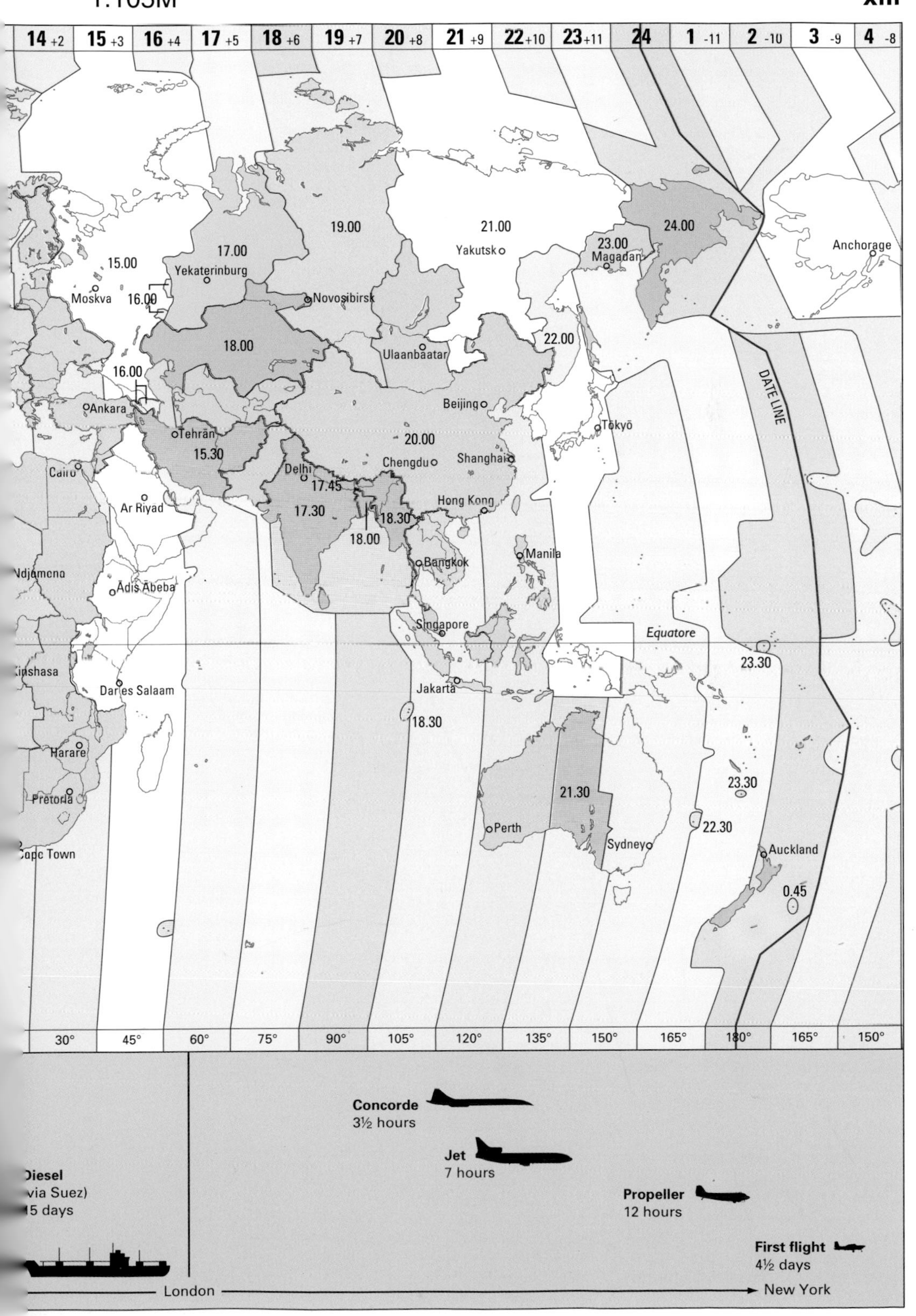

14 +2 **15** +3 **16** +4 **17** +5 **18** +6 **19** +7 **20** +8 **21** +9 **22** +10 **23** +11 **24** **1** -11 **2** -10 **3** -9 **4** -8

19.00 21.00 24.00 Anchorage

23.00
Magadan

17.00
Yekaterinburg

15.00
Moskva 16.00

Novosibirsk

18.00 Ulaanbaatar 22.00

16.00
Ankara DATE LINE

Tehrān Beijing Tōkyō
15.30

Cairo 20.00
Delhi Chengdu Shanghai
17.45
Ar Riyad 17.30 18.30
18.00 Hong Kong

Ndjámena Bangkok Manila

Adis Abeba

Singapore Equatore 23.30

Kinshasa
Dar es Salaam Jakarta

18.30

Harare 21.30 23.30

Pretoria Perth 22.30

Cape Town Sydney Auckland

0.45

30° 45° 60° 75° 90° 105° 120° 135° 150° 165° 180° 165° 150°

Concorde
3½ hours

Jet
7 hours

Diesel
(via Suez)
15 days

Propeller
12 hours

First flight
4½ days

London ———————————————————————————— New York

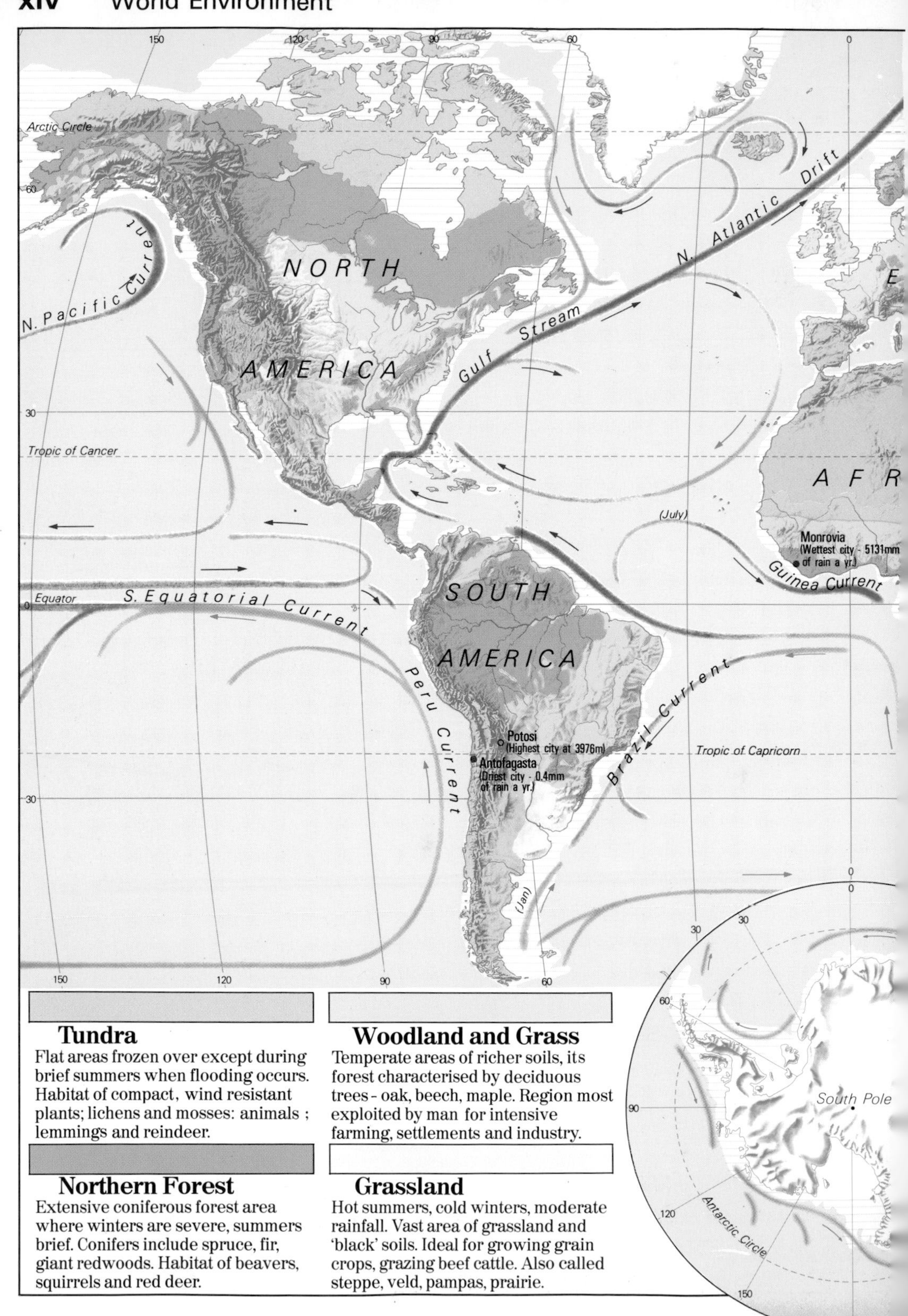

150 120 90 60 0

Arctic Circle

60

N. Pacific Current

NORTH

N. Atlantic Drift

E

AMERICA

Gulf Stream

30

Tropic of Cancer

A F R

(July)

Monrovia
(Wettest city - 5131mm
of rain a yr.)

Guinea Current

Equator　S. Equatorial Current

SOUTH

AMERICA

Peru Current

Potosi
(Highest city at 3976m)

Antofagasta
(Driest city - 0.4mm
of rain a yr.)

Brazil Current

Tropic of Capricorn

30

(Jan)

150 120 90 60

South Pole

60

90

120

Antarctic Circle

150

180

Tundra

Flat areas frozen over except during brief summers when flooding occurs. Habitat of compact, wind resistant plants; lichens and mosses: animals ; lemmings and reindeer.

Northern Forest

Extensive coniferous forest area where winters are severe, summers brief. Conifers include spruce, fir, giant redwoods. Habitat of beavers, squirrels and red deer.

Woodland and Grass

Temperate areas of richer soils, its forest characterised by deciduous trees - oak, beech, maple. Region most exploited by man for intensive farming, settlements and industry.

Grassland

Hot summers, cold winters, moderate rainfall. Vast area of grassland and 'black' soils. Ideal for growing grain crops, grazing beef cattle. Also called steppe, veld, pampas, prairie.

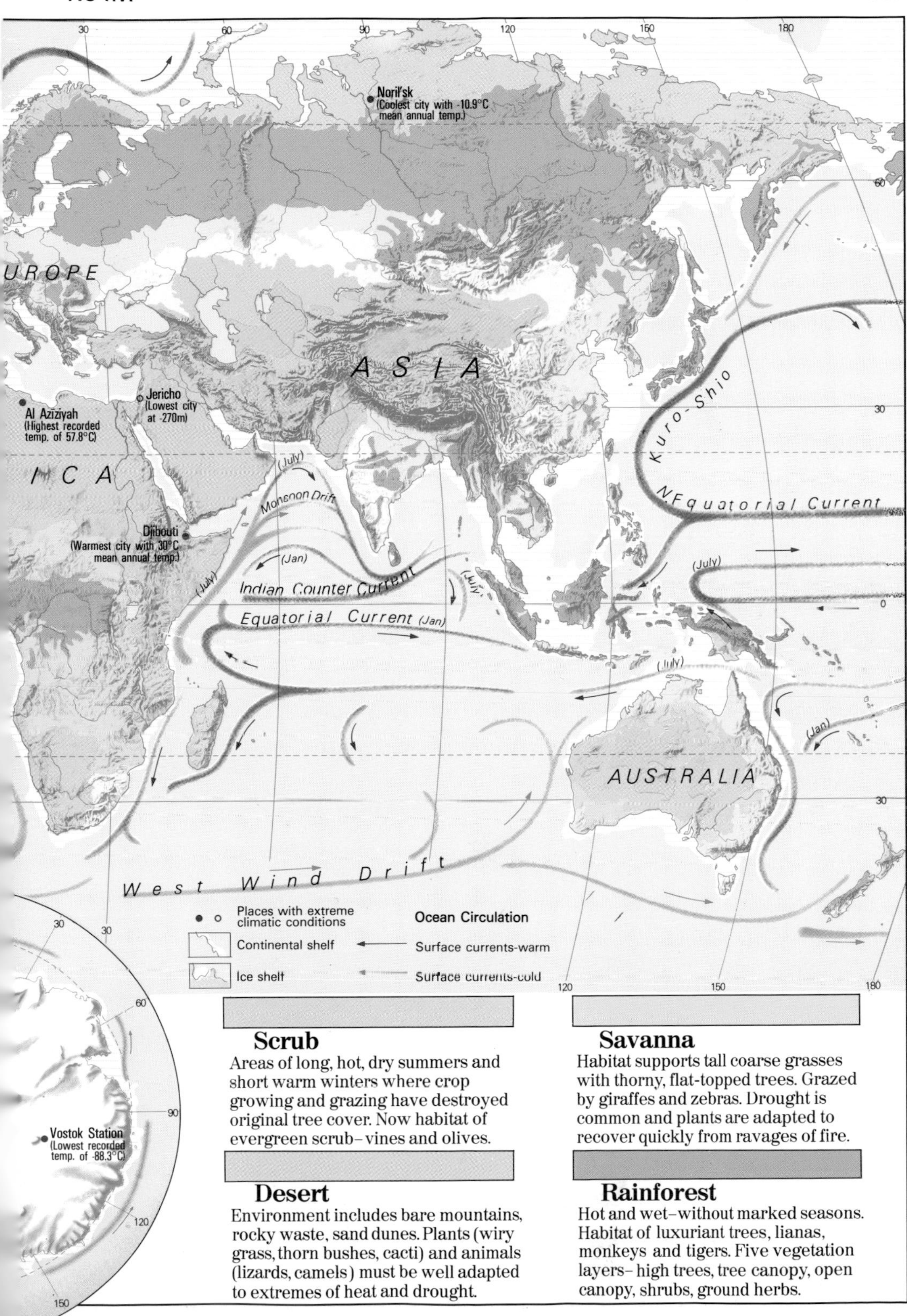

Noril'sk
(Coolest city with -10.9°C
mean annual temp.)

UROPE

ASIA

Al Aziziyah
(Highest recorded
temp. of 57.8°C)

Jericho
(Lowest city
at -270m)

ICA

Djibouti
(Warmest city with 30°C
mean annual temp.)

(July)

Monsoon Drift

(Jan)

(July)

Indian Counter Current

Equatorial Current (Jan)

(July)

Kuro-Shio

N Equatorial Current

(July)

(July)

(Jan)

AUSTRALIA

West Wind Drift

Vostok Station
(Lowest recorded
temp. of -88.3°C)

● ○	Places with extreme climatic conditions
	Continental shelf
	Ice shelf

Ocean Circulation

← Surface currents-warm

← Surface currents-cold

Scrub
Areas of long, hot, dry summers and short warm winters where crop growing and grazing have destroyed original tree cover. Now habitat of evergreen scrub–vines and olives.

Savanna
Habitat supports tall coarse grasses with thorny, flat-topped trees. Grazed by giraffes and zebras. Drought is common and plants are adapted to recover quickly from ravages of fire.

Desert
Environment includes bare mountains, rocky waste, sand dunes. Plants (wiry grass, thorn bushes, cacti) and animals (lizards, camels) must be well adapted to extremes of heat and drought.

Rainforest
Hot and wet–without marked seasons. Habitat of luxuriant trees, lianas, monkeys and tigers. Five vegetation layers– high trees, tree canopy, open canopy, shrubs, ground herbs.

BOUNDARIES

━━━━━	International
━ ━ ━ ━	International under Dispute
▪ ▪ ▪ ▪ ▪	Cease Fire Line
━━━━━	Autonomous or State/ Administrative
━ ━ ━ ━	Maritime (National)
─ ─ ─ ─	International Date Line

COMMUNICATIONS

━━━ ═ ═ ═	Motorway/Under Construction
━━━━━━	Major/Other Road
─ ─ ─ ─	Under Construction
‥‥‥‥‥	Track
⇒⇒═══	Road Tunnel
‥‥‥‥‥	Car Ferry
━━━━━	Main/Other Railway
━ ━ ━ ━	Under Construction
‥‥‥‥‥	Rail Ferry
→─ ─ ─←	Rail Tunnel
⊥⊥⊥⊥⊥	Canal
⊕ ✈	International/Other Airport

LANDSCAPE FEATURES

	Glacier, Ice Cap
	Marsh, Swamp
	Sand Desert, Dunes
	Freshwater
	Saltwater
	Seasonal
	Salt Pan

OTHER FEATURES

	River/Seasonal
≍	Pass, Gorge
	Dam, Barrage
	Waterfall, Rapid
───────	Aqueduct
	Reef
.217 ▲4231	Spot Height, Depth/ Summit, Peak
◡	Well
Δ ▲	Oil/Gas Field
─ Gas / Oil ─	Oil/Natural Gas Pipeline
Gemsbok Nat. Pk	National Park
∴UR	Historic Site

LETTERING STYLES

CANADA	Independent Nation
FLORIDA	State, Province or Autonomous Region
Gibraltar (U.K.)	Sovereignty of Dependent Territory
Lothian	Administrative Area
LANGUEDOC	Historic Region
Loire ***Vosges***	Physical Feature or Physical Region

TOWNS AND CITIES

Square symbols denote capital cities

■	●	**New York**	Major City
■	●	**Montréal**	City
◻	○	Ottawa	Small City
■	●	**Québec**	Large Town
◻	○	St John's	Town
◻	○	Yorkton	Small Town
◻	○	Jasper	Village
			Built-up-area

Depth   Sea Level   Height

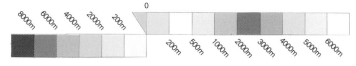

8000m 6000m 4000m 2000m 200m   0   200m 500m 1000m 2000m 3000m 4000m 5000m 6000m

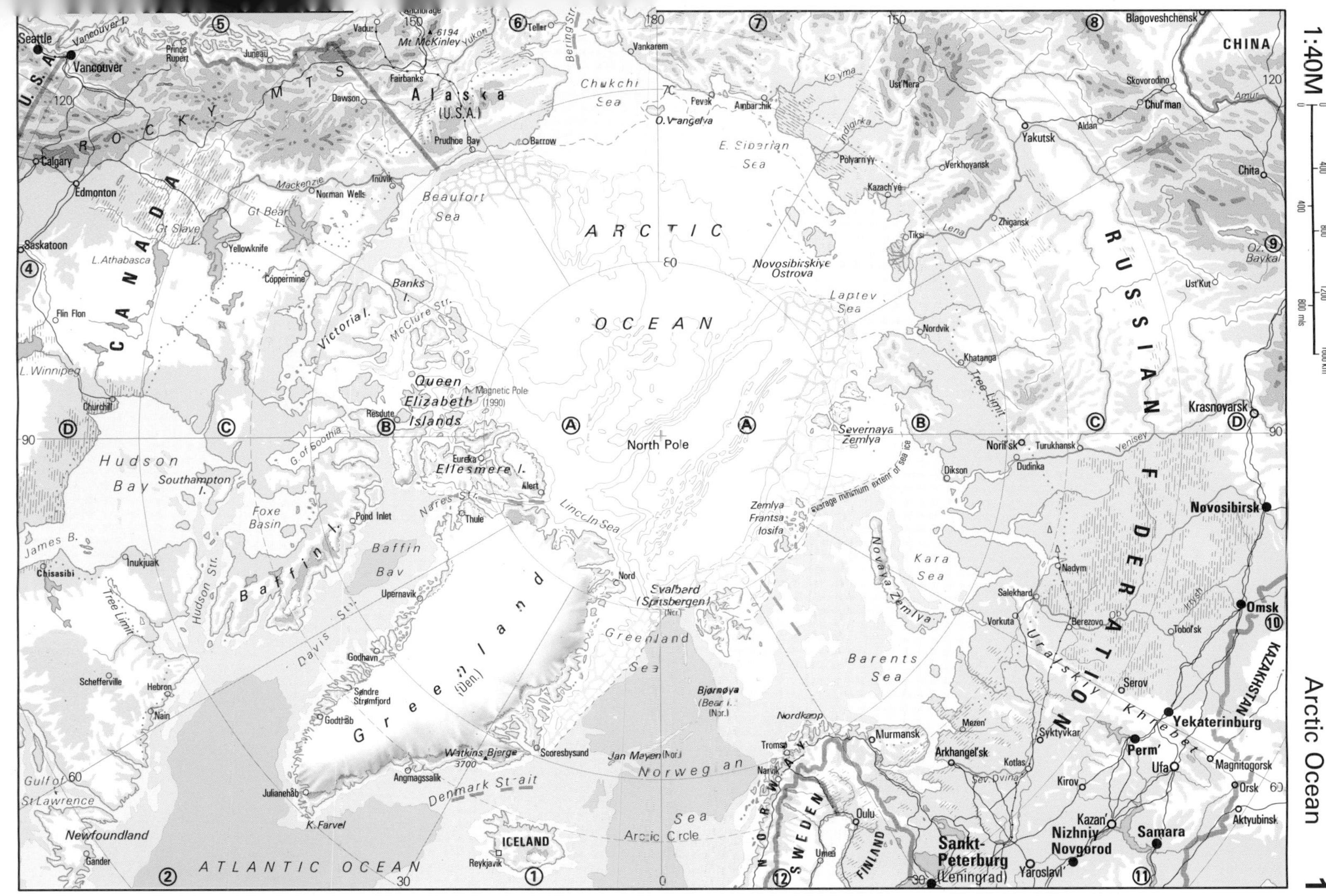
ARCTIC OCEAN
North Pole
RUSSIAN FEDERATION
CANADA
Greenland (Den.)
ICELAND
KAZAKHSTAN
CHINA
FINLAND
SWEDEN
NORWAY
Alaska (U.S.A.)
U.S.A.
ATLANTIC OCEAN
Norwegian Sea
Greenland Sea
Barents Sea
Kara Sea
Laptev Sea
E. Siberian Sea
Chukchi Sea
Beaufort Sea
Lincoln Sea
Baffin Bay
Hudson Bay
Foxe Basin
Davis Str.
Hudson Str.
Denmark Strait
Bering Str.
Nares Str.
McClure Str.
G. of Boothia
Gulf of St Lawrence
James B.
Arctic Circle
Tree Limit
average minimum extent of sea ice
Svalbard (Spitsbergen) (Nor.)
Zemlya Frantsa Iosifa
Novaya Zemlya
Severnaya Zemlya
Novosibirskiye Ostrova
O. Vrangelya
Queen Elizabeth Islands
Ellesmere I.
Banks I.
Victoria I.
Baffin I.
Southampton I.
Newfoundland
Jan Mayen (Nor.)
Bjørnøya (Bear I.) (Nor.)
Nordkapp
Magnetic Pole (1990)
6194 Mt McKinley
Watkins Bjerge 3700
Uralskiy Khrebet
ROCKY MTS
Vancouver I.
Gt Bear L.
Gt Slave L.
L. Athabasca
L. Winnipeg
Oz. Baykal
Yenisey
Lena
Kolyma
Indigirka
Yukon
Amur
Irtysh
Mackenzie
Sev. Dvina
Seattle
Vancouver
Prince Rupert
Juneau
Valdez
Anchorage
Teller
Fairbanks
Dawson
Prudhoe Bay
Barrow
Inuvik
Norman Wells
Calgary
Edmonton
Saskatoon
Yellowknife
Coppermine
Flin Flon
Churchill
Resolute
Eureka
Alert
Thule
Pond Inlet
Inukjuak
Chisasibi
Schefferville
Hebron
Nain
Gander
Upernavik
Godhavn
Søndre Strømfjord
Godthåb
Julianehåb
K. Farvel
Angmagssalik
Scoresbysund
Nord
Reykjavik
Vankarem
Pevek
Ambarchik
Ust'Nera
Polyarnyy
Kazach'ye
Verkhoyansk
Tiksi
Zhigansk
Yakutsk
Aldan
Skovorodino
Chul'man
Blagoveshchensk
Chita
Ust'Kut
Nordvik
Khatanga
Krasnoyarsk
Noril'sk
Turukhansk
Dudinka
Dikson
Novosibirsk
Nadym
Salekhard
Vorkuta
Berezovo
Tobol'sk
Omsk
Serov
Yekaterinburg
Perm'
Ufa
Magnitogorsk
Orsk
Aktyubinsk
Samara
Kazan'
Nizhniy Novgorod
Kirov
Yaroslavl'
Sankt-Peterburg (Leningrad)
Kotlas
Syktyvkar
Mezen'
Arkhangel'sk
Murmansk
Tromsø
Narvik
Oulu
Umeå

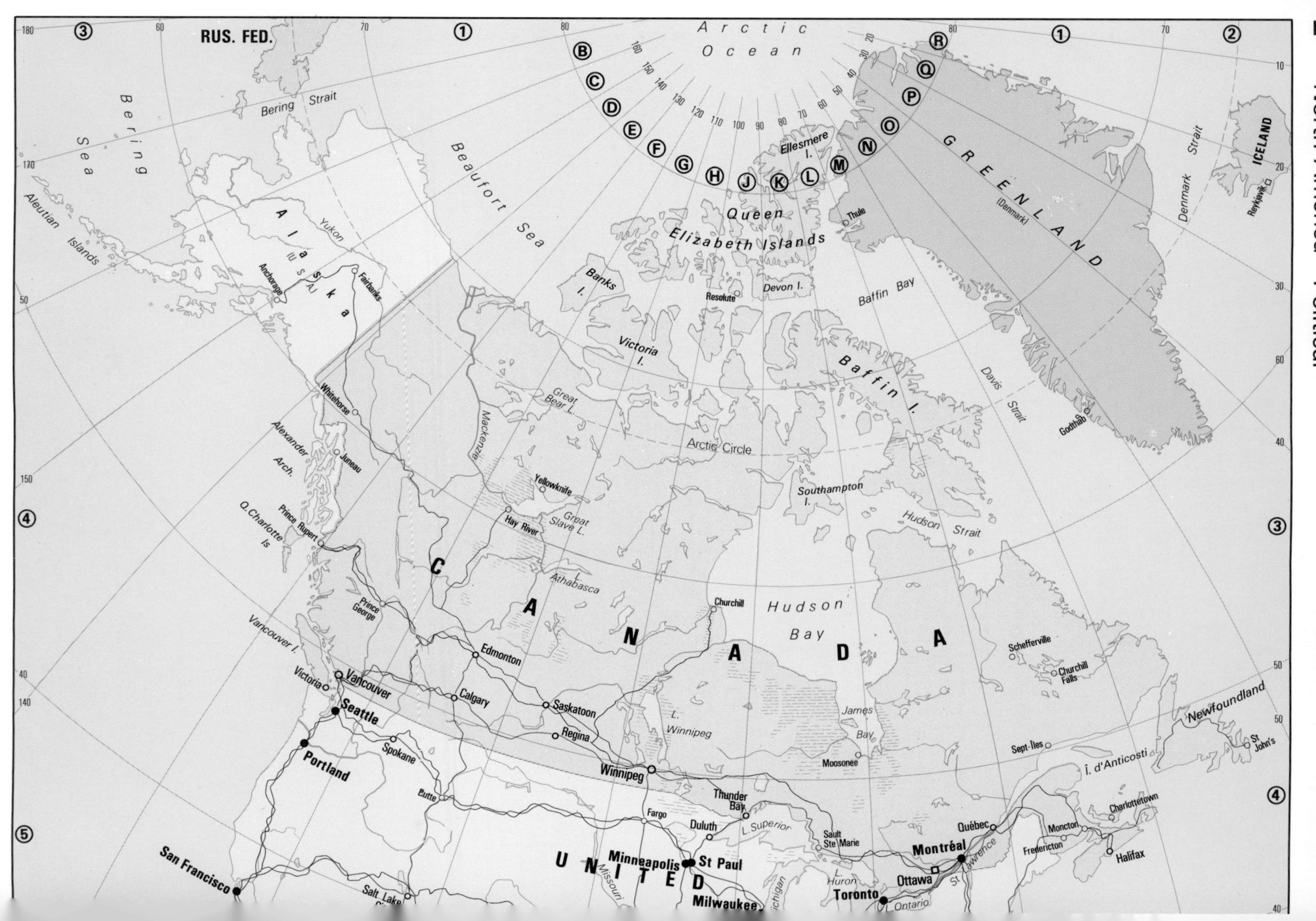

RUS. FED.
Arctic Ocean
ICELAND
Reykjavik
Denmark Strait
GREENLAND
(Denmark)
Thule
Godthåb
Ellesmere I.
Queen Elizabeth Islands
Devon I.
Resolute
Baffin Bay
Baffin I.
Davis Strait
Banks I.
Victoria I.
Beaufort Sea
Bering Strait
Bering Sea
Aleutian Islands
Alaska
(U S A)
Yukon
Fairbanks
Anchorage
Whitehorse
Juneau
Alexander Arch.
Prince Rupert
Q. Charlotte Is
Great Bear L.
Mackenzie
Arctic Circle
Yellowknife
Great Slave L.
Hay River
L. Athabasca
Southampton I.
Hudson Strait
Hudson Bay
Churchill
C A N A D A
Prince George
Vancouver I.
Victoria
Vancouver
Edmonton
Calgary
Saskatoon
Regina
L. Winnipeg
Winnipeg
James Bay
Moosonee
Schefferville
Churchill Falls
Newfoundland
St. John's
Sept-Îles
Î. d'Anticosti
Charlottetown
Québec
Moncton
Fredericton
Halifax
Montréal
St Lawrence
Ottawa
Toronto
L. Ontario
L. Huron
Sault Ste Marie
Thunder Bay
L. Superior
Duluth
Fargo
Minneapolis
St Paul
Milwaukee
Missouri
UNITED
Seattle
Portland
Spokane
Butte
Salt Lake
San Francisco

1:35M

| 0 | 250 | 500 | 750 | 1000 | 1250 km |
| 0 | | 250 | | 500 | 750 mls |

ATLANTIC OCEAN

Bermuda (U.K.)

Boston
New York
Philadelphia
Washington
Buffalo
Cleveland
Baltimore
Detroit
Indianapolis
Nashville
Norfolk
Charleston
Jacksonville

Chicago
St Louis
Memphis
Birmingham
Atlanta
Tampa

UNITED STATES OF AMERICA

Omaha
Kansas City
Dallas
Fort Worth
San Antonio
Houston
New Orleans

Denver
Albuquerque
Phoenix
Tucson
El Paso
Chihuahua

Los Angeles
San Diego
Mazatlán

MEXICO

Monterrey
Torreón
Guadalajara
México
Acapulco
Veracruz
Tarapico
Mérida

Miami
THE BAHAMAS
Nassau

CUBA
Habana

Guantánamo
HAITI
Port-au-Prince
Kingston
JAMAICA

DOMINICAN REP.
Sto Domingo
Pto Rico (U.S.A.)

ST LUCIA
ST VINCENT
GRENADA
TRINIDAD & TOBAGO
BARBADOS
DOMINICA

Netherlands Antilles

CARIBBEAN SEA

BELIZE
Belmopan
GUATEMALA
Guatemala
EL SALVADOR
S.Salvador
HONDURAS
Tegucigalpa
NICARAGUA
Managua
COSTA RICA
S.José
PANAMA
Panamá

Sta Marta
Barranquilla
Maracaibo
Caracas
VENEZUELA

Medellín
Bogotá
COLOMBIA

ECUADOR
Quito
PERU

BRAZIL
Negro

Galápagos Is (Ecu.)

Malpelo (Col.)
I. del Coco (C.R.)

PACIFIC OCEAN

Clipperton (Fr.)
Is Revilla Gigedo (Mex.)
Guadalupe (Mex.)

G. de California
Rio Grande
Colorado
Ohio
Mississippi
Gulf of Mexico
L. Erie

Tropic of Cancer
Equator

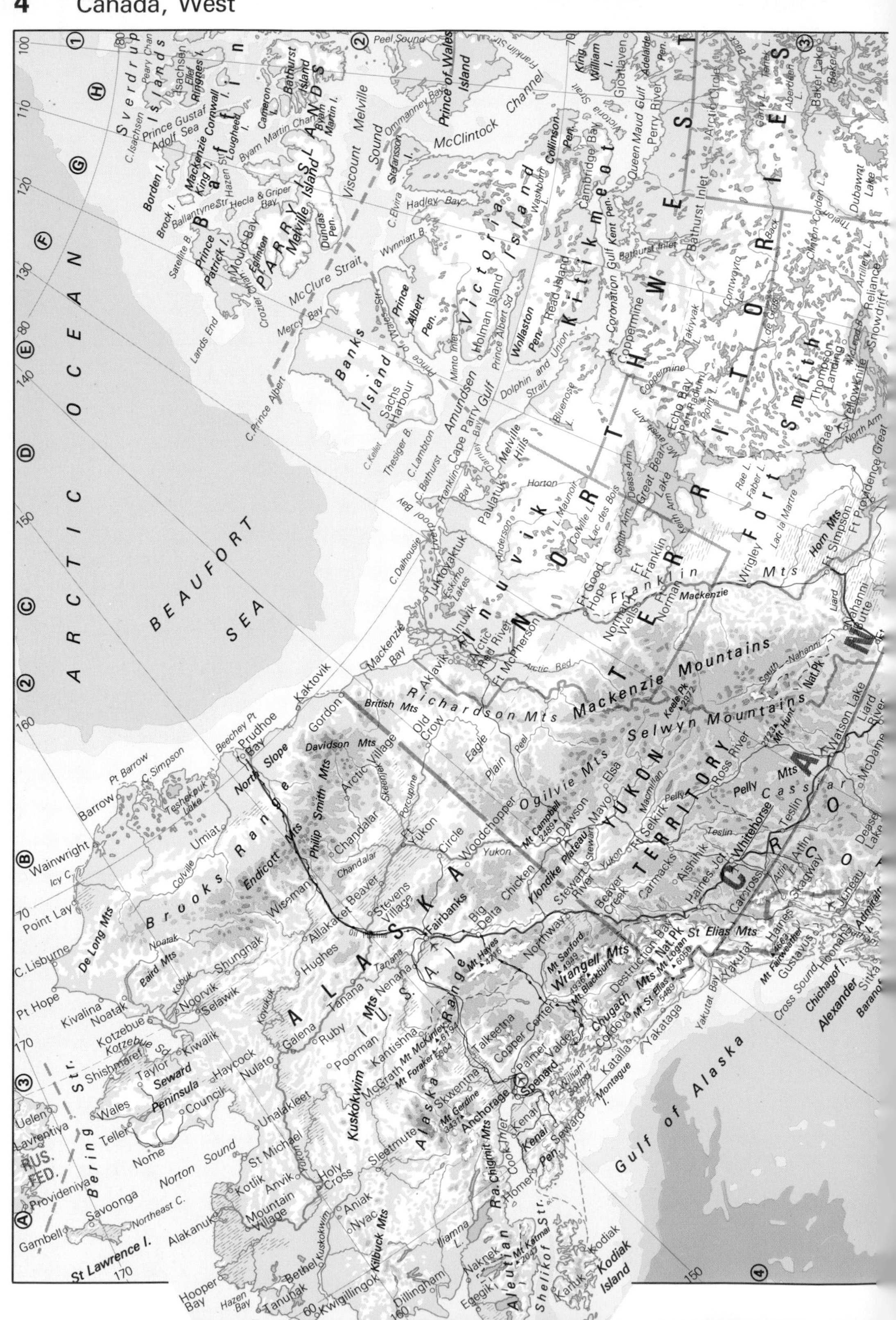
ARCTIC OCEAN
BEAUFORT SEA
Gulf of Alaska
Bering Str.
Norton Sound
ALASKA
U.S.A.
YUKON TERRITORY
NORTHWEST TERRITORIES
Inuvik
Kitikmeot
Fort Smith
Sverdrup Islands
PARRY ISLANDS
Banks Island
Victoria Island
Prince of Wales Island
Melville Island
Prince Patrick I.
Borden I.
Mackenzie King I.
Brock I.
Lougheed I.
Cameron I.
Bathurst Island
Byam Martin I.
Ellef Ringnes I.
Amund Ringnes I.
King William I.
Prince Gustaf Adolf Sea
Viscount Melville Sound
McClintock Channel
McClure Strait
Amundsen Gulf
Coronation Gulf
Queen Maud Gulf
Dolphin and Union Strait
Prince of Wales Str.
Mackenzie Bay
Great Bear Lake
Brooks Range
Mackenzie Mountains
Selwyn Mountains
Richardson Mts
British Mts
Ogilvie Mts
Wrangell Mts
Chugach Mts
St Elias Mts
Alaska Range
Kuskokwim Mts
De Long Mts
Baird Mts
Endicott Mts
Philip Smith Mts
Davidson Mts
Franklin Mts
Cassiar Mts
Pelly Mts
Horn Mts
Klondike Plateau
North Slope
Seward Peninsula
Kenai Pen.
Kodiak Island
St Lawrence I.
Mt McKinley 6194
Mt Foraker 5304
Mt Logan 6050
Mt St Elias 5489
Mt Sanford 4949
Mt Blackburn 4936
Mt Hayes 4216
Mt Fairweather 4663
Mt Campbell 2489
Keele Pk 2972
Mt Hunt 2123
Mt Katmai 2047
Barrow
Pt Barrow
Wainwright
Point Lay
Pt Hope
Kivalina
Kotzebue
Nome
Teller
Wales
Prudhoe Bay
Kaktovik
Fairbanks
Anchorage
Valdez
Cordova
Seward
Homer
Kenai
Bethel
Dillingham
Kodiak
Yakutat
Juneau
Skagway
Haines
Sitka
Whitehorse
Dawson
Mayo
Elsa
Carmacks
Watson Lake
Inuvik
Aklavik
Tuktoyaktuk
Ft McPherson
Arctic Red River
Ft Good Hope
Norman Wells
Ft Franklin
Ft Norman
Wrigley
Ft Simpson
Ft Providence
Rae
Yellowknife
Reliance
Snowdrift
Coppermine
Cambridge Bay
Gjoa Haven
Holman Island
Sachs Harbour
Paulatuk
Old Crow
Circle
Eagle
Tok
Galena
Nulato
Unalakleet
McGrath
Kantishna
Talkeetna
Glennallen
Copper Center
Provideniya
Lavrentiya
Uelen
RUS. FED.
Gambell
Savoonga

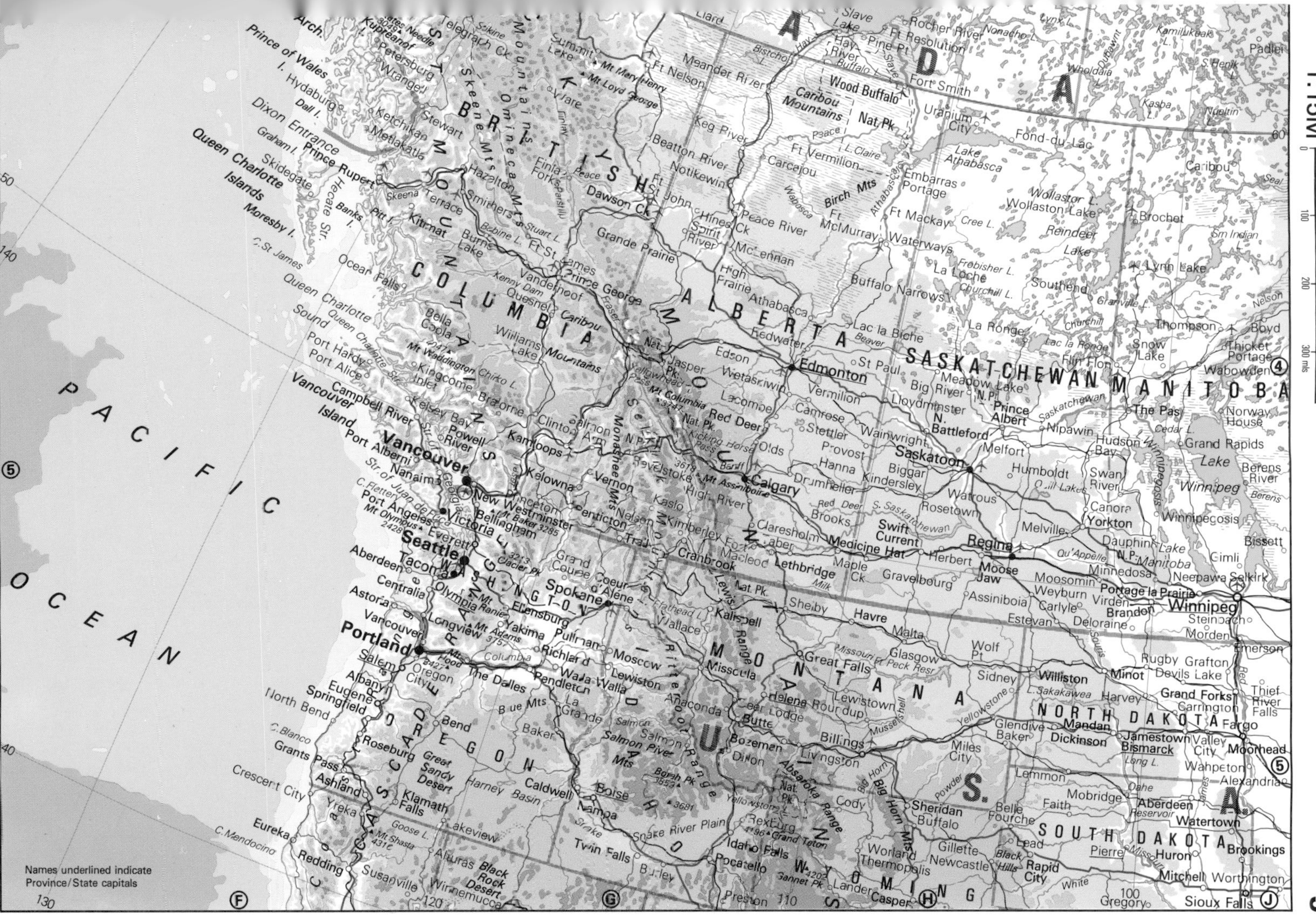
PACIFIC
OCEAN
CANADA
U.S.A.
BRITISH COLUMBIA
ALBERTA
SASKATCHEWAN
MANITOBA
WASHINGTON
OREGON
IDAHO
MONTANA
WYOMING
NORTH DAKOTA
SOUTH DAKOTA
Queen Charlotte Islands
Vancouver Island
Prince of Wales I.
Dixon Entrance
Hecate Str.
Queen Charlotte Sound
Str. of Juan de Fuca
Vancouver
Victoria
Seattle
Tacoma
Olympia
Portland
Salem
Spokane
Boise
Helena
Edmonton
Calgary
Regina
Saskatoon
Winnipeg
Bismarck
Pierre
Fargo
Prince Rupert
Prince George
Kamloops
Kelowna
Lethbridge
Medicine Hat
Red Deer
Great Falls
Billings
Missoula
Butte
Rapid City
Sioux Falls
Eureka
Redding
Eugene
Lake Athabasca
Lake Winnipeg
Winnipegosis
Big Horn Mts
Black Hills
Wood Buffalo Nat Pk
Names underlined indicate Province/State capitals

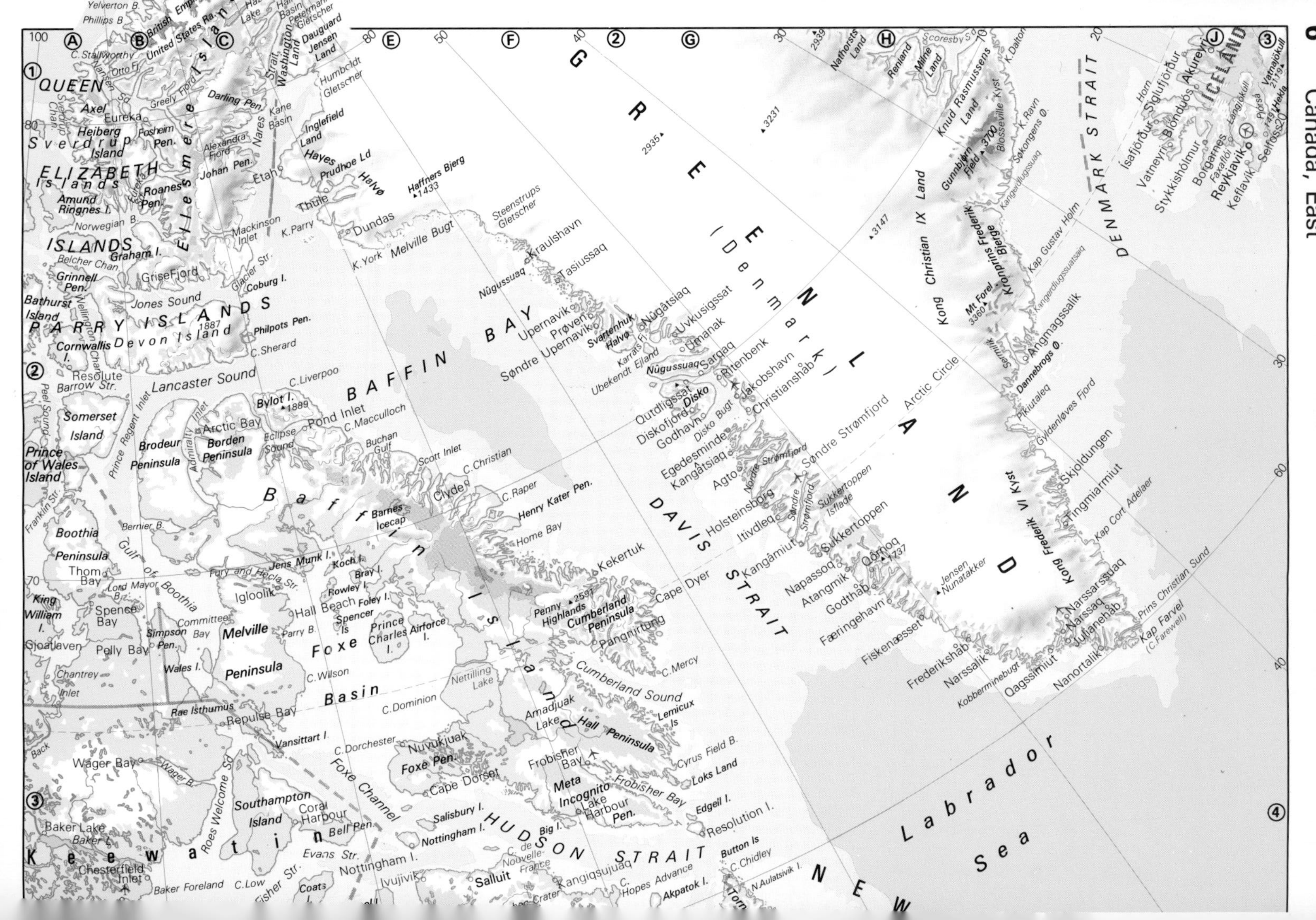
ICELAND
Reykjavík
Keflavík
Akureyri
Ísafjörður
Borgarnes
Stykkishólmur
Blönduós
Siglufjörður
Vatneyri
Selfoss
Hekla
DENMARK STRAIT
GREENLAND
(Denmark)
Kong Christian IX Land
Kong Frederik VI Kyst
Kronprins Frederik Bjerge
Gunnbjørn Fjeld
Knud Rasmussens Land
Blosseville Kyst
Nathorsts Land
Milne Land
Renland
Kap Gustav Holm
Angmagssalik
Dannebrogs Ø.
Mt Forel
Pikiutaleq
Gyldenløves Fjord
Skjoldungen
Tingmiarmiut
Kap Cort Adelaer
Kap Farvel
(C. Farewell)
Prins Christian Sund
Narssarssuaq
Narssaq
Julianehåb
Nanortalik
Qagssimiut
Kobberminebugt
Narssalik
Frederikshåb
Fiskenæsset
Færingehavn
Godthåb
Atangmik
Napassoq
Qôrnoq
Jensen Nunatakker
Kangâmiut
Sukkertoppen
Sukkertoppen Isflade
Søndre Strømfjord
Nordre Strømfjord
Holsteinsborg
Itivdleq
Agto
Kangâtsiaq
Egedesminde
Godhavn
Diskofjord
Qutdligssat
Disko
Disko Bugt
Christianshåb
Jakobshavn
Ritenbenk
Sargaq
Nûgussuaq
Umanak
Uvkusigssat
Nûgâtsiaq
Svartenhuk Halvø
Ubekendt Ejland
Upernavik
Prøven
Søndre Upernavik
Tasiussaq
Kraulshavn
Steenstrups Gletscher
Melville Bugt
K. York
Dundas
Thule
Haffners Bjerg
Prudhoe Ld
Hayes Halvø
Inglefield Land
Humboldt Gletscher
Washington Land
Dauguard Jensen Land
Arctic Circle
DAVIS STRAIT
BAFFIN BAY
Labrador Sea
NEW
Baffin Island
Cumberland Sound
Cumberland Peninsula
Penny Highlands
Pangnirtung
Kekertuk
Cape Dyer
C. Mercy
Lemieux Is
Hall Peninsula
Frobisher Bay
Meta Incognita Pen.
Lake Harbour
Cyrus Field B.
Loks Land
Edgell I.
Resolution I.
Button Is
C. Chidley
Akpatok I.
C. Hopes Advance
Kangiqsujuaq
Salluit
Big I.
Amadjuak Lake
Nettilling Lake
Foxe Basin
Foxe Channel
Foxe Pen.
Nuvukjuak
Cape Dorset
Salisbury I.
Nottingham I.
Ivujivik
Southampton Island
Coral Harbour
Bell Pen.
Evans Str.
Coats I.
HUDSON STRAIT
Melville Peninsula
Igloolik
Hall Beach
Prince Charles I.
Airforce I.
Spencer Is
Foley I.
Rowley I.
Bray I.
Koch I.
Jens Munk I.
Fury and Hecla Str.
Barnes Icecap
Henry Kater Pen.
Home Bay
C. Raper
Clyde
C. Christian
Scott Inlet
Buchan Gulf
C. Macculloch
Pond Inlet
Bylot I.
Eclipse Sound
Arctic Bay
Borden Peninsula
Brodeur Peninsula
Admiralty Inlet
Prince Regent Inlet
Lancaster Sound
C. Liverpool
C. Sherard
Devon Island
Philpots Pen.
PARRY ISLANDS
Jones Sound
Grise Fiord
Coburg I.
Glacier Str.
Mackinson Inlet
K. Parry
Etah
Johan Pen.
Alexandra Fiord
Nares Basin
Kane Basin
Ellesmere Island
Darling Pen.
Greely Fiord
Fosheim Pen.
Eureka
Axel Heiberg Island
Sverdrup Islands
QUEEN ELIZABETH ISLANDS
Amund Ringnes I.
Roanes Pen.
Norwegian B.
Graham I.
Belcher Chan.
Grinnell Pen.
Bathurst Island
Cornwallis I.
Resolute
Barrow Str.
Peel Sound
Somerset Island
Prince of Wales Island
Franklin Str.
Boothia Peninsula
Gulf of Boothia
Bernier B.
Thom Bay
Lord Mayor B.
Spence Bay
Pelly Bay
Committee Bay
Simpson Pen.
Wales I.
King William I.
Gjoa Haven
Chantrey Inlet
Rae Isthmus
Repulse Bay
Vansittart I.
C. Wilson
C. Dominion
C. Dorchester
Wager Bay
Roes Welcome Sd
Baker Lake
Chesterfield Inlet
Baker Foreland
C. Low
Keewatin

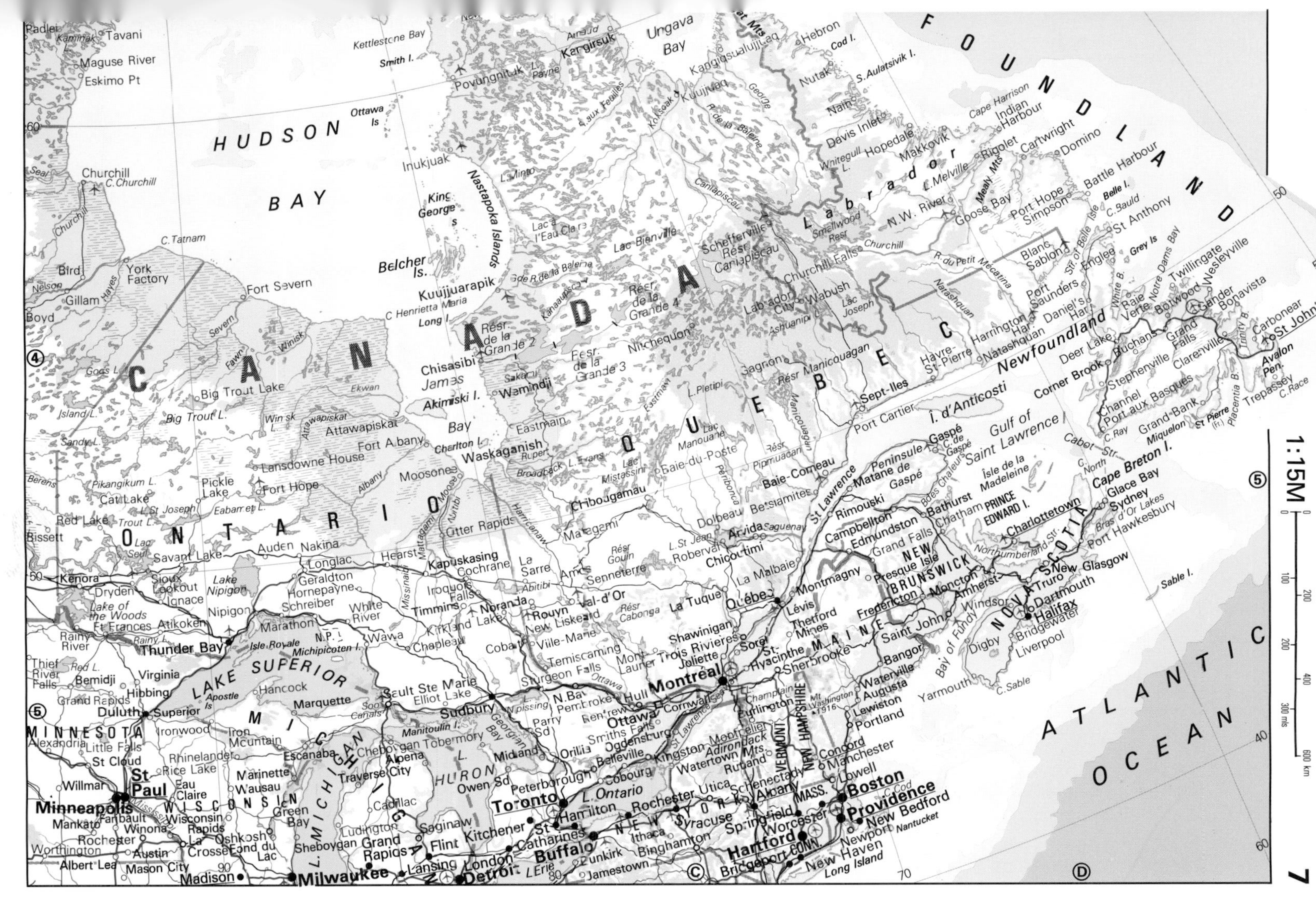
C A N A D A
O N T A R I O
Q U E B E C
N E W F O U N D L A N D
L a b r a d o r
HUDSON BAY
James Bay
Ungava Bay
A T L A N T I C O C E A N
Gulf of Saint Lawrence
LAKE SUPERIOR
HURON
L. Ontario
L. Erie
L. MICHIGAN
NEW BRUNSWICK
NOVA SCOTIA
PRINCE EDWARD I.
MAINE
NEW HAMPSHIRE
VERMONT
MASS.
CONN.
NEW YORK
MICHIGAN
WISCONSIN
MINNESOTA
Montreal
Québec
Ottawa
Toronto
Detroit
Buffalo
Boston
Providence
Hartford
Milwaukee
Minneapolis
St Paul
Thunder Bay
Halifax
Newfoundland
Î. d'Anticosti
Nastapoka Islands
Belcher Is.
Cape Breton I.
Sable I.

1:12.5M

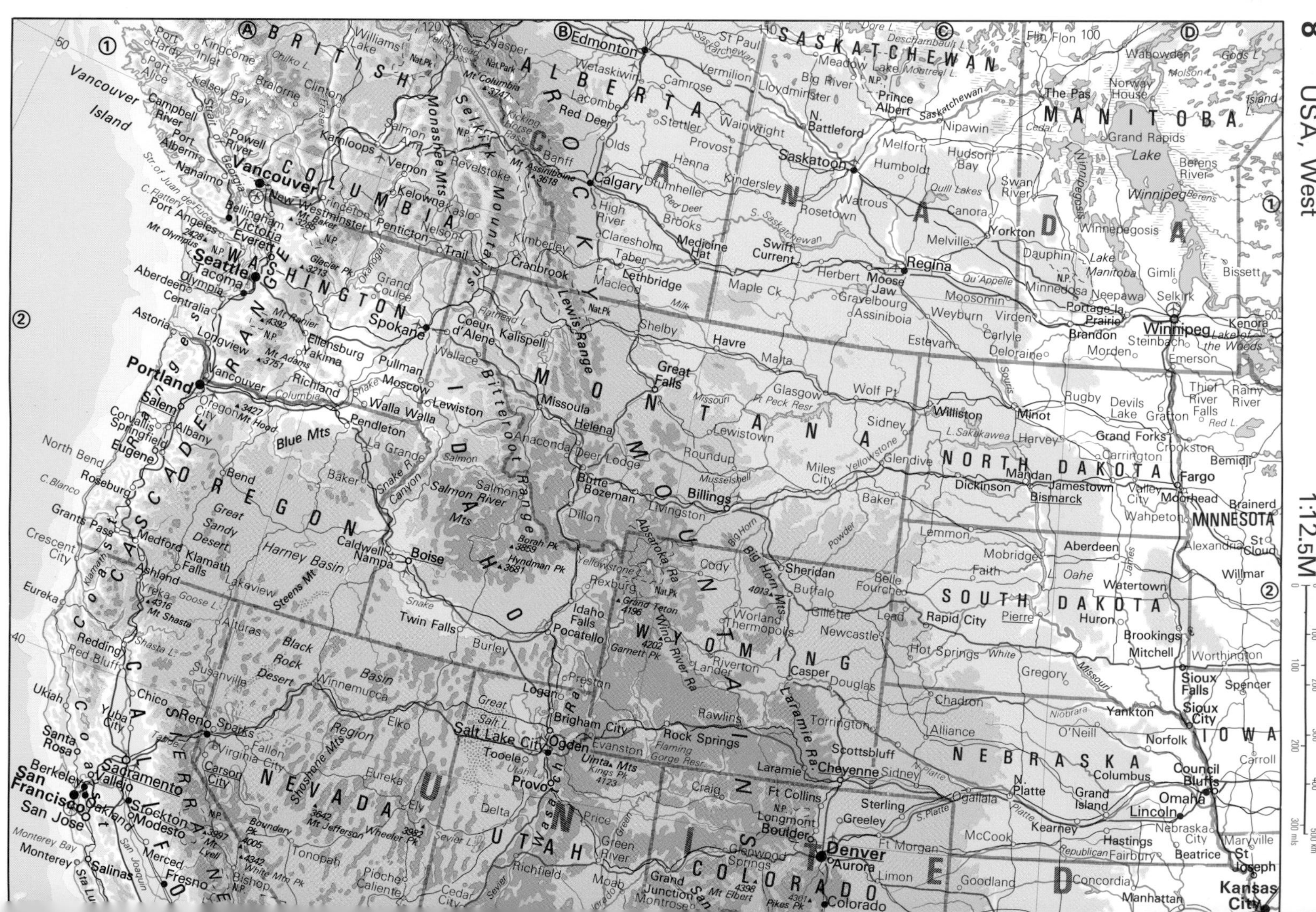
0 100 200 300 400 500 km
0 100 200 300 mls
CANADA
UNITED STATES
BRITISH COLUMBIA
ALBERTA
SASKATCHEWAN
MANITOBA
WASHINGTON
OREGON
IDAHO
MONTANA
NORTH DAKOTA
SOUTH DAKOTA
MINNESOTA
IOWA
NEBRASKA
WYOMING
NEVADA
UTAH
COLORADO
CALIFORNIA
ROCKY MOUNTAINS
CASCADE RANGE
SIERRA NEVADA
COAST RANGES
Vancouver Island
Vancouver
Victoria
Seattle
Tacoma
Olympia
Spokane
Portland
Salem
Eugene
Boise
Edmonton
Calgary
Saskatoon
Regina
Winnipeg
Great Falls
Helena
Missoula
Billings
Bismarck
Fargo
Pierre
Rapid City
Sioux Falls
Omaha
Lincoln
Cheyenne
Denver
Salt Lake City
Ogden
Provo
Reno
Carson City
Sacramento
San Francisco
Oakland
San Jose
Fresno
Kansas City
Selkirk Mountains
Monashee Mts
Lewis Range
Bitterroot Range
Salmon River Mts
Blue Mts
Big Horn Mts
Absaroka Ra
Wind River Ra
Laramie Ra
Uinta Mts
Wasatch Ra
Harney Basin
Great Sandy Desert
Black Rock Desert
Great Salt L.

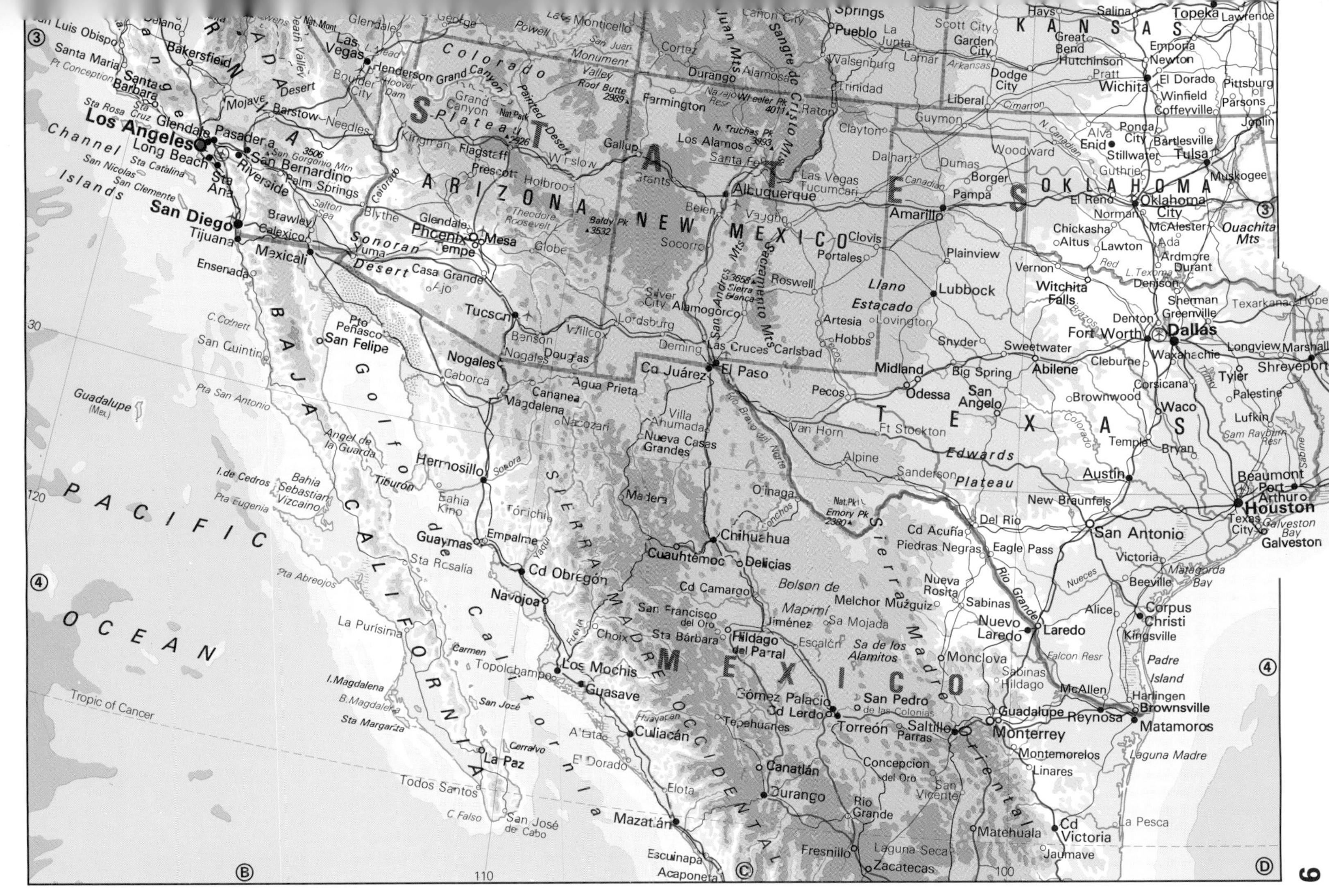

K A N S A S
O K L A H O M A
T E X A S
N E W M E X I C O
A R I Z O N A
S T A T E S
M E X I C O
B A J A C A L I F O R N I A
P A C I F I C
O C E A N
Golfo de California
Sierra Madre Oriental
Sierra Madre Occidental
Llano Estacado
Edwards Plateau
Colorado Plateau
Sonoran Desert
Painted Desert
Mojave Desert
Sangre de Cristo Mts
Sacramento Mts
San Andres Mts
Ouachita Mts
Rio Grande
Rio Bravo del Norte
Bolsón de Mapimí
Channel Islands
Tropic of Cancer
Topeka
Wichita
Tulsa
Oklahoma City
Amarillo
Lubbock
Dallas
Fort Worth
Houston
Galveston
Beaumont
Shreveport
Austin
San Antonio
Corpus Christi
Brownsville
Matamoros
Laredo
Nuevo Laredo
Monterrey
Saltillo
Torreón
Durango
Chihuahua
El Paso
Cd Juárez
Albuquerque
Santa Fe
Tucson
Phoenix
Mesa
Nogales
Hermosillo
Guaymas
Cd Obregón
Los Mochis
Culiacán
Mazatlán
La Paz
Mexicali
Tijuana
San Diego
Los Angeles
Long Beach
San Bernardino
Riverside
Las Vegas
Bakersfield
Santa Barbara
Flagstaff
Pueblo
Midland
Odessa
Abilene
Waco
Zacatecas
Fresnillo
Cd Victoria
Reynosa

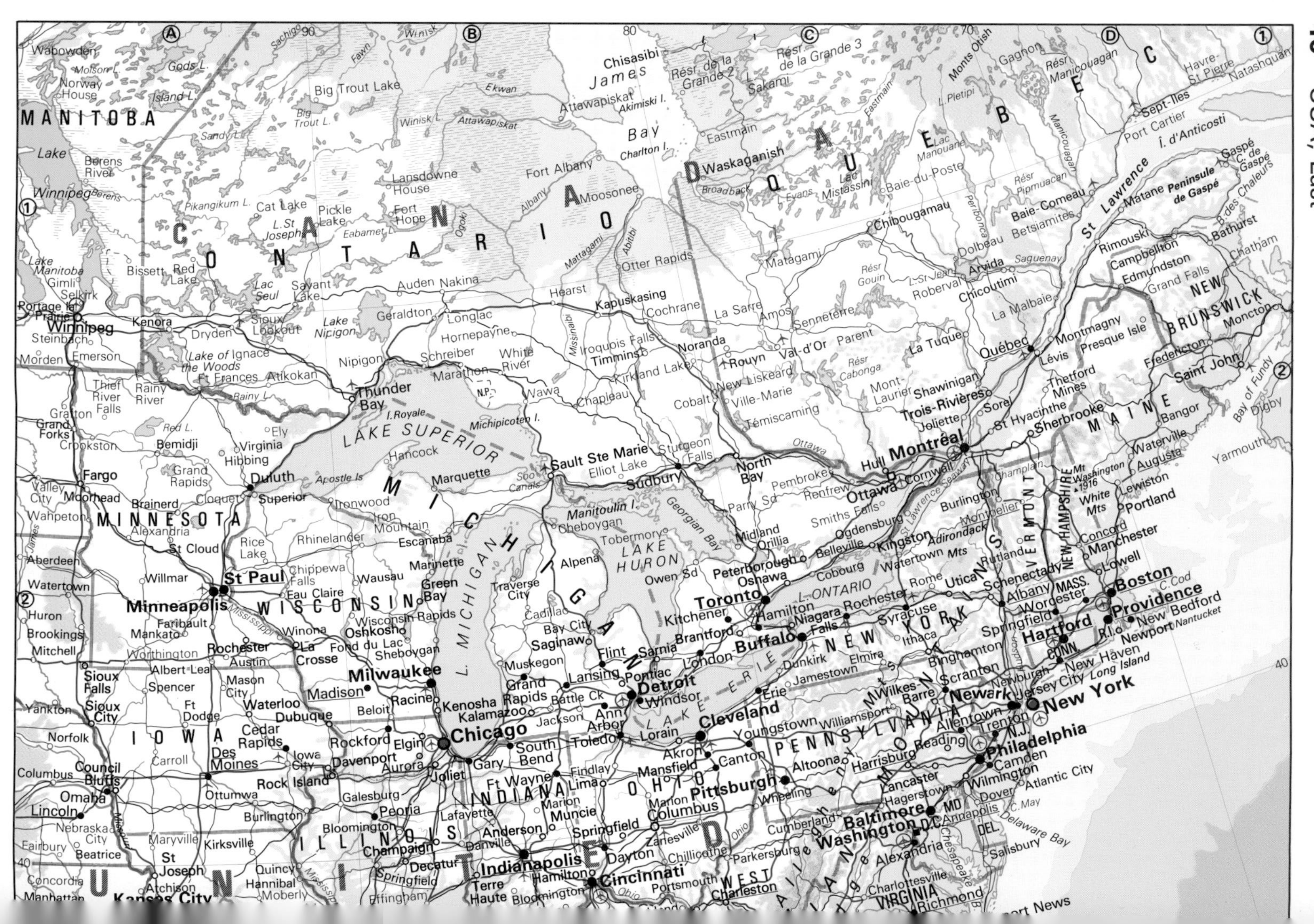

MANITOBA
ONTARIO
QUEBEC
NEW BRUNSWICK
MAINE
VERMONT
NEW HAMPSHIRE
MASS.
CONN.
R.I.
NEW YORK
PENNSYLVANIA
N.J.
MD
DEL.
VIRGINIA
WEST VIRGINIA
OHIO
INDIANA
ILLINOIS
MICHIGAN
WISCONSIN
MINNESOTA
IOWA
James Bay
LAKE SUPERIOR
L. MICHIGAN
LAKE HURON
Georgian Bay
L. ONTARIO
LAKE ERIE
St Lawrence
Bay of Fundy
Long Island
Delaware Bay
Chesapeake
Winnipeg
Lake Winnipeg
Thunder Bay
Duluth
Minneapolis
St Paul
Milwaukee
Chicago
Detroit
Toronto
Buffalo
Cleveland
Pittsburgh
Columbus
Cincinnati
Indianapolis
Ottawa
Montréal
Québec
Boston
Providence
Hartford
New York
Newark
Philadelphia
Baltimore
Washington
Kansas City
Omaha

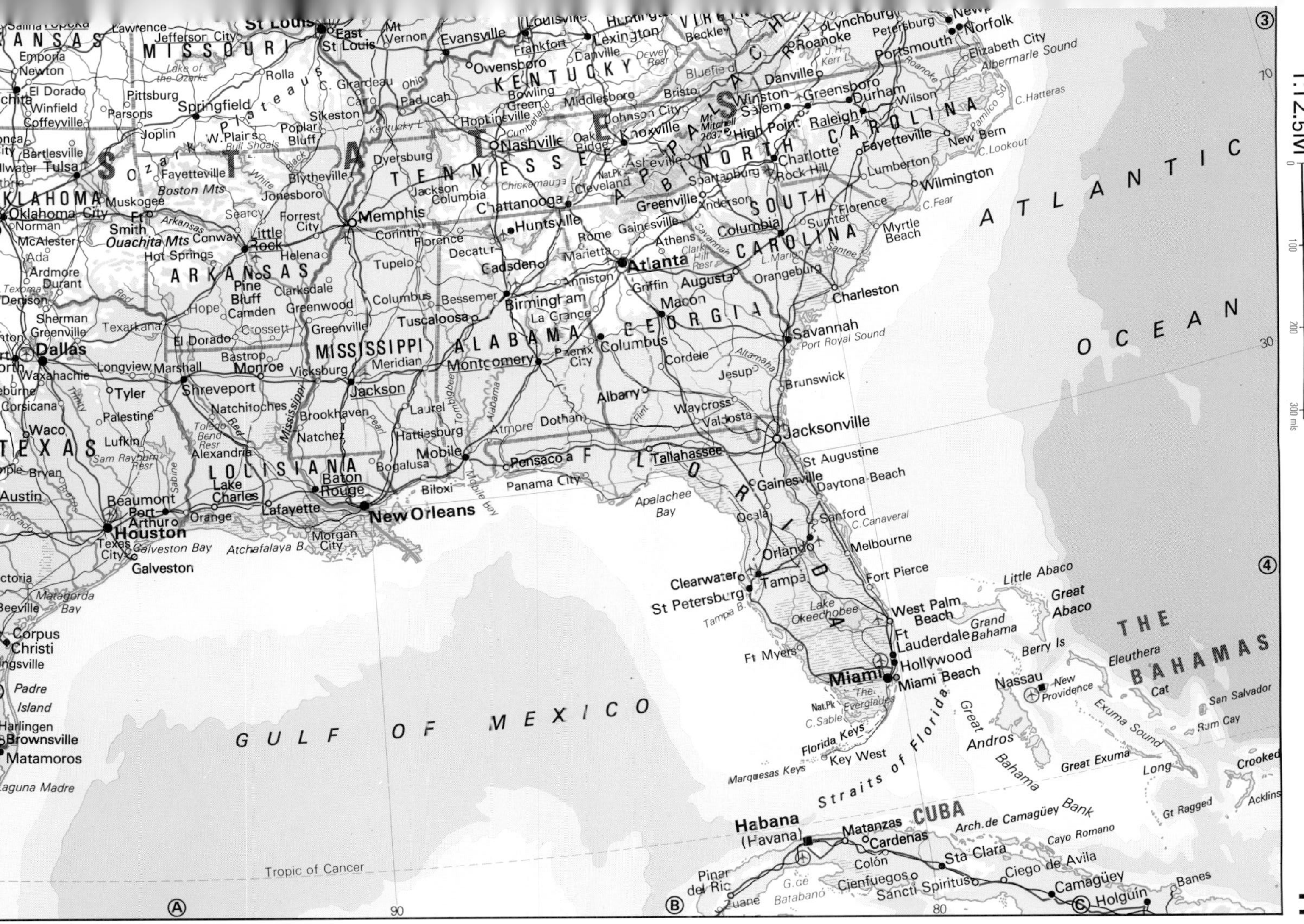

100   200   300   400   500 km
100   200   300 mls

1:10M

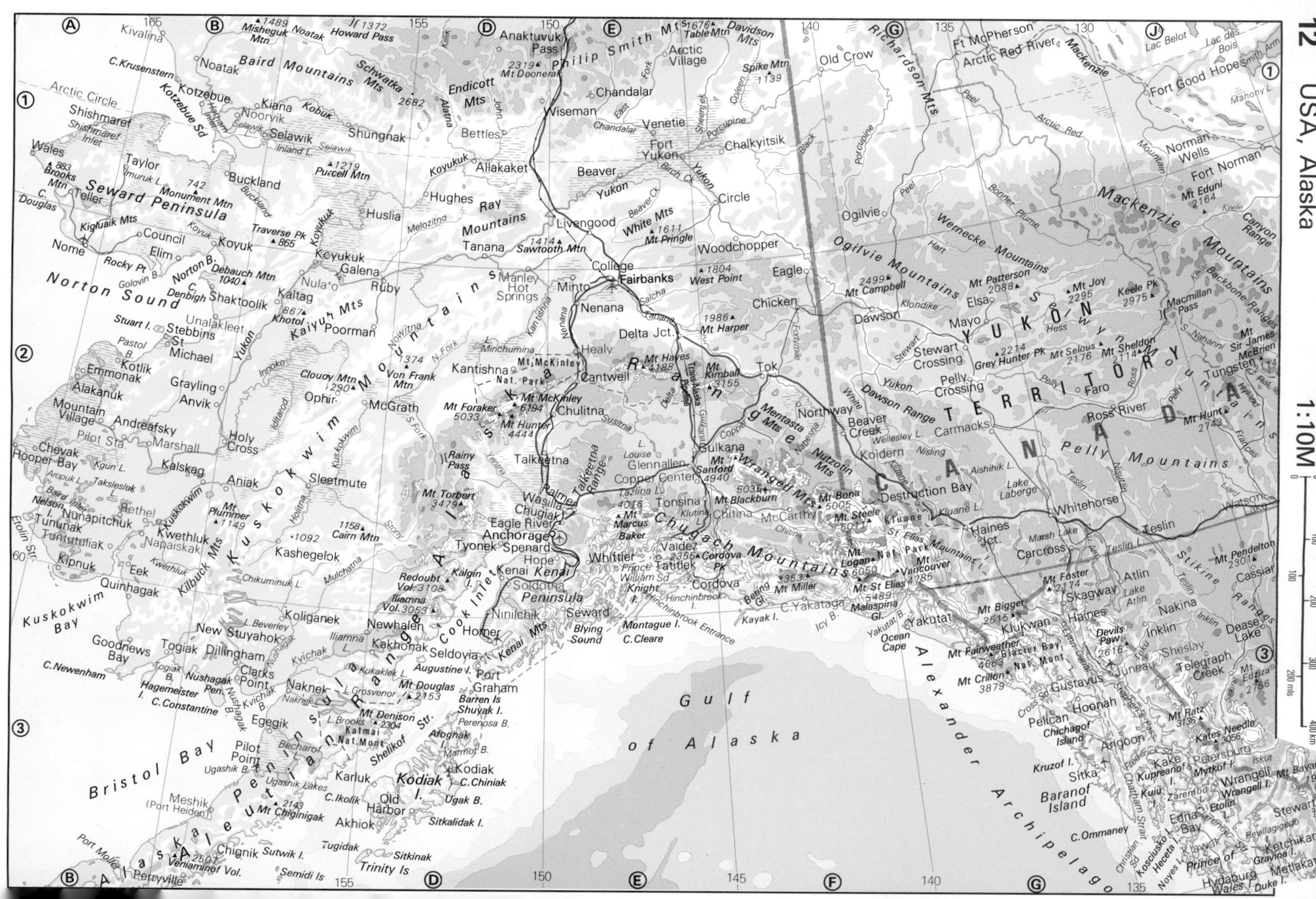

0 100 200 300 400 km
0 100 200 mls
Gulf of Alaska
Alexander Archipelago
Bristol Bay
Norton Sound
Kuskokwim Bay
Kotzebue Sd
Seward Peninsula
Kenai Peninsula
Alaska Peninsula
Baird Mountains
Endicott Mts
Philip Smith Mts
Davidson Mts
Richardson Mts
Mackenzie Mountains
Ogilvie Mountains
Wernecke Mountains
Selwyn Mountains
Pelly Mountains
Cassiar Mountains
Stikine Ranges
St Elias Mountains
Chugach Mountains
Wrangell Mts
Nutzotin Mts
Mentasta Mts
Alaska Range
Talkeetna Range
Kuskokwim Mts
Kilbuck Mts
Kaiyuh Mts
Ray Mountains
White Mts
Dawson Range
YUKON TERRITORY
Trans-Alaska Pipeline
Arctic Circle
Anchorage
Fairbanks
Juneau
Whitehorse
Dawson
Nome
Kotzebue
Kodiak
Valdez
Cordova
Seward
Homer
Kenai
Sitka
Skagway
Haines
Yakutat
Bethel
Dillingham
Tok
Delta Jct.
Tanana
Galena
McGrath
Old Crow
Fort Yukon
Mt McKinley 6194
Mt Foraker 5033
Mt Logan 6050
Mt St Elias 5489
Mt Sanford 4940
Mt Blackburn 5036
Mt Bona 5005
Mt Fairweather 4663
Mt Crillon 3879
Kodiak I.
Baranof Island
Chichagof Island
Prince of Wales I.
Montague I.
Kayak I.
Nunivak I.
Stuart I.

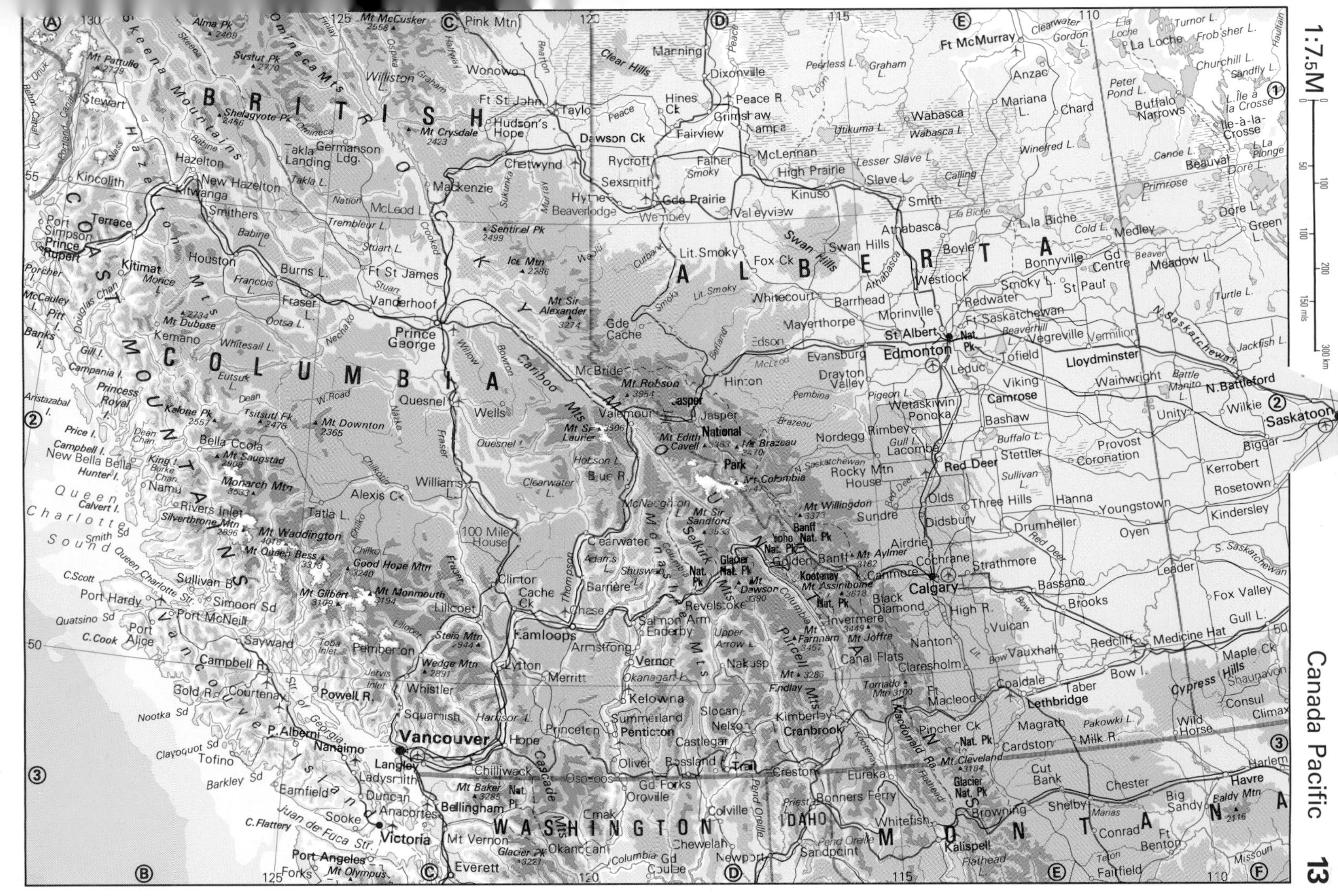

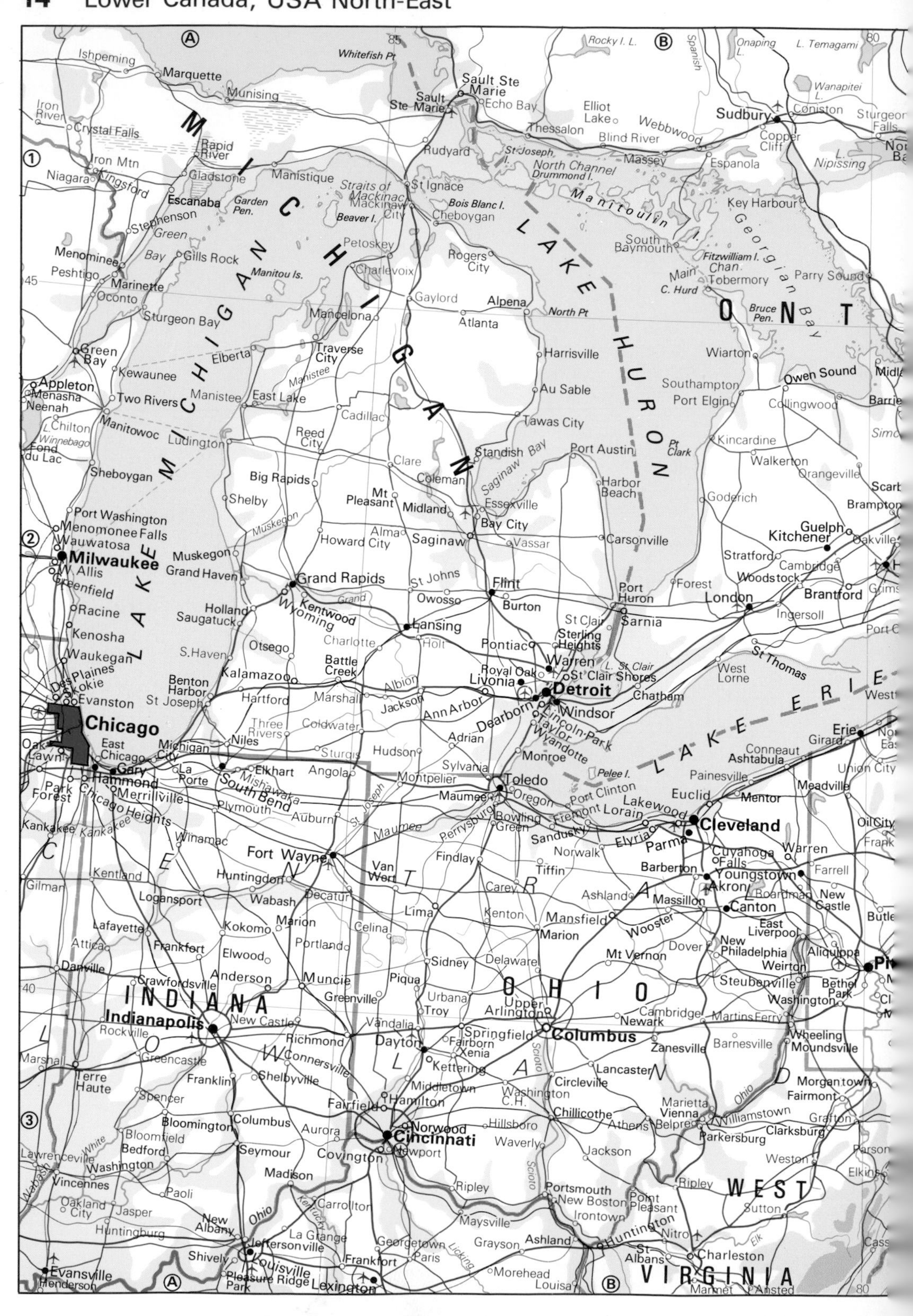

A
B
1
2
3
85
80
45
40
MICHIGAN
LAKE MICHIGAN
LAKE HURON
LAKE ERIE
ONT
INDIANA
OHIO
CENTRAL
LOWLAND
WEST
VIRGINIA
Ishpeming
Marquette
Munising
Whitefish Pt
Sault Ste Marie
Echo Bay
Rocky L. L.
Spanish
Onaping L.
L. Temagami
Wanapitei L.
Sudbury
Coniston
Sturgeon Falls
Copper Cliff
Elliot Lake
Webbwood
Thessalon
Blind River
Massey
Espanola
L. Nipissing
Iron River
Crystal Falls
Rapid River
Iron Mtn
Kingsford
Niagara
Gladstone
Manistique
Rudyard
St Joseph I.
North Channel
Drummond I.
Straits of Mackinac
St Ignace
Mackinaw City
Escanaba
Garden Pen.
Beaver I.
Bois Blanc I.
Cheboygan
Manitoulin I.
Key Harbour
Georgian Bay
Stephenson
Green Bay
Menominee
Gills Rock
Petoskey
Rogers City
South Baymouth
Fitzwilliam I.
Main Chan.
Tobermory
C. Hurd
Parry Sound
Peshtigo
Marinette
Oconto
Manitou Is.
Charlevoix
Gaylord
Alpena
North Pt
Bruce Pen.
Sturgeon Bay
Mancelona
Atlanta
Green Bay
Elberta
Traverse City
Harrisville
Wiarton
Appleton
Menasha
Neenah
Kewaunee
Two Rivers
Manistee
East Lake
Au Sable
Southampton
Port Elgin
Owen Sound
Collingwood
Barrie
Midland
L. Chilton
Winnebago
Fond du Lac
Manitowoc
Ludington
Cadillac
Reed City
Tawas City
Kincardine
Walkerton
Orangeville
Simcoe
Sheboygan
Clare
Standish
Saginaw Bay
Port Austin
Pt Clark
Big Rapids
Coleman
Harbor Beach
Goderich
Scarborough
Brampton
Shelby
Mt Pleasant
Midland
Essexville
Port Washington
Menomonee Falls
Muskegon
Alma
Bay City
Guelph
Kitchener
Oakville
Wauwatosa
Howard City
Saginaw
Vassar
Carsonville
Milwaukee
W. Allis
Greenfield
Grand Haven
Grand Rapids
St Johns
Flint
Stratford
Cambridge
Woodstock
Brantford
Hamilton
Grimsby
Racine
Holland
Saugatuck
Kentwood
Wyoming
Owosso
Burton
Port Huron
Sarnia
Forest
London
Ingersoll
Kenosha
Lansing
St Clair
Port Colborne
Waukegan
S. Haven
Otsego
Charlotte
Holt
Pontiac
Sterling Heights
Warren
St Thomas
Des Plaines
Skokie
Evanston
Benton Harbor
St Joseph
Kalamazoo
Battle Creek
Albion
Royal Oak
Livonia
L. St Clair
St Clair Shores
Detroit
West Lorne
Chatham
Chicago
Hartford
Marshall
Jackson
Ann Arbor
Dearborn
Windsor
Taylor
Lincoln Park
Wyandotte
Oak Lawn
East Chicago
Michigan City
Three Rivers
Coldwater
Adrian
Gary
Hammond
Niles
Sturgis
Hudson
Monroe
Erie
Girard
Conneaut
Ashtabula
Union City
Park Forest
La Porte
Elkhart
Mishawaka
South Bend
Angola
Montpelier
Sylvania
Toledo
Pelee I.
Painesville
Meadville
Chicago Heights
Merrillville
Plymouth
Auburn
Maumee
Oregon
Port Clinton
Euclid
Mentor
Kankakee
Fremont
Lorain
Lakewood
Cleveland
Oil City
Winamac
Fort Wayne
St Joseph
Perrysburg
Bowling Green
Sandusky
Elyria
Parma
Franklin
Van Wert
Findlay
Norwalk
Cuyahoga Falls
Warren
Kentland
Huntingdon
Tiffin
Barberton
Youngstown
Farrell
Gilman
Logansport
Wabash
Decatur
Carey
Ashland
Akron
Boardman
New Castle
Lima
Kenton
Massillon
Canton
Lafayette
Kokomo
Marion
Celina
Mansfield
Marion
Wooster
East Liverpool
Butler
Attica
Frankfort
Portland
Elwood
Delaware
Mt Vernon
Dover
New Philadelphia
Aliquippa
Danville
Crawfordsville
Anderson
Sidney
Weirton
Pittsburgh
Muncie
Piqua
Steubenville
Bethel Park
Greenville
Urbana
Washington
Indianapolis
New Castle
Troy
Upper Arlington
Cambridge
Newark
Martins Ferry
Rockville
Richmond
Vandalia
Dayton
Springfield
Columbus
Wheeling
Moundsville
Marshall
Greencastle
Connersville
Fairborn
Xenia
Zanesville
Barnesville
Terre Haute
Franklin
Shelbyville
Kettering
Lancaster
Middletown
Circleville
Washington C.H.
Scioto
Morgantown
Fairmont
Spencer
Hamilton
Fairfield
Marietta
Vienna
Belpre
Williamstown
Grafton
Bloomington
Columbus
Norwood
Hillsboro
Chillicothe
Athens
Parkersburg
Clarksburg
Bloomfield
White
Bedford
Aurora
Cincinnati
Waverly
Lawrenceville
Washington
Seymour
Covington
Newport
Jackson
Weston
Elkins
Vincennes
Wabash
Madison
Ripley
Ripley
Paoli
Portsmouth
New Boston
Point Pleasant
Oakland City
Jasper
Carrollton
Kentucky
Maysville
Ironton
Sutton
Huntingburg
New Albany
Ohio
La Grange
Huntington
Nitro
Elk
Jeffersonville
Georgetown
Grayson
Ashland
Shively
Louisville
Frankfort
Paris
Licking
St Albans
Charleston
Evansville
Henderson
Pleasure Ridge Park
Lexington
Morehead
Louisa
Marmet
Ansted

1:5M 0 50 100 150 200 km 0 50 100 mls

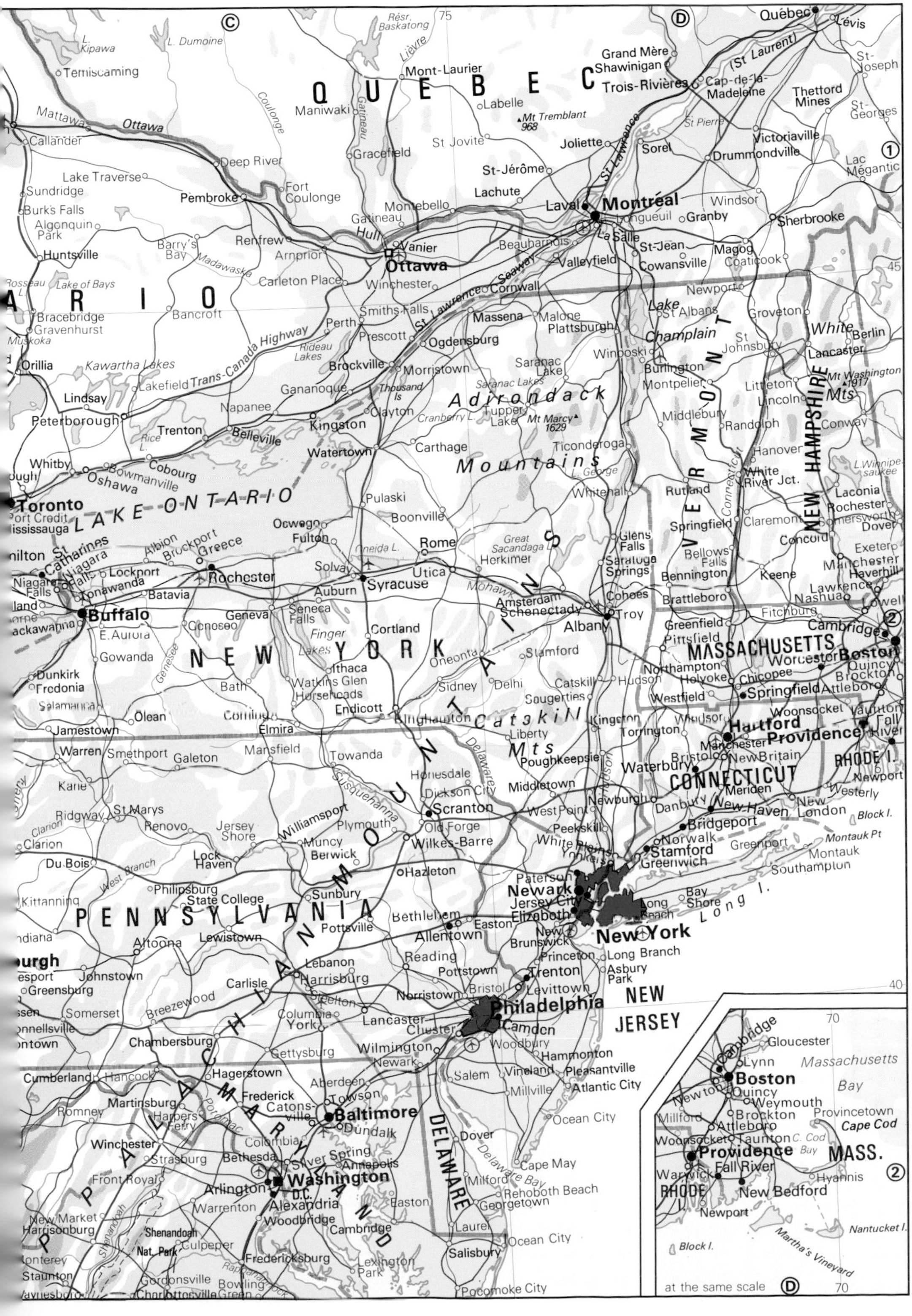

QUEBEC
Québec
Lévis
Grand Mère
Shawinigan
Trois-Rivières
Cap-de-la-Madeleine
Thetford Mines
St-Joseph
St-Georges
Mont-Laurier
Maniwaki
Labelle
Mt Tremblant 968
St Jovite
Joliette
Sorel
Victoriaville
Drummondville
Lac Mégantic
St-Jérôme
Lachute
Laval
Montréal
Longueuil
Granby
Windsor
Sherbrooke
Magog
Coaticook
St-Jean
Cowansville
La Salle
Valleyfield
Beauharnois
Gatineau
Hull
Vanier
Ottawa
Montebello
Gracefield
Temiscaming
L. Kipawa
L. Dumoine
Rés. Baskatong
Mattawa
Callander
Deep River
Lake Traverse
Sundridge
Burk's Falls
Algonquin Park
Pembroke
Fort Coulonge
Huntsville
Barry's Bay
Renfrew
Arnprior
Carleton Place
Winchester
Cornwall
Smiths Falls
Perth
Prescott
Brockville
Ogdensburg
Massena
Malone
Plattsburgh
ONTARIO
Bracebridge
Gravenhurst
Muskoka
Bancroft
Orillia
Kawartha Lakes
Lakefield
Lindsay
Peterborough
Trenton
Belleville
Napanee
Kingston
Gananoque
Thousand Is
Clayton
Morristown
Watertown
Carthage
Whitby
Oshawa
Bowmanville
Cobourg
Toronto
Port Credit
Mississauga
LAKE ONTARIO
Trans-Canada Highway
St Lawrence Seaway
Ottawa
Lake Champlain
Burlington
Winooski
Montpelier
Middlebury
Randolph
Rutland
Springfield
Bellows Falls
Bennington
Brattleboro
VERMONT
St Albans
Newport
St Johnsbury
Groveton
Berlin
Lancaster
White Mts
Mt Washington 1917
Littleton
Lincoln
Conway
Hanover
White River Jct.
Laconia
Rochester
Claremont
Concord
Dover
Exeter
Manchester
Keene
Nashua
Lawrence
Haverhill
Lowell
NEW HAMPSHIRE
L. Winnipesaukee
Adirondack Mountains
Saranac Lake
Tupper Lake
Mt Marcy 1629
Ticonderoga
L. George
Whitehall
Glens Falls
Saratoga Springs
Great Sacandaga L.
Cohoes
Troy
Albany
Schenectady
Amsterdam
Herkimer
Utica
Rome
Oneida L.
Syracuse
Oswego
Fulton
Pulaski
Boonville
Solvay
Auburn
Seneca Falls
Geneva
Rochester
Greece
Brockport
Albion
Lockport
Niagara Falls
St Catharines
Tonawanda
Batavia
Buffalo
Lackawanna
E. Aurora
Gowanda
Geneseo
Finger Lakes
Cortland
Ithaca
Watkins Glen
Horseheads
Bath
Corning
Elmira
Endicott
Binghamton
Oneonta
Sidney
Delhi
Stamford
Catskill
Hudson
Saugerties
Kingston
Catskill Mts
Liberty
Poughkeepsie
Middletown
Newburgh
West Point
Peekskill
White Plains
Yonkers
NEW YORK
Dunkirk
Fredonia
Salamanca
Olean
Jamestown
Warren
Smethport
Galeton
Mansfield
Towanda
Kane
Ridgway
St Marys
Renovo
Jersey Shore
Williamsport
Lock Haven
Muncy
Berwick
Plymouth
Wilkes-Barre
Scranton
Old Forge
Honesdale
Dickson City
Hazleton
Clarion
Du Bois
Philipsburg
State College
Kittanning
Sunbury
Pottsville
Bethlehem
Easton
Allentown
Reading
Pottstown
Norristown
Lebanon
Harrisburg
Carlisle
Steelton
Lewistown
Altoona
Johnstown
Greensburg
Somerset
Connellsville
Breezewood
Chambersburg
Gettysburg
Columbia
York
Lancaster
Chester
Philadelphia
Camden
Bristol
Levittown
Trenton
PENNSYLVANIA
APPALACHIAN MOUNTAINS
Susquehanna
Delaware
Paterson
Newark
Jersey City
Elizabeth
New Brunswick
Princeton
New York
Long Beach
Long Branch
Asbury Park
NEW JERSEY
Woodbury
Hammonton
Pleasantville
Atlantic City
Vineland
Millville
Salem
Ocean City
Cape May
Delaware Bay
Wilmington
Newark
Aberdeen
Towson
Baltimore
Dundalk
Catonsville
Frederick
Hagerstown
Cumberland
Hancock
Martinsburg
Harpers Ferry
Romney
Winchester
Strasburg
Front Royal
Columbia
Bethesda
Silver Spring
Annapolis
Washington D.C.
Arlington
Alexandria
Warrenton
Woodbridge
Fredericksburg
Culpeper
Shenandoah Nat. Park
New Market
Harrisonburg
Staunton
Gordonsville
Charlottesville
Bowling Green
MARYLAND
DELAWARE
Dover
Milford
Rehoboth Beach
Georgetown
Easton
Cambridge
Laurel
Salisbury
Ocean City
Pocomoke City
Lexington Park
MASSACHUSETTS
Greenfield
Pittsfield
Northampton
Holyoke
Chicopee
Springfield
Westfield
Worcester
Fitchburg
Cambridge
Boston
Quincy
Brockton
Attleboro
Woonsocket
Providence
Taunton
Fall River
RHODE I.
Newport
Westerly
Block I.
Hartford
Manchester
New Britain
Bristol
Windsor
Torrington
Waterbury
Meriden
Danbury
New Haven
New London
Bridgeport
Norwalk
Stamford
Greenwich
CONNECTICUT
Greenport
Montauk Pt
Montauk
Southampton
Bay Shore
Long I.
Gloucester
Lynn
Massachusetts Bay
Newton
Weymouth
Millford
Provincetown
Cape Cod
C. Cod Bay
MASS.
Warwick
Hyannis
New Bedford
Nantucket I.
Martha's Vineyard
at the same scale

25 50 75 100 km
25 50 mils

MASSACHUSETTS · **NEW YORK** · **CONNECTICUT** · **RHODE ISLAND** · **NEW JERSEY** · **PENN.** · **MARYLAND** · **NEW JERSEY**

Boston · Cambridge · Worcester · Springfield · Hartford · Providence · Pawtucket · Fall River · New Bedford · Newport · New Haven · Bridgeport · New York · Newark · Jersey City · Elizabeth · Albany · Pittsfield · Poughkeepsie · Stamford

Catskill Mountains · *Long Island Sound* · *Long Island* · *Great South Bay* · *Block Island Sd* · *Block Island* · *Rhode Island Sound* · *Martha's Vineyard* · *Buzzards Bay* · *Vineyard Haven* · *Nomans Land* · *Montauk Pt* · *Montauk* · *Gardiners I.* · *Fishers I.* · Massachusetts Bay · Quincy Bay

ATLANTIC OCEAN

Philadelphia · Camden · Trenton · Baltimore · Washington D.C. · Allentown · Bethlehem · Reading · Lancaster · York · Harrisburg · Wilmington · Atlantic City · Cape May · Arlington · Alexandria

Blue Mtn · *Blue Mtn* · *Delaware Bay* · *Raritan Bay* · *Barnegat Bay* · *Great Bay* · *Little Egg Harbor* · *Great Egg Harbor*

ATLANTIC OCEAN

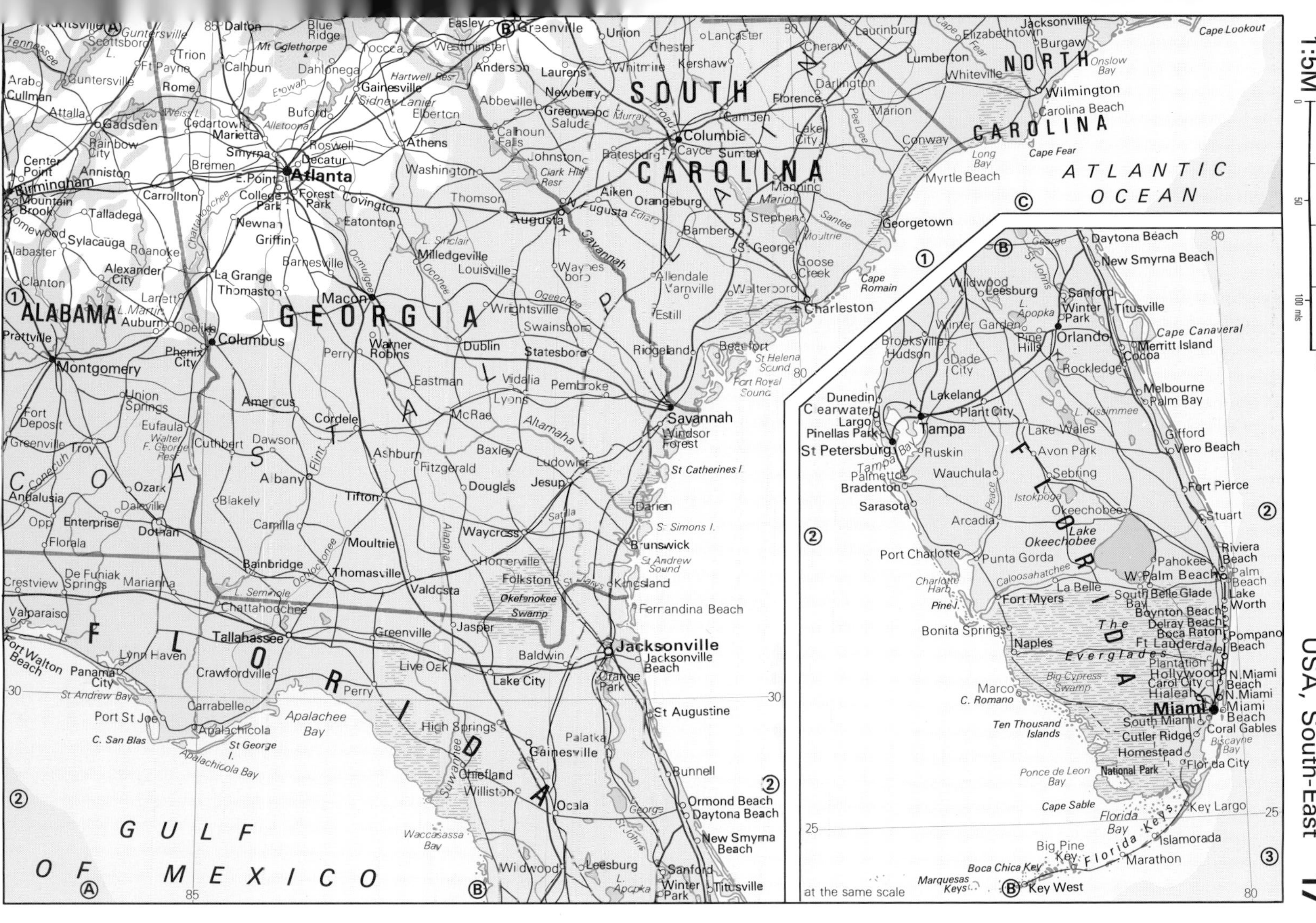
ATLANTIC OCEAN
GULF OF MEXICO
NORTH CAROLINA
SOUTH CAROLINA
GEORGIA
FLORIDA
ALABAMA
COASTAL PLAIN
Cape Lookout
Cape Fear
Onslow Bay
Long Bay
Cape Romain
Jacksonville
Wilmington
Carolina Beach
Burgaw
Elizabethtown
Whiteville
Lumberton
Laurinburg
Myrtle Beach
Conway
Marion
Georgetown
Darlington
Cheraw
Florence
Lake City
Charleston
Goose Creek
Manning
Sumter
Camden
Lancaster
Columbia
Cayce
Orangeburg
Bamberg
St Stephen
St George
Walterboro
Beaufort
St Helena Sound
Port Royal Sound
Allendale
Varnville
Estill
Ridgeland
Savannah
Windsor Forest
St Catherines I.
Aiken
Augusta
Batesburg
Chester
Kershaw
Union
Whitmire
Newberry
Greenwood
Saluda
Laurens
Greenville
Easley
Westminster
Anderson
Abbeville
Calhoun Falls
Johnston
Clark Hill Resr
Hartwell Res.
Athens
Elberton
Washington
Thomson
Milledgeville
Louisville
Wrightsville
Swainsboro
Statesboro
Waynesboro
Pembroke
Vidalia
Lyons
Dublin
Eastman
McRae
Baxley
Jesup
Ludowici
Darien
St Simons I.
Brunswick
St Andrew Sound
Kingsland
Folkston
Okefenokee Swamp
Homerville
Waycross
Douglas
Fitzgerald
Ashburn
Tifton
Moultrie
Valdosta
Thomasville
Bainbridge
Albany
Camilla
Blakely
Dawson
Cuthbert
Americus
Cordele
Perry
Macon
Warner Robins
Atlanta
Decatur
Roswell
Marietta
Smyrna
College Park
Forest Park
E. Point
Covington
Eatonton
Griffin
Barnesville
Newnan
Thomaston
La Grange
Columbus
Dalton
Calhoun
Rome
Cedartown
Carrollton
Bremen
Gainesville
Toccoa
Dahlonega
Blue Ridge
Buford
Mt Oglethorpe
Trion
Birmingham
Gadsden
Anniston
Talladega
Sylacauga
Alexander City
Roanoke
Lanett
Opelika
Auburn
Phenix City
Montgomery
Prattville
Clanton
Cullman
Arab
Attalla
Rainbow City
Center Point
Scottsboro
Guntersville
Troy
Union Springs
Eufaula
Walter F. George Resr
Ozark
Dothan
Daleville
Enterprise
Andalusia
Opp
Florala
Greenville
Fort Deposit
Marianna
Chattahoochee
L. Seminole
Tallahassee
Crawfordville
Apalachicola
Apalachicola Bay
St George I.
Carrabelle
Apalachee Bay
Port St Joe
C. San Blas
St Andrew Bay
Panama City
Lynn Haven
De Funiak Springs
Crestview
Valparaiso
Fort Walton Beach
Perry
Live Oak
Lake City
Jasper
Greenville
High Springs
Gainesville
Chiefland
Williston
Waccasassa Bay
Ocala
Palatka
Baldwin
Jacksonville
Jacksonville Beach
Orange Park
Fernandina Beach
St Augustine
Bunnell
Ormond Beach
Daytona Beach
New Smyrna Beach
Titusville
Sanford
Winter Park
Leesburg
Wildwood
Orlando
Winter Garden
Pine Hills
Cape Canaveral
Merritt Island
Cocoa
Rockledge
Melbourne
Palm Bay
Gifford
Vero Beach
Fort Pierce
Stuart
Riviera Beach
Palm Beach
W. Palm Beach
Lake Worth
Boynton Beach
Delray Beach
Boca Raton
Pompano Beach
Ft Lauderdale
Plantation
Hollywood
Carol City
Hialeah
N. Miami Beach
N. Miami
Miami
Miami Beach
South Miami
Coral Gables
Biscayne Bay
Cutler Ridge
Homestead
Florida City
Key Largo
Florida Bay
Florida Keys
Islamorada
Marathon
Big Pine Key
Boca Chica Key
Key West
Marquesas Keys
Tampa
St Petersburg
Clearwater
Largo
Pinellas Park
Dunedin
Brooksville
Hudson
Dade City
Lakeland
Plant City
Lake Wales
Avon Park
Sebring
Wauchula
Ruskin
Palmetto
Bradenton
Sarasota
Arcadia
Port Charlotte
Punta Gorda
Charlotte Harb.
Pine I.
Fort Myers
La Belle
Okeechobee
Lake Okeechobee
Pahokee
South Bay
Belle Glade
Bonita Springs
Naples
Marco
C. Romano
The Everglades
Big Cypress Swamp
National Park
Cape Sable
Ponce de Leon Bay
Ten Thousand Islands
at the same scale

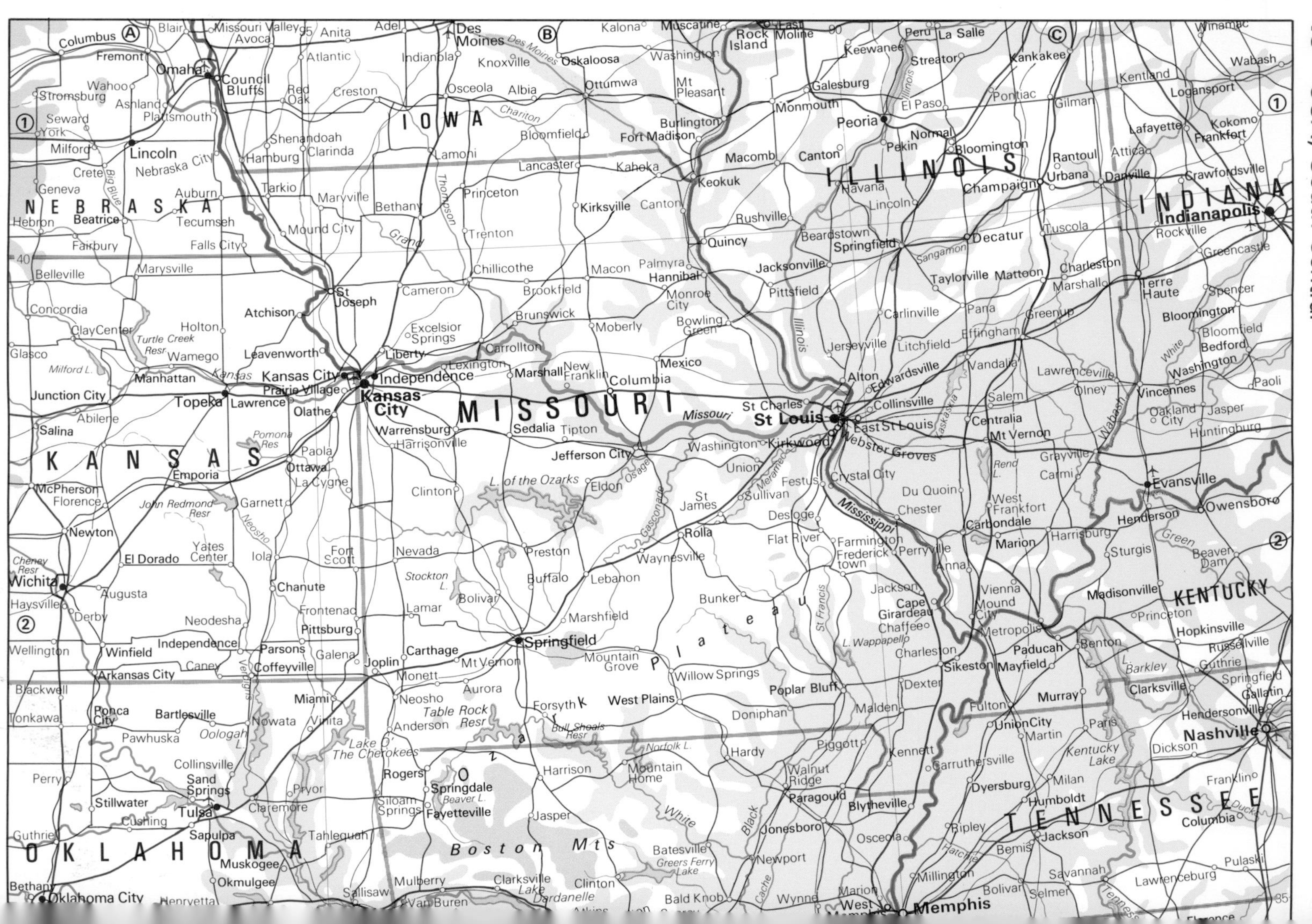

NEBRASKA
IOWA
ILLINOIS
INDIANA
KANSAS
MISSOURI
KENTUCKY
TENNESSEE
OKLAHOMA
Ozark Plateau
Boston Mts
Omaha
Lincoln
Des Moines
Peoria
Springfield
Decatur
Champaign
Indianapolis
Kansas City
Independence
Topeka
St Louis
Columbia
Jefferson City
Evansville
Owensboro
Wichita
Tulsa
Oklahoma City
Memphis
Nashville
Paducah
Mississippi
Missouri
Illinois
Wabash
L. of the Ozarks
Table Rock Resr
Kentucky Lake

Scale bar: 0 50 100 150 200 km / 0 50 100 mils

States

ALABAMA ③
MISSISSIPPI
LOUISIANA
ARKANSAS
TEXAS
OKLAHOMA

Major cities and towns

Athens, Lewis Smith, Birmingham, Bessemer, Centreville, Cullman, Hartselle, Decatur, Tuscumbia, Sheffield, Russellville, Hamilton, Winfield, Jasper, Sipsey, Demopolis, Grove Hill, Marion, Black Warrior, Cahaba, Tombigbee, Alabama

Russellville, New Albany, Tupelo, Aberdeen, West Point, Starkville, Columbus, Louisville, Philadelphia, Meridian, Waynesboro, Jackson, Mt Vernon, Lucedale, Citronelle, Prichard, Mobile, Mobile Bay, Mobile Pt, Dauphin I., Pascagoula, Horn I.

Corinth, Holly Springs, Southaven, Senatobia, Oxford, Pontotoc, Houston, Grenada, Eupora, Winona, Kosciusko, Canton, Forest, Newton, Laurel, Hattiesburg, Collins, Columbia, Purvis, Poplarville, Picayune, Wiggins, Ocean Springs, Biloxi, Gulfport, Breton Sound, Chandeleur Is, Mississippi Delta

Batesville, Clarksdale, Cleveland, Greenwood, Indianola, Leland, Greenville, Yazoo City, Jackson, Hazlehurst, Brookhaven, McComb, Magnolia, Kentwood, Bogalusa, Bude, Natchez, Port Gibson, Vicksburg, Clinton, Ross Barnett Resr, Big Black, Pearl, Yazoo, Leaf, Chickasawhay

Covington, Slidell, Laplace, New Orleans, Gretna, Marrero, Kenner, Metairie, Thibodaux, Houma, Golden Meadow, Lake Pontchartrain, Hammond, Baton Rouge, Port Allen, New Iberia, Jeanerette, Patterson, Morgan City, Breton Sound, Grand Isle, West Bay, East Bay, Fort Sulphur, Pilottown, Timbalier Bay, Terre Bonne Bay, Atchafalaya Bay, Marsh I.

Helena, Brinkley, Forrest City, Stuttgart, De Witt, Clarendon, Monticello, McGehee, Dumas, Lake Village, Tallulah, St Joseph, Ferriday, Jonesville, Pineville, Alexandria, Bunkie, Ville Platte, Opelousas, Lafayette, Abbeville, Kaplan, Crowley, Jennings, Eunice, Kinder, Lake Charles, Sulphur, Leesville, De Ridder, Jasper, Woodville, Livingston, Cleveland, Liberty, Dayton, Beaumont, Orange, Port Arthur, Silsbee, High Island, Galveston Bay, Pecan Island

Little Rock, North Little Rock, Benton, Sheridan, Malvern, Hot Springs, Arkadelphia, Pine Bluff, Warren, Fordyce, Hampton, El Dorado, Camden, Magnolia, Crossett, Hamburg, Bastrop, Monroe, Ruston, Winnfield, Colfax, Natchitoches, Many, Mansfield, Logansport, Pineland, Jasper, Hornbeck, Toledo Bend Resr

Mansfield, McAlester, Hartshorne, Mena, Glenwood, Nashville, Hope, Prescott, Lewisville, Minden, Bossier City, Shreveport, Marshall, Longview, Kilgore, Henderson, Rusk, Nacogdoches, Lufkin, Corrigan, Livingston, Conroe, Huntsville, Madisonville, Crockett, Palestine, Athens, Tyler, Mineola, Canton, Jacksonville

Poteau, Wilburton, McAlester, Atoka, Stonewall, Ada, Sulphur, Tishomingo, Durant, Antlers, Hugo, Broken Bow, Idabel, De Queen, Ashdown, Texarkana, Naples, Mt Pleasant, Paris, Bonham, Sherman, Denison, McKinney, Greenville, Terrell, Dallas, Garland, Mesquite, Richardson, Plano, Fort Worth, Arlington, Grand Prairie, Cleburne, Glen Rose, Waxahachie, Ennis, Corsicana, Hillsboro, Waco, Mexia, Marlin, Temple, Belton, Killeen, Gatesville

Norman, Purcell, Wewoka, Holdenville, Paul's Valley, Ardmore, Marietta, Gainesville, Bowie, Nocona, Bridgeport, Weatherford, Denton, Lake Texoma, Bryan, College Station, Navasota, Hempstead, Brenham, La Grange, Columbus, Houston, Bellaire, Pasadena, Baytown, La Marque, Texas City, Alvin, Angleton, Freeport, Lake Jackson, Bay City, Wharton, El Campo, Edna, Yoakum, Gonzales, Cuero, Luling, Austin, Bastrop, Smithville, Georgetown, Taylor, Cameron, Hearne, Somerville Resr, Brazos, Colorado

Rivers and natural features

Ouachita Mts, Ouachita, Arkansas, Saline, Little, Broken Bow Resr, Eagle Mtn Lake, Garza Little Elm Resr, Lake Lewisville, Lake Texoma, Sam Rayburn Resr, Neches, Sabine, Trinity, Cedar Creek Resr, Navasota, Brazos, Colorado, Guadalupe, Atchafalaya, Calcasieu, Sabine L., White L., Grand L., Pecan Island, Marsh I.

35, 30, 30, 90

1:5M

0 50 100 150 200 km
0 50 100 mls

A (125) (B) (C)

CANADA

Parksville · Gibsons · Vancouver · Princeton · 120 · Okanagan Falls · Keremeos · Castlegar · Salmo
Port Alberni · Horseshoe Bay · Hope · Oliver · Osoyoos · Grand Forks · Trail · Creston
Nanaimo · Vancouver · New Westminster · Agassiz · Chilliwack · Metaline Falls · Bonners Ferry
Ladysmith · Blaine · Abbotsford · North Cascades · Ross L. · Okanagan River Ra. · Ione · Priest · Sandpoint
Cowichan · Ferndale · Bellingham · Mt Baker 3285 · Otoville · Tonasket · Colville · Pend Oreille · Spirit Lake
Duncan · Sidney · Burlington · Nat. · Mt Logan 2733 · Republic · Omak · Franklin D. Roosevelt Lake · Newport · Priest River · Coeur d'Alene
Victoria · Anacortes · Skagit · Concrete · Park · Okanogan · Columbia · Kellogg
Esquimalt · San Juan Is. · Mt Vernon · Glacier Peak 3221 · Brewster · Grand Coulee · Spokane · (1)
C. Flattery · Str. of Juan de Fuca · Port Angeles · Marysville · L. Chelan · Medical Lake · Cheney · Plummer
Forks · Olympic Nat. Park · Everett · Snohomish · Chelan · Banks L. · Wilbur · St Joe
Edmonds · Monroe · **WASHINGTON** · Odessa · Ritzville · Maries
Mt Olympus 2428 · Bellevue · Seattle · Renton · Snoqualmie Pass · Wenatchee · Ephrata · Moses Lake
Bremerton · Kent · Auburn · Colfax · Potlatch
Port Orchard · Tacoma · Puyallup · Ellensburg · Othello · Pullman · Moscow · Kendrick
Shelton · Olympia · Mt Rainier 4392 · Mount Rainier Nat. Park · Yakima · Naches · Selah · Eltopia · Clarkston · Lewiston
Hoquiam · Aberdeen · Centralia · Yakima · Sunnyside · Richland · Pasco · Dayton · Walla Walla
Grays Harb. · Raymond · Chehalis · Toppenish · Kennewick · Wenatchee
Willapa B. · South Bend · Winlock · Cowlitz · Goldendale · Columbia · Umatilla · Blue Mountains
C. Disappointment · Longview · Kelso · Mt St Helens 2950 · Mt Adams 3751 · Wallowa · Riggins
Astoria · Rainier · Woodland · White Salmon · The Dalles · Arlington · Echo · Pendleton · Enterprise · He Devil Mtn 2863
Seaside · St Helens · Vancouver · Camas · Hood River · Ukiah · La Grande · Wallowa Mts · Sacajawea 2997 Pk
Portland · Hillsboro · Gresham · Condon · John Day · Baker · Midvale
45 · Tillamook · Lake Oswego · Oregon City · Mt Hood 3427 · Spray · 45
Lincoln City · Newberg · Woodburn · Mt Wilson 1707 · Long Creek · Weiser
McMinnville · Salem · Deschutes · Mt Jefferson 3199 · Madras · Dayville · Unity · Payette · Ontario
Newport · Corvallis · Stayton · Idanha · Prineville · Canyon City · John Day · Vale · Nyssa
Yachats · Albany · Lebanon · Sweet Home · Redmond · **OREGON** · Emmett
Florence · Eugene · Springfield · Three Sisters 3156 · Bend · Brothers · Long Creek · Caldwell · Nampa
Cottage Grove · Lowell · La Pine · Burns · Crane · Drewsey
Reedsport · Oakridge · Crescent · High Desert · Harney Basin · Jordan Valley · Murphy
125 · Coos Bay · N.Bend · Oakland · Silver Lake · Harney L. · Malheur L. · Owyhee Mts
Myrtle Point · Roseburg · Mt Thielsen 2799 · Columbia · Plateau
C. Blanco · Myrtle Creek · Crater · Steens Mtn · Owyhee
Port Orford · Canyonville · Prospect · Nat. Pk. · Mt Scott 2721 · Chiloquin · Upper Klamath · Valley Falls · Denio · McDermitt
(2) · Gold Beach · Wolf Creek · Grants Pass · McLoughlin 2894 · Bly · Lakeview
Central Point · Medford · Ashland · Klamath Falls · Warner Mts
Brookings · O'Brien · Hornbrook · Dorris · Willow Ranch · Upper L. · Santa Rosa Ra. · Osgood Mts
Pt St George · Crescent City · Yreka · Clear L. Resr · Goose L. · Black Rock Desert · Goleconda
Klamath · Weed · Canby · Middle Alturas · **NEVADA** · Winnemucca
Humboldt Bay · Mt Shasta 4317 · Alkali L. · Humboldt
Eureka · Arcata · Klamath Mts · Mount Shasta · Adin · Rye Patch Resr · Battle Mountain
Fortuna · **CALIFORNIA** · Dunsmuir · Shasta · Pit · Imlay
C. Mendocino · (B) · Weaverville · Redding · Nat. Pk. 3187 · Susanville · (C) · Mt Tobin 2979
Project City · Burney · Lassen Pk · Eagle L. · 120

1:5M

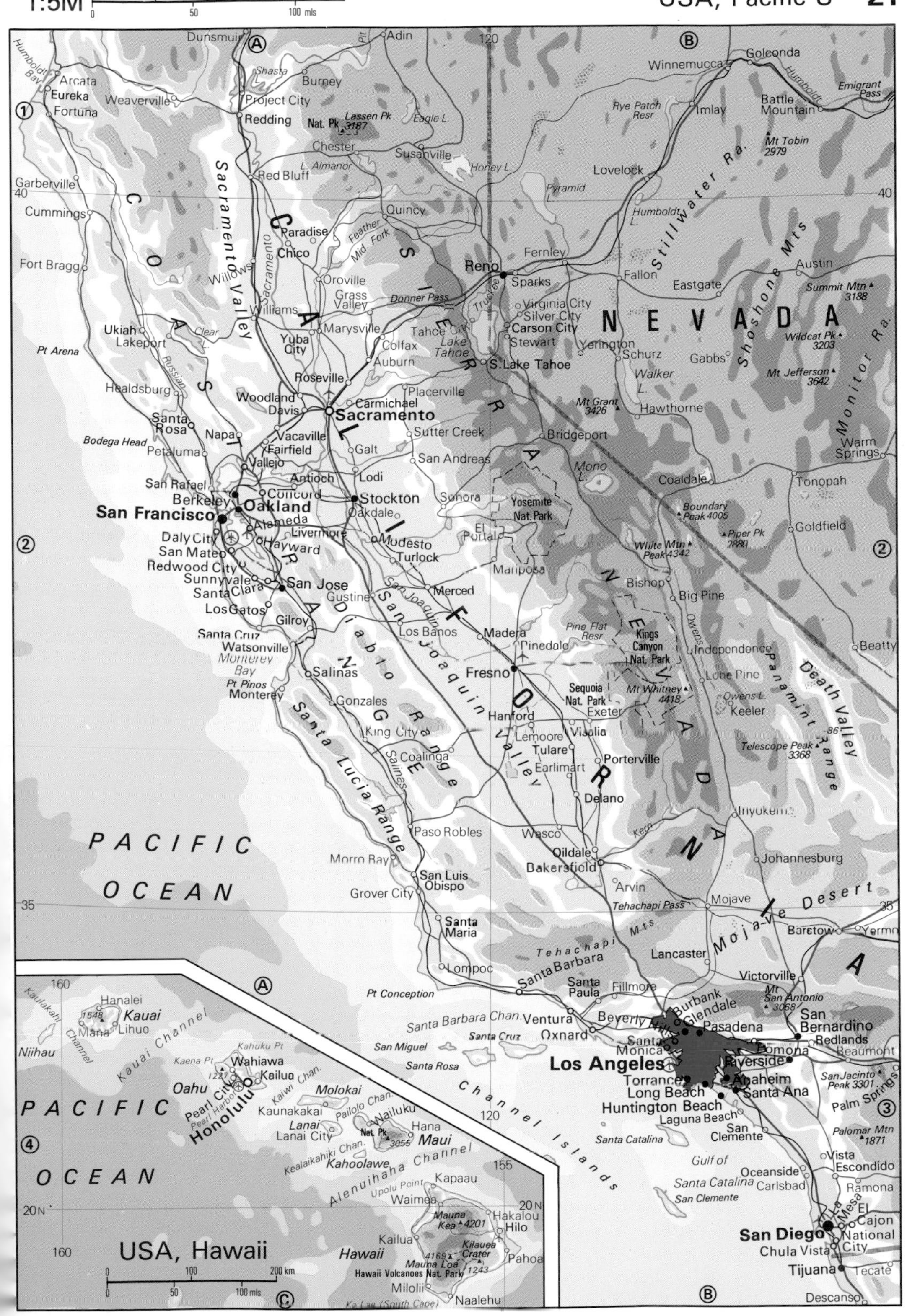

USA, Hawaii

1:2.5M

0 25 50 75 100 km
0 25 50 mls

Lytton Calistoga Woodland Folsom Placerville Camino
Healdsburg L. Berryessa Diamond Springs Folsom Markleeville Topaz
Forestville St Helena Winters Davis **Sacramento** Highland Pk Coleville
Santa Yountville Dixon Elk Grove Plymouth 3333 Devils Gate
Rosa Napa Sutter Ck West Pt Bear Valley 2301
Sebastopol Vacaville Elmira Galt Jackson Dardanelle Bridgeport
Petaluma Fairfield Lodi Mokelumne Arnold Sonora Pass Bridgeport
Novato Vallejo Isleton Clements Hill Murphys Pinecrest Excelsior Mtn
San Rafael S. Pablo B Pittsburg Antioch San Andreas Sonora Tioga
Mill Valley Concord Oakley Bellota Angels Camp Groveland Mt Dana
Berkeley Richmond Mt Diablo Byron Stockton Melones Resr Mather 3978
Golden Gate Oakland 1173 Brentwood Farmington Oakdale Mt Lyell June
San Francisco Alameda San Leandro Tracy Riverbank Modesto 3997 Lake
Daly City San Hayward Ripon Don Pedro Coulterville Mt Ritter 4010
S. San Francisco Francisco Pleasanton Manteca Resr El Portal Devil
San Mateo Bay Livermore Ceres McClure Postpile
Redwood City Fremont Patterson Turlock Snelling Wawona N.M.
Palo Alto Mountain Calaveras Modesto Turlock L Merced Mariposa Fish Camp
Santa Clara View Resr Newman Yosemite Planada Bass Lake
Sunnyvale Mt Hamilton Gustine Merced Mariposa Resr Kaiser Pk
San Gregorio **San Jose** 1284 Los Banos Raymond Lakeshore 3146
Pescadero Coyote (Lick Observatory) Chowchilla Huntingtn L.
Los Gatos Volta Dos Palos Madera Friant Shaver L.
Boulder Creek Morgan Hill S. Luis Berenda Friant Dam Humphreys
Davenport Gilroy Resr Firebaugh Herndon Pine Flat Patterson Mtn
Santa Cruz Laveaga Pk Mendota Pinedale Resr 3489
Watsonville 1154 Clovis Piedra
Monterey Hollister Tres Pinos Kerman Fresno Sanger Minkler
Bay Castroville San Juan Helm Badger
Pacific Grove Salinas Bautista Alisal Selma Reedley
Carmel Seaside Gonzales Kingsburg Dinuba
Monterey Pinnacles N.M.
Carmel Valley

Sta Ynez Los Big Pine Mtn Gorman Rosamond L. Helendale
Lompoc Alamos 2081 Lake Hughes Lancaster Mirage L.
Buellton Los L. Cachuma Castaic Palmdale Adelanto
Pt Arguello Solvang Santa Barbara Ojai Acton Littlerock Victorville
Pt Conception Gaviota Goleta Carpinteria Fillmore Newhall Wrightwood Hesperia
Santa Santa Paula Moorpark San Gabriel Mts 3068
Barbara Ventura Camarillo San Fernando Mt Wilson Mt San Antonio San Bernardino
Santa Barbara Channel Oxnard Burbank 1740 Pasadena Upland
San Miguel Port Hueneme Glendale Pasadena Monrovia Colton Highland
Santa Rosa Anacapa Is **Los Angeles** Hollywood Pomona Ontario Redlands
Sta Cruz Chan. Santa Cruz Santa Monica Beverly Hills Whittier Riverside
Santa Inglewood Fullerton Corona
C h a n n e l Monica Torrance Lakewood Orange Santa Ana Perris
Bay Redondo Garden Santiago Pk
I s l a n d s Beach Long Beach Grove Costa Mesa 1736
Santa Barbara Huntington Beach Santa Ana Mts Elsinore
Newport Beach Elsinore
Santa Catalina Laguna Beach San Clemente
San Nicolas Avalon Gulf of Onofre Fall-
San Clemente Santa Oceanside brook
Outer Santa Barbara Channel Catalina Carlsbad Vista
San Pedro Channel Encinitas
P A C I F I C Del Mar
La Jolla
O C E A N **San Diego**

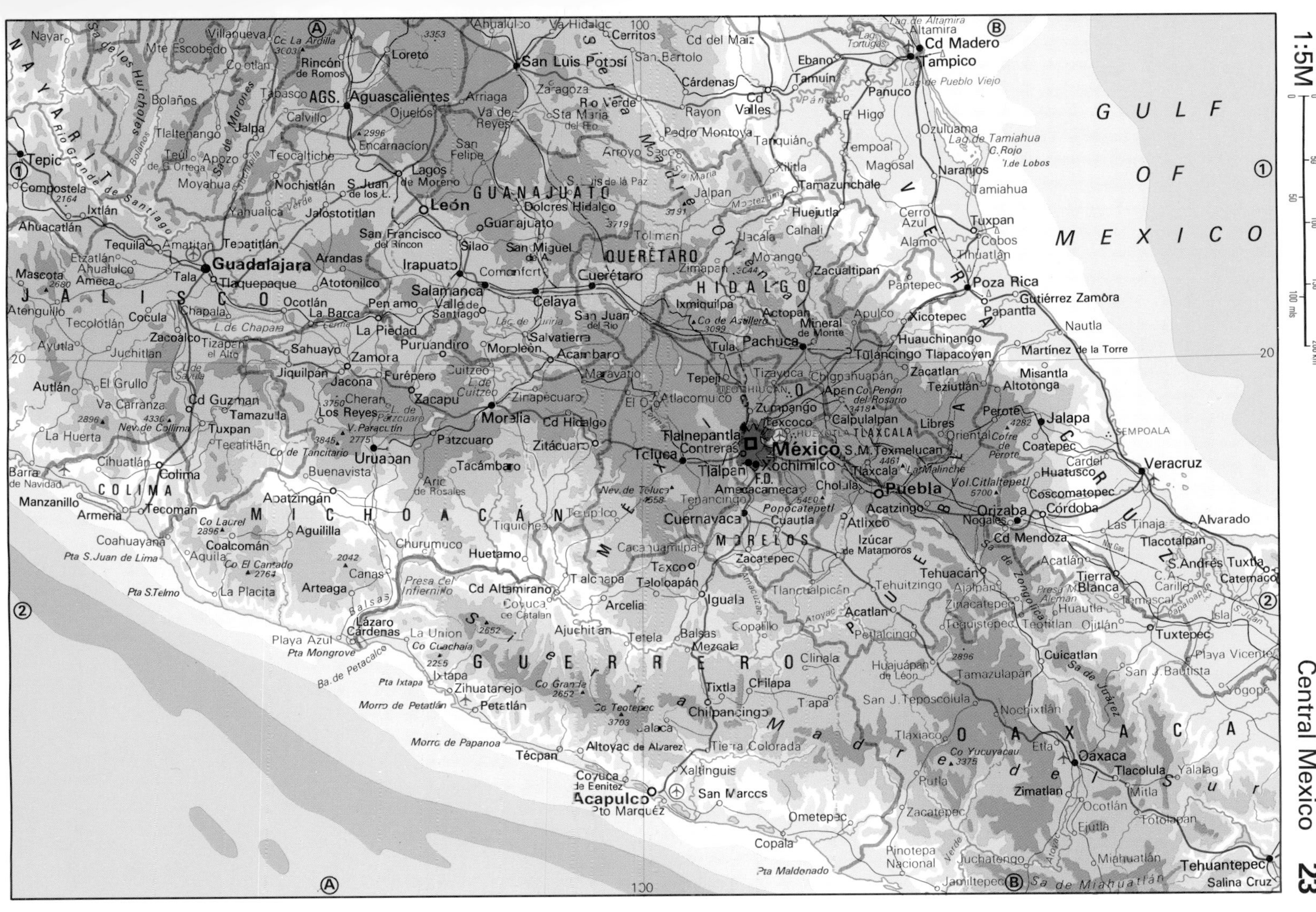

1:5M

50 100 150 200 km
50 100 mls

GULF OF MEXICO

Major cities and places

Tampico
Cd Madero
Veracruz
Tuxpan
Poza Rica
Papantla
Jalapa
Córdoba
Orizaba
Puebla
Tlaxcala
México
Xochimilco
Pachuca
Querétaro
Celaya
Guanajuato
León
Irapuato
Salamanca
Morelia
Uruapan
Guadalajara
Colima
Manzanillo
Acapulco
Chilpancingo
Cuernavaca
Toluca
Oaxaca
Tehuantepec
Salina Cruz
San Luis Potosí
Aguascalientes
Tepic

S I E R R A   M A D R E   O R I E N T A L

S I E R R A   M A D R E   D E L   S U R

J A L I S C O
GUANAJUATO
QUERÉTARO
HIDALGO
MICHOACÁN
MORELOS
GUERRERO
O A X A C A
COLIMA
N A Y A R I T

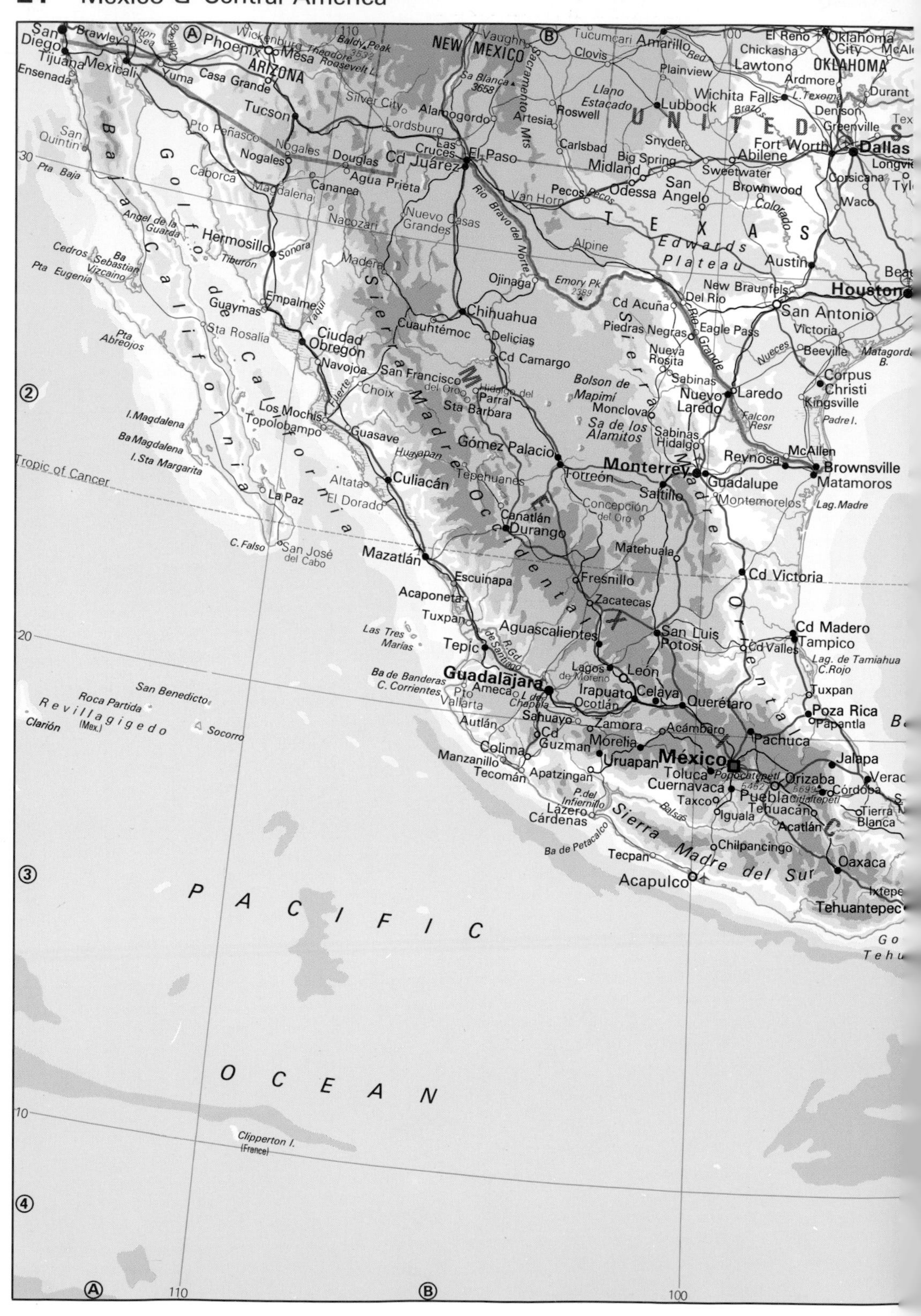
San Diego
Tijuana
Ensenada
Brawley
Salton Sea
Mexicali
Yuma
Phoenix
Mesa
Wickenburg
ARIZONA
Casa Grande
Tucson
Baldy Peak
Theodore Roosevelt L.
NEW MEXICO
Vaughn
Tucumcari
Amarillo
Clovis
Plainview
Chickasha
Lawton
Oklahoma City
OKLAHOMA
Ardmore
El Reno
Wichita Falls
L. Texoma
Durant
Denison
Greenville
Llano Estacado
Lubbock
Roswell
Artesia
Alamogordo
Silver City
Lordsburg
Las Cruces
El Paso
Cd Juárez
Sa Blanca
3658
Sacramento Mts
UNITED STATES
Snyder
Fort Worth
Dallas
Abilene
Sweetwater
Big Spring
Carlsbad
Midland
Odessa
San Angelo
Brownwood
Colorado
Corsicana
Waco
Longview
Tyler
Pecos
Van Horn
TEXAS
Edwards Plateau
Austin
Houston
New Braunfels
San Antonio
Del Rio
Alpine
Emory Pk
2389
Ojinaga
Rio Bravo del Norte
Nuevo Casas Grandes
Nacozari
Agua Prieta
Douglas
Cananea
Nogales
Magdalena
Caborca
Pto Peñasco
San Quintín
Pta Baja
Golfo de California
Baja California
Hermosillo
Sonora
Tiburón
Angel de la Guarda
Cedros
Ba Sebastián Vizcaíno
Pta Eugenia
Guaymas
Empalme
Yaqui
Sta Rosalía
Pta Abreojos
Ciudad Obregón
Navojoa
Madera
Cuauhtémoc
Chihuahua
Delicias
Cd Camargo
Sierra Madre Occidental
Sierra Madre Oriental
MEXICO
Cd Acuña
Piedras Negras
Eagle Pass
Victoria
Nueva Rosita
Sabinas
Beeville
Matagorda B.
Corpus Christi
Kingsville
Nueces
Rio Grande
Nuevo Laredo
Laredo
Falcon Resr
Padre I.
Bolson de Mapimí
Monclova
Sa de los Alamitos
Sabinas Hidalgo
McAllen
Reynosa
Brownsville
Matamoros
Monterrey
Guadalupe
Montemorelos
Lag. Madre
Saltillo
Torreón
Gómez Palacio
San Francisco del Oro
Hidalgo del Parral
Sta Barbara
Choix
Fuerte
Los Mochis
Topolobampo
Guasave
I. Magdalena
Ba Magdalena
I. Sta Margarita
Tropic of Cancer
Altata
Culiacán
Huayapan
Tepehuanes
El Dorado
La Paz
C. Falso
San José del Cabo
Mazatlán
Canatlán
Durango
Concepción del Oro
Matehuala
Cd Victoria
Escuinapa
Fresnillo
Acaponeta
Zacatecas
Tuxpan
Aguascalientes
San Luis Potosí
Cd Valles
Cd Madero
Tampico
Las Tres Marías
Tepic
R. Gde de Santiago
Lag. de Tamiahua
C. Rojo
Ba de Banderas
C. Corrientes
Pto Vallarta
Guadalajara
Ameca
L. de Chapala
Lagos de Moreno
León
Irapuato
Celaya
Ocotlán
Querétaro
Tuxpan
Poza Rica
Papantla
San Benedicto
Roca Partida
Revillagigedo
(Mex.)
Clarión
Socorro
Autlán
Sahuayo
Zamora
Acámbaro
Pachuca
Cd Guzman
Colima
Morelia
Uruapan
México
Jalapa
Manzanillo
Tecomán
Apatzingan
Toluca
Popocatépetl
5452
Orizaba
Citlaltépetl
5699
Veracruz
Córdoba
Cuernavaca
Taxco
Puebla
Tehuacán
Tierra Blanca
P. del Infiernillo
Lázaro Cárdenas
Balsas
Iguala
Acatlán
Sierra Madre del Sur
Ba de Petacalco
Chilpancingo
Tecpan
Acapulco
Oaxaca
Ixtepec
Tehuantepec
Golfo de Tehuantepec
PACIFIC OCEAN
Clipperton I.
(France)
30
20
10
110
100
A
B
2
3
4

1:15M

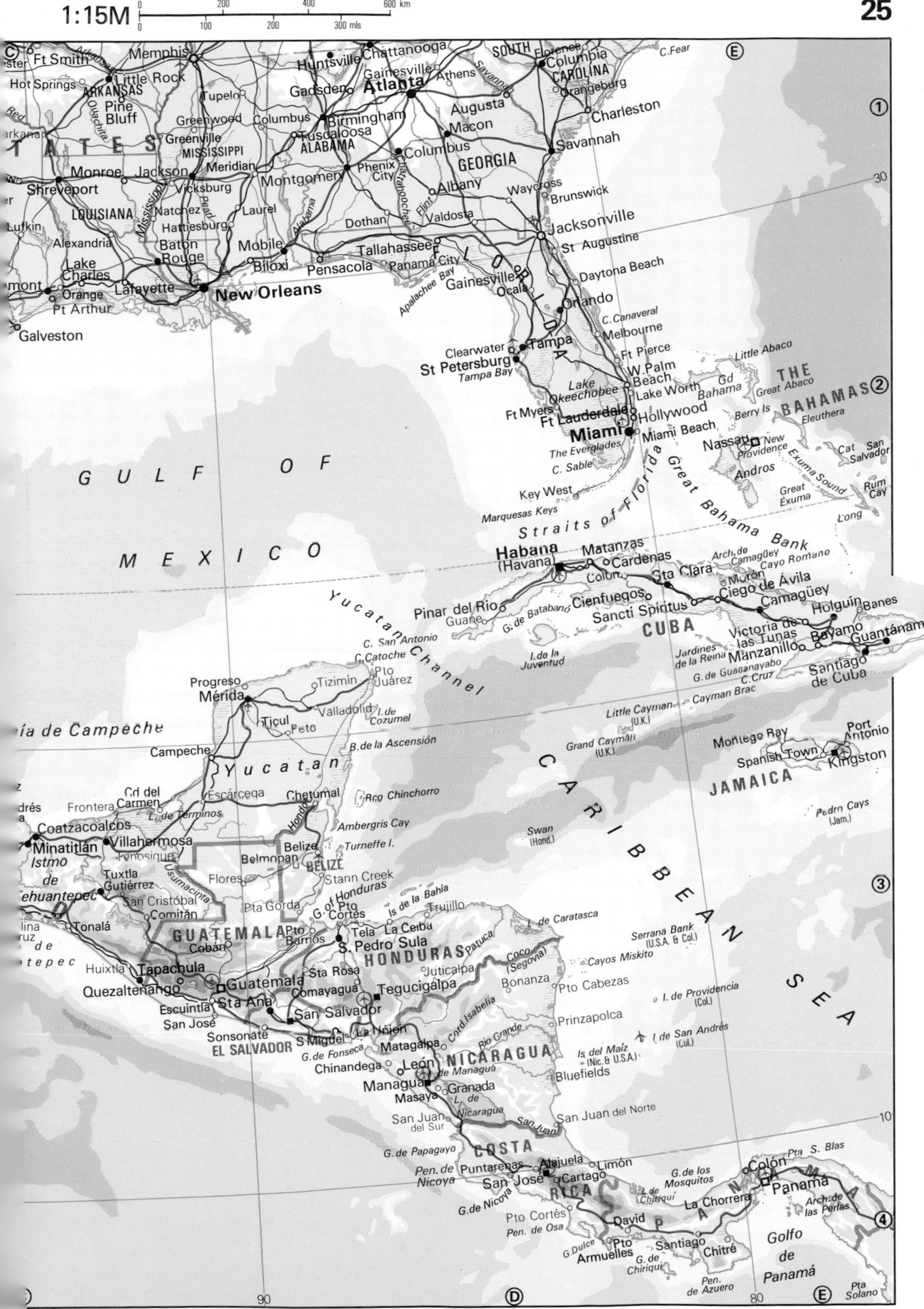

C · Ft Smith · Memphis · Huntsville · Chattanooga · SOUTH · Florence · Columbia · C.Fear · E
Hot Springs · Little Rock · Gainesville · Athens · CAROLINA · Orangeburg
ARKANSAS · Gadsden · Atlanta · Augusta · Charleston · ①
Pine · Greenwood · Birmingham · Macon
Bluff · Tuscaloosa · ALABAMA · Columbus · GEORGIA · Savannah
Monroe · Jackson · Meridian · Montgomery · Phenix · Waycross · Brunswick · 30
Shreveport · Vicksburg · City · Albany
LOUISIANA · Natchez · Laurel · Dothan · Jacksonville · St Augustine
Lufkin · Hattiesburg · Valdosta
Alexandria · Baton · Mobile · Tallahassee · FLORIDA · Daytona Beach
Lake · Rouge · Biloxi · Pensacola · Panama City · Gainesville · Ocala
Charles · New Orleans · Apalachee Bay · Orlando
Orange · Lafayette · C. Canaveral
Pt Arthur · Melbourne
Galveston · Clearwater · Tampa · Ft Pierce · Little Abaco · THE
St Petersburg · Lake · W.Palm · BAHAMAS · ②
Tampa Bay · Okeechobee · Beach · Gd · Great Abaco
Ft Myers · Lake Worth · Bahama
GULF · OF · Ft Lauderdale · Berry Is · Eleuthera
Miami · Hollywood
The Everglades · Miami Beach · Nassau · New · Cat · San
C. Sable · Providence · Salvador
MEXICO · Key West · Andros · Great · Rum
Marquesas Keys · Exuma · Cay
Straits of Florida · Long
Habana · Matanzas · Arch. de · Camagüey · Cayo Romano
(Havana) · Cárdenas · Camagüey · Cayo Romano
Pinar del Rio · Colón · Sta Clara · Morón · Ciego de Ávila
Guane · G. de Batabanó · Cienfuegos · Camagüey
Yucatán Channel · Sancti Spíritus · CUBA · Holguín · Banes
C. San Antonio · I. de · Victoria de · Bayamo · Guantánamo
C. Catoche · Juventud · las Tunas · Manzanillo · Santiago
Progreso · Pto · Jardines · G. de Guacanayabo · de Cuba
Mérida · Juárez · de la Reina · C. Cruz
Tizimín · Little Cayman · Cayman Brac
Valladolid · I. de · Grand Cayman · Montego Bay · Port
Ticul · Cozumel · (U.K.) · Antonio
Peto · (U.K.) · Spanish Town · Kingston
Campeche · B. de la Ascensión · JAMAICA
Bahía de Campeche · Yucatán · Pedro Cays
Cd del · Escárcega · Chetumal · Rio Chinchorro · (Jam.)
Frontera · Carmen · I. de Términos · Hondo · Ambergris Cay
Coatzacoalcos · Villahermosa · Belize · Turneffe I. · Swan
Minatitlán · Tenosique · BELIZE · (Hond.)
Istmo · Tuxtla · Flores · Stann Creek · CARIBBEAN
de · Gutiérrez · Pta Gorda · G. of Honduras · I. de la Bahía
Tehuantepec · San Cristóbal · Pto · Trujillo · I. de Caratasca
Tonalá · Comitán · Cortés · Serrana Bank · SEA
Lina · GUATEMALA · Pto · Tela · La Ceiba · Coco · (U.S.A. & Col.) · ③
de · Cobán · Barrios · S. Pedro Sula · Patuca · Cayos Miskito
Tehuantepec · Huixtla · HONDURAS · Juticalpa · Segovia
Tapachula · Sta Rosa · Comayagua · Bonanza · Pto Cabezas
Quezaltenango · Guatemala · Tegucigalpa · I. de Providencia
Escuintla · Sta Ana · San Salvador · (Col.)
San José · Comayagua · La Unión · Prinzapolca · I. de San Andrés
Sonsonate · S Miguel · (Col.)
EL SALVADOR · G. de Fonseca · Matagalpa · Río Grande · Is del Maíz
Chinandega · León · NICARAGUA · (Nic. & U.S.A.)
Masaya · L. de Managua · Bluefields
Managua · Granada · 10
San Juan · L. de · San Juan del Norte
del Sur · Nicaragua · San Juan
G. de Papagayo · COSTA · Colón · Pta S. Blas
Pen. de · Puntarenas · Alajuela · Limón · G. de los
Nicoya · San José · Cartago · Mosquitos · Panamá
G. de Nicoya · RICA · L. de · La Chorrera · P · Arch. de
Pto Cortés · Chiriquí · David · A · las Perlas
Pen. de Osa · Santiago · N · Golfo · E
G.Dulce · Pto · Chitré · A · de · ④
Armuelles · G. de · M · Panamá
Chiriquí · Pen. · A · Pta
de Azuero · Solano
90 · D · 80 · E

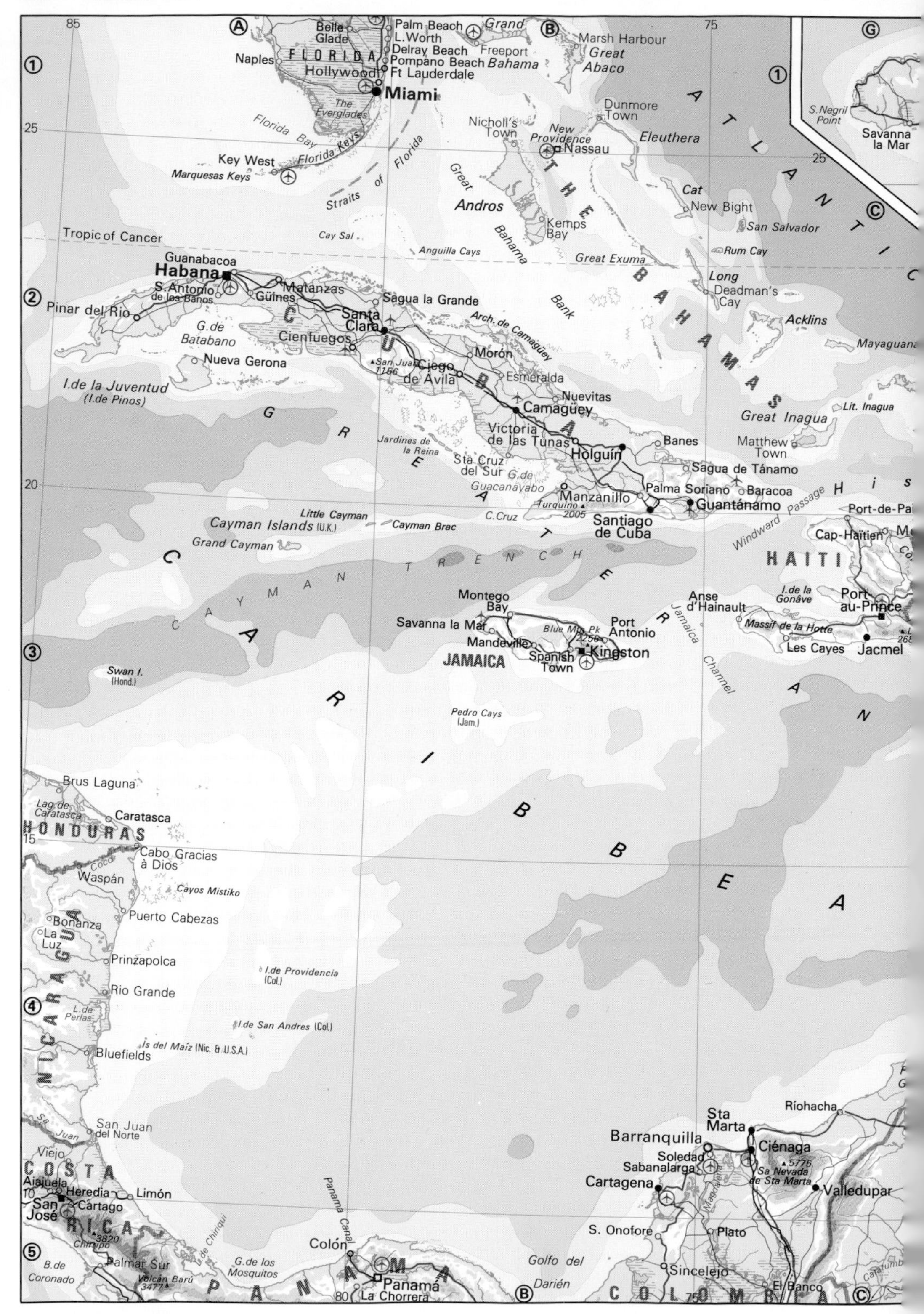

26 Caribbean

85

① A B 75 G ①

Belle
Glade
Naples
FLORIDA
Hollywood
Miami
Palm Beach
L.Worth
Delray Beach
Pompano Beach
Ft Lauderdale
Grand Bahama
Freeport
Marsh Harbour
Great Abaco
S.Negril Point
Savanna la Mar

25

Key West
The Everglades
Florida Bay
Florida Keys
Marquesas Keys
Straits of Florida
Nicholl's Town
New Providence
Nassau
Dunmore Town
Eleuthera
ATLANTIC
25 ①
C

Tropic of Cancer
Cay Sal
Anguilla Cays
Andros
Kemps Bay
Great Bahama Bank
Great Exuma
Cat
New Bight
San Salvador
Rum Cay
Long
Deadman's Cay

② Pinar del Río
Habana
Guanabacoa
S.Antonio de los Baños
Güines
Matanzas
Sagua la Grande
Santa Clara
Cienfuegos
C U B A
G.de Batabano
Nueva Gerona
I.de la Juventud
(I.de Pinos)
Arch. de Camagüey
Morón
Ciego de Ávila
San Juan 1156
Esmeralda
Camagüey
Nuevitas
Victoria de las Tunas
Holguín
Banes
Sagua de Tánamo
Acklins
Mayaguana
Lit. Inagua
Great Inagua
Matthew Town
②

20

Cayman Islands (U.K.)
Little Cayman
Grand Cayman
Cayman Brac
Jardines de la Reina
Sta Cruz del Sur
G.de Guacanáyabo
C.Cruz
Turquino 2005
Manzanillo
Palma Soriano
Santiago de Cuba
Guantánamo
Baracoa
Windward Passage
Port-de-Pa
Cap-Haïtien
His
20

CARIBBEAN
CAYMAN TRENCH
THE
TRENCH
Swan I.
(Hond.)
Montego Bay
Savanna la Mar
Mandeville
JAMAICA
Spanish Town
Kingston
Port Antonio
Blue Mtn Pk 2256
Jamaica Channel
Anse d'Hainault
I.de la Gonâve
Massif de la Hotte
Les Cayes
Port-au-Prince
Jacmel
HAITI
M
L 268
③

Pedro Cays (Jam.)

Brus Laguna
Lag.de Caratasca
Caratasca
HONDURAS
Cabo Gracias à Dios
Cayos Mistiko
Waspán
Bonanza
La Luz
Prinzapolca
Río Grande
Puerto Cabezas
I.de Providencia (Col.)
I.de San Andres (Col.)

15

④

L.de Perlas
Bluefields
Is del Maíz (Nic. & U.S.A.)
④

San Juan del Norte
Viejo
COSTA
Aiajuela
Heredia
Limón
San José
Cártago
RICA
Chirripó 3820
B.de Coronado
Palmar Sur
Volcán Barú 3477
Colón
G.de los Mosquitos
PANAMA
Panamá
La Chorrera
Golfo del Darién
Sta Marta
Ríohacha
Barranquilla
Soledad
Sabanalarga
Cartagena
Ciénaga
5775
Sa Nevada de Sta Marta
Valledupar
S. Onofore
Plato
Sincelejo
El Banco
COLOMBIA

10

⑤ 80 ⑤ B 75 C

20

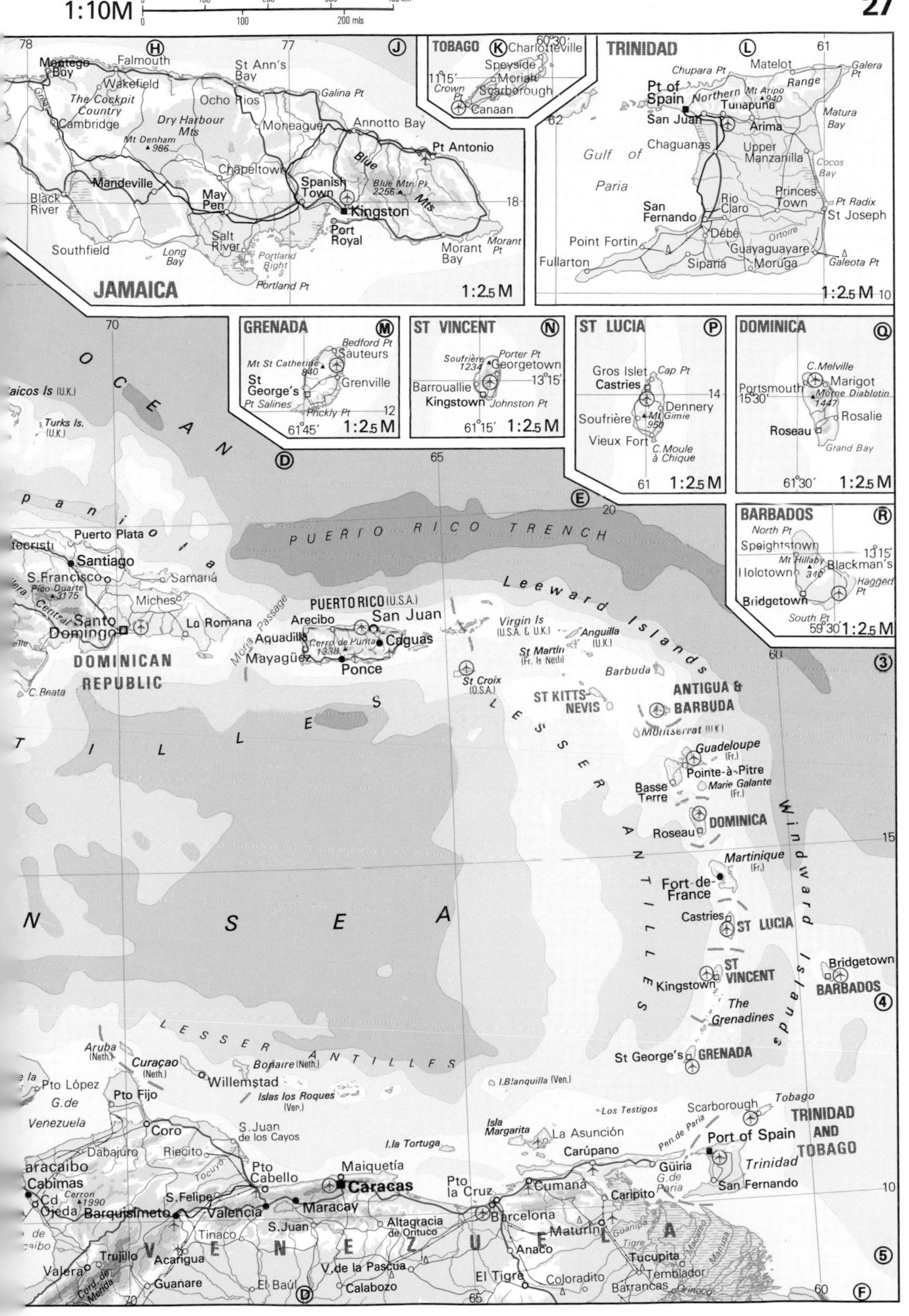

100   200   300   400 km
100   200 mls

TOBAGO
Charlotteville
Speyside
Moriah
Scarborough
Canaan

TRINIDAD
Chupara Pt
Mt Aripo
940
Range
Matelot
Galera Pt
Northern
Pt of
Spain
Tunapuna
San Juan
Arima
Chaguanas
Upper
Manzanilla
Cocos
Bay
San
Fernando
Rio
Claro
Princes
Town
Pt Radix
St Joseph
Point Fortin
Débe
Guayaguayare
Fullarton
Siparia
Moruga
Galeota Pt

Montego
Bay
Falmouth
St Ann's
Bay
Galina Pt
Wakefield
Ocho Rios
The Cockpit
Country
Dry Harbour
Mts
Moneague
Annotto Bay
Cambridge
Mt Denham
986
Chapeltown
Pt Antonio
Mandeville
Spanish
Town
Blue Mtn Pk
2256
Blue
Mts
18
May
Pen
Kingston
Port
Royal
Black
River
Salt
River
Portland
Bight
Morant
Pt
Morant
Bay
Southfield
Long
Bay
Portland Pt
Portland Bight

JAMAICA   1:2.5M

GRENADA
Bedford Pt
Sauteurs
Mt St Catherine
840
St
George's
Grenville
Pt Salines
Prickly Pt
61°45'   1:2.5M   12

ST VINCENT
Porter Pt
Soufrière
1234
Georgetown
Barrouallie
13°15'
Kingstown
Johnston Pt
61°15'   1:2.5M

ST LUCIA
Gros Islet
Cap Pt
Castries
14
Soufrière
Mt
Gimie
950
Dennery
Vieux Fort
C.Moule
à Chique
61   1:2.5M

DOMINICA
C.Melville
Portsmouth
Marigot
15°30'
Morne Diablotin
1447
Roseau
Rosalie
Grand Bay
61°30'   1:2.5M

BARBADOS
North Pt
Speightstown
Mt Hillaby
340
13°15'
Holetown
Blackman's
Bridgetown
Ragged
Pt
South Pt
59°30'   1:2.5M

O C E A N

Turks Is.
(U.K.)
Caicos Is. (U.K.)

P U E R T O   R I C O   T R E N C H

20

Puerto Plata
Santiago
Samana
S.Francisco
Pico Duarte
3175
Miches
Santo
Domingo
La Romana
DOMINICAN
REPUBLIC
C.Beata

Aguadilla
Arecibo
San Juan
PUERTO RICO (U.S.A.)
Mayagüez
Cerro de Punta
1338
Caguas
Ponce
Mona Passage

Virgin Is.
(U.S.A. & U.K.)
Anguilla
(U.K.)
St Martin
(Fr. & Neth.)
St Croix
(U.S.A.)
Barbuda

L e e w a r d   I s l a n d s

ANTIGUA &
BARBUDA
ST KITTS
NEVIS
Montserrat (U.K.)
Guadeloupe
(Fr.)
Pointe-à-Pitre
Basse
Terre
Marie Galante
(Fr.)
Roseau
DOMINICA

15

Martinique
(Fr.)
Fort-de-
France
Castries
ST LUCIA

Kingstown
ST
VINCENT
Bridgetown
BARBADOS

C A R I B B E A N   S E A

L E S S E R

A N T I L L E S

W i n d w a r d   I s l a n d s

The
Grenadines
St George's
GRENADA

Aruba
(Neth.)
Curaçao
(Neth.)
Bonaire
(Neth.)
Willemstad
Islas los Roques
(Ven.)
I.Blanquilla (Ven.)
Los Testigos
Scarborough
Tobago
TRINIDAD
AND
TOBAGO

Pto López
G.de
Venezuela
Pto Fijo
Coro
S.Juan
de los Cayos
I.la Tortuga
Isla
Margarita
La Asunción
Pen.de Paria
Port of Spain
Trinidad

Dabajuro
Riecito
Pto
Cabello
Maiquetía
Carúpano
Güiria
G.de
Paria
San Fernando

Maracaibo
Cabimas
Cd
Ojeda
S.Felipe
CARACAS
Cumaná
Caripito
Barquisimeto
Valencia
Maracay
Pto
la Cruz
Barcelona
Maturín
Tucupita
Temblador

Valera
Trujillo
Acarigua
S.Juan
Altagracia
de Orituco
Anaco
Tigre
Guanipa
Orinoco
Guanare
El Baúl
V.de la Pascua
Calabozo
El Tigre
Coloradito
Barrancas

V E N E Z U E L A

Cerron
1990

1:40M

400 800 1200 1600 km
400 800 mls

NICARAGUA
CARIBBEAN   SEA
ST LUCIA
BARBADOS
COSTA RICA
S.José
Panamá
PANAMA
Sta Marta
Barranquilla
Maracaibo
Caracas
Barcelona
TRINIDAD & TOBAGO
S.Cristóbal
Cd Bolívar
Orinoco
VENEZUELA
Georgetown
Paramaribo
GUYANA
Cayenne
Medellín
Bogotá
Buenaventura
Cali
Popayán
COLOMBIA
Boa Vista
SURINAM
FR. GUIANA
Malpelo (Col.)
S.Lorenzo
Quito
ECUADOR
Negro
Santarem
I. de Marajó
Belém
São Luís
Equator
Guayaquil
Iquitos
Amazonas
Manaus
I.Fernando de Noronha (Brz.)
Trujillo
Ucayali
Purus
Madeira
Tapajós
Xingu
Teresina
Fortaleza
Natal
PERU
Pto Velho
BRAZIL
Recife
Maceió
Callao
Lima
Huancayo
Pto Maldonado
Cuzco
Salvador
Arequipa
La Paz
BOLIVIA
Cuiabá
Goiânia
Brasília
São Francisco
Cochabamba
Sta Cruz
Sucre
Corumbá
Belo Horizonte
Arica
Campo Grande
Paraná
Ribeirão Prêto
Campos
SOUTH
PACIFIC
Antofagasta
PARAGUAY
Asunción
Rio de Janeiro
São Paulo
Santos
Tropic of Capricorn
OCEAN
S.Félix (Chi.)
Salta
S.Miguel de Tucumán
Resistencia
Posadas
Curitiba
CHILE
ARGENTINA
Córdoba
Sante Fe
Paraná
Pto Alegre
Pelotas
SOUTH
Valparaíso
Mendoza
Rosario
URUGUAY
Santiago
Buenos Aires
Montevideo
R.de la Plata
ATLANTIC
Is Juan Fernández (Chi.)
Concepción
Mar del Plata
Bahía Blanca
OCEAN
Valdivia
Pto Montt
Cmd. Rivadavia
G.San Jorge
Falkland Is (U.K.)
Stanley
Río Gallegos
S.Georgia (U.K.)
Punta Arenas
Tierra del Fuego
S.Shetland Is (U.K.)
S.Orkney Is (U.K.)

1:15M

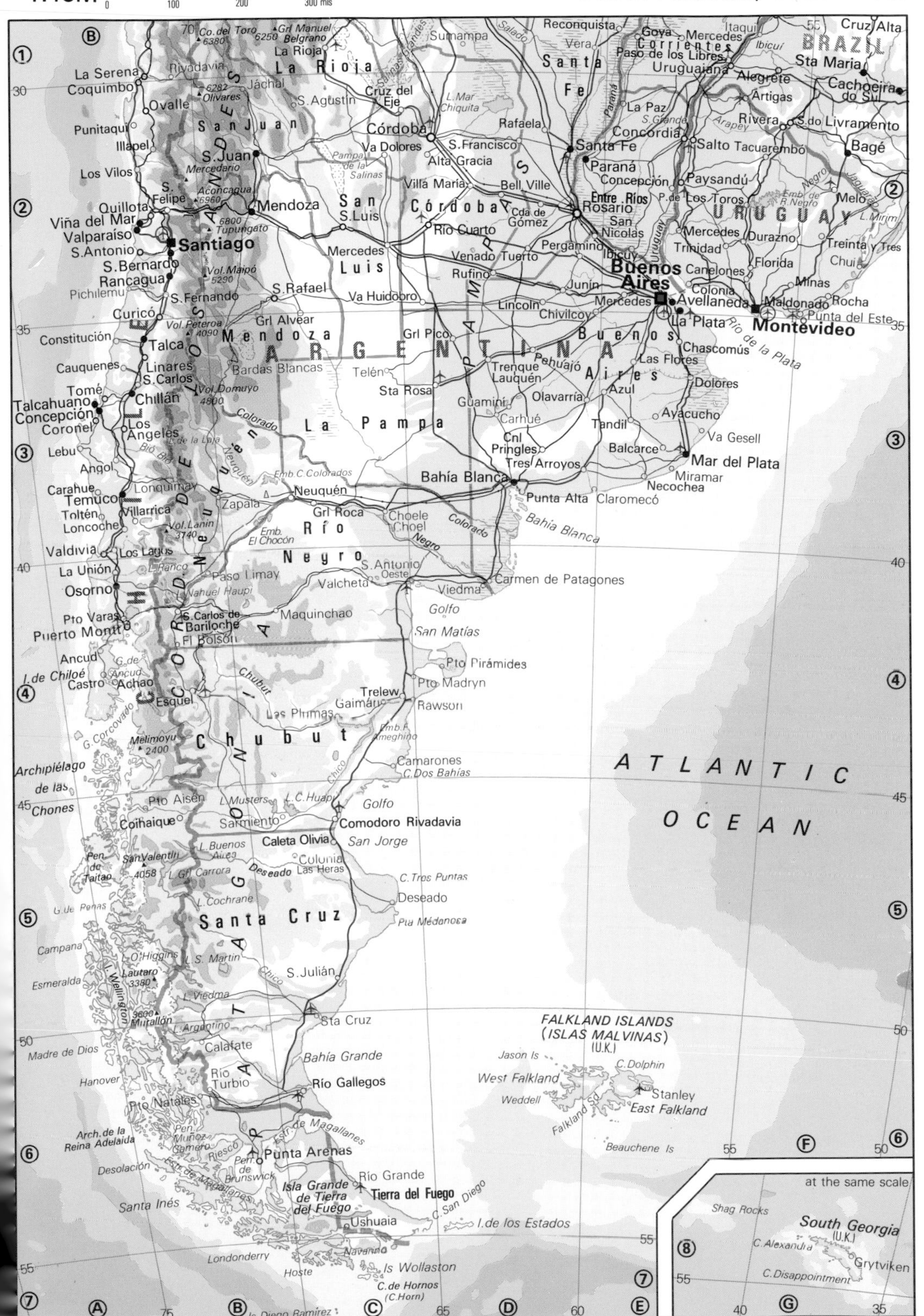

200   400   600 km
100   200   300 mils

ATLANTIC

OCEAN

FALKLAND ISLANDS
(ISLAS MALVINAS)
(U.K.)

Jason Is
C. Dolphin
West Falkland
Weddell
Stanley
East Falkland
Falkland Sd
Beauchene Is

at the same scale

South Georgia
(U.K.)

Shag Rocks
C. Alexandria
C. Disappointment
Grytviken

1:15M

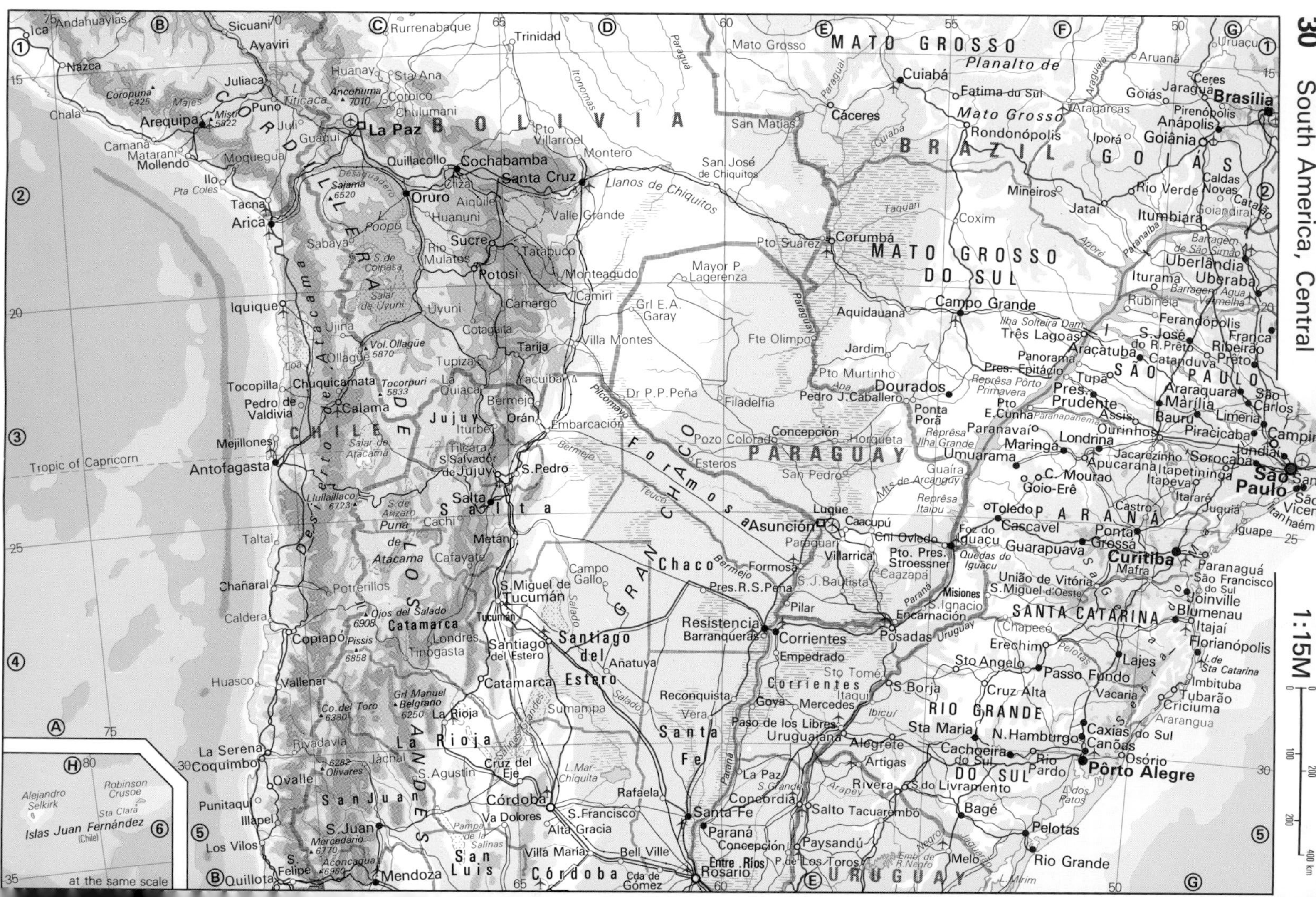

0 200 400 km
0 100 200
MATO GROSSO
Planalto de Mato Grosso
MATO GROSSO DO SUL
GOIÁS
SÃO PAULO
PARANÁ
SANTA CATARINA
RIO GRANDE DO SUL
BRAZIL
BOLIVIA
PARAGUAY
URUGUAY
CHILE
Salta
Jujuy
Catamarca
La Rioja
San Juan
San Luis
Córdoba
Santa Fe
Santiago del Estero
Corrientes
Misiones
Chaco
Formosa
Entre Ríos
GRAN CHACO
CORDILLERA DE LOS ANDES
Desierto de Atacama
Llanos de Chiquitos
Tropic of Capricorn
Brasília
Goiânia
Anápolis
Uberlândia
Uberaba
Ribeirão Prêto
Campinas
São Paulo
Santos
São Vicente
Sorocaba
Jundiaí
Piracicaba
Bauru
Marília
Araraquara
S. José do R. Prêto
Araçatuba
Pres. Prudente
Londrina
Maringá
Curitiba
Ponta Grossa
Paranaguá
Joinville
Blumenau
Florianópolis
Lajes
Passo Fundo
Caxias do Sul
Pôrto Alegre
Pelotas
Rio Grande
Sta Maria
Bagé
Campo Grande
Corumbá
Cuiabá
Cáceres
Rondonópolis
Dourados
Três Lagoas
Asunción
Concepción
Encarnación
Posadas
Corrientes
Resistencia
Formosa
Santa Fe
Paraná
Rosario
Córdoba
Santiago del Estero
Tucumán
Salta
Jujuy
Catamarca
La Rioja
S. Juan
Mendoza
Santa Cruz
Cochabamba
Sucre
Potosí
Oruro
La Paz
Tarija
Trinidad
Arica
Iquique
Antofagasta
Calama
Copiapó
La Serena
Coquimbo
Tacna
Arequipa
Puno
Juliaca
Islas Juan Fernández (Chile)
Robinson Crusoe
Alejandro Selkirk
at the same scale

200 400 600 km
100 200 300 mls

A 50   B   45   C   40   D   35   E

① Equator 0

C. Maguarinho
I. de Marajó
Salinópolis
Bragança
Capanema
Pará
Belém
Abaetetuba
Cametá
Alcântara
Pinheiro
São Luís
Rosário Parnaíba
Camocim Acaraú
② Monção Chapadinha Sobral Itapipoca Caucaia
Coroatá Piripiri Sta Fortaleza (Ceará)
Bacabal Quitéria I. Fernando
Codó Campo Nova Canindé Aracati de Noronha
Caxias Maior Russas Quixadá Areia Branca
Teresina Crateús Morada N. Macaú Pta do Calcanhar
5 Marabá Castelo Mombaça Mossoró Natal 5
Imperatriz Tauá Acopiara RIO GRANDE DO NORTE
Grajaú Iguatu Patu Caicó
Pto Franco Floriano Sousa Patos Cabedelo
③ Araguaína Carolina Oeiras Picos J. do Norte Salgueiro Talhada PARAÍBA João Pessoa
Balsas PIAUÍ Crato Campina Grande
C. do Araguaia Paulistana Ouricuri PERNAMBUCO Olinda Recife (Pernambuco)
S.Raimundo Garanhuns Palmares Jaboatão
Petrolina Nonato Palmeira dos Ind. Barreiros
B R A Z I L Juàzeiro ALAGOAS Maceió
10 Barragem de Propriá Arapiraca Penedo 10
TOCANTINS Sobradinho Sen. do Bonfim SERGIPE
São Barra Jacobina Lagarto Aracajú
Félix Ibotirama Serrinha Estância
B A H I A R. de Jacuípe
④ GOIÁS Barreiras Feira de S. Cachoeira Salvador (Bahia) ④
Bom Jesus Iaçu Castro B. de T. de Santos
da Lapa Alves
Caetité Valença
Uruaçu Vitória da Ipiaú ATLANTIC
15 Aruanã Ceres Formosa Conquista Itabuna Ilhéus OCEAN 15
Goiás Jaraguá Januária Itapetinga Canavieiras
Pirenópolis Brasília Salinas Belmonte
Anápolis São Francisco Porteirinha Pôrto Seguro
Iporá Goiânia Montes Claros Araçuaí Itamaraju
⑤ Caldas Paracatu Piripora Sa do Chifre Nanuque ⑤
Rio Verde Novas João Corinto Teófilo Otôni
Jataí Itumbiara Goiandira Pinheiro Diamantina São Mateus
Barragem Catalão Gov. ESPÍRITO
de São Simão Araguari Curvelo Valadares Linhares
20 Iturama MINAS GERAIS Itabira Cnl SANTO Colatina 20
Uberlândia Uberaba Sete Lagoas Fabriciano Vitória
Rubinéia Araxá Belo Caratinga Carjacica Vila Velha
Fernandópolis Franca Horizonte Con. Ponte Nova
S. José Divinópolis Lafaiete Cachoeiro de Itapemirim
do R. Prêto Barretos Passos Carangola
Catanduva SÃO PAULO S.João del Rei Itaperuna
Araraquara Ribeirão Prêto Lavras Barbacena S.João da Barra
Marília Pôços de Caldas Juiz Campos
Pres. Bauru S. Carlos Volta de Fora Nova Friburgo
Prudente Assis Piracicaba Redonda Petrópolis Magé
Ourinhos Limeira Barra Niterói
Londrina Jacarezinho Jundiaí Campinas Mansa
Apucarana Itapeva Sorocaba São Paulo Tropic of Capricorn
⑥ Itararé Itapetininga Santos Rio de Janeiro ⑥
Juquiá São Vicente
Castro Itanhaém
Ponta Iguape
Grossa Guarapuava Curitiba
União Paranaguá
de Mafra
Vitória São Francisco do Sul 25

45   C   40   D   35   E

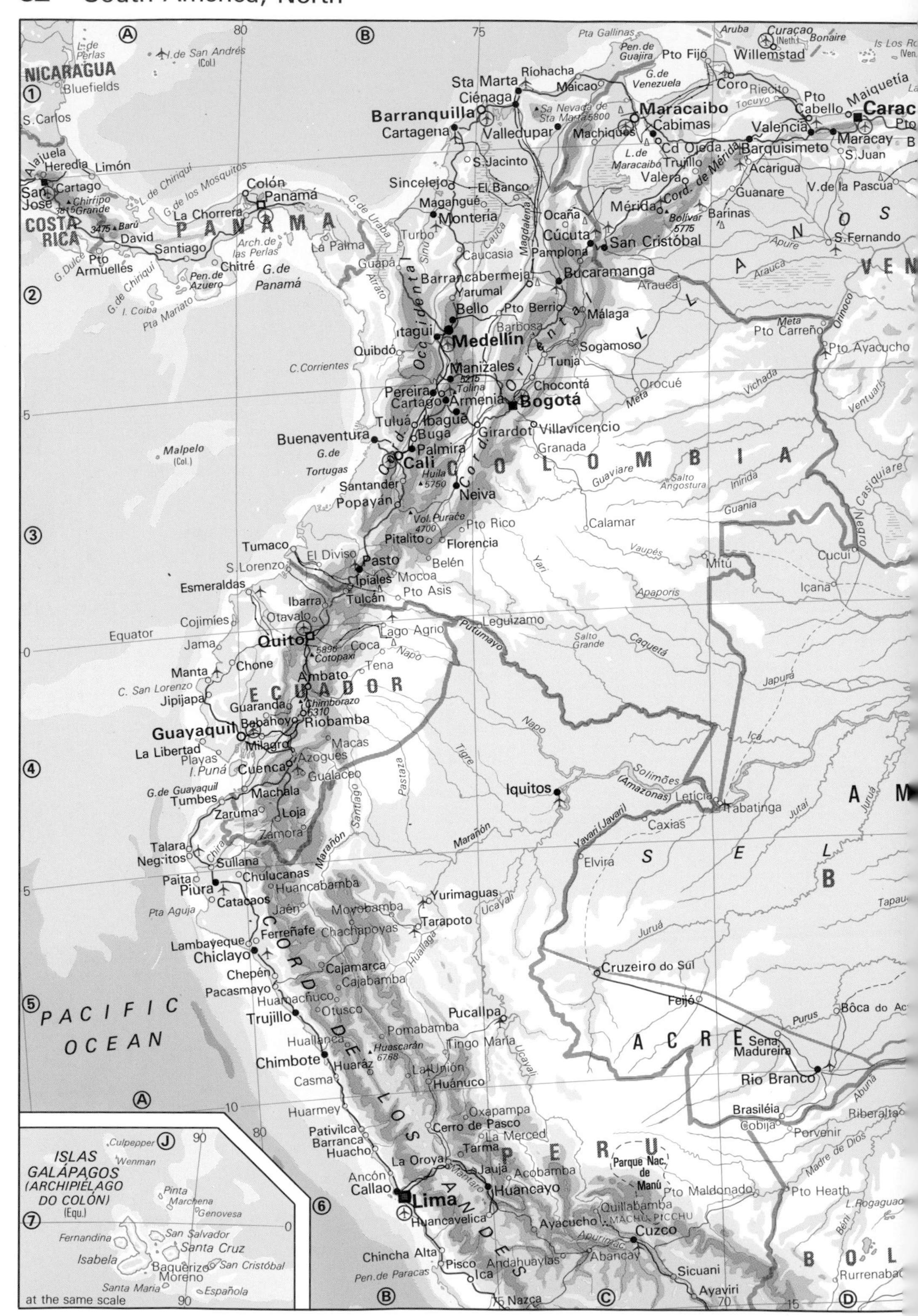
NICARAGUA
Bluefields
S.Carlos
L.de Perlas
I.de San Andrés (Col.)
Alajuela
Heredia
Limón
San José
Cartago
Chirripó Grande 3815
3475 Barú
COSTA RICA
David
G.Dulce
Pto Armuelles
G.de Chiriquí
I. Coiba
Pta Mariato
L.de Chiriquí
G.de los Mosquitos
Santiago
Pen.de Azuero
Chitré
La Chorrera
Colón
Panamá
PANAMA
Arch.de las Perlas
G.de Panamá
La Palma
G.de Uraba
Turbo
Guapá
Atrato
Quibdó
C.Corrientes
Pta Gallinas
Pen.de Guajira
Pto Fijó
Aruba
Curaçao (Neth.)
Bonaire
Willemstad
Is Los Roques (Ven.)
Ríohacha
Sta Marta
Ciénaga
Maicao
G.de Venezuela
Coro
Riecito
Pto Cabello
Maiquetía
Caracas
Barranquilla
Cartagena
Sa Nevada de Sta Marta 5800
Valledupar
Maracaibo
Cabimas
Machiques
L.de Maracaibo
Cd Ojeda
Tocuyo
Valencia
Maracay
Barquisimeto
S.Juan
Acarigua
Trujillo
Valera
Cord. de Mérida
Mérida
Bolívar 5775
Barinas
Guanare
V.de la Pascua
S.Fernando
Apure
Arauca
LLANOS
S.Jacinto
Sincelejo
El Banco
Magangué
Montería
Sinú
Cauca
Magdalena
Caucasia
Ocaña
Cúcuta
San Cristóbal
Pamplona
Bucaramanga
Barrancabermeja
Yarumal
Bello
Pto Berrio
Málaga
Barbosa
Itagüí
Medellín
Sogamoso
Tunja
Manizales
5215 Tolima
Pereira
Cartago
Armenia
Chocontá
Bogotá
Orocué
Meta
Vichada
Pto Carreño
Pto Ayacucho
Orinoco
Ventuari
Tuluá
Ibagué
Buga
Girardot
Villavicencio
Buenaventura
Palmira
Cali
Granada
G.de Tortugas
Malpelo (Col.)
Occidental
Central
Oriental
COLOMBIA
Huila 5750
Santander
Popayán
Neiva
Guaviare
Salto Angostura
Inírida
Guania
Casiquiare
Negro
Vol. Puracé 4700
Pto Rico
Calamar
Pitalito
Florencia
Belén
Yari
Vaupés
Mitú
Cucuí
Içana
Tumaco
El Diviso
Pasto
S.Lorenzo
Ipiales
Mocoa
Esmeraldas
Tulcán
Pto Asis
Apaporis
Ibarra
Otavalo
Cojimíes
Leguízamo
Putumayo
Equator
Quito
5896 Cotopaxi
Coca
Lago Agrio
Napo
Salto Grande
Caquetá
Jama
Tena
Chone
Manta
Ambato
C. San Lorenzo
Jipijapa
ECUADOR
Guaranda
Chimborazo 6310
Japurá
Guayaquil
Babahoyo
Riobamba
Milagro
Macas
La Libertad
Playas
I.Puná
Cuenca
Azogues
Gualaceo
Tigre
Pastaza
G.de Guayaquil
Tumbes
Machala
Santiago
Iquitos
Solimões
(Amazonas)
Letícia
Tabatinga
Zaruma
Loja
Zamora
Yavari (Javari)
Caxias
Jutaí
Juruá
Marañón
Talara
Negritos
Chira
Sullana
Elvira
SELVAS
Paita
Piura
Chulucanas
Huancabamba
Catacaos
Pta Aguja
Jaén
Moyobamba
Yurimaguas
Ucayali
Tapauá
Ferreñafe
Chachapoyas
Tarapoto
Huallaga
Lambayeque
Chiclayo
Chepén
Cajamarca
Cajabamba
Cruzeiro do Sul
Pacasmayo
Huamachuco
Otusco
Feijó
Trujillo
Pucallpa
Purus
Bôca do Acre
PACIFIC OCEAN
Pomabamba
Huallanca
Huascarán 6768
Tingo María
Chimbote
Huaráz
La Unión
ACRE
Sena Madureira
Casma
Huánuco
Rio Branco
Abunã
Huarmey
Oxapampa
Brasiléia
Riberalta
Cobija
Porvenir
Pativilca
Barranca
Huacho
Cerro de Pasco
La Merced
Tarma
PERU
Parque Nac. de Manú
Madre de Dios
La Oroya
Ancón
Callao
Lima
Mantaro
Jauja
Acobamba
Huancayo
Pto Maldonado
Pto Heath
L.Rogaguado
Huancavelica
Ayacucho
Quillabamba
MACHU PICCHU
Cuzco
Beni
Apurímac
Chincha Alta
Abancay
Pisco
Andahuaylas
Pen.de Paracas
Ica
Sicuani
Nazca
Ayaviri
Rurrenabaque
BOLIVIA
CORD. DE LOS ANDES
VENEZUELA
AMAZONAS
ISLAS GALÁPAGOS (ARCHIPIÉLAGO DO COLÓN) (Equ.)
Culpepper
Wenman
Pinta
Marchena
Genovesa
Fernandina
San Salvador
Santa Cruz
Isabela
Baquerizo Moreno
San Cristóbal
Santa María
Española
at the same scale
80
75
70
90
0
5
10
15
A
B
C
D
J
1
2
3
4
5
6
7

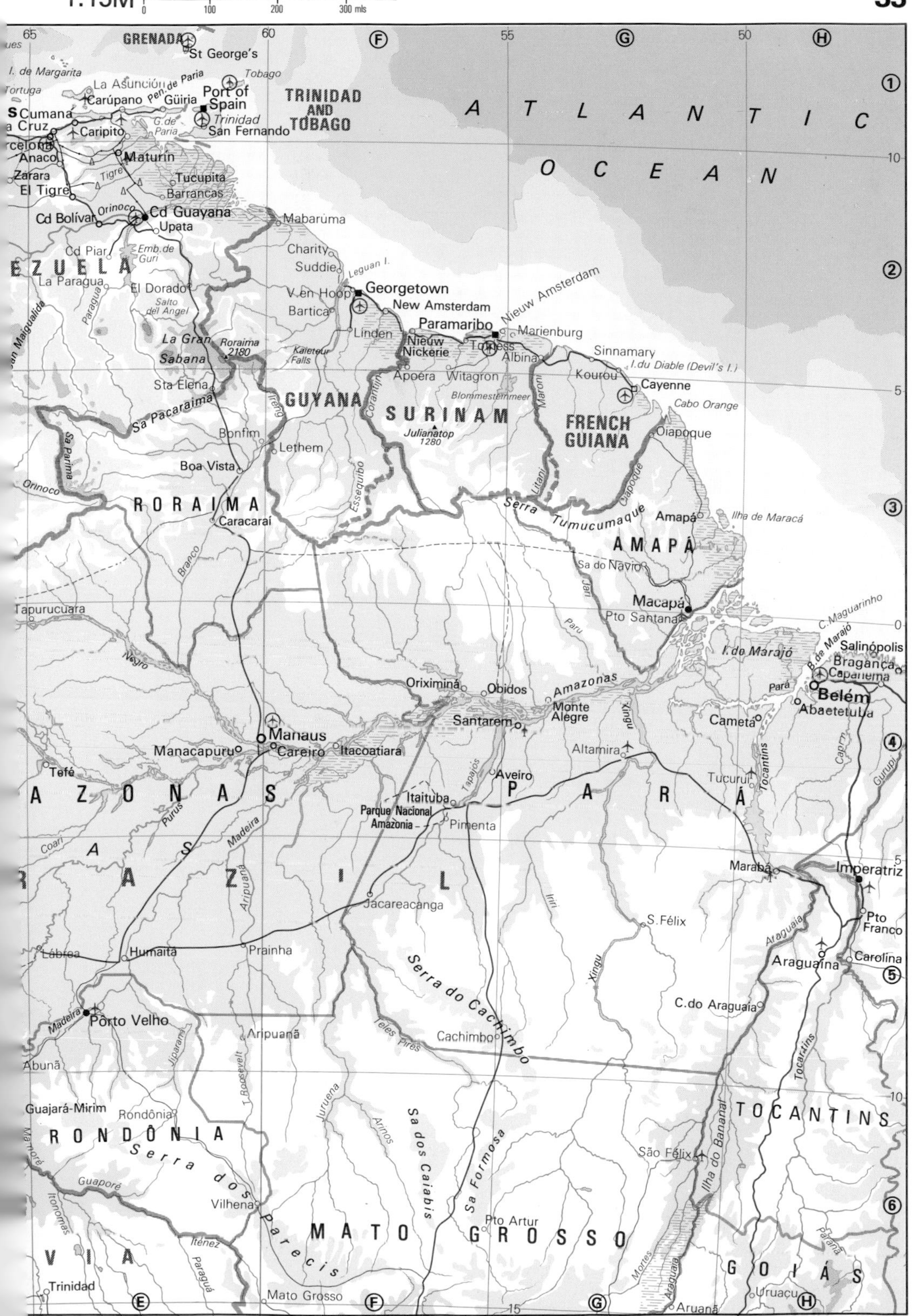

200   400   600 km
100   200   300 mls

65   60   (F)   55   (G)   50   (H)

GRENADA
St George's
I. de Margarita
La Asunción   Pen de Paria   Tobago
Tortuga   TRINIDAD
Carúpano Güiria Port of   AND
S Cumaná   Spain   TOBAGO
a Cruz   Caripito   G. de Paria   Trinidad
celona   Anaco   Maturín   San Fernando
Zarara Anaco
El Tigre   Tucupita
Cd Bolívar   Orinoco   Barrancas
Cd Piar   Upata   Cd Guayana   Mabaruma
ZUELA   Emb. de
La Paragua   Guri   El Dorado   Charity
Salto   Suddie
del Angel   V. en Hoop   Georgetown
Roraima   Bartica   New Amsterdam
La Gran   2180   Linden   Paramaribo
Sabana   Kaletour   Nieuw   Nieuw Amsterdam
Sta Elena   Falls   Nickerie   Totness   Marienburg
Sa Pacaraima   Apoera   Witagron   Albina   Sinnamary
Bonfim   GUYANA   SURINAM   I.du Diable (Devil's I.)
Lethem   Kourou   Cayenne
Boa Vista   Julianatop   FRENCH   Cabo Orange
1280   GUIANA
RORAIMA   Blommestenmeer   Oiapoque
Caracaraí   Serra   Tumucumaque   Amapá   Ilha de Maracá
Tapurucuara   Sa do Navio   AMAPÁ
Manaus   Oriximiná   Óbidos   Amazonas   Macapá   C. Maguarinho
Manacapuru   Careiro   Itacoatiara   Santarém   Monte   Pto Santana   B. de Marajó   Salinópolis
Tefé   Alegre   I. do Marajó   Bragança
A Z O N A S   Aveiro   Altamira   Xingu   Cametá   Pará   Belém   Capanema
Itaituba   Tucuruí   Abaetetuba
Parque Nacional
Amazônia   Pimenta   P A R Á
B R A S I L   Jácareacanga   Marabá   Imperatriz
Lábrea   Humaitá   Prainha   S. Félix   Pto Franco
Pôrto Velho   Aripuanã   Serra do Cachimbo   Carolina
Abunã   Cachimbo   Xingu   C. do Araguaia   Araguaína
Guajará-Mirim   Rondônia   TOCANTINS
RONDÔNIA   Serra dos Parecis   São Félix
Vilhena   Ilha do Bananal
VIA   Guaporé   Pto Artur
Trinidad   Mato Grosso   MATO   GROSSO   GOIÁS   Uruaçu
Aruanã

A T L A N T I C
O C E A N

(1)
10
(2)
5
(3)
0
(4)
5
10
(5)
(6)

(E)   (F)   15   (G)   (H)

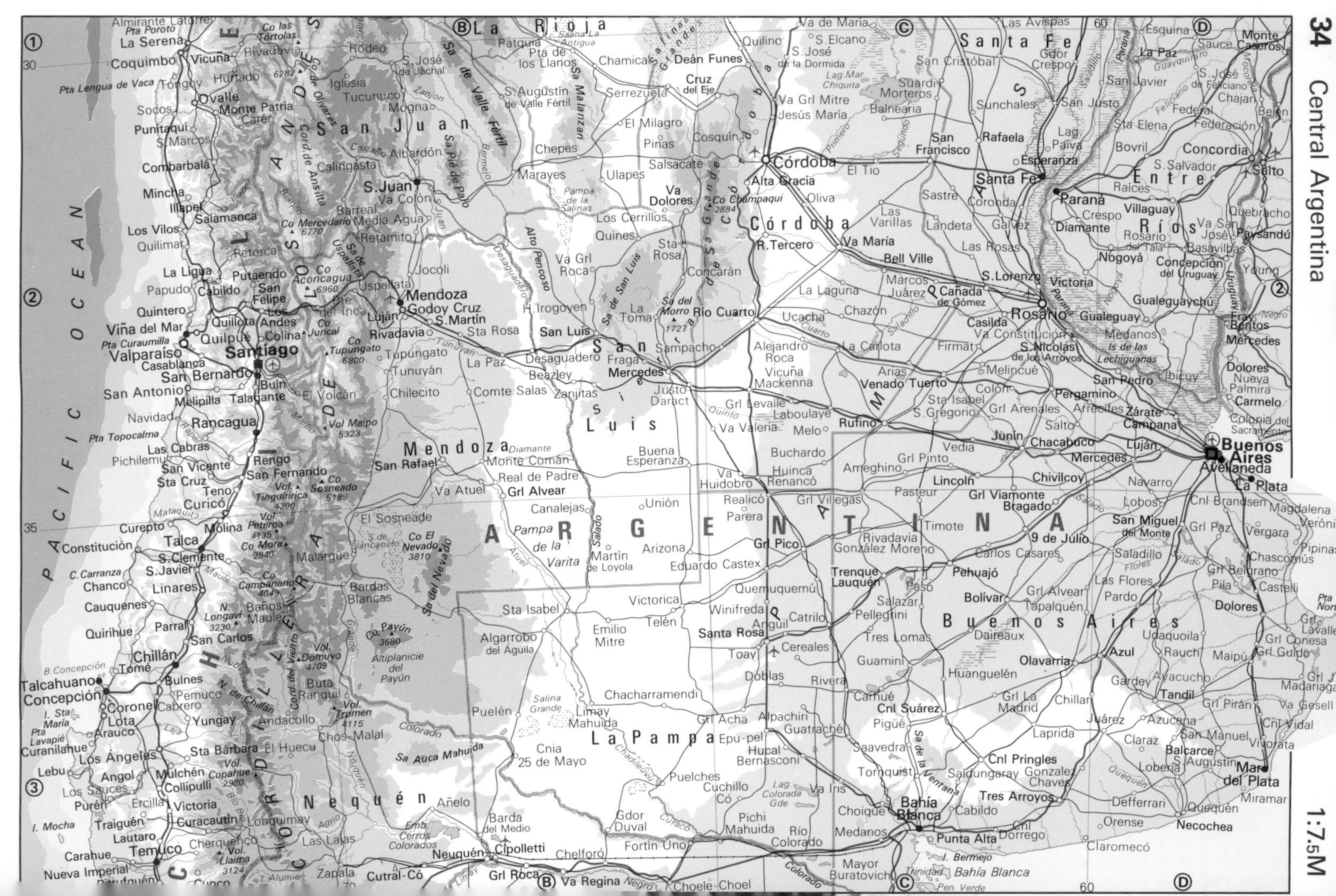
Buenos Aires
La Plata
Avellaneda
Rosario
Santa Fe
Paraná
Córdoba
Mendoza
S.Juan
San Luis
Santiago
Valparaíso
Viña del Mar
Concepción
Talcahuano
Bahía Blanca
Mar del Plata
Santa Rosa
Neuquén
Río Cuarto
Va María
Concordia
Gualeguaychú
Tandil
Olavarría
Necochea
Tres Arroyos
Junín
Pergamino
Venado Tuerto
Rufino
Chillán
Talca
Curicó
Rancagua
Temuco
Los Angeles
La Serena
Coquimbo
Ovalle
San Rafael
Grl Alvear
Cipolletti
Grl Roca
Entre Ríos
Santa Fe
Córdoba
San Luis
Mendoza
San Juan
La Rioja
La Pampa
Nequén
Buenos Aires
A R G E N T I N A
PACIFIC OCEAN
Co Aconcagua 6960
Co Tupungato 6800
Sa de Valle Fértil
Sa de San Luis
Sa del Nevado
Bahía Blanca

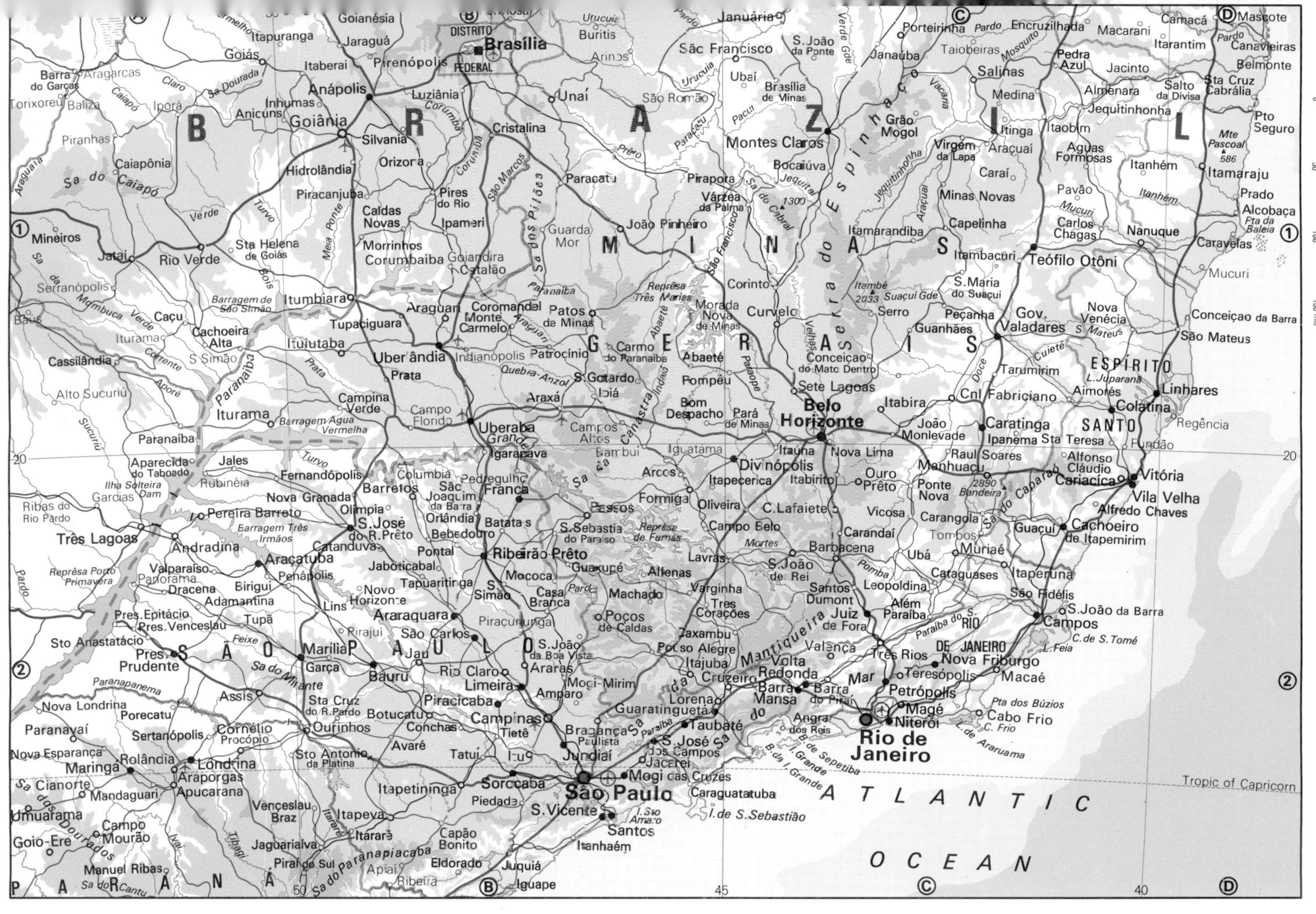
B R A Z I L
M I N A S G E R A I S
S Ã O P A U L O
P A R A N Á
ESPÍRITO SANTO
RIO DE JANEIRO
DISTRITO FEDERAL
A T L A N T I C
O C E A N
Tropic of Capricorn
Brasília
Goiânia
Anápolis
Belo Horizonte
Rio de Janeiro
São Paulo
Vitória
Vila Velha
Niterói
Santos
Campinas
Uberlândia
Uberaba
Ribeirão Prêto
Juiz de Fora
Montes Claros
Gov. Valadares
Teófilo Otôni
Londrina
Maringá
Bauru
Marília
Campos
Três Lagoas
Serra do Espinhaço
Serra da Mantiqueira
Serra da Canastra
São Francisco
Paranaíba
Paraná
Grande
Tietê
Paranapanema
Doce
Jequitinhonha

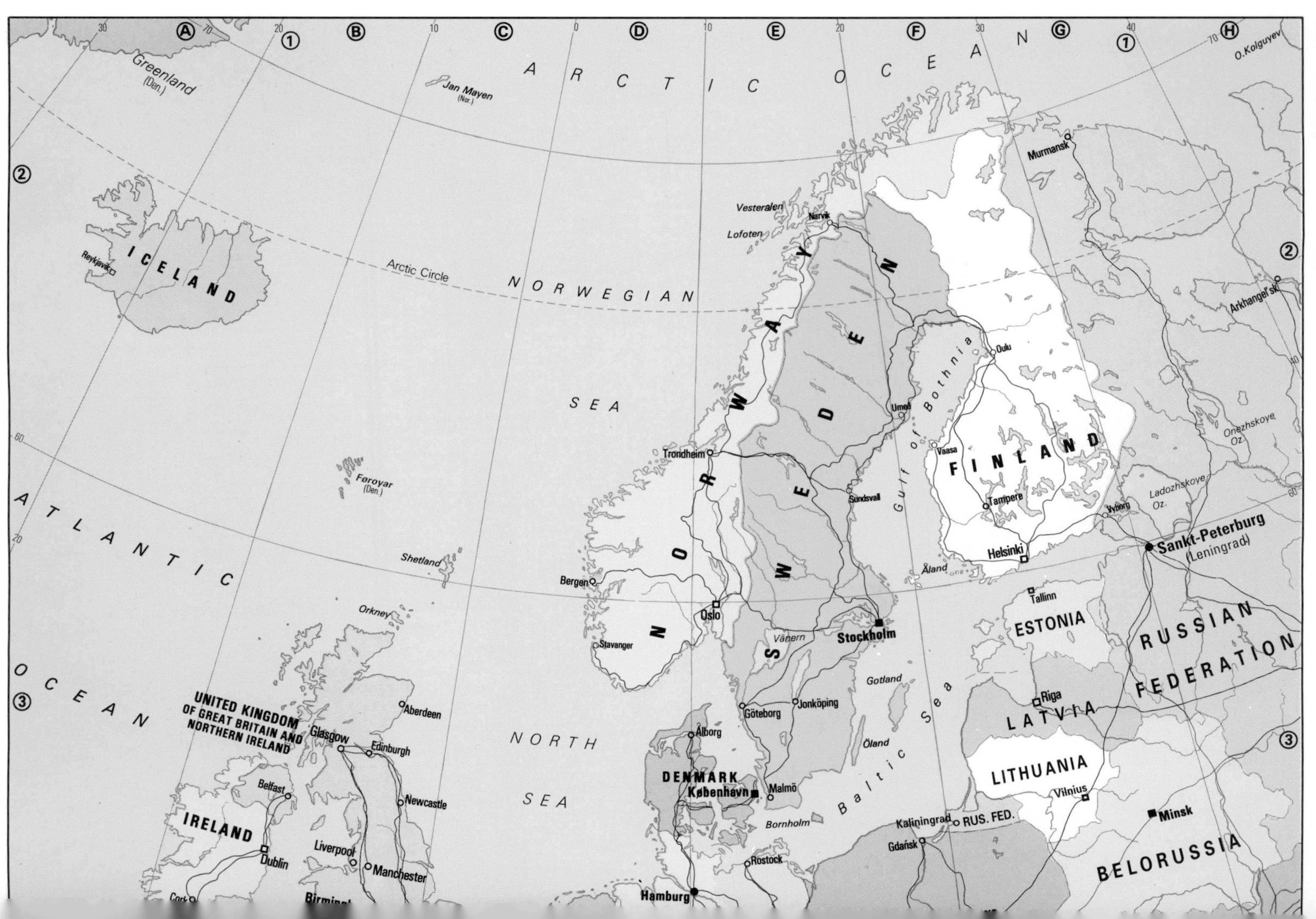
ARCTIC OCEAN
NORWEGIAN SEA
ATLANTIC OCEAN
NORTH SEA
Baltic Sea
Gulf of Bothnia
Arctic Circle
Greenland (Den.)
Jan Mayen (Nor.)
Føroyar (Den.)
Shetland
Orkney
O.Kolguyev
ICELAND
Reykjavik
NORWAY
SWEDEN
FINLAND
DENMARK
ESTONIA
LATVIA
LITHUANIA
BELORUSSIA
RUSSIAN FEDERATION
RUS. FED.
UNITED KINGDOM OF GREAT BRITAIN AND NORTHERN IRELAND
IRELAND
Murmansk
Arkhangel'sk
Onezhskoye Oz.
Ladozhskoye Oz.
Sankt-Peterburg (Leningrad)
Vyborg
Helsinki
Tampere
Oulu
Vaasa
Åland
Tallinn
Riga
Vilnius
Minsk
Kaliningrad
Gdańsk
Umeå
Sundsvall
Stockholm
Gotland
Öland
Jönköping
Vänern
Göteborg
Malmö
Bornholm
Rostock
København
Ålborg
Hamburg
Narvik
Vesterålen
Lofoten
Trondheim
Oslo
Bergen
Stavanger
Aberdeen
Edinburgh
Glasgow
Newcastle
Manchester
Liverpool
Belfast
Dublin
A B C D E F G H
1 2 3

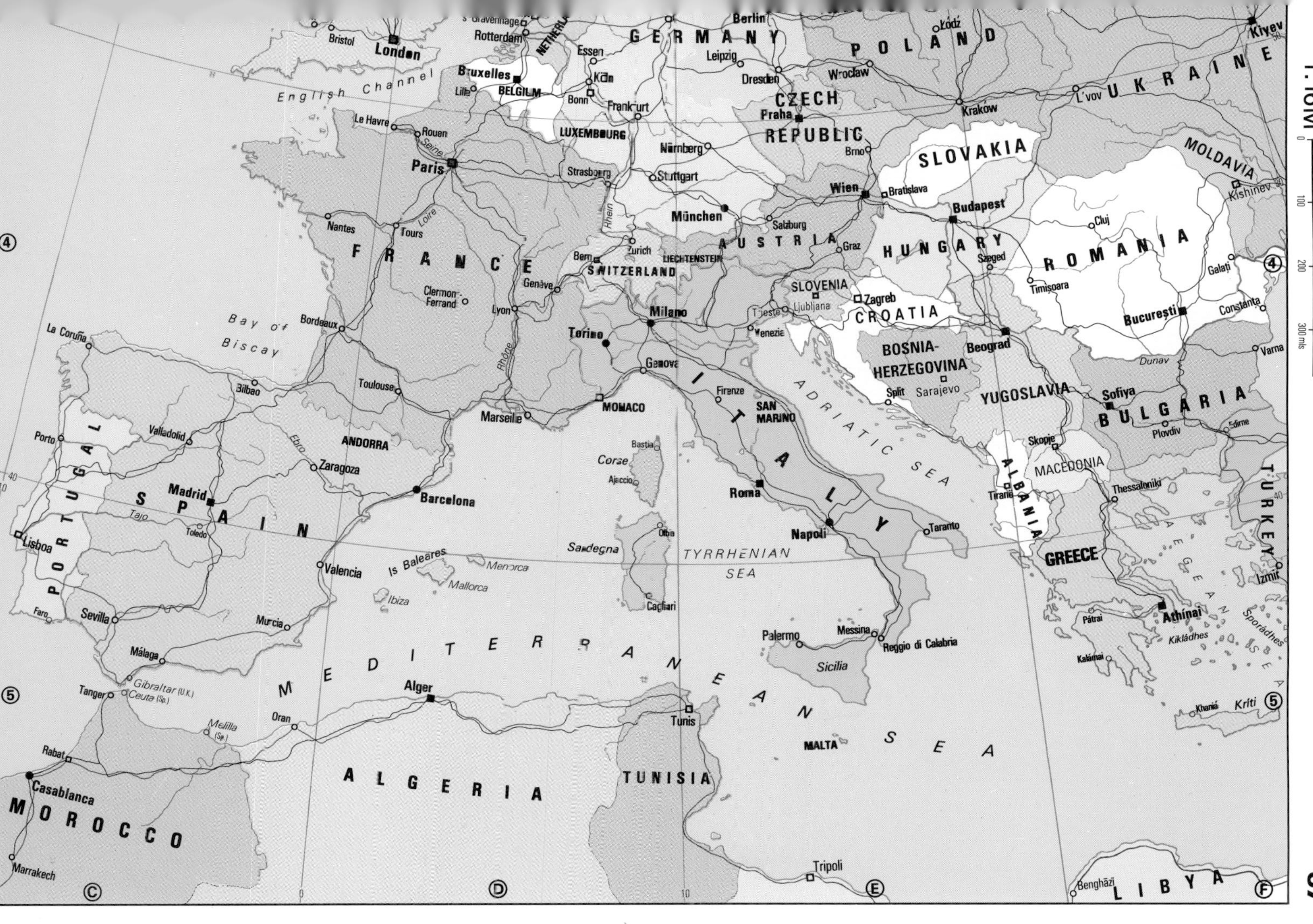

200 400 600km
100 200 300mls

GERMANY
POLAND
UKRAINE
CZECH REPUBLIC
SLOVAKIA
MOLDAVIA
HUNGARY
ROMANIA
AUSTRIA
LIECHTENSTEIN
SWITZERLAND
SLOVENIA
CROATIA
BOSNIA-HERZEGOVINA
YUGOSLAVIA
BULGARIA
MACEDONIA
ALBANIA
GREECE
TURKEY
FRANCE
BELGIUM
LUXEMBOURG
MONACO
ITALY
SAN MARINO
ANDORRA
SPAIN
PORTUGAL
MOROCCO
ALGERIA
TUNISIA
LIBYA
MALTA
English Channel
Bay of Biscay
MEDITERRANEAN SEA
ADRIATIC SEA
TYRRHENIAN SEA
AEGEAN SEA
Bristol
London
Rotterdam
Bruxelles
Lille
Essen
Köln
Bonn
Frankfurt
Berlin
Leipzig
Dresden
Łódź
Wrocław
Praha
Brno
Kraków
L'vov
Kiyev
Kishinev
Le Havre
Rouen
Seine
Paris
Strasbourg
Nürnberg
Stuttgart
München
Salzburg
Wien
Bratislava
Budapest
Cluj
Nantes
Tours
Loire
Zurich
Bern
Graz
Szeged
Timişoara
Galaţi
Constanţa
Genève
Clermont-Ferrand
Lyon
Rhône
Rhein
Milano
Torino
Trieste
Ljubljana
Venezia
Zagreb
Bucureşti
Beograd
Sarajevo
Split
Varna
Dunav
Bordeaux
La Coruña
Bilbao
Toulouse
Genova
Firenze
Marseille
Sofiya
Plovdiv
Edirne
Skopje
Porto
Valladolid
Zaragoza
Ebro
Madrid
Tajo
Toledo
Lisboa
Barcelona
Bastia
Corse
Ajaccio
Roma
Tiranë
Thessaloníki
Napoli
Taranto
Sardegna
Olbia
Valencia
Is Baleares
Menorca
Mallorca
Ibiza
Cagliari
Faro
Sevilla
Murcia
Málaga
Palermo
Messina
Reggio di Calabria
Sicilia
Pátrai
Athínai
Kikládhes
Sporádhes
Kalámai
İzmir
Tanger
Gibraltar (U.K.)
Ceuta (Sp.)
Melilla (Sp.)
Oran
Alger
Tunis
Khaniá
Kríti
Rabat
Casablanca
Marrakech
Tripoli
Benghāzī

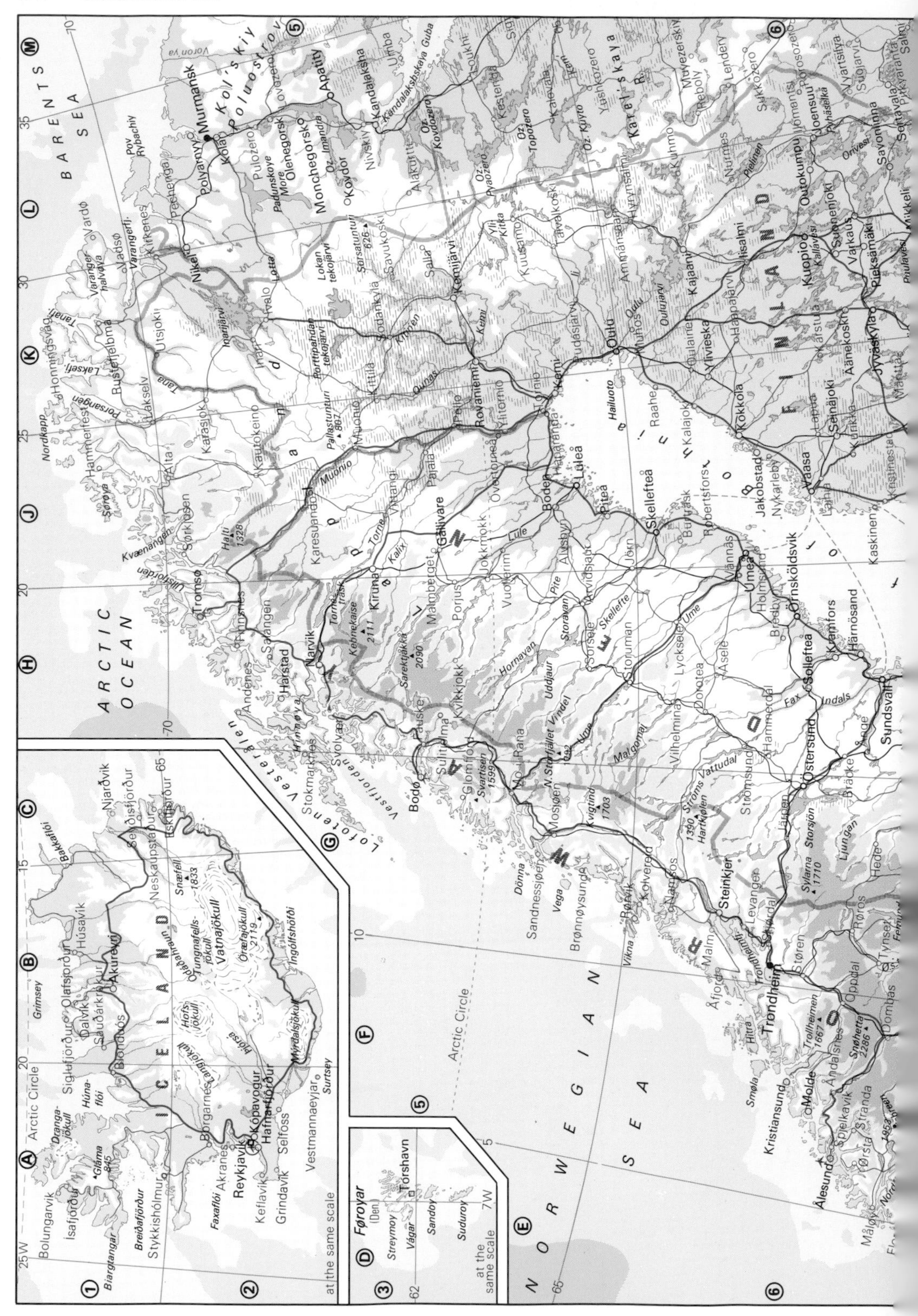
BARENTS SEA
ARCTIC OCEAN
NORWEGIAN SEA
ICELAND
Føroyar (Den.)
at the same scale
Arctic Circle
Kol'skiy Poluostrov
Karel'skaya
Murmansk
Apatity
Kandalaksha
Monchegorsk
Olenegorsk
Kirkenes
Vardø
Vadsø
Hammerfest
Nordkapp
Tromsø
Narvik
Harstad
Bodø
Kiruna
Gällivare
Luleå
Boden
Piteå
Skellefteå
Umeå
Örnsköldsvik
Härnösand
Sundsvall
Östersund
Trondheim
Steinkjer
Molde
Kristiansund
Ålesund
Oulu
Kemi
Tornio
Rovaniemi
Kemijärvi
Kajaani
Kuopio
Joensuu
Jyväskylä
Vaasa
Kokkola
Jakobstad
Reykjavík
Kópavogur
Hafnarfjörður
Akureyri
Húsavík
Ísafjörður
Vatnajökull
Tórshavn
Lofoten
Vesterålen
Vestfjorden
Kebnekaise 2111
Sarektjåkkå 2090
Snøhetta 2286
Sylarna 1710
Kvigtind 1703
Svartisen 1599
Hvannadalshnúkur
Öræfajökull 2119
Snæfell 1833
Gláma 845

1:7.5M

100   200   300 km
50   150 mils

⑦

⑧

RUSSIAN FEDERATION

Sankt-Peter-burg
Leningrad
Kronstadt

Priozersk
Ladozhskoye Ozero

Elisenvaara

Vyborg
Primorsk
Svetogorsk
Kamennogorsk

Imatra
Savonlinna
Lappeenranta
Kouvola
Kotka
Hamina
Porvoo

Heinola
Valkeakoski
Hämeenlinna
Lahti
Riihimäki
Hyvinkää

Helsinki
(Helsingfors)

Tampere
Forssa
Hämeenkyrö
Kokemäki

Turku
Salo
Kerava

Pori
Rauma
Uusikaupunki

Naantali

Mariehamn

Åland

Gulf of Finland

Lomonosov
Gatchina
Luga
Luga

Narva
Zelenogorsk

Kunda
Kohtla-Järve
Tapa
Rakvere

Gdov
Lake Peipus
Pskov
Ostrov

Polotsk
Opochka
Pustoshka

Borisov
Cherven'

Minsk
BELORUSSIA

Daugavpils

Vilnius
Alytus
Kaunas
Marijampole

Panevezys

Siauliai
Mazeikiai

Riga
Jurmala
Jelgava
Saldus
Kuldiga

Tartu
Valga
Võru
Cēsis

Tallinn
ESTONIA
Pärnu
Haapsalu
Paldiski

LATVIA

Ventspils
Liepāja
Klaipeda

Šuwałki
Grodno
Białystok
Volkovysk
Baranovichi
Pinsk

Gdynia
Gdańsk
Sopot
Słupsk
Szczecinek

POLAND

Stockholm
Uppsala
Norrtälje
Södertälje

Gävle
Söderhamn
Hudiksvall

Falun
Borlänge

Västerås
Köping
Sala
Enköping

Örebro
Eskilstuna
Katrineholm
Nyköping

Norrköping
Linköping
Motala

SWEDEN

Jönköping
Borås
Göteborg

Oslo
Drammen
Moss

NORWAY

Bergen
Stavanger

Gotland
Visby

BALTIC SEA

Bornholm
(Den.)

København
Malmö
Helsingborg
DENMARK

Berlin
GERMANY
Hamburg
Lübeck
Rostock

North Sea

Bremen
Hannover

⑦

⑧

55

K

J

H

G

F

M

N

9

1:5M

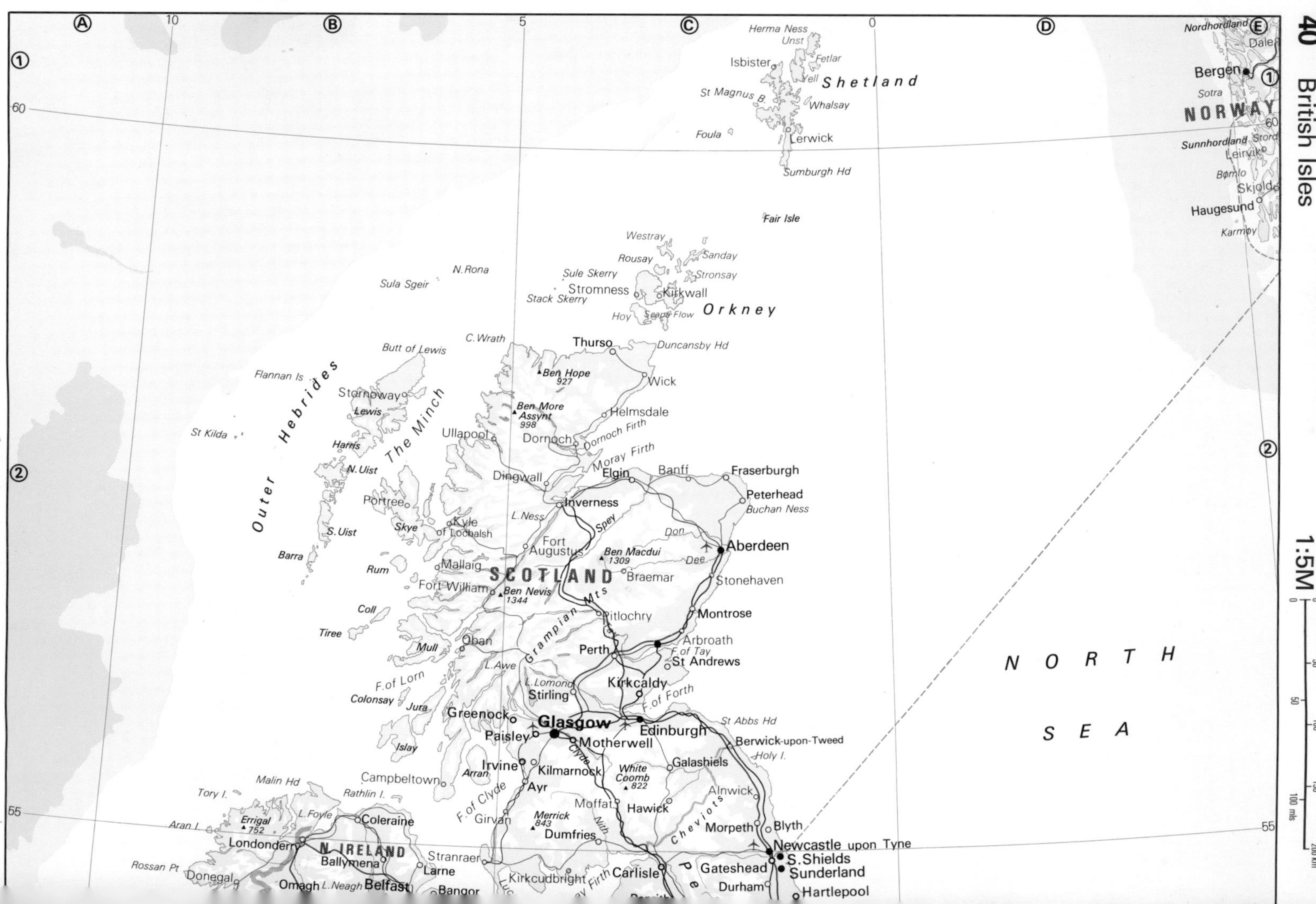

0   50   100   150   200 km
0   50   100 mls

NORWAY

Nordhordland
Bergen
Sotra
Sunnhordland
Bømlo
Skjold
Leirvik
Stord
Karmøy
Haugesund

Dale

NORTH SEA

Herma Ness
Unst
Fetlar
Isbister
Yell
St Magnus B.
Whalsay
Foula
Shetland
Lerwick
Sumburgh Hd

Fair Isle

Westray
Rousay
Sanday
Stronsay
Orkney
Sule Skerry
Stromness
Kirkwall
Hoy
Scapa Flow
Stack Skerry
Duncansby Hd

N. Rona
Sula Sgeir
C. Wrath
Thurso
Wick
Helmsdale

Butt of Lewis
Ullapool
Ben Hope 927
Ben More Assynt 998
Dornoch Firth
Moray Firth
Helmsdale

Flannan Is
Stornoway
Lewis
Harris
N. Uist
The Minch
Portree
Skye
L. Ness
Fort Augustus
Dingwall
Inverness
Elgin
Banff
Fraserburgh
Peterhead
Buchan Ness
Aberdeen
Stonehaven
Dee
Ben Macdui 1309
Braemar
Pitlochry
SCOTLAND

St Kilda
Barra
S. Uist
Rum
Coll
Tiree
Mallaig
Kyle of Lochalsh
Fort William
Ben Nevis 1344
F. of Lorn
Mull
Oban
L. Awe
L. Lomond
Grampian Mts
Perth
F. of Tay
St Andrews
Arbroath
Montrose

Outer Hebrides

Tory I.
Errigal 752
Aran I.
Donegal
Rossan Pt
Colonsay
Jura
Islay
Campbeltown
Arran
F. of Clyde
Irvine
Ayr
Girvan
Kilmarnock
Paisley
Greenock
Glasgow
Motherwell
Stirling
Kirkcaldy
F. of Forth
Edinburgh
Galashiels
White Coomb 822
Hawick
Merrick 843
Dumfries
Nith
Moffat
Berwick-upon-Tweed
St Abbs Hd
Holy I.

Main Hd
L. Foyle
Coleraine
Rathlin I.
Larne
Belfast
Ballymena
Omagh L. Neagh
Londonderry
N IRELAND
Bangor
Stranraer
Kirkcudbright
Kirkcudbright Bay
Carlisle
Durham
Cheviot Hills
Alnwick
Morpeth
Blyth
Newcastle upon Tyne
Gateshead
S. Shields
Sunderland
Hartlepool

60

55

55

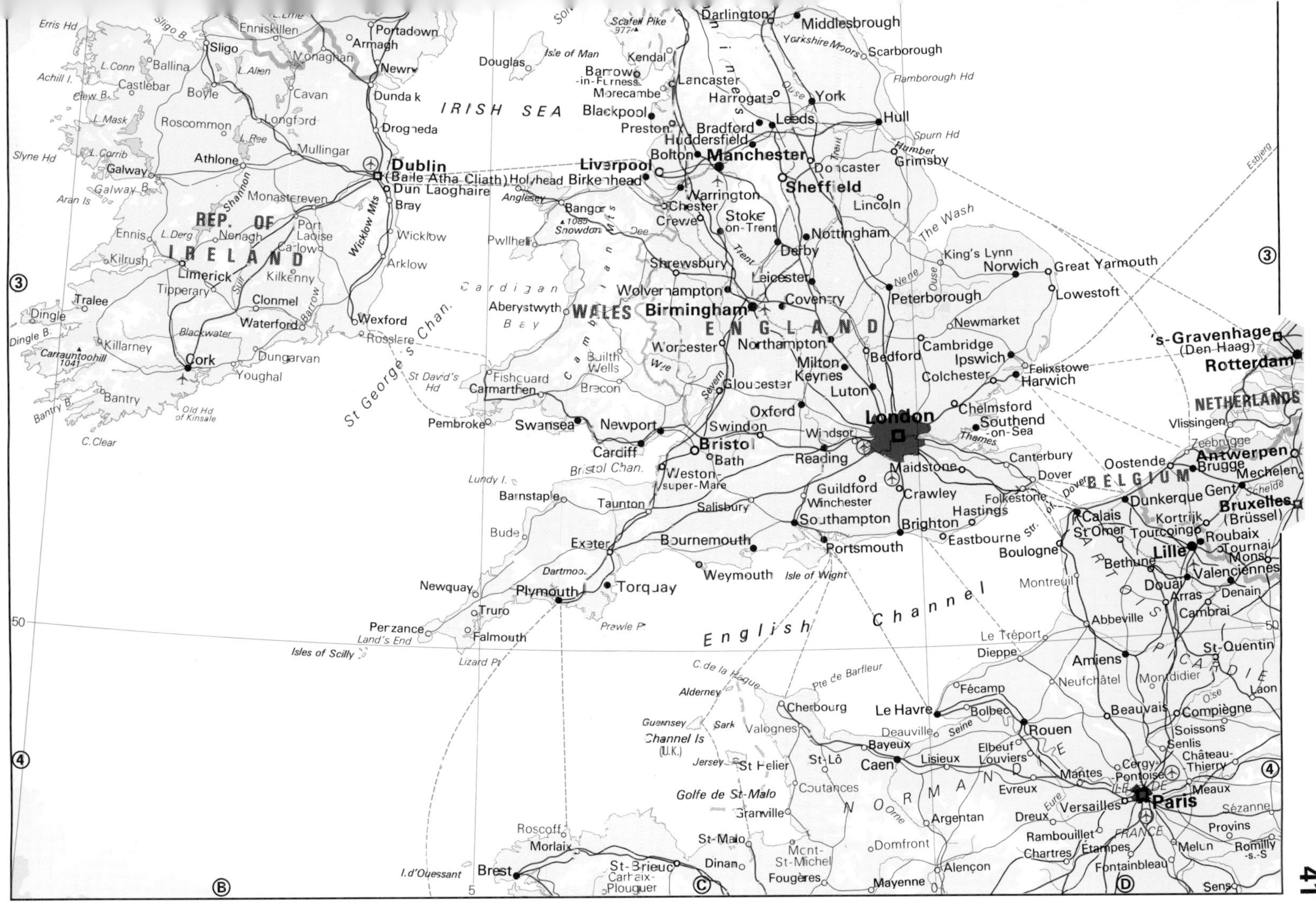
Sligo
Enniskillen
Portadown
Armagh
Monaghan
Newry
Ballina
Castlebar
Boyle
Cavan
Dundalk
Roscommon
Longford
Drogheda
Athlone
Mullingar
Galway
Dublin
(Baile Atha Cliath)
Dun Laoghaire
Bray
Wicklow Mts
REP. OF IRELAND
Monasterevan
Port Laoise
Carlow
Nenagh
Ennis
Kilrush
Limerick
Kilkenny
Tipperary
Clonmel
Tralee
Dingle
Waterford
Wexford
Rosslare
Killarney
Cork
Dungarvan
Youghal
Bantry
Carrauntoohill 1041
Arklow
Wicklow
Shannon
Blackwater
Barrow
Erris Hd
Achill I.
Slyne Hd
Aran Is
Galway B.
Sligo B.
Dingle B.
Bantry B.
C. Clear
Old Hd of Kinsale
L. Conn
L. Mask
L. Corrib
L. Derg
L. Ree
L. Allen
IRISH SEA
Douglas
Isle of Man
St George's Chan.
Cardigan Bay
Holyhead
Anglesey
Bangor
Snowdon 1085
Pwllheli
Aberystwyth
WALES
Fishguard
Carmarthen
Pembroke
St David's Hd
Swansea
Newport
Cardiff
Brecon
Builth Wells
Bristol Chan.
Lundy I.
Barnstaple
Bude
Newquay
Truro
Falmouth
Penzance
Land's End
Isles of Scilly
Lizard Pt
Plymouth
Dartmoor
Torquay
Prawle Pt
Exeter
Taunton
Weston-super-Mare
Bristol
Bath
Swindon
Salisbury
Bournemouth
Weymouth
Southampton
Portsmouth
Isle of Wight
Winchester
Guildford
Reading
Windsor
Oxford
Gloucester
Worcester
Severn
Wye
Birmingham
Wolverhampton
Shrewsbury
Stoke-on-Trent
Crewe
Chester
Warrington
Liverpool
Birkenhead
Bolton
Manchester
Huddersfield
Bradford
Leeds
Preston
Blackpool
Morecambe
Lancaster
Barrow-in-Furness
Kendal
Scafell Pike 977
Darlington
Middlesbrough
Yorkshire Moors
Scarborough
Flamborough Hd
Harrogate
York
Ouse
Hull
Spurn Hd
Humber
Grimsby
Doncaster
Sheffield
Lincoln
Trent
Nottingham
Derby
Leicester
Coventry
ENGLAND
Northampton
Milton Keynes
Luton
Bedford
Peterborough
The Wash
King's Lynn
Norwich
Great Yarmouth
Lowestoft
Newmarket
Cambridge
Ipswich
Felixstowe
Harwich
Colchester
Chelmsford
Southend-on-Sea
Thames
London
Maidstone
Crawley
Brighton
Hastings
Eastbourne
Canterbury
Dover
Folkestone
Str. of Dover
English Channel
Esbjerg
's-Gravenhage
(Den Haag)
Rotterdam
NETHERLANDS
Vlissingen
Zeebrugge
Antwerpen
Brugge
Mechelen
Schelde
Oostende
BELGIUM
Gent
Bruxelles
(Brüssel)
Dunkerque
Kortrijk
Calais
St Omer
Tourcoing
Roubaix
Lille
Tournai
Mons
Bethune
Boulogne
Valenciennes
Douai
Arras
Denain
Cambrai
Montreuil
Abbeville
Le Tréport
Dieppe
Amiens
St-Quentin
PICARDIE
Neufchâtel
Montdidier
Laon
Oise
Fécamp
Le Havre
Bolbec
Seine
Rouen
Beauvais
Compiègne
Soissons
Senlis
Château-Thierry
Cergy-Pontoise
ILE-DE-FRANCE
Meaux
Paris
Versailles
Sézanne
Provins
Mantes
Evreux
Eure
Dreux
Rambouillet
Chartres
Étampes
Melun
Fontainbleau
Romilly-s.-S
Sens
Deauville
Bayeux
Caen
Lisieux
Elbeuf
Louviers
NORMANDIE
Orne
Argentan
Domfront
Alençon
Mayenne
Cherbourg
Pte de Barfleur
C. de la Hague
Alderney
Valognes
Guernsey
Sark
Channel Is
(U.K.)
Jersey
St Helier
St-Lô
Coutances
Golfe de St-Malo
Granville
St-Malo
Dinan
Mont-St-Michel
Fougères
Roscoff
Morlaix
Brest
I.d'Ouessant
St-Brieuc
Carhaix-Plouguer
50
5
3
4
B
C
D

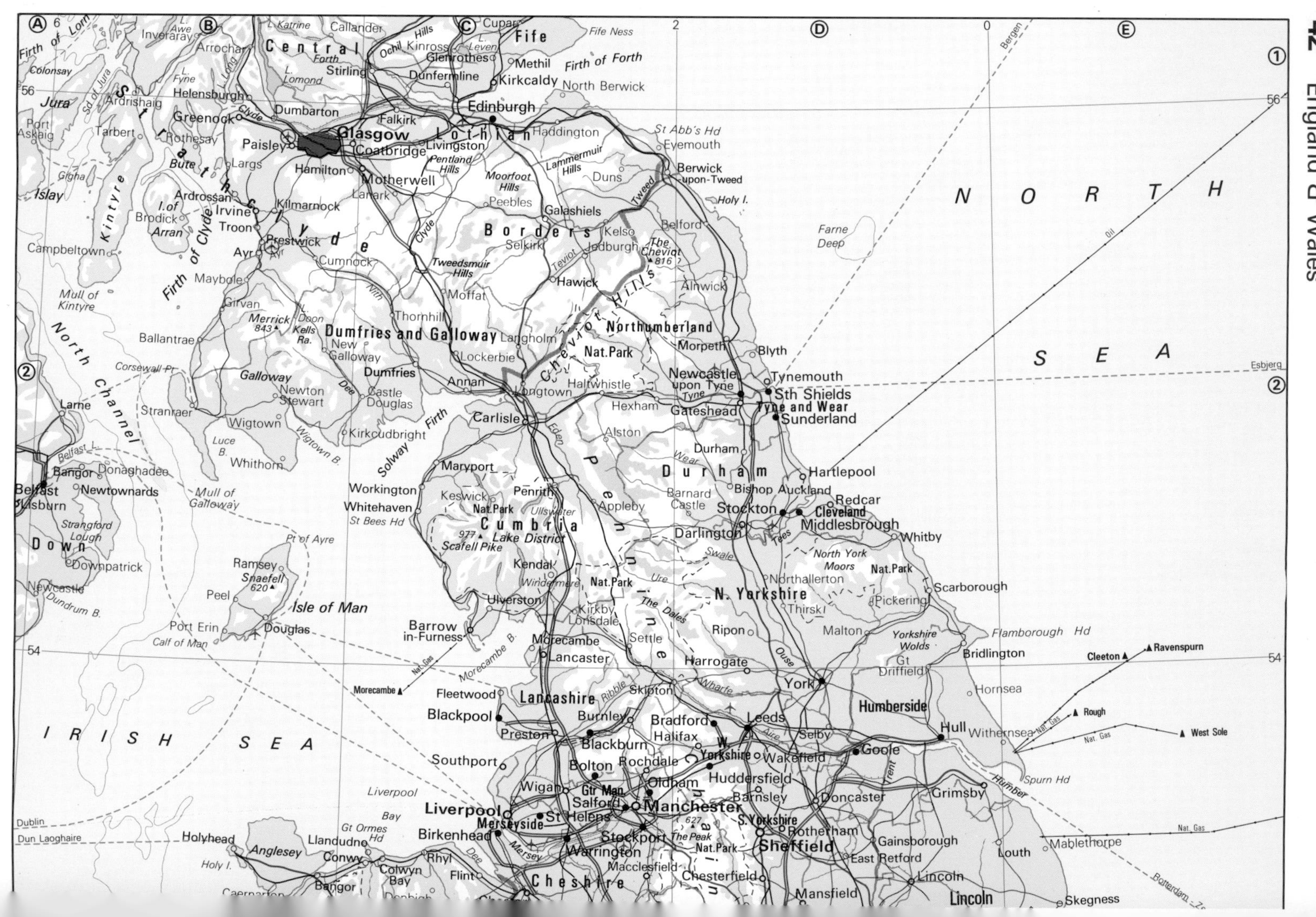
NORTH SEA
IRISH SEA
North Channel
Firth of Clyde
Firth of Forth
Solway Firth
Isle of Man
Central
Fife
Lothian
Borders
Strathclyde
Dumfries and Galloway
Northumberland
Tyne and Wear
Durham
Cumbria
Cleveland
N. Yorkshire
Humberside
Lancashire
Merseyside
Gtr Man
W. Yorkshire
S. Yorkshire
Cheshire
Down
Pennines
Cheviot Hills
Lake District
Galloway
Glasgow
Edinburgh
Stirling
Falkirk
Dunfermline
Kirkcaldy
Glenrothes
Paisley
Greenock
Dumbarton
Motherwell
Hamilton
Coatbridge
Livingston
Kilmarnock
Ayr
Prestwick
Troon
Irvine
Ardrossan
Largs
Girvan
Stranraer
Dumfries
Lockerbie
Annan
Moffat
Hawick
Galashiels
Peebles
Selkirk
Kelso
Jedburgh
Berwick upon-Tweed
Newcastle upon Tyne
Gateshead
Sunderland
Sth Shields
Tynemouth
Blyth
Morpeth
Hexham
Carlisle
Penrith
Keswick
Workington
Whitehaven
Barrow in-Furness
Kendal
Lancaster
Morecambe
Blackpool
Preston
Blackburn
Burnley
Bolton
Wigan
Southport
Liverpool
Birkenhead
St Helens
Warrington
Manchester
Salford
Oldham
Rochdale
Stockport
Bradford
Leeds
Halifax
Huddersfield
Wakefield
Barnsley
Sheffield
Rotherham
Doncaster
York
Harrogate
Ripon
Skipton
Middlesbrough
Stockton
Darlington
Hartlepool
Redcar
Whitby
Scarborough
Bridlington
Hull
Grimsby
Goole
Lincoln
Skegness
Douglas
Ramsey
Peel
Belfast
Bangor
Larne
Newtownards
Downpatrick
Holyhead
Anglesey
Llandudno
Conwy
Colwyn Bay
Rhyl
Flint
Scafell Pike
Snaefell

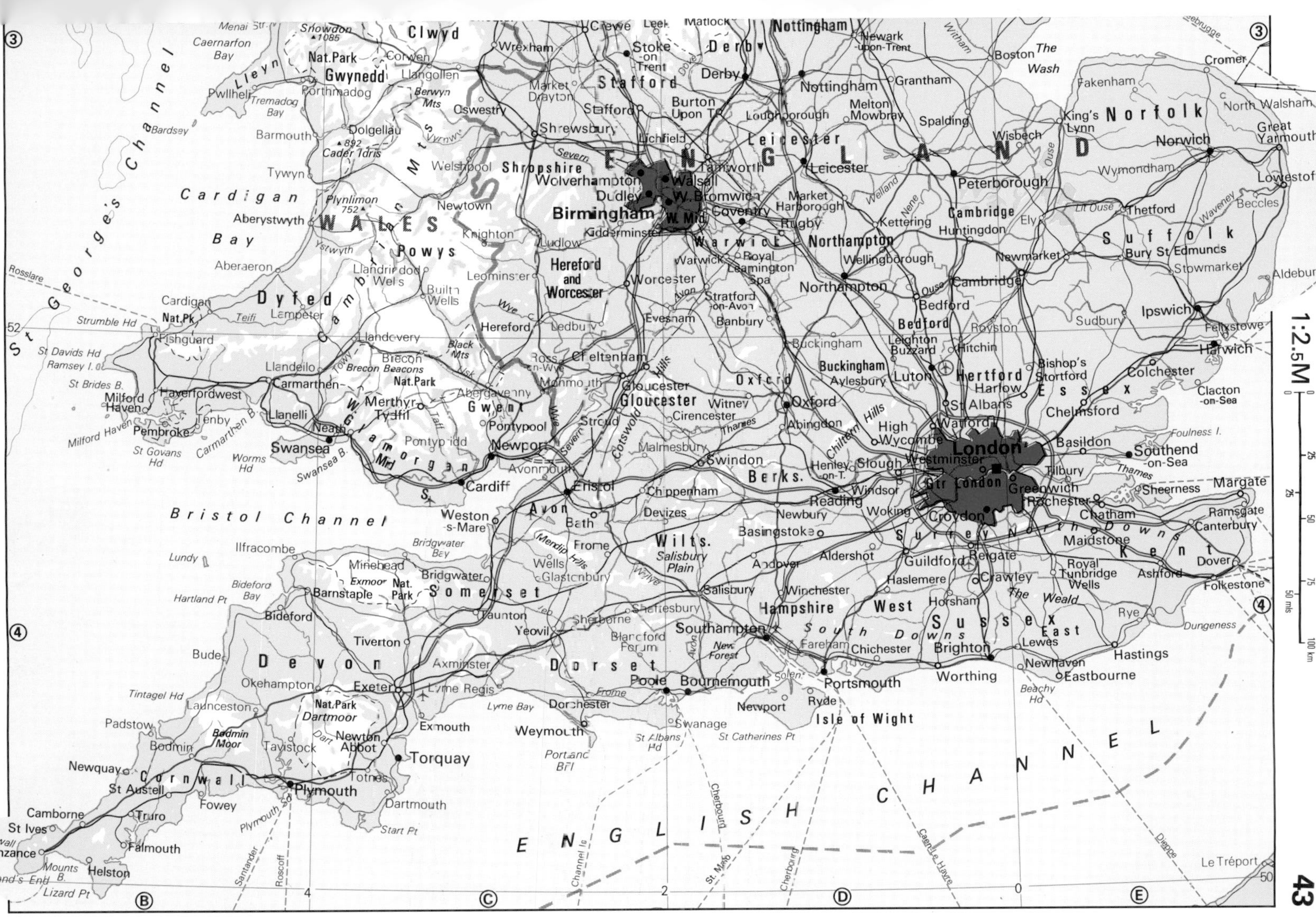
1:2.5M
0 25 50 75 100 km
0 25 50 mls
ENGLISH CHANNEL
ENGLAND
WALES
St George's Channel
Bristol Channel
Cardigan Bay
The Wash
Isle of Wight
Norfolk
Suffolk
Essex
Kent
Surrey
East Sussex
West Sussex
Hampshire
Dorset
Devon
Cornwall
Somerset
Avon
Wilts.
Berks.
Oxford
Buckingham
Bedford
Hertford
Cambridge
Northampton
Leicester
Nottingham
Derby
Stafford
Shropshire
Warwick
Gloucester
Hereford and Worcester
W. Mid.
Gwynedd
Clwyd
Powys
Dyfed
Gwent
Glamorgan
Cambrian Mts
London
Gtr London
Birmingham
Wolverhampton
Coventry
Bristol
Cardiff
Swansea
Newport
Plymouth
Exeter
Southampton
Portsmouth
Brighton
Bournemouth
Poole
Norwich
Ipswich
Peterborough
Oxford
Reading
Northampton
Luton
Southend-on-Sea
Dover
Folkestone
Canterbury
Margate
Ramsgate
Hastings
Eastbourne
Torquay
Penzance
Land's End
Lizard Pt
St Ives
Truro
Falmouth
Newquay
Great Yarmouth
Lowestoft
Cromer
King's Lynn
Boston
Grantham
Stoke-on-Trent
Crewe
Shrewsbury
Hereford
Worcester
Cheltenham
Swindon
Salisbury
Winchester
Basingstoke
Guildford
Croydon
Maidstone
Chelmsford
Colchester
Harwich
Felixstowe
Aberystwyth
Cardigan
Fishguard
Pembroke
Milford Haven
Carmarthen
Brecon
Snowdon 1085
Cader Idris 892
Plynlimon 752
Dieppe
Le Tréport
Cherbourg
Roscoff
Santander
Caen-Le Havre
Channel Is
St Malo
Rosslare

1:2.5M

0 25 50 75 100 km
0 25 50 mls

Shetland
Herma Ness, Unst, The Faither, Isbister, Hillswick, Papa Stour, Foula, St Magnus Bay, Yell, Fetlar, Whalsay, Brae, Voe, Noss, Bressay, Lerwick, Scalloway, Gruthess, Hanstholm-Bergen, Aberdeen, Fitful Hd, Sumburgh Hd, Fair Isle, Stromness

Orkney
Papa Westray, N. Ronaldsay, Westray, Sanday, Eday, Stronsay, Shapinsay, Rousay, Mainland, Stromness, Kirkwall, Burray, Scapa Flow, S. Ronaldsay, Duncansby Hd, John o' Groats, Hoy, Pentland Firth, Dunnet Hd, Thurso

NORTH SEA
Long Forties, Buchan Deep

Burray, S. Ronaldsay, Duncansby Hd, John o' Groats, Hoy, Pentland Firth, Dunnet Hd, C. Wrath, Durness, Eriboll, Tongue, Ben Hope 927, Ben Kilbreck 961, Loch Naver, Brora, Helmsdale, Lybster, Wick, Thurso, Dunnet Hd, Loch Shin, Lairg, Dornoch, Tain, Dornoch Firth, Tarbat Ness, Golspie

Beatrice, Moray Firth, Kinnairds Hd, Fraserburgh, Peterhead, Buchan Ness, Aberdeen, Girdle Ness, Stonehaven, Montrose, Arbroath, Banff, Huntly, Keith, Elgin, Lossiemouth, Forres, Nairn, Inverurie, Don, Deveron, Dufftown, Ythan

Ben More Assynt 998, Ullapool, Loch Broom, Ben Dearg 1087, Ben Wyvis 1045, Dingwall, Beauly, Black Isle, Cromarty, Inverness, Loch Ness, Farrar, Loch Maree, Gairloch, Torridon, Kyle of Lochalsh, Ben Attow 1031, Fort Augustus, Kingussie, Mohadhjath Mts, Findhorn, Grantown-on-Spey, Aviemore, Cairngorms 1310, Ben Macdui 1310, Lochnagar 1155, Braemar, Ballater, Dee, Banchory, Brechin, A. Esk, Forfar, Dundee

Grampian, HIGHLAND, SCOTLAND, Monadhliath Mts, Glen More, TAYSIDE, CENTRAL, FIFE

Stornoway, Lewis, Harris, Tarbert, North Uist, Benbecula, South Uist, Barra, Castlebay, Barra Hd, Lochmaddy, Lochboisdale, WESTERN ISLES, Monach Is, Flannan Is, Scarp, Taransay, Pabbay, Eriskay, Sd of Barra

Little Minch, North Minch, Rubha Hunish, Uig, Portree, Raasay, Sd of Raasay, Isle of Skye, Cuillin Hills, Broadford, Kyleakin, Snizort, L. Snizort, Canna, Rum, Eigg, Muck, Mallaig, Arisaig, L. Morar, L. Shiel, Ardnamurchan Pt, Coll, Tiree, Mull, Tobermory, Ulva, Staffa, Iona, Colonsay

Ben Nevis 1344, Fort William, Loch Lochy, Loch Linnhe, Ballachulish, Glencoe, L. Etive, Oban, L. Awe, Morvern, Firth of Lorn, Sd of Jura, Jura, Islay, Port Askaig

Ben Lawers 1214, L. Rannoch, L. Ericht, Blair Atholl, Pitlochry, Aberfeldy, Garry, L. Tay, L. Earn, Crieff, Perth, L. Katrine, L. Lomond, Callander, Killin, Crianlarich, Stirling, Dunblane, Kinross, L. Leven, Dunfermline, Glenrothes, Cupar, St Andrews, Fife Ness, Methil, Kirkcaldy, North Berwick, Edinburgh, Firth of Forth, Firth of Tay

Arrochar, Inveraray, L. Fyne, Helensburgh, Dumbarton, Greenock, Gourock, Rothesay, Bute, Paisley, GLASGOW, Hamilton, Motherwell, Coatbridge, Livingston, Falkirk, Pentland Hills, Lammermuir Hills, Haddington, Duns, Berwick-upon-Tweed, St Abb's Hd, Eyemouth, Largs, Ardrishaig, Tarbert

St Abb's Hd, Duncansby Hd, John o' Groats, Thurso, Dunnet Hd, Pentland Firth

25 50 75 100 km
25 50 mls

NORTHERN IRELAND
REPUBLIC OF IRELAND

ULSTER · CONNAUGHT · LEINSTER · MUNSTER

Provinces and counties:
Donegal, Londonderry, Antrim, Tyrone, Fermanagh, Monaghan, Armagh, Down, Cavan, Louth, Leitrim, Sligo, Mayo, Roscommon, Longford, Meath, Westmeath, Galway, Offaly, Kildare, Dublin, Wicklow, Laois, Carlow, Clare, Tipperary, Kilkenny, Wexford, Limerick, Kerry, Cork, Waterford

North Channel · St George's Channel

Key towns: Londonderry, Coleraine, Belfast, Newtownards, Bangor, Larne, Lisburn, Lurgan, Portadown, Armagh, Newry, Dundalk, Drogheda, Dublin (Baile Átha Cliath), Dún Laoghaire, Bray, Wicklow, Arklow, Wexford, Rosslare, Waterford, Cork, Cobh, Kinsale, Bantry, Killarney, Tralee, Dingle, Limerick, Galway, Sligo, Ennis, Clonmel

Errigal 752 · Blue Stack 676 · Mts of Nephin 807 · MacGillycuddys Reeks 1041 · Kippure 754

St George's Channel · Fishguard · Cherbourg-le-Havre

1:2.5M

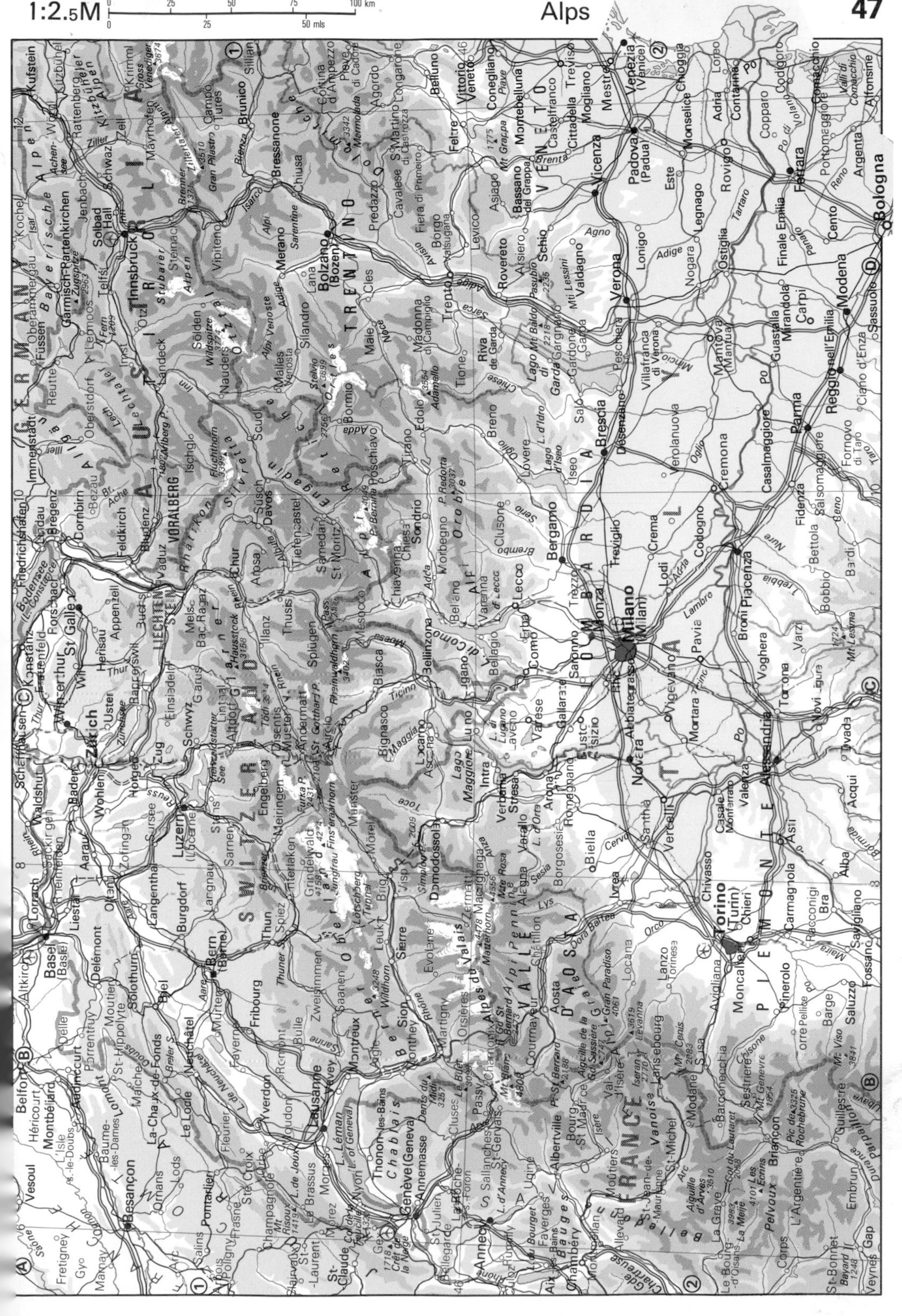
GERMANY
AUSTRIA
TIROL
SWITZERLAND
LIECHTENSTEIN
FRANCE
ITALY
TRENTINO
VENETO
LOMBARDIA
PIEMONTE
VALLE D'AOSTA
VORALBERG
Kufstein
Innsbruck
Bolzano (Bozen)
Merano
Bressanone
Brunico
Trento
Verona
Vicenza
Padova (Padua)
Venezia (Venice)
Treviso
Belluno
Ferrara
Bologna
Modena
Mantova (Mantua)
Parma
Reggio nell'Emilia
Cremona
Piacenza
Brescia
Bergamo
Milano (Milan)
Monza
Como
Lecco
Lugano
Bellinzona
Novara
Vercelli
Alessandria
Asti
Torino (Turin)
Biella
Ivrea
Aosta
Chur
Davos
St Moritz
Zürich
Luzern (Lucerne)
Bern (Berne)
Basel (Basle)
Fribourg
Lausanne
Genève (Geneva)
Annecy
Chambéry
Besançon
Konstanz
St Gallen
Bodensee (L. Constance)
Lago Maggiore
Lago di Garda
L. Léman (L. of Geneva)
Mt Blanc 4808
Bregenz
Feldkirch
Vaduz
Landeck
Garmisch-Partenkirchen
Füssen
Domodossola
Sion
Sierre
Montreux
Neuchâtel
Chamonix
Briançon
Gap
Saluzzo
Pinerolo
Cuneo

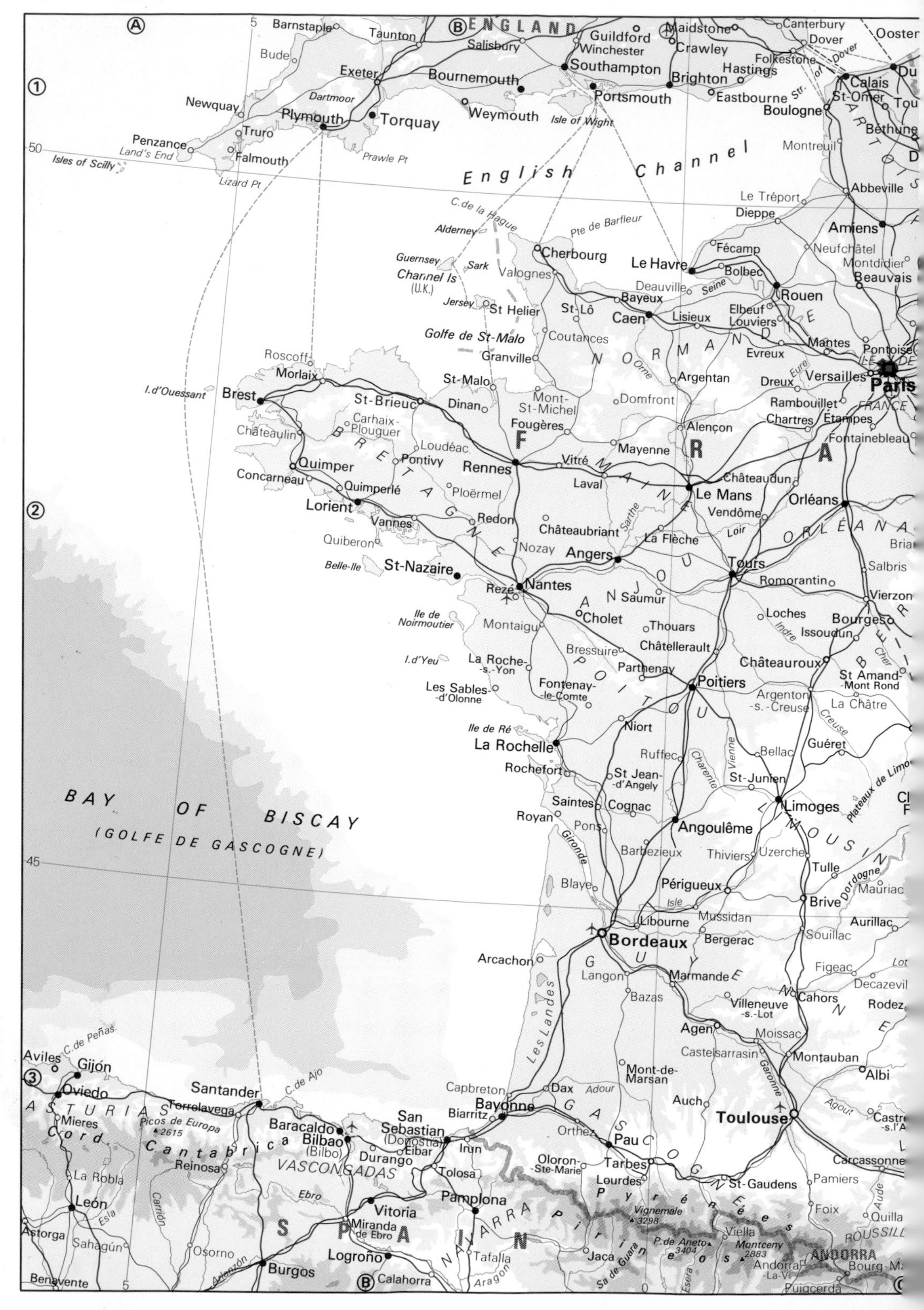
A
B
ENGLAND
Barnstaple
Taunton
Bude
Exeter
Salisbury
Guildford
Winchester
Maidstone
Canterbury
Dover
Crawley
Oosten
Southampton
Bournemouth
Brighton
Hastings
Folkestone
Str. of Dover
Calais
St-Omer
Eastbourne
Boulogne
Newquay
Dartmoor
Plymouth
Torquay
Weymouth
Portsmouth
Isle of Wight
Penzance
Truro
Land's End
Falmouth
Isles of Scilly
Prawle Pt
Lizard Pt
Béthune
Montreuil
English Channel
Abbeville
Le Tréport
Dieppe
C. de la Hague
Alderney
Pte de Barfleur
Amiens
Fécamp
Neufchâtel
Montdidier
Guernsey
Sark
Cherbourg
Le Havre
Bolbec
Beauvais
Channel Is (U.K.)
Valognes
Deauville
Seine
Rouen
Jersey
St Helier
Bayeux
St-Lô
Caen
Lisieux
Elbeuf
Louviers
Golfe de St-Malo
Coutances
Granville
Mantes
Pontoise
Evreux
Roscoff
Morlaix
NORMANDIE
Orne
Argentan
Dreux
Eure
Versailles
Paris
I. d'Ouessant
Brest
St-Malo
St-Brieuc
Dinan
Mont-St-Michel
Domfront
Rambouillet
ÎLE-DE-FRANCE
Carhaix-Plouguer
Fougères
Chartres
Étampes
Châteaulin
Alençon
Fontainebleau
Loudéac
Mayenne
BRETAGNE
F
R
A
Pontivy
Rennes
Vitré
Quimper
Concarneau
Quimperlé
Ploërmel
Laval
Châteaudun
MAINE
Le Mans
Lorient
Orléans
Vannes
Redon
Vendôme
Sarthe
Châteaubriant
Quiberon
La Flèche
Loir
ORLÉANAIS
Nozay
Angers
Belle-Ile
St-Nazaire
Tours
Salbris
Rezé
Nantes
ANJOU
Romorantin
Saumur
Vierzon
Ile de Noirmoutier
Cholet
Loches
Bourges
Montaigu
Thouars
Indre
Issoudun
Bressuire
Châtellerault
I. d'Yeu
La Roche-s.-Yon
POITOU
Parthenay
Châteauroux
Cher
St Amand-Mont Rond
Poitiers
Les Sables-d'Olonne
Fontenay-le-Comte
Argenton-s.-Creuse
La Châtre
Creuse
Ile de Ré
Niort
La Rochelle
Ruffec
Bellac
Guéret
Rochefort
St Jean-d'Angely
Charente
Vienne
St-Junien
BAY OF BISCAY
(GOLFE DE GASCOGNE)
Saintes
Cognac
Limoges
Plateaux de Limo
Royan
Pons
Angoulême
LIMOUSIN
Gironde
Barbezieux
Thiviers
Uzerche
Tulle
Dordogne
Blaye
Périgueux
Mauriac
Isle
Brive
Libourne
Mussidan
Aurillac
Bordeaux
Bergerac
Souillac
Arcachon
GUYENNE
Langon
Marmande
Figeac
Lot
Decazeville
Bazas
Cahors
Villeneuve-s.-Lot
Rodez
Les Landes
Agen
Moissac
Castelsarrasin
Montauban
Albi
C. de Peñas
Aviles
Gijón
Mont-de-Marsan
Garonne
Oviedo
Santander
C. de Ajo
Capbreton
Dax
Adour
Agout
ASTURIAS
Torrelavega
Auch
Bayonne
Toulouse
Castres
Mieres
Picos de Europa 2615
Baracaldo
San Sebastian (Donostia)
Biarritz
GASCOGNE
Cord. Cantabrica
Bilbao (Bilbo)
Eibar
Orthez
Pau
Reinosa
Durango
Irun
Carcassonne
VASCONGADAS
Oloron-Ste-Marie
Tarbes
La Robla
Tolosa
Lourdes
St-Gaudens
Pamiers
Carrión
Ebro
Pyrénées
León
Vitoria
Pamplona
Vignemale 3298
Foix
Esla
NAVARRA
Aude
Quillan
Astorga
Miranda de Ebro
Viella
Sahagún
SPAIN
Pirineos
P. de Aneto 3404
Montceny 2883
ROUSSILLON
Osorno
Tafalla
Jaca
ANDORRA
Sa de Guara
Esera
Andorra-La-V.
Logroño
Bourg-Madame
Arlanzón
Burgos
Aragon
Benavente
Calahorra
Puigcerdá
50
45
5

0 50 100 150 200 km
50 100 mls

①
②
③

Vlissingen
Zeebrugge
Eindhoven
Erfurt
Jena
Gera
Zwickau
Brugge
Antwerpen
(Anvers)
Mönchen-
gladbach
Düsseldorf
WESTFALEN
Köln
Siegen
Bad
Hersfeld
Eisenach
Plauen
Gent
Mechelen
Hasselt
Bruxelles
(Brüssel)
Leuven
Maastricht
St Truiden
Aachen
Bonn
Bad Godesberg
Marburg
Alsfeld
Giessen
Fulda
HESSEN
Coburg
Hof
Cheb
Kortrijk
Lille
Roubaix
Tournai
Liège
Euskirchen
Limburg
GERMANY
Schweinfurt
Bayreuth
Weiden
Valenciennes
Mons
Namur
Charleroi
Andernach
Koblenz
Würzburg
Bamberg
Denain
Maubeuge
Marche
Bitburg
Frankfurt
Offenbach
Aschaffenburg
Kitzingen
Erlangen
Amberg
Arras
Cambrai
Fourmies
Ardennes
Bastogne
LUXEM-
BOURG
RHEINLAND
PFALZ
Wiesbaden
Mainz
Darmstadt
Würzburg
Fürth
Nürnberg
Parsberg
St-Quentin
Charleville-
Mézières
Sedan
Arlon
Trier
Luxembourg
SAAR
LAND
Worms
Ludwigshafen
Mannheim
Heidelberg
Speyer
Ansbach
Crailsheim
Regensburg
BAYERN
Compiègne
Laon
Soissons
Verdun
Thionville
Saarlouis
Saarbrücken
Kaiserslautern
Pirmasens
Karlsruhe
Pforzheim
Heilbronn
Ludwigsburg
Esslingen
Donauwörth
Ingolstadt
Château-
Thierry
Reims
Épernay
Châlons
-s.-M.
Metz
Sarreguemines
Rastatt
Baden-Baden
Stuttgart
Heidenheim
Landshut
Meaux
Sézanne
Vitry-l.-F.
St-Dizier
Nancy
Sarrebourg
Strasbourg
Offenburg
Tübingen
Reutlingen
Ulm
Augsburg
Dachau
München
Provins
Melun
Troyes
Bar-s.-A.
Chaumont
Épinal
St Dié
Colmar
Freiburg
WÜRTEMBERG
Biberach
Ravensburg
Landsberg
Memmingen
Kempten
Bad Tölz
Starnberg
Rosenheim
Kufstein
Garmisch-P.
Sens
Joigny
Langres
Vesoul
Mulhouse
Lörrach
Schaffhausen
Konstanz
Friedrichshafen
Lindau
Winterthur
Dornbirn
AUSTRIA
Innsbruck
Brenner
Montargis
Auxerre
Avallon
Belfort
Montbéliard
Basel
Zürich
St Gallen
Feldkirch
Bludenz
Landeck
Wildspitze
Brunico
Besançon
Biel
Luzern
Zug
LIECHTEN-
STEIN
Vaduz
Chur
Arosa
Merano
Bolzano
Marmolada
Dijon
Dole
Neuchâtel
Bern
Schwyz
St Gotthard
St Moritz
Edolo
Trento
Rovereto
Beaune
Autun
Chalon-s.-S.
Pontarlier
Fribourg
Thun
Interlaken
Jungfrau
Rhein
Bellinzona
Domodossola
Lugano
Sondrio
Bassano
Le Creusot
Moncean-
l.-M.
Lons-
l.-S.
Lausanne
Vevey
Montreux
SWITZERLAND
Brig
Simplon
L. Maggiore
Lecco
Lovere
Vicenza
Moulins
Montluçon
Lapalisse
Digoin
Mâcon
Bourg
Bellegarde
Genève
L. Léman
Martigny
Col du Gd
St Bernard
Matterhorn
Aosta
Varese
Como
Biella
Bergamo
Verona
Vichy
Roanne
Villefranche
Annecy
Aix-
l.-B.
Mt Blanc
Gran Paradiso
Novara
Busto
Arsizio
Monza
Brescia
Mantova
Rovigo
Thiers
Tarare
Lyon
Villeurbanne
Chambéry
Ivrea
Vercelli
Milano
(Milan)
Lodi
Cremona
Adige
St-Chamond
Vienne
Voiron
Albertville
Gran Paradiso
Col du
Mt Cenis
Casale
Monf.
Pavia
Piacenza
Carpi
Ferrara
St-Étienne
Annonay
Romans-s.-I.
Grenoble
Susa
Torino
(Turin)
Asti
Alessandria
Novi Ligure
Parma
Reggio
n.-E.
Modena
Bologna
Le Puy
en-Velay
Bourg
-s.-I.
Valence
Massif
du Pelvoux
Briançon
Corps
Mte Viso
Ovada
Alba
Mondovi
Appennino
Genova
(Genoa)
Massif
Central
Mt Mézenc
Aubenas
Montélimar
Nyons
Gap
Durance
Mt Pelat
Digne-
les-B.
Cuneo
C. de Tende
Savona
Rapallo
La Spezia
Massa
Carrara
Mte Cimone
Pistoia
Prato
Firenze
(Florence)
Mende
Alès
Bagnols
-s.-Cèze
Orange
Carpentras
Cavaillon
Sisteron
Castellane
Nice
San Remo
Imperia
Alassio
LIGURIAN
Viareggio
Lucca
Pontedera
Pisa
Siena
Mt Aigoual
Nîmes
Avignon
Arles
Salon-d.-P.
Draguignan
Grasse
Aix-en-Provence
Cannes
St Raphaël
MONACO
Monte Carlo
Côte d'Azur
SEA
Livorno
Cecina
Montpellier
Sète
Martigues
Aubagne
Toulon
Hyères
St Tropez
Cap Corse
G. de
St Florent
Portoferraio
Elba
Piombino
Follonica
Grosseto
Narbonne
Golfe du Lion
Marseille
Îles d'Hyères
Perpignan
Calvi
Mt Cinto
CORSE
(CORSICA)
Ponte Lecca
Corte
Montecristo
Pianosa
Giglio
Orbetello
Ajaccio
C. Rosso
Caterraggio

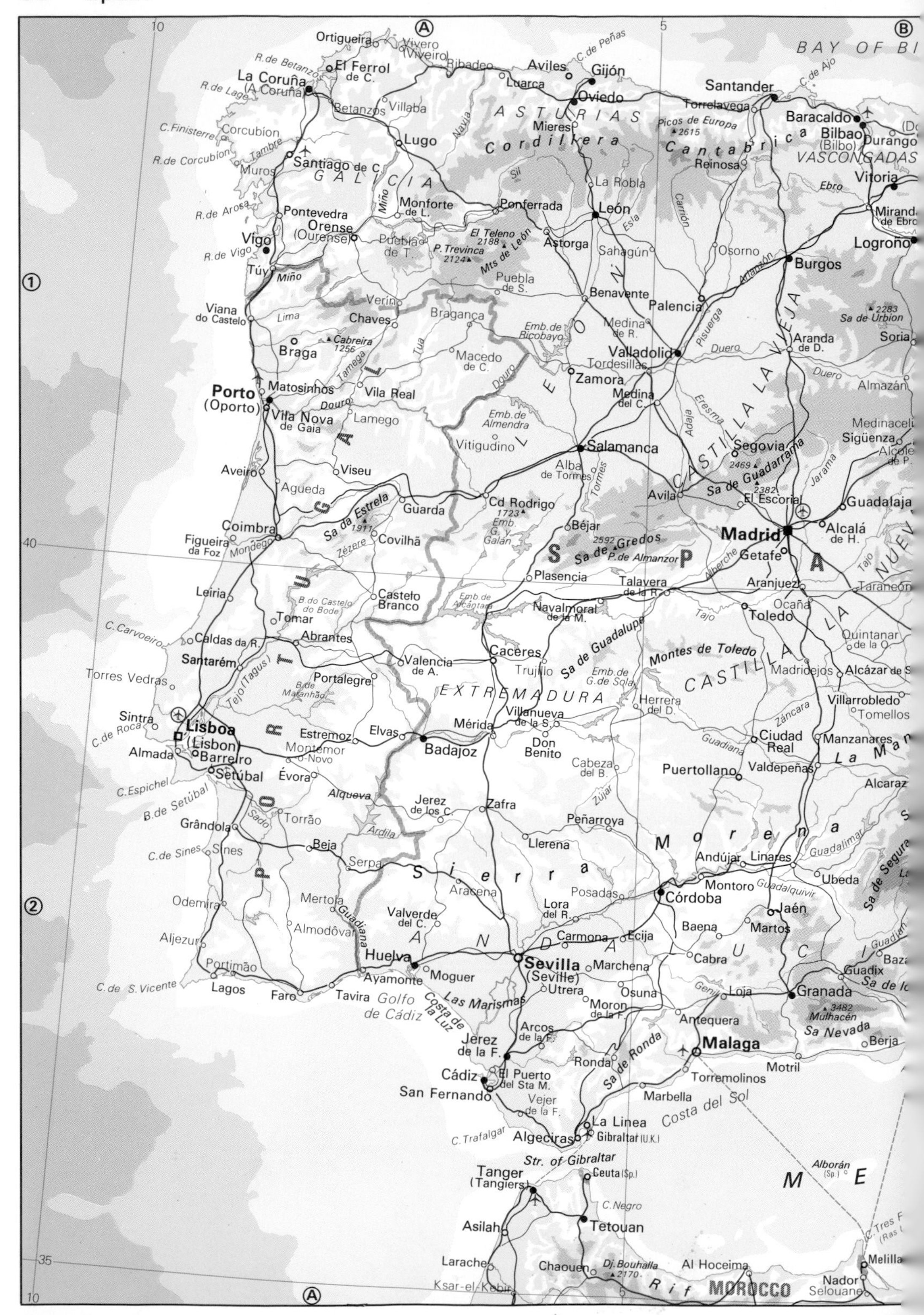

BAY OF BI
Ortigueira
Vivero (Viveiro)
Ribadeo
C. de Peñas
Aviles
Gijón
C. de Ajo
R. de Betanzos
El Ferrol de C.
La Coruña (A Coruña)
R. de Lage
Luarca
Oviedo
Santander
Torrelavega
Baracaldo
Bilbao (Bilbo)
Durango
Betanzos
Villaba
A S T U R I A S
Mieres
Picos de Europa
2615
C. Finisterre
Corcubion
Tambre
Lugo
Navia
C o r d i l l e r a
C a n t a b r i c a
VASCONGADAS
R. de Corcubion
Muros
Santiago de C.
G A L I C I A
La Robla
Reinosa
Sil
Ebro
Vitoria
Miño
Monforte de L.
Ponferrada
León
Carrión
Miranda de Ebro
R. de Arosa
Pontevedra
Orense (Ourense)
Puebla de T.
El Teleno 2188
P. Trevinca 2124
Mts de León
Astorga
Esla
Sahagún
Osorno
Logroño
Vigo
R. de Vigo
Túy
Miño
Burgos
Puebla de S.
Benavente
Palencia
Arlanzón
Viana do Castelo
Lima
Verín
Chaves
Bragança
Emb. de Ricobayo
Medina de R.
2283 Sa de Urbion
Soria
Cabreira 1256
Braga
Tamega
Tua
Macedo de C.
Douro
Valladolid
Pisuerga
Aranda de D.
Duero
Tordesillas
Zamora
Almazán
Porto (Oporto)
Matosinhos
Vila Real
Douro
Medina del C.
Eresma
Vila Nova de Gaia
Lamego
Emb. de Almendra
Medinaceli
Sigüenza
Adaja
Vitigudino
Salamanca
Segovia
Alcolea de P.
Aveiro
Viseu
Alba de Tormes
Tormes
2469
Sa de Guadarrama
Jarama
Agueda
2382
Avila
El Escorial
Guadalajara
Cd Rodrigo
Guarda
Sa da Estrela 1911
1723
Emb. G. y Galán
Coimbra
Béjar
Madrid
Alcalá de H.
Covilhã
Zêzere
2592 Gredos
Sa de P. de Almanzor
Getafe
Figueira da Foz
Mondego
Alberche
Tajo
Plasencia
Talavera de la R.
Aranjuez
Tarancón
Leiria
Castelo Branco
Emb. de Alcántara
Navalmoral de la M.
Ocaña
B. do Castelo do Bode
Toledo
Tomar
Tajo
C. Carvoeiro
Caldas da R.
Abrantes
Quintanar de la O.
Sa de Guadalupe
Montes de Toledo
Santarém
Valencia de A.
Caceres
Trujillo
Emb. de G. de Sola
Madridejos
Alcázar de S
Torres Vedras
Tejo (Tagus)
Portalegre
B. de Marañhão
E X T R E M A D U R A
C A S T I L L A
Herrera del D.
Villarrobledo
Záncara
Tomellos
Sintra
Lisboa (Lisbon)
C. de Roca
Villanueva de la S.
Mérida
Estremoz
Elvas
Badajoz
Don Benito
Guadiana
Ciudad Real
Manzanares
La Man
Almada
Barreiro
Montemor o-Novo
Cabeza del B.
Puertollano
Valdepeñas
Setúbal
Évora
C. Espichel
Alcaraz
B. de Setúbal
Alqueva
Jerez de los C.
Zafra
Zújar
Sado
Torrão
Grândola
Ardila
Peñarroya
Llerena
M o r e n a
Beja
C. de Sines
Sines
Serpa
Andújar
Linares
Guadalimar
S i e r r a
Posadas
Montoro
Ubeda
Sa de Segura
Aracena
Guadalquivir
Córdoba
Odemira
Mertola
Lora del R.
Jaén
Valverde del C.
Almodôvar
Guadiana
A N D A L U C I A
Baena
Martos
Aljezur
Carmona
Ecija
Huelva
Sevilla (Seville)
Marchena
Cabra
Guadiana
Baza
Portimão
Guadix
Ayamonte
Moguer
C. de S. Vicente
Lagos
Faro
Tavira
Golfo de Cádiz
Utrera
Osuna
Genil
Loja
Granada
Sa de los
Costa de la Luz
Las Marismas
Moron de la F.
Antequera
3482 Mulhacén
Sa Nevada
Arcos de la F.
Jerez de la F.
Malaga
Berja
Sa de Ronda
Ronda
Motril
Cádiz
El Puerto del Sta M.
San Fernando
Torremolinos
Marbella
Vejer de la F.
La Linea
Costa del Sol
C. Trafalgar
Algeciras
Gibraltar (U.K.)
Str. of Gibraltar
Tanger (Tangiers)
Ceuta (Sp.)
Alborán (Sp.)
M E
C. Negro
Asilah
Tetouan
C. Tres F (Ras
Larache
Chaouen
Dj. Bouhalla 2170
Al Hoceima
Melilla
Ksar-el-Kebir
R i f
MOROCCO
Nador
Selouane
10
5
40
35
A
B
1
2

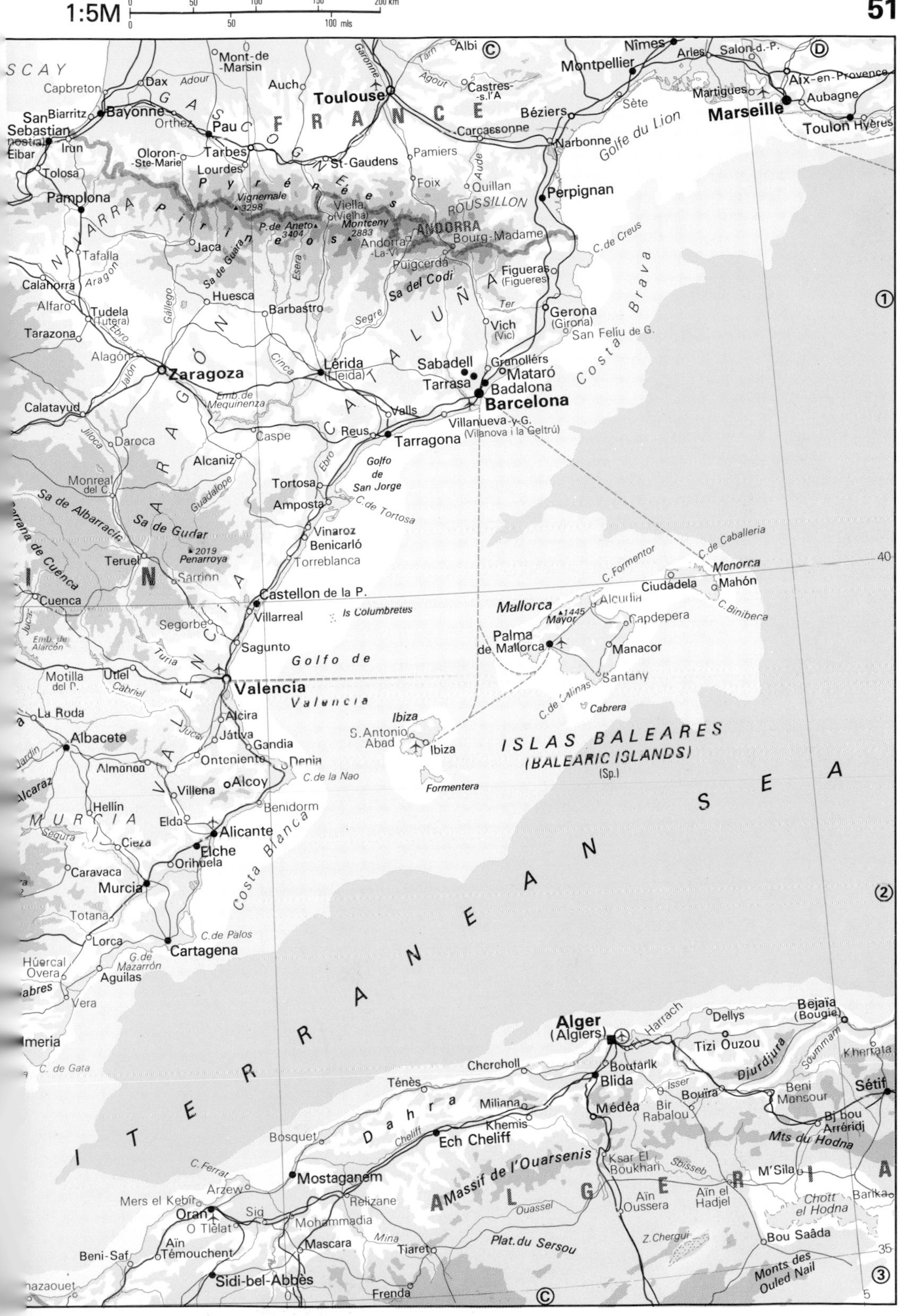

1:5M

0   50   100   150   200 km
0   50   100 mls

SCAY
Capbreton
San Sebastian
postial
Eibar
Tolosa
Biarritz
Bayonne
Irun
Pamplona
Tafalla
Calahorra
Alfaro
Tarazona
Alagón
Tudela
(Tutera)
Calatayud
Daroca
Mont-de-Marsin
Dax
Orthez
Pau
Oloron-Ste-Marie
Lourdes
Tarbes
Jaca
Huesca
Barbastro
Auch
Albi
Castres-s-l'A
St-Gaudens
Pamiers
Foix
Quillan
Vignemale
3298
Andorra-La-Vella
P. de Aneto
3404
Viella
(Vielha)
Montceny
2883
Bourg-Madame
Figueras
(Figueres)
Gerona
(Girona)
San Felíu de G.

Toulouse
F R A N C E
Carcassonne
Narbonne
Perpignan
ANDORRA
Puigcerdá

Montpellier
Béziers
Sète
Golfe du Lion
Nîmes
Arles
Salon-d.-P
Martigues
Marseille
Aix-en-Provence
Aubagne
Toulon
Hyères

Zaragoza
Lérida
(Leida)
Sabadell
Tarrasa
Granollérs
Mataró
Badalona
Barcelona
Vich
(Vic)
San Felíu de G.
C. de Creus
Costa Brava

Calaf
Caspe
Reus
Valls
Villanueva-y-G.
(Vilanova i la Geltrú)
Tarragona
C. Reus

Monreal del C
Alcaniz
Tortosa
Amposta
Vinaroz
Benicarló
Torreblanca

Teruel
Penarroya
2019
Sartrin
Cuenca

Castellon de la P.
Villarreal
Segorbe
Sagunto
Is Columbretes

Motilla del P.
Utiel
La Roda
Albacete
Almodo
Alcira
Játiva
Gandia
Ontoniente
Denia
Alcoy
C. de la Nao
Villena
Benidorm

Valencia
Golfo de Valencia
Ibiza
S. Antonio Abad
Ibiza
Formentera

Hellín
Elda
Villena
Alicante
Elche
Orihuela
Caravaca
Murcia
Totana
Lorca
Cartagena
C. de Palos
G. de Mazarrón
Aguilas
Vera
Húercal Overa

ISLAS BALEARES
(BALEARIC ISLANDS)
(Sp.)

Mallorca
Palma de Mallorca
Manacor
Santany
Alcudia
Ciudadela
Mahón
Monorca
C. Formentor
C. de Caballeria
C. Binibeca
C. de Salinas
Cabrera
1445 Mayor

40

MEDITERRANEAN SEA

Alger
(Algiers)
Dellys
Bejaïa
(Bougie)
Tizi Ouzou
Cheroholl
Boutärlk
Blida
Tizi Ouzou
Djurdjura
Khertata
Sétif
Ténès
Miliana
Médéa
Bir Rabalou
Bouira
Beni Monsour
Bj bou Arréridj
Bosquet
Khemis
Ech Cheliff
Ksar El Boukhan
Sbisseb
Mts du Hodna
M'Sila
C. Ferrat
Dahra
Massif de l'Ouarsenis
Aïn el Hadjel
Chott el Hodna
Barika
Mostaganem
Arzew
Relizane
Ouassel
Aïn Oussera
Bou Saâda
Mers el Kebir
Oran
O Tlélat
Sig
Mohammadia
Mascara
Tiareto
Plat. du Sersou
Z. Chergut
Monts des Ouled Nail
Beni-Saf
Aïn Témouchent
Mina
A L G E R I A
Frenda
hazaouet
Sidi-bel-Abbès
35
5

Emb. de Mequinenza
Emb. de Alarcón
Golfo de San Jorge
C. de Tortosa
C. de Gata

NAVARRA
ARAGON
CATALUÑA
Pirineos
Pyrénées
ROUSSILLON
Ebro
Segre
Cinca
Gállego
Jalón
Jiloca
Guadalope
Sa. de Gudar
Sa de Albarracín
Serranía de Cuenca
Júcar
Cabriel
Turia
VALENCIA
MURCIA
Costa Blanca
Segura
Jardin
Alcaraz
Almonaa
Cieza

① ② ③

40 35

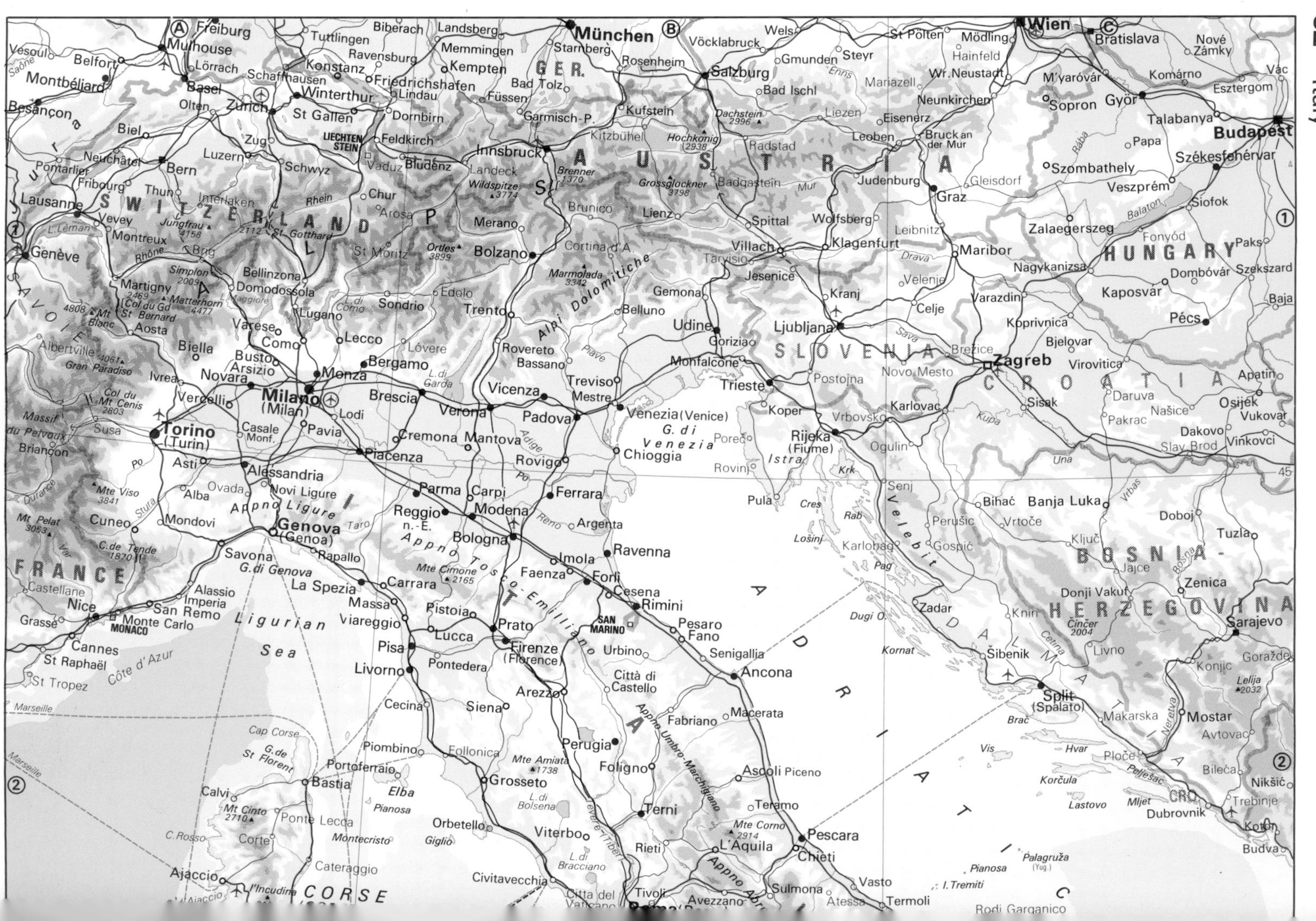
HUNGARY
CROATIA
SLOVENIJA
AUSTRIA
SWITZERLAND
BOSNIA
HERZEGOVINA
FRANCE
CORSE
ADRIATIC
DALMATIA
GER.
LIECHTENSTEIN
SAN MARINO
MONACO
Wien
Bratislava
Budapest
Győr
Sopron
Szombathely
Veszprém
Székesfehérvár
Siófok
Balaton
Pécs
Kaposvár
Nagykanizsa
Zalaegerszeg
Zagreb
Sisak
Karlovac
Rijeka (Fiume)
Pula
Zadar
Šibenik
Split (Spalato)
Mostar
Sarajevo
Zenica
Tuzla
Banja Luka
Dubrovnik
Kotor
Budva
Osijek
Vukovar
Maribor
Ljubljana
Kranj
Celje
Koper
Trieste
Graz
Klagenfurt
Villach
Salzburg
Wels
St Pölten
Mödling
Wr. Neustadt
München
Kempten
Landsberg
Memmingen
Friedrichshafen
Lindau
Konstanz
Schaffhausen
Winterthur
St Gallen
Zürich
Basel
Freiburg
Mulhouse
Belfort
Montbéliard
Besançon
Bern
Luzern
Biel
Neuchâtel
Fribourg
Lausanne
Genève
Montreux
Martigny
Chur
Vaduz
Feldkirch
Bludenz
Bolzano
Merano
Trento
Rovereto
Bassano
Belluno
Udine
Gorizia
Monfalcone
Venezia (Venice)
Chioggia
Mestre
Treviso
Padova
Vicenza
Verona
Mantova
Rovigo
Ferrara
Ravenna
Rimini
Pesaro
Fano
Senigallia
Ancona
Macerata
Pescara
Chieti
L'Aquila
Teramo
Vasto
Termoli
Bologna
Modena
Reggio
Parma
Carpi
Piacenza
Cremona
Brescia
Bergamo
Milano (Milan)
Monza
Como
Varese
Novara
Vercelli
Torino (Turin)
Asti
Alessandria
Cuneo
Aosta
Biella
Ivrea
Genova (Genoa)
Savona
La Spezia
Massa
Carrara
Viareggio
Pisa
Livorno
Lucca
Pistoia
Prato
Firenze (Florence)
Arezzo
Siena
Grosseto
Perugia
Terni
Foligno
Viterbo
Civitavecchia
Tivoli
Rieti
Avezzano
Sulmona
Nice
Cannes
Monte Carlo
San Remo
Imperia
Bastia
Ajaccio
Calvi
Corte
Elba
Piombino
Ligurian Sea
Mt Blanc 4808
Matterhorn 4477
Jungfrau 4158
Gran Paradiso 4061
Grossglockner 3798
Marmolada 3342
Mte Viso 3841

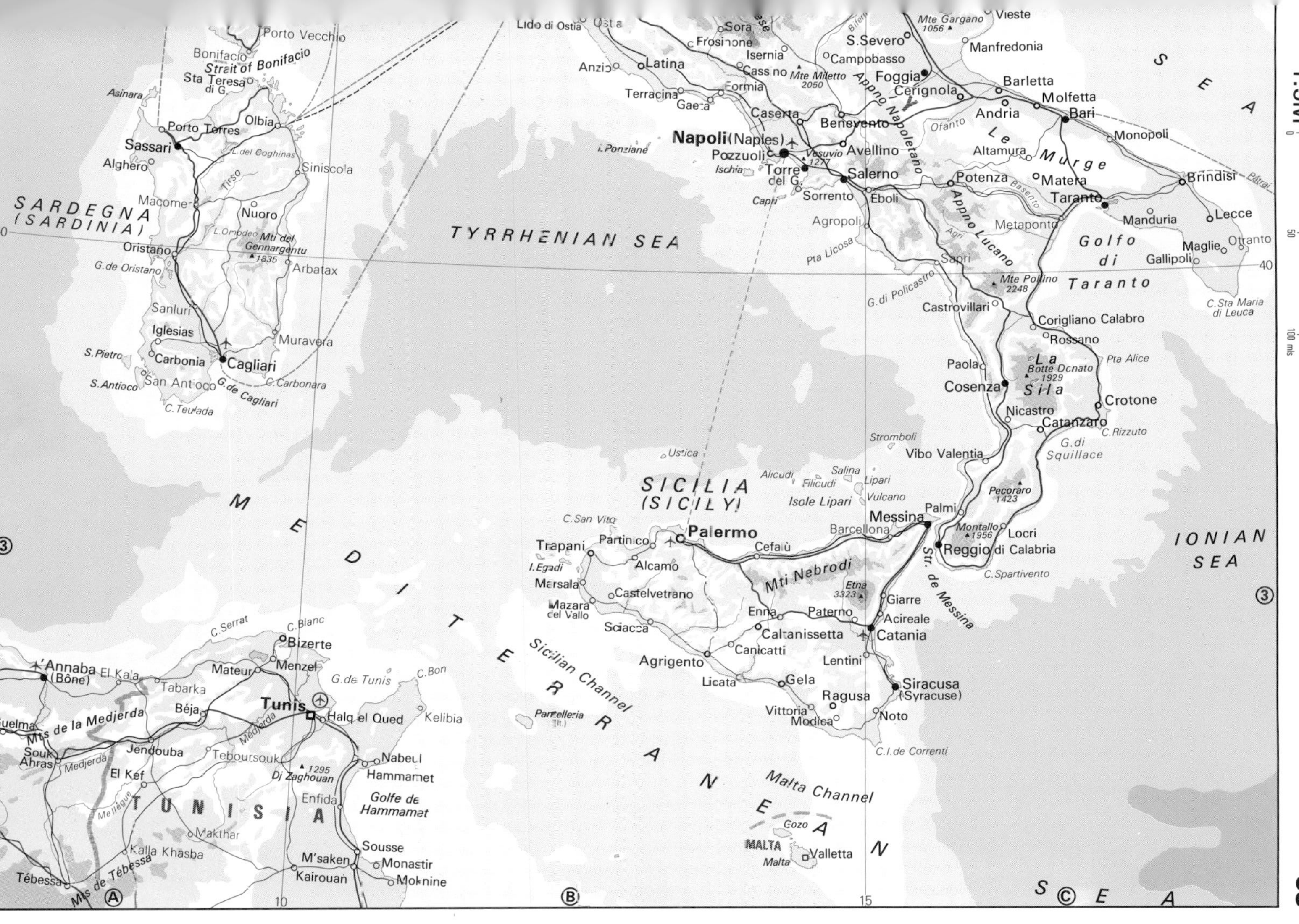

0   50   100   150   200 km
0   50   100 mls

③

IONIAN SEA

S   E   A

I O N I A N   S E A

S E A

Vieste
Mte Gargano
1056 ▲
Manfredonia
S. Severo
Campobasso
Foggia
Cerignola
Isernia
Cass no Mte Miletto
2050
Benevento
Avellino
Sorrento
Caserta
Vesuvio
Napoli (Naples)
Pozzuoli
Torre del G.
Capri
Ischia
Sora
Frosinone
Latina
Terracina
Gaeta
Formia
Anzio
L. Ponziane
Lido di Ostia
Ostia

Monopoli
Molfetta
Bari
Barletta
Andria
Matera
Altamura
Potenza
Appno Lucano
Eboli
Salerno
Agropoli

Brindisi
Lecce
Maglie Otranto
Manduria
Gallipolo
Taranto
C. Sta Maria di Leuca
Golfo di Taranto
Le Murge
Meiaponto
Bradano
Basento
Mte Pollino
2248
Castrovillari
Sapri
Pta Licosa
Agropoli
G. di Policastro
Stromboli

Crotone
Rossano
Corigliano Calabro
La Sila
La Botte Donato
1929
Nicastro
Catanzaro
Pta Alice
C. Rizzuto
G. di Squillace
C. Spartivento
Locri
Pecoraro
1423
Reggio di Calabria
Montalto
1956
Palmi
Vibo Valentia
Paola
Cosenza
Str. de Messina

Alicudi
Filicudi
Salina
Lipari
Isole Lipari
Vulcano
Panarea
Ustica

Messina
Barcellona
Milazzo
Giarre
Acireale
Catania
Mti. Nebrodi
Etna
3323 ▲
Paterno
Lentini
Siracusa
(Syracuse)
Noto
C.I. de Correnti

SICILIA
(SICILY)
Cefalù
Palermo
Partinico
Alcamo
Castelvetrano
Enna
Caltanissetta
Canicatti
Licata
Agrigento
Gela
Vittoria
Modica
Ragusa
C. San Vito
Trapani
I. Egadi
Marsala
Mazara del Vallo
Sciacca
Sicilian Channel
Pantelleria

C. Bon
Kelibia
Nabeul
Hammamet
Golfe de Hammamet
Sousse
Monastir
Mohnine
M'saken
Enfida
Dj Zaghouan
1295
Kairouan
Tunis
Halq el Oued
G. de Tunis
Bizerte
Menzel
Mateur
C. Blanc
C. Serrat
Tabarka
Béja
Mejerda
Jendouba
Medjerda
El Kef
El Kala
Annaba
(Bône)
Guelma
Souk Ahras
Tébessa
Mts de Tébessa

Malta Channel
Gozo
MALTA
Valletta
Malta

M E D I T E R R A N E A N   S E A

T Y R R H E N I A N   S E A

S E A

Porto Vecchio
Bonifacio
Strait of Bonifacio
Sta Teresa di G.
Porto Torres
Sassari
Alghero
Asinara
SARDEGNA
(SARDINIA)
Olbia
Nuoro
Mti del Gennargentu
1835
Arbatax
Muravera
Oristano
G. di Oristano
Iglesias
Carbonia
S. Antioco
S. Pietro
C. Carbonara
Cagliari
G. de Cagliari
C. Teulada
C. Blanc
Siniscola

T U N I S I A

15

10

③

Ⓐ

Ⓑ

Ⓒ

40

40

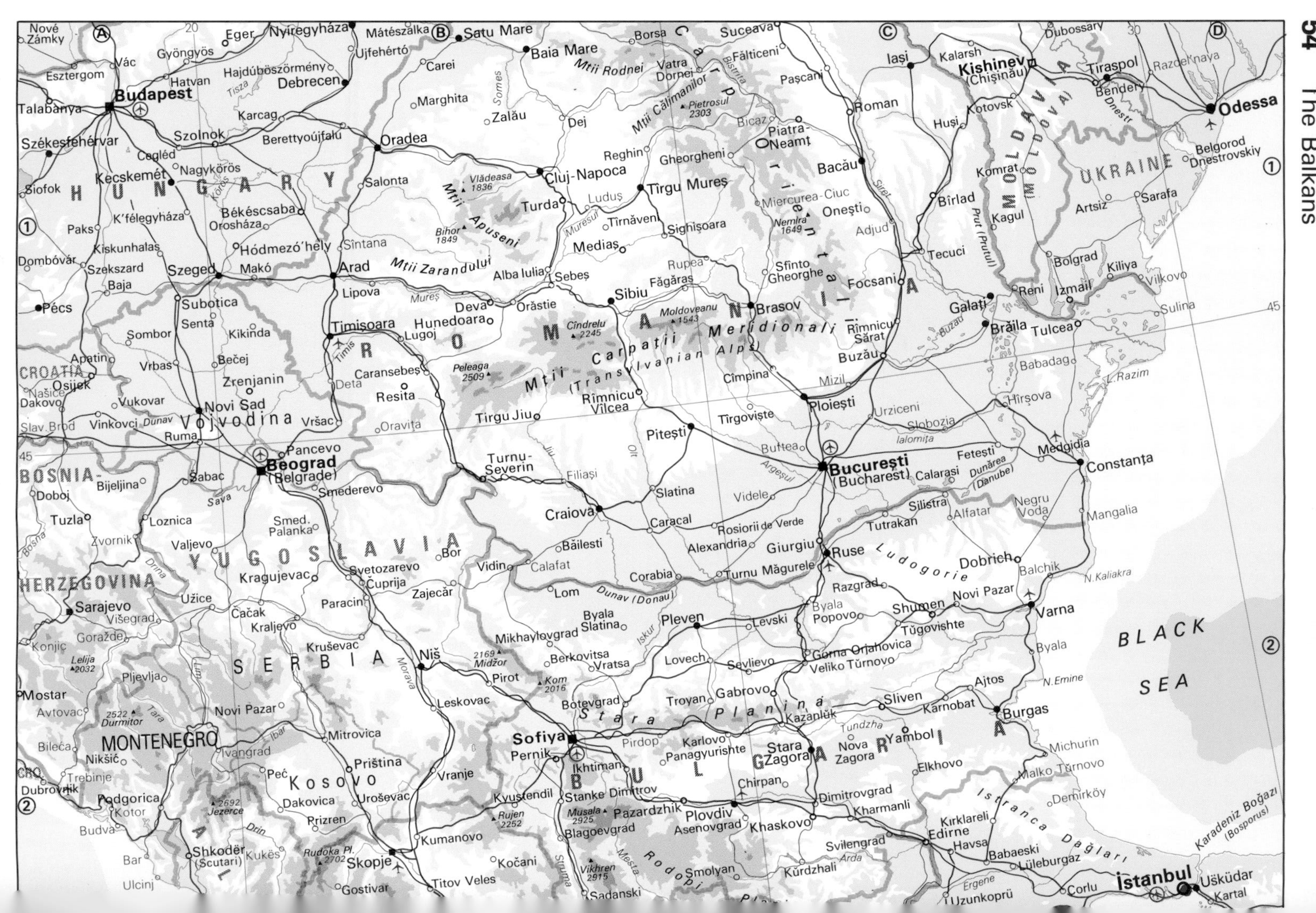

Nové Zámky
Esztergom
Vác
Budapest
Talabánya
Székesfehérvár
Siófok
Paks
Dombóvár
Pécs
Gyöngyös
Hatvan
Eger
Nyíregyháza
Hajdúböszörmény
Debrecen
Tisza
Karcag
Szolnok
Cegléd
Nagykőrös
Kecskemét
HUNGARY
K'félegyháza
Kiskunhalas
Szekszard
Baja
Békéscsaba
Orosháza
Hódmezó'hely
Szeged
Makó
Berettyóújfalu
Mátészalka
Újfehértó
Satu Mare
Carei
Marghita
Zalău
Someş
Oradea
Salonta
Sîntana
Arad
Lipova
Mureş
Timişoara
Timiş
Deta
Lugoj
Caransebeş
Resita
Oraviţa
Vršac
Pancevo
Beograd (Belgrade)
Smederevo
Ruma
Šabac
Sava
Vojvodina
Novi Sad
Zrenjanin
Bečej
Kikinda
Senta
Subotica
Sombor
Vrbas
Apatin
Osijek
Našice
Dakovo
Vukovar
Vinkovci
Dunav
Slav. Brod
CROATIA
BOSNIA-HERZEGOVINA
Bijeljina
Doboj
Tuzla
Bosna
Zvornik
Loznica
Drina
Valjevo
Sarajevo
Višegrad
Goražde
Konjic
Lelija 2032
Mostar
Avtovac
Bileća
Trebinje
Dubrovnik
Nikšić
2522 Durmitor
Tara
Pljevlja
Lim
MONTENEGRO
Podgorica
Kotor
Budva
Bar
Ulcinj
Shkodër (Scutari)
2692 Jezerce
Kukës
Drin
Užice
Čačak
Kraljevo
Kragujevac
YUGOSLAVIA
Smed. Palanka
Paraćin
Svetozarevo
Ćuprija
Zaječar
Bor
Kruševac
SERBIA
Novi Pazar
Ibar
Ivangrad
Mitrovica
Peć
Kosovo
Priština
Dakovica
Uroševac
Prizren
Rudoka Pl. 2702
Skopje
Gostivar
Kumanovo
Titov Veles
Kočani
Vranje
Leskovac
Niš
Morava
Pirot
2169 Midžor
Kom 2016
Kyustendil
Rujen 2252
Struma
Baia Mare
Mţii Rodnei
Borsa
Vatra Dornei
Mţii Călimanilor
Pietrosul 2303
Dej
Reghin
Cluj-Napoca
Vlădeasa 1836
Mţii Apuseni
Bihor 1849
Turda
Luduş
Mureşul
Tîrnăveni
Mediaş
Mţii Zarandului
Alba Iulia
Sebeş
Orăştie
Deva
Hunedoara
Cîndrelu 2245
Peleaga 2509
Mţii Carpaţii Meridionali
(Transylvanian Alps)
Tîrgu Jiu
Rîmnicu Vîlcea
Turnu-Severin
Jiu
Filiaşi
Olt
Craiova
Băilesti
Calafat
Vidin
Lom
Dunav (Donau)
Corabia
Slatina
Caracal
Piteşti
Sibiu
Făgăraş
Rupea
Sighişoara
Tîrgu Mureş
Gheorgheni
Miercurea-Ciuc
Nemira 1649
Sfînto Gheorghe
Braşov
Moldoveanu 1543
Cîmpina
Tîrgovişte
Bicaz
Piatra-Neamţ
Suceava
Fălticeni
Bistriţa
Paşcani
Roman
Bacău
Oneşti
Adjud
Siret
Focsani
Rîmnicu Sărat
Buzău
Mizil
Ploieşti
Urziceni
Slobozia
Ialomiţa
Buftea
Argeşul
Bucureşti (Bucharest)
Videle
Rosiorii de Verde
Alexandria
Giurgiu
Turnu Măgurele
Calarasi
Dunărea (Danube)
Feteşti
Iaşi
Kalarsh
Kishinev (Chişinău)
Dubossary
Tiraspol
Bendery
Dnestr
Razdel'naya
Odessa
Belgorod Dnestrovskiy
UKRAINE
MOLDOVA
Kotovsk
Huşi
Komrat
Bîrlad
Kagul
Prut (Prutul)
Tecuci
Artsiz
Sarafa
Bolgrad
Kiliya
Vilkovo
Reni
Izmail
Sulina
Galaţi
Brăila
Tulcea
Babadag
L. Razim
Hîrşova
Medgidia
Constanţa
Mangalia
Negru Vodă
Alfatar
Silistra
Tutrakan
Ruse
Ludogorie
Dobrich
Balchik
N. Kaliakra
Razgrad
Novi Pazar
Shumen
Varna
Byala
Popovo
Tŭgovishte
Levski
Pleven
Iskur
Byala Slatina
Mikhaylovgrad
Berkovitsa
Vratsa
Lovech
Sevlievo
Gorna Orjahovica
Veliko Tŭrnovo
Gabrovo
Troyan
Botevgrad
Stara Planina
Kazanlŭk
Sliven
Karnobat
Ajtos
N. Emine
Burgas
BLACK SEA
Sofiya
Pernik
Ikhtiman
Pirdop
Karlovo
Panagyurishte
Stara Zagora
Tundzha
Nova Zagora
Yambol
BULGARIA
Elkhovo
Chirpan
Stanke Dimitrov
Musala 2925
Pazardzhik
Blagoevgrad
Plovdiv
Asenovgrad
Khaskovo
Dimitrovgrad
Kharmanli
Mesta
Rodopi
Vikhren 2915
Sadanski
Smolyan
Kŭrdzhali
Arda
Svilengrad
Michurin
Malko Tŭrnovo
Demirköy
Istranca Dağları
Kırklareli
Edirne
Havsa
Babaeski
Lüleburgaz
Ergene
Uzunköprü
Çorlu
İstanbul
Üsküdar
Kartal
Karadeniz Boğazı (Bosporus)

0 50 100 150 200 km
0 50 100 mls

Sea of Marmara / Turkey / Aegean

İznik G.
Bursa
Yalova
Gemlik
Karacabey
Mustafa-Kemalpaşa
Simav
Tavşanlı
Ak Dağ 2089
Gediz
Denizli ③

Tekirdağ
Marmara Adı
Bandırma
Gönen
Biga
Orhaneli
Kütahya
Bigadiç
Akhisar
Kula
Buldan
Nazilli

Makara
Keşan
Edremit
Balıkesir
Manisa
Salihli
Alaşehir
Ödemiş

İpsala
Gelibolu
(Gallipoli)
Çanakkale
Edremit K.
Ayvalık
Bergama
Menemen
Bornova
İzmir
Urla
Tire
Torbalı
Selçuk
Söke
Aydın

Alexandroúpolis
Ezine
Bozcaada
Çandarlı K.
İzmir Körfezi
Kuşadası K.
Sámos

Komotiní
Xánthi
Gökçeada
Ayvacık
Mitilíni
Khíos
Sisam

Kavála
Thásos
Límnos
Lésvos
Psará
Ikaría
Pátmos
Léros

Dráma
Sérrai
Áyios Evstrátios
Skíros
Psará
Sámos
Kálimnos

Nigríta
K. Strimonikós
Kandárli
Ándros
Síros
Páros
Náxos
Kós
Nísiros

Thessaloníki (Salonica)
Khalkidhikí
K. Sirgitikós
K. Toronéos
Skíathos
Skópelos
Kím
Tínos
Míkonos
Páros
Íos
Thíra
Astipálaia

Kilkís
Thermaïkós Kólpos
Vólos
Skópelos
Évvoie
Kéa
Kíthnos
Sérifos
Sífnos
Mílos
Síkinos

Édhessa
Véroia
Katerini
Ólimbos (Olympus) 2917
Lárisa
Tírnavos
Lamía
Khalkís
Athínai (Athens)
Piraiévs

Ptolemaïs
Kozáni
Kalabáka
Tríkala
Othris 1726
Lamía
Levádhia
Thívai
Akharnaí
Mégara

Kastoría
Grevená
Kardhítsa
Dhomokós 2500
Timfristós 2315
Amfíklia
Ávios
Koríthos
Sikión
Náfplion
Idhra

Flórina
Kónitsa
Áartia
Timfi 2409
Pínós
Dhomokós
Navpaktos
Pátrai
Kórinthos
Árgos
Spétsai

Ioánnina
Mésolóngion
Zákinthos
Kalíni 2376
Trípolis
Messíni

Préveza
Levkás
Agrínion
Navpak os
Aíyion
Pirgos
Kalamái

Igoumenítsa
Árta
Amfilokhía
Argostólion
Zákinthos
Amaliás
Kiparissía
Megalópolis

Kérkira (Corfu)
IÓNIOI NÍSOI (Ionian Islands)
Kefallinía
Pilos
Filiatrá K.
Yíthion

Tiranë
Fier
Berat
Vlorë
Gjirokastër
Sarandë

Durrës
Kavajë
Lushnje
Strait of Otranto
Lecce
Brindisi
Maglie
Otranto
C. Sta Maria di Leuca
Gallipoli

Seas
AEGEAN SEA
SPORÁDHES (DODECÁNESE)
Sea of Crete
Kikládhes (Cyclades)
Mírtoan Sea
Lakonikós Kólpos
Messiniakós Kólpos
IONIAN SEA
Argolikós K.
Saronikós K.
Korinthiakós K.

Crete / Kríti
Khaniá
Réthimnon
Iráklion
Dhíkti Óri 2148
Lévka Óri 2452
Ídhi Óros 2456
Timbákion
Akr. Spátha
Akr. Sídheros
Ierápetra
Akr. Líthinon

Ródhos
Ródhos
Líndos
Kárpathos
Kásos
Sími
Khálki
Alimniá
Tílos

MACEDONIA
GREECE
ÍPIROS

② ③ ④
35 25 20 40

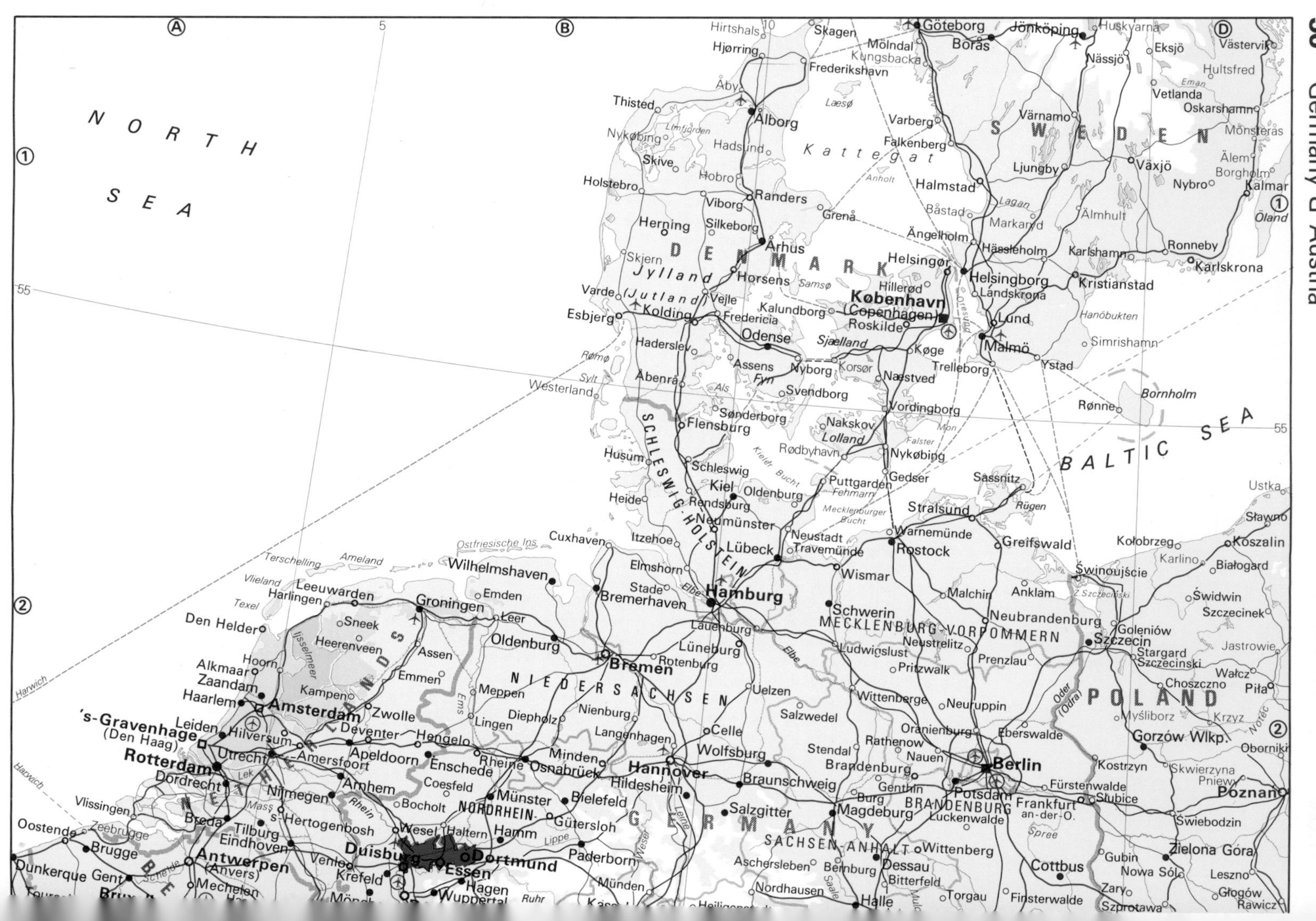
NORTH SEA
BALTIC SEA
SWEDEN
DENMARK
POLAND
GERMANY
NIEDERSACHSEN
SCHLESWIG-HOLSTEIN
MECKLENBURG-VORPOMMERN
BRANDENBURG
SACHSEN-ANHALT
NORDRHEIN-
Kattegat
Jylland (Jutland)
Sjælland
Fyn
Lolland
Bornholm
Rügen
Fehmarn
Öland
Ijsselmeer
Göteborg
Borås
Jönköping
Helsingborg
Malmö
Lund
Kristianstad
Karlskrona
Kalmar
Växjö
Halmstad
København (Copenhagen)
Roskilde
Odense
Århus
Ålborg
Esbjerg
Kolding
Herning
Randers
Hamburg
Bremen
Bremerhaven
Kiel
Lübeck
Rostock
Stralsund
Greifswald
Szczecin
Berlin
Potsdam
Frankfurt an-der-O.
Cottbus
Magdeburg
Dessau
Halle
Braunschweig
Hannover
Wolfsburg
Salzgitter
Hildesheim
Bielefeld
Osnabrück
Münster
Dortmund
Essen
Duisburg
Oldenburg
Wilhelmshaven
Groningen
Leeuwarden
Amsterdam
Utrecht
Rotterdam
's-Gravenhage (Den Haag)
Antwerpen (Anvers)
Brugge
Gent
Oostende
Dunkerque
Gorzów Wlkp.
Poznań
Zielona Góra
Koszalin

③

CZECH REP.

Wołów Świdnica Bielawa Kłodzko Zabrze
Bolesławiec Legnica Wałbrzych Brno Břeclav
Jelenia Góra Śnieżka 1602 Hradec Králové Blansko Bratislava
Görlitz Zittau Liberec Jablonec n.N. Pardubice Svitavy Sopron Wien (Vienna)
Bautzen Labe Ústí n.L. Mladá Boleslav Svitava Hollabrunn Znojmo Mikulov Stockerau Szombathely Zalaegerszeg
Teplice Kolín Kutná Hora Jihlava Trebíč Znojmo Korneuburg Hainfeld Wr Neustadt Glesdorf Maribor
Dresden Chomutov Chemnitz Praha (Prague) Brandýs n.L. Havlíčkův Brod Třebíč Horn Krems Klosterneuburg Mödling Neunkirchen Leibnitz Varaždin Koprivnica Bjelovar Sisak
SACHSEN Most Kladno Benešov Písek České Budějovice Gmünd Freistadt St Pölten Mariazell Eisenerz Leoben Graz Drava Celje Velenje Novo Mesto Karlovac Ogulin CROATIA
Zwickau Karlovy Vary Plzeň Klatovy Kaplice Linz Steyr Liezen Judenburg Wolfsberg Klagenfurt Kranj Ljubljana SLOVENIA Rijeka (Fiume)
Gera Cheb Brd Böhmer wald Passau Schärding Wels Bad Ischl Hochkönig Spittal Villach Jesenice Gorizia Trieste
Erfurt Hof Bayreuth Weiden Vltava Regensburg Landshut Vöcklabruck Salzburg Dachstein 2996 Badgastein Lienz Gemona Udine Monfalcone Venezia (Venice)
THÜRINGER WALD Coburg Bamberg Amberg Cham Straubing München (Munich) Rosenheim Kufstein Kitzbühel Grossglockner 3798 Cortina d'A. Belluno Treviso Mestre
Eisenach Plauen Nürnberg Fürth Ingolstadt Dachau Starnberg Bad Tölz Garmisch-P. Innsbruck Brenner P. Brunico Dolomites Bassano Vicenza Padova Rovigo
Fulda Schweinfurt Würzburg Kitzingen Ansbach Donauwörth Augsburg Landsberg Kempten Füssen Wildspitze 3772 Meran Bolzano Trento Rovereto Verona Mantova
Frankfurt Offenbach Aschaffenburg Crailsheim Ulm Memmingen Lindau Dornbirn Feldkirch Ortles 3899 Edolo Bergamo Brescia Cremona
Wiesbaden Mainz Darmstadt Heilbronn Ludwigsburg Heidenheim Biberach Ravensburg Friedrichshafen Bregenz Chur Sondrio Lecco Como Monza Lodi
Koblenz Heidelberg Mannheim Stuttgart Esslingen Reutlingen Tübingen Konstanz St Gallen LIECHTEN. SIEN Schwyz Rhein Bellinzona Domodossola Varese Busto Arsizio Milano (Milan) Pavia
Bonn Bad Godesberg Worms Pforzheim Baden-Baden Offenburg Winterthur Schaffhausen Zürich Zug Gotthard Lecco Novara Vercelli Alessandria
Köln Andernach Kaiserslautern Karlsruhe Freiburg Lörrach Basel Olten Luzern Simplon Biella Casale Mont. Asti
Aachen Bonn Trier Pirmasens Rastatt Mulhouse Belfort Biel Neuchâtel Bern Thun Jungfrau 4158 Matterhorn 4477 Novara Vercelli Torino (Turin) Po
Euskirchen Bitburg Saarbrücken Strasbourg Colmar Montbéliard Fontaine Fribourg Simplon Martigny Aosta Ivrea Gran Paradiso 4061
Liège Luxembourg Saarlouis Sarrebourg Nancy Vesoul Besançon Lausanne Vevey Montreux Sion St Bernard Col du Mt Cenis Susa Alessandria
Namur Marche Arlon Longwy Thionville Metz Épinal Lons-le-S. St Claude Genève Annecy Chambéry Albertville Briançon Grenoble
Charleroi Bastogne Sedan Verdun Bar-le-Duc Chaumont Langres Dijon Bourg Villeurbanne Voiron Vienne Valence
Mons Charleville-Mézières Reims Châlons-s-M. Vitry-le-F. Beaune Chalon-s-S. Mâcon Lyon St-Étienne Annonay
St-Quentin Laon Soissons Château-Thierry Sézanne Troyes Sens Joigny Auxerre Avallon Autun Le Creusot Roanne Tarare St-Chamond Aubenas Montélimar
Cambrai Arras Provins Montereau Montbard Châtillon Digoin ③ ④ ⑧

FRANCE

GERMANY

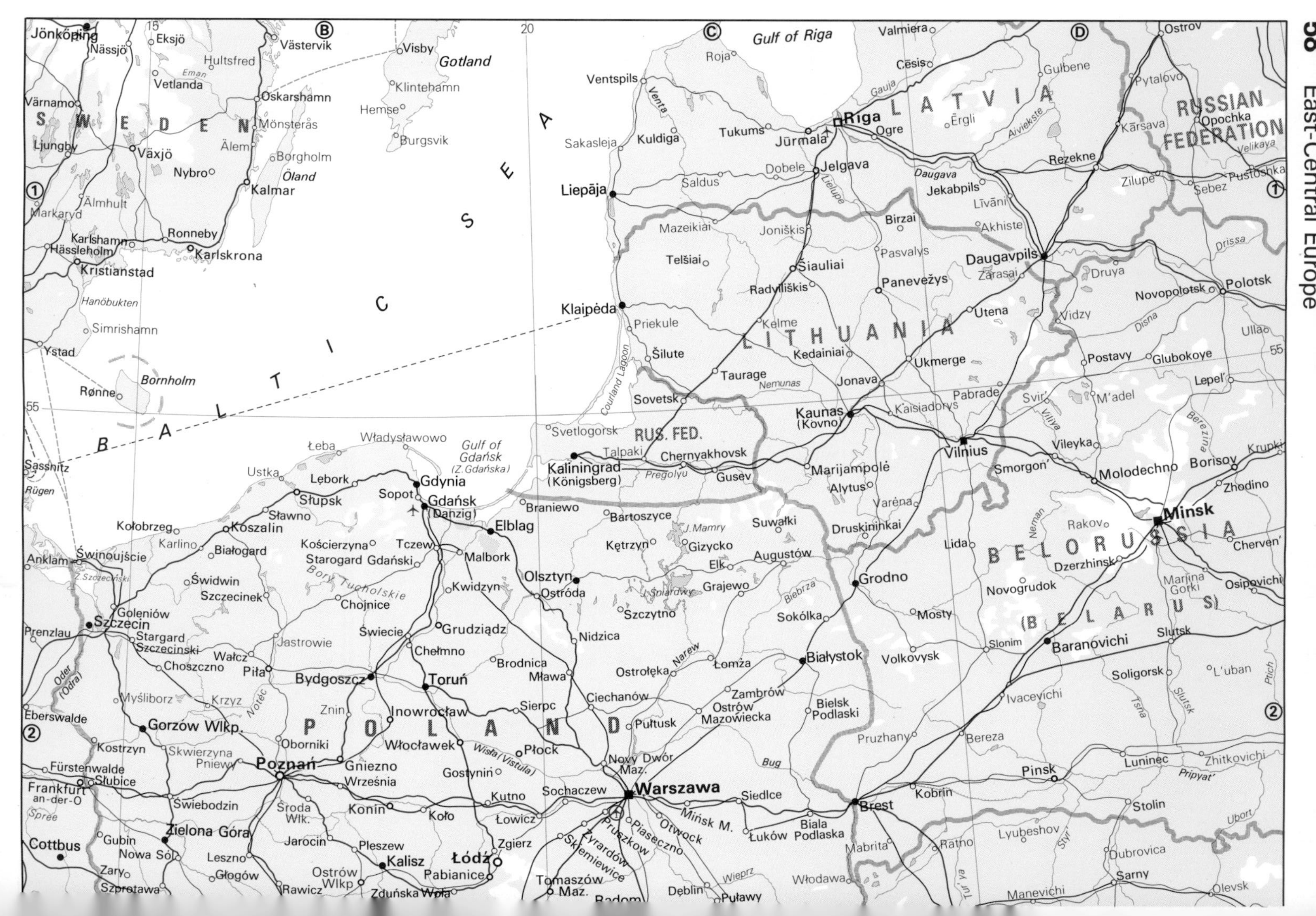
RUSSIAN FEDERATION
LATVIA
LITHUANIA
BELORUSSIA
(BELARUS')
POLAND
SWEDEN
BALTIC SEA
RUS. FED.
Gulf of Riga
Gulf of Gdańsk (Z. Gdańska)
Courland Lagoon
Hanöbukten
Gotland
Öland
Bornholm
Rügen
Riga
Minsk
Vilnius
Warszawa
Kaunas (Kovno)
Kaliningrad (Königsberg)
Gdańsk (Danzig)
Gdynia
Sopot
Klaipėda
Liepāja
Ventspils
Daugavpils
Jelgava
Jūrmala
Šiauliai
Panevėžys
Grodno
Białystok
Brest
Baranovichi
Pinsk
Polotsk
Novopolotsk
Borisov
Molodechno
Olsztyn
Elbląg
Toruń
Bydgoszcz
Poznań
Łódź
Szczecin
Gorzów Wlkp.
Zielona Góra
Kalisz
Płock
Włocławek
Cottbus
Frankfurt an-der-O
Kalmar
Karlskrona
Växjö
Jönköping
Visby
Kristianstad
Ystad
Rønne
Sassnitz
Chernyakhovsk
Sovetsk
Gusev
Marijampolė
Alytus
Ukmerge
Utena
Jonava
Kedainiai
Taurage
Šilute
Telšiai
Mazeikiai
Tukums
Dobele
Ogre
Jekabpils
Rezekne
Valmiera
Cēsis
Ostrov
Wisła (Vistula)
Oder (Odra)
Nemunas
Neman
Daugava
Berezina
Pripyat'
Bug
Narew
Noteć
Venta
Lielupe
Gauja
Slutsk
Lida
Slonim
Novogrudok
Kobrin
Siedlce
Radom
Koszalin
Słupsk
Kołobrzeg
Świnoujście
Łomża
Suwałki
Augustów
Ełk
Ciechanów
Ostrołęka
Mława
Kutno
Konin
Gniezno
Leszno
Piła
Grudziądz
Malbork
Kwidzyn
Chełmno
Inowrocław
Mińsk M.
Puławy
Dęblin
Pruszków
Żyrardów
Skierniewice
Tomaszów Maz.
1
2
B
C
D
15
20
55

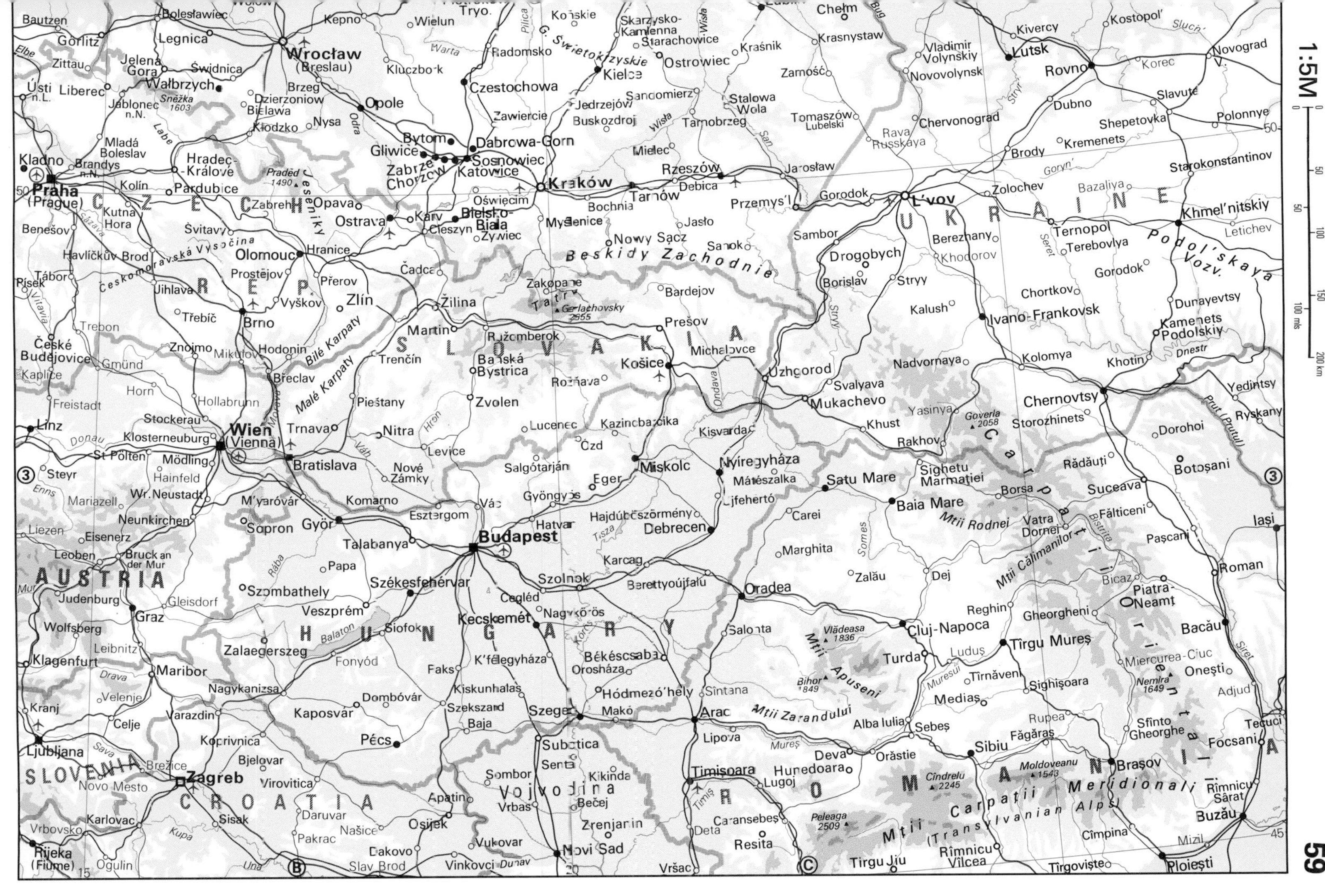
C Z E C H R E P.
S L O V A K I A
U K R A I N E
H U N G A R Y
R O M A N I A
A U S T R I A
C R O A T I A
S L O V E N I A
Vojvodina
Carpații Meridionali
(Transylvanian Alps)
Mtii Apuseni
Mtii Zarandului
Mtii Rodnei
Mtii Călimanilor
Beskidy Zachodnie
G. Świetokrzyskie
Tatry
Podol'skaya Vozv.
Bílé Karpaty
Malé Karpaty
Jeseníky
Českomoravská Vysočina
Gerlachovsky 2655
Goverla 2058
Moldoveanu 2543
Cîndrelu 2245
Peleaga 2509
Vlădeasa 1836
Bihor 1849
Nemira 1649
Praděd 1490
Sněžka 1603
Bautzen
Görlitz
Zittau
Ústi n.L.
Liberec
Jablonec n.N.
Bolesławiec
Legnica
Jelena Gora
Świdnica
Wałbrzych
Wrocław (Breslau)
Kepno
Wielun
Kluczbork
Brzeg
Dzierzoniow
Bielawa
Kłodzko
Nysa
Opole
Radomsko
Czestochowa
Zawiercie
Bytom
Gliwice
Zabrze
Chorzow
Dabrowa-Gorn
Sosnowiec
Katowice
Końskie
Skarzysko-Kamienna
Starachowice
Ostrowiec
Kielce
Jedrzejów
Buskozdroj
Sandomierz
Stalowa Wola
Tarnobrzeg
Mielec
Kraśnik
Krasnystaw
Chełm
Zamość
Tomaszów Lubelski
Rzeszów
Debica
Jarosław
Przemyśl
Kraków
Tarnów
Bochnia
Oświęcim
Bielsko-Biała
Cieszyn
Żywiec
Myślenice
Nowy Sacz
Jasło
Sanok
Zakopane
Kladno
Praha (Prague)
Brandys n.N.
Mladá Boleslav
Hradec-Králové
Pardubice
Kolín
Kutná Hora
Benešov
Havlíčkův Brod
Svitavy
Zabreh
Opava
Ostrava
Karv
Olomouc
Hranice
Prostějov
Přerov
Vyškov
Zlín
Jihlava
Třebíč
Brno
Tábor
Písek
České Budějovice
Kaplice
Trebon
Gmünd
Freistadt
Znojmo
Mikulov
Hodonin
Břeclav
Horn
Hollabrunn
Stockerau
Klosterneuburg
Wien (Vienna)
Mödling
Hainfeld
St Pölten
Linz
Steyr
Enns
Mariazell
Wr. Neustadt
Neunkirchen
Liezen
Eisenerz
Leoben
Bruck an der Mur
Judenburg
Gleisdorf
Graz
Wolfsberg
Leibnitz
Klagenfurt
Drava
Maribor
Velenje
Kranj
Celje
Ljubljana
Sava
Brežice
Novo Mesto
Karlovac
Vrbovsko
Rijeka (Fiume)
Ogulin
Zagreb
Sisak
Kupa
Una
Varazdin
Koprivnica
Bjelovar
Virovitica
Daruvar
Pakrac
Našice
Dakovo
Slav Brod
Osijek
Vukovar
Vinkovci
Dunav
Apatin
Sombor
Vrbas
Senta
Subotica
Kikinda
Bečej
Zrenjanin
Novi Sad
Vršac
Čadca
Žilina
Martin
Ružomberok
Banská Bystrica
Trenčín
Piešťany
Trnava
Bratislava
Nitra
Hron
Váh
Levice
Nové Zámky
Zvolen
Lucenec
Rožňava
Košice
Prešov
Bardejov
Michalovce
Ondava
Kazincbarcika
Ózd
Miskolc
Salgótarján
Eger
Gyöngyös
Hatvan
Vác
Esztergom
Komarno
M'yaróvár
Sopron
Györ
Talabanya
Budapest
Papa
Rába
Szombathely
Székesfehérvár
Veszprém
Balaton
Siofok
Zalaegerszeg
Fonyód
Nagykanizsa
Kaposvár
Dombóvár
Pécs
Faks
Kiskunhalas
Szekszard
Baja
Cegléd
Kecskemét
Nagykőrös
K'félegyháza
Szolnok
Karcag
Tisza
Hajdúböszörmény
Debrecen
Berettyóújfalu
Nyíregyháza
Mátészalka
Újfehértó
Kisvarda
Békéscsaba
Orosháza
Hódmezó'hely
Szeged
Makó
Sîntana
Arad
Lipova
Timișoara
Timiș
Deta
Lugoj
Caransebeș
Resita
Uzhgorod
Mukachevo
Svalyava
Khust
Rakhov
Yasinya
Nadvornaya
Kolomya
Ivano-Frankovsk
Kalush
Stryy
Drogobych
Borislav
Sambor
Gorodok
L'vov
Berezhany
Khodorov
Vladimir Volynskiy
Novovolynsk
Chervonograd
Rava Russkaya
Lutsk
Kivercy
Kostopol'
Rovno
Korec
Novograd V.
Slavuta
Polonnye
Dubno
Shepetovka
Kremenets
Brody
Zolochev
Starokonstantinov
Bazaliya
Khmel'nitskiy
Letichev
Ternopol
Terebovlya
Gorodok
Chortkov
Dunayevtsy
Kamenets Podolskiy
Dnestr
Khotin
Chernovtsy
Storozhinets
Yedintsy
Ryskany
Prut (Prutul)
Dorohoi
Botoșani
Rădăuți
Suceava
Fălticeni
Pașcani
Iași
Roman
Sighetu Marmației
Borșa
Vatra Dornei
Bistrița
Satu Mare
Baia Mare
Carei
Marghita
Someș
Zalău
Dej
Oradea
Salonta
Cluj-Napoca
Reghin
Gheorgheni
Bicaz
Piatra-Neamț
Bacău
Siret
Tîrgu Mureș
Luduș
Mureșul
Turda
Tîrnăveni
Sighișoara
Mediaș
Miercurea-Ciuc
Onești
Adjud
Alba Iulia
Sebeș
Deva
Hunedoara
Orăștie
Mureș
Rupea
Făgăraș
Sibiu
Sfînto Gheorghe
Brașov
Tecuci
Focsani
Rîmnicu Sărat
Buzău
Mizil
Ploiești
Cîmpina
Tîrgoviște
Rîmnicu Vîlcea
Tirgu Jiu

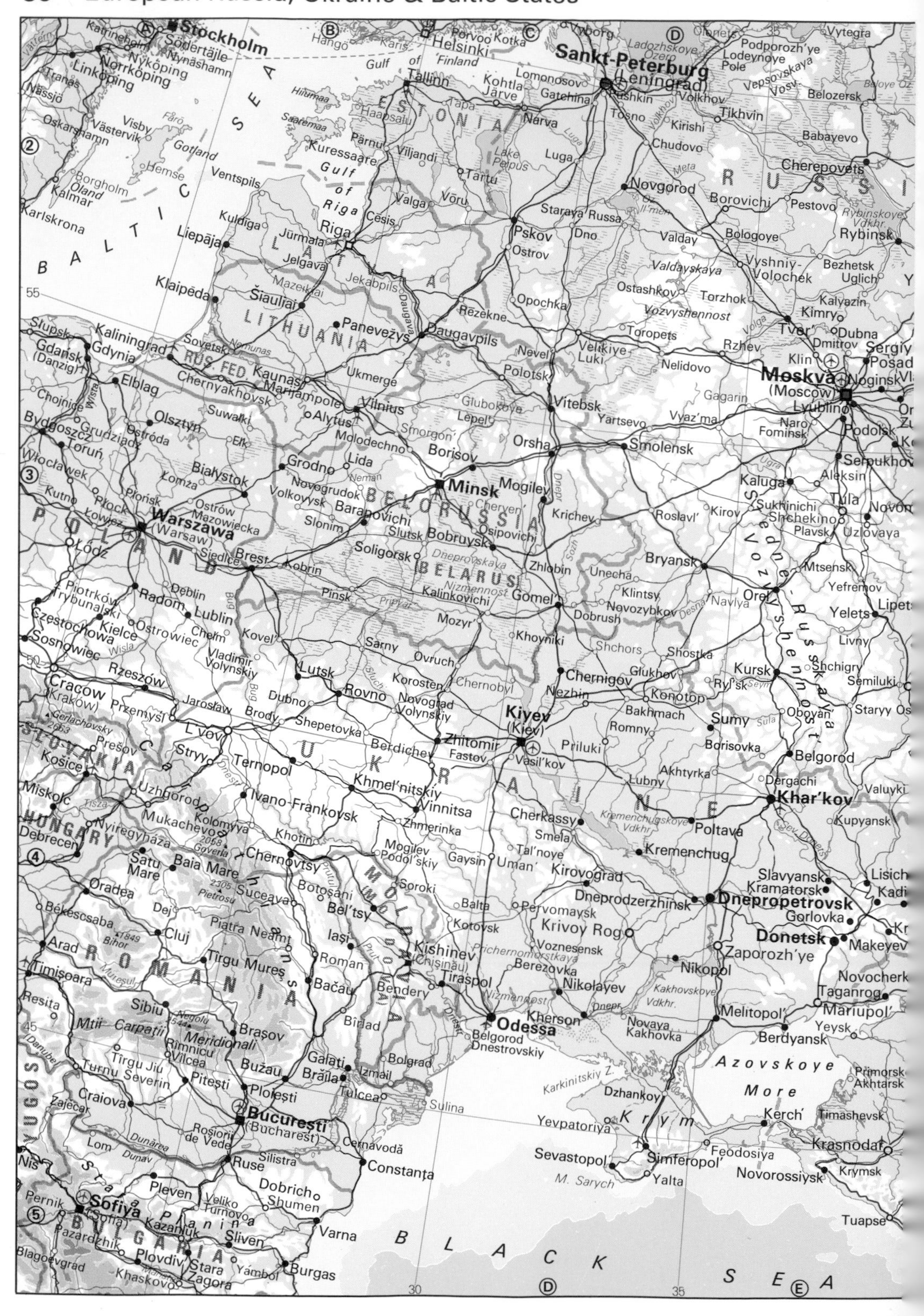
Stockholm
Södertälje
Nynäshamn
Nyköping
Norrköping
Linköping
Katrineholm
Tranås
Nässjö
Västervik
Oskarshamn
Visby
Fårö
Gotland
Hemse
Borgholm
Öland
Kalmar
Karlskrona
BALTIC SEA
Hangö
Helsinki
Porvoo
Kotka
Karis
Gulf of Finland
Tallinn
Hiiumaa
Saaremaa
Haapsalu
Kohtla-Järve
Lomonosov
Gatchina
Narva
ESTONIA
Pärnu
Viljandi
Kuressaare
Gulf of Riga
Tartu
Lake Peipus
Valga
Võru
Cēsis
Riga
Jūrmala
Jelgava
Ventspils
Kuldīga
Liepāja
LATVIA
Jēkabpils
Daugava
Mazeikiai
Šiauliai
Klaipėda
LITHUANIA
Panevežys
Daugavpils
Rezekne
Słupsk
Kaliningrad
Sovetsk
Nemunas
RUS. FED.
Chernyakhovsk
Gdańsk (Danzig)
Gdynia
Elblag
Kaunas
Marijampole
Ukmerge
Vilnius
Alytus
Chojnice
Wisła
Bydgoszcz
Grudziądz
Toruń
Olsztyn
Ostróda
Suwałki
Ełk
Włocławek
Kutno
Płock
Płońsk
Łomża
Białystok
Ostrów Mazowiecka
Grodno
Lida
Neman
Novogrudok
Volkovysk
Molodechno
Smorgon'
Glubokoye
Lepel'
Borisov
Minsk
Baranovichi
Slonim
Slutsk
Bobruysk
BELORUSSIA
Cherven'
Osipovichi
Mogilev
Warszawa (Warsaw)
POLAND
Łódź
Łowicz
Siedlce
Brest
Kobrin
Soligorsk
Dneprovskaya
BELARUS
Nizmennost'
Pinsk
Pripyat
Kalinkovichi
Mozyr'
Zhlobin
Gomel'
Piotrków Trybunalski
Radom
Deblin
Lublin
Kielce
Ostrowiec
Częstochowa
Sosnowiec
Wisła
Chełm
Kovel'
Vladimir Volynskiy
Rzeszów
Cracow (Kraków)
Przemyśl
Jarosław
Lutsk
Sarny
Ovruch
Korosten'
Chernobyl
Dubno
Rovno
Novograd Volynskiy
Brody
Shepetovka
Berdichev
Zhitomir
Fastov
Kiyev (Kiev)
Vasil'kov
L'vov
Stryy
Ternopol
Gerlachovský 2663
SLOVAKIA
Prešov
Košice
Uzhgorod
Mukachevo
Miskolc
Tisza
HUNGARY
Nyíregyháza
Debrecen
Ivano-Frankovsk
Kolomyya
2058 Goverla
Khmel'nitskiy
Vinnitsa
Zhmerinka
Khotin
Chernovtsy
Mogilev Podol'skiy
Gaysin
Uman'
Satu Mare
Baia Mare
2305 Pietrosu
Suceava
Botoşani
Oradea
Dej
Békéscsaba
Bel'tsy
Soroki
MOLDOVA
Balta
Kotovsk
Piatra Neamţ
Iaşi
Prut
Kishinev (Chişinău)
Cluj
1849 Bihor
ROMANIA
Roman
Arad
Tîrgu Mureş
Timişoara
Mureşul
Bacău
Bendery
Tiraspol
Reşiţa
Sibiu
Negoiu 2544
Carpaţii Meridionali
Mtii
Braşov
Bîrlad
Rîmnicu Vîlcea
Tîrgu Jiu
Turnu Severin
Piteşti
Buzău
Galaţi
Brăila
Bolgrad
Izmail
Craiova
Ploieşti
Tulcea
Sulina
Zaječar
Bucureşti (Bucharest)
Roşiori de Vede
Dunărea
Cernavodă
Lom
Dunav
Ruse
Silistra
Constanţa
Niš
Pleven
Dobrich
Shumen
Veliko Turnovo
Pernik
Sofiya (Sofia)
Kazanluk
BULGARIA
Stara Planina
Sliven
Varna
Pazardzhik
Plovdiv
Stara Zagora
Yambol
Burgas
Blagoevgrad
Khaskovo
Vyborg
Ladozhskoye Ozero
Sankt-Peterburg (Leningrad)
Pushkin
Tosno
Volkhov
Kirishi
Tikhvin
Luga
Chudovo
Novgorod
Staraya Russa
Il'men
Pskov
Ostrov
Dno
Opochka
Velikiye Luki
Nevel
Polotsk
Vitebsk
Orsha
Yartsevo
Smolensk
Krichev
Dnepr
Sozh
Olonets
Podporozh'ye
Lodeynoye Pole
Vepsovskaya Vozv.
Vytegra
Beloye Oz.
Belozersk
Babayevo
Cherepovets
Borovichi
Pestovo
Rybinskoye Vdkhr.
Rybinsk
Valday
Bologoye
Valdayskaya
Vyshniy-Volochek
Bezhetsk
Uglich
Ostashkov
Torzhok
Vozvyshennost
Kalyazin
Kimry
Tver'
Dubna
Toropets
Rzhev
Dmitrov
Sergiy Posad
Nelidovo
Klin
Moskva (Moscow)
Noginsk
Lyublino
Gagarin
Vyaz'ma
Naro Fominsk
Podolsk
Serpukhov
Aleksin
Kaluga
Ugra
Tula
Novomoskovsk
Sukhinichi
Shchekino
Kirov
Roslavl'
Plavsk
Uzlovaya
Bryansk
Unecha
Mtsensk
Yefremov
Klintsy
Novozybkov
Desna
Navlya
Orel
Yelets
Lipetsk
Dobrush
Khoyniki
Livny
Shchors
Shostka
Chernigov
Glukhov
Kursk
Shchigry
Seym
Sredne-Russkaya Vozvyshennost'
Nezhin
Konotop
Bakhmach
Ryl'sk
Romny
Sumy
Sula
Oboyan'
Staryy Oskol
Priluki
Borisovka
Belgorod
Lubny
Akhtyrka
Dergachi
Valuyki
Khar'kov
UKRAINE
Cherkassy
Kremenchugskoye Vdkhr.
Poltava
Kupyansk
Smela
Tal'noye
Kremenchug
Sev. Donets
Kirovograd
Slavyansk
Kramatorsk
Lisichansk
Pervomaysk
Dneprodzerzhinsk
Dnepropetrovsk
Gorlovka
Krivoy Rog
Donetsk
Makeyevka
Voznesensk
Prichernomorskaya
Berezovka
Zaporozh'ye
Nikopol
Nikolayev
Kakhovskoye Vdkhr.
Novocherkassk
Taganrog
Mariupol'
Odessa
Nizmennost
Kherson
Novaya Kakhovka
Melitopol'
Yeysk
Berdyansk
Belgorod Dnestrovskiy
Dnestr
Karkinitskiy Z.
Azovskoye More
Primorsko-Akhtarsk
Dzhankoy
Krym
Kerch'
Timashevsk
Yevpatoriya
Feodosiya
Krasnodar
Sevastopol'
Simferopol'
Yalta
M. Sarych
Novorossiysk
Krymsk
Tuapse
BLACK SEA
55
50
45
30
35

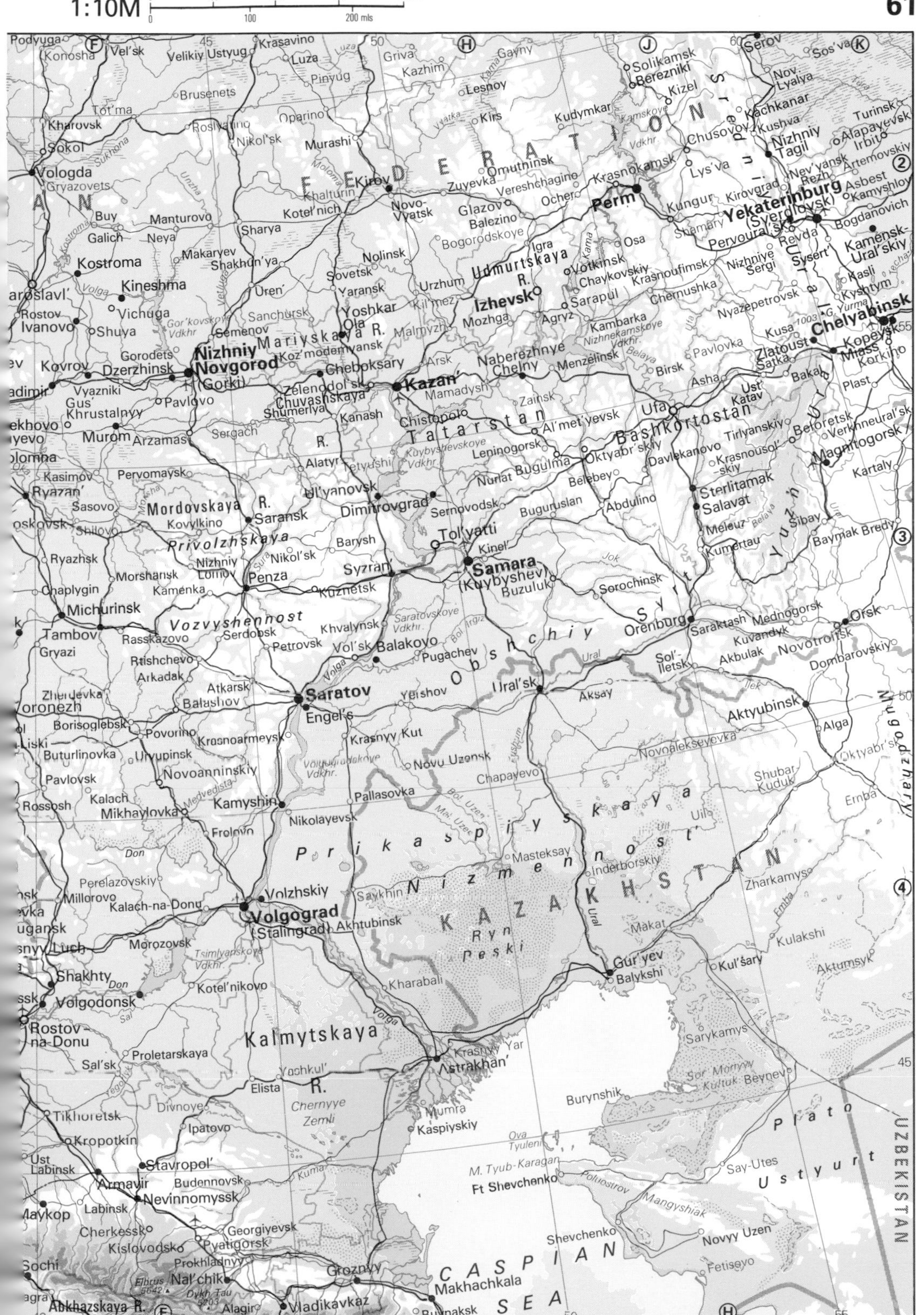

1:10M

100   200   300   400 km

100

200 mls

F   H   J   K

Podyuga   Vel'sk   Velikiy Ustyug   Krasavino   Griva   Gayny   Serov   Sos'va   2
Konosha   Luza   Kazhim   Solikamsk   Nov.   Sos'va
Brusenets   Pinyug   Lesnoy   Berezniki   Kizel   Lyalya   Turinsk
Tot'ma   Nikol'sk   Kirs   Kudymkar   Kamskoye   Nizhniy   Alapayevsk   Irbito
Kharovsk   Oparino   Vatka   Kushva   Tagil   Artemovskiy
Sokol   Roslatino   Omutninsk   Chusovoy   Vekaterinburg   Asbest   Myashyloy
Vologda   Kirov   Zuyevka   Vereshchagino   Ocher   Perm   Kungur   (Syerdlovsk)   Bogdanovich
Gryazovets   Novo-   Glazov   Krasnokamsk   Lys'va   Rezh.   Nev'yansk   Kamensk-
Buy   Manturovo   Vyatsk   Pervoural'sk   Nizhniye   Ural'skiy
aroslavl'   Galich   Neya   Balezino   Osa   Votkinsk   Shamary   Kirovgrad   Revda   Sysert'   Kasli
Kostroma   Makaryev   Bogorodskoye   Sergi   Zlatoust   Kyshtym
Kineshma   Shakhun'ya   Nolinsk   Udmurtskaya   Igra   Kama   Krasnoufimsk   Nyazepetrovsk   Chelyabinsk
Rostov   Vichuga   Uren'   Yaransk   Izhevsk   R.   Chaykovskiy   Chernushka   Kusa 1003 G.Yurma   Kopeysk
Ivanovo   Shuya   Sanchursk   Yoshkar   Votkinsk   Sarapul   Nizhneka mskoye   Satka   Miass   Korkino
Ola   Kil'mez   Mozhga   Agryz   Kambarka   Vdkhr.   Bakal   Plast
Kovrov   Gorodets   Mariyskaya R.   Koz'modem'yansk   Malmyzh   Birsk   Pavlovka   Asha   Ust'
adimir   Dzerzhinsk   Nizhniy   Cheboksary   Arsk   Naberezhnye   Menzelinsk   Belaya   Ufa   Katay
Vyazniki   Novgorod   Kazan   Chelny   Bashkortostan   Yuzh.
ekhovo   Gus'   (Gorki)   Zelenodol'sk   Mamadysh   Al'met'yevsk   Ufa   Verkhneural'sk
Khrustalnyy   Pavlovo   Chuvashskaya   Shumerlya   Chistopolo   Zainsk   Sterlitamak   Beloretsk
olomna   Murom   Arzamas   Sergach   Kanash   Leninogorsk   Davlekanovo   Salavat   Magnitogorsk
Kasimov   Pervomaysk   Alatyr'   Tetyushi   Kuybyshevskoye   Oktyabr'skiy   Krasnousol'   Kartaly
Ryazan'   Sasovo   Mordovskaya R.   Dimitrovgrad   Vdkhr.   Bugulma   Belebey   Kumertau   Baymak Bredy
oskovsk   Shilovo   Kovylkino   Saransk   Nurlat   Abdulino   Sibay
Ryazhsk   Privolzhskaya   Ul'yanovsk   Sernovodsk   Buguruslan   Meleuz
Chaplygin   Morshansk   Nikol'sk   Tol'yatti   Kinel'   Sorochinsk   Mednogorsk
Michurinsk   Kamenka   Penza   Syzran'   Samara   Buzuluk   Orenburg   Orsk
Tambov   Vozvyshennost   Kuznetsk   (Kuybyshev)   Saraktash   Novotroitsk
Gryazi   Rasskazovo   Serdobsk   Khvalynsk   Saratovskoye   Bol. Irgiz   Sol'   Akbulak   Dombarovskiy
Zherdevka   Rtishchevo   Petrovsk   Vdkhr.   Pugachev   Ural   Iletsk
oronezh   Arkadak   Atkarsk   Vol'sk   Balakovo   Ural'sk   Aksay   Aktyubinsk   Alga
Borisoglebsk   Balashov   Volga   Ybishov   Novoalekseyevka   50
Liski   Buturlinovka   Povorino   Krasnoarmeysk   Krasnyy Kut   Chapayevo   Shubar-
Pavlovsk   Uryupinsk   Engel's   Novu Uzensk   Kuduk
Rossosh   Kalach   Novoanninskiy   Saratov   Mln.Uzen   Erna
Mikhaylovka   Kamyshin   Pallasovka   Inderborskiy   Zharkamys
nsk   Medveditsa   Frolovo   Bol.Uzen   Uila   4
evka   Perelazovskiy   Millorovo   Nikolayevsk   Prikaspiyskaya   Masteksay   Nizmennost
uganск   Kalach-na-Donu   Volzhskiy   Saykhin   Kazakhstan   Kulakshi
snyy Luch   Morozovsk   Volgograd   Akhtubinsk   Ryn   Makat
Shakhty   Don   (Stalingrad)   Peski   Gur'yev   Kul'sary   Aktumsyk
Volgodonsk   Kotel'nikovo   Tsimlyanskoye   Kharabali   Balykshi   Sarykamys
Rostov-   Sal   Vdkhr.   Kalmytskaya   Krasnyy Yar   Plato
na-Donu   Proletarskaya   R.   Astrakhan'   Sor Mortsyy   Ustyurt   45
Sal'sk   Yashkul   Volga   Kultuk Beyneu
Tikhoretsk   Divnoye   Elista   Chernyye   Mumra   Burynshik   Say-Utes   Uzbekistan
Kropotkin   Ipatovo   Zemli   Kaspiyskiy   Ova   Novvy Uzen
Ust   Stavropol'   Kuma   M.Tyub-Karagan   Tyuleni   Poluostrov   Mangyshlak
Labinsk   Armavir   Budennovsk   Ft Shevchenko   Fetiseyo
Maykop   Labinsk   Nevinnomyssk   Georgiyevsk   Shevchenko
Cherkessk   Pyatigorsk   CASPIAN
Sochi   Kislovodsk   Prokhladnyy   Elbrus 5642   Nal'chik   SEA   H
agra   Abkhazskaya R.   Dykh Tau   Grozny   Makhachkala   Buynaksk
Alagir   Vladikavkaz   50   55

1:45M
0 600 1200 1800 km
0 300 600 900 mls

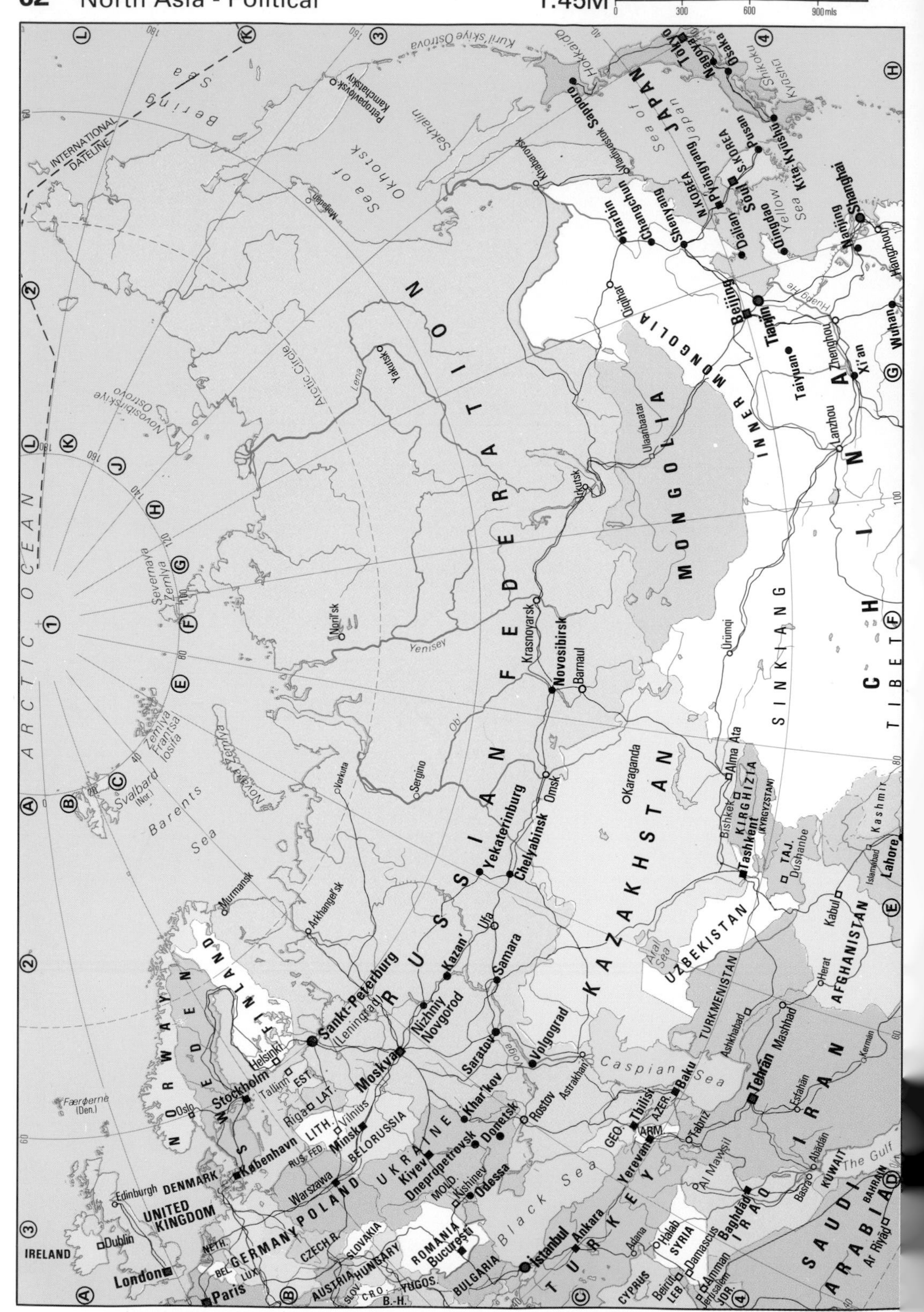

1:20M

200 400 600 800 km

200 400 mls

RUSSIAN FEDERATION

SAKHALIN

Sikhote Alin'

SEA OF JAPAN

YELLOW SEA

KOREA

NORTH KOREA

SOUTH KOREA

Seoul

Beijing / Peking

MONGOLIA

CHINA

Ulaanbaatar

Harbin

Changchun

Shenyang

Dalian

Tianjin

Vladivostok

Nakhodka

Khabarovsk

Komsomol'sk-na-Amure

Nikolayevsk

Yuzhno-Sakhalinsk

Yakutsk

Bratsk

Irkutsk

Ulan-Ude

Chita

Krasnoyarsk

Abakan

Novokuznetsk

Kemerovo

Tomsk

Stanovoy Khrebet

Da Hinggan Ling

Proliv Tatarskiy

Arctic Circle

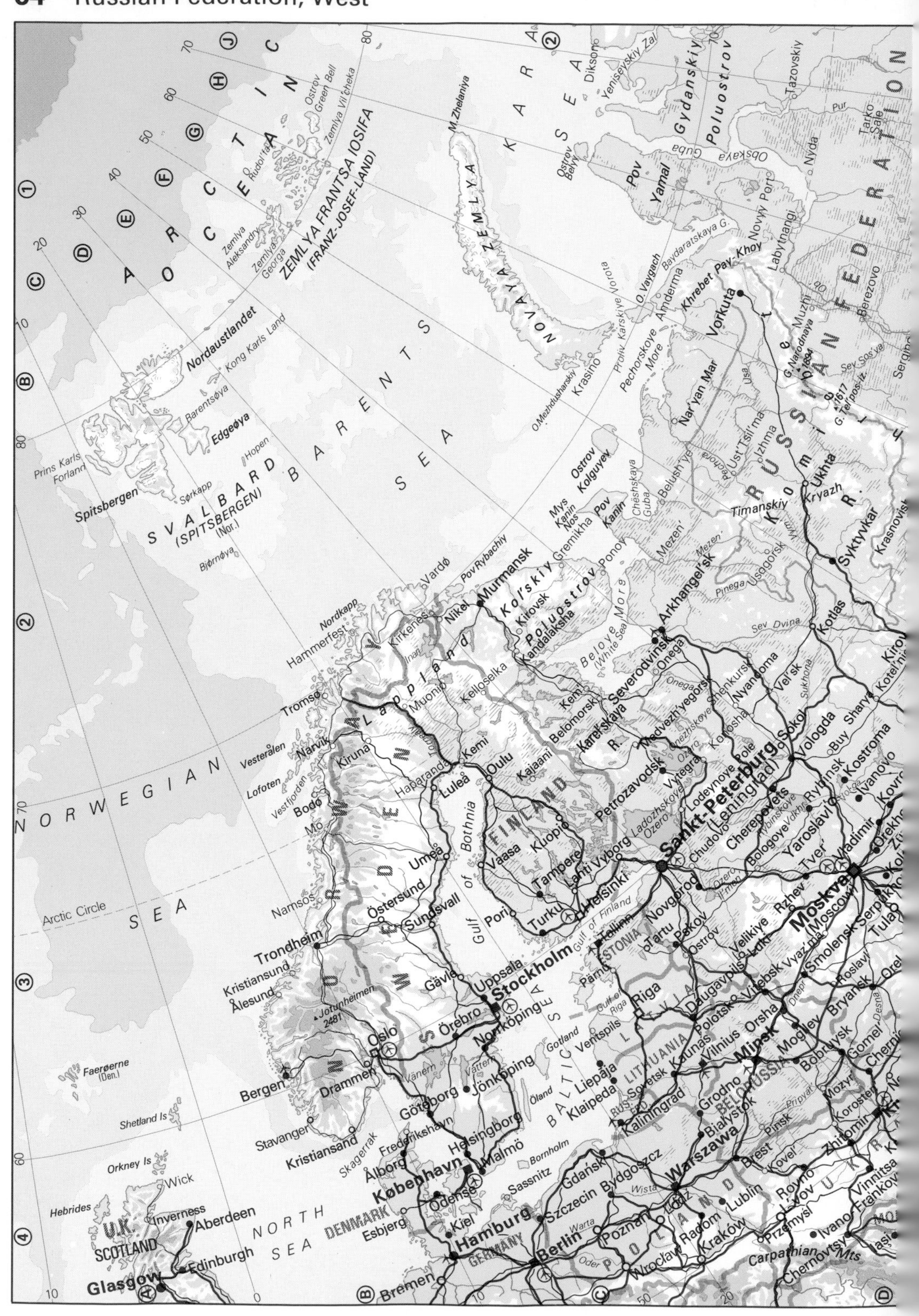
ARCTIC OCEAN
BARENTS SEA
KARA SEA
NORWEGIAN SEA
NORTH SEA
BALTIC SEA
SVALBARD (SPITSBERGEN) (Nor.)
ZEMLYA FRANTSA IOSIFA (FRANZ-JOSEF-LAND)
NOVAYA ZEMLYA
RUSSIAN FEDERATION
FINLAND
SWEDEN
NORWAY
DENMARK
ESTONIA
LATVIA
LITHUANIA
BELORUSSIA
POLAND
GERMANY
U.K.
SCOTLAND
Spitsbergen
Nordaustlandet
Edgeøya
Murmansk
Arkhangel'sk
Sankt-Peterburg (Leningrad)
Moskva (Moscow)
Helsinki
Stockholm
Oslo
København
Berlin
Warszawa
Minsk
Riga
Hamburg
Glasgow
Aberdeen
Edinburgh
Arctic Circle

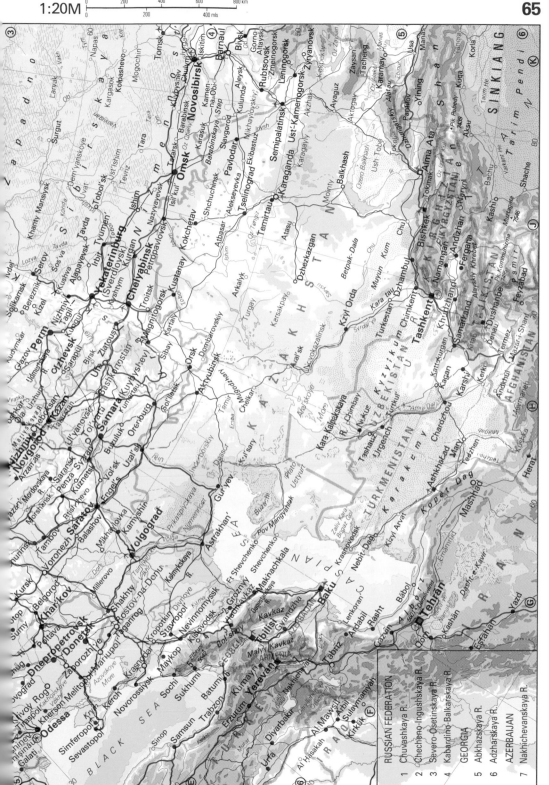

RUSSIAN FEDERATION
1 Chuvashskaya R.
2 Checheno-Ingushskaya R.
3 Severo-Osetinskaya R.
4 Kabardino-Balkarskaya R.

GEORGIA
5 Abkhazskaya R.
6 Adzharskaya R.

AZERBAIJAN
7 Nakhichevanskaya R.

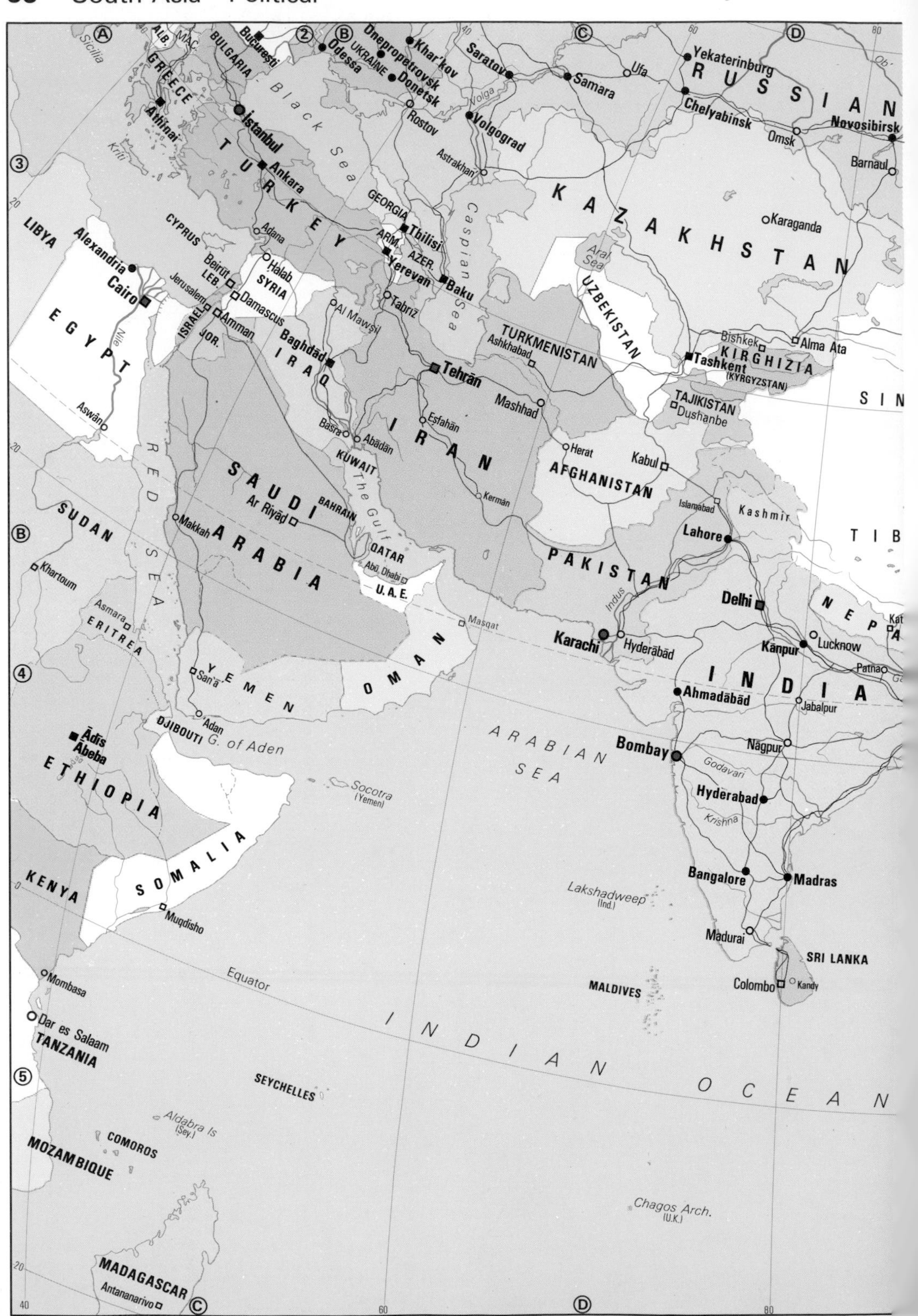
RUSSIAN
KAZAKHSTAN
TURKEY
GREECE
BULGARIA
UKRAINE
GEORGIA
ARM.
AZER.
CYPRUS
LEB.
SYRIA
ISRAEL
JOR.
IRAQ
IRAN
TURKMENISTAN
UZBEKISTAN
KIRGHIZIA (KYRGYZSTAN)
TAJIKISTAN
AFGHANISTAN
PAKISTAN
INDIA
NEPAL
SRI LANKA
MALDIVES
LIBYA
EGYPT
SUDAN
ERITREA
ETHIOPIA
DJIBOUTI
SOMALIA
KENYA
TANZANIA
MOZAMBIQUE
MADAGASCAR
COMOROS
SEYCHELLES
SAUDI ARABIA
KUWAIT
BAHRAIN
QATAR
U.A.E.
OMAN
YEMEN
Black Sea
Caspian Sea
Aral Sea
RED SEA
The Gulf
G. of Aden
ARABIAN SEA
INDIAN OCEAN
Bucureşti
Odessa
Dnepropetrovsk
Khar'kov
Donetsk
Rostov
Saratov
Samara
Ufa
Yekaterinburg
Chelyabinsk
Omsk
Novosibirsk
Barnaul
Volgograd
Astrakhan'
Karaganda
Athínai
İstanbul
Ankara
Adana
Halab
Tbilisi
Yerevan
Baku
Tabrīz
Alexandria
Cairo
Beirūt
Damascus
Jerusalem
Amman
Al Mawşil
Baghdād
Tehrān
Ashkhabad
Mashhad
Eşfahān
Başra
Abādān
Kermān
Herat
Kabul
Islamabad
Kashmir
Lahore
Delhi
Bishkek
Alma Ata
Tashkent
Dushanbe
Ar Riyāḑ
Makkah
Abū Dhabi
Masqat
Karachi
Hyderābād
Indus
Kānpur
Lucknow
Patna
Ahmadābād
Jabalpur
Bombay
Nāgpur
Godavari
Hyderabad
Krishna
Bangalore
Madras
Madurai
Colombo
Kandy
Lakshadweep (Ind.)
Aswân
Nile
Khartoum
Asmara
San'ā
Adan
Ādīs Ābeba
Socotra (Yemen)
Muqdisho
Mombasa
Dar es Salaam
Equator
Aldabra Is (Sey.)
Chagos Arch. (U.K.)
Antananarivo
Sicilia
Kríti
ALB.
MAC.
Volga
Ob'
TIB
SIN
Kat
A
B
C
D
2
3
4
5
20
40
60
80
0

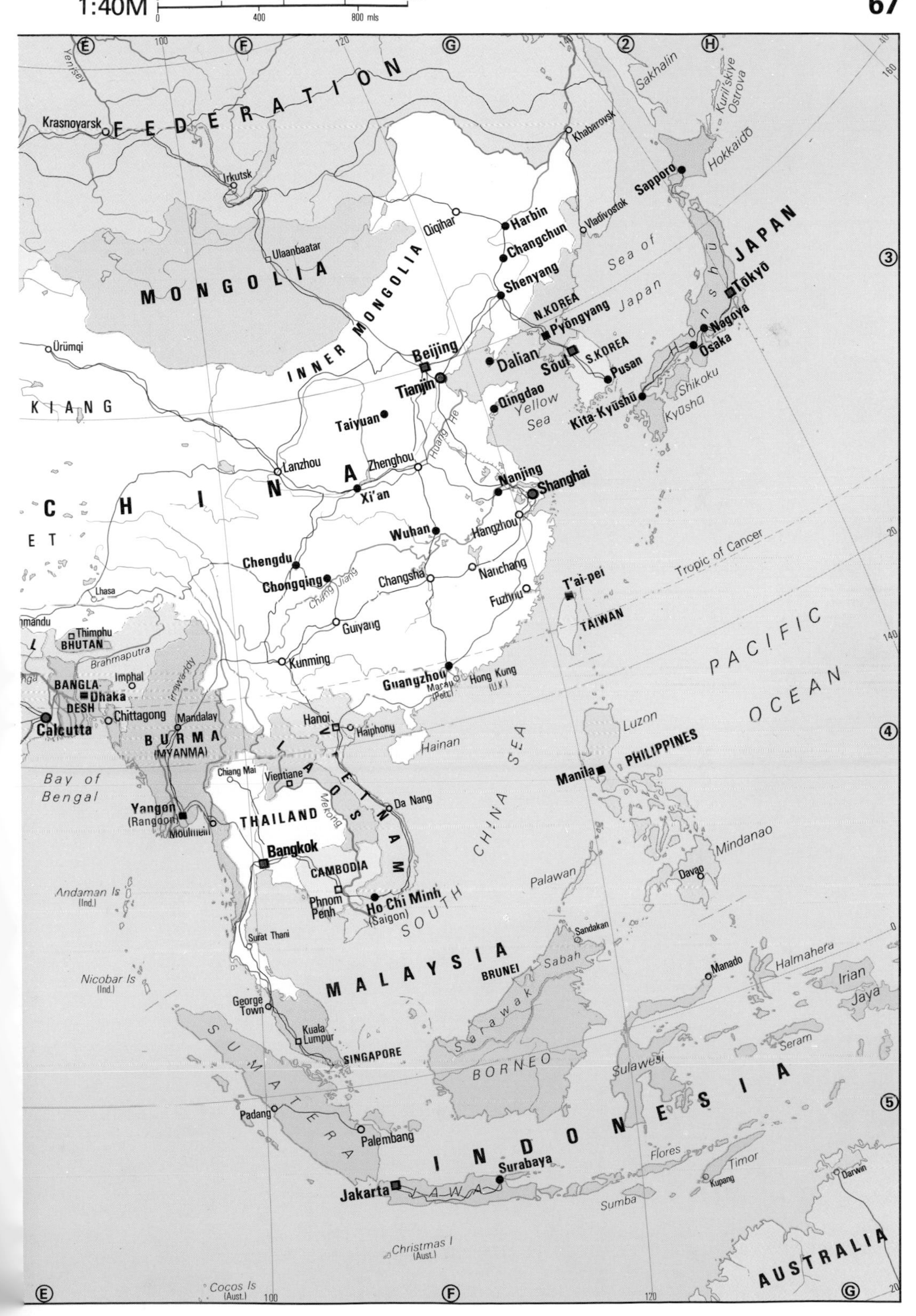
E
F
G
2
H
3
4
5
100
120
140
160
40
20
0
Yenisey
Krasnoyarsk
F E D E R A T I O N
Irkutsk
Sakhalin
Kuril'skiye Ostrova
Khabarovsk
Hokkaidō
Sapporo
Vladivostok
Harbin
Qiqihar
Ulaanbaatar
Changchun
Shenyang
M O N G O L I A
INNER MONGOLIA
JAPAN
Honshu
Tokyō
Sea of Japan
N.KOREA
Pyongyang
S.KOREA
Sŏul
Pusan
Nagoya
Ōsaka
Shikoku
Kyūshū
Kita-Kyūshū
Ürümqi
Beijing
Tianjin
Dalian
Qingdao
Yellow Sea
K I A N G
Taiyuan
Huang He
Lanzhou
Zhenghou
Nanjing
Shanghai
Xi'an
C H I N A
E T
Hangzhou
Wuhan
Chengdu
Chongqing
Chang Jiang
Changsha
Nanchang
Fuzhou
T'ai-pei
TAIWAN
Tropic of Cancer
Lhasa
Guiyang
Thimphu
BHUTAN
Brahmaputra
Kunming
Guangzhou
Macau (Port.)
Hong Kong (U.K.)
PACIFIC
OCEAN
BANGLADESH
Dhaka
Imphal
Chittagong
Mandalay
Irrawaddy
Calcutta
BURMA (MYANMA)
Hanoi
Haiphong
LAOS
VIETNAM
Hainan
Luzon
PHILIPPINES
Manila
Bay of Bengal
Chiang Mai
Vientiane
Mekong
Da Nang
SOUTH CHINA SEA
Yangon (Rangoon)
Moulmein
THAILAND
Bangkok
CAMBODIA
Phnom Penh
Ho Chi Minh (Saigon)
Mindanao
Palawan
Davao
Andaman Is (Ind.)
Surat Thani
Sandakan
Sabah
BRUNEI
Sarawak
M A L A Y S I A
Manado
Halmahera
Irian Jaya
Nicobar Is (Ind.)
George Town
Kuala Lumpur
SINGAPORE
Seram
SUMATERA
BORNEO
Sulawesi
Padang
Palembang
I N D O N E S I A
Flores
Timor
Surabaya
Kupang
Darwin
Jakarta
JAWA
Sumba
Christmas I (Aust.)
AUSTRALIA
Cocos Is (Aust.)

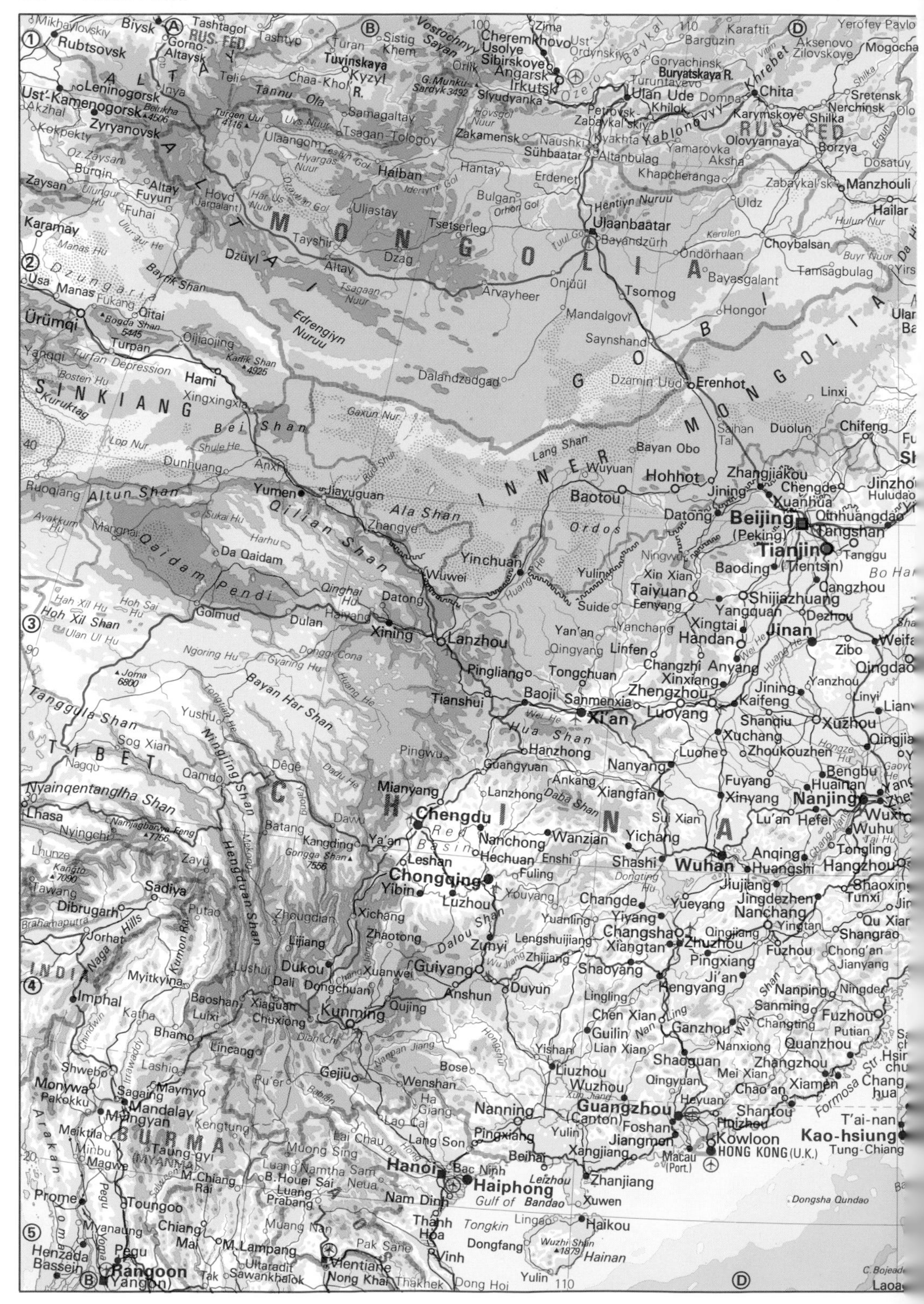
Mikhaylovskiy
Biysk
Tashtagol
Rubtsovsk
Gorno-Altaysk
RUS. FED.
Tashtyp
Turan
Sistig Khem
Vostochnyy Sayan
Cheremkhovo
Zima
Usolye Sibirskoye
Angarsk
Irkutsk
Ust'-Ordynskiy
Barguzin
Karaftit
Aksenovo
Zilovskoye
Yerofey Pavlov
Mogocha
Tuvinskaya
Kyzyl
Teli
Chaa-Khol
Orlik
G. Munku-Sardyk 3492
Slyudyanka
Ozero Baykal
Goryachinsk
Buryatskaya R.
Turuntayevo
Vitim
Khrebet
Chita
Leninogorsk
Ust'-Kamenogorsk
Akzhal
ALTAI
Inya
Tannu Ola
Ulan Ude
Domna
Khilok
Sretensk
Nerchinsk
Shilka
Belukha 4506
Turgen Uul 4116
Uvs Nuur
Samagaltay
Hovsgol Nuur
Petrovsk-Zabaykal'skiy
Yablonovyy
Karymskoye
Zyryanovsk
Kokpekty
Tsagan-Tologoy
Zakamensk
Naushki
Kyakhta
Olovyannaya
Borzya
Ulaangom
Sühbaatar
Altanbulag
Yamarovka
Aksha
Oz. Zaysan
Hyargas Nuur
Tesiyn Gol
Haiban
Hantay
Erdenet
Khapcheranga
Dosatuy
Burqin
Zaysan
Ulungur Hu
Altay
Fuyun
Hovd (Jargalant)
Har Us Nuur
Dzavhan Gol
Ideriyn Gol
Bulgan
Orhon Gol
Hentiyn Nuruu
Uldz
Zabaykal'sk
Manzhouli
Hailar
Fuhai
Uliastay
Tsetserleg
Ulaanbaatar
Kerulen
Hulun Nur
Karamay
Manas Hu
Ulungur He
MONGOLIA
Tayshir
Dzag
Tuul Gol
Bayandzürh
Öndörhaan
Choybalsan
Buyr Nuur
Dzungaria
Bayrik Shan
Dzüyl
Altay
Arvayheer
Onjüül
Tsomog
Bayasgalant
Tamsagbulag
Usa
Manas
Fukang
Qitai
Tsagaan Nuur
Mandalgovi
Hongor
Ürümqi
Bogda Shan 5445
Edrengiyn Nuruu
Saynshand
GOBI
Turpan
Qijiaojing
Yanqqi
Turfan Depression
Karlik Shan 4925
Bosten Hu
Hami
Dalandzadgad
Dzamin Uud
Erenhot
Linxi
SINKIANG
Kuruktag
Xingxingxia
Gaxun Nur
INNER MONGOLIA
Bei Shan
Saihan Tal
Duolun
Chifeng
Lop Nur
Shule He
Lang Shan
Bayan Obo
Dunhuang
Anxi
Ruo Shui
Wuyuan
Hohhot
Zhangjiakou
Chengde
Jinzhou
Huludao
Ruoqiang
Altun Shan
Yumen
Jiayuguan
Baotou
Jining
Xuanhua
Qinhuangdao
Qilian Shan
Ala Shan
Datong
Beijing (Peking)
Tangshan
Ayakkum Hu
Sukai Hu
Mangnai
Qaidam Pendi
Harhu
Zhangye
Ordos
Tianjin (Tientsin)
Tanggu
Da Qaidam
Yinchuan
Ningwu
Yulin
Xin Xian
Baoding
Bo Hai
Wuwei
Huang He
Taiyuan
Fenyang
Cangzhou
Qinghai Hu
Datong
Shijiazhuang
Hah Xil Hu
Hoh Sai Hu
Golmud
Haiyang
Suide
Yangquan
Dezhou
Hoh Xil Shan
Ulan Ul Hu
Dulan
Xining
Yan'an
Yanchang
Xingtai
Handan
Jinan
Weifang
Lanzhou
Ngoring Hu
Donggi Cona
Gyaring Hu
Qingyang
Linfen
Zibo
Joma 6800
Bayan Har Shan
Pingliang
Tongchuan
Changzhi
Anyang
Qingdao
Tanggula Shan
Xinxiang
Jining
Yanzhou
Tianshui
Baoji
Sanmenxia
Zhengzhou
Kaifeng
Linyi
Yushu
Tongtian He
Xi'an
Luoyang
Lianyungang
Wei He
Hua Shan
Shangqiu
Xuzhou
Xuchang
TIBET
Sog Xian
Ningjing Shan
Pingwu
Hanzhong
Luohe
Zhoukouzhen
Qingjiang
Nagqu
Qamdo
Dêgê
Dadu He
Guangyuan
Nanyang
Bengbu
Nyainqentanglha Shan
Yalong
Mianyang
Ankang
Daba Shan
Xiangfan
Fuyang
Huainan
Lhasa
CHINA
Lanzhong
Xinyang
Nanjing
Namjagbarwa Feng 7756
Dawu
Chengdu
Sui Xian
Lu'an
Hefei
Wuxi
Nyingchi
Batang
Kangding
Red Basin
Nanchong
Wanzian
Yichang
Wuhu
Gongga Shan 7556
Ya'an
Tongling
Lhunze
Zayu
Leshan
Hechuan
Enshi
Shashi
Wuhan
Anqing
Huangshi
Hangzhou
Kangto 7090
Hengduan Shan
Chongqing
Fuling
Dongting Hu
Jiujiang
Shaoxing
Tawang
Sadiya
Yibin
Luzhou
Youyang
Changde
Yueyang
Jingdezhen
Tunxi
Dibrugarh
Putao
Dalou Shan
Yuanling
Yiyang
Nanchang
Qu Xian
Brahmaputra
Zhougdian
Xichang
Qingjiang
Yingtan
Shangrao
Jorhat
Naga Hills
Kumon Ra.
Zhaotong
Changsha
Zhuzhou
Lijiang
Zunyi
Lengshuijiang
Xiangtan
Fuzhou
Chong'an
INDIA
Lushui
Dukou
Guiyang
Zhijiang
Wu Jiang
Shaoyang
Pingxiang
Jianyang
Myitkyina
Dali
Dongchuan
Xuanwei
Ji'an
Imphal
Baoshan
Xiaguan
Anshun
Duyun
Hengyang
Wuyi Shan
Nanping
Ningde
Luixi
Chuxiong
Kunming
Qujing
Lingling
Sanming
Katha
Chen Xian
Nan Ling
Fuzhou
Bhamo
Lincang
Dian Chi
Guilin
Ganzhou
Changting
Putian
Chindwin
Irrawaddy
Hongshui
Lian Xian
Nanxiong
Quanzhou
Shwebo
Lashio
Nanpan Jiang
Yishan
Bose
Shaoguan
Zhangzhou
Hsinchu
Monywa
Sagaing
Maymyo
Gejiu
Liuzhou
Mei Xian
Pakokku
Pu'er
Wenshan
Qingyuan
Wuzhou
Chao'an
Xiamen
Changhua
Mandalay
Xun Jiang
Heyuan
Formosa Str.
Arakan
Myingyan
Ha Giang
Nanning
Guangzhou (Canton)
Shantou
T'ai-nan
Meiktila
BURMA
Kengtung
Lao Cai
Yulin
Huizhou
Minbu
Taung-gyi
Lang Son
Pingxiang
Foshan
Kowloon
Kao-hsiung
Magwe
(MYANMA)
Muong Sing
Bai Chau
Beihai
Jiangmen
HONG KONG (U.K.)
Tung-Chiang
Luang Namtha
Sam Neua
Xangjiang
Macau (Port.)
M. Chiang Rai
B. Houei Sai
Hanoi
Bac Ninh
Haiphong
Leizhou
Zhanjiang
Pegu
Luang Prabang
Nam Dinh
Gulf of Tongkin
Bandao
Xuwen
Prome
Toungoo
Dongsha Qundao
Thanh Hoa
Lingao
Haikou
Chiang Mai
Muang Nan
Myanaung
Pegu
M. Lampang
Pak Sane
Dongfang
Wuzhi Shan 1879
Hainan
Henzada
Bassein
Rangoon (Yangon)
Tak
Uttaradit
Sawankhalok
Vientiane
Nong Khai
Thakhek
Vinh
Dong Hoi
Yulin
C. Bojeador
Laoag

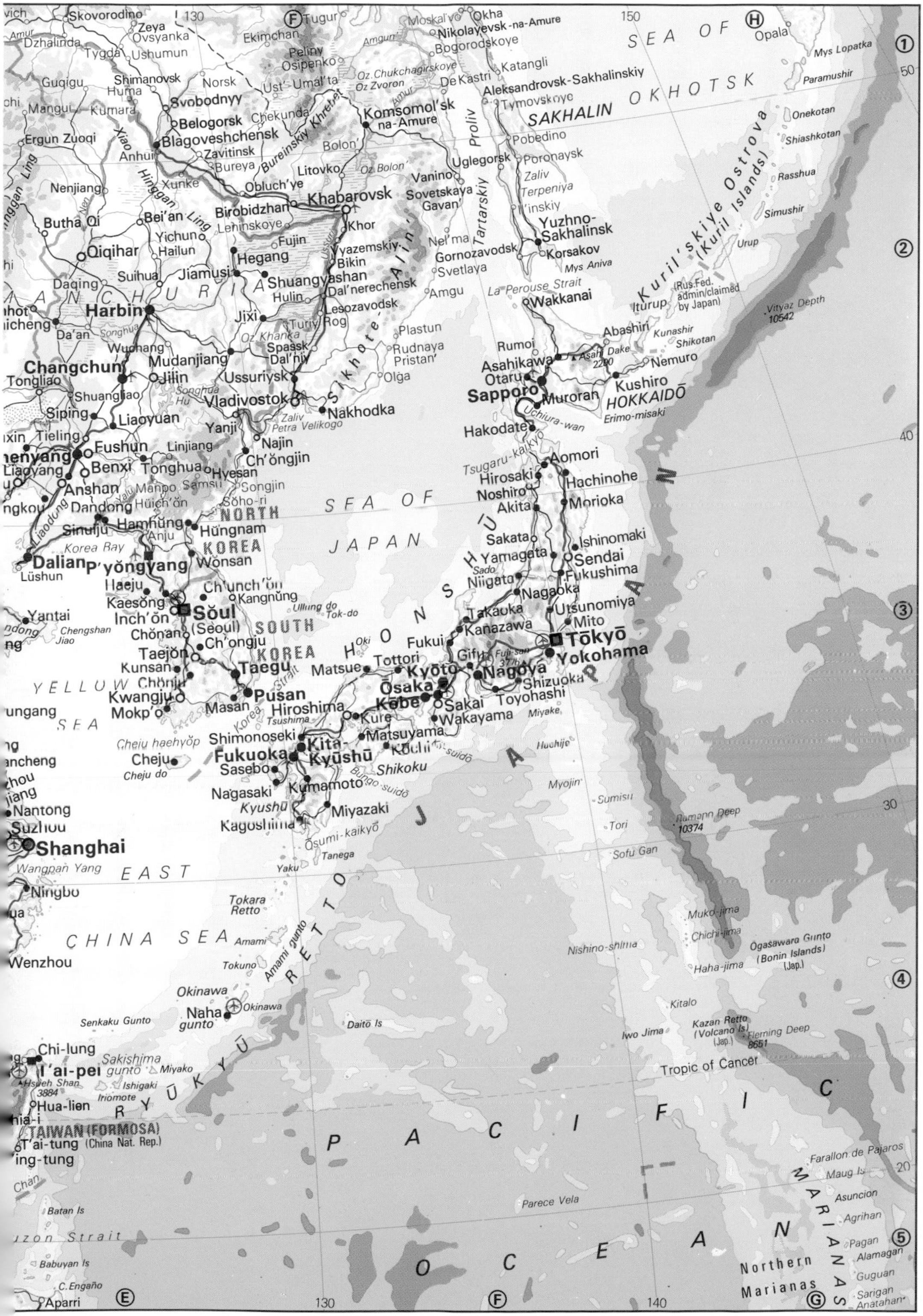
SEA OF OKHOTSK
SAKHALIN
Kuril'skiye Ostrova (Kuril Islands)
(Rus.Fed. admin/claimed by Japan)
Skovorodino
Zeya
Ovsyanka
Dzhalinda
Tygda
Ushumun
Tugur
Okha
Moskal'vo
Nikolayevsk-na-Amure
Bogorodskoye
Opala
Mys Lopatka
Paramushir
Onekotan
Shiashkotan
Rasshua
Simushir
Urup
Iturup
Kunashir
Shikotan
Vityaz Depth 10542
Ekimchan
Peliny Osipenko
Oz. Chukchagirskoye
Oz Zvoron
De Kastri
Katangli
Aleksandrovsk-Sakhalinskiy
Tymovskoye
Pobedino
Poronaysk
Zaliv Terpeniya
Uglegorsk
Yuzhno-Sakhalinsk
Korsakov
Mys Aniva
Tartarskiy Proliv
Guqigu
Shimanovsk
Huma
Norsk
Ust'-Umal'ta
Komsomol'sk na-Amure
Mangui
Kumara
Svobodnyy
Belogorsk
Chekunda
Bureinskiy Khrebet
Ergun Zuoqi
Blagoveshchensk
Zavitinsk
Bureya
Bolon'
Oz. Bolon'
Litovko
Vanino
Sovetskaya Gavan'
Anhui
Xunke
Obluch'ye
Nenjiang
Birobidzhan
Khabarovsk
Leninskoye
Khor
Butha Qi
Bei'an
Yichun
Hailun
Fujin
Qiqihar
Hegang
Vyazemskiy
Bikin
Nel'ma
Gornozavodsk
Svetlaya
Daqing
Suihua
Jiamusi
Shuangyashan
Dal'nerechensk
Hulin
Amgu
La Perouse Strait
Wakkanai
Harbin
Lesozavodsk
Jixi
Turiy Rog
Oz Khanka
Plastun
Sikhote Alin'
Spassk Dal'niy
Rudnaya Pristan'
Da'an
Wuchang
Mudanjiang
Changchun
Jilin
Ussuriysk
Olga
Tongliao
Shuangliao
Vladivostok
Nakhodka
Siping
Liaoyuan
Zaliv Petra Velikogo
Tieling
Fushun
Linjiang
Yanji
Najin
Ch'ongjin
Shenyang
Benxi
Tonghua
Hyesan
Liaoyang
Anshan
Manpo
Samsu
Songjin
Dandong
Hŭich'ŏn
Sŏho-ri
NORTH KOREA
Sinŭiju
Hamhŭng
Hŭngnam
Anju
Korea Bay
Dalian
Lüshun
P'yŏngyang
Wŏnsan
Haeju
Ch'unch'ŏn
Kaesŏng
Kangnŭng
Yantai
Inch'ŏn
Sŏul (Seoul)
SOUTH KOREA
Ullŭng do
Tok-do
Chengshan Jiao
Chŏnan
Ch'ŏngju
Taejŏn
Taegu
Kunsan
Chŏnju
Kwangju
Pusan
Masan
Mokp'o
YELLOW SEA
Korea Strait
Tsushima
Cheju haehyŏp
Cheju
Cheju do
SEA OF JAPAN
Rumoi
Asahikawa
Asahi Dake 2290
Abashiri
Nemuro
Otaru
Sapporo
Muroran
Kushiro
HOKKAIDŌ
Erimo-misaki
Uchiura-wan
Hakodate
Tsugaru-kaikyō
Aomori
Hirosaki
Hachinohe
Noshiro
Morioka
Akita
Sakata
Ishinomaki
Yamagata
Sendai
Sado
Niigata
Fukushima
Nagaoka
HONSHŪ
Utsunomiya
Takaoka
Mito
Kanazawa
Oki
Fukui
Tōkyō
Yokohama
Tottori
Gifu
Fuji-san 3776
Matsue
Kyōto
Nagoya
Ōsaka
Shizuoka
Kōbe
Sakai
Toyohashi
Hiroshima
Kure
Wakayama
Miyake
Shimonoseki
Kita-Kyūshū
Matsuyama
Kōchi
Fukuoka
Kyūshū
Shikoku
Hachijō
Sasebo
Bungo-suidō
Nagasaki
Kumamoto
Myojin
Kyushu
Miyazaki
Sumisu
Kagoshima
Ōsumi-kaikyō
Tori
Ramapo Deep 10374
Tanega
Sofu Gan
Yaku
JAPAN
Shanghai
Suzhou
Nantong
Wangpan Yang
EAST CHINA SEA
Ningbo
Tokara Retto
Wenzhou
Amami
Amami gunto
Tokuno
Muko-jima
Chichi-jima
Nishino-shima
Ogasawara Gunto (Bonin Islands) (Jap.)
Haha-jima
Okinawa
Naha
Okinawa gunto
Senkaku Gunto
Daitō Is
Kitalo
Iwo Jima
Kazan Retto (Volcano Is) (Jap.)
Fleming Deep 8651
Tropic of Cancer
Chi-lung
T'ai-pei
Sakishima gunto
Miyako
Ishigaki
Iriomote
Hsueh Shan 3884
Hua-lien
RYŪKYŪ RETTO
TAIWAN (FORMOSA) (China Nat. Rep.)
T'ai-tung
P'ing-tung
PACIFIC OCEAN
Farallon de Pajaros
Maug Is
MARIANAS
Asuncion
Parece Vela
Agrihan
Batan Is
Luzon Strait
Pagan
Alamagan
Babuyan Is
Guguan
Northern Marianas
C. Engaño
Aparri
Sarigan
Anatahan
130
140
150
40
30
20
50
E
F
G
H
1
2
3
4
5

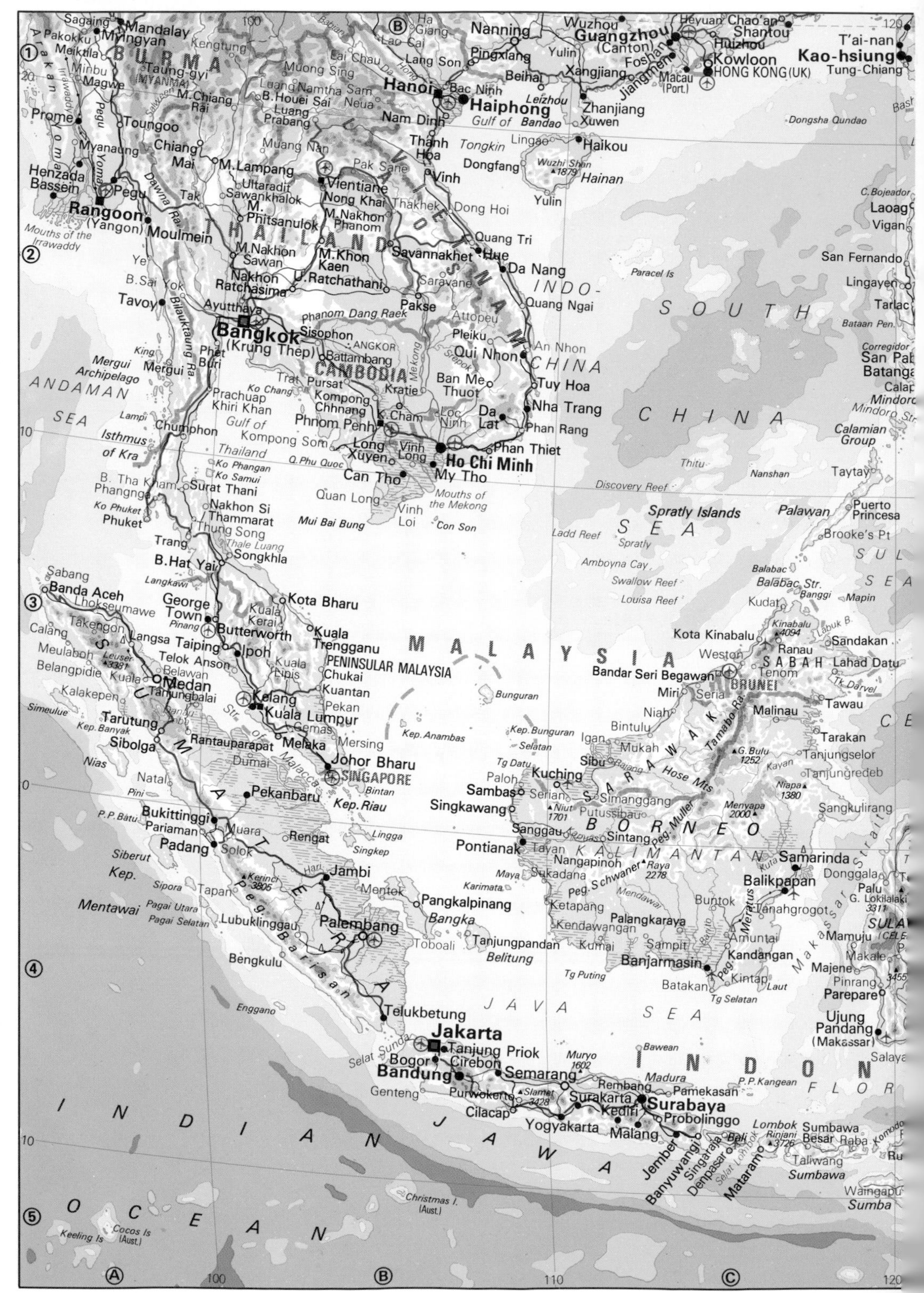
BURMA (MYANMA)
Sagaing
Mandalay
Pakokku
Myingyan
Meiktila
Minbu
Magwe
Taung-gyi
Kengtung
Arakan Yoma
Irrawaddy
Prome
Pegu Yoma
Toungoo
Myanaung
Henzada
Bassein
Pegu
Rangoon (Yangon)
Mouths of the Irrawaddy
Moulmein
Dawna Ra.
Tak
Ye
B. Sai Yok
Tavoy
Bilauktaung Ra.
King
Mergui
Mergui Archipelago
ANDAMAN SEA
Lampi
Isthmus of Kra
Chumphon
M.Chiang Rai
Chiang Mai
M.Lampang
Uttaradit
Sawankhalok
M. Phitsanulok
M.Nakhon Sawan
Nakhon Ratchasima
Ayutthaya
Bangkok (Krung Thep)
Phet Buri
Prachuap Khiri Khan
THAILAND
Gulf of Thailand
Ko Phangan
Ko Samui
B. Tha Kham
Phangnga
Ko Phuket
Phuket
Surat Thani
Nakhon Si Thammarat
Thung Song
Thale Luang
Trang
Songkhla
B.Hat Yai
Langkawi
Muong Sing
Luang Namtha
B.Houei Sai
Sam Neua
Luang Prabang
Muang Nan
Pak Sane
Vientiane
Nong Khai
Thakhek
M.Nakhon Phanom
Savannakhet
M.Khon Kaen
U.Ratchathani
Saravane
Pakse
Attopeu
Phanom Dang Raek
Sisophon
ANGKOR
Battambang
CAMBODIA
Trat
Pursat
Ko Chang
Kompong Chhnang
Kratie
Mekong
K.Cham
Phnom Penh
Kompong Som
Q.Phu Quoc
Long Xuyen
Vinh Long
Can Tho
My Tho
Quan Long
Vinh Loi
Mui Bai Bung
Mouths of the Mekong
Con Son
Ha Giang
Lao Cai
Lai Chau
Lang Son
Hanoi
Bac Ninh
Haiphong
Nam Dinh
Thanh Hoa
Vinh
Dong Hoi
Quang Tri
Hue
Da Nang
VIETNAM
Quang Ngai
Pleiku
Qui Nhon
An Nhon
Ban Me Thuot
Tuy Hoa
Nha Trang
Da Lat
Loc Ninh
Phan Rang
Phan Thiet
Ho Chi Minh
Gulf of Tongkin
Nanning
Pingxiang
Beihai
Yulin
Wuzhou
Guangzhou (Canton)
Foshan
Jiangmen
Xangjiang
Heyuan
Chao'an
Shantou
Huizhou
Kowloon
HONG KONG (UK)
Macau (Port.)
Leizhou Bandao
Zhanjiang
Xuwen
Lingao
Haikou
Dongfang
Wuzhi Shan 1879
Hainan
Yulin
T'ai-nan
Kao-hsiung
Tung-Chiang
Dongsha Qundao
C.Bojeador
Laoag
Vigan
San Fernando
Lingayen
Tarlac
Bataan Pen.
Corregidor
San Pablo
Batangas
Calapan
Mindoro
Mindoro Str.
Calamian Group
Paracel Is
INDO-CHINA
SOUTH CHINA SEA
Thitu
Nanshan
Taytay
Discovery Reef
Spratly Islands
Palawan
Puerto Princesa
Brooke's Pt
Ladd Reef
Spratly
Amboyna Cay
Swallow Reef
Louisa Reef
Balabac
Balabac Str.
Banggi
Mapin
SULU SEA
Kudat
Kinabalu 4094
Labuk B.
Kota Kinabalu
Ranau
Sandakan
Weston
SABAH
Lahad Datu
Tenom
Bandar Seri Begawan
BRUNEI
Tk.Darvel
Miri
Seria
Tawau
Niah
Malinau
Bintulu
Tarakan
Mukah
SARAWAK
Tamabo Ra.
G. Bulu 1252
Tanjungselor
Kayan
Tanjungredeb
Hose Mts
Niapa 1380
Sibu
Kuching
Serian
Simanggang
Putussibau
Menyapa 2000
Sangkulirang
Peg. Muller
BORNEO
Sintang
KALIMANTAN
Samarinda
Nangapinoh
Raya 2278
Peg. Schwaner
Balikpapan
Donggala
Palu
G. Lokilalaki 3311
Kuta
Mendawai
Buntok
Tanahgrogot
Ketapang
Palangkaraya
Meratus
Kendawangan
Sampit
Amuntai
Mamuju
Kumai
Barito
Banjarmasin
Kandangan
Majene
Makale
Peg. Meratus
Kintap
Pinrang
Batakan
Laut
Parepare
Tg Puting
Tg Selatan
Makassar Str.
Ujung Pandang (Makassar)
Salayar
Sabang
Banda Aceh
Lhokseumawe
Calang
Takengon
Meulaboh
Leuser 3381
Belangpidie
Kuala
Langsa
Medan
Belawan
Tanjungbalai
Kalakepen
Simeulue
Tarutung
Kep. Banyak
Sibolga
Nias
Natal
Pini
Rantauparapat
Dumai
Pekanbaru
P.P. Batu
Bukittinggi
Pariaman
Muara
Padang
Solok
Siberut
Kep. Mentawai
Sipora
Pagai Utara
Pagai Selatan
Tapan
Kerinci 3805
Lubuklinggau
Bengkulu
Peg. Barisan
SUMATERA
Enggano
Rengat
Jambi
Hari
Palembang
Telukbetung
George Town
Pinang
Butterworth
Kuala Kerai
Kota Bharu
Kuala Trengganu
Taiping
Ipoh
Telok Anson
Kuala Lipis
PENINSULAR MALAYSIA
Chukai
Kuantan
Kelang
Kuala Lumpur
Pekan
Gemas
Melaka
Mersing
Str. of Malacca
Johor Bharu
SINGAPORE
Bintan
Kep. Riau
Lingga
Singkep
MALAYSIA
Kep. Anambas
Bunguran
Kep. Bunguran Selatan
Tg Datu
Paloh
Sambas
Singkawang
Niut 1701
Sanggau
Pontianak
Tayan
Maya
Sukadana
Karimata
Mentok
Pangkalpinang
Bangka
Toboali
Tanjungpandan
Belitung
JAVA SEA
Selat Sunda
Jakarta
Tanjung Priok
Bogor
Cirebon
Bandung
Muryo 1602
Semarang
Bawean
Madura
Rembang
Pamekasan
P.P. Kangean
Genteng
Purwokerto
Slamet 3428
Surakarta
Surabaya
Cilacap
Kediri
Yogyakarta
Probolinggo
Malang
JAWA
Jember
Banyuwangi
Singaraja
Denpasar
Bali
Selat Lombok
Lombok
Mataram
Rinjani 3726
Sumbawa Besar
Raba
Komodo
Taliwang
Sumbawa
Waingapu
Sumba
INDONESIA
FLORES
INDIAN OCEAN
Christmas I. (Aust.)
Cocos Is (Aust.)
Keeling Is
SULAWESI (CELEBES)
A
B
C
1
2
3
4
5
10
0
100
110
120

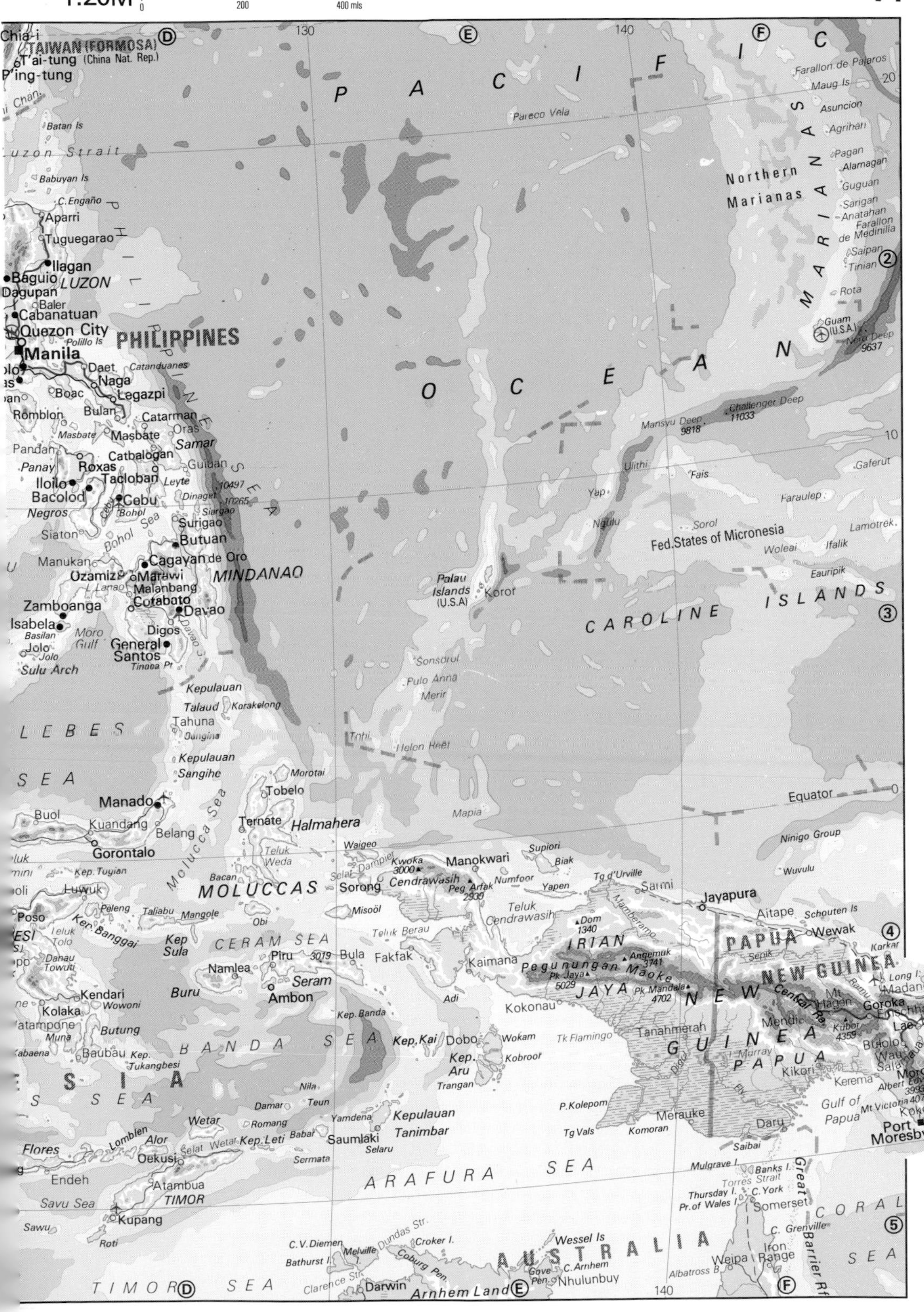

1:20M

200   400   600   800 km

200   400 mls

Chia-i
TAIWAN (FORMOSA)
T'ai-tung (China Nat. Rep.)
P'ing-tung

P A C I F I C

Pareco Vela

Farallon de Pajaros
Maug Is

Asuncion

Agrihan

Pagan
Alamagan
Guguan
Sarigan
Anatahan
Farallon
de Medinilla
Saipan
Tinian

Rota

Guam
(U.S.A)   Nero Deep
9637

N
o
r
t
h
e
r
n

M
a
r
i
a
n
a
s

O C E A N

M
A
R
I
A
N
A

Luzon Strait
Batan Is
Babuyan Is
C. Engaño
Aparri
Tuguegarao
Ilagan
Baguio   LUZON
Dagupan
Baler
Cabanatuan
Quezon City
Manila   PHILIPPINES
Polillo Is
Boac
Bulan   Legazpi
Romblon
Pandan
Panay   Roxas
Iloilo   Tacloban
Bacolod
Negros
Siaton
Manukan
Ozamiz
Zamboanga
Isabela
Jolo
Jolo   General
Sulu Arch   Santos
Cebu
Bohol
Surigao
Butuan
Cagayan de Oro
Marawi
Cotabato
Digos
Davao
MINDANAO
Daet   Catanduanes
Naga
Catarman
Oras
Masbate   Masbate
Catbalogan
Samar
Guiuan
Leyte
10497
Dinagat   11055
Siargao
Bohol Sea
Lanao
Malanbang
Moro
Gulf
Basilan
Moro Gulf

Ulithi
Yap
Ngulu
Palau
Islands
(U.S.A)   Koror
Sonsorol
Pulo Anna
Merir
Tobi
Helen Reef
Waigeo

Fais
Faraulep
Sorol
Woleai   Ifalik
Eauripik
Mapia

Gaferut

Fed.States of Micronesia

Lamotrek

C A R O L I N E   I S L A N D S

Challenger Deep
11033

Mansyu Deep
9818

Kuandang
Manado
Belang
Gorontalo
Buol

LEBES
SEA

Kepulauan
Talaud   Karakelong
Tahuna
Sangihe
Morotai
Tobelo
Ternate   Halmahera

Teluk
Weda

Waigeo
Kwoka
3000   Manokwari
Selat Dampier   Peg.Arfak
2930
Cendrawasih
Teluk
Cendrawasih

Supiori
Biak
Numfoor
Yapen   Sarmi
Mamberamo

Ninigo Group

Wuvulu

Equator

Jayapura

Aitape   Schouten Is

Wewak

MOLUCCAS   Sorong
Bacan   Misool
Obi
Paleng
Taliabu
Mangole

Sula   Piru
Namlea   Bula   Fakfak
Seram
Ambon   Adi
Kep.Banda
Buru
Butung
Kep.Kai
Dobo
Kep.
Aru
Wokam
Kobroor
Trangan

Kep.
Tukangbesi

Nila

Teun

Wetar
Lomblen   Romang
Alor   Selat Wetar
Kep.Leti   Babar
Sermata   Selaru

Kendari
Kolaka
Muna
Baubau

Damar

BANDA   SEA

CERAM SEA
5019
Teluk Berau
Kaimana
Dom
1340   Angemuk
3741
Pegunungan Maoke
Pk.Jaya   Pk.Mandala
5029   4702
Kokonau
Tanahmerah

Tk Flamingo

Yamdena
Kepulauan
Saumlaki   Tanimbar

P.Kolepom

Merauke
Komoran

P.Vals
Tg Vals

IRIAN

JAYA

N E W

G U I N E A

PAPUA

Karkar
Madang
Long I.
Kubor
4359
Central
Mt
Hagen
Goroka

Bolobo

Mendi

P A P U A

Gulf of
Papua

Kikori

Kerema

Mt Victoria
4073
Daru
Saibai

Kokoda

Port
Moresby

Morobe
Wau
Salar

Lae

4073

A R A F U R A   S E A

C O R A L

Mulgrave I.
Banks I.
Torres Strait
Thursday I.   C.York
Pr.of Wales I.   Somerset

S E A

Flores
Endeh
Atambua   TIMOR
Sawu   Oekusi
Kupang
Roti
Sawu Sea

C.V.Diemen   Croker I.
Melville I.   Dundas Str.
Bathurst I.   Coburg Pen.
Clarence Str.
Darwin

Wessel Is

Gove
C.Arnhem   Nhulunbuy
Arnhem Land

A U S T R A L I A

Weipa

Iron
Range
Albatross B.

C. Grenville

Great Barrier Rf.

TIMOR   SEA

130   140   140

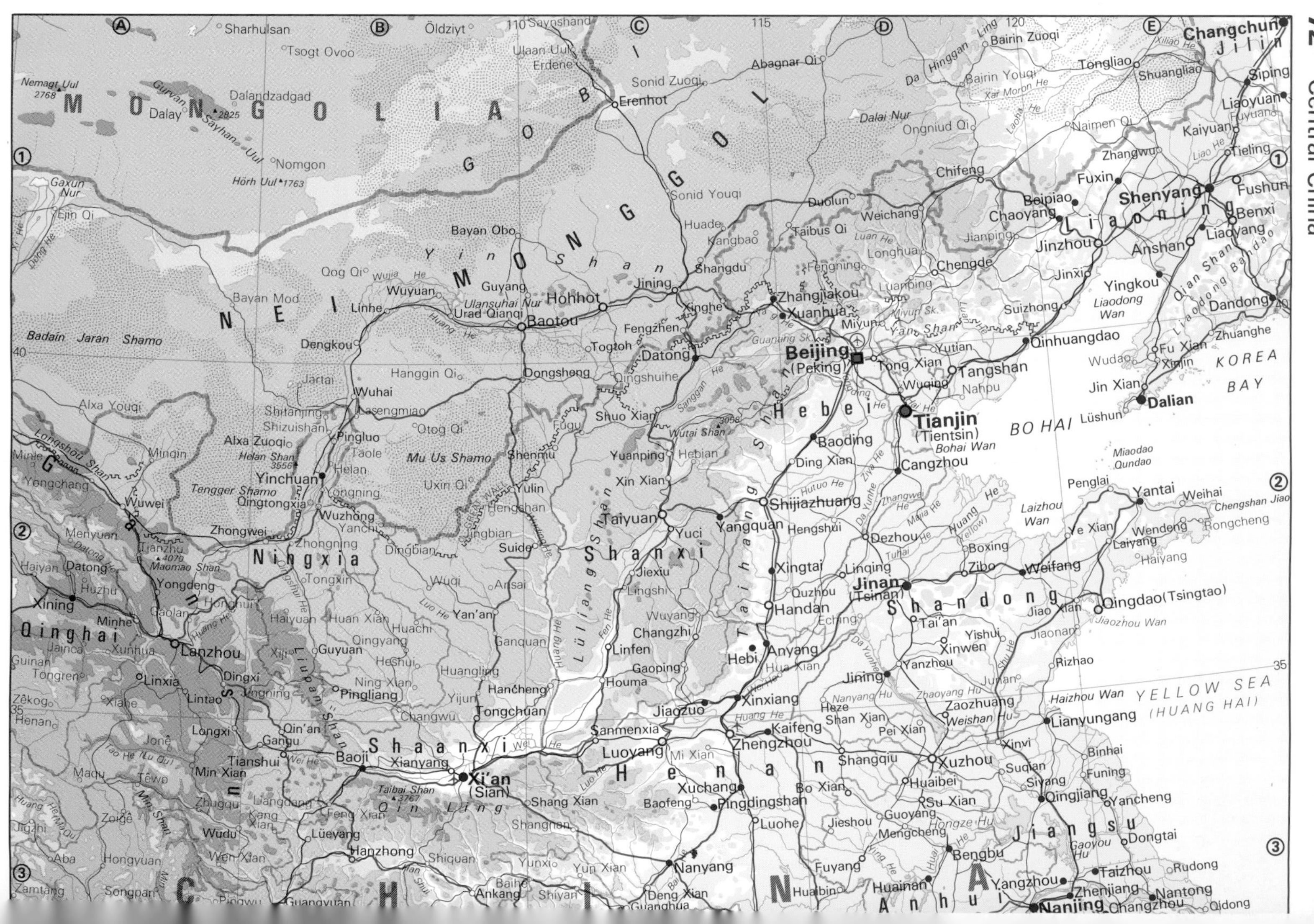

MONGOLIA
GOBI
NEI MONGGOL
Yin Shan
Ningxia
Qinghai
Shaanxi
Shanxi
Hebei
Henan
Shandong
Jiangsu
Anhui
Liaoning
Jilin
CHINA
Taihang Shan
Lüliang Shan
Qin Ling
Liupan Shan
Da Hinggan Ling
Yan Shan
Qian Shan
Liaodong Bandao
BO HAI
Bohai Wan
Liaodong Wan
Laizhou Wan
KOREA BAY
YELLOW SEA (HUANG HAI)
Haizhou Wan
Badain Jaran Shamo
Tengger Shamo
Mu Us Shamo
Changchun
Shenyang
Dalian
Beijing (Peking)
Tianjin (Tientsin)
Jinan (Tsinan)
Qingdao (Tsingtao)
Taiyuan
Shijiazhuang
Zhengzhou
Luoyang
Xi'an (Sian)
Lanzhou
Yinchuan
Xining
Hohhot
Baotou
Datong
Zhangjiakou
Tangshan
Qinhuangdao
Nanjing
Xuzhou
Kaifeng
Anshan
Fushun
Benxi
Dandong
Yantai
Weifang
Zibo
Lianyungang
Handan
Anyang
Baoding
Xinxiang
Baoji
Tianshui
Yan'an
Yulin
Wuhai
Erenhot
Jining
Chifeng
Jinzhou
Huang He
Wei He
Fen He
Luan He
Hutuo He
Da Yunhe

1:10M

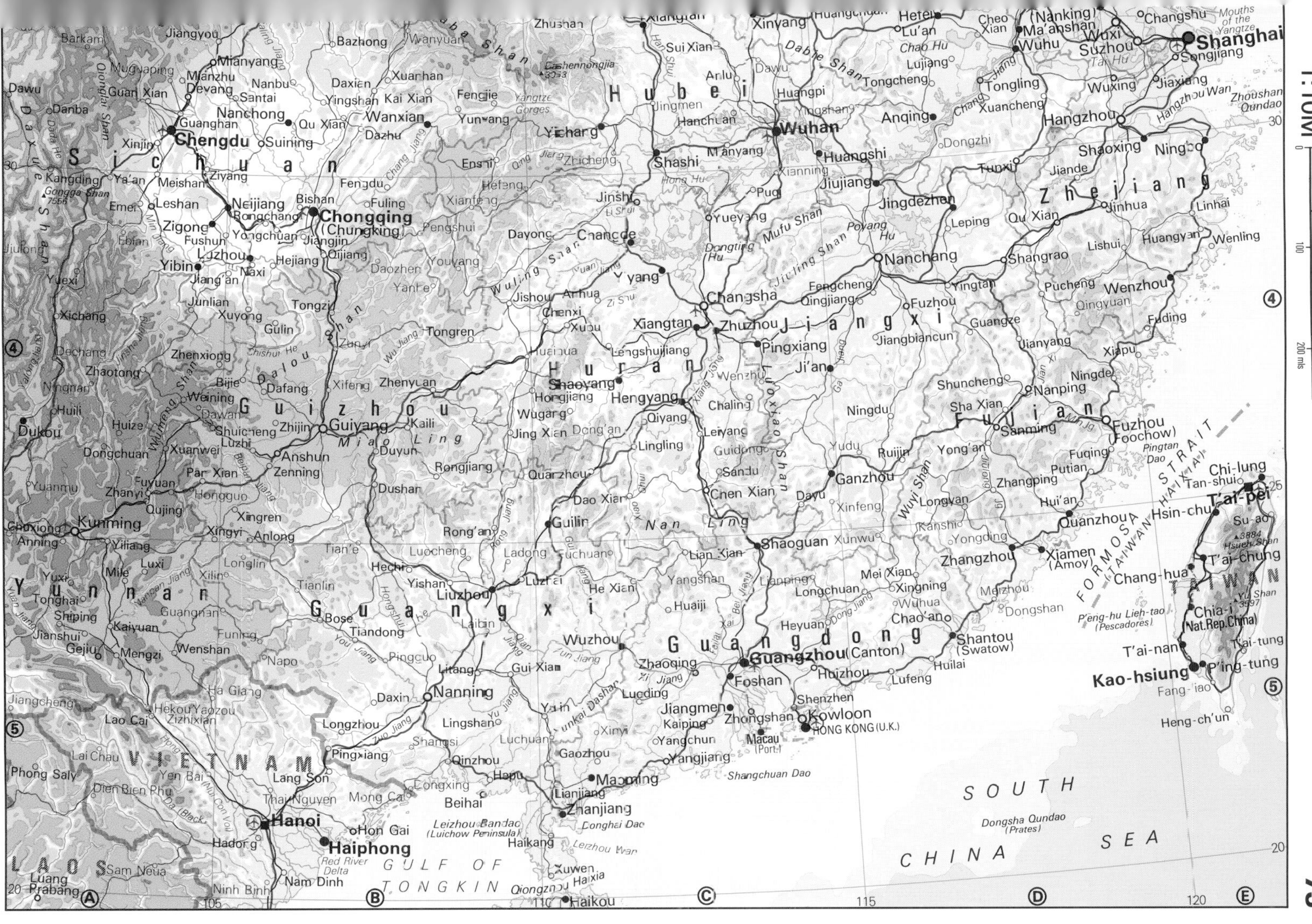

100   200   300   400 km
100   200 mls

SOUTH CHINA SEA

GULF OF TONGKING

FORMOSA (TAIWAN)

HAI-NAN STRAIT

Shanghai
Chongqing
Chengdu
Wuhan
Guangzhou (Canton)
Kowloon
HONG KONG (U.K.)
Kao-hsiung
T'ai-pei
Hanoi
Haiphong
Nanning
Kunming
Guiyang
Changsha
Nanchang
Fuzhou (Foochow)
Xiamen (Amoy)
Shantou (Swatow)

Sichuan
Yunnan
Guizhou
Guangxi
Guangdong
Hunan
Hubei
Jiangxi
Fujian
Zhejiang
Henan

VIETNAM
LAOS

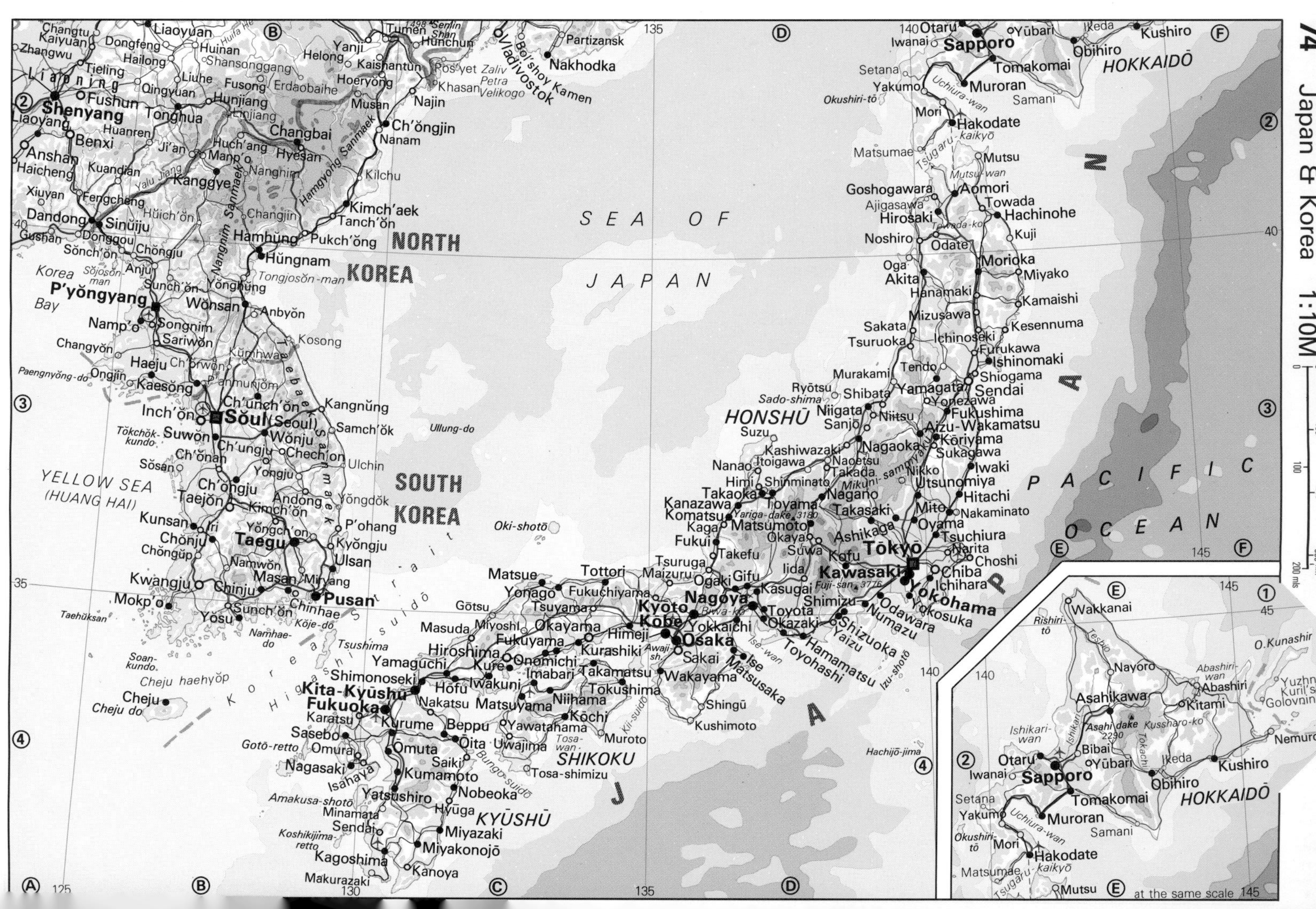
0 100 200 300 km
0 100 200 mls
SEA OF JAPAN
PACIFIC OCEAN
NORTH KOREA
SOUTH KOREA
YELLOW SEA (HUANG HAI)
Korea Bay
Korea Strait
HONSHŪ
SHIKOKU
KYŪSHŪ
HOKKAIDŌ
Tōkyō
Yokohama
Kawasaki
Nagoya
Kyōto
Kōbe
Ōsaka
Sapporo
Kita-Kyūshū
Fukuoka
Hiroshima
Sendai
Sŏul (Seoul)
P'yŏngyang
Pusan
Taegu
Inch'ŏn
Vladivostok
Nakhodka
Shenyang
Fushun
Liaoning
Oki-shotō
Ullung-do
Cheju do
Tsushima
Sado-shima
Amakusa-shotō
Gotō-retto
Koshikijima-retto
Hachijō-jima
Izu-shotō
Fuji-san 3776
Yariga-dake 3180
Asahi dake 2290
at the same scale

1:5M

0 50 100 150 200 km
0 50 100 mls

SEA OF JAPAN

PACIFIC OCEAN

Sendai, Yamagata, Fukushima, Niigata, Tokyo, Yokohama, Kawasaki, Chiba, Nagoya, Kyoto, Osaka, Kobe, Sakai, Okayama, Hiroshima, Fukuoka, Kita-Kyūshū

HONSHŪ
SHIKOKU
KYŪSHŪ

Sado-shima, Oki-shotō, Awa-shima, Noto-hantō, Izu-shotō, Bōsō-hantō, Hachijō-jima

Iwaki, Hitachi, Mito, Utsunomiya, Takasaki, Maebashi, Nagano, Matsumoto, Kōfu, Shizuoka, Hamamatsu, Toyohashi, Toyota, Gifu, Kanazawa, Toyama, Fukui, Tsuruga, Tottori, Matsue, Kurashiki, Kōchi, Matsuyama, Tokushima, Ōita, Kumamoto, Kagoshima, Nagasaki, Saga, Kurume

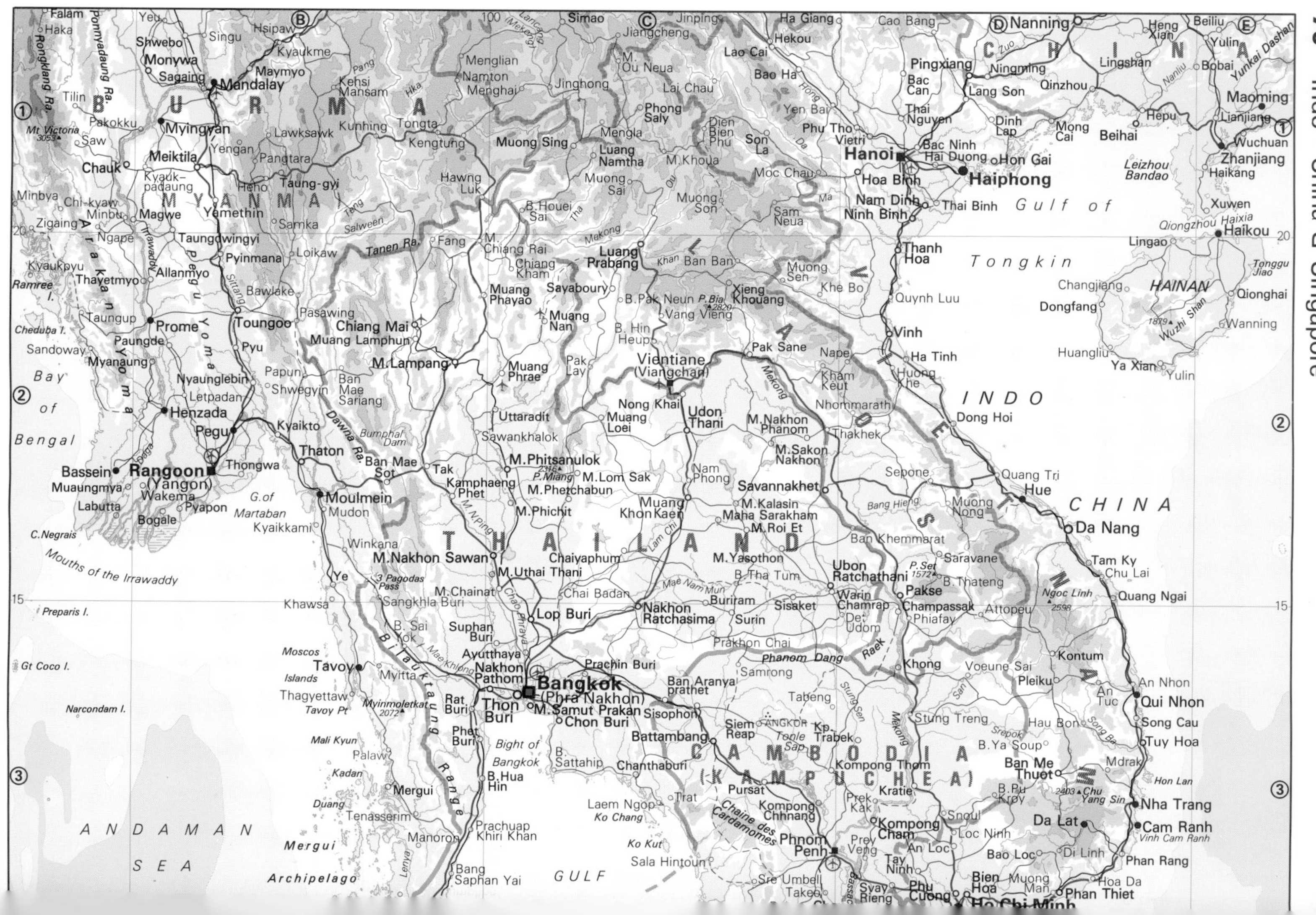

BURMA
MYANMAR
THAILAND
LAOS
VIETNAM
CAMBODIA (KAMPUCHEA)
CHINA
INDO CHINA
HAINAN
Gulf of Tongkin
Bay of Bengal
ANDAMAN SEA
GULF
Bight of Bangkok
G. of Martaban
Mergui Archipelago
Mouths of the Irrawaddy
Arakan Yoma
Pegu Yoma
Bilauktaung Range
Dawna Ra.
Tanen Ra.
Phanom Dang
Chaine des Cardamomes
Ponnyadaung Ra.
Rongklang Ra.
Mekong
Irrawaddy
Sittang
Salween
Chao Phraya
Rangoon (Yangon)
Mandalay
Bangkok (Phra Nakhon)
Thon Buri
Hanoi
Haiphong
Vientiane (Viangchan)
Phnom Penh
Da Nang
Hue
Qui Nhon
Nha Trang
Cam Ranh
Da Lat
Phan Thiet
Nanning
Haikou
Zhanjiang
Maoming
Moulmein
Bassein
Henzada
Prome
Toungoo
Pegu
Tavoy
Mergui
Chiang Mai
Luang Prabang
Savannakhet
Pakse
Ubon Ratchathani
Nakhon Ratchasima
Udon Thani
Battambang
Kompong Thom
Siem Reap
Kontum
Pleiku
Ban Me Thuot
Vinh
Thanh Hoa
Dong Hoi
Nam Dinh
Lang Son
Lao Cai
Monywa
Meiktila
Myingyan
Magwe
Taung-gyi
Sagaing
Chauk
Hsipaw
Maymyo
Yamethin
Pyinmana
Thaton
Kyaikto
Gt Coco I.
Preparis I.
Narcondam I.
Cheduba I.
Ramree I.
C.Negrais
Moscos Islands
Ko Chang
Ko Kut
Mt Victoria 3053

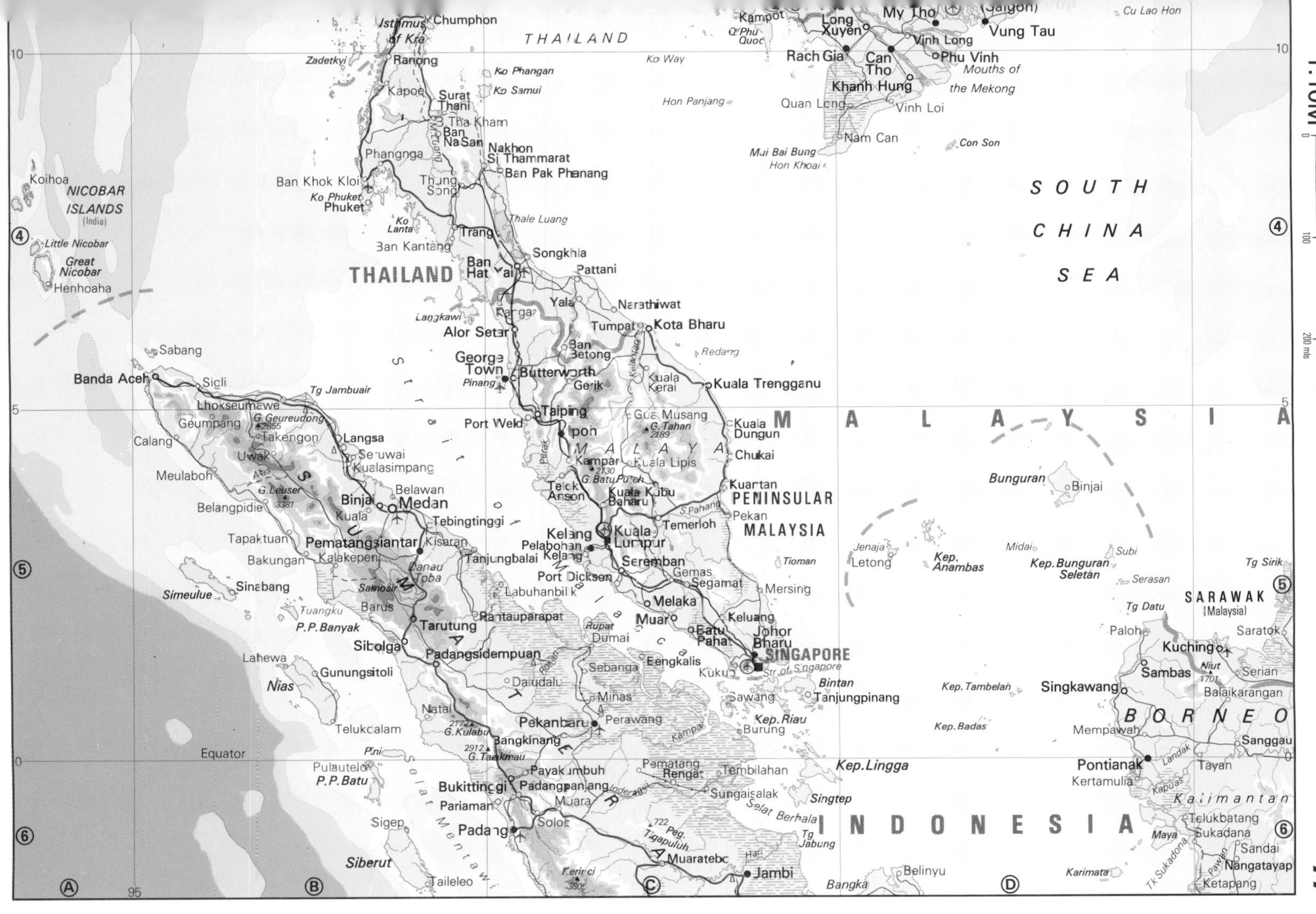

0   100   200   300   400 km
0   100   200 mls

④

S A L A Y S I A

SARAWAK
(Malaysia)

B O R N E O

Kuching
Serian
Tg Sirik
Saratok
Balaikarangan
Tayan
Sanggau
Sandai
Nangatayap
Ketapang

Kalimantan

Niut
Sambas
Singkawang
Pontianak
Kertamulia
Mempawah
Paloh
Tg Datu

S O U T H

Cu Lao Hon
Vung Tau
Phu Vinh
Mouths of
the Mekong
Vinh Long
My Tho
(Saigon)
Long
Kuyen
Rach Gia
Can
Tho
Kampot
Phu Quoc
Khanh Hung
Quan Long
Nam Can
Vinh Loi
Con Son
Hon Khoai

C H I N A

Binjai
Subi
Midai
Kep. Bunguran
Selatan

Bunguran

Kep.
Anambas

Serasan

Kep. Tambelan

Kep. Badas

S E A

Jenaja
Letong

I N D O N E S I A

Belinyu
Bangka

Singkep
Tg
Jabung
Kep. Lingga
Kep. Riau
Tanjungpinang
Bintan
Tembilahan
Sungaisalak
Rengat
Tg Berhala
Jambi
Muaratebo

THAILAND

Isthmus
of Kra
Chumphon
Ranong
Kapoe
Surat
Thani
Ko Phangan
Ko Samui
Nakhon
Si Thammarat
Ban
Na San
Ban
Tha Kham
Thung
Song
Ban Kantang
Trang
Phatthalung
Songkhla
Hat Yai
Yala
Betong
Pattani
Narathiwat
Tumpat
Kota Bharu
Kuala Trengganu
Redang
Kuala
Dungun
Chukai
Kuartan
Pekan
Tioman
Mersing
Kuala Lipis
Temenioh
Kelang
Kuala
Lumpur
Seremban
Melaka
Muar
Segamat
Gemas
Keluang
Kota Tinggi
Johor
Bahru
SINGAPORE
Str. of Singapore

Banda Aceh
Sabang
Sigli
Lhokseumawe
Meulaboh
Calang
Langsa
Medan
Binjai
Belawan
Tebingtinggi
Pematangsiantar
Kisaran
Tanjungbalai
Rantauparapat
Sibolga
Padangsidempuan
Bukittinggi
Padang
Pariaman
Pekanbaru
Bangkinang
Payakumbuh

NICOBAR
ISLANDS
(India)
Little Nicobar
Great
Nicobar

Equator

Simeulue
Nias
Siberut
Selat Mentaw

100 200 300 400 km
100 200 mils

Celebes Sea

Tarakan
Maratua
G. Bulu
Tanjungselor
Kayan
Kengkemu
G. Niapa
Tanjungredeb
Seguntur
Sangkulirang
Mangkalihat
Tg

Equator

SULAWESI (CELEBES)
Karossa
Pasangkayu
Mamuju
Bk Gandangdewata
Pewali
Onang
Majene
Polewali

Ujung Pandang
(Makassar)
Pattallassang

Flores Sea

P.P. Postiljon
Kep. Sabalana
Sabalana

Samboja
Samarinda
Balikpapan

Tanahgrogot

Sumenep
Pamekasan
Madura
Sampang
Gresik
Surabaya
Pasuruan
Probolinggo
Situbondo
Banyuwangi
Malang
Jember
Bali
Singaraja
Denpasar
Mataram
Praya
Lombok

Makassar Str.

Muaratewah
Tintu
Merah
Barabbi
Tanjung
Amuntai
Kandangan
Banjarmasin
Martapura
Batakan
Jorong
Kintap
Kalembau
Kadapongan
Matasiri

Laut Sea

BORNEO
KALIMANTAN

Semitau
Sintang
Putussibau
Bt Batubrok
Longnawan
Batukelau
Tewah
Buntok
Palangkaraya
Mendawai
Sampit
Seruyan
Kumai
Pangkalanbuun

Java Sea

Bawean
Salembu Besar
Rembang
Blora
Cepu
Madiun
Kediri
Blitar
Tuiungagung
Pacitan

Mojokerto
Semarang
Surakarta
Yogyakarta
Magelang
Purworejo
Cilacap

JAWA (JAVA)

Kuching
Sibu
Sarikei
Simanggang
Balaikarangan
Sanggau
Tayan
Nangapinoh
Sandai
Nangatayap
Ketapang
Kendawangan
Sukaraya
Sukadana

Pontianak
Singkawang
Sambas
Kertamulia
Mempawah
Paloh

Indramayu
Cirebon
Tegal
Pekalongan
Brebes
Tasikmalaya
Bandung
Garut
Ciamis
Sukabumi
Bogor
Jakarta
Tanjung Priok
Serang
Labuhan
Telukbetung
Kalianda
Pameungpeuk

MALAYSIA
Kuala Lumpur
Kelang
Seremban
Melaka
Port Dickson
Batu Pahat
Johor Bahru
SINGAPORE
Tanjungpinang
Bintan
Kep. Riau

Kep. Anambas
Kep. Tambelan
Kep. Badas
Kep. Lingga
Singtep

Pangkalpinang
Bangka
Belinyu
Mentok
Koba
Toboali
Manggar
Tanjungpandan
Belitung

Palembang
Jambi
Talangbetutu
Prabumulih
Muaraenim
Lahat
Lubuklinggau
Bangko
Sarolangun
Bengkulu
Manna
Tais
Krui
Kotaagung
Teginengeng

SUMATERA
Pegunungan Barisan

Pekanbaru
Rengat
Tembilahan
Bengkalis
Dumai

Enggano

INDONESIA

BRUNEI
Bandar Seri Begawan
SABAH
Kota Kinabalu
Victoria
Labuan
Westori
Tenom
Bingkor
Pensiangan
Keningau
Llawas
Tawau

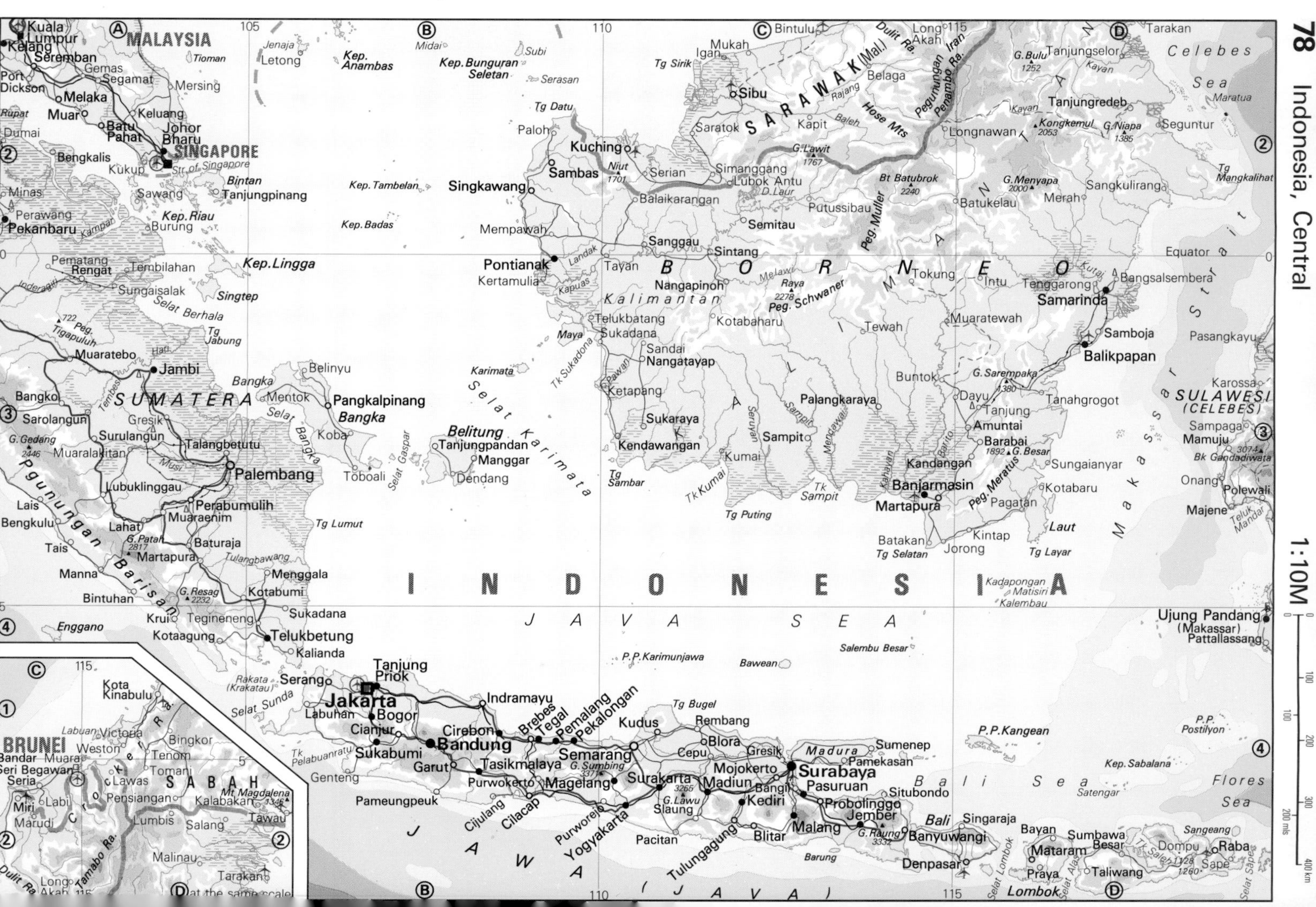

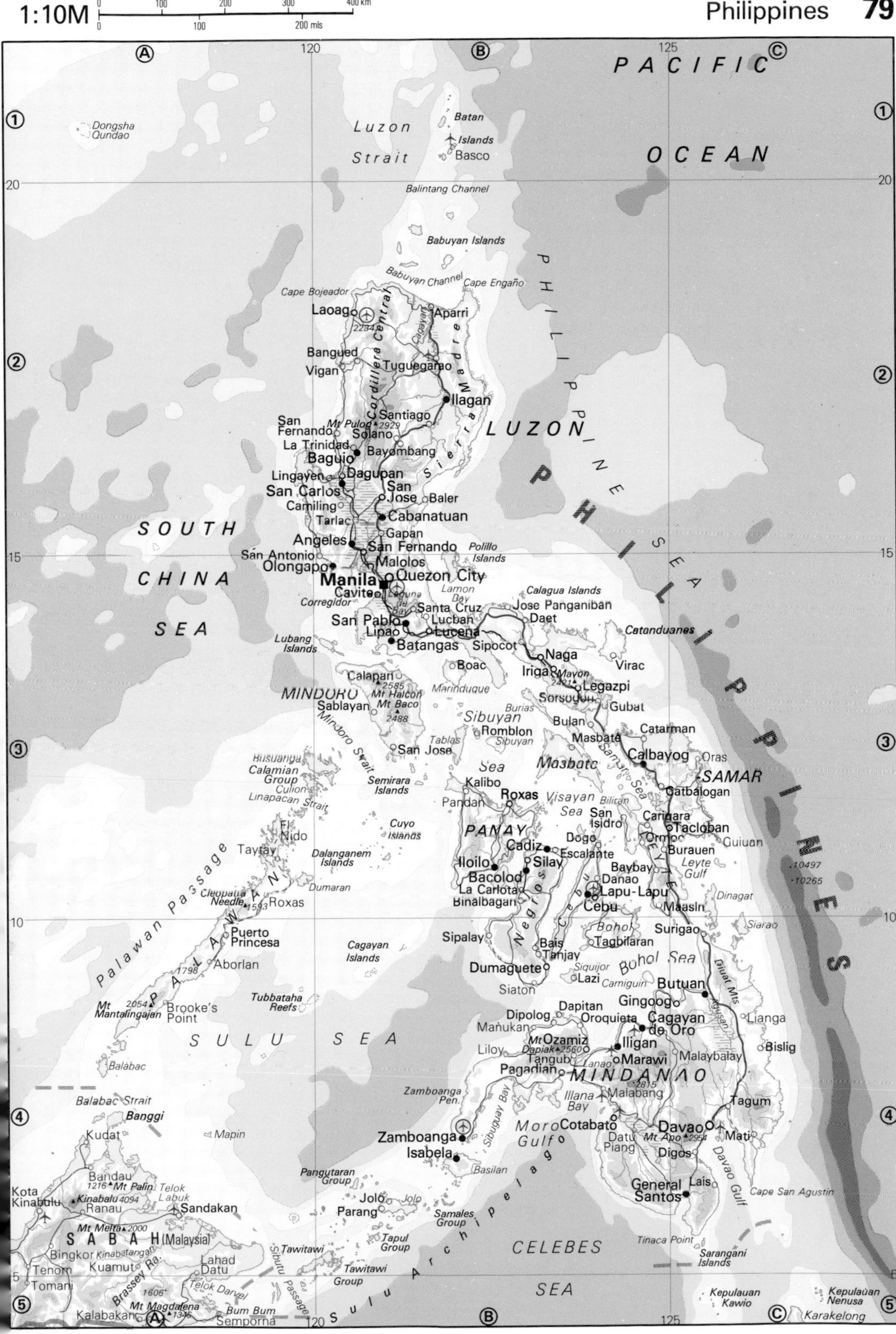

0   100   200   300   400 km
0   100   200 mls

P A C I F I C

O C E A N

Luzon Strait

Batan Islands
Basco

Dongsha Qundao

Balintang Channel

Babuyan Islands

Babuyan Channel
Cape Bojeador
Cape Engaño

Laoag
Aparri
2234

Bangued
Tuguegarao
Vigan
Ilagan

Cordillera Central
Santiago
Solano

L U Z O N

San Fernando
Mt Pulog 2929
La Trinidad
Baguio
Bayombang
Lingayen
Dagupan
San Carlos
San Jose
Baler
Camiling
Tarlac
Cabanatuan
Angeles
Gapan
San Antonio
San Fernando
Malolos
Olongapo
Quezon City
Corregidor
Manila
Cavite
Laguna Bay
Polillo Islands

Calagua Islands

S O U T H

C H I N A

S E A

Santa Cruz
San Pablo
Lucban
Jose Panganiban
Daet
Lipa
Lucena
Batangas
Sipocot
Naga
Lubang Islands
Boac
Iriga
Mayon 2421
Virac
Catanduanes
Legazpi
Calapan
Marinduque
Sorsogon
Gubat
Mindoro
2585
Mt Halcon
Sablayan
Mt Baco
2488
Sibuyan
Burias
Bulan
San Jose
Tablas
Romblon
Sibuyan
Masbate
Catarman
Calbayog
Oras
SAMAR

Busuanga
Calamian Group
Culion
Linapacan Strait
Semirara Islands
Kalibo
Masbate
Catbalogan
Pandan
Roxas
Visayan Sea
Biliran
Carigara
Tacloban
Taytay
Cuyo Islands
PANAY
San Isidro
Ormoc
Guiuan
Nido
Dalanganem Islands
Cadiz
Dogo
Burauen
Cleopatra Needle 1593
Roxas
Dumaran
Iloilo
Silay
Escalante
Baybay
Leyte Gulf
Bacolod
La Carlota
Danao
Lapu-Lapu
Maasin
Binalbagan
Cebu
Dinagat
10497
Puerto Princesa
Cagayan Islands
Sipalay
Bais
Tagbilaran
Surigao
Siarao
10265
Aborlan
Bohol
Tanjay
Bohol Sea
Butuan
Palawan Passage
Tubbataha Reefs
Dumaguete
Siaton
Lazi
Camiguin
Gingoog
Lianga
Mt Mantalingajan 2054
Brooke's Point
1798
Siquijor
Dapitan
Cagayan de Oro
Dipolog
Oroquieta
Malaybalay
Bislig
Balabac
Mt Ozamiz
Iligan
Liloy
Dapiak 2600
Mañukan
Tangub
Marawi
Malabang
Tagum
Balabac Strait
Pagadian
MINDANAO
Banggi
Kudat
Mapin
Zamboanga Pen.
Illana Bay
Cotabato
Davao
Mati
Pangutaran Group
Zamboanga
Moro Gulf
Datu Piang
Mt Apo 2954
Bandau
Isabela
Basilan
Digos
Davao Gulf
Cape San Agustin
Kota Kinabalu
Mt Palin 1216
Kinabalu 4094
Ranau
Sandakan
Jolo
Jolo
Samales Group
General Santos
Lais
S A B A H (Malaysia)
Mt Melita 2000
Lahad Datu
Tapul Group
Tinaca Point
Sarangani Islands
Bingkor
Kinabatangan
Tawitawi Group
C E L E B E S
Tenom
Kuamut
Telok Darvel
Kepulauan Kawio
Kepulauan Nenusa
Tomani
Brassey Ra.
Mt Magdalena 1606
Bum Bum
Semporna
S E A
Karakelong
Kalabakan

S U L U   S E A

Sulu Archipelago

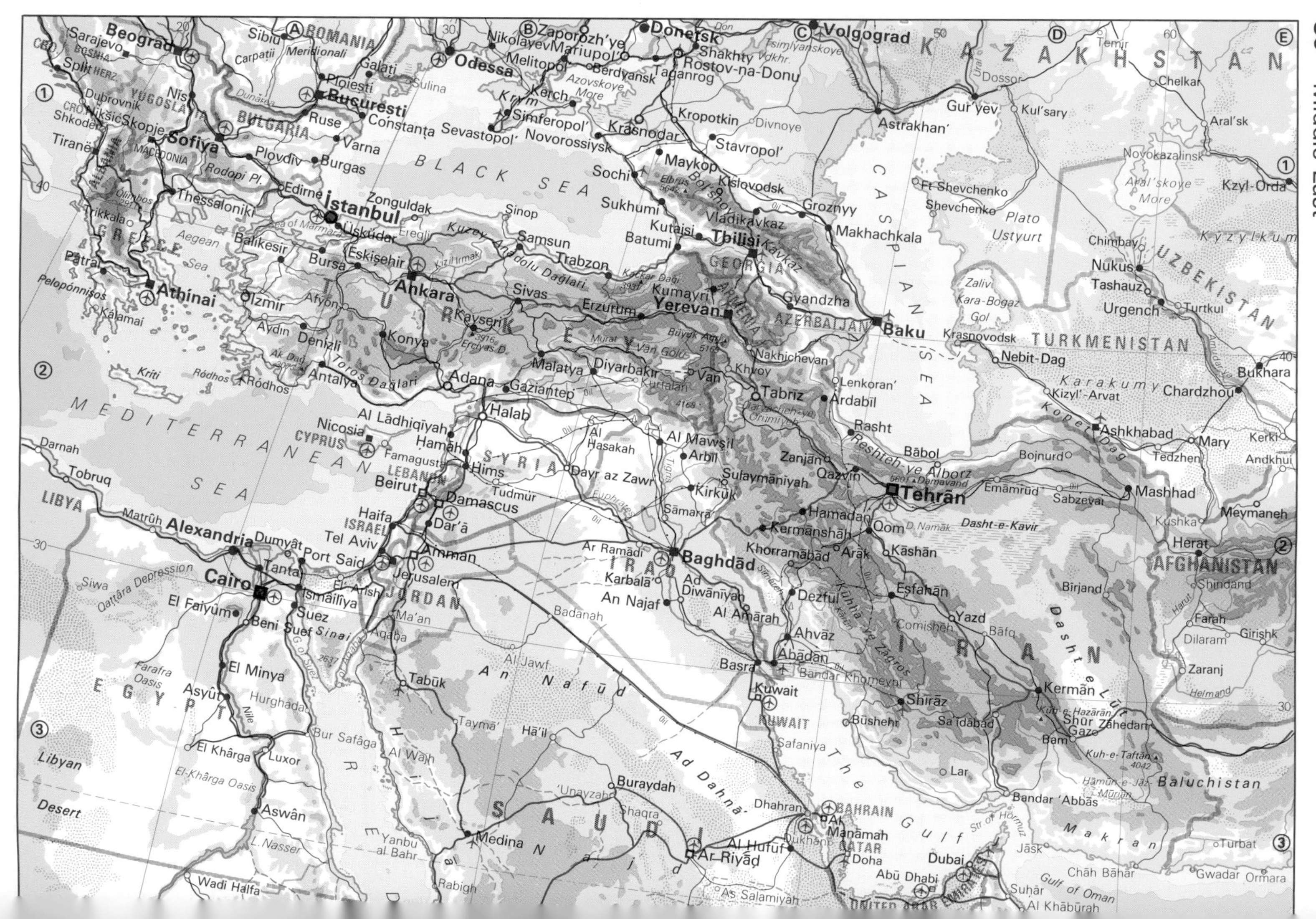
BLACK SEA
CASPIAN SEA
MEDITERRANEAN SEA
The Gulf
Gulf of Oman
Aegean Sea
KAZAKHSTAN
TURKMENISTAN
UZBEKISTAN
AFGHANISTAN
GEORGIA
ARMENIA
AZERBAIJAN
TURKEY
SYRIA
IRAQ
IRAN
LEBANON
ISRAEL
JORDAN
KUWAIT
BAHRAIN
QATAR
CYPRUS
SAUDI
EGYPT
LIBYA
ROMANIA
BULGARIA
GREECE
Beograd
Sofiya
Bucureşti
Odessa
Donetsk
Volgograd
Istanbul
Ankara
Athínai
Tbilisi
Yerevan
Baku
Tehrān
Baghdād
Damascus
Beirut
Amman
Jerusalem
Nicosia
Cairo
Alexandria
Kuwait
Ar Riyād
Medina
Dubai
Abū Dhabi
Doha
Manāmah
Dasht-e-Kavir
Dasht-e Lūt
Baluchistan
Makran
An Nafūd
Ad Dahnā'
Libyan Desert
Plato Ustyurt
Karakumy
Kopet Dag
Kūhha-ye Zagros
Reshteh-ye Alborz
Toros Dağları
Anadolu Dağları
Aral'skoye More
Zaliv Kara-Bogaz Gol
Azovskoye More
Kriti
Ródhos

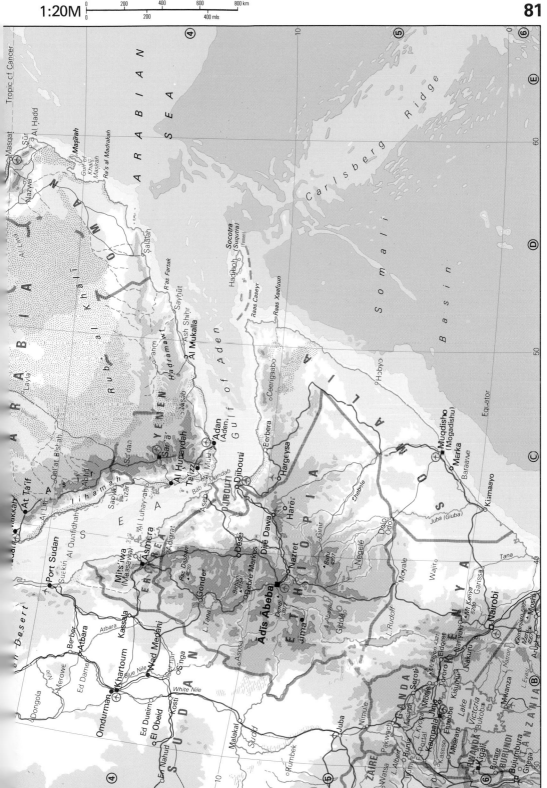

1:20M

200   400   600   800 km
200   400 mls

Tropic of Cancer

Masqat
Sūr
Ra's al Hadd

A R A B I A N   S E A

Masīrah
Gulf of Khalīj Masīrah
Ra's al Madrakah

Nazwā

Y E M E N

Al Luwā'

Ṣalālah

Ras Fartak
Sayḥūt
Ash Shiḥr

R u b '   a l   K h ā l ī

Laylā

H a d r a m a w t

Al Mukalla

Socotra
(Suquṭrā)

Haḍboh
Raas Caseyr
Raas Xaafuun

C a r l s b e r g   R i d g e

S o m a l i   B a s i n

Qal'at Bīshah

Gulf of Aden

Najrān

Sa'dah

Ṣan'ā'

Al Ḥudaydah

Ta'izz

Al Mukhā

Ceerigaabo

Berbera

Bab al Mandab

Hobyo

50

Jīzān

'Adan
(Aden)

Djibouti

Hargeysa

Muqdisho
(Mogadishu)

Marka

At Ṭā'if

Al Liṭḥ

Saḥwah

'Al Luḥayyah

I H ā m a h

ERITREA

Aseb

Dese

Dirē Dawa

Harē

SOMALIA

Baraawe

Kiamaayo

Makkah

Port Sudan

Sūakin

Al Qunfidhah

Mitsiwa
(Massawa)

Adīgrat

Asmera

Ras Dashan

Djibouti

Hārer

Chebele

Ginir

Dolo

Juba (Giuba)

Baardheere

Tana

Equator

40

S U D A N

Ber Ber

Atbara

Kassala

Wad Medani

Gonder

L. Tana

Birhan

Gebre Markos

Ādīs Ābeba

Nazret

E T H I O P I A

Jīma

Banu

Negēlē

Moyale

Wajir

K E N Y A

Mt Kenya

Nairobi

Aden Desert

Dongola

Merowe

Ed Damer

Atbara

Khartoum

Omdurman

Blue Nile

White Nile

Kosti

Ed Dueim

El Obeid

Er Nahud

Nile

Dema

Os'nga

Asosa

Malakal

Sudd

Juba

Nimule

Rumbek

Pakwach

L. Albert

ZAIRE

UGANDA

Kampala

Jinja

Lake Victoria

Bukoba

Kisumu

Eldoret

Nakuru

Naivasha

Kampala

RWANDA

Kigali

BURUNDI

Bujumbura

Gitega

T A N Z A N I A

Mwanza

Mosi

Nairobi

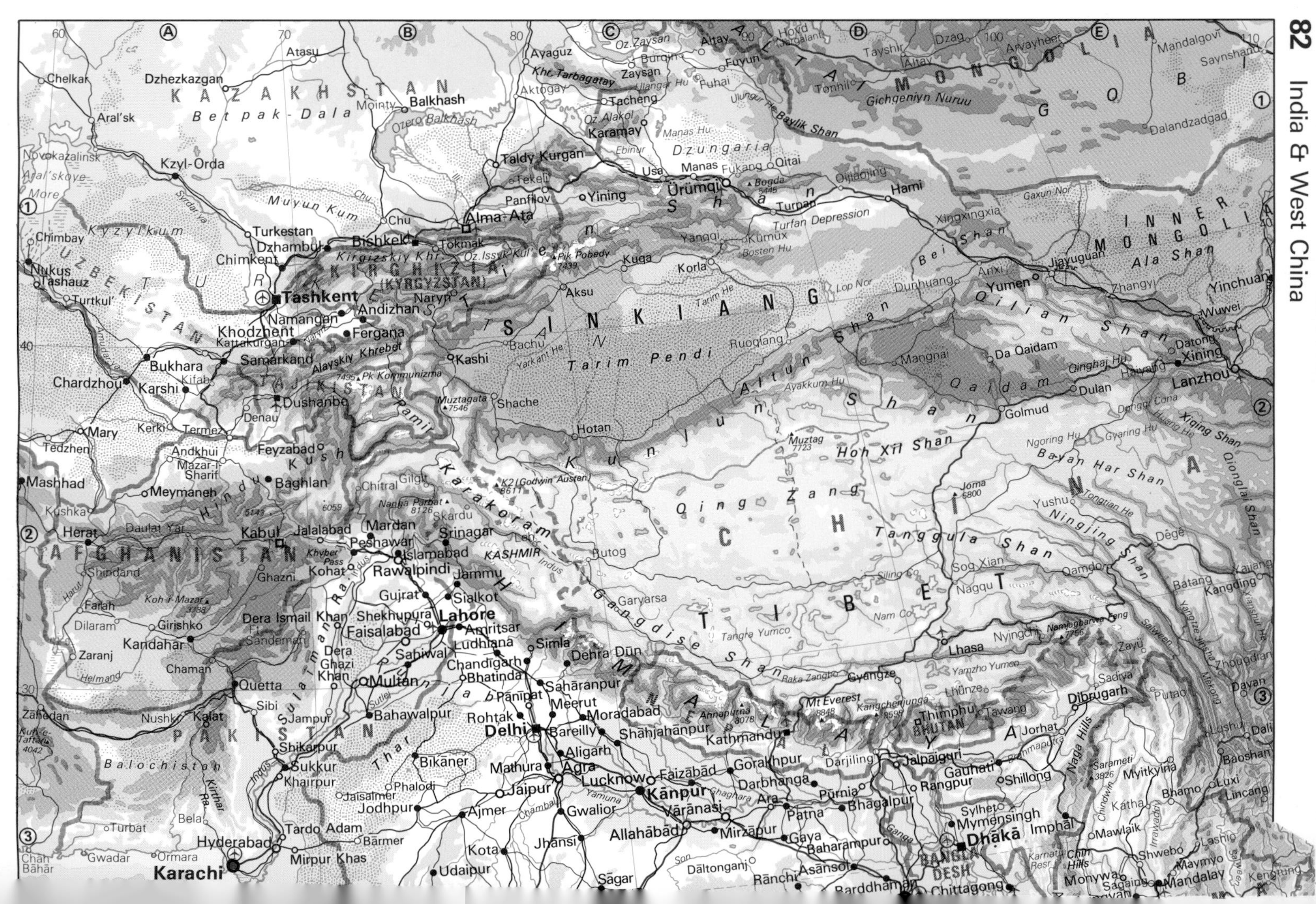
KAZAKHSTAN
MONGOLIA
INNER MONGOLIA
SINKIANG
CHINA
TIBET
UZBEKISTAN
KIRGHIZIA (KYRGYZSTAN)
TAJIKISTAN
AFGHANISTAN
PAKISTAN
KASHMIR
BHUTAN
BANGLADESH
Tashkent
Alma-Ata
Bishkek
Dushanbe
Kabul
Islamabad
Lahore
Karachi
Delhi
Kathmandu
Thimphu
Dhaka
Lhasa
Ürümqi
Lanzhou
Xining
Kashi
Hotan
Aksu
Korla
Hami
Golmud
Samarkand
Bukhara
Kandahar
Herat
Quetta
Peshawar
Rawalpindi
Faisalabad
Multan
Hyderabad
Amritsar
Jaipur
Agra
Kanpur
Lucknow
Varanasi
Allahabad
Patna
Balkhash
Kzyl-Orda
Chimkent
Mashhad
Mary
Tarim Pendi
Kunlun Shan
Altun Shan
Qilian Shan
Karakoram
Hindu Kush
Pamir
Tanggula Shan
Gangdise Shan
Bayan Har Shan
Qaidam
Turfan Depression
Dzungaria
Betpak-Dala
Kyzylkum
Muyun Kum
Thar
Balochistan
Mt Everest 8848
K2 (Godwin Austen) 8611
Nanga Parbat 8126
Kangchenjunga 8598
Annapurna 8078
Indus
Ganga
Brahmaputra
Yangtze
Mekong
Salween
Irrawaddy
Amudar'ya
Syrdar'ya

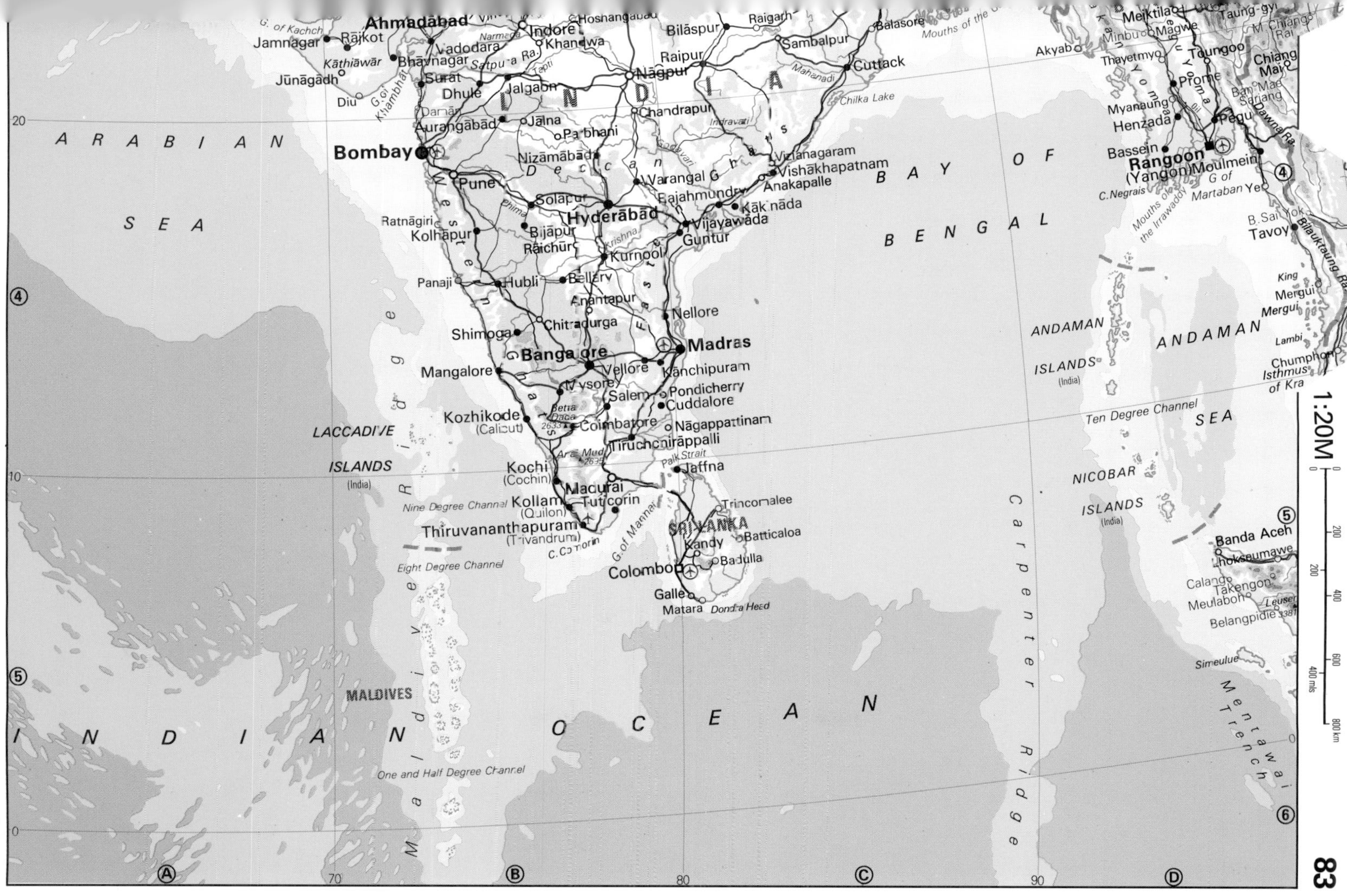

1:20M

0   200   400   600   800 km
0   200   400 mls

D

C

B

A

4   5   6

90

80

70

20

10

ARABIAN SEA

BAY OF BENGAL

ANDAMAN SEA

Carpenter Ridge

INDIAN OCEAN

Mentawai Trench

Bombay

Ahmadābad

Rājkot

Jamnagar

Jūnāgadh

Diu

Bhāvnagar

Vadodara

Surat

Dhule

Khambhāt

G. of Kachchh

Kāthiāwār

G. of Khambhat

Nagpur

Indore

Bilāspur

Raigarh

Sambalpur

Cuttack

Balasore

Raipur

Chandrapur

Jalgaon

Aurangābād

Jālna

Pune

Kolhāpur

Ratnagiri

Panaji

Hubli

Shimoga

Mangalore

Kozhikode
(Calicut)

Bangalore

Mysore

Salem

Madras

Kānchipuram

Pondicherry

Cuddalore

Nāgappattinam

Tiruchchirāppalli

Madurai

Tuticorin

C. Comorin

Kollam
(Quilon)

Kochi
(Cochin)

Thiruvananthapuram
(Trivandrum)

Coimbatore

Vellore

Chitradurga

Anantapur

Bellary

Kurnool

Rāichūr

Bijāpur

Solāpur

Bidar

Hyderābad

Nizāmābad

Warangal

Guntūr

Vijayawāda

Eluru

Rājahmundry

Kākināda

Anakapalle

Vishākhapatnam

Vizianagaram

Srīkākulam

Nellore

DECCAN

Western Ghats

Eastern Ghats

Nārmada

Tāpti

Godāvari

Krishna

Tungabhadra

Penner

Kāveri

Palk Strait

G. of Mannar

SRI LANKA

Jaffna

Trincomalee

Batticaloa

Kandy

Colombo

Galle

Matara

Dondra Head

Bā-dulla

MALDIVES

LACCADIVE ISLANDS
(India)

Nine Degree Channel

Eight Degree Channel

One and Half Degree Channel

NICOBAR ISLANDS
(India)

ANDAMAN ISLANDS
(India)

Ten Degree Channel

C. Negrais

Mouths of the Irrawaddy

Rangoon (Yangon)

Moulmein

Bassein

Henzada

Myanaung

Thayetmyo

Prome

Toungoo

Pegu

Tavoy

Mergui

King I.

Lambi

Chumphon
Isthmus of Kra

Banda Aceh

Lhokseumawe

Meulaboh

Simeulue

Tungoo

Yoma

Dawna Ra.

Bilauktaung Ra.

Chiang Mai

B. Salween

Akyab

Mouths of the Ganges

Chilka Lake

Chhindwāra

Khandwa

Damān

INDIA

I N D I A

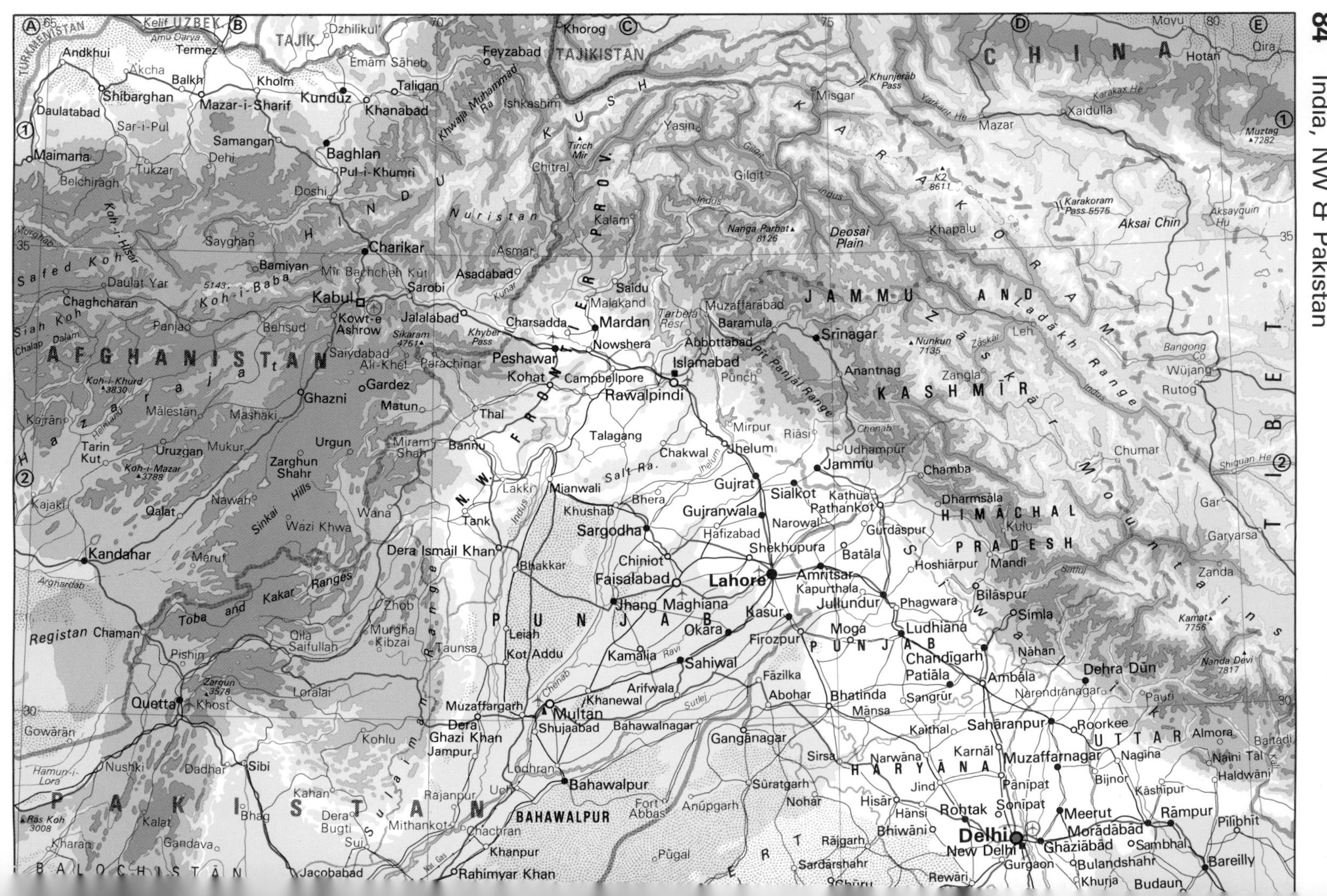
C H I N A
Hotan
Qira
Moyu
Muztag 7282
Xaidulla
Karakax He
Yarkant He
Mazar
Khunjerab Pass
Misgar
K2 8611
Karakoram Pass 5575
Aksai Chin
Aksayquin Hu
Khapalu
Deosai Plain
Nanga Parbat 8126
Gilgit
Yasin
Tirich Mir
Chitral
Ishkashim
Khorog
TAJIKISTAN
TAJIK
Dzhilikul'
Feyzabad
Emam Saheb
Taliqan
Khanabad
Kunduz
Kholm
Khwaja Muhammad Ra.
Kelif
UZBEK
TURKMENISTAN
Amu Darya
Termez
Andkhui
Akcha
Balkh
Shibarghan
Mazar-i-Sharif
Daulatabad
Sar-i-Pul
Samangan
Baghlan
Pul-i-Khumri
Maimana
Dehi
Tukzar
Belchiragh
Doshi
Koh-i-Hisar
Murghab
Saighan
Charikar
Bamiyan
Safed Koh
Daulat Yar
Koh-i-Baba
Mir Bachcheh Kut
Sarobi
Asadabad
Asmar
Nuristan
Kunar
Kabul
Kowt-e Ashrow
Jalalabad
Chaghcharan
Siah Koh
Chalap Dalan
Panjao
Behsud
A F G H A N I S T A N
Hazarajat
Sikaram 4761
Khyber Pass
Saydabad
Ali-Khel
Parachinar
Gardez
Koh-i-Khurd 3830
Ghazni
Malestan
Mashaki
Helmand
Matun
Kajran
Tarin Kut
Uruzgan
Mukur
Urgun
Miram Shah
Zarghun Shahr
Koh-i-Mazar 3788
Nawah
Sinkai Hills
Qalat
Wazi Khwa
Wana
Kajaki
Kandahar
Maruf
Arghandab
Toba and Kakar Ranges
Zhob
Registan
Chaman
Qila Saifullah
Murgha Kibzai
Pishin
Zargun 3578
Quetta
Khost
Loralai
Gowaran
Kohlu
Hamun-i-Lora
Nushki
Dadhar
Sibi
Kahan
Bhag
Dera Bugti
Sui
Ras Koh 3008
Kalat
Gandava
Kharan
B A L O C H I S T A N
P A K I S T A N
Jacobabad
Sulaiman Range
Taunsa
N.W. FRONTIER PROV.
Saidu
Malakand
Kalam
Charsadda
Mardan
Nowshera
Peshawar
Kohat
Campbellpore
Rawalpindi
Islamabad
Abbottabad
Tarbela Resr.
Muzaffarabad
Baramula
Punch
Pir Panjal Range
Srinagar
Anantnag
Thal
Bannu
Talagang
Mirpur
Riasi
Chakwal
Jhelum
Salt Ra.
Lakki
Mianwali
Tank
Indus
Khushab
Bhera
Gujrat
Sialkot
Jammu
Udhampur
Chenab
Gujranwala
Sargodha
Hafizabad
Narowal
Kathua
Pathankot
Gurdaspur
Dera Ismail Khan
Bhakkar
Chiniot
Shekhupura
Batala
Faisalabad
Lahore
Amritsar
Kapurthala
Jhang Maghiana
Kasur
Jullundur
Phagwara
Leiah
P U N J A B
Okara
Firozpur
Moga
Ludhiana
Kot Addu
Kamalia
Ravi
Sahiwal
Chandigarh
Fazilka
Patiala
Arifwala
Khanewal
Sutlej
Abohar
Bhatinda
Sangrur
Mansa
Muzaffargarh
Multan
Shujaabad
Dera Ghazi Khan
Jampur
Bahawalnagar
Ganganagar
Lodhran
Bahawalpur
BAHAWALPUR
Rajanpur
Uch
Mithankot
Chachran
Khanpur
Rahimyar Khan
Fort Abbas
Anupgarh
Suratgarh
Nohar
Pugal
Rajgarh
Sardarshahr
Sirsa
Narwana
H A R Y A N A
Kaithal
Karnal
Jind
Hisar
Hansi
Bhiwani
Rohtak
Sonipat
Panipat
Delhi
New Delhi
Gurgaon
Rewari
Ghaziabad
Bulandshahr
Khurja
Budaun
Meerut
Moradabad
Sambhal
Rampur
Bareilly
Pilibhit
Bijnor
Kashipur
Nagina
Muzaffarnagar
Saharanpur
Roorkee
U T T A R
Almora
Naini Tal
Haldwani
Baitadi
Kali
Ambala
Narendranagar
Pauri
Dehra Dun
Nahan
Simla
Bilaspur
Hoshiarpur
Mandi
Kulu
Dharmsala
H I M A C H A L P R A D E S H
Chamba
Nanda Devi 7817
Kamet 7756
Zanda
Garyarsa
Gar
Siwalik
Satluj
J A M M U A N D K A S H M I R
Zaskar Range
Nunkun 7135
Zaskar
Leh
Zangla
Ladakh Range
K A R A K O R A M
Chumar
Bangong Co
Wujang
Rutog
Shiquan He
T I B E T
Himalaya Mountains
H I N D U K U S H

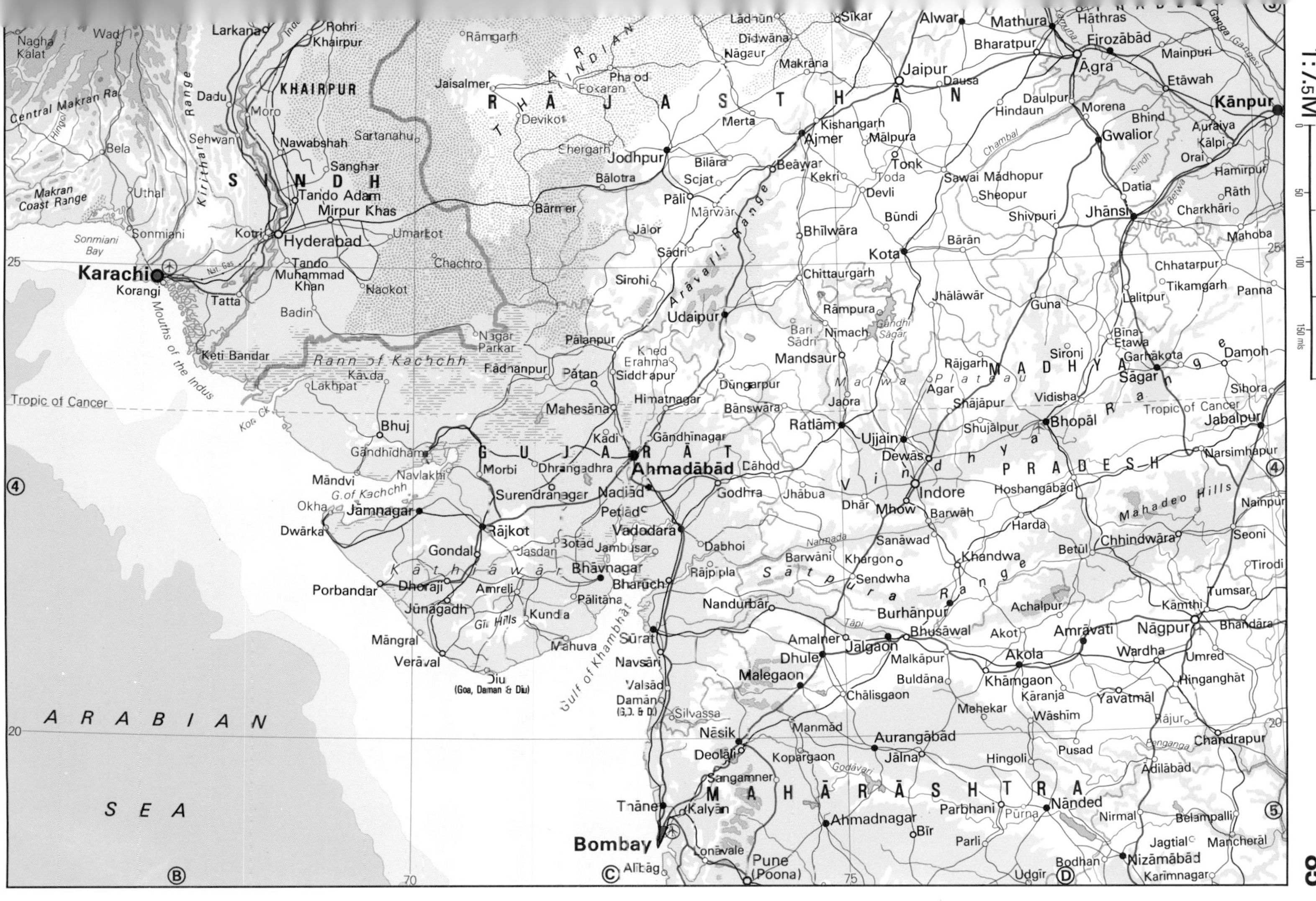

1:7.₅M

100   200   300 km

50   100   150 mls

1:7.5M

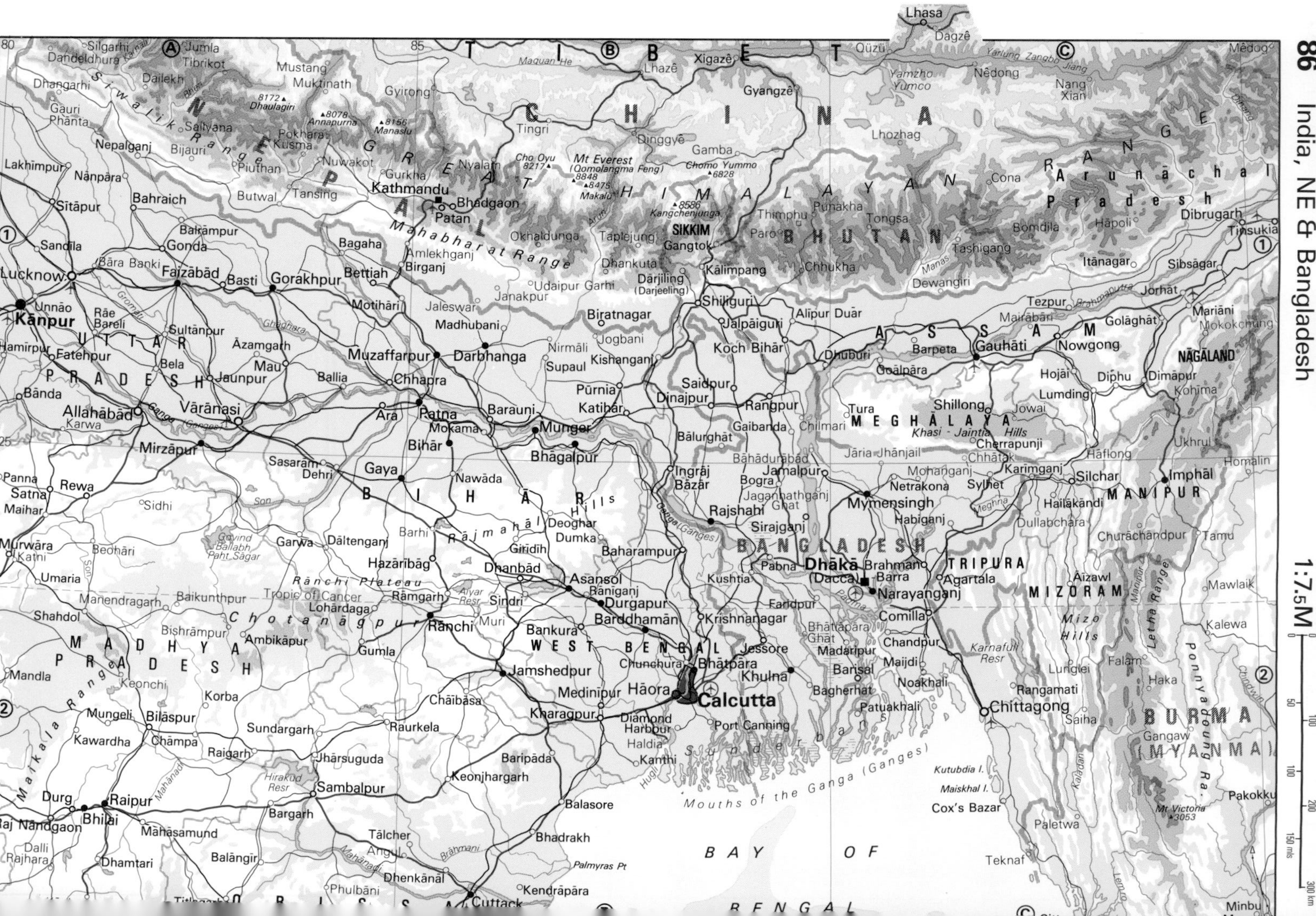
0 100 200 300 km
0 50 100 150 mls
T I B E T
C H I N A
G R E A T H I M A L A Y A N R A N G E
N E P A L
Arunāchal Pradesh
B H U T A N
SIKKIM
NĀGĀLAND
A S S A M
M E G H Ā L A Y A
M A N I P U R
M I Z O R A M
T R I P U R A
B A N G L A D E S H
WEST BENGAL
B I H Ā R
U T T A R P R A D E S H
M A D H Y A P R A D E S H
B U R M A (M Y A N M A R)
BAY OF BENGAL
Mouths of the Ganga (Ganges)
Lhasa
Xigazê
Mt Everest (Qomolangma Feng) 8848
Kathmandu
Patan
Bhadgaon
Thimphu
Gangtok
Dārjiling (Darjeeling)
Shillong
Imphāl
Dhākā (Dacca)
Calcutta
Hāora
Chittagong
Patna
Vārānasi
Allahābād
Lucknow
Kānpur
Gorakhpur
Gaya
Ranchi
Jamshedpur
Asansol
Durgapur
Cuttack
Raipur
Bilāspur
Sambalpur
Dibrugarh
Gauhāti
Silchar
Sylhet
Comilla
Khulna
Rajshahi
Jessore
Mymensingh
Cox's Bazar
Chota Nāgpur
Rānchi Plateau
Tropic of Cancer
Rājmahāl Hills
Mahabharat Range
Siwalik Range
Khasi - Jaintia Hills
Mizo Hills
Letha Range
Ponnyadoung Ra.
Maikala Range
Mt Victoria 3053

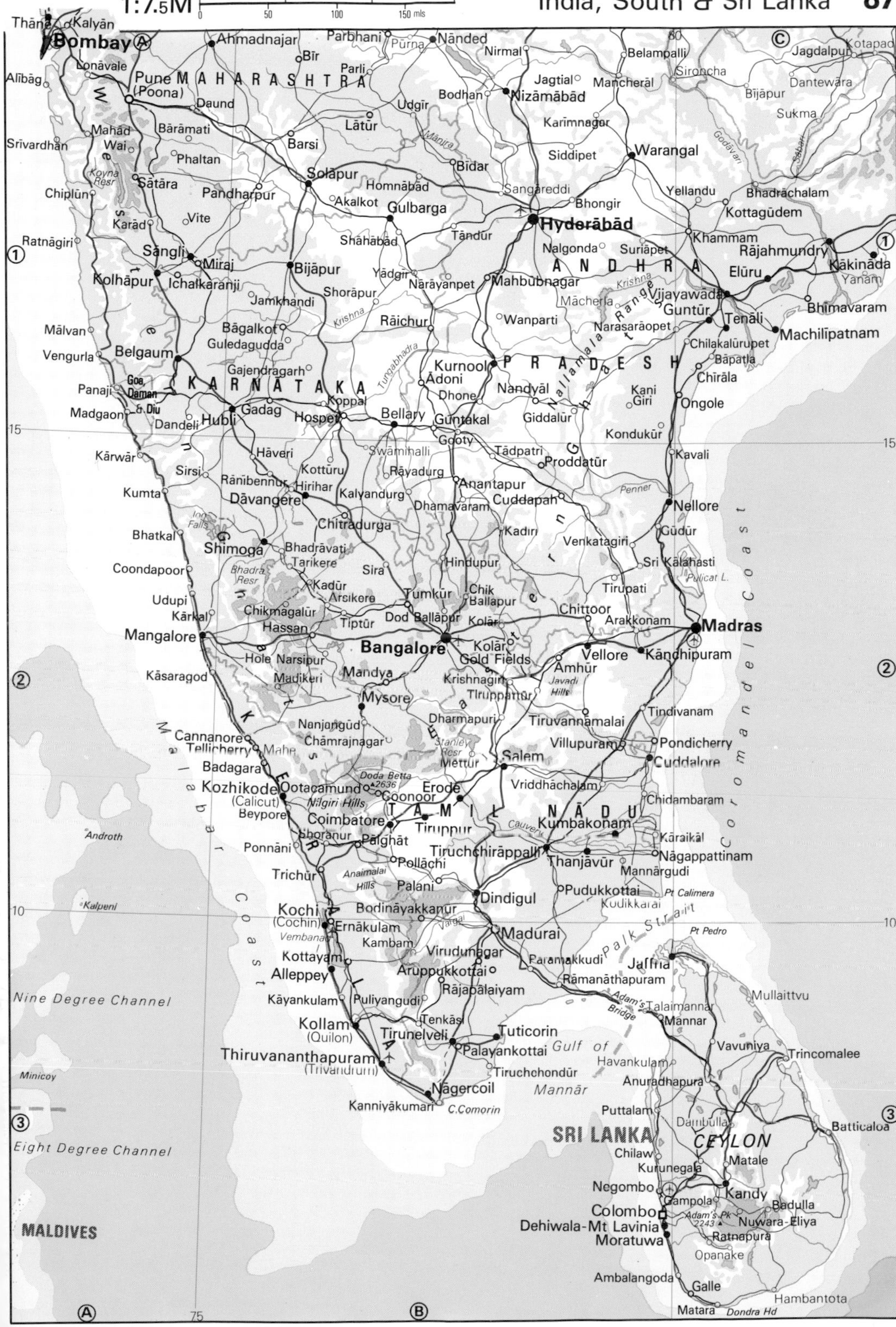

1:7.5M

100   200   300 km
50   100   150 mls

Thāna Kalyān
Bombay Ⓐ   Ahmadnajar   Parbhani   Purna   Nānded   Ⓒ   Jagdalpur   Kotapad
Lonāvale   Bīr   Parli   Nirmal   Belampalli   Sironcha   Dantewāra
Alībāg   **Pune** MAHARASHTRA   Jagtial   Mancherāl   Bījapur   Sukma
(Poona)   Daund   Bodhan   **Nizāmābad**   Karimnagar
Srivardhān   Mahād   Bārāmati   Lātūr   Udgir   Siddipet   Warangal   Bhadrāchalam
Wai   Phaltan   Barsi   Bidar   Sangāreddi   Bhongir   Yellandu   Kottagūdem
Chiplūn   Sātāra   Homnābād   Bhongir   Khammam   Rājahmundry   ①
① Ratnāgiri   Sāngli   Akalkot   **Gulbarga**   **Hyderābād**   Nalgonda   Suriāpet   Eluru   Kākināda
Kolhāpur   Miraj   Shāhābād   ANDHRA   Rājahmundry   Yānam
Ichalkaranji   Bijāpur   Shorāpur   Nārāyanpet   Māhbubnagar   Vijayawāda   Bhīmavaram
Mālvan   Jamkhandi   Yādgir   Mācherla   Guntūr   Machilīpatnam
Vengurla   Bāgalkot   Rāichur   Wanparti   Narasarāopet   Tenāli
Belgaum   Guledagudda   PRADESH   Chilakalūrupet   Bāpatla
Panaji   Gajendragarh   Kurnool   Nandyāl   Kani   Chīrāla
Goa   KARNATAKA   Koppal   Adoni   Giri   Ongole
Daman   Gadag   Dhone   Giddalūr   Kondukūr
Madgaon   Diu   Dandeli   Hubli   Bellary   Guntakal   Kavali   15
15   Kārwār   Hāveri   Hospet   Gooty   Tādpatri   Proddatūr
Sirsi   Kottūru   Rāyadurg   Anantapur   Nellore
Kumta   Rānibennur   Swāminalli   Cuddapah   Gūdūr
Bhatkal   Hirihar   Kalyandurg   Dhamavaram   Kadiri   Venkatagiri   Sri Kālahasti
Coondapoor   Dāvangere   Chitrādurga   Hindupur   Tirupati   Pulicat L.
Udupi   Shimoga   Tarikere   Sira   Chik   Chittoor   Arakkonam   **Madras**
Kārkal   Chikmāgalūr   Kadūr   Arsikere   Dod Ballāpur   Ballāpur   Kolār   Vellore   Kāndhipuram
Mangalore   Hassan   Tiptūr   **Bangalore**   Gold Fields   Amhūr   Coromandel Coast
Kāsaragod   Hole Narsipur   Mandya   Kolār   Krishnagiri   Javādi   ②
②   Cannanore   Madikeri   Mysore   Tiruppattūr   Hills   Tindivanam
Tellicherry   Mahe   Nanjangūd   Dharmapuri   Tiruvannāmalai   Pondicherry
Badagara   Chāmrajnagar   Mettūr   Villupuram   Cuddalore
Kozhikode   Ootacamund   Doda Betta   Salem   Vriddhāchalam   Chidambaram
(Calicut)   Coonoor   Erode   Kumbakonam
Beypore   Coimbatore   TAMIL   Kāraikāl
Ponnāni   Sholapur   Tiruppur   NĀDU   Tiruchchirāppalli   Nāgappattinam
Trichūr   Pālghāt   Pollāchi   Thanjāvūr   Mannārgudi
Palani   Pudukkottai   Pt Calimera
Kochi   Bodināyakkanūr   Dindigul   Kudikkarai
(Cochin)   Kambam   Madurai   Pt Pedro
10   Ernakulam   Virudunagar   Paramakkudi   Jaffna   10
Kottayam   Arūppukkottai   Rāmanāthapuram   Mullaittvu
Allepey   Rājapālaiyam   Adam's   Talaimannar
Kāyankulam   Puliyangudi   Bridge   Mannār
Nine Degree Channel   Tenkāsi   Tuticorin   Gulf of   Vavuniya   Trincomalee
Kollam   Tirunelveli   Havankulam
(Quilon)   Palayankottai   Mannār   Anurādhapura
Thiruvananthapuram   Tiruchchondūr   Puttalam
(Trivandrum)   Nāgercoil   Batticaloa   ③
③   Kanniyākumari   C.Comorin   SRI LANKA   Dambulla   CEYLON
Minicoy   Chilaw   Matale
Eight Degree Channel   Kurunegala   Kandy   Badulla
Negombo   Gampola   Nuwara-Eliya
Colombo   Adam's Pk   Ratnapura
MALDIVES   Dehiwala-Mt Lavinia   Opanake
Moratuwa   Ambalangoda   Galle
Ⓐ   75   Ⓑ   Matara   Dondra Hd   Hambantota

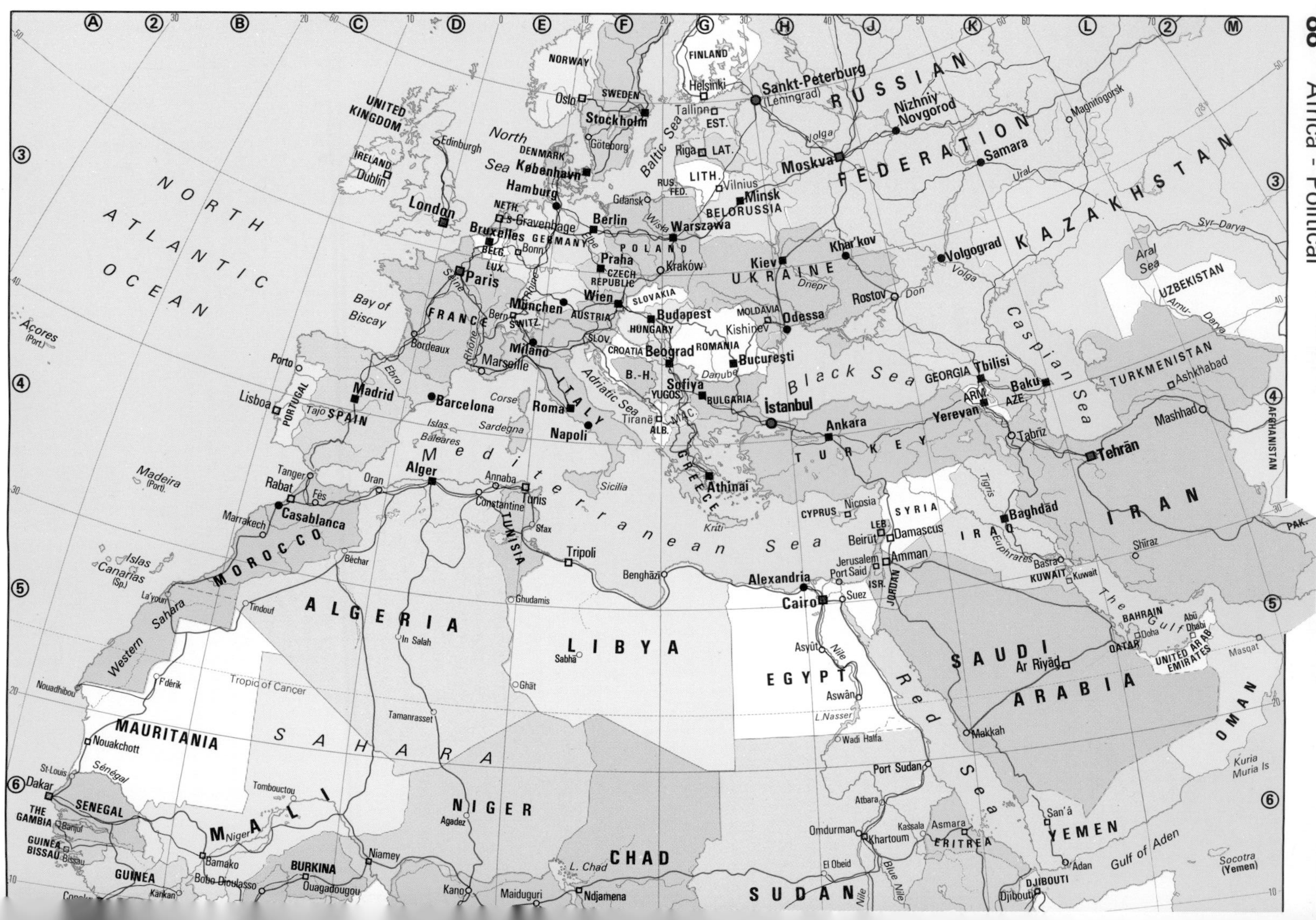
NORTH ATLANTIC OCEAN
UNITED KINGDOM
IRELAND
NORWAY
SWEDEN
FINLAND
DENMARK
NETH.
BELG.
LUX.
GERMANY
POLAND
CZECH REPUBLIC
SLOVAKIA
AUSTRIA
SWITZ.
HUNGARY
SLOV.
CROATIA
B.-H.
YUGOS.
ALB.
ROMANIA
MOLDAVIA
BULGARIA
GREECE
FRANCE
SPAIN
PORTUGAL
ITALY
EST.
LAT.
LITH.
RUS. FED.
BELORUSSIA
UKRAINE
RUSSIAN FEDERATION
KAZAKHSTAN
UZBEKISTAN
TURKMENISTAN
AFGHANISTAN
PAK.
IRAN
IRAQ
SYRIA
LEB.
ISR.
JORDAN
CYPRUS
TURKEY
GEORGIA
ARM.
AZE.
KUWAIT
BAHRAIN
QATAR
UNITED ARAB EMIRATES
OMAN
SAUDI ARABIA
YEMEN
DJIBOUTI
ERITREA
SUDAN
EGYPT
LIBYA
TUNISIA
ALGERIA
MOROCCO
Western Sahara
MAURITANIA
MALI
NIGER
CHAD
SENEGAL
THE GAMBIA
GUINEA-BISSAU
GUINEA
BURKINA
SAHARA
North Sea
Baltic Sea
Bay of Biscay
Mediterranean Sea
Adriatic Sea
Black Sea
Caspian Sea
Aral Sea
Red Sea
The Gulf
Gulf of Aden
Tropic of Cancer
London
Paris
Madrid
Roma
Berlin
Moskva
Sankt-Peterburg (Leningrad)
Kiev
Ankara
İstanbul
Cairo
Alexandria
Tehrān
Baghdād
Ar Riyāḍ
Alger
Tunis
Tripoli
Casablanca
Dakar
Nouakchott
Bamako
Niamey
Ndjamena
Khartoum
Madeira (Port.)
Islas Canarias (Sp.)
Açores (Port.)
Socotra (Yemen)
Kuria Muria Is

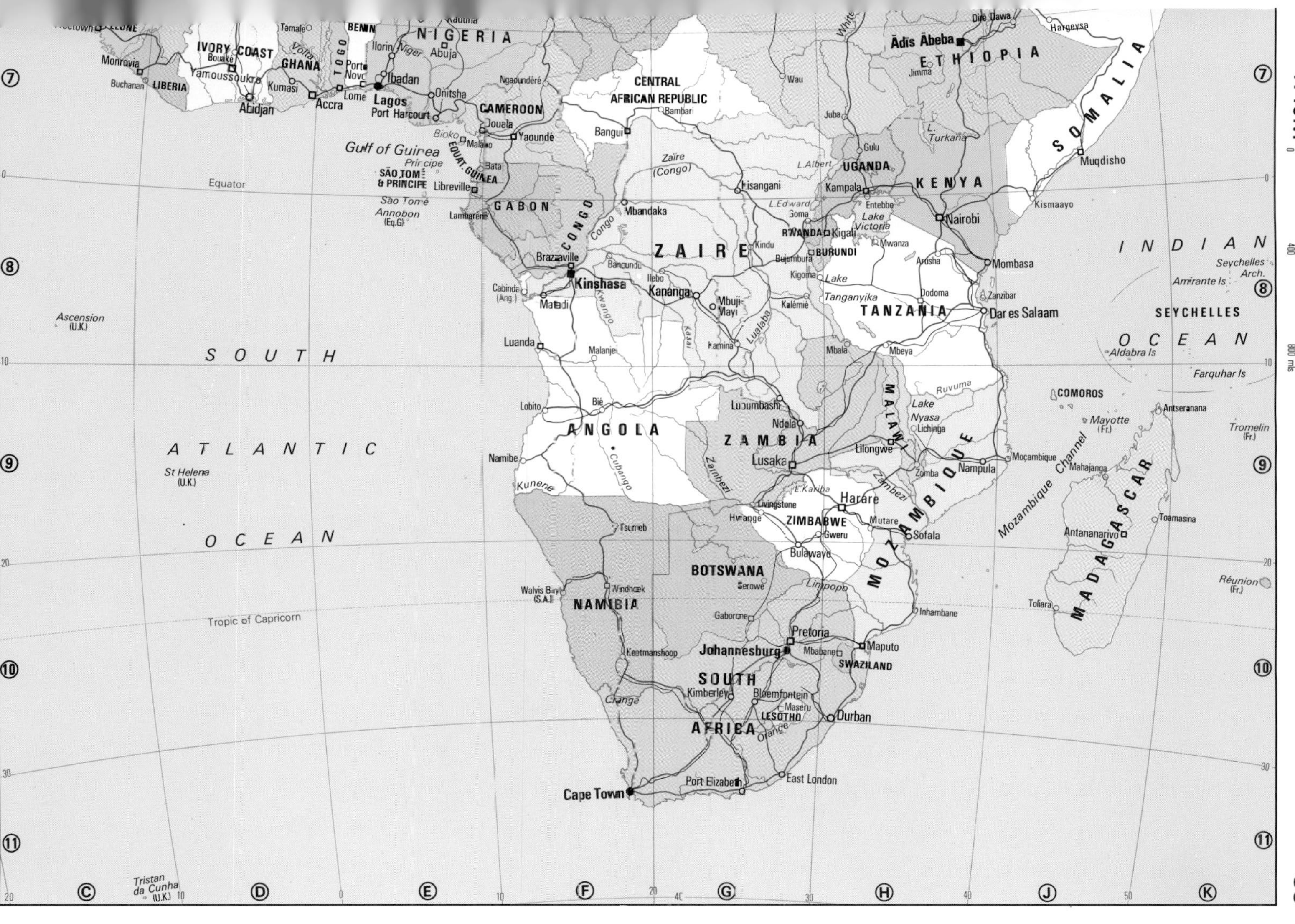
INDIAN OCEAN
SOUTH ATLANTIC OCEAN
SOMALIA
ETHIOPIA
KENYA
UGANDA
TANZANIA
RWANDA
BURUNDI
ZAIRE
CENTRAL AFRICAN REPUBLIC
CONGO
GABON
CAMEROON
NIGERIA
BENIN
TOGO
GHANA
IVORY COAST
LIBERIA
EQUAT. GUINEA
SÃO TOMÉ & PRINCIPE
ANGOLA
ZAMBIA
MALAWI
MOZAMBIQUE
ZIMBABWE
BOTSWANA
NAMIBIA
SOUTH AFRICA
LESOTHO
SWAZILAND
MADAGASCAR
COMOROS
SEYCHELLES
Ādis Ābeba
Dire Dawa
Hargeysa
Jimma
Nairobi
Mombasa
Muqdisho
Kismaayo
Dar es Salaam
Zanzibar
Dodoma
Arusha
Mwanza
Kampala
Entebbe
Gulu
Juba
Wau
Kigali
Goma
Bujumbura
Kigoma
Kalémié
Kisangani
Kindu
Mbandaka
Bangui
Bambari
Kinshasa
Brazzaville
Bandundu
Ilebo
Matadi
Kananga
Mbuji Mayi
Kamina
Lubumbashi
Ndola
Lusaka
Lilongwe
Lichinga
Zomba
Harare
Bulawayo
Gweru
Mutare
Livingstone
Hwange
Maputo
Mbabane
Pretoria
Johannesburg
Bloemfontein
Maseru
Kimberley
Durban
East London
Port Elizabeth
Cape Town
Keetmanshoop
Windhoek
Walvis Bay (S.A.)
Tsumeb
Gaborone
Serowe
Luanda
Lobito
Bié
Namibe
Malanje
Cabinda (Ang.)
Libreville
Lambaréné
Bata
Malabo
Douala
Yaoundé
Ngaoundéré
Lagos
Ibadan
Ilorin
Abuja
Onitsha
Port Harcourt
Porto Novo
Lomé
Accra
Kumasi
Tamale
Abidjan
Yamoussoukro
Bouaké
Monrovia
Buchanan
Antananarivo
Toliara
Toamasina
Antseranana
Mahajanga
Moçambique
Nampula
Mbeya
Mbala
Sofala
Inhambane
Gulf of Guinea
Mozambique Channel
Equator
Tropic of Capricorn
Lake Victoria
Lake Tanganyika
Lake Nyasa
L. Turkana
L. Albert
L. Edward
L. Kariba
Zaire (Congo)
Congo
Kasai
Kwango
Lualaba
Zambezi
Cubango
Kunene
Limpopo
Orange
Niger
Volta
Ruvuma
White
Bioko
Principe
São Tomé
Annobon (Eq.G)
Ascension (U.K.)
St Helena (U.K.)
Tristan da Cunha (U.K.)
Réunion (Fr.)
Tromelin (Fr.)
Mayotte (Fr.)
Aldabra Is
Farquhar Is
Amirante Is
Seychelles Arch.

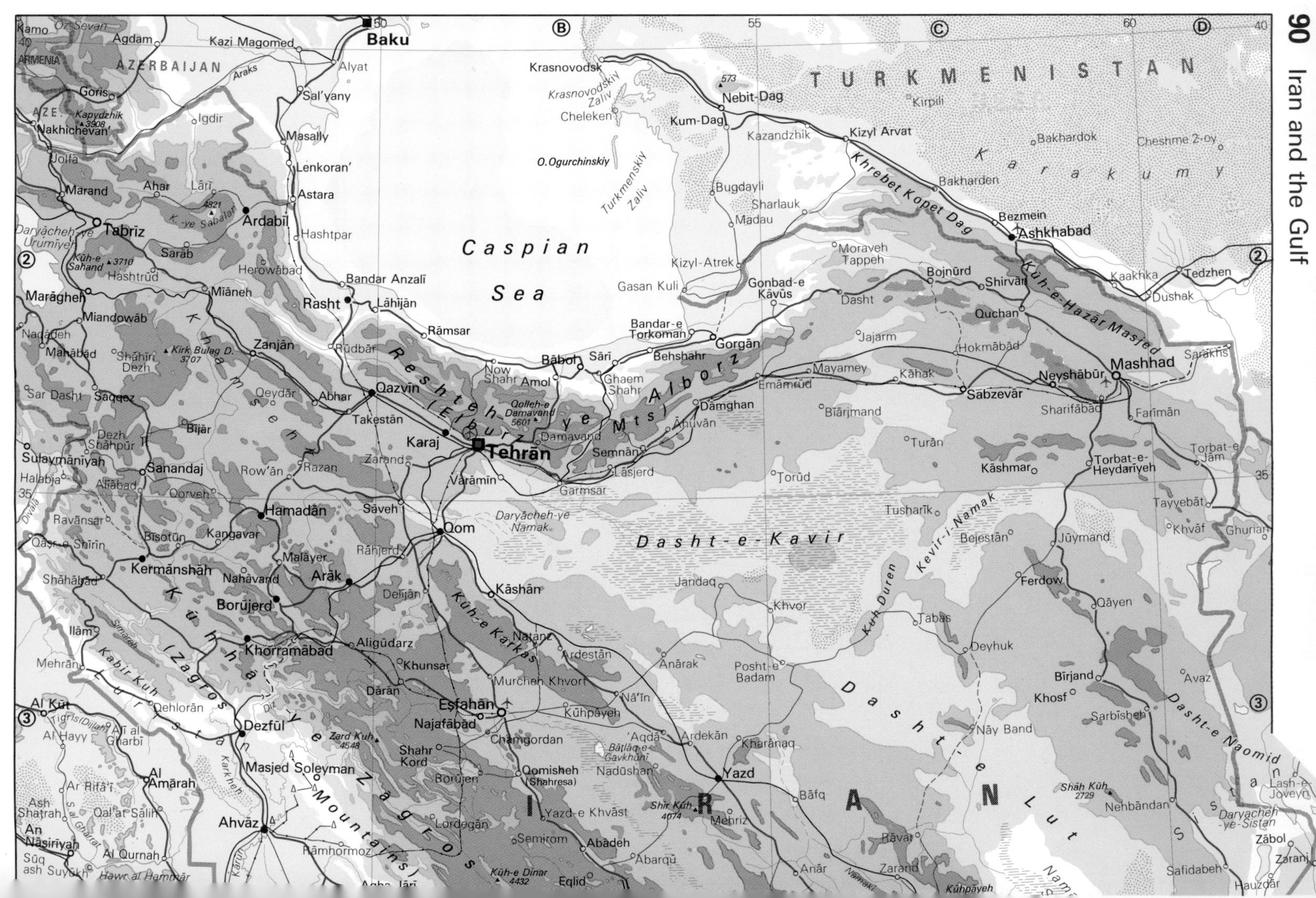
T U R K M E N I S T A N
K a r a k u m y
A Z E R B A I J A N
ARMENIA
AZE.
I R A N
Caspian Sea
Krasnovodskiy Zaliv
Turkmenskiy Zaliv
O. Ogurchinskiy
Khrebet Kopet Dag
Kūh-e Hazār Masjed
Reshteh-ye Alborz (Elburz Mts)
Qolleh-ye Damāvand 5601
Dasht-e Kavīr
Dasht-e Lut
Dasht-e Naomid
Kevir-i-Namak
Kuh Duren
Kūh-e Karkas
Kūhhā-ye Zagros (Zagros Mountains)
Luristan
Daryācheh-ye Namak
Daryācheh-ye Orūmīyeh
Daryācheh-ye Sīstān
Bātlāq-e Gavkhūnī
Kūh-e Sahand 3710
Kapydzhik 3908
K. ye Sabalān 4821
Kirk Bulag D. 3707
Zard Kūh 4548
Kūh-e Dīnār 4432
Shīr Kūh 4074
Shāh Kūh 2729
Kabir Kuh
Baku
Tehrān
Mashhad
Tabrīz
Eşfahān
Yazd
Ashkhabad
Nebit-Dag
Krasnovodsk
Kum-Dag
Kizyl Arvat
Kizyl-Atrek
Gasan Kuli
Cheleken
Tedzhen
Dushak
Kaakhka
Bakhardok
Bakharden
Bezmein
Kazandzhik
Bugdayli
Madau
Sharlauk
Kirpili
Cheshme 2-oy
Lenkoran'
Astara
Masally
Sal'yany
Alyat
Kazi Magomed
Agdam
Goris
Nakhichevan'
Igdir
Julfa
Marand
Ahar
Ardabīl
Sarāb
Mīāneh
Marāgheh
Miandowāb
Mahābād
Saqqez
Sanandaj
Kermānshāh
Hamadān
Zanjān
Qazvīn
Karaj
Rasht
Bandar Anzalī
Lāhījān
Rāmsar
Now Shahr
Amol
Bābol
Sārī
Behshahr
Bandar-e Torkoman
Gorgān
Gonbad-e Kāvūs
Bojnūrd
Shīrvān
Quchan
Neyshābūr
Sabzevār
Dāmghan
Semnān
Garmsar
Varāmīn
Qom
Kāshān
Arāk
Malāyer
Borūjerd
Khorramābād
Dezfūl
Ahvāz
Masjed Soleyman
Shahr Kord
Najafābād
Nā'īn
Ardekān
Bāfq
Anār
Rāvar
Zarand
Kūhpāyeh
Ṭabas
Ferdow
Bīrjand
Qāyen
Torbat-e Heydarīyeh
Torbat-e Jām
Kāshmar
Farīmān
Tayyebāt
Khvāf
Nehbandān
Zābol
Zaranj
Abādeh
Eqlīd
Semīrom
Sarakhs
Al Kūt
Al 'Amārah
An Nāşirīyah
Sūq ash Suyūkh
Ilām
Mehrān
Qaşr-e Shīrīn
Sulaymānīyah
Halabja
Ar Rifā'ī
Al Qurnah
Hawr al Hammār
Tigris (Dijlah)
Araks
Karkheh
Kārūn

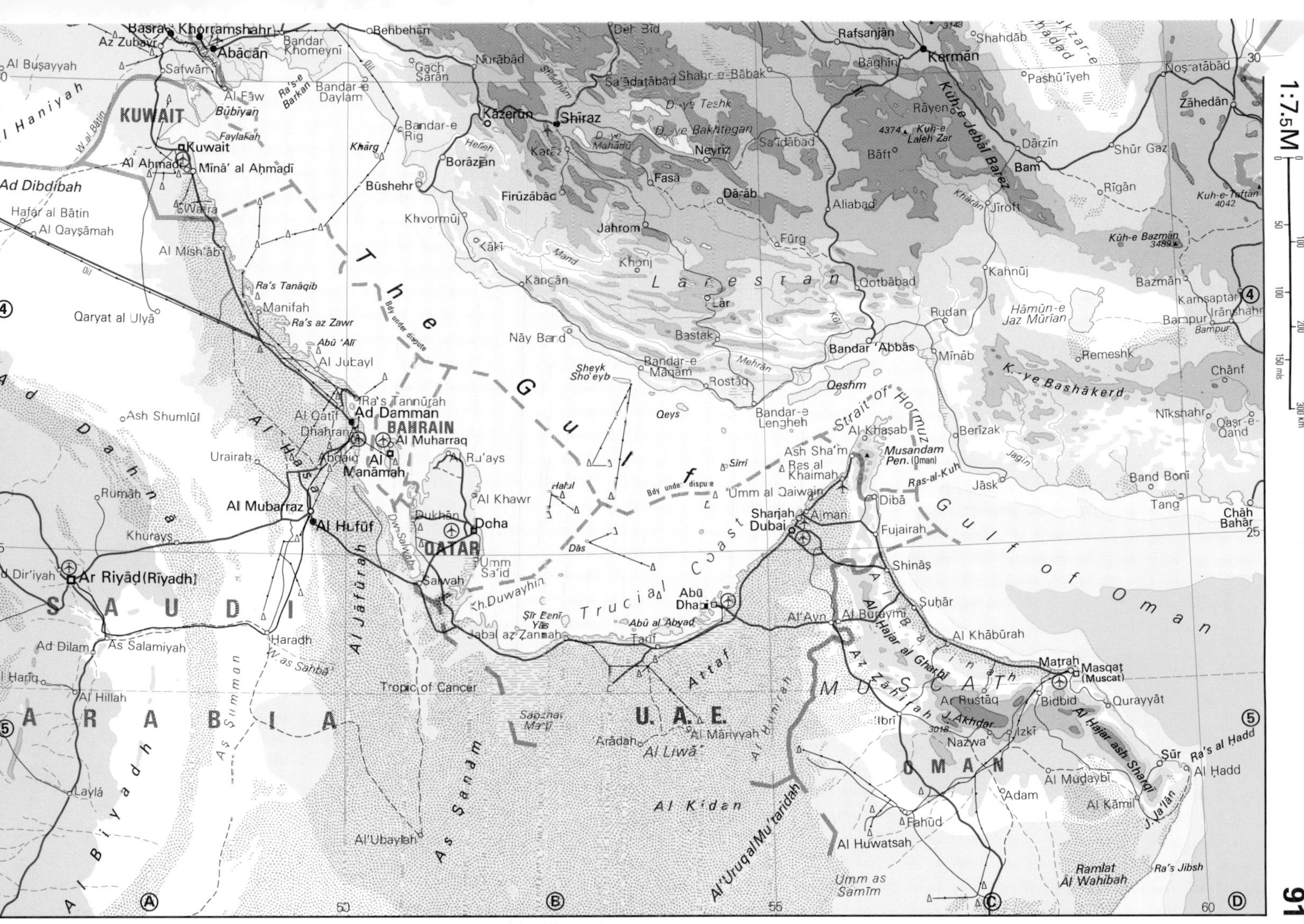

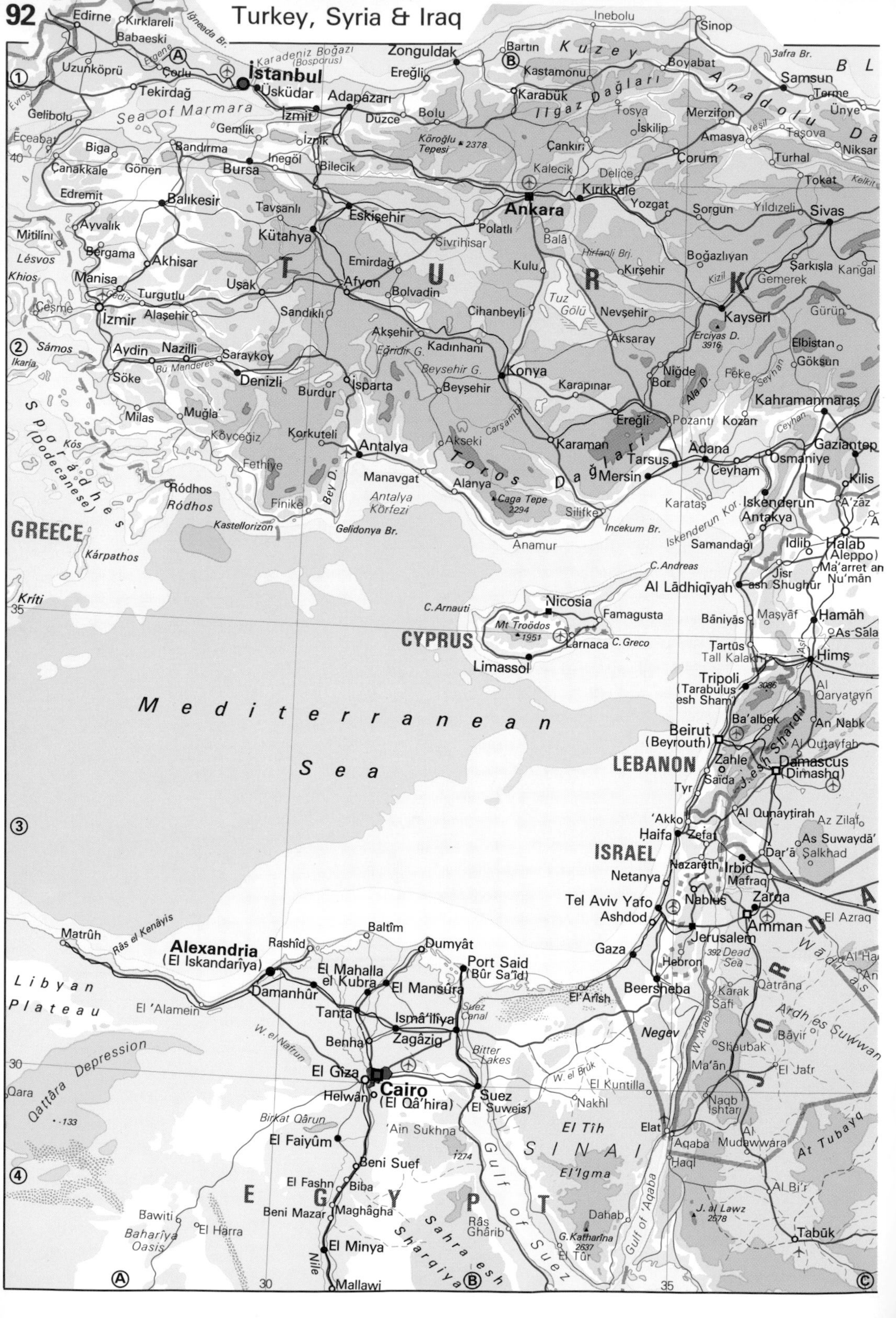

GREECE

TURKEY

Mediterranean Sea

CYPRUS

Libyan Plateau

EGYPT

Qattâra Depression

LEBANON

ISRAEL

JORDAN

SINAI

Edirne
Kırklareli
Babaeski
İğneada Br.
Uzunköprü
Çorlu
Istanbul
Üsküdar
Tekirdağ
Adapazarı
İzmit
Karadeniz Boğazı (Bosporus)
Gelibolu
Sea of Marmara
Gemlik
İznik
Bandırma
İnegöl
Bilecik
Eceabat
Biga
Bursa
Çanakkale
Gönen
Edremit
Balıkesir
Tavşanlı
Kütahya
Eskişehir
Mitilíni
Ayvalık
Lésvos
Bergama
Akhisar
Manisa
Khios
Turgutlu
Uşak
Afyon
Bolvadin
Çeşme
İzmir
Alaşehir
Sandıklı
Aydın
Nazilli
Sarayköy
Sámos
Ikaría
Söke
Denizli
Burdur
Isparta
Milas
Muğla
Korkuteli
Köyceğiz
Ródhos
Ródhos
Kárpathos
Fethiye
Antalya
Kastellórizon
Finike
Bey D.
Manavgat
Alanya
Kaş
Anamur
Kriti

Zonguldak
Ereğli
Bartın
Kastamonu
Karabük
Kuzey Anadolu Dağları
İlgaz Dağları
Tosya
Bolu
Düzce
Köroğlu Tepesi 2378
Çankırı
Kalecik
Delice
Çorum
Ankara
Kırıkkale
Yozgat
Sorgun
Polatlı
Sivrihisar
Bala
Hirfanli Brj.
Kırşehir
Kulu
Cihanbeyli
Nevşehir
Aksaray
Tuz Gölü
Konya
Akşehir
Eğridir G.
Kadınhanı
Beyşehir G.
Beyşehir
Karapınar
Karaman
Ereğli
Akseki
Çarşamba
Toros Dağları
Silifke
İncekum Br.
Caga Tepe 2294
Gelidonya Br.
Antalya Körfezi

İnebolu
Sinop
Boyabat
Safra Br.
Samsun
Terme
Ünye
Merzifon
Amasya
Taşova
Niksar
Turhal
Yeşil
Tokat
Kelkit
Sivas
Yıldızeli
Boğazlıyan
Şarkışla
Kangal
Gemerek
Kayseri
Gürün
Erciyas D. 3916
Niğde
Bor
Ala D.
Elbistan
Göksun
Pozantı
Kozan
Feke
Seyhan
Kahramanmaraş
Tarsus
Adana
Ceyhan
Osmaniye
Mersin
Karataş
Ceyhan
Gaziantep
Kilis
A'zâz
İskenderun
Antakya
İskenderun Kör.
Samandağı
İdlib
Halab (Aleppo)
Ma'arret an Nu'mân
Jisr esh Shughûr
C. Andreas
Al Lâdhiqîyah
Bâniyâs
Maşyâf
As-Sála
Hamâh
Hims
Al Qaryatayn

C. Arnauti
Nicosia
Famagusta
Mt Troödos 1951
Larnaca
C. Greco
Limassol
Tartûs
Tall Kalah
Tripoli (Tarabulus esh Sham)
3086
Ba'albek
An Nabk
Al Qutayfab
Beirut (Beyrouth)
Zahle
Jebel esh Sharqi
Damascus (Dimashq)
Saïda
Tyr
'Akko
Zefat
Al Qunaytirah
Az Zilaf
Haifa
Dar'â
Şalkhad
Netanya
Nazareth
Irbid
As Suwaydâ'
Tel Aviv Yafo
Nablus
Mafraq
Zarqa
Ashdod
Al Azraq
Jerusalem
Amman
Gaza
392 Dead Sea
Wâdi el Ha
Hebron
Beersheba
Kârak
Safi
El 'Arîsh
Qatrâna
Ardh es Suwwan
Bâyir
Negev
Ma'ân
Shaubak
El Jafr

Matrûh
Râs el Kenâyis
Rashîd
Baltîm
Dumyât
Alexandria (El Iskandariya)
El Mahalla el Kubra
El Mansûra
Port Said (Bûr Sa'îd)
El 'Alamein
Damanhûr
Tanta
İsmâ'îliya
Suez Canal
W. el Nafrun
Benha
Zagâzig
Bitter Lakes
El Qunfilla
W. el Brûk
Qara
El Giza
Cairo (El Qâ'hira)
Helwan
Suez (El Suweis)
Nakhl
El Faiyûm
'Ain Sukhna
El Tîh
Birkat Qârun
El Fashn
Beni Suef
1274
El Igma
Biba
Maghâgha
Bawiti
El Harra
Beni Mazar
Baharîya Oasis
El Minya
Mallawi
Sahra esh Sharqîya
Nile
Dahab
Gulf of Aqaba
Naqb Ishtar
Elat
Aqaba
Mudawwara
At Tubayq
Haql
J. al Lawz 2578
Râs Ghârib
G. Katharîna 2637
El Tûr
Gulf of Suez
Tabûk
El Bi'r
Al Hi

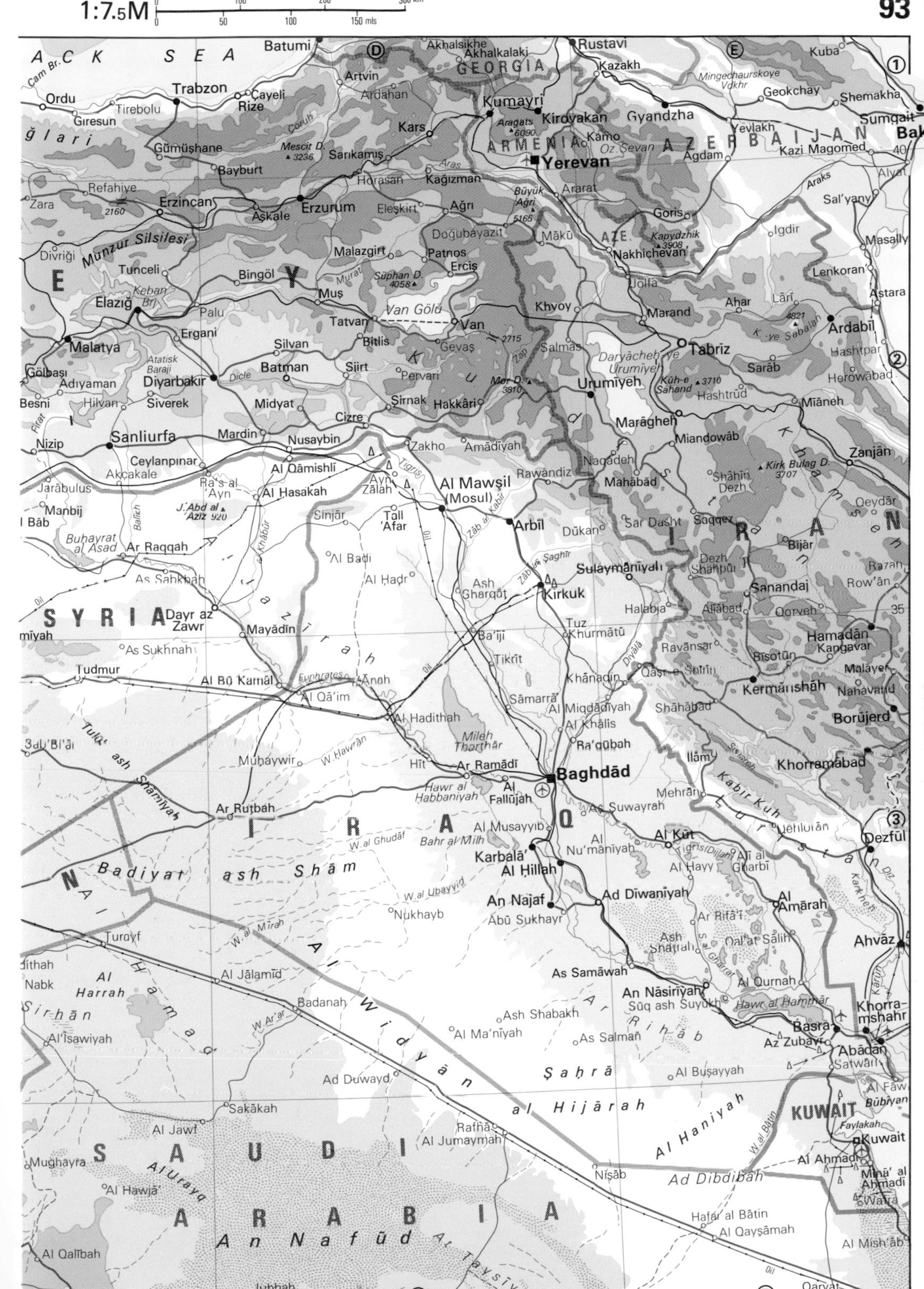

100 200 300 km
0 50 100 150 mls

ACK SEA

Batumi
Ordu Tirebolu Trabzon Çayeli Rize Artvin Akhalsikhe Akhalkalaki Rustavi Kuba (E)
Giresun Ardahan GEORGIA Kazakh Kumayri Kiroyakan Gyandzha Geokchay Shemakha
ğları Gümüşhane Kars Aragats Kamo Sumgait Bak
Çoruh Bayburt Sarıkamış 6050 ARMENIA Oz Sevan AZERBAIJAN Kazi Magomed 40
Refahiye Mescit D. Horasan Yerevan Agdam
Zara 2160 Erzincan Aşkale Erzurum Eleşkirt Ağrı Kağızman Büyük Ağrı Ararat AZE Goris Igdir Sal'yany Masally
Divriği 3236 Malazgirt Doğubayazıt 5165 Nakhichevan 3908 Astara
Tunceli Bingöl Mus Patnos Erciş Süphan D. Makü Jolfa Ahar Ları Lenkoran'
Elazığ Keban Palu Y 4058 Van Gölü Khvoy Marand 4821 k-ye Sabalan Ardabil
Malatya Baraj Ergani Tatvan Bitlis Gevaş Van 2715 Salmas Tabriz Sarab Hashtpar
Gölbaşı Atatisk Silvan Siirt Pervari Mer D. Urumiyeh Daryacheh-ye Kühl-e 3710 Herowabad (2)
Adıyaman Hilvan Diyarbakir Batman K 3910 Urümiyeh Sahand Hashtrud Mianeh
Besni Siverek Midyat Cizre Hakkâri U Marãgheh Miandowãb Zanjan
Nizip Sanliurfa Mardin Nusaybin Zakho Amadiyah Rawãndiz Naqadeh Kirk Bulag D.
Jarabulus Ceylanpınar Ra's al Al Qamishli Ayn Rawãndiz Mahãbãd Shahin 3707 Qeydar
l Bâb Akçakale 'Ayn Zalah Al Hasakah Al Mawşil Dezh Bijãr Razan
Manbij J.'Abd al Sinjãr Tall (Mosul) Dükan Sar Dasht Saqqez I Row'ãn
Buhayrat Aziz 920 'Afar Arbil R Dezh Sanandaj 35
al Asad Ar Raqqah Al Badi Al Hadr Ash Sulaymaniyah Shahpur A Qorveh
As Sabkhah Gharqut Kirkuk Halabja Aliabad N Hamadãn Kangavar
SYRIA Mayãdin Ba'ji Tuz Ravãnsar Kapydzhik Kermanshãh Malãyer
Dayr az As Sukhnah Khurmãtu Qasr-e Shirin Bisotun Nahãvanú Borüjerd
mîyah Zawr Tikrit Khãnaqin Shãhabad
Tudmur Al Bu Kamãl 'Anah Sãmarrã' Diyala Khorramãbad
Al Qã'im Al Haditha Al Miqdãdiyah Ilãm
3ál Bl'ái Muhaywir Mileh Al Khãlis Mehrãn
Tulut ash Shamiya Hit Tharthãr Ar Ramãdi Ra'dubah Kabir Kuh
Ar Rutbah W.Hawran Al Baghdãd L
Habbaniyah Al u Dezful (3)
Fallujah As Suwayrah r Dezful
IRAQ Al Musayyib Al Ali al
Badiyat ash Shãm W.al Ghudaf Bahr al Milh Nu'maniyah Al Hayy Gharbi
Karbalã' Ahvãz
Al Hillah Al Kut Al Amãrah
N W.al Ubayyiq An Najaf Tigris/Dijlah Khorram-
Turayf Ad Diwãniyah shahr
A Nukhayb Abu Sukhayr Ar Rifã'i Basra Abãdan
Jithah Badanah As Samãwah Ash Al Qurnah Az Zubayr Satwari
Nabk Al W.Ar'ar Shaffãh Hawr al Hammãr
Sirhãn Harrah Al Jãlamid An Nãsiriyah Qal'at Sãlih Al Faw
Al Ísawiya Süq ash Suyükh As Salmãn KUWAIT Bübiyan
Mughayra Ad Duwayd Al Ma'nîyah Ar Rihãb Al Ahmadi Faylakah
Al Jawf Ash Shabakh Sahrã Al Buşayyah Kuwait Minã' al
Al Hawja' Sakãkah SAUDI Al Widyãn Al Haniyah Mina al Ahmadi
Rafhã' Nişãb Ad Dibdibah Al Wafra
Al 'Uraya Al Jumaymah Ş a h r ã al Hijãrah Al Mish'ãb
Al Qalibah ARABIA An Nafüd Hafar al Bãtin Al Qayşãmah
Jubbah (D) Al Taysiyah (E) Qaryat al Ulyã

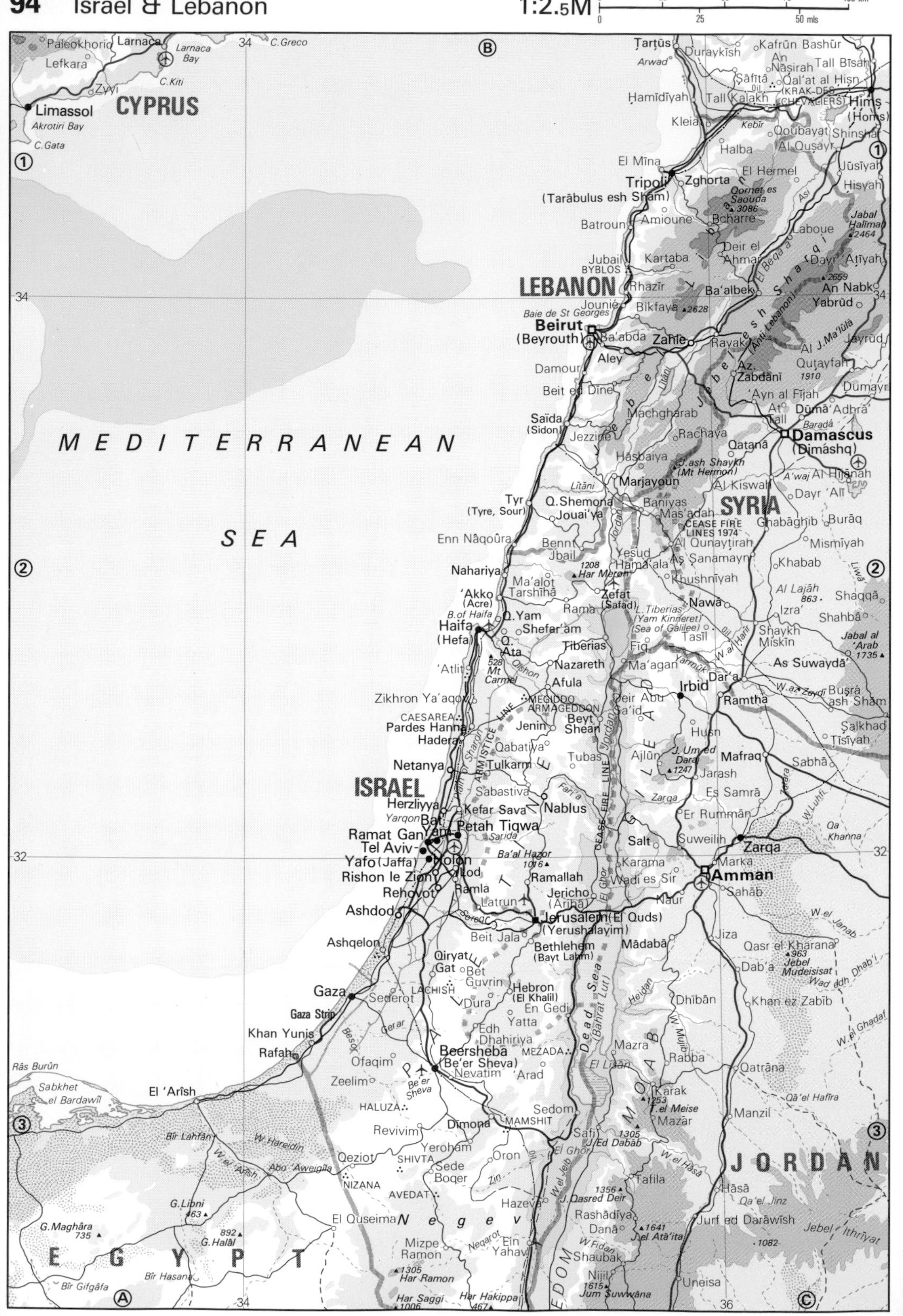

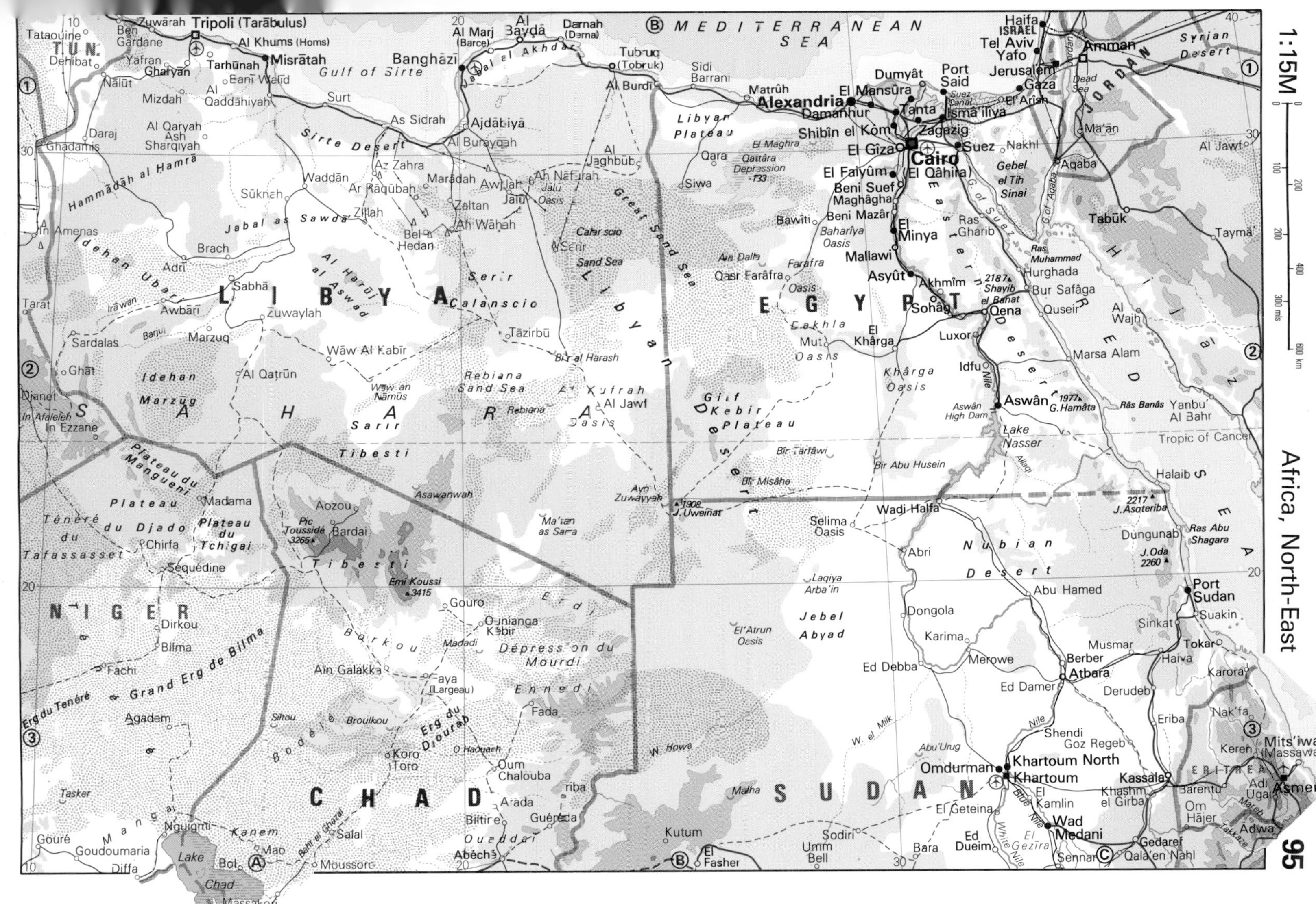
MEDITERRANEAN SEA
Tripoli (Tarābulus)
Zuwārah
Al Khums (Homs)
Misrātah
Tarhūnah
Gharyān
Banghāzī
Gulf of Sirte
Sirte Desert
Surt
As Sidrah
Tubruq (Tobruk)
Darnah (Derna)
Al Bayḑā
Al Marj (Barce)
Alexandria
Matrûh
Sidi Barrani
El Mansûra
Dumyât
Port Said
Tanta
Damanhur
Shibîn el Kôm
Cairo (El Qâhira)
El Gîza
Suez
Ismâ'ilîya
Zagazig
Haifa
ISRAEL
Tel Aviv Yafo
Jerusalem
Gaza
El Arîsh
Amman
JORDAN
Dead Sea
Syrian Desert
Ma'ān
Tabūk
Taymā'
Al Jawf
Aqaba
G. of Aqaba
G. of Suez
Gebel el Tih
Sinai
Nakhl
El Faiyûm
Beni Suef
Maghâgha
Beni Mazâr
El Minya
Mallawi
Asyût
Akhmîm
Sohâg
Qena
Luxor
Idfu
Aswân
Aswân High Dam
Lake Nasser
Nile
Hurghada
Bur Safâga
Quseir
Marsa Alam
Kharga Oasis
El Khârga
Dakhla Oasis
Farafra Oasis
Qasr Farâfra
Bahariya Oasis
Bawiti
Siwa
Qara
Qattâra Depression
Libyan Plateau
Great Sand Sea
Libyan Desert
Gilf Kebir Plateau
EGYPT
Tropic of Cancer
Halaib
Port Sudan
Suakin
Tokar
Wadi Halfa
Nubian Desert
Abu Hamed
Dongola
Karima
Merowe
Atbara
Berber
Ed Damer
Kassala
Khartoum
Khartoum North
Omdurman
Wad Medani
Gedaref
Blue Nile
White Nile
El Fasher
SUDAN
Selima Oasis
Jebel Abyad
Mits'iwa (Massawa)
Asmera
Keren
Adwa
LIBYA
Ajdābiyā
Jalū
Al Jawf
Al Kufrah Oasis
Rebiana Sand Sea
Calanscio Sand Sea
Serir Calanscio
Sabhā
Marzuq
Idehan Marzūq
Ghāt
Ghadāmis
Hammādah al Hamrā
Al Harūj al Aswad
Tibesti
Emi Koussi 3415
Pic Toussidé 3265
Bardai
Aozou
aya (Largeau)
Fada
Abéché
CHAD
Lake Chad
Bol
Mao
NIGER
Bilma
Dirkou
Grand Erg de Bilma
Ténéré du Tafassasset
Agadem
Madama
Plateau du Djado
Diffa
T U N.
J. Uweinat 1908

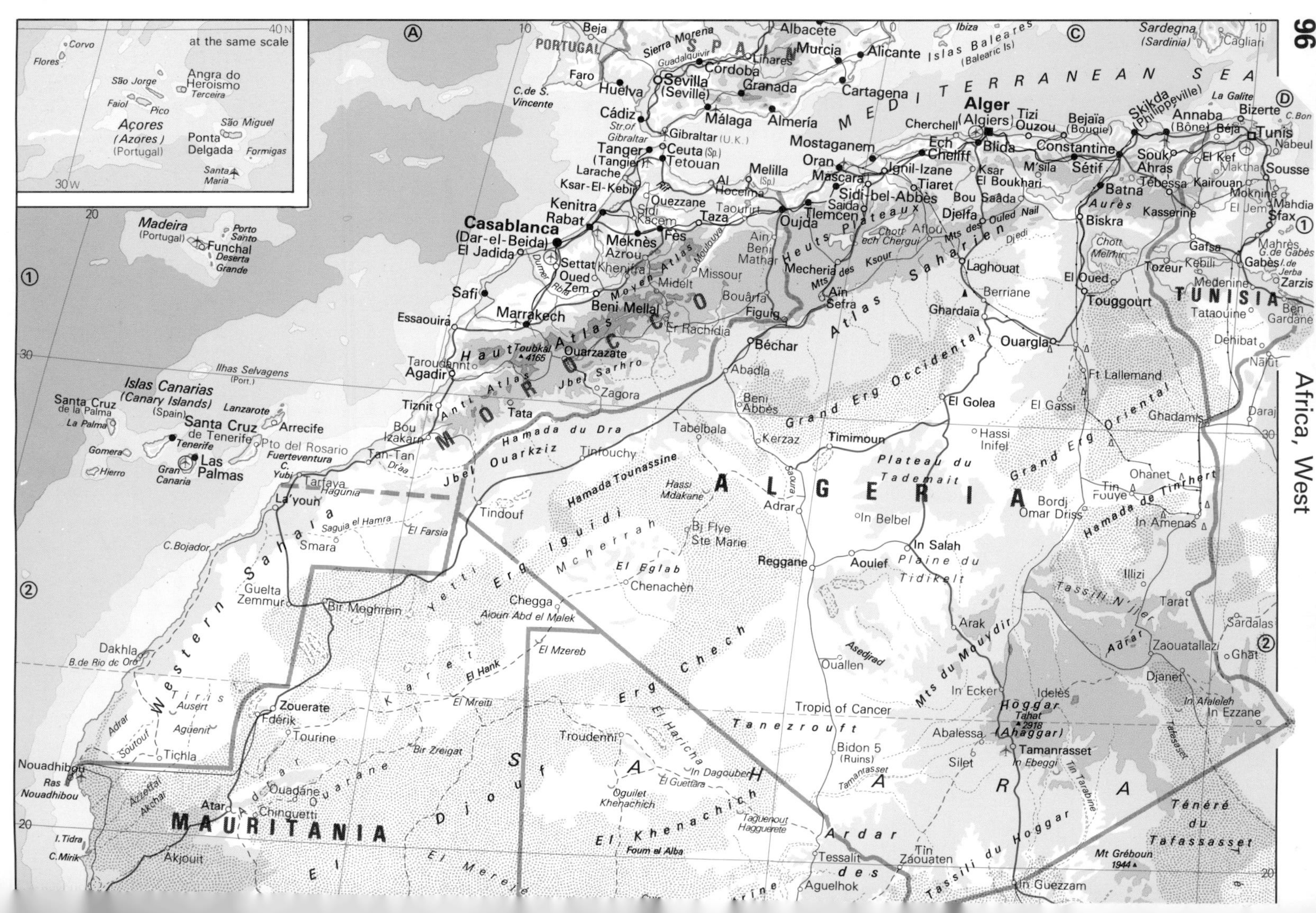
M E D I T E R R A N E A N S E A
Sardegna (Sardinia)
Cagliari
Islas Baleares (Balearic Is)
Ibiza
La Galite
C. Bon
S P A I N
PORTUGAL
Beja
Faro
C. de S. Vicente
Huelva
Cádiz
Sevilla (Seville)
Córdoba
Linares
Granada
Málaga
Almería
Murcia
Albacete
Cartagena
Alicante
Gibraltar (U.K.)
Str. of Gibraltar
Ceuta (Sp.)
Melilla (Sp.)
Tanger (Tangier)
Tetouan
Larache
Ksar-El-Kebir
Kenitra
Rabat
Casablanca (Dar-el-Beida)
El Jadida
Safi
Essaouira
Agadir
Taroudannt
Tiznit
Bou Izakarn
Tan-Tan
Marrakech
Settat
Oued Zem
Beni Mellal
Meknès
Fès
Azrou
Khenifra
Midelt
Taza
Oujda
Ouezzane
Al Hoceima
Missour
Er Rachidia
Ouarzazate
Zagora
Tata
Toubkal 4165
Haut Atlas
Moyen Atlas
Anti Atlas
M O R O C C O
Hamada du Dra
Jbel Ouarkziz
Tindouf
Tinfouchy
Figuig
Béchar
Abadla
Beni Abbès
Kerzaz
Adrar
Reggane
Timimoun
In Salah
Aoulef
Tabelbala
Oran
Mostaganem
Tlemcen
Sidi-bel-Abbès
Mascara
Saida
Tiaret
Ighil-Izane
Ech Cheliff
Cherchell
Alger (Algiers)
Blida
Tizi Ouzou
Bejaïa (Bougie)
Sétif
Constantine
Skikda (Philippeville)
Annaba (Bône)
Batna
Biskra
M'sila
Bou Saâda
Djelfa
Laghouat
Ghardaïa
Ouargla
El Golea
Touggourt
El Oued
Ft Lallemand
El Gassi
Hassi Inifel
Grand Erg Occidental
Grand Erg Oriental
Plateau du Tademait
Tassili N'Ajjer
Illizi
Djanet
Tamanrasset
Hoggar (Ahaggar) Tahat 2918
Ideles
In Ecker
Abalessa
Silet
Tin Zaouaten
Tessalit
Aguelhok
Bidon 5 (Ruins)
Ouallen
Tropic of Cancer
Tanezrouft
Erg Chech
Taoudenni
El Haricha
In Dagouber
Ghadamis
In Amenas
Bordj Omar Driss
In Guezzam
Mt Gréboun 1944
Ténéré du Tafassasset
A L G E R I A
T U N I S I A
Tunis
Bizerte
Béja
Nabeul
Sousse
Mahdia
Sfax
Kairouan
El Kef
Kasserine
Gafsa
Tozeur
Gabès
Medenine
Tataouine
Zarzis
Dehibat
Nalut
Ghat
Chegga
Bir Moghrein
Tarfaya
La'youn
Smara
Guelta Zemmur
Zouerate
F'dérik
Atar
Chinguetti
Ouadane
Akjoujt
Tichla
Dakhla
Nouadhibou
Ras Nouadhibou
C. Bojador
B. de Rio de Oro
W e s t e r n S a h a r a
M A U R I T A N I A
Islas Canarias (Canary Islands) (Spain)
Lanzarote
Arrecife
Fuerteventura
Pto del Rosario
Gran Canaria
Las Palmas
Tenerife
Santa Cruz de Tenerife
Gomera
Hierro
La Palma
Santa Cruz de la Palma
Ilhas Selvagens (Port.)
Madeira (Portugal)
Porto Santo
Funchal
Açores (Azores) (Portugal)
at the same scale
Corvo
Flores
Faial
Pico
São Jorge
Terceira
Angra do Heroismo
São Miguel
Ponta Delgada
Santa Maria
Formigas
40 N
30 W

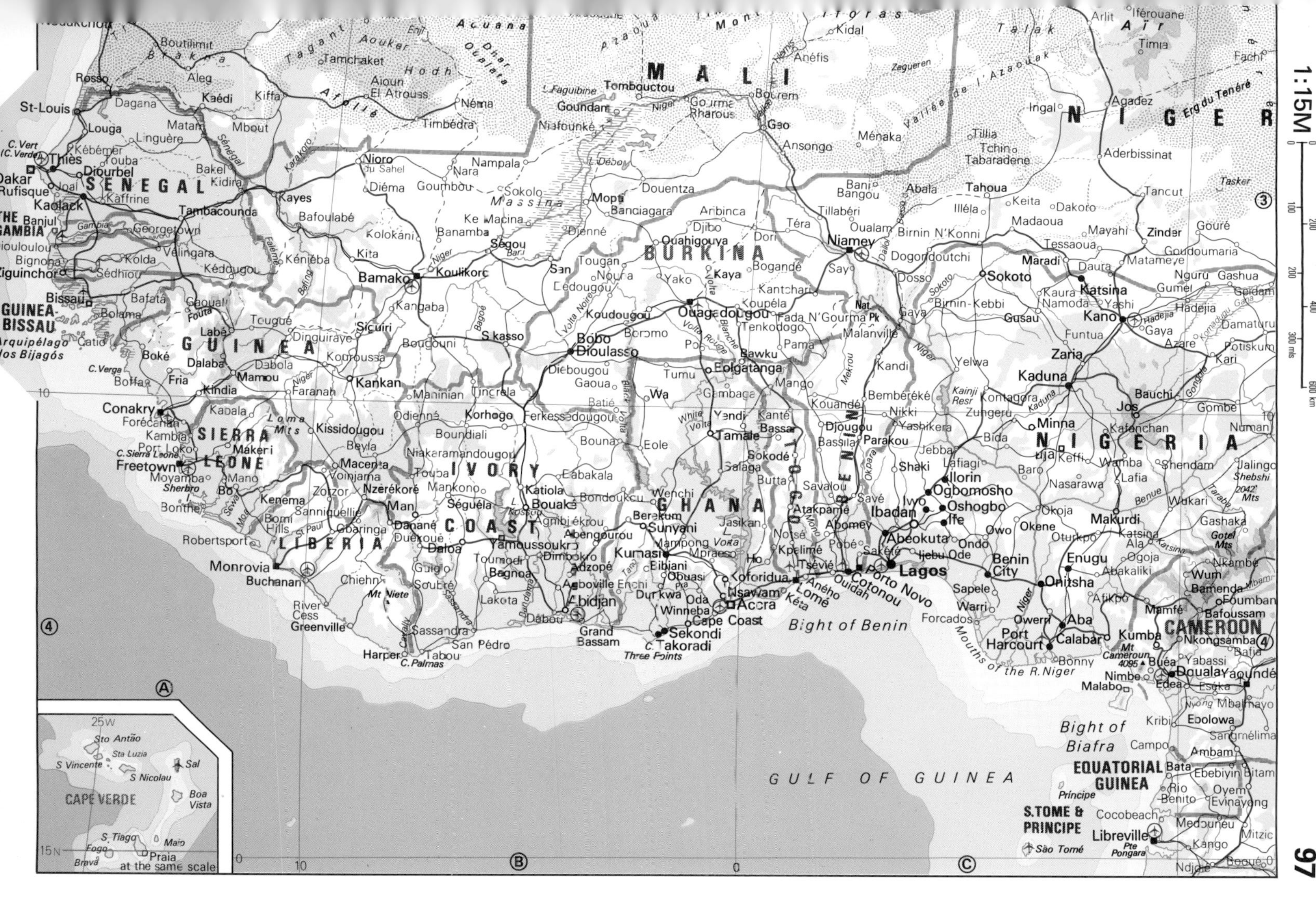
MALI
NIGER
BURKINA
NIGERIA
GHANA
IVORY COAST
LIBERIA
SIERRA LEONE
GUINEA
GUINEA-BISSAU
SENEGAL
THE GAMBIA
CAMEROON
EQUATORIAL GUINEA
S.TOME & PRINCIPE
CAPE VERDE
GULF OF GUINEA
Bight of Benin
Bight of Biafra
at the same scale

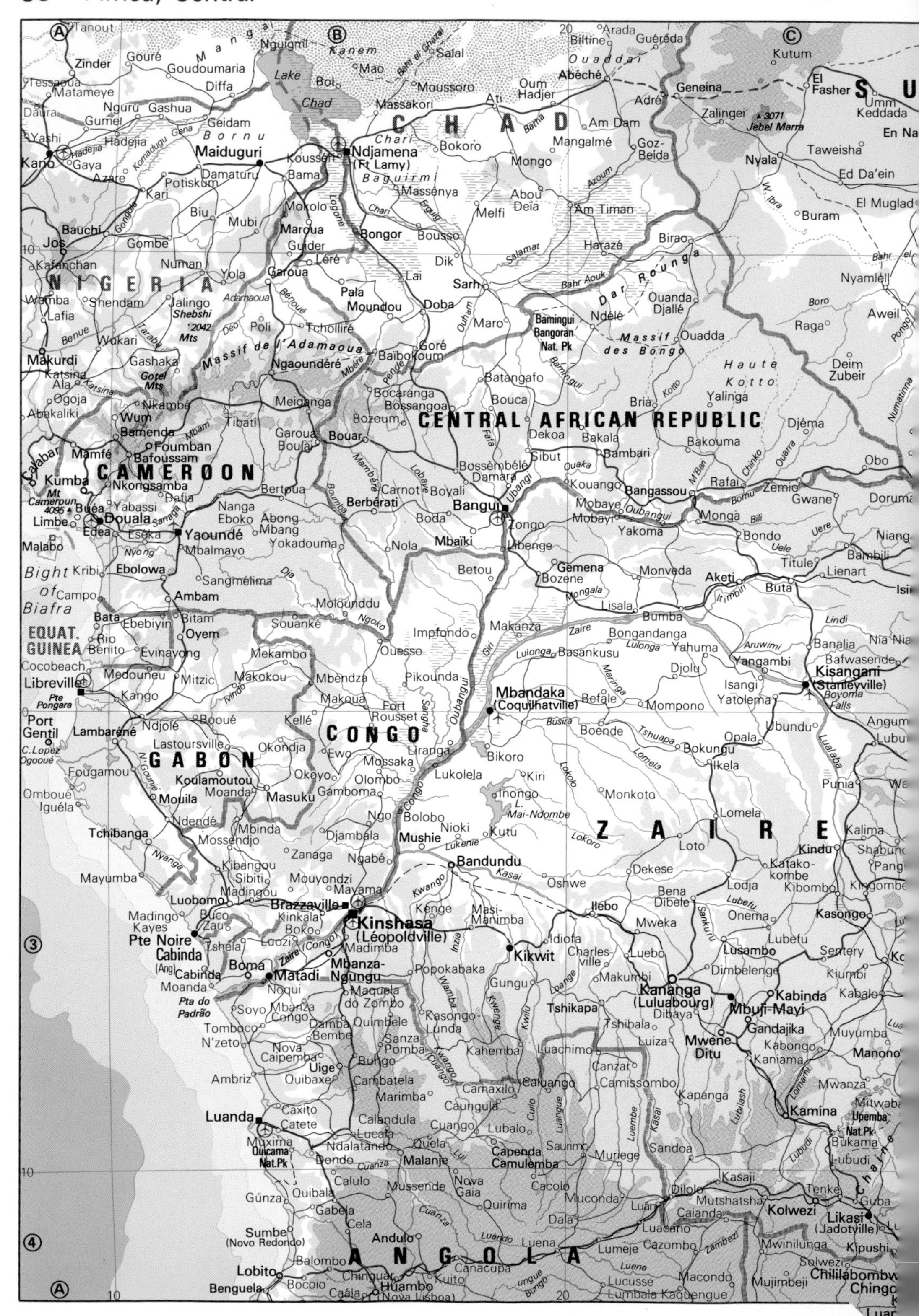
CHAD
NIGERIA
CAMEROON
CENTRAL AFRICAN REPUBLIC
EQUAT. GUINEA
GABON
CONGO
ZAIRE
ANGOLA
Lake Chad
Ndjamena (Ft Lamy)
Maiduguri
Kano
Jos
Abéché
Bangui
Yaoundé
Douala
Libreville
Brazzaville
Kinshasa (Léopoldville)
Mbandaka (Coquilhatville)
Kisangani (Stanleyville)
Luanda
Kananga (Luluabourg)
Lubumbashi
Likasi (Jadotville)
Kolwezi
Matadi
Bandundu
Kikwit
Mbuji-Mayi
Kamina
Huambo (Nova Lisboa)
Lobito
Benguela
Malabo
Bight of Biafra
Massif de l'Adamaoua
Ubangi
Zaire
Congo
Kasai
Lualaba

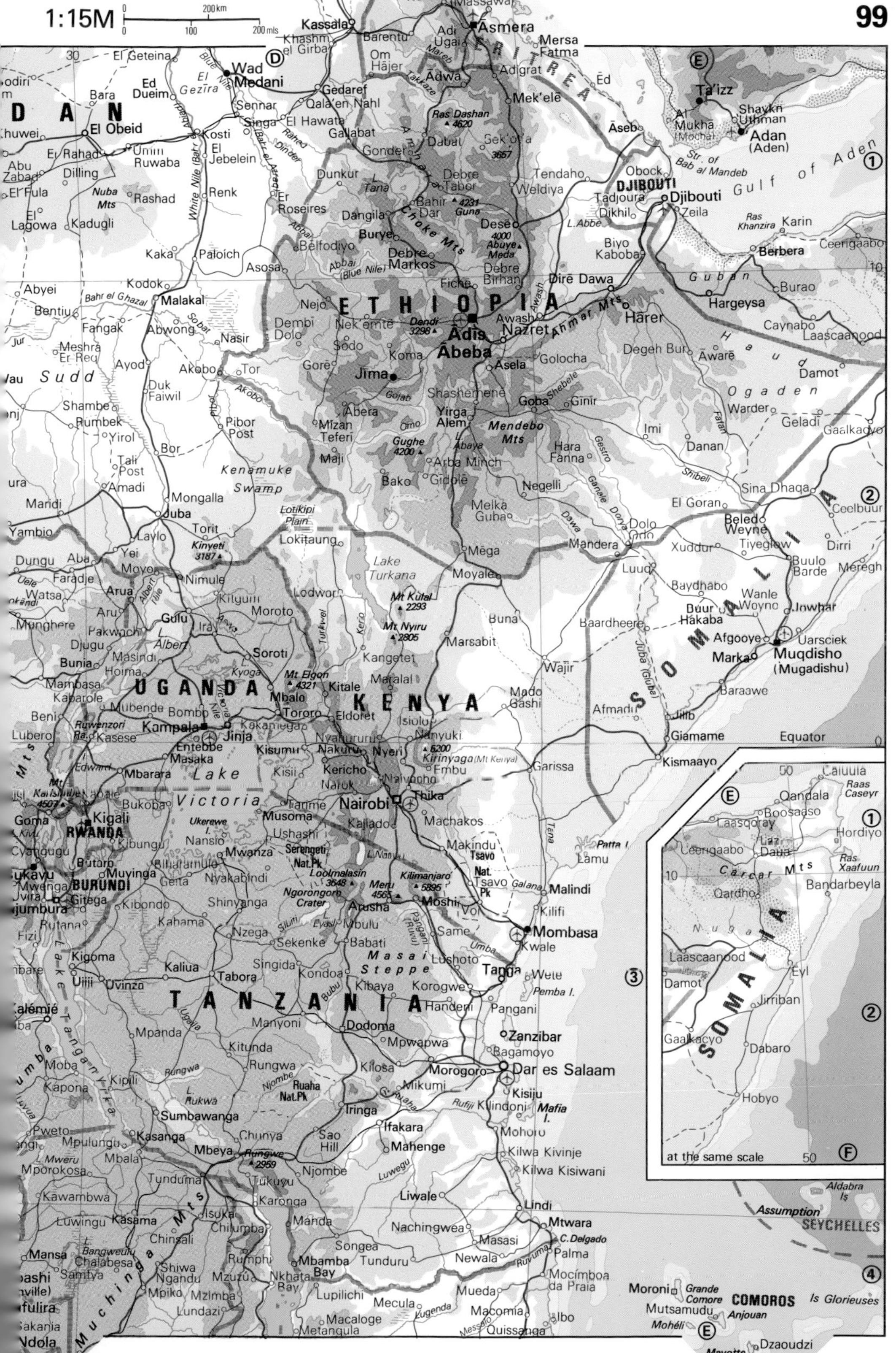
0 200 km
0 100 200 mls
ETHIOPIA
ERITREA
DJIBOUTI
SOMALIA
KENYA
UGANDA
TANZANIA
RWANDA
BURUNDI
SEYCHELLES
COMOROS
Gulf of Aden
Str. of Bab al Mandeb
Keren
Mits'iwa (Massawa)
Asmera
Kassala
Khashm el Girba
Barentu
Adi Ugai
Mersa Fatma
Om Hājer
Ādwa
Ādīgrat
Mek'elē
Ed
Āseb
Ta'izz
Al Mukhā (Mocha)
Shaykh Uthman
Adan (Aden)
Obock
Tadjoura
Djibouti
Dikhil
Zeila
Wad Medani
El Geteina
Ed Dueim
Bara
El Obeid
Gezira
Blue Nile
Sennar
Singa
Gedaref
Qala'en Nahl
El Hawata
Gallabat
Kosti
El Jebelein
Umm Ruwaba
Er Rahad
Abu Zabad
Dilling
El Fula
El Lagowa
Kadugli
Nuba Mts
Rashad
Renk
White Nile (Bahr el Abiad)
Er Roseires
Ras Dashan 4620
Dabat
Gonder
L. Tana
Bahir Dar
Debre Tabor
4231 Guna
Sek'ota
3657
Tendaho
Weldiya
Dunkur
Dangila
Choke Mts
Burye
Desē
4000 Abuye Meda
Debre Markos
Debre Birhan
Fichē
Belfodiyo
Abbai (Blue Nile)
Asosa
Kaka
Paloich
Kodok
Malakal
Abyei
Bentiu
Bahr el Ghazal
Sobat
Fangak
Abwong
Nasir
Meshra Er Req
Jur
Wau
Sudd
Ayod
Akobo
Tor
Duk Faiwil
Pibor
Pibor Post
Shambe
Rumbek
Yirol
Tali Post
Amadi
Bor
Kenamuke Swamp
Mongalla
Juba
Maridi
Yambio
Torit
Laylo
Kinyeti 3187
Yei
Lotikipi Plain
Lokitaung
Nejo
Dembī Dolo
Nek'emtē
Dendi 3298
Ādīs Ābeba
Awash
Nazret
Ahmar Mts
Dirē Dawa
Hārer
Biyo Kaboba
L. Abbe
Sodo
Gorē
Koma
Jīma
Asela
Golocha
Degeh Bur
Āwarē
Shashemenē
Goba
Gīnīr
Shebele
Ogaden
Haud
Mīzan Teferī
Abera
Yirga Alem
Mendebo Mts
Omo
Gughe 4200
Arba Minch
Hara Fanna
Imī
Danan
Warder
Geladi
Gaalkacyo
Maji
Bako
Gidolē
Negelli
Melka Guba
El Goran
Sina Dhaqa
Ceelbuur
Beled Weyne
Tiyeglow
Xuddur
Dolo Odo
Mandera
Mēga
Luuq
Moyale
Buulo Barde
Dirri
Meregh
Baydhabo
Wanle Woyno
Buur Hakaba
Jowhar
Afgooye
Uarsciek
Muqdisho (Mugadishu)
Marka
Baraawe
Baardheere
Juba (Giuba)
Wajir
Mado Gashi
Afmadu
Jilib
Giamame
Equator
Kismaayo
Garissa
Lake Turkana
Mt Kulal 2293
Mt Nyiru 2805
Buna
Marsabit
Lodwar
Turkwel
Kerio
Kangetet
Maralal
Isiolo
Nanyuki
5200 Kirinyaga (Mt Kenya)
Embu
Nyeri
Nyahururu
Eldoret
Kitale
Mt Elgon 4321
Mbalo
Tororo
Soroti
Moroto
Kitgum
Gulu
L. Kyoga
Lira
Dungu
Aba
Faradje
Uele
Watsa
Arua
Moyo
Nimule
Albert Nile
Aru
Pakwach
Mungbere
Djugu
Masindi
L. Albert
Bunia
Hoima
Mambasa
Kabarole
Mubende
Bombo
Beni
Lubero
Ruwenzori Ra.
Kasese
Kampala
Jinja
Entebbe
Masaka
Kisumu
Nakuru
Kericho
Kisii
Narok
Naivasha
Nairobi
Thika
Machakos
Kajiado
L. Edward
Mbarara
Lake Victoria
Mt Karisimbi 4507
Kabale
Goma
L. Kivu
Kigali
Bukoba
Ukerewe I.
Nansio
Tarime
Musoma
Ushashi
Mwanza
Serengeti Nat.Pk
Loolmalasin 3648
Ngorongoro Crater
Meru 4565
Kilimanjaro 5895
Arusha
Moshi
Makindu
Tsavo
Tsavo Nat. Pk
Voi
Galana
Malindi
Kilifi
Mombasa
Kwale
Lamu
Patta I.
Tana
Cyangugu
Bukavu
Butare
Muyinga
Bujumbura
Gitega
Biharamulo
Geita
Nyakabindi
Shinyanga
Kibondo
Kahama
Rutana
Fizi
Nzega
Sekenke
Mbulu
Babati
Same
Lushoto
Tanga
Wete
Pemba I.
Kigoma
Ujiji
Uvinza
Kaliua
Tabora
Singida
Kondoa
Masai Steppe
Kibaya
Korogwe
Handeni
Pangani
Bubu
Kalémié
Lake Tanganyika
Ugalla
Manyoni
Dodoma
Mpwapwa
Zanzibar
Bagamoyo
Dar es Salaam
Mpanda
Kitunda
Rungwa
Moba
Kapona
Kipili
L. Rukwa
Ruaha Nat.Pk
Kilosa
Morogoro
Mikumi
Kisiju
Rufiji
Kilindoni
Mafia I.
Mohoro
Sumbawanga
Iringa
Ifakara
Mahenge
Pweto
Mpulungu
Kasanga
Chunya
Sao Hill
L. Mweru
Mbala
Mbeya
Rungwe 2959
Njombe
Mporokosa
Tunduma
Tukuyu
Kawambwa
Karonga
Isoka
Kilwa Kivinje
Kilwa Kisiwani
Luwegu
Liwale
Lindi
Luwingu
Kasama
Chilumba
Manda
Nachingwea
Mtwara
Masasi
C. Delgado
Chinsali
L. Bangweulu
Mansa
Chalabesa
Samfya
Shiwa Ngandu
Muchinga Mts
Rumphi
Mzuzu
Songea
Tunduru
Mbamba Bay
Newala
Ruvuma
Palma
Mocímboa da Praia
Nkhata Bay
Mzimba
Mpika
Lundazi
Lupilichi
Mueda
Mecula
Lugenda
Macomia
Macaloge
Metangula
Messalo
Quissanga
Ibo
Ndola
Luanshya
Mufulira
Mukhya
Ceerigaabo
Ras Khanzira
Karin
Berbera
Guban
Burao
Hargeysa
Caynabo
Laascaanood
Damot
Ras Dashan
Aldabra Is
Assumption
Moroni
Grande Comore
Mutsamudu
Anjouan
Mohéli
Mayotte (Fr.)
Dzaoudzi
Is Glorieuses
Caluula
Raas Caseyr
Qandala
Boosaaso
Laasqoray
Hordiyo
Ceengaabo
Dahar
Ras Xaafuun
Carcar Mts
Bandarbeyla
Qardho
Nugaal
Eyl
Jirriban
Dabaro
Hobyo
at the same scale

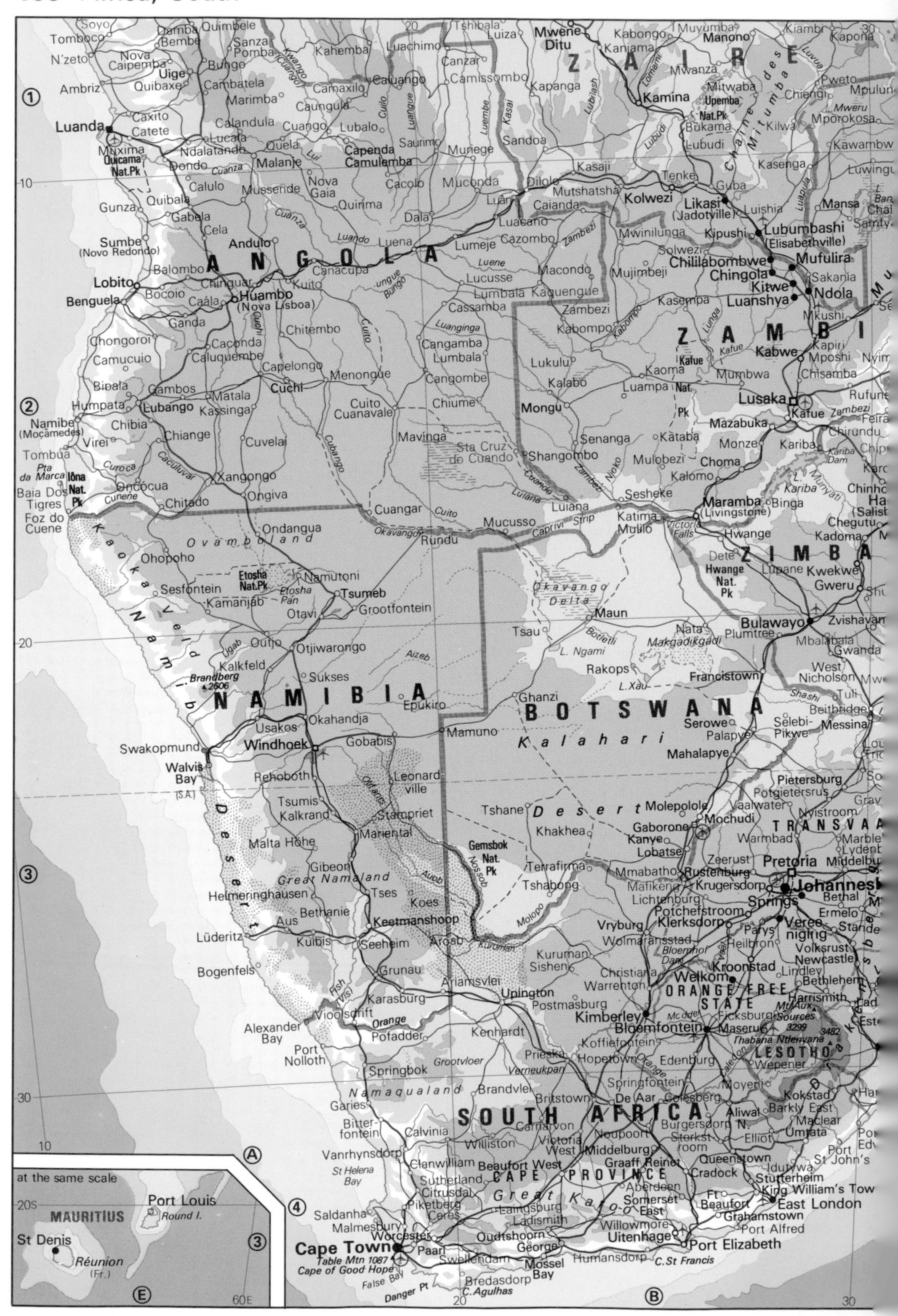

Soyo Camba Quimbele Tshibala Luiza Mwene Kabongo Muyumba Kiambi
Tomboco Nova Bembe Sanza Kahemba Luachimo Ditu Kaniama Manono Kapona
N'zeto Caipemba Pomba Camaxilo Canzar Kaniama Z A I R E Mpulung
Ambriz Uige Quibaxe Cambatela Marimba Camissombo Kapanga Mwanza Chiengi Mpulung
① Luanda Caxito Catete Calandula Caungula Kamina Mitwaba Pweto Mporokosa
Mixima Quicama Ndalatando Cuango Lubalo Saurimo Sandoa Bukama Kasenga Kawambw
Nat.Pk Dondo Malanje Quela Capenda Camulemba Kasaji Kasenga Luwingu
10 Calulo Mussende Nova Cacolo Muconda Dilolo Tenke Guba
Gunza Quibala Gaia Quirima Dala Luacano Caianda Kolwezi Likasi Luishia Mansa Bangw
Gabela Cela Andulo Cazombo Mutshatsha (Jadotville) Kipushi Lubumbashi Chili
Sumbe Balombo Chinguar Lumeje Luena Mwinilunga Solwezi (Elisabethville) Mufulira
(Novo Redondo) Lobito Huambo Kuito Cangamba Lumbala Kaguengue Mujimbeji Chililabombwe Ndola
Benguela Bocoio Caála (Nova Lisboa) Chitembo Cassamba Zambezi Kasempa Chingola Sakania Kitwe Luanshya
Ganda Chongoroi Caconda Capelongo Luanginga Kabompo ZAMBI Mushi Luanshya
Camucuio Caluquembe Menongue Cangamba Lumbala Cangombe Lukulu Mumbwa Chisamba Mposhi
Bipala Matala Cuchi Kalabo Luampa Nat. Kabwe Kapiri Nyi
② Namibe Humpata Gambos Kassinga Cuito Chiume Mongu Pk Mazabuka Kafue Zambezi Feira
(Moçâmedes) Lubango Chibia Cuanavale Sta Cruz Shangombo Senanga Kataba Monze Kariba Chirundu Chip
Virei Chiange Cuvelai do Cuando Mavinga Mulobezi Choma Kariba Dam
Tômbua Curoca Xangongo Cuito Luiana Sesheke Maramba Kariba Chinh
Pta Caculuvar Ongiva Cuando Luiana Strip Katima (Livingstone) Binga Ha(Salis
da Marca Iôna Onbocua Cuangar Caprivi Mulilo Victoria Hwange Chegutu
Baia Dos Nat. Cunene Chitado Mucusso Falls Dete ZIMBA Kadoma
Tigres Pk Ohopoho Rundu Okavango Hwange Lupane Kwekwe
Foz do Ondangwa Namutoni Delta Nat. Gweru
Cuene Etosha Etosha Nata Pk Zvishavan
Sesfontein Nat.Pk Pan Maun Makgadikgadi Bulawayo
Kamanjab Tsumeb Botleti Mbalabala Gwanda
Otavi Grootfontein L. Ngami West Beitbridge
Outjo Tsau Rakops L.Xau Francistown Nicholson Mw
Otjiwarongo Ghanzi Serowe Sélebi- Messina
Kalkfeld Sukses Pikwe Ful
Brandberg B O T S W A N A Palapye Sir
△2606 Okahandja Mahalapye
N A M I B I A Epukiro K a l a h a r i
Usakos Gobabis Tshane Molepolole Pietersburg
Swakopmund Windhoek Leonard- D e s e r t Mochudi Potgietersrus Grav
Walvis Rehoboth ville Gaborone Warmbad Nylstroom So
Bay Tsumis Mamuno Khakhea Kanye TRANSVAA Marble
(S.A.) Kalkrand Stampriet Lobatse Zeerust Lydent
Malta Hohe Mariental Terrafirma Mmabatho Rustenburg Pretoria Middelbu
Gibeon Gemsbok Tshabong Mafikeng Krugersdorp Johannes!
Helmeringhausen Great Namaland Nat. Lichtenburg Klerksdorp Springs
Lüderitz Aus Tses Pk Potchefstroom Vereen Bethal
Bethanie Koes Kuruman Vryburg Parys niglng Ermelo Stande
Keetmanshoop Aroab Sishen Wolmaransstad Heilbron Volksrust
Kuibis Christiana Warrenton Bloemhof Kroonstad Newcastle
Bogenfels Seeheim Dam Lindley Bethlehem
Grunau Upington Postmasburg ORANGE FREE Harrismith
Alexander Karasburg Kimberley McDona STATE Ficksburg Sources
Bay Vioolsdrift Prieska Maseru 3299 Est
Port Orange Koffiefontein Bloemfontein LESOTHO 3482
Nolloth Pofadder Kenhardt Hopetown Edenburg Thabana Ntlenyana K
Springbok De Aar Colesberg Moyeni Wepener
30 Garies Brandvlei Britstown Springfontein Kokstad
Bitter- Calvinia SOUTH AFRICA Aliwal Barkly East
fontein Carnarvon Burgersdorp N Maclear Umtata Po
Namaqualand Williston Victoria Middelburg Dordrecht King William's Tow
Vanrhynsdorp West Elliot Indutwa East London
St Helena Clanwilliam Beaufort West Graaff-Reinet Cradock Queenstown Stutterheim
Bay Sutherland CAPE PROVINCE Aberdeen Somerset E Port Alfred
Saldanha Citrusdal Piketberg Great Karoo Willowmore Grahamstown St John's
Malmesbury Ceres Ladismith Oudtshoorn Uitenhage Port Elizabeth
Cape Town Worcester George Humansdorp
Table Mtn 1087 Paarl Swellendam Mossel C.St Francis
Cape of Good Hope Bredasdorp Bay
False Bay Danger Pt C.Agulhas

200 400 600 km
100 200 300 mls

L. Rukwa
Ruaha Nat.Pk.
Sumbawanga
Chunya
Iringa
Ifakara
Mikumi
Rufiji
Kilindoni
Mafia I.
Kisiju

SEYCHELLES

Providence

Mbeya
Rungwe ▲2959
Sao Hill
Mahenge
Kilwa Kivinje
Kilwa Kisiwani

Aldabra Is
Assumption
Cosmoledo Is

Farquhar Is

Njombe
Liwale
Lindi
Mtwara

Is Glorieuses

Tundama
Karonga
Nachingwea
Masasi
C.Delgado
Mocímboa da Praia

Moroni
Grande Comore
COMOROS

Tj. Babaomby
Antseranana

Isoka
Chitumbai
Mbamba Bay
Songea
Tunduru
Newala
Palma

Mutsamudu
Anjouan

C. St Sébastien
▲1478 Mgne d'Ambre

Rumphi
Nkhata Bay
Lupilichi
Mecula
Macomia
Ibo

Mohéli
Mayotte (Fr.)
Dzaoudzi

Ambilobe
Nosy Be
Ambanja

Massif du Tsaratanana ▲2876

Vohimarina

Lichinga
Maúa
Namuno
Namapa
Memba

Analalava

Bealanana
Sambava

MADAGASCAR
(MALAGASY REP.)

Antse) Antsohihy
Antalaha
Maroantsetra
C.Masoala

MOZAMBIQUE

Nampula
Mahajanga (Majunga)
Marovoay
Mampikony
Mananara

Mozambique Channel

Quelimane

Tanjona Vilanandro
Besalampy

Juan de Nova (Fr.)

Maintirano
Nosy Barren

Tsiroanomandidy
Moramanga
Antananarivo (Tananarive)

Toamasina (Tamatave)

Sofala (Beira)

Morondava
Manabo
Antsirabe
Mahanoro

Nova Mambone
Bartolomeu Dias

Bassas da India (Fr.)

Fianarantsoa

Vilanculos
Pta de Barra Falsa

Europa (Fr.)

Morombe
Tanjona Ankaboa

Ankazoabo

Manakara

Funhalouro

Massinga
Morrumbene
Inhambane
Inharrime

Toliara
B.de St Augustin

Betioky
Bekily
Isoanala

Tropic of Capricorn

Xai Xai
Manhica

Ampanihy
Beloha
Tshombe
Ambovombe
Tanjona Vohimena

Maputo (Lourenço Marques)

1:7.5M

Pretoria
Johannesburg
Krugersdorp
Soweto
Springs
Vereeniging
Klerksdorp

Maputo
SWAZILAND
Manzini

Potchefstroom

ORANGE FREE STATE
Kimberley
Bloemfontein

NATAL
Durban
Pietermaritzburg
LESOTHO
Maseru

Welkom
Ladysmith
Richard's Bay
L.St Lucia

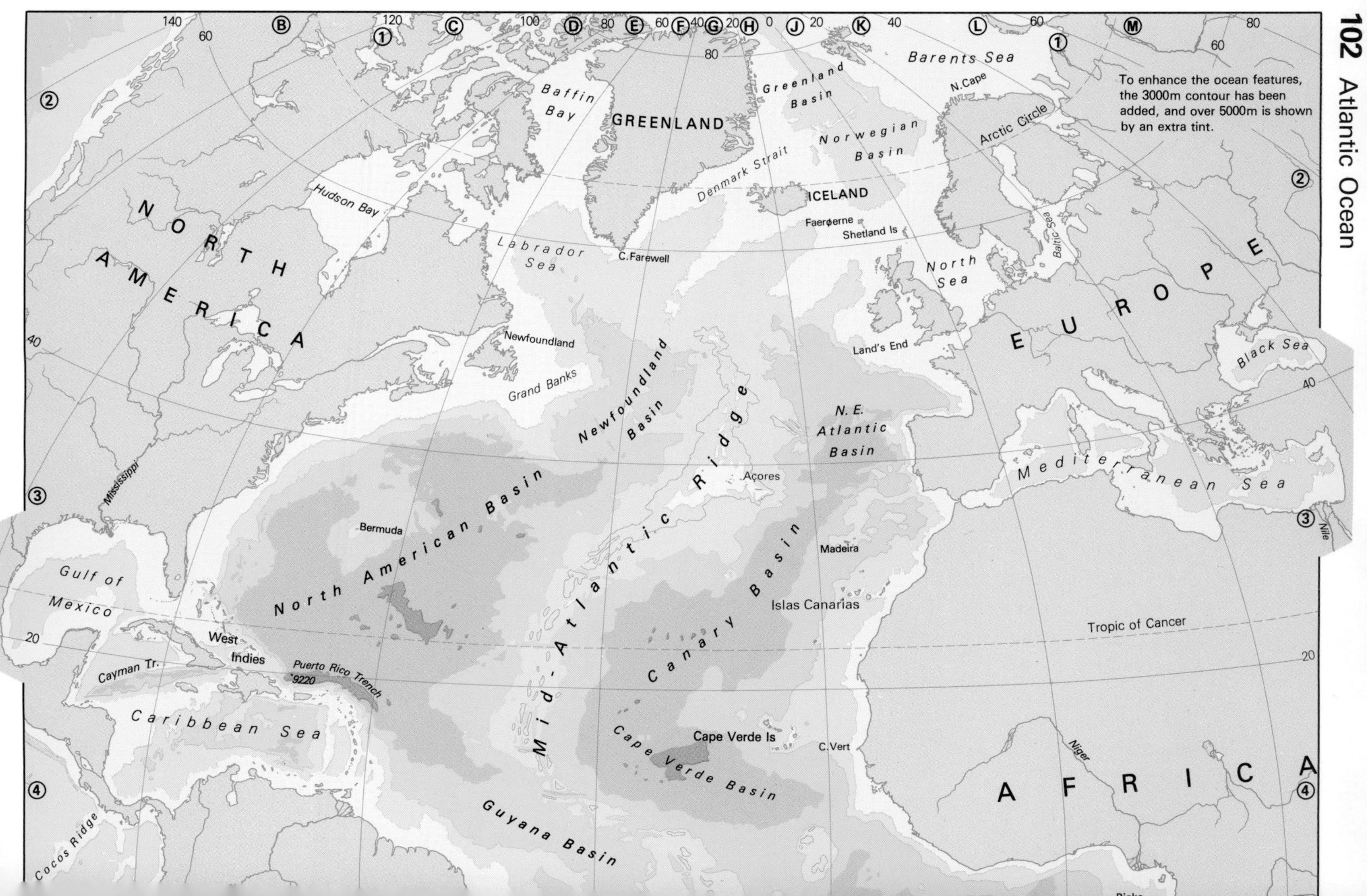

To enhance the ocean features, the 3000m contour has been added, and over 5000m is shown by an extra tint.

EUROPE

AFRICA

NORTH AMERICA

GREENLAND

ICELAND

Black Sea

Baltic Sea

North Sea

Barents Sea

Mediterranean Sea

Nile

Niger

Binke

Tropic of Cancer

Arctic Circle

N.Cape

Greenland Basin

Norwegian Basin

Denmark Strait

C.Farewell

Faeröerne

Shetland Is

Land's End

N.E. Atlantic Basin

Madeira

Islas Canarias

C.Vert

Cape Verde Is

Cape Verde Basin

Canary Basin

Mid-Atlantic Ridge

Açores

Newfoundland Basin

Baffin Bay

Labrador Sea

Newfoundland

Grand Banks

North American Basin

Bermuda

Guyana Basin

Puerto Rico Trench

9220

West Indies

Caribbean Sea

Hudson Bay

Mississippi

Gulf of Mexico

Cayman Tr.

Cocos Ridge

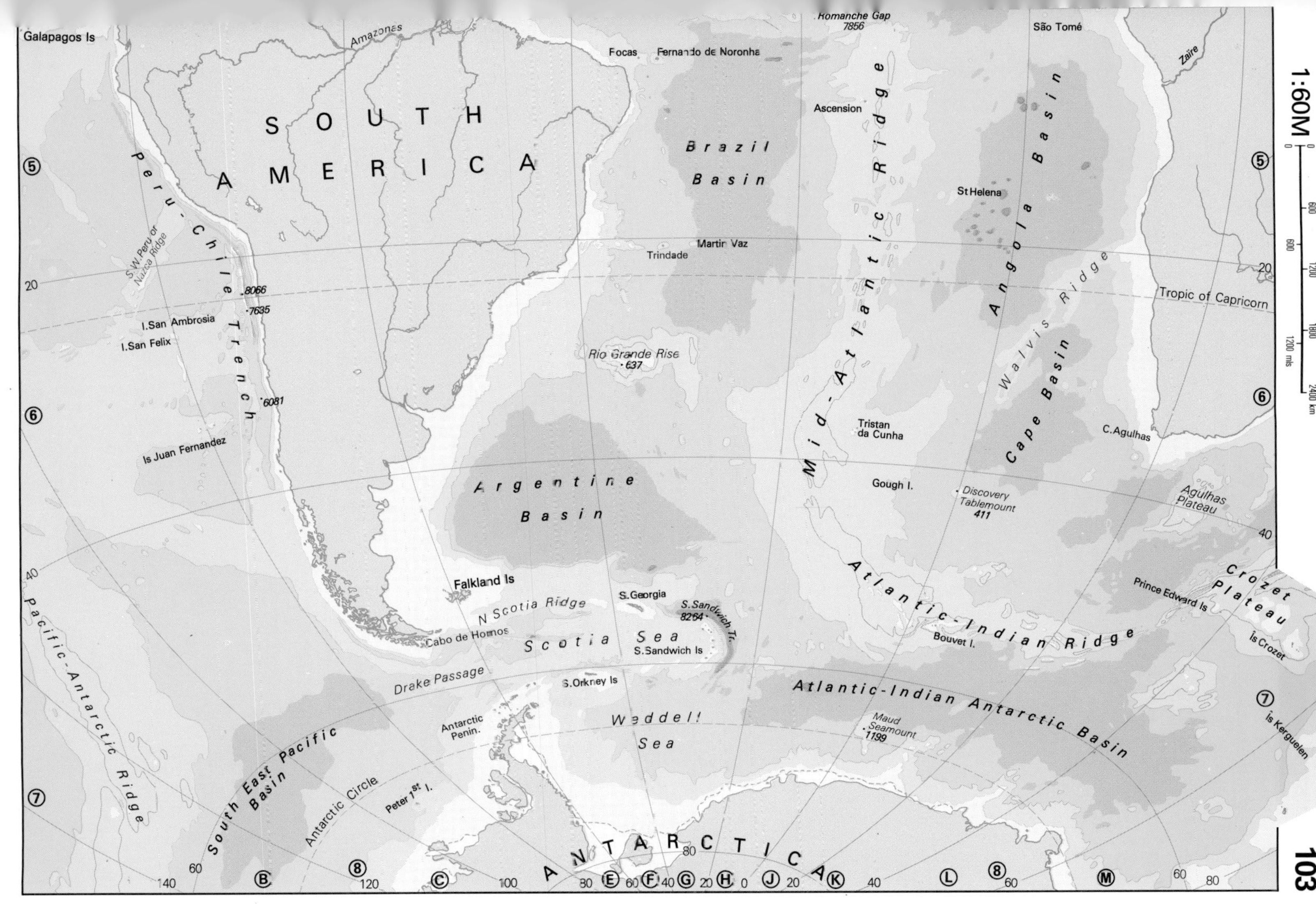

0   600   1200   1800   2400 km
0   600   1200 mls

Zaire

São Tomé

Tropic of Capricorn

Agulhas Plateau

Crozet Plateau

Is Crozet

Prince Edward Is

C.Agulhas

Is Kerguelen

Angola Basin

Walvis Ridge

Cape Basin

St Helena

Atlantic–Indian Ridge

Discovery Tablemount 411

Bouvet I.

Atlantic–Indian Antarctic Basin

Maud Seamount 1159

Homanche Gap 7856

Mid-Atlantic Ridge

Ascension

Tristan da Cunha

Gough I.

Brazil Basin

Fernando de Noronha

Martin Vaz

Trindade

Rio Grande Rise 637

S. Sandwich Tr. 8264

S. Georgia

S. Sandwich Is

Focas

Waddell Sea

Argentine Basin

Scotia Sea

S.Orkney Is

Amazones

SOUTH AMERICA

Falkland Is

N Scotia Ridge

Cabo de Hornos

Drake Passage

Antarctic Penin.

ANTARCTICA

Peter I. Is

Antarctic Circle

Galapagos Is

Peru–Chile Trench

I.San Ambrosia

I.San Felix

Is Juan Fernandez

S.W.Peru or Nazca ridge

8066

7635

6081

South East pacific Basin

Pacific–Antarctic Ridge

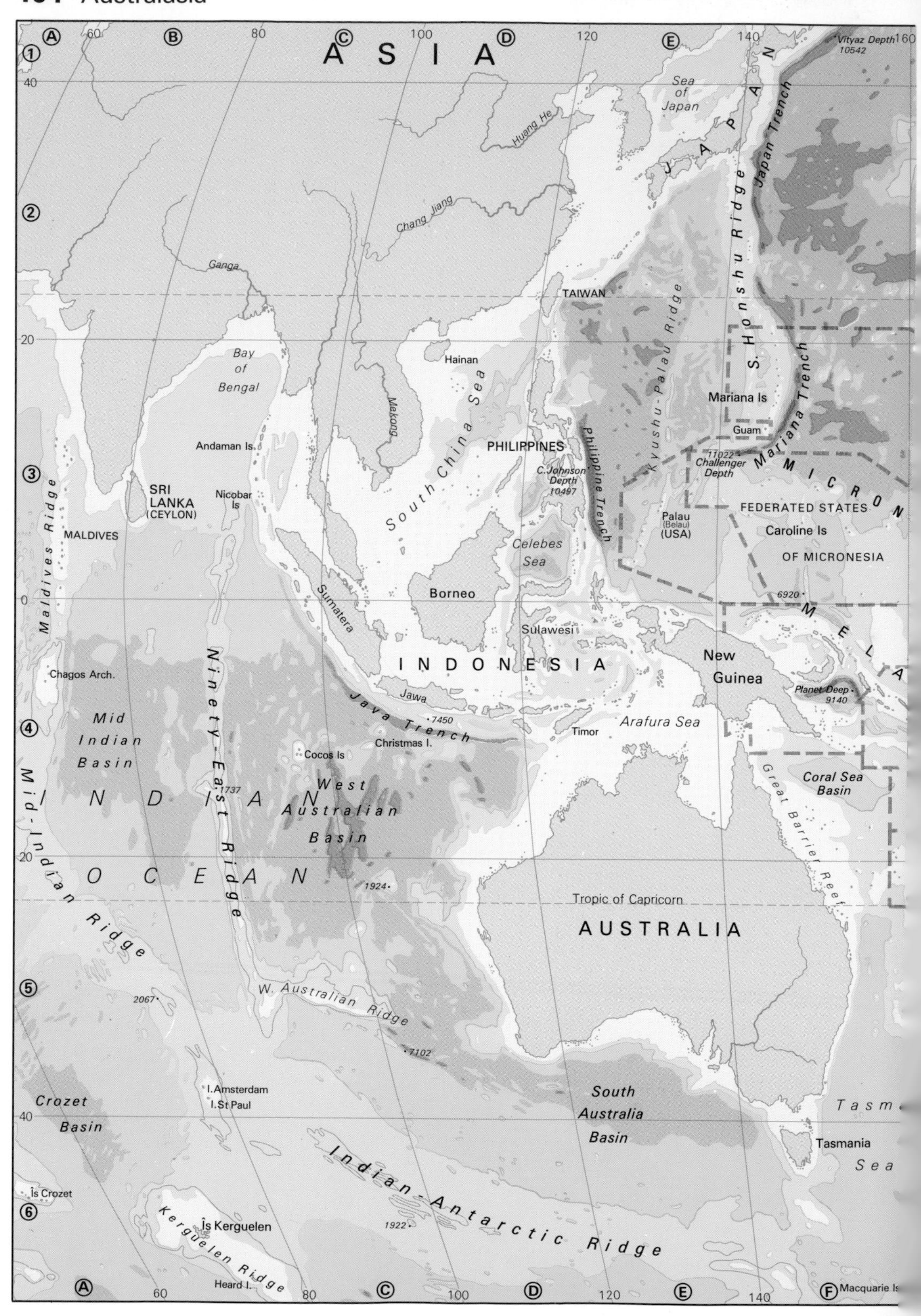

A S I A

Vityaz Depth 160
10542

Sea of Japan

Huang He

Chang Jiang

Ganga

40

① Ⓐ 60 Ⓑ 80 Ⓒ 100 Ⓓ 120 Ⓔ 140

②

20

TAIWAN

Hainan

Bay of Bengal

Mekong

Andaman Is.

③

SRI LANKA (CEYLON)   Nicobar Is

Maldives Ridge

MALDIVES

Chagos Arch.

South China Sea

PHILIPPINES

C. Johnson Depth 10497

Philippine Trench

Kyushu-Palau Ridge

S. Honshu Ridge

Japan Trench

J A P A N

Mariana Is

Mariana Trench

Guam

11022 Challenger Depth

Palau (Belau) (USA)

M I C R O N

FEDERATED STATES

Caroline Is

OF MICRONESIA

6920

M E L A

Celebes Sea

Borneo

Sulawesi

New Guinea

Planet Deep 9140

④

Mid Indian Basin

Ninety-East Ridge

I N D I A N

Sumatera

Java Trench

Jawa

7450

Christmas I.

Cocos Is

West Australian Basin

1737

I N D I A N

O C E A N

Timor

Arafura Sea

INDONESIA

Great Barrier Reef

Coral Sea Basin

1924

Tropic of Capricorn

AUSTRALIA

⑤

2067

W. Australian Ridge

7102

I. Amsterdam
I. St Paul

South Australia Basin

T a s m

Tasmania

Sea

Crozet Basin

40

Is Crozet

⑥

Kerguelen Ridge

Is Kerguelen

Indian-Antarctic Ridge

1922

Heard I.

Macquarie Is

Ⓐ 60 Ⓑ 80 Ⓒ 100 Ⓓ 120 Ⓔ 140 Ⓕ

600   1200   1800   2400 km
0   600   1200 mls

G   180   H   160   J   140   K   120   L   100   ①   40

NORTH
AMERICA

Mendocino Seascarp   2926

Murray Seascarp   ②

18°   Midway Is   Tropic of Cancer   C.Falso
104°

Hawaiian
Islands   20   Is Revilla
Gigedo

Mid-Pacific Mountains   1477·   *Clarion Fracture Zone*   ③

P   Marshall
Is   ·6150

KIRIBATI   Line Is   Equator   0

NAURU   E S I A   French Polynesia   East Pacific Ridge   ④

Phoenix Is   Îs Marquises

SOLOMON
ISLANDS   TUVALU

Tokelau
(N.Z.)   American
Samoa
WRN.   Samoa
Wallis &   SAMOA   Cook   Îs de la   Îs Tuamotu
VANUATU   (Fr.) Futuna   Is.   Société
FIJI   TONGA   (N.Z.)   Tahiti
Niue   Cook Is   20

Nouvelle   Îs Tubuai   Îs Gambier
Calédonie   Horizon Depth
(Fr.)   10882

S. Fiji   Pitcairn (U.K.)   Gala y Gómez
Basin   1044   I.de Pascua   ⑤

Norfolk I.   10047   S o u t h W e s t
P a c i f i c
N.Cape   B a s i n

NEW   Pacific-Antarctic Ridge   40
ZEALAND

Chatham Is   ⑥

New Zealand
Plateau
Auckland Is   732
Campbell I.
G   180   H   160   J   140   K   120   L   100   M

PACIFIC OCEAN   POLYNESIA   MELANESIA   Emperor Seamount Chain   International Date Line   Tonga Trench   Kermadec Trench   Lord Howe Rise   Norfolk I. Ridge

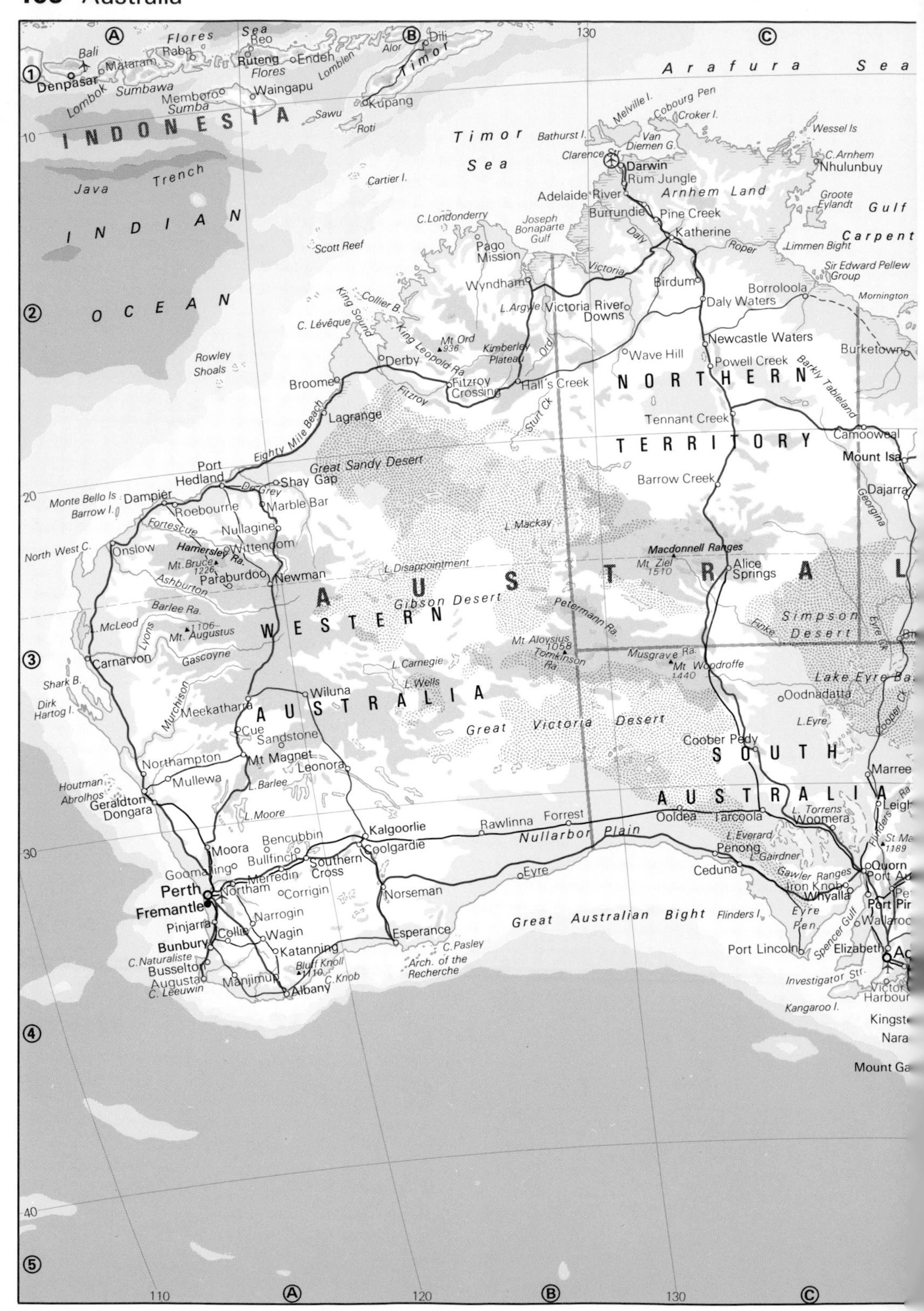
Flores Sea
Bali
Mataram
Denpasar
Lombok
Sumbawa
Raba
Reo
Ruteng
Endeh
Flores
Memboro
Sumba
Waingapu
Alor
Dili
Timor
Lomblen
Kupang
Sawu
Roti
INDONESIA
Java Trench
INDIAN OCEAN
Arafura Sea
Timor Sea
Melville I.
Cobourg Pen
Croker I.
Wessel Is
Bathurst I.
Van Diemen G.
Clarence Str.
Darwin
C.Arnhem
Nhulunbuy
Rum Jungle
Arnhem Land
Adelaide River
Groote Eylandt
Gulf of Carpentaria
Cartier I.
Burrundie
Pine Creek
C.Londonderry
Joseph Bonaparte Gulf
Katherine
Daly
Roper
Limmen Bight
Scott Reef
Pago Mission
Victoria
Sir Edward Pellew Group
Wyndham
Birdum
Borroloola
Mornington
King Sound
Collier B.
L.Argyle
Victoria River Downs
Daly Waters
C. Lévêque
King Leopold Ra
Mt Ord 936
Kimberley Plateau
Ord
Newcastle Waters
Rowley Shoals
Derby
Wave Hill
Powell Creek
Burketown
Broome
Fitzroy Crossing
Hall's Creek
NORTHERN TERRITORY
Barkly Tableland
Fitzroy
Sturt Ck
Eighty Mile Beach
Lagrange
Tennant Creek
Camooweal
Mount Isa
Port Hedland
Great Sandy Desert
Shay Gap
De Grey
Barrow Creek
Monte Bello Is
Barrow I.
Dampier
Roebourne
Marble Bar
Dajarra
Fortescue
Nullagine
L.Mackay
Georgina
North West C.
Onslow
Hamersley Ra.
Wittenoom
Macdonnell Ranges
Mt. Bruce 1226
Paraburdoo
Newman
L. Disappointment
Mt Ziel 1510
Alice Springs
Ashburton
AUSTRALIA
Gibson Desert
Barlee Ra.
Petermann Ra.
Simpson Desert
L.McLeod
Lyons
1106 Mt. Augustus
WESTERN AUSTRALIA
Finke
Eyre Ck
Mt Aloysius 1058
Tomkinson Ra.
Musgrave Ra.
Mt Woodroffe 1440
Carnarvon
Gascoyne
L. Carnegie
Shark B.
L.Wells
Lake Eyre Basin
Dirk Hartog I.
Wiluna
Oodnadatta
Murchison
Meekatharra
Cooper Ck
Great Victoria Desert
L.Eyre
Cue
Sandstone
Coober Pedy
SOUTH AUSTRALIA
Northampton
Mt Magnet
Leonora
Marree
Mullewa
Houtman Abrolhos
L. Barlee
Geraldton
Dongara
Leigh
Flinders Ra.
L.Moore
Ooldea
Tarcoola
L. Torrens
Woomera
Rawlinna
Forrest
Kalgoorlie
Nullarbor Plain
L.Everard
St Ma 1189
Moora
Bencubbin
Coolgardie
Penong
L. Gairdner
Bullfinch
Southern Cross
Quorn
Goomalling
Merredin
Eyre
Ceduna
Gawler Ranges
Perth
Northam
Corrigin
Norseman
Iron Knob
Whyalla
Fremantle
Narrogin
Great Australian Bight
Flinders I.
Eyre Pen.
Port Pir
Pinjarra
Collie
Wagin
Esperance
Spencer Gulf
Wallaroo
Bunbury
Katanning
C.Pasley
Port Lincoln
Elizabeth
C.Naturaliste
Busselton
Bluff Knoll 1110
Arch. of the Recherche
Augusta
C. Leeuwin
Manjimup
Albany
C.Knob
Investigator Str.
Victor Harbour
Kangaroo I.
Kingst
Nara
Mount Ga
110
120
130
10
20
30
40
A
B
C
1
2
3
4
5

200 400 600 800 km
200 400 mls

140

E PAPUA SOLOMON

Darnu New Georgia Santa Isabel ISLANDS
Gulf of Papua Popondetta Kokoda Florida Is Malaita Stewart Is
Port Moresby Tobriand Is Woodlark Guadalcanal Honiara Maramasike
NEW GUINEA D'Entrecasteaux Islands San Cristobal
Kupiano Alotau Misima Louisiade Rennell
Samarai Arch.
Torres Strait Saibai Tagula Rossel
Pr.of Wales I. C. York Récifs
Somerset d'Entrecasteaux
Weipa Cape Îles Chesterfield Îles Bélep
York C. Grenville (Fr.)
Coen Coral Sea
Peninsula Princess Charlotte B. Island Territories Mueo Uvéa
Mitchell River Laura Willis Group Nouvelle Lifu
Wellesley Is Cooktown Calédonie Bourail
Normanton Mt Bartle Frere Cairns Coringa Is (Fr.) Nouméa
Croydon Ravenshoe Innisfail Île des Pins
Forsayth Palm Is Marion Reef
Ingham Bellona
Townsville Ayr Reefs
Cloncurry Richmond Charters Towers Swain Tropic of Capricorn
Hughenden Bowen Proserpine Reefs
Selwyn Collinsville Cato PACIFIC
QUEENSLAND Mackay Sarina Northumberland Is
Winton Clermont Marlborough OCEAN
Longreach Emerald Rockhampton
Barcaldine Mount Morgan
Blackall Gladstone
Windorah Theodore Bundaberg Fraser or
Charleville Taroom Gt Sandy I.
Quilpie Roma Maryborough
Milparinka Miles Dalby Gympie
St George Toowoomba Brisbane
Cunnamulla Goondiwindi Ipswich
Bourke Walgett Stanthorpe Warwick
Narrabri Moree Glen Innes Lismore Norfolk I.
Tamworth Armidale Casino (Aust.)
Cobar Grafton
Wilcannia Nyngan Port Macquarie
Menindee Dubbo Lord Howe I.
Broken Hill Ivanhoe NEW SOUTH Taree (Aust.)
Gondobolin WALES Maitland
Orange Cessnock
Griffith Bathurst Newcastle
Remark Hay Lachlan Lithgow
Mildura Cootamundra Sydney
Baranald Riverina Wollongong
Murray Bridge Wagga Wagga Goulburn
Deniliquin Yass
VICTORIA Albury Canberra
Shepparton A.C.T.
Horsham Bendigo Mt Kosciusko Bombala
Ararat Australian Alps
Hamilton Ballarat Melbourne Orbost
Portland Geelong Morwell Bairnsdale C. Howe
Port Fairy Colac Sale
Warrnambool Wonthaggi TASMAN
Wilson's Prom.
King I. Bass Strait Furneaux
C. Grim Group
Smithton Burnie C. Barren SEA
Devonport Launceston NEW
Queenstown Mt Ossa St Mary's ZEALAND
Hobart Nelson
Geeveston TASMANIA Westport
South West C. South East C. South Island Greymouth

140 150 160

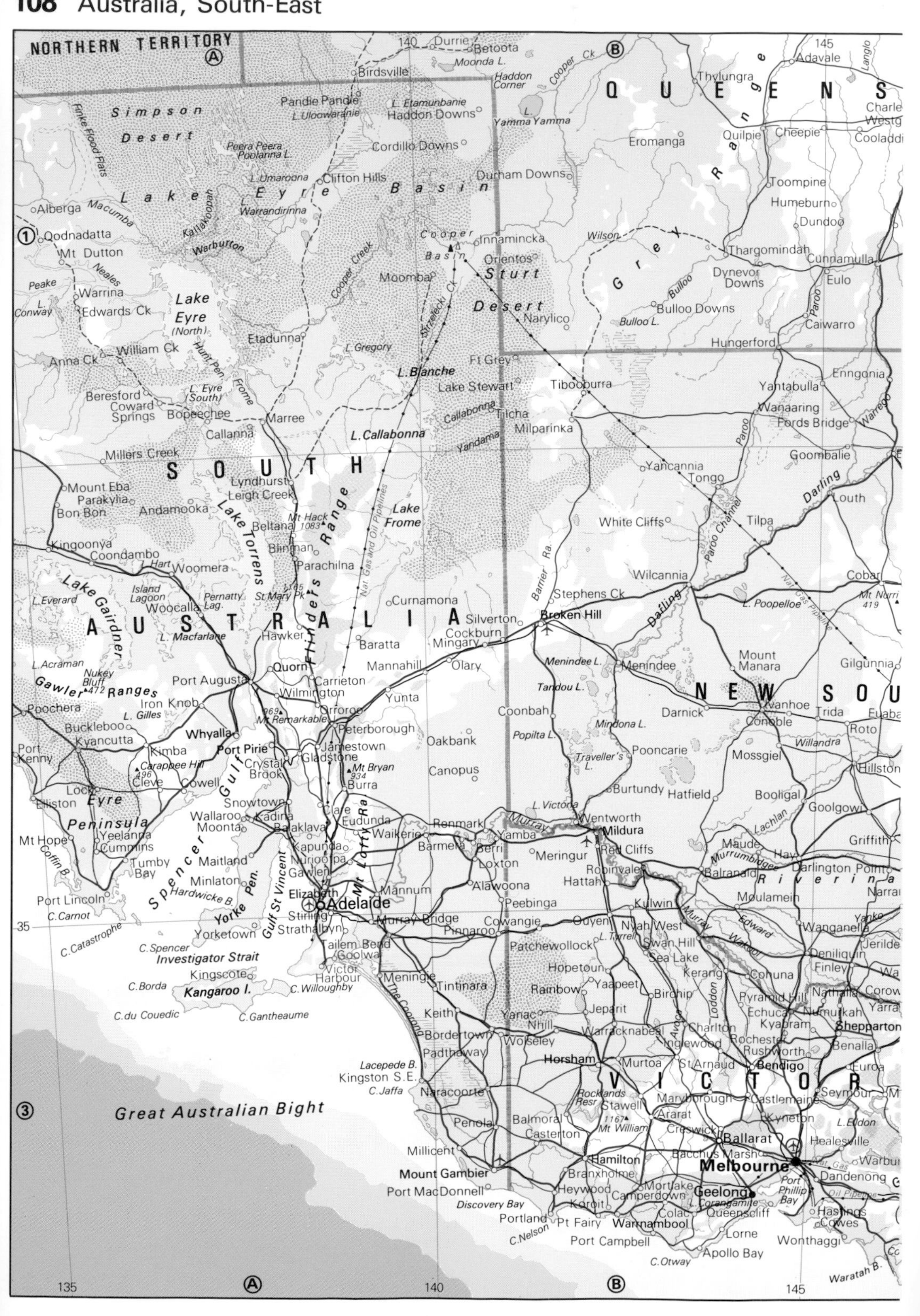

NORTHERN TERRITORY Ⓐ

QUEENS B

Durrie 140 Betoota
Moonda L.
Birdsville
Haddon
Corner
Pandie Pandie
L. Uloowaranie Haddon Downs
L. Etamunbanie
Yamma Yamma
Cordillo Downs
Simpson
Desert
Peera Peera
Poolanna L.
Durham Downs
Umaroona Clifton Hills
Eromanga
Thylungra
Adavale 145
Cooper Ck
Langlo
Charle
Westg
Quilpie
Cheepie
Cooladdi

Ⓐ
L A K E
E Y R E
B A S I N
Innamincka
Wilson
Grey
Humeburn
Dundoo
Eulo
Toompine
Range

Oodnadatta
Mt Dutton
Alberga
Macumba
Warrandirinna
Cooper
Basin
Moomba
Orientos
Sturt
Narylico
Thargomindah
Dynevor
Downs
Bulloo
Cunnamulla

① Peake
Warrina
Edwards Ck
L.
Conway
Lake
Eyre
(North)
Etadunna
L. Gregory
Ft Grey
L. Blanche
Lake Stewart
Tibooburra
Bulloo Downs
Bulloo L.
Hungerford
Caiwarro
Enngonia

Anna Ck
William Ck
Beresford
Coward
Springs
Bopeechee
Callanna
Marree
L. Eyre
(South)
Hunt Pen
Frome
L. Callabonna
Callabonna
Ticha
Yandama
Milparinka
Yancannia
Tongo
Wanaaring
Fords Bridge
Goombalie
Warre

Millers Creek
S O U T H
Lyndhurst
Leigh Creek
Mt Hack
1083
Lake
Frome
White Cliffs
Tilpa
Darling
Louth

Mount Eba
Parakylia
Bon Bon
Andamooka
Beltana
Blinman
Parachilna
Wilcannia
Cobar
Mt Narri
419

Kingoonya
Coondambo
Hart
Woomera
Flinders
Range
Curnamona
Stephens Ck
Darling
L. Poopelloe

Lake Gairdner
L. Everard
Island
Lagoon
Pernatty
Lag.
St Mary Pk
Woocalla
Hawker
Silverton
Cockburn
Mingary
Broken Hill
Menindee L.
Menindee
Mount
Manara
Gilgunnia

A U S T R A L I A
L. Acraman
Nukey
Bluff
472
Gawler Ranges
Poochera
Iron Knob
L. Gilles
L. Macfarlane
Quorn
Wilmington
Baratta
Mannahill
Olary
Tandou L.
Darnick
Ivanhoe
Trida
Fuab
Roto
N E W S O U

Buckleboo
Kyancutta
Kimba
Carapee Hill
496
Cowell
Whyalla
Port Pirie
Crystal
Brook
Peterborough
Jamestown
Gladstone
Mt Remarkable
969
Orroroo
Yunta
Carrieton
Port Augusta
Coonbah
Popilta L.
Mindona L.
Mossgiel
Willandra
Hillston

Port
Kenny
Cleve
Snowtown
Mt Bryan
934
Burra
Oakbank
Canopus
Traveller's
L.
Pooncarie
Hatfield
Booligal
Goolgow

Locks
Eyre
Peninsula
Elliston
Wallaroo
Moonta
Kadina
Balaklava
Cafe
Eudunda
Renmark
Yamba
Murray
L. Victoria
Wentworth
Mildura
Maude
Hay
Lachlan
Griffith

Mt Hope
Yeelanna
Cummins
Waikerie
Barmera
Berri
Loxton
Meringur
Red Cliffs
Robinvale
Murrumbidgee
Balranald
Darlington Point
Riverina
Narra

Tumby
Bay
Minlaton
Maitland
Kapunda
Nuriootpa
Gawler
Mannum
Alawoona
Hattah
Kulwin
Moulamein

Port Lincoln
Hardwicke B.
Yorke Pen.
Elizabeth
Stirling
Adelaide
Strathalbyn
Murray Bridge
Peebinga
Odyen
Nyah West
Swan Hill
Edward
Wanganella
Jerilde

C. Carnot
35
C. Catastrophe
Yorketown
Goolwa
Tailem Bend
Cowangie
Pinnaroo
Patchewollock
L. Tyrrell
Sea Lake
Cohuna
Deniliquin
Finley
Wa

Investigator Strait
Kingscote
Meningie
Tintinara
Hopetoun
Kerang
Pyramid Hill
Echuca
Numurkah
Yarra
Corow

C. Borda
Kangaroo I.
C. Willoughby
Victor
Harbour
Rainbow
Yaapeet
Birchip
Charlton
Rochester
Kyabram
Shepparton

C. du Couedic
C. Gantheaume
Keith
Yanac
Nhill
Warracknabeal
Inglewood
Rushworth
Benalla
Euroa

Ⓐ
Great Australian Bight
Bordertown
Padthaway
Wolseley
Murtoa
Horsham
St Arnaud
Maryborough
Castlemaine
Seymour

Lacepede B.
Kingston S.E.
C. Jaffa
Naracoorte
Rocklands
Resr
Stawell
1167
Mt William
Ararat
Creswick
Kyneton
L. Eldon

Penola
Balmoral
Casterton
Ballarat
Healesville

Millicent
Hamilton
Branxholme
Bacchus Marsh
Melbourne
Dandenong

Mount Gambier
Heywood
Camperdown
Korumburra
Geelong
Port
Phillip
Bay
Hastings

Port MacDonnell
Discovery Bay
Portland
Pt Fairy
Warrnambool
Colac
Queenscliff

C. Nelson
Port Campbell
Lorne
Wonthaggi

C. Otway
Apollo Bay
Waratah B.

135 Ⓐ 140 B 145

VICTORIA

1:7.5M 0 100 200 300 km 0 50 100 150 mls

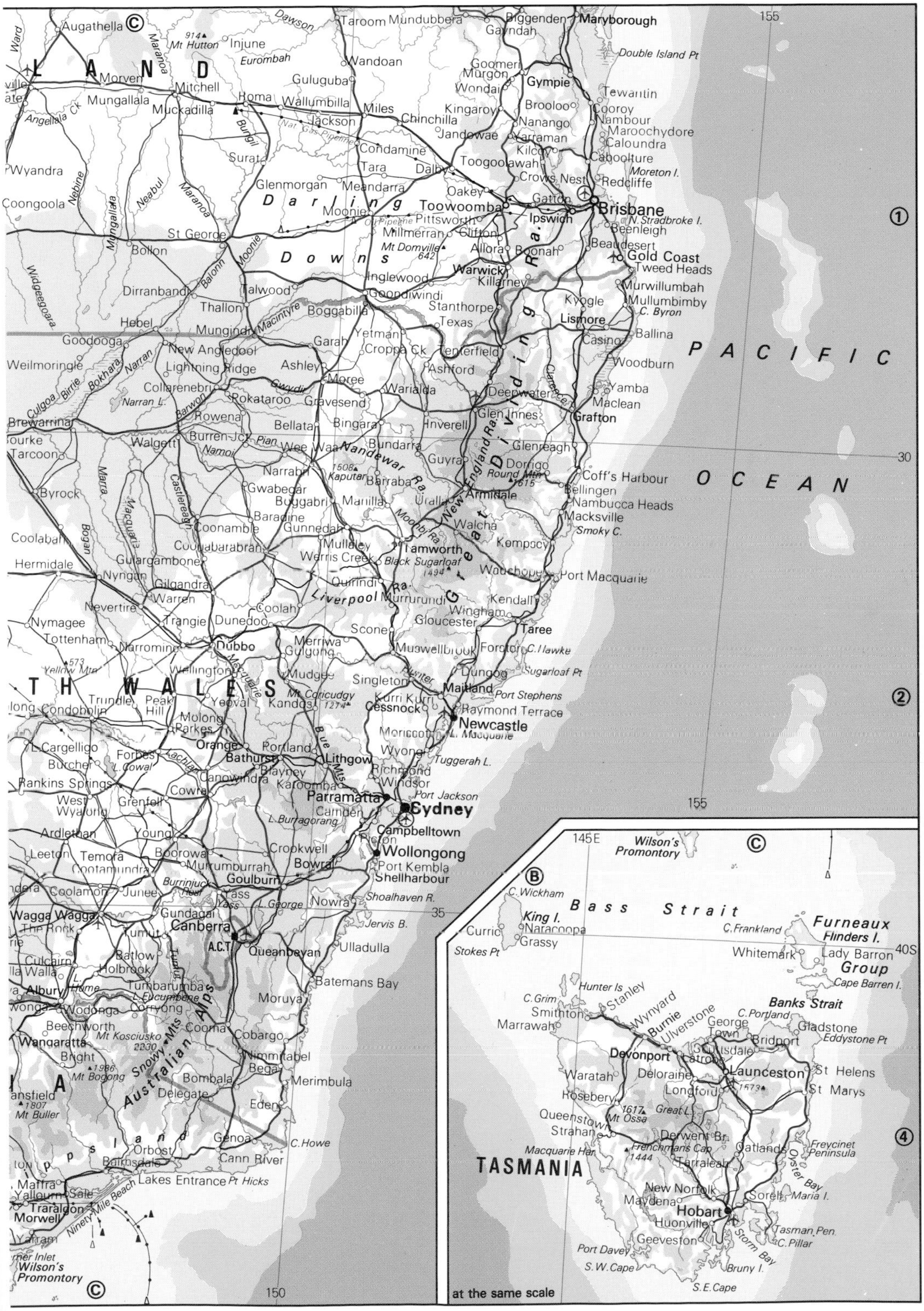

Augathella
Mt Hutton 914
Injune
Eurombah
Dawson
Taroom
Mundubbera
Biggenden
Gayndah
Maryborough
Double Island Pt
Wandoan
Goomeri
Murgon
Wondai
Gympie
Guluguba
Morven
Mitchell
Roma
Wallumbilla
Miles
Mungallala
Muckadilla
Jackson
Chinchilla
Kingaroy
Nanango
Jandowae
Yarraman
Kilcoy
Brooloo
Tewantin
Cooroy
Nambour
Maroochydore
Caloundra
Caboolture
Moreton I.
Redcliffe
Bungil
Nat Gas Pipeline
Condamine
Surat
Tara
Dalby
Toogoolawah
Crows Nest
Wyandra
Nebine
Neabul
Maranoa
Glenmorgan
Meandarra
Oakey
Cungoola
Mungallala
Darling
Downs
Moonie
Toowoomba
Gatton
Brisbane
Ipswich
N. Stradbroke I.
Beenleigh
Oil Pipeline
Pittsworth
Millmerran
Clifton
St George
Bollon
Mt Domville 642
Allora
Boonah
Beaudesert
Gold Coast
Tweed Heads
Widgeegoara
Balonn
Moonie
Warwick
Killarney
Dirranbandi
Talwood
Inglewood
Goondiwindi
Murwillumbah
Mullumbimby
C. Byron
Thallon
Boggabilla
Stanthorpe
Kyogle
Hebel
Macintyre
Texas
Lismore
Goodooga
Mungindi
Yetman
Garah
Casino
Ballina
New Angledool
Croppa Ck
Tenterfield
PACIFIC
OCEAN
Weilmoringle
Lightning Ridge
Ashley
Woodburn
Narran
Bokhara
Birrie
Culgoa
Ashford
Collarenebri
Gwydir
Moree
Warialda
Deepwater
Clarence
Yamba
Maclean
Narran L.
Pokataroo
Gravesend
Glen Innes
Grafton
Brewarrina
Rowena
Barwon
Bellata
Bingara
Inverell
Bourke
Walgett
Burren Jct
Pian
Namoi
Wee Waa
Bundarra
Glenreagh
Tarcoon
Nandewar Ra.
Guyra
Dorrigo
Round Mtn 1615
Kaputar 1508
Narrabri
Barraba
Coff's Harbour
Byrock
Marra
Castlereagh
Gwabegar
Armidale
Bellingen
Nambucca Heads
Macquarie
Boggabri
Manilla
Uralla
New England Ra.
Baradine
Macksville
Smoky C.
Bogan
Coonamble
Gunnedah
Moonbi Ra.
Walcha
Coolabah
Mullaley
Coonabarabran
Tamworth
Kempsey
Hermidale
Gulargambone
Werris Creek
Black Sugarloaf 1494
Great Dividing Ra.
Nyngan
Gilgandra
Quirindi
Wauchope
Port Macquarie
Warren
Liverpool Ra.
Murrurundi
Kendall
Nevertire
Trangie
Dunedoo
Coolah
Wingham
Nymagee
Gloucester
Taree
Tottenham
Narromine
Dubbo
Scone
Merriwa
Gulgong
Muswellbrook
Forster
C. Hawke
Yellow Mtn 573
Wellington
Mudgee
Dungog
Sugarloaf Pt
THWALES
Trundle
Peak Hill
Yeoval
Mt Coricudgy 1274
Kandos
Singleton
Hunter
Maitland
Port Stephens
Condobolin
Molong
Kurri Kurri
Cessnock
Raymond Terrace
Parkes
Newcastle
Morisset
L. Macquarie
Orange
Portland
Blue Mts
L. Cargelligo
Forbes
Lachlan
Bathurst
Lithgow
Wyong
Burcher
L. Cowal
Blayney
Richmond
Tuggerah L.
Rankins Springs
Canowindra
Karoomba
Windsor
Cowra
Parramatta
Port Jackson
West Wyalong
Grenfell
Sydney
Camden
L. Burragorang
Ardlethan
Young
Campbelltown
Picton
Leeton
Temora
Boorowa
Crookwell
Wollongong
Cootamundra
Murrumburrah
Port Kembla
Bowral
Shellharbour
Coolamon
Junee
Burrinjuck Res.
Goulburn
Yass
L. George
Nowra
Shoalhaven R.
Wagga Wagga
The Rock
Gundagai
Canberra
Jervis B.
Tumut
A.C.T.
Queanbeyan
Ulladulla
Culcairn
Batlow
Holbrook
Tumut
Albury
L. Hume
Tumbarumba
Batemans Bay
Wodonga
L. Eucumbene
Corryong
Moruya
Beechworth
Snowy Mts
Wangaratta
Mt Kosciusko 2230
Cooma
Cobargo
Australian Alps
Bright
Nimmitabel
Mt Bogong 1986
Bega
Bombala
Merimbula
Mansfield
Mt Buller 1807
Delegate
Eden
Gippsland
Genoa
C. Howe
Orbost
Cann River
Bairnsdale
Lakes Entrance
Pt Hicks
Maffra
Sale
Yallourn
Traralgon
Ninety Mile Beach
Morwell
Yarram
Corner Inlet
Wilson's Promontory
150
155
30
35
145E
40S
Wilson's Promontory
Bass Strait
C. Wickham
King I.
Naracoopa
Currie
Grassy
Stokes Pt
C. Frankland
Furneaux
Flinders I.
Whitemark
Lady Barron
Group
Cape Barren I.
Hunter Is
C. Grim
Stanley
Smithton
Wynyard
Marrawah
Burnie
Ulverstone
Banks Strait
C. Portland
George Town
Gladstone
Eddystone Pt
Devonport
Latrobe
Bridport
Scottsdale
Waratah
Deloraine
Launceston
St Helens
Longford
1573
St Marys
Rosebery
1617
Mt Ossa
Great L.
Queenstown
Strahan
Derwent Br.
Macquarie Har.
Frenchmans Cap 1444
Tarraleah
Oatlands
Freycinet Peninsula
TASMANIA
Oyster Bay
New Norfolk
Maydena
Sorell
Maria I.
Hobart
Huonville
Tasman Pen.
C. Pillar
Geeveston
Storm Bay
Port Davey
S.W. Cape
Bruny I.
S.E. Cape
at the same scale

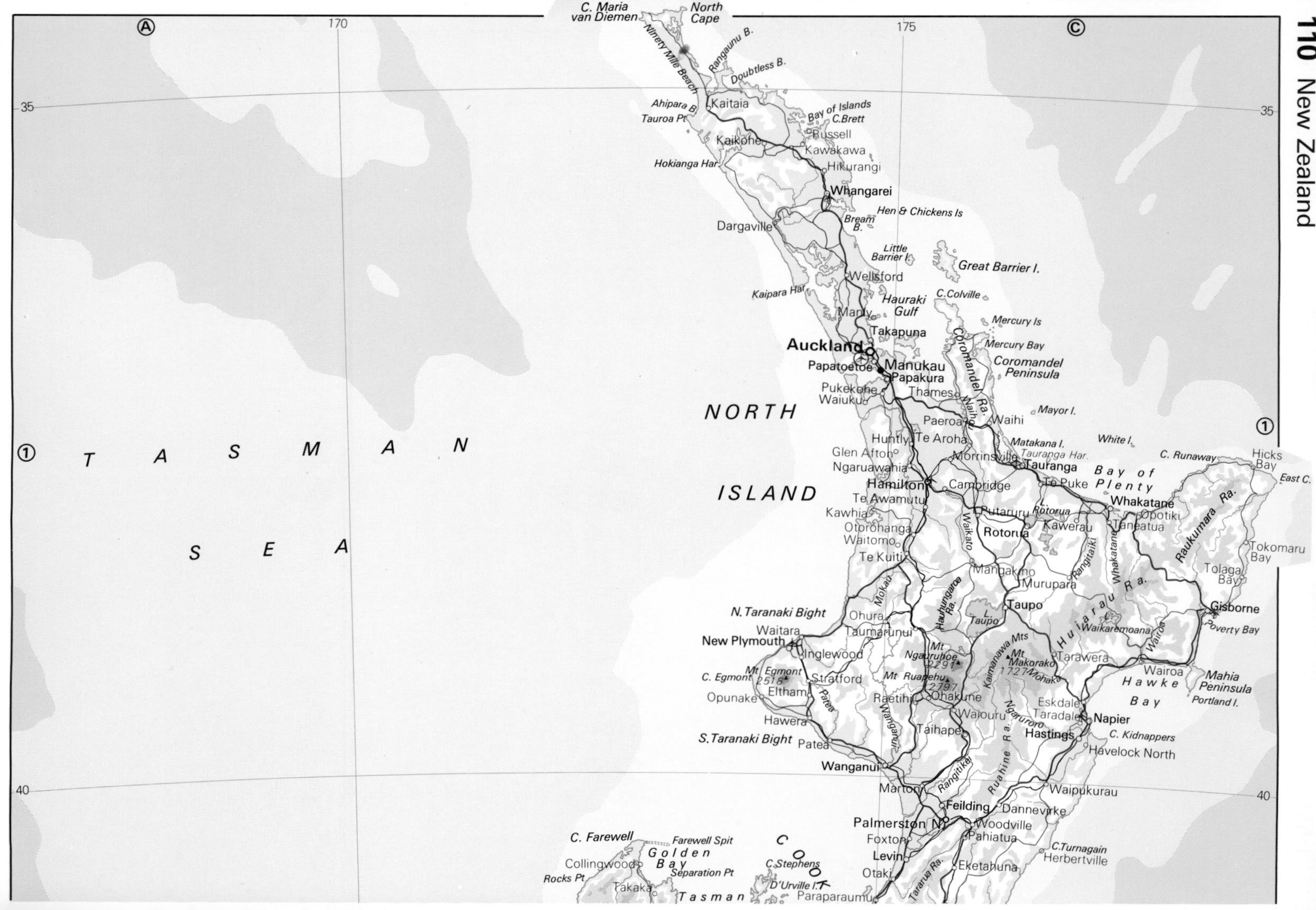

C. Maria van Diemen
North Cape
Ninety Mile Beach
Rangaunu B.
Doubtless B.
Kaitaia
Ahipara B.
Tauroa Pt
Kaikohe
Hokianga Har.
Bay of Islands
C.Brett
Russell
Kawakawa
Hikurangi
Whangarei
Dargaville
Bream B.
Hen & Chickens Is
Little Barrier I.
Great Barrier I.
Wellsford
Kaipara Har.
Hauraki Gulf
C.Colville
Manly
Takapuna
Auckland
Manukau
Papakura
Papatoetoe
Pukekohe
Waiuku
Thames
Coromandel Ra.
Coromandel Peninsula
Mercury Is
Mercury Bay
Mayor I.
Waihou
Waihi
Paeroa
Te Aroha
Huntly
Glen Afton
Ngaruawahia
Hamilton
Cambridge
Morrinsville
Matakana I.
Tauranga Har.
Tauranga
Te Puke
Bay of Plenty
White I.
Whakatane
Opotiki
Taneatua
C. Runaway
Hicks Bay
East C.
Raukumara Ra.
Tokomaru Bay
Tolaga Bay
Gisborne
Poverty Bay
Mahia Peninsula
Portland I.
Wairoa
Hawke Bay
C. Kidnappers
Napier
Havelock North
Hastings
Taradale
Eskdale
Tarawera
Huiarau Ra.
Waikaremoana
Mt Makorako 1727
Mohaka
Kaimanawa Mts
Ngaruroro
Taupo
L. Taupo
Murupara
Rangitaiki
Kawerau
L. Rotorua
Rotorua
Putaruru
Waikato
Mangakino
Hauhungaroa Ra.
Te Awamutu
Kawhia
Otorohanga
Waitomo
Te Kuiti
Mokau
Ohura
Taumarunui
Mt Ngauruhoe 2291
Mt Ruapehu 2797
Ohakune
Waiouru
Taihape
Raetihi
Wanganui
Marton
Rangitikei
Ruahine Ra.
Feilding
Palmerston N.
Foxton
Levin
Otaki
Paraparaumu
Tararua Ra.
Dannevirke
Woodville
Pahiatua
Eketahuna
Waipukurau
C.Turnagain
Herbertville
N.Taranaki Bight
S.Taranaki Bight
Waitara
New Plymouth
Inglewood
Stratford
Eltham
Hawera
Patea
Opunake
Mt Egmont 2518
C. Egmont
NORTH ISLAND
TASMAN SEA
C. Farewell
Farewell Spit
Golden Bay
Separation Pt
Collingwood
Takaka
Rocks Pt
C.Stephens
D'Urville I.
COOK
Tasman

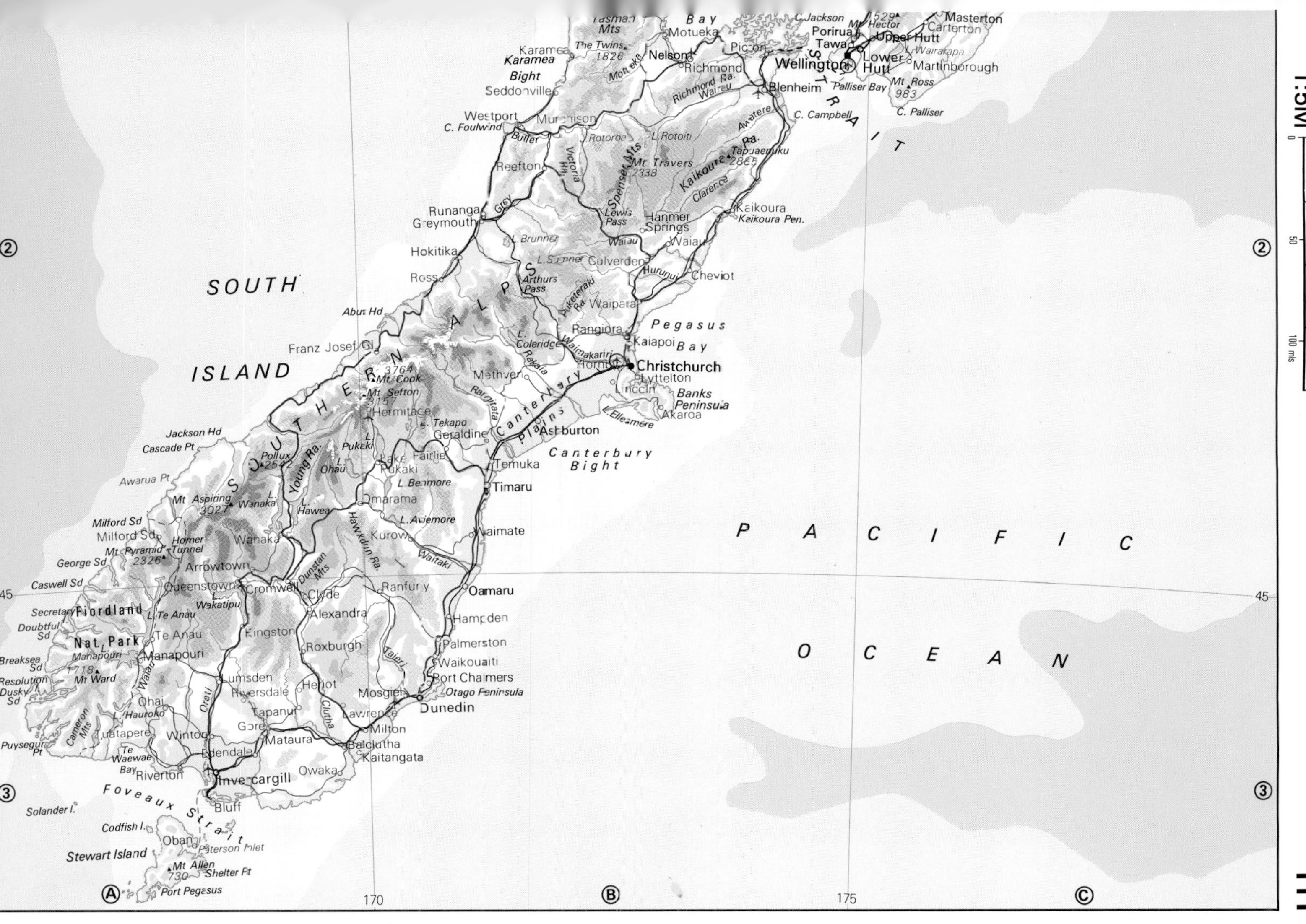

0   50   100   150   200 km
0   50   100 mls

P A C I F I C

O C E A N

S T R A I T

S O U T H

I S L A N D

S O U T H E R N

A L P S

Masterton
Carterton
Wairarapa
Lower Hutt
Upper Hutt
Mt Ross 963
C. Palliser
Palliser Bay
Tawa
Porirua
Mt Hector
Wellington
Jackson Mt 1529
C. Campbell
Blenheim
Picton
C. Koamaru
Motueka
Nelson
Richmond
Tasman Mts
The Twins 1826
Takaka
Riwaka R
Mot. R
Buller R
Murchison
Westport
C. Foulwind
Seddonville
Karamea
Karamea Bight
Tasman Bay
Keikoura Pen.
Kaikoura
Kaikoura Pen.
Cheviot
Waiau
Hanmer Springs
Lewis Pass
Spenser Mts
Mt Travers 2265
L. Rotoiti
L. Rotoroa
Victoria Ra
Brunner
Arthurs Pass
Reefton
Runanga
Greymouth
Hokitika
Ross
Pegasus Bay
Christchurch
Lyttelton
Banks Peninsula
Akaroa
Kaiapoi
Rakaia R
Rangiora
Oxford
Ellesmere
Darfield
Waimakariri R
Culverden
Waiau R
Rotherham
Hurunui R
Waipara
Methven
Coleridge
Rakaia
Geraldine
Ashburton
Canterbury Bight
Temuka
Timaru
Rangitata R
Mt Serton
Fairlie
Pukeki
L. Tekapo
Franz Josef Gl
Mt Cook 3764
Abut Hd
Waitaki R
Waimate
Oamaru
Hampden
Palmerston
Waikouaiti
Port Chalmers
Dunedin
Otago Peninsula
Mosgiel
Milton
Kaitangata
Balclutha
Clutha R
Lawrence
Waihola
Roxburgh
Heriot
Tapanui
Clyde
Alexandra
Cromwell
Ranfurly
L. Aviemore
L. Benmore
Kurow
Omarama
Hawkdun Ra
L. Ohau
Twizel
Hermitage
Taieri R
Gore
Mataura
Owaka
Nuggets Pt
Kaitangata
Milton
Oreti R
Lumsden
Riversdale
Balfour
Winton
Invercargill
Bluff
Foveaux Strait
Riverton
Ohai
Nightcaps
Mataura R
Gore
Wyndham
Wallacetown
Orepuki
Tuatapere
Waiau R
Manapouri
L. Manapouri
Te Anau
L. Te Anau
Young Ra
Pembroke
L. Wanaka
Wanaka
Cardrona
Arrowtown
Queenstown
L. Wakatipu
Kingston
Mt Aspiring 3027
Jackson Hd
Cascade Pt
Awarua Pt
Milford Sd
Mt Pembroke
Homer Tunnel
Mitre Pk 1692
George Sd
Caswell Sd
Secretary I.
Doubtful Sd
Breaksea Sd
Dusky Sd
Resolution I.
Fiordland Nat. Park
Puyseguer Pt
Solander I.
Cameron Mts
Codfish I.
Stewart Island
Obata
Mt Allen 730
Shelter Pt
Pierson Inlet
Port Pegasus

45

175

170

45

②

③

Ⓒ

Ⓑ

Ⓐ

②

③

1:40M

0 400 800 1200 1600 km
0 400 800 mls

Heard I. (Aust.)

INDIAN OCEAN

ATLANTIC OCEAN

PACIFIC OCEAN

Antarctic Circle

C. Darnley
Amery Ice Shelf
Davis (Aust.)
Zhongshan China
Mawson (Aust.)
Molodezhnaya (Former USSR)
Syowa (Jap.)
Enderby Land
Mac. Robertson Land
Pt. Charles
3355
Lambert Gl.
American Highland
Queen Mary Land
Knox Coast
C. Poinsett
Casey (Aust.)
Mirny (Former USSR)
Shackleton Ice Shelf
S. Magnetic Pole (1990)
Dumont d'Urville (Fr.)
Adélie
Terre Adélie
George V Land
Wilkes Land
Oates Land
Balleny Is
Sturge I.
Scott I.
Leningradskaya (Former USSR)
C. Adare
Victoria Land
Transantarctic Mts
GREATER ANTARCTICA
Vostok (Former USSR)
Mühlig (Jap.)
Dronning Maud Land
Prinsesse Ragnhild Kyst
Prinsesse Astrid Kyst
Maitri India
Georg Forster Germany
Neumayer (Former USSR)
Novolazarevskaya (Former USSR)
C. Norvegia
Sanae (S.A.)
Coats Land
Pensacola Mts
Halley (U.K.)
Grl Belgrano (Arg.)
Ronne Berkner I. Ice Shelf
Filchner Ice Shelf
Vinson Massif 5140
Ellsworth Land
3022 Mt Seelig
South Pole
Amundsen-Scott (U.S.)
Q. Maud Mts
Mt Kirkpatrick 4528
Mt Markham 4351
Scott (N.Z.)
McMurdo (U.S.)
Ross Ice Shelf
Roosevelt I.
Ross Sea
C. Colbeck
LESSER ANTARCTICA
Marie Byrd Land
Mt Sidley 4181
Walgreen Coast
Siple I.
Amundsen Sea
Thurston I.
Peter I Øy (Nor.)
Bellingshausen Sea
Alexander I.
Charcot I.
Palmer Land
Graham Land
Antarctic Peninsula
Palmer Arch.
S. Shetland Is (U.K.)
S. Orkney Is
Orcadas (Arg.)
Signy (U.K.)
Weddell Sea
Scotia Sea
Drake Passage
Falkland Is (U.K.)
Tierra del Fuego
ARGENTINA CHILE

Antarctic Research Stations
1 Artigas (Uruguay)
2 Teniente Rodolfo Marsh Martin (Chile)
3 Bellingshausen (Former USSR)
4 Great Wall (China)
5 Comandante Ferraz (Brazil)
6 Henryk Arctowski (Poland)
7 Teniente Jubany (Arg.)
8 King Sejong (Korea)
9 Capitan Arturo Prat (Chile)
10 General Bernardo O'Higgins (Arg.)
11 Esperanza (Arg.)
12 Vicecomodoro Marambio (Arg.)
13 Palmer (USA)
14 Faraday (UK)
15 Rothera (UK)
16 General San Martin (Arg.)

Index

In the index, the first number refers to the page, and the following letter and number to the section of the map in which the index entry can be found. For example, 48C2 **Paris** means that Paris can be found on page 48 where column C and row 2 meet.

Abbreviations used in the index

Abbreviation	Meaning
Afghan	Afghanistan
Alb	Albania
Alg	Algeria
Ant	Antarctica
Arg	Argentina
Aust	Australia
Bang	Bangladesh
Belg	Belgium
Bol	Bolivia
Bulg	Bulgaria
Burk	Burkina
Camb	Cambodia
Can	Canada
CAR	Central African Republic
Den	Denmark
Dom Rep	Dominican Republic
El Sal	El Salvador
Eng	England
Eq Guinea	Equatorial Guinea
Eth	Ethiopia
Fin	Finland
Germ	Germany
Hung	Hungary
Ind	Indonesia
Irish Rep	Ireland
Leb	Lebanon
Lib	Liberia
Liech	Liechtenstein
Lux	Luxembourg
Madag	Madagascar
Malay	Malaysia
Maur	Mauritania
Mor	Morocco
Mozam	Mozambique
Neth	Netherlands
NZ	New Zealand
Nic	Nicaragaua
N Ire	Northern Ireland
Nig	Nigeria
Nor	Norway
Pak	Pakistan
PNG	Papua New Guinea
Par	Paraguay
Phil	Philippines
Pol	Poland
Port	Portugal
Rom	Romania
Russian Fed	Russian Federation
S Arabia	Saudi Arabia
Scot	Scotland
Sen	Senegal
S Africa	South Africa
Switz	Switzerland
Tanz	Tanzania
Thai	Thailand
Turk	Turkey
USA	United States of America
Urug	Uruguay
Ven	Venezuela
Viet	Vietnam
Yugos	Yugoslavia
Zim	Zimbabwe
Arch	Archipelago
B	Bay
C	Cape
Chan	Channel
Gl	Glacier
I(s)	Island(s)
Lg	Lagoon
L	Lake
Mt(s)	Mountain(s)
O	Ocean
P	Pass
Pen	Peninsula
Plat	Plateau
Pt	Point
Res	Reservoir
R	River
S	Sea
Sd	Sound
Str	Strait
V	Valley

A

57B2 **Aachen** Germany
46C1 **Aalst** Belg
38K6 **Äänekoski** Fin
47C1 **Aarau** Switz
47B1 **Aare** *R* Switz
72A3 **Aba** China
97C4 **Aba** Nig
99D2 **Aba** Zaïre
91A3 **Ābādān** Iran
90B3 **Ābādeh** Iran
96B1 **Abadla** Alg
35B1 **Abaeté** Brazil
35B1 **Abaeté** *R* Brazil
31B2 **Abaetetuba** Brazil
72D1 **Abagnar Qi** China
97C4 **Abakaliki** Nig
63B2 **Abakan** Russian Fed
97C3 **Abala** Niger
96C2 **Abalessa** Alg
32C6 **Abancay** Peru
90B3 **Abarqū** Iran
74E2 **Abashiri** Japan
74E2 **Abashiri-wan** *B* Japan
71F4 **Abau** PNG
99D2 **Abaya** *L* Eth
99D1 **Abbai** *R* Eth
99E1 **Abbe** *L* Eth
48C1 **Abbeville** France
19B4 **Abbeville** Louisiana, USA
17B1 **Abbeville** S Carolina, USA
45B2 **Abbeyfeale** Irish Rep
47C2 **Abbiategrasso** Italy
20B1 **Abbotsford** Can
84C2 **Abbottabad** Pak
61H3 **Abdulino** Russian Fed
98C1 **Abéché** Chad
39F7 **Åbenrå** Den
97C4 **Abeokuta** Nig
99D2 **Abera** Eth
43B3 **Aberaeron** Wales
15C3 **Aberdeen** Maryland, USA
100B4 **Aberdeen** S Africa
44C3 **Aberdeen** Scot
8D2 **Aberdeen** S Dakota, USA
8A2 **Aberdeen** Washington, USA
4J3 **Aberdeen L** Can
44C3 **Aberfeldy** Scot
43C4 **Abergavenny** Wales
43B3 **Aberystwyth** Wales
81C4 **Abhā** S Arabia
90A2 **Abhar** Iran
97B4 **Abidjan** Ivory Coast
18A2 **Abilene** Kansas, USA
9D3 **Abilene** Texas, USA
43D4 **Abingdon** Eng
7B4 **Abitibi** *R* Can
7C5 **Abitibi,L** Can
61F5 **Abkhazskaya Respublika,** Georgia
84C2 **Abohar** India
97C4 **Abomey** Benin
98B2 **Abong Mbang** Cam
79A4 **Aborlan** Phil
98B1 **Abou Deïa** Chad
91A4 **Abqaiq** S Arabia
50A2 **Abrantes** Port
95C2 **Abri** Sudan
106A3 **Abrolhos** *Is* Aust
8B2 **Absaroka Range** *Mts* USA
91B5 **Abū al Abyad** *I* UAE
91A4 **Abū 'Ali** *I* S Arabia
91B5 **Abū Dhabi** UAE
95C3 **Abu Hamed** Sudan
97C4 **Abuja** Nig
33D5 **Abunã** Brazil
32D6 **Abuna** *R* Bol
93D3 **Abú Sukhayr** Iraq
111B2 **Abut Head** *C* NZ
95C3 **Abu 'Urug** *Well* Sudan
99D1 **Abuye Meda** *Mt* Eth
99C1 **Abu Zabad** Sudan
99D2 **Abwong** Sudan
56B1 **Åby** Den
94B3 **Aby 'Aweigîla** *Well* Egypt
99C2 **Abyei** Sudan
24B2 **Acambaro** Mexico
24B2 **Acaponeta** Mexico
24B3 **Acapulco** Mexico
31D2 **Acaraú** Brazil
32D2 **Acarigua** Ven
24C3 **Acatlán** Mexico
23B2 **Acatzingo** Mexico
97B4 **Accra** Ghana
85D4 **Achalpur** India
29B4 **Achao** Chile
47D1 **Achensee** *L* Austria
46E2 **Achern** Germany
41A3 **Achill** *I* Irish Rep
63B2 **Achinsk** Russian Fed
53C3 **Acireale** Italy
26C2 **Acklins** *I* Caribbean S
32C6 **Acobamba** Peru
29B2 **Aconcagua** *Mt* Chile
31D3 **Acopiara** Brazil
88B4 **Açores** *Is* Atlantic O
A Coruña = La Coruña
47C2 **Acqui** Italy
108A2 **Acraman,L** Aust
Acre = 'Akko
32C5 **Acre** State, Brazil
22C3 **Acton** USA
23B1 **Actopan** Mexico
19A3 **Ada** USA
50B1 **Adaja** *R* Spain
91C5 **Adam** Oman
35A2 **Adamantina** Brazil
98B2 **Adamaoua** Region, Nig/Cam
47D1 **Adamello** *Mt* Italy
16C1 **Adams** USA
87B3 **Adam's Bridge** India/Sri Lanka
13D2 **Adams L** Can
8A2 **Adams,Mt** USA
87C3 **Adam's Peak** *Mt* Sri Lanka
81C4 **'Adan** Yemen
92C2 **Adana** Turk
60D5 **Adapazari** Turk
112B7 **Adare,C** Ant
108B1 **Adavale** Aust
47C2 **Adda** *R* Italy
91A4 **Ad Dahna'** Region, S Arabia
96A2 **Ad Dakhla** Mor
81C4 **Ad Dālī'** Yemen
91B4 **Ad Damman** S Arabia
91A4 **Ad Dibdibah** Region, S Arabia
91A5 **Ad Dilam** S Arabia
91A5 **Ad Dir'iyah** S Arabia
93D3 **Ad Dīwanīyah** Iraq
93D3 **Ad Duwayd** S Arabia
106C4 **Adelaide** Aust
4J3 **Adelaide Pen** Can
22D3 **Adelanto** USA
Aden = 'Adan
81C4 **Aden,G of** Yemen/Somalia
97C3 **Aderbissinat** Niger
94C2 **Adhra** Syria
71E4 **Adi** *I* Indon
52B1 **Adige** *R* Italy
99D1 **Adigrat** Eth
85D5 **Adilābād** India
20B2 **Adin** USA
15D2 **Adirondack Mts** USA
99D2 **Ādīs Ābeba** Eth
95C3 **Adi Ugai** Eritrea
93C2 **Adıyaman** Turk
54C1 **Adjud** Rom
4E4 **Admiralty I** USA
6B2 **Admiralty Inlet** *B* Can
87B1 **Adoni** India
48B3 **Adour** *R* France
96A2 **Adrar** Region, Maur
96C2 **Adrar** *Mts* Alg
96A2 **Adrar Soutouf** Region, Mor
98C1 **Adré** Chad
95A2 **Adri** Libya
47E2 **Adria** Italy

Adrian

91C5 **Al Hajar al Gharbī** *Mts* Oman
91C5 **Al Hajar ash Sharqī** *Mts* Oman
93C3 **Al Hamad** *Desert Region* Jordan/S Arabia
93E4 **Al Haniyah** *Desert Region* Iraq
91A5 **Al Harīq** S Arabia
93C3 **Al Harrah** *Desert Region* S Arabia
95A2 **Al Harūj al Aswad** *Upland* Libya
91A4 **Al Hasa** Region, S Arabia
93D2 **Al Hasakah** Syria
93C4 **Al Hawjā'** S Arabia
93E3 **Al Hayy** Iraq
94C2 **Al Hījānah** Syria
93D3 **Al Hillah** Iraq
91A5 **Al Hillah** S Arabia
96B1 **Al Hoceima** Mor
91A4 **Al Hufūf** S Arabia
91B5 **Al Humrah** Region, UAE
91C5 **Al Huwatsah** Oman
90A2 **Alīābad** Iran
91C4 **Aliabad** Iran
55B2 **Aliákmon** *R* Greece
93E3 **Alī al Gharbī** Iraq
87A1 **Alībāg** India
51B2 **Alicante** Spain
9D4 **Alice** USA
106C3 **Alice Springs** Aust
53B3 **Alicudi** *I* Italy
84D3 **Aligarh** India
90A3 **Aligūdarz** Iran
84B2 **Ali-Khel** Afghan
55C3 **Alimniá** *I* Greece
86B1 **Alīpur Duār** India
14B2 **Aliquippa** USA
22B2 **Alisal** USA
93C3 **Al' Isawiyah** S Arabia
100B4 **Aliwal North** S Africa
95B2 **Al Jaghbūb** Libya
93D3 **Al Jālamīd** S Arabia
95B2 **Al Jawf** Libya
93C4 **Al Jawf** S Arabia
93D2 **Al Jazīrah** *Desert Region* Syria/Iraq
50A2 **Aljezur** Port
91A4 **Al Jubayl** S Arabia
91C5 **Al Kāmil** Oman
93D2 **Al Khābūr** *R* Syria
91C5 **Al Khabūrah** Oman
93D3 **Al Khālis** Iraq
91C4 **Al Khasab** Oman
91B4 **Al Khawr** Qatar
95A1 **Al Khums** Libya
91B5 **Al Kidan** Region, S Arabia
94C2 **Al Kiswah** Syria
56A2 **Alkmaar** Neth
95B2 **Al Kufrah Oasis** Libya
93E3 **Al Kūt** Iraq
92C2 **Al Lādhiqīyah** Syria
86A1 **Allahābād** India
94C2 **Al Lajāh** *Mt* Syria
12D1 **Allakaket** USA
76B2 **Allanmyo** Burma
95C2 **'Allaqi** *Watercourse* Egypt
17B1 **Allatoona L** USA
15C2 **Allegheny** *R* USA
10C3 **Allegheny Mts** USA
17B1 **Allendale** USA
111A3 **Allen,Mt** NZ
16C2 **Allentown** USA
87B3 **Alleppey** India
49C2 **Aller** *R* France
47D1 **Allgäu** *Mts* Germany
8C2 **Alliance** USA
81C3 **Al Līth** S Arabia
91B5 **Al Liwā** Region, UAE
109D1 **Allora** Aust
14B2 **Alma** Michigan, USA
82B1 **Alma Ata** Kazakhstan
50A2 **Almada** Port
Al Madinah = Medina
71F2 **Almagan** *I* Pacific O
91B4 **Al Manāmah** Bahrain
93D3 **Al Ma'nīyah** Iraq
21A1 **Almanor,L** USA
51B2 **Almansa** Spain
13B1 **Alma Peak** *Mt* Can
91B5 **Al Māriyyah** UAE
95B1 **Al Marj** Libya
Almaty = Alma Ata
93D2 **Al Mawşil** Iraq
50B1 **Almazán** Spain
35C1 **Almenara** Brazil
50B2 **Almeria** Spain
61H3 **Al'met'yevsk** Russian Fed
56C1 **Älmhult** Sweden
93E3 **Al Miqdādīyah** Iraq
112C3 **Almirante Brown** *Base* Ant
34A1 **Almirante Latorre** Chile
55B3 **Almirós** Greece
91A4 **Al Mish'āb** S Arabia
50A2 **Almodôvar** Port
84D3 **Almora** India
91A4 **Al Mubarraz** S Arabia
92C4 **Al Mudawwara** Jordan
91C5 **Al Mudaybi** Oman
91B4 **Al Muharraq** Bahrain
81C4 **Al Mukallā** Yemen
81C4 **Al Mukhā** Yemen
93D3 **Al Musayyib** Iraq
44B3 **Alness** Scot
93E3 **Al Nu'mānīyah** Iraq
42D2 **Alnwick** Eng
71D4 **Alor** *I* Indon
77C4 **Alor Setar** Malay
Alost = Aalst
107E2 **Alotau** PNG
106B3 **Aloysius,Mt** Aust
34C3 **Alpachiri** Arg
14B1 **Alpena** USA
47B2 **Alpes du Valais** *Mts* Switz
52B1 **Alpi Dolomitiche** *Mts* Italy
47B2 **Alpi Graie** *Mts* Italy
9C3 **Alpine** Texas, USA
47C1 **Alpi Orobie** *Mts* Italy
47B2 **Alpi Pennine** *Mts* Italy
47C1 **Alpi Retiche** *Mts* Switz
47D1 **Alpi Venoste** *Mts* Italy
52A1 **Alps** *Mts* Europe
95A1 **Al Qaddāhiyah** Libya
94C1 **Al Qadmūs** Syria
93D3 **Al Qa'im** Iraq
93C4 **Al Qalībah** S Arabia
93D2 **Al Qāmishlī** Syria
95A1 **Al Qaryah Ash Sharqiyah** Libya
92C3 **Al Qaryatayn** Syria
91A4 **Al Qātif** S Arabia
95A2 **Al Qatrūn** Libya
91A4 **Al Qayşāmah** S Arabia
94C2 **Al Quatayfah** Syria
50A2 **Alqueva** *R* Port
92C3 **Al Qunayţirah** Syria
81C4 **Al Qunfidhah** S Arabia
93E3 **Al Qurnah** Iraq
94C1 **Al Quşayr** Syria
92C3 **Al Qutayfah** Syria
56B1 **Als** *I* Den
49D2 **Alsace** Region, France
57B2 **Alsfeld** Germany
42C2 **Alston** Eng
38J5 **Alta** Nor
29D2 **Alta Gracia** Arg
27D5 **Altagracia de Orituco** Ven
68A2 **Altai** *Mts* Mongolia
17B1 **Altamaha** *R* USA
33G4 **Altamira** Brazil
23B1 **Altamira** Mexico
53C2 **Altamura** Italy
68C1 **Altanbulag** Mongolia
71F4 **Altape** PNG
24B2 **Altata** Mexico
63A3 **Altay** China
63B3 **Altay** Mongolia
63A2 **Altay** *Mts* Russian Fed
47C1 **Altdorf** Switz
46D1 **Altenkirchen** Germany
34B3 **Altiplanicie del Payún** *Plat* Arg
47B1 **Altkirch** France
101C2 **Alto Molócue** Mozam
10A3 **Alton** USA
15C2 **Altoona** USA
34B2 **Alto Pencoso** *Mts* Arg
35A1 **Alto Sucuriú** Brazil
23B2 **Altotonga** Mexico
23A2 **Altoyac de Alvarez** Mexico
82C2 **Altun Shan** *Mts* China
20B2 **Alturas** USA
9D3 **Altus** USA
91B5 **Al'Ubaylah** S Arabia
93C4 **Al Urayq** *Desert Region* S Arabia
91B5 **Al'Uruq al Mu'taridah** Region, S Arabia
9D2 **Alva** USA
23B2 **Alvarado** Mexico
19A3 **Alvarado** USA
39G6 **Älvdalen** Sweden
19A4 **Alvin** USA
38J5 **Alvsbyn** Sweden
80B3 **Al Wajh** S Arabia
85D3 **Alwar** India
93D3 **Al Widyān** *Desert Region* Iraq/S Arabia
72A2 **Alxa Yougi** China
93E2 **Alyat** Azerbaijan
39J8 **Alytus** Lithuania
46E2 **Alzey** Germany
23B2 **Amacuzac** *R* Mexico
99D2 **Amadi** Sudan
93D2 **Amādīyah** Iraq
6C3 **Amadjuak L** Can
74B4 **Amakusa-shotō** *I* Japan
39G7 **Åmål** Sweden
63D2 **Amalat** *R* Russian Fed
55B3 **Amaliás** Greece
85D4 **Amalner** India
69E4 **Amami** *I* Japan
69E4 **Amami gunto** *Arch* Japan
100C4 **Amanzimtoti** S Africa
33G3 **Amapá** Brazil
33G3 **Amapá** State, Brazil
9C3 **Amarillo** USA
60E5 **Amasya** Turk
23A1 **Amatitan** Mexico
Amazonas = Solimões
32D4 **Amazonas** State, Brazil
28C3 **Amazonas** *R* Brazil
84D2 **Ambāla** India
87C3 **Ambalangoda** Sri Lanka
101D3 **Ambalavao** Madag
98B2 **Ambam** Cam
101D2 **Ambanja** Madag
1C7 **Ambarchik** Russian Fed
32B4 **Ambato** Ecuador
101D2 **Ambato-Boeny** Madag
101D2 **Ambatolampy** Madag
101D2 **Ambatondrazaka** Madag
57C3 **Amberg** Germany
25D3 **Ambergris Cay** *I* Belize
86A2 **Ambikāpur** India
101D2 **Ambilobe** Madag
101D3 **Amboasary** Madag
101D2 **Ambodifototra** Madag
101D3 **Ambohimahasoa** Madag
71D4 **Ambon** Indon
101D3 **Ambositra** Madag
101D3 **Ambovombe** Madag
98B3 **Ambriz** Angola
98C1 **Am Dam** Chad
64H3 **Amderma** Russian Fed
24B2 **Ameca** Mexico
23B2 **Amecameca** Mexico
34C2 **Ameghino** Arg
56B2 **Ameland** *I* Neth
16C2 **Amenia** USA
112B10 **American Highland** *Upland* Ant
105H4 **American Samoa** *Is* Pacific O
17B1 **Americus** USA
101G1 **Amersfoort** S Africa
112C10 **Amery Ice Shelf** Ant
55B3 **Amfilokhía** Greece
55B3 **Amfissa** Greece
63F1 **Amga** Russian Fed
63F1 **Amgal** *R* Russian Fed
69F2 **Amgu** Russian Fed
69F1 **Amgun'** *R* Russian Fed
99D1 **Amhara** *Region* Eth
7D5 **Amherst** Can
16C1 **Amherst** Massachusetts, USA
Amherst = Kyaikkami
87B2 **Amhūr** India
48C2 **Amiens** France
75B1 **Amino** Japan
94B1 **Amioune** Leb
89K8 **Amirante Is** Indian O
86B1 **Amlekhgan** Nepal
92C3 **Amman** Jordan
38K6 **Ämmänsaario** Fin
56B2 **Ammersfoort** Neth
90B2 **Amol** Iran
55C3 **Amorgós** *I* Greece
7C5 **Amos** Can
Amoy = Xiamen
101D3 **Ampanihy** Madag
35B2 **Amparo** Brazil
51C1 **Amposta** Spain
85D4 **Amrāvati** India
85C4 **Amreli** India
84C2 **Amritsar** India
56A2 **Amsterdam** Neth
101H1 **Amsterdam** S Africa
15D2 **Amsterdam** USA
98C1 **Am Timan** Chad
88L3 **Amu Darya** *R* Uzbekistan
6A2 **Amund Ringes I** Can
4F2 **Amundsen G** Can
112B4 **Amundsen S** Ant
80E **Amundsen-Scott** *Base* Ant
78D3 **Amuntai** Indon
63E2 **Amur** *R* Russian Fed
33E2 **Anaco** Ven
8B2 **Anaconda** USA
20B1 **Anacortes** USA
55C3 **Anáfi** *I* Greece
93D3 **'Anah** Iraq
21B3 **Anaheim** USA
87B2 **Anaimalai Hills** India
83C4 **Anakapalle** India
12E1 **Anaktuvuk P** USA
101D2 **Analalaya** Madag
92B2 **Anamur** Turk
75A2 **Anan** Japan
87B2 **Anantapur** India
84D2 **Anantnag** India
31B5 **Anápolis** Brazil
90C3 **Anār** Iran
90B3 **Anārak** Iran
71F2 **Anatahan** *I* Pacific O
30D4 **Añatuya** Arg
74B3 **Anbyŏn** N Korea
22C4 **Ancapa Is** USA
4D3 **Anchorage** USA
30C2 **Ancohuma** *Mt* Bol
32B6 **Ancón** Peru
52B2 **Ancona** Italy
16C1 **Ancram** USA
29B4 **Ancud** Chile
34A3 **Andacollo** Arg
108A1 **Andado** Aust
32C6 **Andahuaylas** Peru
38F6 **Andalsnes** Nor
50A2 **Andalucia** Region, Spain
17A1 **Andalusia** USA

Andaman Is

83D4 **Andaman Is** Burma
83D4 **Andaman S** Burma
108A2 **Andamooka** Aust
38H5 **Andenes** Nor
47C1 **Andermatt** Switz
57B2 **Andernach** Germany
14A2 **Anderson** Indiana, USA
18B2 **Anderson** Missouri, USA
17B1 **Anderson** S Carolina, USA
4F3 **Anderson** *R* Can
87B1 **Andhra Pradesh** State, India
55B3 **Andikíthira** *I* Greece
65J5 **Andizhan** Uzbekistan
65H6 **Andkhui** Afghan
74B3 **Andong** S Korea
51C1 **Andorra** Principality, SW Europe
51C1 **Andorra-La-Vella** Andorra
43D4 **Andover** Eng
35A2 **Andradina** Brazil
12B2 **Andreafsky** USA
92B2 **Andreas,C** Cyprus
53C2 **Andria** Italy
11C4 **Andros** *I* The Bahamas
55B3 **Ándros** *I* Greece
87A2 **Androth** *I* India
50B2 **Andújar** Spain
100A2 **Andulo** Angola
97C4 **Anécho** Togo
97C3 **Anéfis** Mali
34B3 **Añelo** Arg
63C2 **Angarsk** Russian Fed
38H6 **Ånge** Sweden
24A2 **Angel de la Guarda** *I* Mexico
79B2 **Angeles** Phil
39G7 **Angelholm** Sweden
109C1 **Angellala Creek** *R* Aust
22B1 **Angels Camp** USA
71E4 **Angemuk** *Mt* Indon
48B2 **Angers** France
76C3 **Angkor** *Hist Site* Camb
41C3 **Anglesey** *I* Wales
19A4 **Angleton** USA
6G3 **Angmagssalik** Greenland
101D2 **Angoche** Mozam
29B3 **Angol** Chile
14B2 **Angola** Indiana, USA
100A2 **Angola** Republic, Africa
103H6 **Angola Basin** Atlantic O
12H3 **Angoon** USA
48C2 **Angoulême** France
96A1 **Angra do Heroismo** Açores
35C2 **Angra dos Reis** Brazil
34C3 **Anguil** Arg
27E3 **Anguilla** *I* Caribbean S
26B2 **Anguilla Cays** *Is* Caribbean S
86B2 **Angul** India
99C3 **Angumu** Zaïre
56C1 **Anholt** *I* Den
73C4 **Anhua** China
72D3 **Anhui** Province, China
12C2 **Aniak** USA
35B1 **Anicuns** Brazil
46B2 **Anizy-le-Château** France
4C3 **Anjak** USA
48B2 **Anjou** Region, France
101D2 **Anjouan** *I* Comoros
101D2 **Anjozorobe** Madag
74B3 **Anju** N Korea
72B3 **Ankang** China
92B2 **Ankara** Turk
101D2 **Ankaratra** *Mt* Madag
101D3 **Ankazoabo** Madag
101D2 **Ankazobe** Madag
56C2 **Anklam** Germany
76D3 **An Loc** Viet

73B4 **Anlong** China
73C3 **Anlu** China
18C2 **Anna** USA
96C1 **'Annaba** Alg
92C3 **An Nabk** S Arabia
92C3 **An Nabk** Syria
108A1 **Anna Creek** Aust
80C3 **An Nafūd** *Desert* S Arabia
93D3 **An Najaf** Iraq
42C2 **Annan** Scot
15C3 **Annapolis** USA
86A1 **Annapurna** *Mt* Nepal
14B2 **Ann Arbor** USA
94C1 **An Nāsirah** Syria
93E3 **An Nāsiriyah** Iraq
47B2 **Annecy** France
47B1 **Annemasse** France
76D3 **An Nhon** Viet
73A5 **Anning** China
17A1 **Anniston** USA
89E8 **Annobon** *I* Eq Guinea
49C2 **Annonay** France
27J1 **Annotto Bay** Jamaica
73D3 **Anqing** China
72B2 **Ansai** China
57C3 **Ansbach** Germany
26C3 **Anse d'Hainault** Haiti
72E1 **Anshan** China
73B4 **Anshun** China
97C3 **Ansongo** Mali
14B3 **Ansted** USA
92C2 **Antakya** Turk
101E2 **Antalaha** Madag
92B2 **Antalya** Turk
92B2 **Antalya Körfezi** *B* Turk
101D2 **Antananarivo** Madag
112C1 **Antarctic Circle** Ant
112C3 **Antarctic Pen** Ant
50B2 **Antequera** Spain
96B2 **Anti-Atlas** *Mts* Mor
7D5 **Anticosti, Î. d'** Can
27E3 **Antigua** *I* Caribbean S
Anti Lebanon = Jebel esh Sharqi
21A2 **Antioch** USA
19A3 **Antlers** USA
30B3 **Antofagasta** Chile
45C1 **Antrim** County, N Ire
45C1 **Antrim** N Ire
45C1 **Antrim Hills** N Ire
101D2 **Antseranana** Madag
101D2 **Antsirabe** Madag
101D2 **Antsohihy** Madag
76D3 **An Tuc** Viet
46C1 **Antwerpen** Belg
45C2 **An Uaimh** Irish Rep
84C3 **Anupgarh** India
87C3 **Anuradhapura** Sri Lanka
Anvers = Antwerpen
4B3 **Anvik** USA
63B3 **Anxi** China
72C2 **Anyang** China
72A3 **A'nyêmaqên Shan** *Upland* China
47C2 **Anza** *R* Italy
13E1 **Anzac** Can
65K4 **Anzhero-Sudzhensk** Russian Fed
53B2 **Anzio** Italy
74E2 **Aomori** Japan
52A1 **Aosta** Italy
97B3 **Aoukâr** *Desert Region* Maur
96C2 **Aoulef** Alg
95A2 **Aozou** Chad
30E3 **Apa** *R* Brazil/Par
11B4 **Apalachee B** USA
17B2 **Apalachicola** USA
17A2 **Apalachicola B** USA
23B2 **Apan** Mexico
64E3 **Apatity** Russian Fed
32C3 **Apaporis** *R* Colombia
35A2 **Aparecida do Taboado** Brazil
79B2 **Aparri** Phil
54A1 **Apatin** Croatia

64E3 **Apatity** Russian Fed
24B3 **Apatzingan** Mexico
56B2 **Apeldoorn** Neth
35B2 **Apiai** Brazil
33F2 **Apoera** Surinam
108B3 **Apollo Bay** Aust
79C4 **Apo,Mt** *Mt* Phil
17B2 **Apopka,L** USA
30F2 **Aporé** *R* Brazil
10A2 **Apostle Is** USA
10A2 **Apostle L** USA
23A1 **Apozol** Mexico
11B3 **Appalachian Mts** USA
52B2 **Appennino Abruzzese** *Mts* Italy
52A2 **Appennino Ligure** *Mts* Italy
53C2 **Appennino Lucano** *Mts* Italy
53B2 **Appennino Napoletano** *Mts* Italy
52B2 **Appennino Tosco-Emilliano** *Mts* Italy
52B2 **Appennino Umbro-Marchigiano** *Mts* Italy
47C1 **Appenzell** Switz
42C2 **Appleby** Eng
14A2 **Appleton** Wisconsin, USA
30F3 **Apucarana** Brazil
23B1 **Apulco** Mexico
32D2 **Apure** *R* Ven
32C6 **Apurimac** *R* Peru
92C4 **'Aqaba** Jordan
92B4 **'Aqaba,G of** Egypt/ S Arabia
90B3 **'Aqdā** Iran
30E3 **Aquidauana** Brazil
23A2 **Aquila** Mexico
86A1 **Ara** India
17A1 **Arab** USA
81D4 **Arabian S** Asia/ Arabian Pen
31D4 **Aracajú** Brazil
30E3 **Aracanguy, Mts de** Par
31D2 **Aracati** Brazil
30F3 **Araçatuba** Brazil
50A2 **Aracena** Spain
31C5 **Araçuai** Brazil
94B3 **Arad** Israel
60B4 **Arad** Rom
98C1 **Arada** Chad
91B5 **'Arādah** UAE
106C1 **Arafura S** Indon/Aust
30F2 **Aragarças** Brazil
51B1 **Aragón** Region, Spain
50B1 **Aragón** *R* Spain
33G6 **Araguaia** *R* Brazil
31B3 **Araguaina** Brazil
31B5 **Araguari** Brazil
35B1 **Araguari** *R* Brazil
75B1 **Arai** Japan
96C2 **Arak** Alg
90A3 **Arak** Iran
76A2 **Arakan Yoma** *Mts* Burma
87B2 **Arakkonam** India
65G5 **Aral Sea** Kazakhstan/ Uzbekistan
80E1 **Aral'sk** Kazakhstan
Aral'skoye More = Aral S
40B2 **Aran I** Irish Rep
50B1 **Aranda de Duero** Spain
23A1 **Arandas** Mexico
50B1 **Aranjuez** Spain
75A2 **Arao** Japan
97B3 **Araouane** Mali
29E2 **Arapey** *R* Urug
31D4 **Arapiraca** Brazil
35A2 **Araporgas** Brazil
30G4 **Ararangua** Brazil
31B6 **Araraquara** Brazil
35B2 **Araras** Brazil
107D4 **Ararat** Aust
93D2 **Ararat** Armenia
93E2 **Aras** *R* Azerbaijan
75C1 **Arato** Japan
32D2 **Arauca** *R* Ven

34A3 **Arauco** Chile
32C2 **Arauea** Colombia
85C4 **Arávalli Range** *Mts* India
31B5 **Araxá** Brazil
99D2 **Arba Minch** Eth
53A3 **Arbatax** Sardegna
93D2 **Arbīl** Iraq
47A1 **Arbois** France
39H6 **Arbrå** Sweden
44C3 **Arbroath** Scot
47A1 **Arc** France
47B2 **Arc** *R* France
48B3 **Arcachon** France
17B2 **Arcadia** USA
20B2 **Arcata** USA
23A2 **Arcelia** Mexico
26B2 **Archipiélago de Camaguey** *Arch* Cuba
29B6 **Archipiélago de la Reina Adelaida** *Arch* Chile
29B4 **Archipiélago de las Chones** *Arch* Chile
32B2 **Archipiélago de las Perlas** *Arch* Panama
35B2 **Arcos** Brazil
50A2 **Arcos de la Frontera** Spain
6B2 **Arctic Bay** Can
1C1 **Arctic Circle**
4E3 **Arctic Red** Can
4E3 **Arctic Red R** Can
4D3 **Arctic Village** USA
54C2 **Arda** *R* Bulg
65F6 **Ardabīl** Iran
93D1 **Ardahan** Turk
39F6 **Ardal** Nor
96C2 **Ardar des Iforas** *Upland* Alg/Mali
45C2 **Ardee** Irish Rep
90B3 **Ardekān** Iran
46C2 **Ardennes** Department, France
57A2 **Ardennes** Region, Belg
90B3 **Ardestan** Iran
92C3 **Ardh es Suwwan** *Desert Region* Jordan
50A2 **Ardila** *R* Port
109C2 **Ardlethan** Aust
9D3 **Ardmore** USA
44A3 **Ardnamurchan** *Pt* Scot
46A1 **Ardres** France
44B3 **Ardrishaig** Scot
42B2 **Ardrossan** Scot
27D3 **Arecibo** Puerto Rico
31D2 **Areia Branca** Brazil
21A2 **Arena,Pt** USA
39F7 **Arendal** Nor
30B2 **Arequipa** Peru
52B2 **Arezzo** Italy
52B2 **Argenta** Italy
49C2 **Argentan** France
46B2 **Argenteuil** France
28C7 **Argentina** Republic, S America
103F7 **Argentine Basin** Atlantic O
48C2 **Argenton-sur-Creuse** France
54C2 **Argeş** *R* Rom
84B2 **Arghardab** *R* Afghan
55B3 **Argolikós Kólpos** *G* Greece
46C2 **Argonne** Region, France
55B3 **Argos** Greece
55B3 **Argostólion** Greece
22B3 **Arguello,Pt** USA
106B2 **Argyle,L** Aust
56C1 **Arhus** Den
100A3 **Ariamsvlei** Namibia
50B1 **Arian zón** *R* Spain
34C2 **Arias** Arg
97B3 **Aribinda** Burkina
30B2 **Arica** Chile
84C2 **Arifwala** Pak
Arihã = Jericho
27L1 **Arima** Trinidad
35B1 **Arinos** Brazil

33F6	**Arinos** *R* Brazil
23A2	**Ario de Rosales** Mexico
27L1	**Aripo,Mt** Trinidad
33E5	**Aripuana** Brazil
33E5	**Aripuaná** *R* Brazil
44B3	**Arisaig** Scot
87B2	**Ariskere** India
13B2	**Aristazabal I** Can
34B3	**Arizona** Arg
9B3	**Arizona** State, USA
39G7	**Arjäng** Sweden
61F3	**Arkadak** Russian Fed
19B3	**Arkadelphia** USA
65H4	**Arkaly** Kazakhstan
11A3	**Arkansas** State, USA
11A3	**Arkansas** *R* USA
18A2	**Arkansas City** USA
64F3	**Arkhangel'sk** Russian Fed
41B3	**Arklow** Irish Rep
47D1	**Arlberg P** Austria
49C3	**Arles** France
19A3	**Arlington** Texas, USA
15C3	**Arlington** Virginia, USA
20B1	**Arlington** Washington, USA
97C3	**Arlit** Niger
57B3	**Arlon** Belg
	Armageddon = Megiddo
45C1	**Armagh** County, N Ire
45C1	**Armagh** N Ire
61F5	**Armavir** Russian Fed
23A2	**Armena** Mexico
32B3	**Armenia** Colombia
65F5	**Armenia** Republic, Europe
107E4	**Armidale** Aust
13D2	**Armstrong** Can
7C3	**Arnaud** *R* Can
92B2	**Arnauti** *C* Cyprus
56B2	**Arnhem** Neth
106C2	**Arnhem,C** Aust
106C2	**Arnhem Land** Aust
22B1	**Arnold** USA
15C1	**Arnprior** Can
46E1	**Arnsberg** Germany
100A3	**Aroab** Namibia
47C2	**Arona** Italy
12B2	**Aropuk L** USA
52A1	**Arosa** Switz
97A3	**Arquipélago dos Bijagós** *Arch* Guinea-Bissau
93D3	**Ar Ramadi** Iraq
42B2	**Arran** *I* Scot
93C2	**Ar Raqqah** Syria
95A2	**Ar Rāqūbah** Libya
49C1	**Arras** France
96A2	**Arrecife** Canary Is
34C2	**Arrecifes** Arg
23A1	**Arriaga** Mexico
93E3	**Ar Rifa't** Iraq
93E3	**Ar Rihāb** *Desert Region* Iraq
91A5	**Ar Riyāḍ** S Arabia
44B3	**Arrochar** Scot
111A2	**Arrowtown** NZ
23B1	**Arroyo Seco** Mexico
91B4	**Ar Ru'ays** Qatar
91C5	**Ar Rustaq** Oman
93D3	**Ar Rutbah** Iraq
47D2	**Arsiero** Italy
49D2	**Arsizio** Italy
61G2	**Arsk** Russian Fed
55B3	**Árta** Greece
23A2	**Arteaga** Mexico
63B2	**Artemovsk** Russian Fed
63D2	**Artemovskiy** Russian Fed
9C3	**Artesia** USA
111B2	**Arthurs P** NZ
112C2	**Artigas** *Base* Ant
29E2	**Artigas** Urug
4H3	**Artillery L** Can
48C1	**Artois** Region, France
112C2	**Arturo Prat** *Base* Ant
93D1	**Artvin** Turk
99D2	**Aru** Zaïre
33G6	**Aruanã** Brazil
27C4	**Aruba** *I* Caribbean S
86B1	**Arun** *R* Nepal
86C1	**Arunāchal Pradesh** Union Territory, India
87B3	**Aruppukkottai** India
99D3	**Arusha** Tanz
98C2	**Aruwimi** *R* Zaïre
68C2	**Arvayheer** Mongolia
47B2	**Arve** *R* France
7C5	**Arvida** Can
38H5	**Arvidsjaur** Sweden
39G7	**Arvika** Sweden
21B2	**Arvin** USA
94B1	**Arwad** *I* Syria
61F2	**Arzamas** Russian Fed
84C2	**Asadabad** Afghan
75A2	**Asahi** *R* Japan
74E2	**Asahi dake** *Mt* Japan
74E2	**Asahikawa** Japan
86B2	**Asansol** India
95A2	**Asawanwah** *Well* Libya
61K2	**Asbest** Russian Fed
15D2	**Asbury Park** USA
103H5	**Ascension** *I* Atlantic O
57B3	**Aschaffenburg** Germany
56C2	**Aschersleben** Germany
52B2	**Ascoli Piceno** Italy
47C1	**Ascona** Switz
99E1	**Aseb** Eritrea
96C2	**Asedjirad** *Upland* Alg
99D2	**Asela** Eth
38H6	**Åsele** Sweden
54B2	**Asenovgrad** Bulg
46C2	**Asfeld** France
61J2	**Asha** Russian Fed
17B1	**Ashburn** USA
111B2	**Ashburton** NZ
106A3	**Ashburton** *R* Aust
92B3	**Ashdod** Israel
19B3	**Ashdown** USA
11B3	**Asheville** USA
109D1	**Ashford** Aust
43E4	**Ashford** Eng
	Ashgabat = Ashkhabad
74D3	**Ashikaga** Japan
75A2	**Ashizuri-misaki** *Pt* Japan
65G6	**Ashkhabad** Turkmenistan
10B3	**Ashland** Kentucky, USA
18A1	**Ashland** Nebraska, USA
14B2	**Ashland** Ohio, USA
8A2	**Ashland** Oregon, USA
109C1	**Ashley** Aust
16B2	**Ashokan Res** USA
94B3	**Ashqelon** Israel
93D3	**Ash Shabakh** Iraq
91C4	**Ash Sha'm** UAE
93D2	**Ash Sharqāt** Iraq
93E3	**Ash Shatrah** Iraq
81C4	**Ash Shihr** Yemen
91A4	**Ash Shumlul** S Arabia
14B2	**Ashtabula** USA
7D4	**Ashuanipi L** Can
92C3	**'Aşi** *R* Syria
47D2	**Asiago** Italy
53A2	**Asinara** *I* Medit S
65K4	**Asino** Russian Fed
93D2	**Aşkale** Turk
39G7	**Askersund** Sweden
84C1	**Asmar** Afghan
95C3	**Asmera** Eritrea
75A2	**Aso** Japan
99D1	**Asosa** Eth
111A2	**Aspiring,Mt** NZ
93C2	**As Sabkhah** Syria
91A5	**As Salamiyah** S Arabia
92C2	**As Salamīyah** Syria
93D3	**As Salmān** Iraq
86C1	**Assam** State, India
93E3	**As Samāwah** Iraq
91B5	**As Şanām** Region, S Arabia
94C2	**As Sanamayn** Syria
56B2	**Assen** Neth
56B1	**Assens** Den
95A1	**As Sidrah** Libya
5H5	**Assiniboia** Can
5G4	**Assiniboine,Mt** Can
30F3	**Assis** Brazil
93C3	**As Sukhnah** Syria
93E2	**As Sulaymānīyah** Iraq
91A5	**As Summan** Region, S Arabia
99E3	**Assumption** *I* Seychelles
92C3	**As Suwaydā'** Syria
93D3	**As Suwayrah** Iraq
93E2	**Astara** Azerbaijan
52A2	**Asti** Italy
55C3	**Astipálaia** *I* Greece
50A1	**Astorga** Spain
8A2	**Astoria** USA
61G4	**Astrakhan'** Russian Fed
50A1	**Asturias** Region, Spain
30E4	**Asunción** Par
99D2	**Aswa** *R* Uganda
80B3	**Aswân** Egypt
95C2	**Aswân High Dam** Egypt
95C2	**Asyût** Egypt
92C3	**As Zilaf** Syria
97C4	**Atakpamé** Togo
71D4	**Atambua** Indon
6E3	**Atangmik** Greenland
96A2	**Atar** Maur
65J5	**Atasu** Kazakhstan
95C3	**Atatisk Baraji** *Res* Turkmenistan
95C3	**Atbara** Sudan
65H4	**Atbasar** Kazakhstan
11A4	**Atchafalaya B** USA
10A3	**Atchison** USA
16B3	**Atco** USA
23A1	**Atenguillo** Mexico
52B2	**Atessa** Italy
46B1	**Ath** Belg
13E2	**Athabasca** Can
5G4	**Athabasca** *R* Can
5H4	**Athabasca L** Can
45D2	**Athenry** Irish Rep
	Athens = Athínai
11B3	**Athens** Georgia, USA
14B3	**Athens** Ohio, USA
19A3	**Athens** Texas, USA
55B3	**Athínai** Greece
41B3	**Athlone** Irish Rep
16C1	**Athol** USA
55B3	**Athos** *Mt* Greece
45C2	**Athy** Irish Rep
98B1	**Ati** Chad
7A5	**Atikoken** Can
61F3	**Atkarsk** Russian Fed
18B2	**Atkins** USA
23B2	**Atlacomulco** Mexico
11B3	**Atlanta** Georgia, USA
14B2	**Atlanta** Michigan, USA
18A1	**Atlantic** USA
10C3	**Atlantic City** USA
16B2	**Atlantic Highlands** USA
103H8	**Atlantic Indian Basin** Atlantic O
103H7	**Atlantic Indian Ridge** Atlantic O
96C1	**Atlas Saharien** *Mts* Alg
4E4	**Atlin** Can
4E4	**Atlin L** Can
94B2	**'Atlit** Israel
23B2	**Atlixco** Mexico
11B3	**Atmore** USA
101D3	**Atofinandrahana** Madag
12D3	**Atognak I** USA
19A3	**Atoka** USA
23A1	**Atotonilco** Mexico
23B2	**Atoyac** *R* Mexico
32B2	**Atrato** *R* Colombia
91B5	**Attaf** Region, UAE
81C3	**At Tā'if** S Arabia
94C2	**At Tall** Syria
17A1	**Attalla** USA
7B4	**Attauapiskat** Can
7B4	**Attauapiskat** *R* Can
93D3	**At Taysīyah** *Desert Region* S Arabia
14A2	**Attica** Indiana, USA
46C2	**Attigny** France
15D2	**Attleboro** Massachusetts, USA
76D3	**Attopeu** Laos
92C4	**At Tubayq** *Upland* S Arabia
34B3	**Atuel** *R* Arg
39H7	**Atvidaberg** Sweden
22B2	**Atwater** USA
49D3	**Aubagne** France
46C2	**Aube** Department, France
49C3	**Aubenas** France
17A1	**Auburn** Alabama, USA
21A2	**Auburn** California, USA
14A2	**Auburn** Indiana, USA
18A1	**Auburn** Nebraska, USA
15C2	**Auburn** New York, USA
20B1	**Auburn** Washington, USA
48C3	**Auch** France
110B1	**Auckland** NZ
105G6	**Auckland Is** NZ
48C3	**Aude** *R* France
7B4	**Auden** Can
47B1	**Audincourt** France
109C1	**Augathella** Aust
57C3	**Augsburg** Germany
106A4	**Augusta** Aust
11B3	**Augusta** Georgia, USA
18A2	**Augusta** Kansas, USA
10D2	**Augusta** Maine, USA
12D3	**Augustine I** USA
58C2	**Augustów** Pol
106A3	**Augustus,Mt** Aust
46A2	**Aumale** France
85D3	**Auraiya** India
85D5	**Aurangābād** India
96C1	**Aurès** *Mts* Alg
48C3	**Aurillac** France
8C3	**Aurora** Colorado, USA
10B2	**Aurora** Illinois, USA
14B3	**Aurora** Indiana, USA
18B2	**Aurora** Mississippi, USA
100A3	**Aus** Namibia
14B2	**Au Sable** USA
10A2	**Austin** Minnesota, USA
21B2	**Austin** Nevada, USA
9D3	**Austin** Texas, USA
106C3	**Australia** Fed. State/ Monarchy
107D4	**Australian Alps** *Mts* Aust
37E4	**Austria** Federal Republic, Europe
46A1	**Authie** *R* France
24B3	**Autlán** Mexico
49C2	**Autun** France
49C2	**Auvergne** Region, France
49C2	**Auxerre** France
46B1	**Auxi-le-Château** France
49C2	**Avallon** France
22C4	**Avalon** USA
7E5	**Avalon Pen** Can
35B2	**Avaré** Brazil
90D3	**Avaz** Iran
94B3	**Avedat** *Hist Site* Israel
33F4	**Aveiro** Brazil
50A1	**Aveiro** Port
29E2	**Avellaneda** Arg
53B2	**Avellino** Italy
46B1	**Avesnes-sur-Helpe** France

Avesta

39H6 **Avesta** Sweden
52B2 **Avezzano** Italy
44C3 **Aviemore** Scot
111B2 **Aviemore,L** NZ
47B2 **Avigliana** Italy
49C3 **Avignon** France
50B1 **Avila** Spain
50A1 **Aviles** Spain
47D1 **Avisio** *R* Italy
108B3 **Avoca** *R* Aust
43C4 **Avon** County, Eng
43D4 **Avon** *R* Dorset, Eng
43D3 **Avon** *R* Warwick, Eng
43C4 **Avonmouth** Wales
17B2 **Avon Park** USA
46B2 **Avre** *R* France
54A2 **Avtovac** Bosnia-Herzegovina
94C2 **A'waj** *R* Syria
74D4 **Awaji-shima** *B* Japan
99E2 **Awarē** Eth
111A2 **Awarua Pt** NZ
99E2 **Awash** Eth
99E2 **Awash** *R* Eth
75B1 **Awa-shima** *I* Japan
111B2 **Awatere** *R* NZ
95A2 **Awbārī** Libya
98C2 **Aweil** Sudan
95B2 **Awjilah** Libya
96A2 **Awserd** *Well* Mor
6A2 **Axel Heiburg I** Can
43C4 **Axminster** Eng
75B1 **Ayabe** Japan
29E3 **Ayacucho** Arg
32C6 **Ayacucho** Peru
65K5 **Ayaguz** Kazakhstan
82C2 **Ayakkum Hu** *L* China
50A2 **Ayamonte** Spain
63F2 **Ayan** Russian Fed
32C6 **Ayauiri** Peru
92A2 **Aydin** Turk
55C3 **Áyios Evstrátios** *I* Greece
43D4 **Aylesbury** Eng
13D2 **Aylmer,Mt** Can
94C2 **'Ayn al Fijah** Syria
93D2 **Ayn Zālah** Iraq
95B2 **Ayn Zuwayyah** *Well* Libya
99D2 **Ayod** Sudan
107D2 **Ayr** Aust
42B2 **Ayr** Scot
42B2 **Ayr** *R* Scot
42B2 **Ayre,Pt of** Eng
54C2 **Aytos** Bulg
76C3 **Aytthaya** Thai
23A1 **Ayutla** Mexico
55C3 **Ayvacık** Turk
55C3 **Ayvalik** Turk
86A1 **Azamgarh** India
97B3 **Azaouad** *Desert Region* Mali
97D3 **Azare** Nig
92C2 **A'Zāz** Syria
Azbine = Aïr
65F5 **Azerbaijan** Republic, Russian Fed
32B4 **Azogues** Ecuador
Azores = Açores
98C1 **Azoum** *R* Chad
60E4 **Azov, Sea of** Russian Fed/Ukraine
Azovskoye More = Azov, Sea of
96B1 **Azrou** Mor
34D3 **Azucena** Arg
32A2 **Azuero,Pen de** Panama
29E3 **Azúl** Arg
94C2 **Az-Zabdānī** Syria
91C5 **Az Zāhirah** *Mts* Oman
95A2 **Az Zahra** Iraq
96A2 **Azzeffal** *R* Maur
93E3 **Az Zubayr** Iraq

B

94B2 **Ba'abda** Leb
92C3 **Ba'albek** Leb
94B3 **Ba'al Hazor** *Mt* Israel

99E2 **Baardheere** Somalia
54C2 **Babadag** Rom
92A1 **Babaeski** Turk
32B4 **Babahoyo** Ecuador
81C4 **Bāb al Mandab** *Str* Djibouti/Yemen
71D4 **Babar** *I* Indon
99D3 **Babati** Tanz
60E2 **Babayevo** Russian Fed
14B2 **Baberton** USA
13B1 **Babine** *R* Can
5F4 **Babine L** Can
90B2 **Bābol** Iran
79B2 **Babuyan Chan** Phil
79B2 **Babuyan Is** Phil
31C2 **Bacabal** Brazil
71D4 **Bacan** *I* Indon
60C4 **Bačau** Rom
76D1 **Bac Can** Viet
108B3 **Bacchus Marsh** Aust
82B2 **Bachu** China
4J3 **Back** *R* Can
12J2 **Backbone Ranges** *Mts* Can
76D1 **Bac Ninh** Viet
79B3 **Bacolod** Phil
79B3 **Baco,Mt** Phil
87B2 **Badagara** India
72A1 **Badain Jaran Shamo** *Desert* China
50A2 **Badajoz** Spain
51C1 **Badalona** Spain
93D3 **Badanah** S Arabia
46D2 **Bad Bergzabern** Germany
46D1 **Bad Ems** Germany
47C1 **Baden** Switz
57B3 **Baden-Baden** Germany
57B3 **Baden-Württemberg** State, Germany
57C3 **Badgastein** Austria
22C2 **Badger** USA
57B2 **Bad-Godesberg** Germany
57B2 **Bad Hersfeld** Germany
46D1 **Bad Honnef** Germany
85B4 **Badin** Pak
52B1 **Bad Ischl** Austria
93C3 **Badiyat ash Sham** *Desert Region* Jordan/Iraq
57B3 **Bad-Kreuznach** Germany
46D1 **Bad Nevenahr-Ahrweiler** Germany
47C1 **Bad Ragaz** Switz
57C3 **Bad Tolz** Germany
87C3 **Badulla** Sri Lanka
50B2 **Baena** Spain
97A3 **Bafatá** Guinea-Bissau
4H2 **Baffin** *Region* Can
6C2 **Baffin B** Greenland/Can
6C2 **Baffin I** Can
98B2 **Bafia** Cam
97A3 **Bafing** *R* Mali
97A3 **Bafoulabé** Mali
98B2 **Bafoussam** Cam
90C3 **Bāfq** Iran
60E5 **Bafra Burun** *Pt* Turk
91C4 **Bāft** Iran
98C2 **Bafwasende** Zaïre
86A1 **Bagaha** India
87B1 **Bāgalkot** India
99D3 **Bagamoyo** Tanz
29F2 **Bagé** Brazil
93D3 **Baghdād** Iraq
86B2 **Bagherhat** Bang
91C3 **Bāghīn** Iran
84B1 **Baghlan** Afghan
49C3 **Bagnols-sur-Cèze** France
97B3 **Bagoé** *R* Mali
Bagu = Pegu
79B2 **Baguio** Phil
86B1 **Bāhādurābād** India
11C4 **Bahamas,The** *Is* Caribbean S
86B2 **Baharampur** India
92A4 **Baharīya Oasis** Egypt

84C3 **Bahawalpur** Pak
84C3 **Bahawalpur** Province, Pak
85C3 **Bahawathagar** Pak
Bahia = Salvador
31C4 **Bahia** State, Brazil
29D3 **Bahía Blanca** Arg
29D3 **Bahía Blanca** *B* Arg
34A3 **Bahía Concepción** *B* Chile
35C2 **Bahia da Ilha Grande** *B* Brazil
24B2 **Bahia de Banderas** *B* Mexico
24C2 **Bahia de Campeche** *B* Mexico
25D3 **Bahia de la Ascension** *B* Mexico
24B3 **Bahia de Petacalco** *B* Mexico
96A2 **Bahia de Rio de Oro** *B* Mor
35C2 **Bahía de Sepetiba** *B* Brazil
29C6 **Bahía Grande** *B* Arg
9B4 **Bahia Kino** Mexico
24A2 **Bahia Magdalena** *B* Mexico
24A2 **Bahia Sebastia Vizcaino** *B* Mexico
99D1 **Bahar Dar** Eth
86A1 **Bahraich** India
80D3 **Bahrain** Sheikdom, Arabian Pen
93D3 **Bahr al Milh** *L* Iraq
98C2 **Bahr Aouk** *R* Chad/CAR
Bahrat Lut = Dead S
98C2 **Bahr el Arab** *Watercourse* Sudan
99D2 **Bahr el Ghazal** *R* Sudan
98B1 **Bahr el Ghazal** *Watercourse* Chad
101H1 **Baia de Maputo** *B* Mozam
31B2 **Baia de Marajó** *B* Brazil
101D2 **Baiá de Pemba** *B* Mozam
31C2 **Baia de São Marcos** *B* Brazil
50A2 **Baia de Setúbal** *B* Port
31D4 **Baia de Todos os Santos** *B* Brazil
100A2 **Baia dos Tigres** Angola
60B4 **Baia Mare** Rom
98B2 **Baïbokoum** Chad
69E2 **Baicheng** China
101E2 **Baie Antongila** *B* Madag
7D5 **Baie-Comeau** Can
101D2 **Baie de Bombetoka** *B* Madag
101D2 **Baie de Mahajamba** *B* Madag
101D3 **Baie de St Augustin** *B* Madag
94B2 **Baie de St Georges** *B* Leb
10D2 **Baie des Chaleurs** *B* Can
7C4 **Baie-du-Poste** Can
72B3 **Baihe** China
72C3 **Bai He** *R* China
93D3 **Ba'īji** Iraq
86A2 **Baikunthpur** India
Baile Atha Cliath = Dublin
54B2 **Băilesti** Rom
46B1 **Bailleul** France
72A3 **Baima** China
17B1 **Bainbridge** USA
12B2 **Baird Inlet** USA
4B3 **Baird Mts** USA
72D1 **Bairin Youqi** China
72D1 **Bairin Zuoqi** China
107D4 **Bairnsdale** Aust
79B4 **Bais** Phil
54A1 **Baja** Hung
9B3 **Baja California** State, Mexico

24A1 **Baja California** *Pen* Mexico
61J2 **Bakal** Russian Fed
98C2 **Bakala** CAR
97A3 **Bakel** Sen
8C2 **Baker** Montana, USA
8B2 **Baker** Oregon, USA
6A3 **Baker Foreland** *Pt* Can
4J3 **Baker L** Can
4J3 **Baker Lake** Can
8A2 **Baker,Mt** USA
9B3 **Bakersfield** USA
90C2 **Bakharden** Turkmenistan
90C2 **Bakhardok** Turkmenistan
60D3 **Bakhmach** Ukraine
38C1 **Bakkaflói** *B* Iceland
99D2 **Bako** Eth
98C2 **Bakouma** CAR
65F5 **Baku** Azerbaijan
Baky = Baku
92B2 **Balā** Turk
79A4 **Balabac** *I* Phil
70C3 **Balabac** *Str* Malay
78C2 **Balaikarangan** Indon
108A2 **Balaklava** Aust
61G3 **Balakovo** Russian Fed
86A2 **Balāngīr** India
61F3 **Balashov** Russian Fed
86B2 **Balasore** India
80A3 **Balât** Egypt
52C1 **Balaton** *L* Hung
45C2 **Balbriggan** Irish Rep
29E3 **Balcarce** Arg
54C2 **Balchik** Bulg
111B3 **Balclutha** NZ
18B2 **Bald Knob** USA
17B1 **Baldwin** USA
9C3 **Baldy Peak** *Mt* USA
Balearic Is = Islas Baleares
78C2 **Baleh** *R* Malay
79B2 **Baler** Phil
61H2 **Balezino** Russian Fed
106A1 **Bali** *I* Indon
92A2 **Balıkesir** Turk
93C2 **Balīkh** *R* Syria
78D3 **Balikpapan** Indon
79B2 **Balintang Chan** Phil
78C4 **Bali S** Indon
35A1 **Baliza** Brazil
84B1 **Balkh** Afghan
65J5 **Balkhash** Kazakhstan
44B3 **Ballachulish** Scot
45B2 **Ballaghaderreen** Irish Rep
42B2 **Ballantrae** Scot
4G2 **Ballantyne Str** Can
87B2 **Ballapur** India
107D4 **Ballarat** Aust
44C3 **Ballater** Scot
112C7 **Balleny Is** Ant
86A1 **Ballia** India
109D1 **Ballina** Aust
41B3 **Ballina** Irish Rep
45B2 **Ballinasloe** Irish Rep
45B2 **Ballinrobe** Irish Rep
55A2 **Ballsh** Alb
45B1 **Ballycastle** Irish Rep
45C1 **Ballycastle** N Ire
45C1 **Ballymena** N Ire
45C1 **Ballymoney** N Ire
45B1 **Ballyshannon** Irish Rep
45B2 **Ballyvaghan** Irish Rep
108B3 **Balmoral** Aust
34C2 **Balnearia** Arg
84B3 **Balochistān** Region, Pak
100A2 **Balombo** Angola
109C1 **Balonn** *R* Aust
85C3 **Balotra** India
86A1 **Balrāmpur** India
107D4 **Balranald** Aust
31B3 **Balsas** Brazil
23B2 **Balsas** Mexico
24B3 **Balsas** *R* Mexico
60C4 **Balta** Ukraine
39H7 **Baltic S** N Europe

92B3 **Baltîm** Egypt
45B3 **Baltimore** Irish Rep
10C3 **Baltimore** USA
86B1 **Bālurghāt** India
61H4 **Balykshi** Kazakhstan
91C4 **Bam** Iran
98B1 **Bama** Nig
97B3 **Bamako** Mali
98C2 **Bambari** CAR
17B1 **Bamberg** USA
57C3 **Bamberg** Germany
98C2 **Bambili** Zaïre
35B2 **Bambui** Brazil
98B2 **Bamenda** Cam
13C3 **Bamfield** Can
98B2 **Bamingui** *R* CAR
98B2 **Bamingui Bangoran** *National Park* CAR
84B2 **Bamiyan** Afghan
91D4 **Bampur** Iran
91D4 **Bampur** *R* Iran
98C2 **Banalia** Zaïre
97B3 **Banamba** Mali
76C3 **Ban Aranyaprathet** Thai
76C2 **Ban Ban** Laos
77C4 **Ban Betong** Thai
45C1 **Banbridge** N Ire
43D3 **Banbury** Eng
44C3 **Banchory** Scot
25D3 **Banco Chinchorro** *Is* Mexico
15C1 **Bancroft** Can
86A1 **Bānda** India
70A3 **Banda Aceh** Indon
97B4 **Bandama** *R* Ivory Coast
91C4 **Bandar Abbās** Iran
90A2 **Bandar Anzalī** Iran
99F2 **Bandarbeyla** Somalia
91B4 **Bandar-e Daylam** Iran
91B4 **Bandar-e Lengheh** Iran
91B4 **Bandar-e Māqām** Iran
91B4 **Bandar-e Rig** Iran
90B2 **Bandar-e Torkoman** Iran
91A3 **Bandar Khomeynī** Iran
78C2 **Bandar Seri Begawan** Brunei
71D4 **Banda S** Indon
91C4 **Band Bonī** Iran
35C2 **Bandeira** *Mt* Brazil
97B3 **Bandiagara** Mali
60C5 **Bandirma** Turk
45B3 **Bandon** Irish Rep
98B3 **Bandundu** Zaïre
78B4 **Bandung** Indon
25E2 **Banes** Cuba
13D2 **Banff** Can
44C3 **Banff** Scot
5G4 **Banff** *R* Can
13D2 **Banff Nat Pk** Can
87B2 **Bangalore** India
98C2 **Bangassou** CAR
70C3 **Banggi** *I* Malay
95B1 **Banghāzī** Libya
76D2 **Bang Hieng** *R* Laos
78B3 **Bangka** *I* Indon
78A3 **Bangko** Indon
76C3 **Bangkok** Thai
82C3 **Bangladesh** Republic, Asia
84D2 **Bangong Co** *L* China
10D2 **Bangor** Maine, USA
45D1 **Bangor** N Ire
16B2 **Bangor** Pennsylvania, USA
42B3 **Bangor** Wales
78D3 **Bangsalsembera** Indon
76B3 **Bang Saphan Yai** Thai
79B2 **Bangued** Phil
98B2 **Bangui** CAR
100C2 **Bangweulu** *L* Zambia
77C4 **Ban Hat Yai** Thai
76C2 **Ban Hin Heup** Laos
76C1 **Ban Houei Sai** Laos
76B3 **Ban Hua Hin** Thai
97B3 **Bani** *R* Mali
97C3 **Bani Bangou** Niger
95A1 **Banī Walīd** Libya
92C2 **Bāniyās** Syria
94B2 **Baniyas** Syria
52C2 **Banja Luka** Bosnia-Herzegovina
78C3 **Banjarmasin** Indon
97A3 **Banjul** The Gambia
77B4 **Ban Kantang** Thai
76D2 **Ban Khemmarat** Laos
77B4 **Ban Khok Kloi** Thai
71F5 **Banks I** Aust
5E4 **Banks I** British Columbia, Can
4F2 **Banks I** Northwest Territories, Can
20C1 **Banks L** USA
111B2 **Banks Pen** NZ
109C4 **Banks Str** Aust
86B2 **Bankura** India
76B2 **Ban Mae Sariang** Thai
76B2 **Ban Mae Sot** Thai
76D3 **Ban Me Thuot** Viet
45C1 **Bann** *R* N Ire
77B4 **Ban Na San** Thai
84C2 **Bannu** Pak
34A3 **Baños Maule** Chile
76C2 **Ban Pak Neun** Laos
77C4 **Ban Pak Phanang** Thai
76D3 **Ban Ru Kroy** Camb
76B3 **Ban Sai Yok** Thai
76C3 **Ban Sattahip** Thai
59B3 **Banská Bystrica** Slovakia
85C4 **Bānswāra** India
77B4 **Ban Tha Kham** Thai
76D2 **Ban Thateng** Laos
76C2 **Ban Tha Tum** Thai
41B3 **Bantry** Irish Rep
41A3 **Bantry** *B* Irish Rep
76D3 **Ban Ya Soup** Viet
78C4 **Banyuwangi** Indon
72C3 **Baofeng** China
76C1 **Bao Ha** Viet
72B3 **Baoji** China
76D3 **Bao Loc** Viet
68B4 **Baoshan** China
72C1 **Baotou** China
87C1 **Bāpatla** India
46B1 **Bapaume** France
93D3 **Ba'Qūbah** Iraq
32J7 **Baquerizo Moreno** Ecuador
54A2 **Bar** Montenegro, Yugos
99D1 **Bara** Sudan
99E2 **Baraawe** Somalia
78D3 **Barabai** Indon
86A1 **Bāra Banki** India
65J4 **Barabinsk** Russian Fed
65J4 **Barabinskaya Step** *Steppe* Kazakhstan/ Russian Fed
50B1 **Baracaldo** Spain
26C2 **Baracoa** Cuba
94C2 **Baradá** *R* Syria
109C2 **Baradine** Aust
87A1 **Bārāmati** India
84C2 **Baramula** Pak
85D3 **Bārān** India
79B3 **Barangas** Phil
4E4 **Baranof I** USA
60C3 **Baranovichi** Belorussia
108A2 **Baratta** Aust
86B1 **Barauni** India
31C6 **Barbacena** Brazil
27F4 **Barbados** *I* Caribbean S
51C1 **Barbastro** Spain
101H1 **Barberton** S Africa
48B2 **Barbezieux** France
32C2 **Barbòsa** Colombia
27E3 **Barbuda** *I* Caribbean S
107D3 **Barcaldine** Aust
Barce = Al Marj
53C3 **Barcellona** Italy
51C1 **Barcelona** Spain
33E1 **Barcelona** Ven
107D3 **Barcoo** *R* Aust
34B3 **Barda del Medio** Arg
95A2 **Bardai** Chad
29C3 **Bardas Blancas** Arg
86B2 **Barddhamān** India
59C3 **Bardejov** Slovakia
47C2 **Bardi** Italy
47B2 **Bardonecchia** Italy
43B3 **Bardsey** *I* Wales
84D3 **Bareilly** India
64D2 **Barentsøya** *I* Barents S
64E2 **Barents S** Russian Fed
95C3 **Barentu** Eritrea
86A2 **Bargarh** India
47B2 **Barge** Italy
63D2 **Barguzin** Russian Fed
63D2 **Barguzin** *R* Russian Fed
86B2 **Barhi** India
53C2 **Bari** Italy
51D2 **Barika** Alg
32C2 **Barinas** Ven
86B2 **Baripāda** India
85C4 **Bari Sādri** India
86C2 **Barisal** Bang
78C3 **Barito** *R* Indon
95A2 **Barjuj** *Watercourse* Libya
73A3 **Barkam** China
18C2 **Barkley,L** USA
13B3 **Barkley Sd** Can
100B4 **Barkly East** S Africa
106C2 **Barkly Tableland** *Mts* Aust
46C2 **Bar-le-Duc** France
106A3 **Barlee,L** Aust
106A3 **Barlee Range** *Mts* Aust
53C2 **Barletta** Italy
85C3 **Barmer** India
108B2 **Barmera** Aust
43B3 **Barmouth** Wales
42D2 **Barnard Castle** Eng
65K4 **Barnaul** Russian Fed
16B3 **Barnegat** USA
16B3 **Barnegat B** USA
6C2 **Barnes Icecap** Can
17B1 **Barnesville** Georgia, USA
14B3 **Barnesville** Ohio USA
42D3 **Barnsley** Eng
43B4 **Barnstaple** Eng
97C4 **Baro** Nig
86C1 **Barpeta** India
32D1 **Barquisimeto** Ven
31C4 **Barra** Brazil
44A3 **Barra** *I* Scot
109D2 **Barraba** Aust
23A2 **Barra de Navidad** Mexico
35C2 **Barra de Piraí** Brazil
35A1 **Barragem de São Simão** *Res* Brazil
35A1 **Barra do Garças** Brazil
35B1 **Barragem Agua Vermelha** *Res* Brazil
50A2 **Barragem do Castelo do Bode** *Res* Port
50A2 **Barragem do Maranhão** *Res* Port
35A2 **Barragem Três Irmãos** *Res* Brazil
44A3 **Barra Head** *Pt* Scot
31C6 **Barra Mansa** Brazil
32B6 **Barranca** Peru
32C2 **Barrancabermeja** Colombia
33E2 **Barrancas** Ven
30E4 **Barranqueras** Arg
32C1 **Barranquilla** Colombia
44A3 **Barra,Sound of** *Chan* Scot
16C1 **Barre** USA
34B2 **Barreal** Arg
31C4 **Barreiras** Brazil
50A2 **Barreiro** Port
31D3 **Barreiros** Brazil
107D5 **Barren,C** Aust
12D3 **Barren Is** USA
31B6 **Barretos** Brazil
13E2 **Barrhead** Can
14C2 **Barrie** Can
13C2 **Barrière** Can
108B2 **Barrier Range** *Mts* Aust
107E4 **Barrington,Mt** Aust
27N2 **Barrouaillie** St Vincent and the Grenadines
4C2 **Barrow** USA
45C2 **Barrow** *R* Irish Rep
106C3 **Barrow Creek** Aust
106A3 **Barrow I** Aust
42C2 **Barrow-in-Furness** Eng
4C2 **Barrow,Pt** USA
6A2 **Barrow Str** Can
15C1 **Barry's Bay** Can
87B1 **Barsi** India
9B3 **Barstow** USA
49C2 **Bar-sur-Aube** France
33F2 **Bartica** Guyana
92B1 **Bartın** Turk
107D2 **Bartle Frere,Mt** Aust
9D3 **Bartlesville** USA
101C3 **Bartolomeu Dias** Mozam
58C2 **Bartoszyce** Pol
78C4 **Barung** *I* Indon
85D4 **Barwāh** India
85C4 **Barwāni** India
109C1 **Barwon** *R* Aust
61G3 **Barysh** Russian Fed
98B2 **Basankusu** Zaïre
34D2 **Basavilbas** Arg
79B1 **Basco** Phil
52A1 **Basel** Switz
53C2 **Basento** *R* Italy
13E2 **Bashaw** Can
79B1 **Bashi Chan** Phil
61H3 **Bashkortostan** Russian Fed
79B4 **Basilan** *I* Phil
43E4 **Basildon** Eng
43D4 **Basingstoke** Eng
8B2 **Basin Region** USA
93E3 **Basra** Iraq
46D2 **Bas-Rhin** Department, France
76D3 **Bassac** *R* Camb
13E2 **Bassano** Can
52B1 **Bassano** Italy
47D2 **Bassano del Grappa** Italy
97C4 **Bassari** Togo
101C3 **Bassas da India** *I* Mozam Chan
76A2 **Bassein** Burma
27E3 **Basse Terre** Guadeloupe
97C4 **Bassila** Benin
22C2 **Bass Lake** USA
107D4 **Bass Str** Aust
39G7 **Båstad** Sweden
91B4 **Bastak** Iran
86A1 **Basti** India
52A2 **Bastia** Corse
57B3 **Bastogne** Belg
19B3 **Bastrop** Louisiana, USA
19A3 **Bastrop** Texas, USA
98A2 **Bata** Eq Guinea
78C3 **Batakan** Indon
84D2 **Batala** India
68B3 **Batang** China
98B2 **Batangafo** CAR
79B1 **Batan Is** Phil
35B2 **Batatais** Brazil
15C2 **Batavia** USA
109D3 **Batemans Bay** Aust
17B1 **Batesburg** USA
18B2 **Batesville** Arkansas, USA
19C3 **Batesville** Mississippi, USA
43C4 **Bath** Eng
15C2 **Bath** New York, USA
98B1 **Batha** *R* Chad
107D4 **Bathurst** Aust
7D5 **Bathurst** Can

4F2	Bathurst,C Can
106C2	Bathurst I Aust
4H2	Bathurst I Can
4H3	Bathurst Inlet *B* Can
97B3	Batié Burkina
90B3	Bātlāq-e-Gavkhūnī Salt Flat Iran
109C3	Batlow Aust
93D2	Batman Turk
96C1	Batna Alg
11A3	Baton Rouge USA
94B1	Batroun Leb
76C3	Battambang Camb
87C3	Batticaloa Sri Lanka
13F2	Battle *R* Can
10B2	Battle Creek USA
7E4	Battle Harbour Can
20C2	Battle Mountain USA
78D2	Batukelau Indon
65F5	Batumi Georgia
77C5	Batu Pahat Malay
78A3	Baturaja Indon
94B2	Bat Yam Israel
71D4	Baubau Indon
97C3	Bauchi Nig
47B2	Bauges *Mts* France
7E4	Bauld,C Can
47B1	Baumes-les-Dames France
63D2	Baunt Russian Fed
31B6	Bauru Brazil
35A1	Baus Brazil
57C2	Bautzen Germany
78C4	Baween *I* Indon
95B2	Bawiti Egypt
97B3	Bawku Ghana
76B2	Bawlake Burma
108A2	Bawlen Aust
17B1	Baxley USA
25E2	Bayamo Cuba
78D4	Bayan Indon
68C2	Bayandzürh Mongolia
68B3	Bayan Har Shan *Mts* China
72A1	Bayan Mod China
72B1	Bayan Obo China
47A2	Bayard *P* France
12J3	Bayard,Mt Can
63D3	Bayasgalant Mongolia
79B3	Baybay Phil
93D1	Bayburt Turk
10B2	Bay City Michigan, USA
19A4	Bay City Texas, USA
92B2	Bay Dağlari Turk
64H3	Baydaratskaya Guba *B* Russian Fed
99E2	Baydhabo Somalia
48B2	Bayeux France
47D1	Bayerische Alpen *Mts* Germany
57C3	Bayern State, Germany
92C3	Bāyir Jordan
63C2	Baykalskiy Khrebet *Mts* Russian Fed
63B1	Baykit Russian Fed
63B3	Baylik Shan *Mts* China/Mongolia
61J3	Baymak Russian Fed
79B2	Bayombang Phil
48B3	Bayonne France
57C3	Bayreuth Germany
19C3	Bay St Louis USA
15D2	Bay Shore USA
15C1	Bays,L of Can
68A2	Baytik Shan *Mts* China
	Bayt Lahm = Bethlehem
19B4	Baytown USA
50B2	Baza Spain
59D3	Bazaliya Ukraine
48B3	Bazas France
73B3	Bazhong China
91D4	Bazmān Iran
94C1	Bcharre Leb
16B3	Beach Haven USA
43E4	Beachy Head Eng
16C2	Beacon USA
101D2	Bealanana Madag
18B1	Beardstown USA

	Bear I = Bjørnøya
22B1	Bear Valley USA
8D2	Beatrice USA
44C2	Beatrice Oilfield N Sea
13C1	Beatton *R* Can
5F4	Beatton River Can
29E6	Beauchene Is Falkland Is
109D1	Beaudesert Aust
1B5	Beaufort S Can
100B4	Beaufort West S Africa
15D1	Beauharnois Can
44B3	Beauly Scot
21B3	Beaumont California, USA
11A3	Beaumont Texas, USA
49C2	Beaune France
48C2	Beauvais France
13F1	Beauval Can
12E1	Beaver Alaska, USA
13F2	Beaver *R* Saskatchewan, Can
4D3	Beaver Creek Can
12E1	Beaver Creek USA
18C2	Beaver Dam Kentucky, USA
13E2	Beaverhill L Can
14A1	Beaver I USA
18B2	Beaver L USA
13D1	Beaverlodge Can
85C3	Beawar India
34B2	Beazley Arg
35B2	Bebedouro Brazil
43E3	Beccles Eng
54B1	Bečej Serbia, Yugos
96B1	Béchar Alg
12C3	Becharof L USA
11B3	Beckley USA
43D3	Bedford County, Eng
43D3	Bedford Eng
14A3	Bedford Indiana, USA
27M2	Bedford Pt Grenada
4D2	Beechey Pt USA
109C3	Beechworth Aust
109D1	Beenleigh Aust
92B3	Beersheba Israel
	Beër Sheva = Beersheba
94B3	Beér Sheva *R* Israel
9D4	Beeville USA
98C2	Befale Zaïre
101D2	Befandriana Madag
109C3	Bega Aust
91B3	Behbehān Iran
12H3	Behm Canal *Sd* USA
90B2	Behshahr Iran
84B2	Behsud Afghan
69E2	Bei'an China
73B5	Beihai China
72D2	Beijing China
76E1	Beiliu China
73B4	Beipan Jiang *R* China
72E1	Beipiao China
	Beira = Sofala
92C3	Beirut Leb
68B2	Bei Shan *Mts* China
94B2	Beit ed Dīne Leb
94B3	Beit Jala Israel
50A2	Beja Port
96C1	Beja Tunisia
96C1	Bejaïa Alg
50A1	Béjar Spain
90C3	Bejestān Iran
59C3	Békéscsaba Hung
101D3	Bekily Madag
86A1	Bela India
85B3	Bela Pak
78C2	Belaga Malay
16A3	Bel Air USA
87B1	Belamoalli India
71D3	Belang Indon
70A3	Belangpidie Indon
	Belarus = Belorussia
	Belau = Palau Is.
101C3	Bela Vista Mozam
70A3	Belawan Indon
61J2	Belaya *R* Ukraine
6A2	Belcher Chan Can
7C4	Belcher Is Can

84B1	Belchiragh Afghan
61H3	Belebey Russian Fed
99E2	Beled Weyne Somalia
31B2	Belém Brazil
32B3	Belén Colombia
34D2	Belén Urug
9C3	Belen USA
45D1	Belfast N Ire
101H1	Belfast S Africa
45D1	Belfast Lough Estuary N Ire
99D1	Bēlfodiyo Eth
42D2	Belford Eng
49D2	Belfort France
87A1	Belgaum India
56A2	Belgium Kingdom, N W Europe
60E3	Belgorod Russian Fed
60D4	Belgorod Dnestrovskiy Ukraine
	Belgrade = Beograd
95A2	Bel Hedan Libya
78B3	Belinyu Indon
78B3	Belitung *I* Indon
25D3	Belize Belize
25D3	Belize Republic, Cent America
48C2	Bellac France
5F4	Bella Coola Can
47C2	Bellagio Italy
19A4	Bellaire USA
47C1	Bellano Italy
87B1	Bellary India
109C1	Bellata Aust
47B2	Belledonne *Mts* France
8C2	Belle Fourche USA
49D2	Bellegarde France
17B2	Belle Glade USA
7E4	Belle I Can
48B2	Belle-Ile *I* France
7E4	Belle Isle,Str of Can
7C5	Belleville Can
18A2	Belleville Kansas, USA
20B1	Bellevue Washington, USA
109D2	Bellingen Aust
8A2	Bellingham USA
112C2	Bellingshausen *Base* Ant
112C3	Bellingshausen S Ant
52A1	Bellinzona Switz
32B2	Bello Colombia
107E3	Bellona Reefs Nouvelle Calédonie
22B1	Bellota USA
15D2	Bellows Falls USA
6B3	Bell Pen Can
52B1	Belluno Italy
29D2	Bell Ville Arg
31D5	Belmonte Brazil
25D3	Belmopan Belize
45B1	Belmullet Irish Rep
69E1	Belogorsk Russian Fed
101D3	Beloha Madag
31C5	Belo Horizonte Brazil
10B2	Beloit Wisconsin, USA
64E3	Belomorsk Russian Fed
61J3	Beloretsk Russian Fed
60C3	Belorussia Republic, Europe
101D2	Belo-Tsiribihina Madag
64E3	Beloye More *S* Russian Fed
60E1	Beloye Ozero *L* Russian Fed
60E1	Belozersk Russian Fed
14B3	Belpre USA
108A2	Beltana Aust
19A3	Belton USA
59D3	Bel'tsy Moldavia
16B2	Belvidere New Jersey, USA
98B3	Bembe Angola

97C3	Bembéréke Benin
10A2	Bemidji USA
39G6	Bena Nor
98C3	Bena Dibele Zaïre
108C3	Benalla Aust
44B3	Ben Attow *Mt* Scot
50A1	Benavente Spain
44A3	Benbecula *I* Scot
106A4	Bencubbin Aust
8A2	Bend USA
44B3	Ben Dearg *Mt* Scot
60C4	Bendery Moldavia
107D4	Bendigo Aust
57C3	Benešov Czech Republic
53B2	Benevento Italy
83C4	Bengal,B of Asia
96D1	Ben Gardane Tunisia
72D3	Bengbu China
78A2	Bengkalis Indon
78A3	Bengkulu Indon
100A2	Benguela Angola
92B3	Benha Egypt
44B2	Ben Hope *Mt* Scot
99C2	Beni Zaïre
32D6	Béni *R* Bol
96B1	Beni Abbes Alg
51C1	Benicarló Spain
7A5	Benidji USA
51B2	Benidorm Spain
51C2	Beni Mansour Alg
95C2	Beni Mazar Egypt
96B1	Beni Mellal Mor
97C4	Benin Republic, Africa
97C4	Benin City Nig
95C2	Beni Suef Egypt
44B2	Ben Kilbreck *Mt* Scot
44B3	Ben Lawers *Mt* UK
109C4	Ben Lomond *Mt* Aust
44C3	Ben Macdui *Mt* Scot
44B2	Ben More Assynt *Mt* Scot
111B2	Benmore,L NZ
44B3	Ben Nevis *Mt* Scot
15D2	Bennington USA
94B2	Bennt Jbail Leb
98B2	Bénoué *R* Cam
9B3	Benson Arizona, USA
99C2	Bentiu Sudan
19B3	Benton Arkansas, USA
18C2	Benton Kentucky, USA
14A2	Benton Harbor USA
97C4	Benue *R* Nig
45B1	Benwee Hd *C* Irish Rep
44B3	Ben Wyvis *Mt* Scot
72E1	Benxi China
54B2	Beograd Serbia, Yugos
86A2	Beohāri India
74C4	Beppu Japan
55A2	Berat Alb
95C3	Berber Sudan
99E1	Berbera Somalia
98B2	Berbérati CAR
46A1	Berck France
60C4	Berdichev Ukraine
60E4	Berdyansk Ukraine
97B4	Berekum Ghana
22B2	Berenda USA
5J4	Berens *R* Can
5J4	Berens River Can
108A1	Beresford Aust
59C3	Berettyóújfalu Hung
58D2	Bereza Belorussia
59C3	Berezhany Ukraine
65G4	Berezniki Russian Fed
60D4	Berezovka Ukraine
64H3	Berezovo Russian Fed
92A2	Bergama Turk
52A1	Bergamo Italy
39F6	Bergen Nor
46C1	Bergen op Zoom Neth
48C3	Bergerac France
46D1	Bergisch-Gladbach Germany
12F2	Bering Gl USA

1C6 Bering Str USA/Russian Fed
91C4 Berizak Iran
50B2 Berja Spain
8A3 Berkeley USA
112B2 Berkner I Ant
54B2 Berkovitsa Bulg
43D4 Berkshire County, Eng
16C1 Berkshire Hills USA
13D2 Berland R Can
56C2 Berlin Germany
56C2 Berlin State, Germany
15D2 Berlin New Hampshire, USA
30D3 Bermejo Bol
30D4 Bermejo R Arg
3M5 Bermuda I Atlantic O
52A1 Bern Switz
16B2 Bernardsville USA
34C3 Bernasconi Arg
56C2 Bernburg Germany
47B1 Berner Oberland Mts Switz
6B2 Bernier B Can
57C3 Berounka R Czech Republic
108B2 Berri Aust
96C1 Berriane Alg
48C2 Berry Region, France
22A1 Berryessa,L USA
11C4 Berry Is The Bahamas
98B2 Bertoua Cam
45B2 Bertraghboy B Irish Rep
15C2 Berwick USA
42C2 Berwick-upon-Tweed Eng
43C3 Berwyn Mts Wales
101D2 Besalampy Madag
49D2 Besançon France
59C3 Beskidy Zachodnie Mts Pol
93C2 Besni Turk
94B3 Besor R Israel
11B3 Bessemer USA
101D2 Betafo Madag
50A1 Betanzos Spain
94B3 Bet Guvrin Israel
101G1 Bethal S Africa
100A3 Bethanie Namibia
18B1 Bethany Missouri, USA
18A2 Bethany Oklahoma, USA
4B3 Bethel Alaska, USA
16C2 Bethel Connecticut, USA
14B2 Bethel Park USA
15C3 Bethesda USA
94B3 Bethlehem Israel
101G1 Bethlehem S Africa
15C2 Bethlehem USA
48C1 Bethune France
101D3 Betioky Madag
108B1 Betoota Aust
98B2 Betou Congo
82A1 Betpak Dala Steppe Kazakhstan
101D3 Betroka Madag
7D5 Betsiamites Can
86A1 Bettiah India
12D1 Bettles USA
47C2 Béttola Italy
85D4 Bétul India
85D3 Betwa R India
46D1 Betzdorf Germany
12C3 Beverley,L USA
16D1 Beverly USA
21B3 Beverly Hills USA
97B4 Beyla Guinea
87B2 Beypore India
Beyrouth = Beirut
92B2 Beyşehir Turk
92B2 Beyşehir Gölü L Turk
94B2 Beyt Shean Israel
47C1 Bezau Austria
60E2 Bezhetsk Russian Fed
49C3 Béziers France
90C2 Bezmein Turkmenistan

63C2 Beznosova Russian Fed
86B1 Bhadgaon Nepal
87C1 Bhadrachalam India
86B2 Bhadrakh India
87B2 Bhadra Res India
87B2 Bhadravati India
84B3 Bhag Pak
86B1 Bhagalpur India
84C2 Bhakkar Pak
82D3 Bhamo Burma
85D4 Bhandara India
85D3 Bharatpur India
85C4 Bharuch India
86B2 Bhatiapara Ghat Bang
84C2 Bhatinda India
87A2 Bhatkal India
86B2 Bhatpara India
85C4 Bhavnagar India
84C2 Bhera Pak
86A1 Bheri R Nepal
86A2 Bhilai India
85C3 Bhilwara India
87C1 Bhimavaram India
85D3 Bhind India
84D3 Bhiwani India
87B1 Bhongir India
85D4 Bhopal India
86B2 Bhubaneshwar India
85B4 Bhuj India
85D4 Bhusawal India
82C3 Bhutan Kingdom, Asia
71E4 Biak I Indon
58C2 Biala Podlaska Pol
58B2 Bialograd Pol
58C2 Bialystok Pol
38A1 Biargtangar C Iceland
90C2 Biarjmand Iran
48B3 Biarritz France
47C1 Biasca Switz
92B4 Biba Egypt
74E2 Bibai Japan
100A2 Bibala Angola
57B3 Biberach Germany
97R4 Bibiani Ghana
54C1 Bicaz Rom
97C4 Bida Nig
87B1 Bidar India
91C5 Bidbid Oman
43B4 Bideford Eng
43B4 Bideford B Eng
96C2 Bidon 5 Alg
58C2 Biebrza Pol
52A1 Biel Switz
59B2 Bielawa Pol
56B2 Bielefeld Germany
47B1 Bieler See L Switz
52A1 Biella Italy
58C2 Bielsk Podlaski Pol
76D3 Bien Hoa Viet
53B2 Biferno R Italy
92A1 Biga Turk
55C3 Bigadiç Turk
19C3 Big Black R USA
18A1 Big Blue R USA
17B2 Big Cypress Swamp USA
4D3 Big Delta USA
49D2 Bigent Germany
13F2 Biggar Can
5H4 Biggar Kindersley Can
109D1 Biggenden Aust
12G3 Bigger,Mt Can
8C2 Bighorn R USA
76C3 Bight of Bangkok B Thai
97C4 Bight of Benin B W Africa
97C4 Bight of Biafra B Cam
6C3 Big I Can
47C1 Bignasco Switz
97A3 Bignona Sen
21B2 Big Pine USA
17B2 Big Pine Key USA
22C3 Big Pine Mt USA
14A2 Big Rapids USA
5H4 Big River Can
9C3 Big Spring USA
7A4 Big Trout L Can

7B4 Big Trout Lake Can
52C2 Bihać Bosnia-Herzegovina
86B1 Bihar India
86B2 Bihar State, India
99D3 Biharamulo Tanz
60B4 Bihor Mt Rom
87B1 Bijapur India
87C1 Bijapur India
90A2 Bijar Iran
86A1 Bijauri Nepal
54A2 Bijeljina Bosnia-Herzegovina
73B4 Bijie China
84D3 Bijnor India
84C3 Bijnot Pak
84C3 Bikaner India
94B2 Bikfaya Leb
69F2 Bikin Russian Fed
98B3 Bikoro Zaïre
85C3 Bilara India
84D2 Bilaspur India
86A2 Bilaspur India
76B3 Bilauktaung Range Mts Thai
50B1 Bilbao Spain
Bilbo = Bilbao
59B3 Bilé R Czech Republic
54A2 Bileća Bosnia-Herzegovina
92B1 Bilecik Turk
98C2 Bili R Zaïre
79B3 Biliran I Phil
8C2 Billings USA
95A3 Bilma Niger
11B3 Biloxi USA
98C1 Biltine Chad
85D4 Bina-Etawa India
79B3 Binalbagan Phil
101C2 Bindura Zim
100B2 Binga Zim
101C2 Binga Mt Zim
109D1 Bingara Aust
57B3 Bingen Germany
10C2 Binghamton USA
78D1 Bingkor Malay
93D2 Bingöl Turk
72D3 Binhai China
78A2 Bintan I Indon
78A3 Bintuhan Indon
78C2 Bintulu Malay
29B3 Bió Bió R Chile
102J4 Bioko I Atlantic O
87B1 Bir India
95B2 Bir Abu Husein Well Egypt
95B2 Bi'r al Harash Well Libya
98C1 Birao CAR
86B1 Biratnagar Nepal
12E1 Birch Creek USA
108B3 Birchip Aust
5G4 Birch Mts Can
7A4 Bird Can
106C3 Birdsville Aust
106C2 Birdum Aust
86A1 Birganj Nepal
91A3 Bir Gifgafa Well Egypt
94A3 Bir Hasana Well Egypt
35A2 Birigui Brazil
90C3 Birjand Iran
92B4 Birkat Qarun L Egypt
46D2 Birkenfeld Germany
42C3 Birkenhead Eng
60C4 Birlad Rom
94A3 Bir Lahfan Well Egypt
43C3 Birmingham Eng
11B3 Birmingham USA
95B2 Bir Misaha Well Egypt
96A2 Bir Moghrein Maur
97C3 Birnin Kebbi Nig
97C3 Birni N'Konni Nig
69F2 Birobidzhan Russian Fed
45C2 Birr Irish Rep
51C2 Bir Rabalou Alg
109C1 Birrie R Aust
44C2 Birsay Scot
61J2 Birsk Russian Fed

95B2 Bîr Tarfâwi Well Egypt
63B2 Biryusa Russian Fed
39J7 Biržai Lithuania
96B2 Bir Zreigat Well Maur
48A2 Biscay,B of France/Spain
17B2 Biscayne B USA
46D2 Bischwiller France
73B4 Bishan China
82B1 Bishkek Kirghizia
8B3 Bishop USA
42D2 Bishop Auckland Eng
43E4 Bishop's Stortford Eng
86A2 Bishrampur India
96C1 Biskra Alg
79C4 Bislig Phil
8C2 Bismarck USA
90A3 Bisotün Iran
97A3 Bissau Guinea-Bissau
10A1 Bissett Can
5G4 Bistcho L Can
54C1 Bistrita R Rom
98B2 Bitam Gabon
57B3 Bitburg Germany
46D2 Bitche France
93D2 Bitlis Turk
55B2 Bitola Macedonia
56C2 Bitterfeld Germany
100A4 Bitterfontein S Africa
92B3 Bitter Lakes Egypt
8B2 Bitteroot Range Mts USA
74D3 Biwa-ko L Japan
99E1 Biyo Kaboba Eth
65K4 Biysk Russian Fed
96C1 Bizerte Tunisia
51C2 Bj bou Arréridj Alg
52C1 Bjelovar Croatia
96B2 Bj Flye Ste Marie Alg
64C2 Bjørnøya I Barents S
12F1 Black R USA
18B2 Black R USA
107D3 Blackall Aust
42C3 Blackburn Eng
4D3 Blackburn,Mt USA
13E2 Black Diamond Can
5H5 Black Hills USA
44B3 Black Isle Pen Scot
27R3 Blackman's Barbados
43C4 Black Mts Wales
43C3 Blackpool Eng
27H1 Black River Jamaica
8B2 Black Rock Desert USA
66E6 Black S Asia/Europe
45A1 Blacksod B Irish Rep
109D2 Black Sugarloaf Mt Aust
97B3 Black Volta R Ghana
41B3 Blackwater R Irish Rep
18A2 Blackwell USA
54B2 Blagoevgrad Bulg
63E2 Blagoveshchensk Russian Fed
20B1 Blaine USA
44C3 Blair Atholl Scot
44C3 Blairgowrie Scot
17B1 Blakely USA
108A1 Blanche,L Aust
34A2 Blanco R Arg
34B1 Blanco R Arg
8A2 Blanco,C USA
7E4 Blanc Sablon Can
43C4 Blandford Forum Eng
46A2 Blangy-sur-Bresle France
46B1 Blankenberge Belg
101C2 Blantyre Malawi
48B2 Blaye France
109C2 Blayney Aust
111B2 Blenheim NZ
96C1 Blida Alg
14B1 Blind River Can
108A2 Blinman Aust
78C4 Blitar Indon
15D2 Block I USA
16D2 Block Island Sd USA

Bloemfontein

101G1 **Bloemfontein** S Africa	6H3 **Bogarnes** Iceland	7E5 **Bonavista** Can	54B2 **Botevgrad** Bulg
101G1 **Bloemhof** S Africa	92C2 **Boğazlıyan** Turk	108A2 **Bon Bon** Aust	101G1 **Bothaville** S Africa
101G1 **Bloemhof Dam** *Res* S Africa	61K2 **Bogdanovich** Russian Fed	98C2 **Bondo** Zaïre	64C3 **Bothnia,G of** Sweden/Fin
33F3 **Blommesteinmeer** *L* Surinam	68A2 **Bogda Shan** *Mt* China	97B4 **Bondoukou** Ivory Coast	100B3 **Botletli** *R* Botswana
38A1 **Blonduós** Iceland	100A3 **Bogenfels** Namibia	Bône = 'Annaba	60C4 **Botosani** Rom
45B1 **Bloody Foreland** *C* Irish Rep	109D1 **Boggabilla** Aust	33E3 **Bonfim** Guyana	100B3 **Botswana** Republic, Africa
14A3 **Bloomfield** Indiana, USA	109C2 **Boggabri** Aust	98C2 **Bongandanga** Zaïre	53C3 **Botte Donato** *Mt* Italy
18B1 **Bloomfield** Iowa, USA	45B2 **Boggeragh Mts** Irish Rep	98B1 **Bongor** Chad	46D1 **Bottrop** Germany
10B2 **Bloomington** Illinois, USA	79B3 **Bogo** Phil	19A3 **Bonham** USA	35B2 **Botucatu** Brazil
14A3 **Bloomington** Indiana, USA	109C3 **Bogong,Mt** Aust	53A2 **Bonifacio** Corse	7E5 **Botwood** Can
16A2 **Bloomsburg** USA	78B4 **Bogor** Indon	52A2 **Bonifacio,Str of** *Chan* Medit S	89D7 **Bouaké** Ivory Coast
78C4 **Blora** Indon	61H2 **Bogorodskoye** Russian Fed	Bonin Is = Ogasawara Gunto	98B2 **Bouar** CAR
6H3 **Blosseville Kyst** *Mts* Greenland	32C3 **Bogotá** Colombia	17B2 **Bonita Springs** USA	96B1 **Bouârfa** Mor
57B3 **Bludenz** Austria	63A2 **Bogotol** Russian Fed	57B2 **Bonn** Germany	98B2 **Bouca** CAR
11B3 **Bluefield** USA	86B2 **Bogra** Bang	20C1 **Bonners Ferry** USA	51C2 **Boufarik** Alg
32A1 **Bluefields** Nic	72D2 **Bo Hai** *B* China	12H1 **Bonnet Plume** *R* Can	Bougie = Bejaïa
26B3 **Blue Mountain Peak** *Mt* Jamaica	46B2 **Bohain-en-Vermandois** France	13E2 **Bonnyville** Can	97B3 **Bougouni** Mali
16A2 **Blue Mt** USA	72D2 **Bohai Wan** *B* China	97A4 **Bonthe** Sierra Leone	46C2 **Bouillon** France
109D2 **Blue Mts** Aust	57C3 **Böhmer-Wald** *Upland* Germany	99E1 **Booaaso** Somalia	96B2 **Bou Izakarn** Mor
27J1 **Blue Mts** Jamaica	79B4 **Bohol** *I* Phil	108B2 **Booligal** Aust	46D2 **Boulay-Moselle** France
8A2 **Blue Mts** USA	79B4 **Bohol S** Phil	109D1 **Boonah** Aust	8C2 **Boulder** Colorado, USA
Blue Nile = Bahr el Azraq	35A1 **Bois** *R* Brazil	15C2 **Boonville** USA	9B3 **Boulder City** USA
99D1 **Blue Nile** *R* Sudan	14B1 **Bois Blanc I** USA	109C2 **Boorowa** Aust	22A2 **Boulder Creek** USA
4G3 **Bluenose L** Can	8B2 **Boise** USA	6A2 **Boothia,G of** Can	48C1 **Boulogne** France
11B3 **Blue Ridge Mts** USA	96A2 **Bojador,C** Mor	6A2 **Boothia Pen** Can	98B2 **Boumba** *R* CAR
13D2 **Blue River** Can	79B2 **Bojeador,C** Phil	98B3 **Booué** Gabon	97B4 **Bouna** Ivory Coast
45B1 **Blue Stack** *Mt* Irish Rep	90C2 **Bojnürd** Iran	108A1 **Bopeechee** Aust	8B3 **Boundary Peak** *Mt* USA
111A3 **Bluff** NZ	97A3 **Boké** Guinea	99D2 **Bor** Sudan	97B4 **Boundiali** Ivory Coast
106A4 **Bluff Knoll** *Mt* Aust	109C1 **Bokhara** *R* Aust	92B2 **Bor** Turk	107F3 **Bourail** Nouvelle Calédonie
30G4 **Blumenau** Brazil	39F7 **Boknafjord** *Inlet* Nor	54B2 **Bor** Serbia, Yugos	
49D2 **Blundez** Austria	98B3 **Boko** Congo	8B2 **Borah Peak** *Mt* USA	97B3 **Bourem** Mali
20B2 **Bly** USA	76C3 **Bokor** Camb	39G7 **Borås** Sweden	49D2 **Bourg** France
12E3 **Blying Sd** USA	98C3 **Bokungu** Zaïre	91B4 **Borāzjän** Iran	49D2 **Bourg de Péage** France
42D2 **Blyth** Eng	98B1 **Bol** Chad	108A3 **Borda,C** Aust	
9B3 **Blythe** USA	23A1 **Bolaānos** Mexico	48B3 **Bordeaux** France	48C2 **Bourges** France
11B3 **Blytheville** USA	97A3 **Bolama** Guinea-Bissau	4G2 **Borden I** Can	48C3 **Bourg-Madame** France
97A4 **Bo** Sierra Leone	23A1 **Bolanos** Mexico	6B2 **Borden Pen** Can	49C2 **Bourgogne** Region, France
79B3 **Boac** Phil	48C2 **Bolbec** France	16B2 **Bordentown** USA	47B2 **Bourg-St-Maurice** France
72D2 **Boading** China	97B4 **Bole** Ghana	42C2 **Borders** Region, Scot	
14B2 **Boardman** USA	59B2 **Boleslawiec** Pol	108B3 **Bordertown** Aust	108C2 **Bourke** Aust
63C3 **Boatou** China	97B3 **Bolgatanga** Ghana	96C2 **Bordj Omar Dris** Alg	43D4 **Bournemouth** Eng
33E3 **Boa Vista** Brazil	60C4 **Bolgrad** Ukraine	8D1 **Borens River** Can	96C1 **Bou Saâda** Alg
97A4 **Boa Vista** *I* Cape Verde	34C3 **Bolívar** Arg	38A2 **Borgarnes** Iceland	98B1 **Bousso** Chad
76E1 **Bobai** China	18B2 **Bolívar** Missouri, USA	9C3 **Borger** USA	97A3 **Boutilmit** Maur
47C2 **Bóbbio** Italy	18C2 **Bolívar** Tennessee, USA	39H7 **Borgholm** Sweden	103J7 **Bouvet I** Atlantic O
97B3 **Bobo Dioulasso** Burkina	30C2 **Bolivia** Republic, S America	47C2 **Borgosia** Italy	34D2 **Bovril** Arg
60C3 **Bobruysk** Belorussia	38H6 **Bollnas** Sweden	47D1 **Borgo Valsugana** Italy	13E2 **Bow** *R* Can
17B2 **Boca Chica Key** *I* USA	109C1 **Bollon** Aust	59C3 **Borislav** Ukraine	107D2 **Bowen** Aust
32D5 **Bôca do Acre** Brazil	32C2 **Bollvar** *Mt* Ven	61F3 **Borisoglebsk** Russian Fed	19A3 **Bowie** Texas, USA
35C1 **Bocaiúva** Brazil	52B2 **Bologna** Italy	60C3 **Borisov** Belorussia	13E2 **Bow Island** Can
98B2 **Bocaranga** CAR	60D2 **Bologoye** Russian Fed	60E3 **Borisovka** Russian Fed	11B3 **Bowling Green** Kentucky, USA
17B2 **Boca Raton** USA	69F2 **Bolon'** Russian Fed	95A3 **Borkou** Region Chad	18B2 **Bowling Green** Missouri, USA
59C3 **Bochnia** Pol	61G3 **Bol'shoy Irgiz** *R* Russian Fed	39H6 **Borlänge** Sweden	14B2 **Bowling Green** Ohio, USA
56B2 **Bocholt** Germany	74C2 **Bol'shoy Kamen** Russian Fed	47C2 **Bormida** Italy	15C3 **Bowling Green** Virginia, USA
46D1 **Bochum** Germany	Bol'shoy Kavkaz =Caucasus	47D1 **Bormio** Italy	15C2 **Bowmanville** Can
100A2 **Bocoio** Angola	61G4 **Bol'shoy Uzen** *R* Kazakhstan	67F5 **Borneo** *I* Malay/ Indon	109D2 **Bowral** Aust
98B2 **Boda** CAR	9C4 **Bolson de Mapimi** *Desert* Mexico	39H7 **Bornholm** *I* Den	13C2 **Bowron** *R* Can
63D2 **Bodaybo** Russian Fed	43C3 **Bolton** Eng	55C3 **Bornova** Turk	72D3 **Bo Xian** China
21A2 **Bodega Head** *Pt* USA	92B1 **Bolu** Turk	98C2 **Boro** *R* Sudan	72D2 **Boxing** China
95A3 **Bodélé** *Region* Chad	38A1 **Bolungarvik** Iceland	97B3 **Boromo** Burkina	92B1 **Boyabat** Turk
38J5 **Boden** Sweden	92B2 **Bolvadin** Turk	60D2 **Borovichi** Russian Fed	98B2 **Boyali** CAR
47C1 **Bodensee** *L* Switz/ Germany	52B1 **Bolzano** Italy	106C2 **Borroloola** Aust	5J4 **Boyd** Can
87B1 **Bodhan** India	98B3 **Boma** Zaïre	54B1 **Borsa** Rom	16B2 **Boyertown** USA
87B2 **Bodinäyakkanür** India	107D4 **Bombala** Aust	90A3 **Borūjed** Iran	13E2 **Boyle** Can
43B4 **Bodmin** Eng	87A1 **Bombay** India	90B3 **Borūjen** Iran	41B3 **Boyle** Irish Rep
43B4 **Bodmin Moor** *Upland* Eng	99D2 **Bombo** Uganda	58B2 **Bory Tucholskie** Region, Pol	45C2 **Boyne** *R* Irish Rep
38G5 **Bodø** Nor	35B1 **Bom Despacho** Brazil	63D2 **Borzya** Russian Fed	17B2 **Boynoton Beach** USA
55C3 **Bodrum** Turk	86C1 **Bomdila** India	73B5 **Bose** China	98C2 **Boyoma Falls** Zaïre
98C3 **Boende** Zaïre	97A4 **Bomi Hills** Lib	101G1 **Boshof** S Africa	55C3 **Bozca Ada** *I* Turk
97A3 **Boffa** Guinea	31C4 **Bom Jesus da Lapa** Brazil	54A2 **Bosna** *R* Bosnia-Herzegovina	55C3 **Boz Dağlari** *Mts* Turk
76B2 **Bogale** Burma	63E2 **Bomnak** Russian Fed	37E4 **Bosnia-Herzegovina** Republic, Europe	8B2 **Bozeman** USA
19C3 **Bogalusa** USA	99C2 **Bomokandi** *R* Zaïre	75C1 **Bōsō-hantō** *B* Japan	Bozen = Bolzano
109C2 **Bogan** *R* Aust	98C2 **Bomu** *R* CAR/Zaïre	Bosporus = Karadeniz Boğazi	98B2 **Bozene** Zaïre
97B3 **Bogandé** Burkina	27D4 **Bonaire** *I* Caribbean S	51C2 **Bosquet** Alg	98B2 **Bozoum** CAR
	12F2 **Bona,Mt** USA	98B2 **Bossangoa** CAR	47B2 **Bra** Italy
	25D3 **Bonanza** Nic	98B2 **Bossèmbélé** CAR	52C2 **Brač** *I* Croatia
		19B3 **Bossier City** USA	15C1 **Bracebridge** Can
		65K5 **Bosten Hu** *L* China	95A2 **Brach** Libya
		43D3 **Boston** Eng	38H6 **Bräcke** Sweden
		10C2 **Boston** USA	17B2 **Bradenton** USA
		11A3 **Boston Mts** USA	
		85C4 **Botād** India	

Burhaniye

55C3	**Burhaniye** Turk
85D4	**Burhānpur** India
79B3	**Burias** *I* Phil
76C2	**Buriram** Thai
35B1	**Buritis** Brazil
13B2	**Burke Chan** Can
106C2	**Burketown** Aust
97B3	**Burkina** Republic, Africa
15C1	**Burks Falls** Can
8B2	**Burley** USA
10A2	**Burlington** Iowa, USA
16B2	**Burlington** New Jersey, USA
10C2	**Burlington** Vermont, USA
20B1	**Burlington** Washington, USA
83D3	**Burma** Republic, Asia
20B2	**Burney** USA
16A2	**Burnham** USA
107D5	**Burnie** Aust
42C3	**Burnley** Eng
20C2	**Burns** USA
5F4	**Burns Lake** Can
82C1	**Burqin** China
108A2	**Burra** Aust
109D2	**Burragorang,L** Aust
44C2	**Burray** *I* Scot
109C2	**Burren Junction** Aust
109C2	**Burrinjuck Res** Aust
60C5	**Bursa** Turk
80B3	**Bur Safâga** Egypt
	Bûr Sa'îd = Port Said
14B2	**Burton** USA
43D3	**Burton upon Trent** Eng
38J6	**Burtrask** Sweden
108B2	**Burtundy** Aust
71D4	**Buru** Indon
99C3	**Burundi** Republic, Africa
78A2	**Burung** Indon
63D2	**Buryatskaya Respublika,** Russian Fed
99D1	**Burye** Eth
61H4	**Burynshik** Kazakhstan
43E3	**Bury St Edmunds** Eng
91B4	**Büshehr** Iran
98B3	**Busira** *R* Zaïre
58C2	**Buskozdroj** Pol
94C2	**Busrā ash Shām** Syria
106A4	**Busselton** Aust
49D2	**Busto** Italy
52A1	**Busto Arsizio** Italy
79A3	**Busuanga** *I* Phil
98C2	**Buta** Zaïre
34B3	**Buta Ranquil** Arg
99C3	**Butare** Rwanda
42B2	**Bute** *I* Scot
69E2	**Butha Qi** China
14C2	**Butler** USA
8B2	**Butte** USA
77C4	**Butterworth** Malay
40B2	**Butt of Lewis** *C* Scot
6D3	**Button Is** Can
79C4	**Butuan** Phil
71D4	**Butung** *I* Indon
61F3	**Buturlinovka** Russian Fed
86A1	**Butwal** Nepal
99E2	**Buulo Barde** Somalia
99E2	**Buur Hakaba** Somalia
61F2	**Buy** Russian Fed
72B1	**Buyant Ovvo** Mongolia
61G5	**Buynaksk** Russian Fed
63D3	**Buyr Nuur** *L* Mongolia
93D2	**Büyük Ağri** *Mt* Turk
92A2	**Büyük Menderes** *R* Turk
54C1	**Buzău** Rom
54C1	**Buzau** *R* Rom
61H3	**Buzuluk** Russian Fed

16D2	**Buzzards B** USA
54C2	**Byala** Bulg
54B2	**Byala Slatina** Bulg
4H2	**Byam Martin** *Chan* Can
4H2	**Byam Martin I** Can
	Byblos = Jubail
94B1	**Byblos** Hist Site, Leb
58B2	**Bydgoszcz** Pol
39F7	**Bygland** Nor
6C2	**Bylot I** Can
109C2	**Byrock** Aust
22B2	**Byron** USA
109D1	**Byron,C** Aust
59B2	**Bytom** Pol

C

30E4	**Caacupé** Par
100A2	**Caála** Angola
13B2	**Caamano Sd** Can
30E4	**Caazapá** Par
79B2	**Cabanatuan** Phil
31E3	**Cabedelo** Brazil
50A2	**Cabeza del Buey** Spain
34C3	**Cabildo** Arg
34A2	**Cabildo** Chile
32C1	**Cabimas** Ven
98B3	**Cabinda** Angola
98B3	**Cabinda** Province, Angola
27C3	**Cabo Beata** Dom Rep
51C2	**Cabo Binibeca** *C* Spain
53A3	**Cabo Carbonara** *C* Sardegna
34A3	**Cabo Carranza** *C* Chile
50A2	**Cabo Carvoeiro** *C* Port
9B3	**Cabo Colnett** *C* Mexico
32B2	**Cabo Corrientes** *C* Colombia
24B2	**Cabo Corrientes** *C* Mexico
26B3	**Cabo Cruz** *C* Cuba
50B1	**Cabo de Ajo** *C* Spain
51C1	**Cabo de Caballeria** *C* Spain
51C1	**Cabo de Creus** *C* Spain
50B2	**Cabo de Gata** *C* Spain
29C7	**Cabo de Hornos** *C* Chile
51C2	**Cabo de la Nao** *C* Spain
50A1	**Cabo de Peñas** *C* Spain
50A2	**Cabo de Roca** *C* Port
51C2	**Cabo de Salinas** *C* Spain
35C2	**Cabo de São Tomé** *C* Brazil
50A2	**Cabo de São Vicente** *C* Port
50A2	**Cabo de Sines** *C* Port
51C1	**Cabo de Tortosa** *C* Spain
29C4	**Cabo Dos Bahias** *C* Arg
50A2	**Cabo Espichel** *C* Port
9B4	**Cabo Falso** *C* Mexico
51B2	**Cabo Ferrat** *C* Alg
50A1	**Cabo Finisterre** *C* Spain
51C1	**Cabo Formentor** *C* Spain
35C2	**Cabo Frio** Brazil
35C2	**Cabo Frio** *C* Brazil
26A4	**Cabo Gracias à Dios** Honduras
31B2	**Cabo Maguarinho** *C* Brazil
50A2	**Cabo Negro** *C* Mor
109D1	**Caboolture** Aust
33G3	**Cabo Orange** *C* Brazil
21B3	**Cabo Punta Banda** *C* Mexico
101C2	**Cabora Bassa Dam** Mozam

24A1	**Caborca** Mexico
24C2	**Cabo Rojo** *C* Mexico
23B1	**Cabos** Mexico
29C6	**Cabo San Diego** *C* Arg
32A4	**Cabo San Lorenzo** *C* Ecuador
53A3	**Cabo Teulada** *C* Sardegna
50A2	**Cabo Trafalgar** *C* Spain
50B2	**Cabo Tres Forcas** *C* Mor
29C5	**Cabo Tres Puntas** *C* Arg
7D5	**Cabot Str** Can
50B2	**Cabra** Spain
50A1	**Cabreira** *Mt* Port
51C2	**Cabrera** *I* Spain
34A3	**Cabrero** Chile
51B2	**Cabriel** *R* Spain
23B2	**Cacahuamilpa** Mexico
54B2	**Čačak** Serbia, Yugos
23B2	**C A Carillo** Mexico
30E2	**Cáceres** Brazil
50A2	**Caceres** Spain
18B2	**Cache** *R* USA
13C2	**Cache Creek** Can
30C4	**Cachi** Arg
33G5	**Cachimbo** Brazil
31D4	**Cachoeira** Brazil
35A1	**Cachoeira Alta** Brazil
31D3	**Cachoeira de Paulo Alfonso** *Waterfall* Brazil
29F2	**Cachoeira do Sul** Brazil
31C6	**Cachoeiro de Itapemirim** Brazil
22C3	**Cachuma,L** USA
100A2	**Cacolo** Angola
100A2	**Caconda** Angola
35A1	**Caçu** Brazil
100A2	**Çaculuvar** *R* Angola
59B3	**Čadca** Slovakia
43C3	**Cader Idris** *Mts* Wales
10B2	**Cadillac** USA
79B3	**Cadiz** Phil
50A2	**Cadiz** Spain
48B2	**Caen** France
42B3	**Caernarfon** Wales
43B3	**Caernarfon B** Wales
94B2	**Caesarea** *Hist Site* Israel
31C4	**Caetité** Brazil
30C4	**Cafayate** Arg
92B2	**Caga Tepe** Turk
79B2	**Cagayan** *R* Phil
79B4	**Cagayan de Oro** Phil
79B4	**Cagayan Is** Phil
53A3	**Cagliari** Sardegna
27D3	**Caguas** Puerto Rico
45B3	**Caha Mts** Irish Rep
45A3	**Cahersiveen** Irish Rep
45C2	**Cahir** Irish Rep
45C2	**Cahone Pt** Irish Rep
48C3	**Cahors** France
101C2	**Caia** Mozam
100B2	**Caianda** Angola
35A1	**Caiapó** *R* Brazil
35A1	**Caiapônia** Brazil
31D3	**Caicó** Brazil
26C2	**Caicos Is** Caribbean S
11C4	**Caicos Pass** The Bahamas
12C2	**Cairn Mt** USA
44C3	**Cairngorms** *Mts* Scot
107D2	**Cairns** Aust
92B3	**Cairo** Egypt
11B3	**Cairo** USA
108B1	**Caiwarro** Aust
32B5	**Cajabamba** Peru
32B5	**Cajamarca** Peru
27D5	**Calabozo** Ven
54B2	**Calafat** Rom
29B6	**Calafate** Arg
79B3	**Calagua Is** Phil
51B1	**Calahorra** Spain
48C1	**Calais** France

30C3	**Calama** Chile
32C3	**Calamar** Colombia
79A3	**Calamian Group** *Is* Phil
98B3	**Calandula** Angola
70A3	**Calang** Indon
95B2	**Calanscio Sand Sea** Libya
79B3	**Calapan** Phil
54C2	**Calarasi** Rom
51B1	**Calatayud** Spain
22B2	**Calaveras Res** USA
79B3	**Calbayog** Phil
19B4	**Calcasieu L** USA
86B2	**Calcutta** India
50A2	**Caldas da Rainha** Port
31B5	**Caldas Novas** Brazil
30B4	**Caldera** Chile
8B2	**Caldwell** USA
29C5	**Caleta Olivia** Arg
9B3	**Calexico** USA
5G4	**Calgary** Can
17B1	**Calhoun** USA
17B1	**Calhoun Falls** USA
32B3	**Cali** Colombia
87B2	**Calicut** India
8B3	**Caliente** Nevada, USA
8A3	**California** State, USA
22C3	**California Aqueduct** USA
87B2	**Calimera,Pt** India
34B2	**Calingasta** Arg
22A1	**Calistoga** USA
108B1	**Callabonna** *R* Aust
108A1	**Callabonna,L** Aust
15C1	**Callander** Can
44B3	**Callander** Scot
108A1	**Callanna** Aust
32B6	**Callao** Peru
13E1	**Calling L** Can
23B1	**Calnali** Mexico
17B2	**Caloosahatchee** *R* USA
109D1	**Caloundra** Aust
23B2	**Calpulalpan** Mexico
53B3	**Caltanissetta** Italy
98B3	**Caluango** Angola
100A2	**Calulo** Angola
100A2	**Caluquembe** Angola
99F1	**Caluula** Somalia
13B2	**Calvert I** Can
52A2	**Calvi** Corse
23A1	**Calvillo** Mexico
100A4	**Calvinia** S Africa
25E2	**Camagüey** Cuba
25E2	**Camagüey,Arch de** *Is* Cuba
30B2	**Camaná** Peru
30C3	**Camargo** Bol
22C3	**Camarillo** USA
29C4	**Camarones** Arg
20B1	**Camas** USA
98B3	**Camaxilo** Angola
98B3	**Cambatela** Angola
76C3	**Cambodia** Republic, S E Asia
43B4	**Camborne** Eng
49C1	**Cambrai** France
43C3	**Cambrian Mts** Wales
14B2	**Cambridge** Can
43D3	**Cambridge** County, Eng
43E3	**Cambridge** Eng
27H1	**Cambridge** Jamaica
15C3	**Cambridge** Maryland, USA
15D2	**Cambridge** Massachussets, USA
110C1	**Cambridge** NZ
14B2	**Cambridge** Ohio, USA
4H3	**Cambridge Bay** Can
60E5	**Cam Burun** *Pt* Turk
11A3	**Camden** Arkansas, USA
109D2	**Camden** Aust
15D3	**Camden** New Jersey, USA
17B1	**Camden** South Carolina, USA
18B2	**Cameron** Missouri, USA

19A3 **Cameron** Texas, USA
4H2 **Cameron I** Can
111A3 **Cameron Mts** NZ
98A2 **Cameroon** Federal Republic, Africa
98A2 **Cameroun** *Mt* Cam
31B2 **Cametá** Brazil
79B4 **Camiguin** *I* Phil
79B2 **Camiling** Phil
17B1 **Camilla** USA
22B1 **Camino** USA
30D3 **Camiri** Bol
31C2 **Camocim** Brazil
98C3 **Camissombo** Angola
106C2 **Camooweal** Aust
34D2 **Campana** Arg
29A5 **Campana** *I* Chile
13B2 **Campania I** Can
111B2 **Campbell,C** NZ
13B2 **Campbell I** Can
105G6 **Campbell I** NZ
4E3 **Campbell,Mt** Can
84C2 **Campbellpore** Pak
5F5 **Campbell River** Can
7D5 **Campbellton** Can
109D2 **Campbelltown** Aust
42B2 **Campbeltown** Scot
25C3 **Campeche** Mexico
108B3 **Camperdown** Aust
31D3 **Campina Grande** Brazil
31B6 **Campinas** Brazil
35B1 **Campina Verde** Brazil
98A2 **Campo** Cam
53B2 **Campobasso** Italy
35B2 **Campo Belo** Brazil
35B1 **Campo Florido** Brazil
30D4 **Campo Gallo** Arg
30F3 **Campo Grande** Brazil
31C2 **Campo Maior** Brazil
30F3 **Campo Mourão** Brazil
35C3 **Campos** Brazil
35B1 **Campos Altos** Brazil
47D1 **Campo Tures** Italy
70D3 **Cam Ranh** Viet
5G4 **Camrose** Can
100A2 **Camuculo** Angola
27K1 **Canaan** Tobago
16C1 **Canaan** USA
100A2 **Canacupa** Angola
2F3 **Canada** Dominion, N America
29D2 **Cañada de Gomez** Arg
9C3 **Canadian** *R* USA
60C5 **Canakkale** Turk
34B3 **Canalejas** Arg
13D2 **Canal Flats** Can
24A1 **Cananea** Mexico
102G3 **Canary Basin** Atlantic O
Canary Is = Islas Canarias
23A2 **Canas** Mexico
24B2 **Canatlán** Mexico
11B4 **Canaveral,C** USA
31D5 **Canavieiras** Brazil
107D4 **Canberra** Aust
20B2 **Canby** California, USA
55C3 **Çandarli Körfezi** *B* Turk
16C2 **Candlewood,L** USA
29E2 **Canelones** Urug
18A2 **Caney** USA
100A2 **Cangamba** Angola
100B2 **Cangombe** Angola
72D2 **Cangzhou** China
7D4 **Caniapiscau** *R* Can
53B3 **Canicatti** Italy
31D2 **Canindé** Brazil
92B1 **Çankırı** Turk
13D2 **Canmore** Can
44A3 **Canna** *I* Scot
87B2 **Cannanore** India
49D3 **Cannes** France
109C3 **Cann River** Aust
30F4 **Canõas** Brazil
13F1 **Canoe L** Can
9C3 **Canon City** USA
108B2 **Canopus** Aust
5H4 **Canora** Can
109C2 **Canowindra** Aust
45C2 **Cansore Pt** Irish Rep
43E4 **Canterbury** Eng
111B2 **Canterbury Bight** *B* NZ
111B2 **Canterbury Plains** NZ
77D4 **Can Tho** Viet
Canton = Guangzhou
19C3 **Canton** Mississippi, USA
18B1 **Canton** Missouri, USA
10B2 **Canton** Ohio, USA
12E2 **Cantwell** USA
20C2 **Canyon City** USA
12J2 **Canyon Range** *Mts* Can
20B2 **Canyonville** USA
98C3 **Canzar** Angola
76D1 **Cao Bang** Viet
31B2 **Capanema** Brazil
35B2 **Capão Bonito** Brazil
48B3 **Capbreton** France
24B2 **Cap Corrientes** *C* Mexico
52A2 **Cap Corse** *C* Corse
48B2 **Cap de la Hague** *C* France
15D1 **Cap-de-la-Madeleine** Can
6C3 **Cap de Nouvelle-France** *C* Can
51C2 **Capdepera** Spain
23A2 **Cap de Tancitiario** *C* Mexico
109C4 **Cape Barren I** Aust
103J6 **Cape Basin** Atlantic O
7E5 **Cape Breton I** Can
97B4 **Cape Coast** Ghana
15D2 **Cape Cod B** USA
6C3 **Cape Dorset** Can
17C1 **Cape Fear** *R* USA
18C2 **Cape Girardeau** USA
6B3 **Cape Henrietta Maria** Can
Cape Horn = Cabo de Hornos
104E3 **Cape Johnston Depth** Pacific O
35C1 **Capelinha** Brazil
4B3 **Cape Lisburne** USA
100A2 **Capelongo** Angola
15D3 **Cape May** USA
5F5 **Cape Mendocino** USA
98B3 **Capenda Camulemba** Angola
4F2 **Cape Perry** Can
100B4 **Cape Province** S Africa
7A4 **Cape Tatnam** Can
100A4 **Cape Town** S Africa
102G4 **Cape Verde** *Is* Atlantic O
102G4 **Cape Verde Basin** Atlantic O
12F3 **Cape Yakataga** USA
107D2 **Cape York Pen** Aust
46A1 **Cap Gris Nez** *C* France
26C3 **Cap-Haitien** Haiti
31B2 **Capim** *R* Brazil
112C2 **Capitán Arturo Prat** *Base* Ant
27P2 **Cap Moule à Chique** *C* St Lucia
53C3 **Capo Isola de Correnti** *C* Italy
53C3 **Capo Rizzuto** *C* Italy
55A3 **Capo Santa Maria di Leuca** *C* Italy
53B3 **Capo San Vito** Italy
53C3 **Capo Spartivento** *C* Italy
27P2 **Cap Pt** St Lucia
53B2 **Capri** *I* Italy
100B2 **Caprivi Strip** Region, Namibia
52A2 **Cap Rosso** *C* Corse
102H4 **Cap Vert** *C* Sen
32C4 **Caquetá** *R* Colombia
54B2 **Caracal** Rom
33E3 **Caracaraí** Brazil
32D1 **Caracas** Ven
35B2 **Caraguatatuba** Brazil
29B3 **Carahue** Chile
35C1 **Caraí** Brazil
35C2 **Carandaí** Brazil
31C6 **Carangola** Brazil
54B1 **Caransebeş** Rom
108A2 **Carappee Hill** *Mt* Aust
26A3 **Caratasca** Honduras
35C1 **Caratinga** Brazil
51B2 **Caravaca** Spain
35D1 **Caravelas** Brazil
18C2 **Carbondale** Illinois, USA
53A3 **Carbonia** Sardegna
7E5 **Carborear** Can
5G4 **Carcaion** Can
99E1 **Carcar Mts** Somalia
48C3 **Carcassonne** France
4E3 **Carcross** Can
23B2 **Cardel** Mexico
25D2 **Cardenas** Cuba
23B1 **Cárdenas** Mexico
43C4 **Cardiff** Wales
43B3 **Cardigan** Wales
43B3 **Cardigan B** Wales
13E2 **Cardston** Can
54B1 **Carei** Rom
33F4 **Careiro** Brazil
34A2 **Carén** Chile
14B2 **Carey** USA
48B2 **Carhaix-Plouguer** France
29D3 **Carhué** Arg
31C6 **Cariacica** Brazil
5J4 **Caribou** Can
5G4 **Caribou Mts** Alberta, Can
5F4 **Caribou Mts** British Columbia, Can
79B3 **Carigara** Phil
46C2 **Carignan** France
33E1 **Caripito** Ven
15C1 **Carleton Place** Can
101G1 **Carletonville** S Africa
18C2 **Carlinville** USA
42C2 **Carlisle** Eng
15C2 **Carlisle** USA
34C3 **Carlos** Arg
35C1 **Carlos Chagas** Brazil
45C2 **Carlow** County, Irish Rep
45C2 **Carlow** Irish Rep
21B3 **Carlsbad** California, USA
9C3 **Carlsbad** New Mexico, USA
5H5 **Carlyle** Can
12G2 **Carmacks** Can
47B2 **Carmagnola** Italy
43B4 **Carmarthen** Wales
43B4 **Carmarthen B** Wales
22B2 **Carmel** California, USA
16C2 **Carmel** New York, USA
94B2 **Carmel,Mt** Israel
34D2 **Carmelo** Urug
22B2 **Carmel Valley** USA
9B4 **Carmen** *I* Mexico
29D4 **Carmen de Patagones** Arg
18C2 **Carmi** USA
21A2 **Carmichael** USA
35B1 **Carmo do Paranaiba** Brazil
50A2 **Carmona** Spain
106A3 **Carnarvon** Aust
100B4 **Carnarvon** S Africa
35D1 **Carncacá** Brazil
45C1 **Carndonagh** Irish Rep
106B3 **Carnegi,L** Aust
98B2 **Carnot** CAR
108A2 **Carnot,C** Aust
17B2 **Carol City** USA
31B3 **Carolina** Brazil
101H1 **Carolina** S Africa
17C1 **Carolina Beach** USA
104F3 **Caroline Is** Pacific O
60B4 **Carpathians** *Mts* E Europe
59D3 **Carpatii Orientali** *Mts* Rom
106C2 **Carpentaria,G of** Aust
83C5 **Carpenter Ridge** Indian O
49D3 **Carpentras** France
52B2 **Carpi** Italy
22C3 **Carpinteria** USA
17B2 **Carrabelle** USA
52B2 **Carrara** Italy
41B3 **Carrauntoohill** *Mt* Irish Rep
45C2 **Carrickmacross** Irish Rep
45B2 **Carrick on Shannon** Irish Rep
45C2 **Carrick-on-Suir** Irish Rep
108A2 **Carrieton** Aust
8D2 **Carrington** USA
50B1 **Carrión** *R* Spain
10A2 **Carroll** USA
17A1 **Carrollton** Georgia, USA
14A3 **Carrollton** Kentucky, USA
18B2 **Carrollton** Missouri, USA
18C2 **Carruthersville** USA
60E5 **Carsamba** Turk
92B2 **Carsamba** *R* Turk
8B3 **Carson City** USA
14B2 **Carsonville** USA
26B4 **Cartagena** Colombia
51B2 **Cartagena** Spain
32B3 **Cartago** Colombia
25D4 **Cartago** Costa Rica
111C2 **Carterton** NZ
18B2 **Carthage** Missouri, USA
15C2 **Carthage** New York, USA
19B3 **Carthage** Texas, USA
106B2 **Cartier I** Timor S
7E4 **Cartwright** Can
31D3 **Caruaru** Brazil
33E1 **Carúpano** Ven
46B1 **Carvin** France
34A2 **Casablanca** Chile
96B1 **Casablanca** Mor
35B2 **Casa Branca** Brazil
9B3 **Casa Grande** USA
52A1 **Casale Monferrato** Italy
47D2 **Casalmaggiore** Italy
34C3 **Casares** Arg
13C3 **Cascade Mts** Can/USA
111A2 **Cascade Pt** NZ
8A2 **Cascade Range** *Mts* USA
30F3 **Cascavel** Brazil
53B2 **Caserta** Italy
112C9 **Casey** *Base* Ant
45C2 **Cashel** Irish Rep
34C2 **Casilda** Arg
107E3 **Casino** Aust
32B5 **Casma** Peru
51B1 **Caspe** Spain
8C2 **Casper** USA
61G4 **Caspian Depression** *Region* Kazakhstan
65G6 **Caspian S** Asia/Europe
14C3 **Cass** USA
100B2 **Cassamba** Angola
46B1 **Cassel** France
12J3 **Cassiar** Can
4E3 **Cassiar Mts** Can
35A1 **Cassilândia** Brazil
53B2 **Cassino** Italy
22C3 **Castaic** USA
34B2 **Castaño** *R* Arg
47D2 **Castelfranco** Italy
49D3 **Castellane** France
34D3 **Castelli** Arg
51B2 **Castellon de la Plana** Spain
31C3 **Castelo** Brazil
50A2 **Castelo Branco** Port
48C3 **Castelsarrasin** France
53B3 **Castelvetrano** Italy
108B3 **Casterton** Aust

50B2 **Castilla La Nueva** Region, Spain
50B1 **Castilla La Vieja** Region, Spain
41B3 **Castlebar** Irish Rep
44A3 **Castlebay** Scot
42C2 **Castle Douglas** Scot
20C1 **Castlegar** Can
45B2 **Castleisland** Irish Rep
108B3 **Castlemaine** Aust
45B2 **Castlerea** Irish Rep
109C2 **Castlereagh** Aust
48C3 **Castres-sur-l'Agout** France
27E4 **Castries** St Lucia
29B4 **Castro** Arg
30F3 **Castro** Brazil
31D4 **Castro Alves** Brazil
53C3 **Castrovillari** Italy
22B2 **Castroville** Italy
111A2 **Caswell Sd** NZ
25E2 **Cat** I The Bahamas
79B3 **Catabalogan** Phil
32A5 **Catacaos** Peru
35C2 **Cataguases** Brazil
19B3 **Catahoula L** USA
35B1 **Catalão** Brazil
51C1 **Cataluña** Region, Spain
30C4 **Catamarca** Arg
30C4 **Catamarca** State, Arg
101C2 **Catandica** Mozam
79B3 **Catanduanes** I Phil
31B6 **Catanduva** Brazil
53C3 **Catania** Italy
53C3 **Catanzaro** Italy
79B3 **Catarman** Phil
108A2 **Catastrophe,C** Aust
26C5 **Catatumbo** R Ven
16A2 **Catawissa** USA
23B2 **Catemaco** Mexico
49D3 **Cater** Corse
52A2 **Cateraggio** Corse
98B3 **Catete** Angola
97A3 **Catio** Guinea-Bissau
7A4 **Cat Lake** Can
13D3 **Catlegar** Can
107E3 **Cato** I Aust
25D2 **Catoche,C** Mexico
16A3 **Catoctin Mt** USA
15C3 **Catonsville** USA
34C3 **Catrilo** Arg
15D2 **Catskill** USA
15D2 **Catskill Mts** USA
32C2 **Cauca** R Colombia
31D2 **Caucaia** Brazil
32B2 **Caucasia** Colombia
65F5 **Caucasus** Mts Georgia
46B1 **Caudry** France
98B3 **Caungula** Angola
29B3 **Cauquenes** Chile
87B2 **Cauvery** R India
49D3 **Cavaillon** France
47D1 **Cavalese** Italy
97B4 **Cavally** R Lib
45C2 **Cavan** County, Irish Rep
45C2 **Cavan** Irish Rep
79B3 **Cavite** Phil
31C2 **Caxias** Brazil
32C4 **Caxias** Brazil
30F4 **Caxias do Sul** Brazil
98B3 **Caxito** Angola
17B1 **Cayce** USA
93D1 **Çayeli** Turk
33G3 **Cayenne** French Guiana
46A1 **Cayeux-sur-Mer** France
25E3 **Cayman Brac** I Caribbean S
26A3 **Cayman Is** Caribbean S
26A3 **Cayman Trench** Caribbean S
99E2 **Caynabo** Somalia
25E2 **Cayo Romana** I Cuba
25D3 **Cayos Miskitos** Is Nic
26A2 **Cay Sal** I Caribbean S
100B2 **Cazombo** Angola
Ceará = Fortaleza

31C3 **Ceara** State, Brazil
79B3 **Cebu** Phil
79B3 **Cebu** I Phil
16B3 **Cecilton** USA
52B2 **Cecina** Italy
8B3 **Cedar City** USA
19A3 **Cedar Creek Res** USA
5J4 **Cedar L** Can
10A2 **Cedar Rapids** USA
17A1 **Cedartown** USA
24A2 **Cedros** I Mexico
106C4 **Ceduna** Aust
99E2 **Ceelbuur** Somalia
99E1 **Ceerigaabo** Somalia
53B3 **Cefalù** Italy
59B3 **Cegléd** Hung
100A2 **Cela** Angola
24B2 **Celaya** Mexico
Celebes = Sulawesi
70C3 **Celebes S** S E Asia
14B2 **Celina** USA
52C1 **Celje** Slovenia
56C2 **Celle** Germany
71E4 **Cendrawasih** Pen Indon
47C2 **Ceno** R Italy
19B3 **Center** USA
16C2 **Center Moriches** USA
17A1 **Center Point** USA
47D2 **Cento** Italy
44B3 **Central** Region, Scot
98B2 **Central African Republic** Africa
16D2 **Central Falls** USA
18C2 **Centralia** Illinois, USA
8A2 **Centralia** Washington, USA
20B2 **Central Point** USA
71F4 **Central Range** Mts PNG
16A3 **Centreville** Maryland, USA
78C4 **Cepu** Indon
Ceram = Seram
71D4 **Ceram Sea** Indon
34C3 **Cereales** Arg
31B5 **Ceres** Brazil
100A4 **Ceres** S Africa
22B2 **Ceres** USA
48C2 **Cergy-Pontoise** France
53C2 **Cerignola** Italy
60C5 **Cernavodă** Rom
9C4 **Cerralvo** I Mexico
23A1 **Cerritos** Mexico
34B2 **Cerro Aconcagua** Mt Arg
23B1 **Cerro Azul** Mexico
34A3 **Cerro Campanario** Mt Chile
34C2 **Cerro Champaqui** Mt Arg
23A2 **Cerro Cuachaia** Mt Mexico
23B1 **Cerro de Astillero** Mexico
34B2 **Cerro de Olivares** Mt Arg
32B6 **Cerro de Pasco** Peru
27D3 **Cerro de Punta** Mt Puerto Rico
23A2 **Cerro El Cantado** Mt Mexico
34B3 **Cerro El Nevado** Mt Arg
23A2 **Cerro Grande** Mts Mexico
34A2 **Cerro Juncal** Mt Arg/Chile
23A1 **Cerro la Ardilla** Mts Mexico
34B1 **Cerro las Tortolas** Mt Chile
23A2 **Cerro Laurel** Mt Mexico
34A2 **Cerro Mercedario** Mt Arg
34A3 **Cerro Mora** Mt Chile
27C4 **Cerron** Mt Ven
34B3 **Cerro Payún** Mt Arg

23B2 **Cerro Penón del Rosario** Mt Mexico
34B2 **Cerro Sosneado** Mt Arg
23A2 **Cerro Teotepec** Mt Mexico
34B2 **Cerro Tupungato** Mt Arg
23B2 **Cerro Yucuyacau** Mt Mexico
47C2 **Cervo** R Italy
52B2 **Cesena** Italy
60B2 **Cēsis** Latvia
57C3 **České Budejovice** Czech Republic
59B3 **Českomoravská Vysocina** Mts Czech Republic
55C3 **Çeşme** Turk
107E4 **Cessnock** Aust
52C2 **Cetina** R Croatia
96B1 **Ceuta** N W Africa
92C2 **Ceyham** Turk
92C2 **Ceyhan** R Turk
93C2 **Ceylanpınar** Turk
Ceylon = Sri Lanka
63B2 **Chaa-Khol** Russian Fed
48C2 **Chaâteaudun** France
47B1 **Chablais** Region, France
34C2 **Chacabuco** Arg
32B5 **Chachapoyas** Peru
34B3 **Chacharramendi** Arg
84C3 **Chachran** Pak
30D4 **Chaco** State, Arg
98B1 **Chad** Republic, Africa
98B1 **Chad** L C Africa
34B3 **Chadileuvu** R Arg
8C2 **Chadron** USA
18C2 **Chaffee** USA
85A3 **Chagai** Pak
63F2 **Chagda** Russian Fed
84B2 **Chaghcharan** Afghan
104B4 **Chagos Arch** Indian O
27L1 **Chaguanas** Trinidad
91D4 **Chāh Bahār** Iran
76C2 **Chai Badan** Thai
76C3 **Chaine des Cardamomes** Mts Camb
98C4 **Chaine des Mitumba** Mts Zaïre
76C2 **Chaiyaphum** Thai
34D2 **Chajari** Arg
84C2 **Chakwal** Pak
30B2 **Chala** Peru
100C2 **Chalabesa** Zambia
84A2 **Chalap Dalam** Mts Afghan
73C4 **Chaling** China
85C4 **Chālisgaon** India
12F1 **Chalkyitsik** USA
46C2 **Challerange** France
46C2 **Châlons sur Marne** France
49C2 **Chalon sur Saône** France
57C3 **Cham** Germany
84B2 **Chaman** Pak
84D2 **Chamba** India
85D3 **Chambal** R India
15C3 **Chambersburg** USA
49D2 **Chambéry** France
46B2 **Chambly** France
85A3 **Chambor Kalat** Pak
90B3 **Chamgordan** Iran
34B2 **Chamical** Arg
47B2 **Chamonix** France
86A2 **Champa** India
49C2 **Champagne** Region, France
101G1 **Champagne Castle** Mt Lesotho
47A1 **Champagnole** France
10B2 **Champaign** USA
76D3 **Champassak** Laos
10C2 **Champlain,L** USA
87B2 **Chāmrājnagar** India
30B4 **Chañaral** Chile
34A3 **Chanco** Chile
4D3 **Chandalar** USA

4D3 **Chandalar** R USA
84D2 **Chandīgarh** India
86C2 **Chandpur** Bang
85D5 **Chandrapur** India
91D4 **Chänf** Iran
101C2 **Changara** Mozam
74B2 **Changbai** China
69E2 **Changchun** China
73C4 **Changde** China
68E4 **Chang-hua** Taiwan
76D2 **Changjiang** China
73D3 **Chang Jiang** R China
74B2 **Changjin** N Korea
73C4 **Changsha** China
72E3 **Changshu** China
74A2 **Changtu** China
72B2 **Changwu** China
74B3 **Changyŏn** N Korea
72C2 **Changzhi** China
73E3 **Changzhou** China
48B2 **Channel Is** Europe
9B3 **Channel Is** USA
7E5 **Channel Port-aux-Basques** Can
76C3 **Chanthaburi** Thai
46B2 **Chantilly** France
18A2 **Chanute** USA
73D5 **Chaoàn** China
73D5 **Chao'an** China
73D3 **Chao Hu** L China
76C3 **Chao Phraya** R Thai
72E1 **Chaoyang** China
31C4 **Chapada Diamantina** Mts Brazil
31C2 **Chapadinha** Brazil
23A1 **Chapala** Mexico
23A1 **Chapala,Lac de** L Mexico
61H3 **Chapayevo** Kazakhstan
30F4 **Chapecó** Brazil
27H1 **Chapeltown** Jamaica
7B5 **Chapleau** Can
61E3 **Chaplygin** Russian Fed
112C3 **Charcot I** Ant
80E2 **Chardzhou** Turkmenistan
48C2 **Charente** R France
98B1 **Chari** R Chad
98B1 **Chari Baguirmi** Region, Chad
84B1 **Charikar** Afghan
18B1 **Chariton** R USA
33F2 **Charity** Guyana
85D3 **Charkhāri** India
46C1 **Charleroi** Belg
18C2 **Charleston** Illinois, USA
18C2 **Charleston** Missouri, USA
11C3 **Charleston** S Carolina, USA
10B3 **Charleston** W Virginia, USA
98C3 **Charlesville** Zaïre
107D3 **Charleville** Aust
49C2 **Charleville-Mézières** France
14A1 **Charlevoix** USA
14B2 **Charlotte** Michigan, USA
11B3 **Charlotte** N Carolina, USA
17B2 **Charlotte Harbor** B USA
10C3 **Charlottesville** USA
7D5 **Charlottetown** Can
27K1 **Charlotteville** Tobago
108B3 **Charlton** Aust
10C1 **Charlton I** Can
84C2 **Charsadda** Pak
107D3 **Charters Towers** Aust
48C2 **Chartres** France
29E3 **Chascomús** Arg
13D2 **Chase** Can
48B2 **Châteaubriant** France
48C2 **Châteaudun** France
48B2 **Châteaulin** France
48C2 **Châteauroux** France

46D2 **Château-Salins** France
49C2 **Château-Thierry** France
46C1 **Châtelet** Belg
48C2 **Châtellerault** France
43F4 **Chatham** Eng
7D5 **Chatham** New Brunswick, Can
16C1 **Chatham** New York, USA
14B2 **Chatham** Ontario, Can
13A2 **Chatham Sd** Can
12H3 **Chatham Str** USA
49C2 **Châtillon** France
47B2 **Châtillon** Italy
16B3 **Chatsworth** USA
17B1 **Chattahoochee** USA
17A1 **Chattahoochee** R USA
11B3 **Chattanooga** USA
76A1 **Chauk** Burma
49D2 **Chaumont** France
46B2 **Chauny** France
77D3 **Chau Phu** Viet
50A1 **Chaves** Port
61H2 **Chaykovskiy** Russian Fed
50B2 **Chazaouet** Alg
34C2 **Chazón** Arg
32C2 **Chcontá** Colombia
57C2 **Cheb** Czech Republic
65F4 **Cheboksary** Russian Fed
10B2 **Cheboygan** USA
74B3 **Chech'on** S Korea
85C3 **Chechro** Pak
18A2 **Checotah** USA
76A2 **Cheduba** I Burma
108B1 **Cheepie** Aust
96B2 **Chegga** Maur
100C2 **Chegutu** Zim
20B1 **Chehalis** USA
74B4 **Cheju** S Korea
74B4 **Cheju do** I S Korea
74B4 **Cheju-haehyŏp** Str S Korea
63F2 **Chekunda** Russian Fed
20B1 **Chelan,L** USA
90B2 **Cheleken** Turkmenistan
34B3 **Chelforo** Arg
80D1 **Chelkar** Kazakhstan
59C2 **Chelm** Pol
58B2 **Chelmno** Pol
43E4 **Chelmsford** Eng
43C4 **Cheltenham** Eng
65H4 **Chelyabinsk** Russian Fed
101C2 **Chemba** Mozam
57C2 **Chemnitz** Germany
84D2 **Chenab** R India/Pak
96B2 **Chenachane** Alg
20C1 **Cheney** USA
18A2 **Cheney Res** USA
72D1 **Chengda** China
73A3 **Chengdu** China
72E2 **Chengshan Jiao** Pt China
73C4 **Chenxi** China
73C4 **Chen Xian** China
73D3 **Cheo Xian** China
32B5 **Chepén** Peru
34B2 **Chepes** Arg
48C2 **Cher** R France
23A2 **Cheran** Mexico
17C1 **Cheraw** USA
48B2 **Cherbourg** France
96C1 **Cherchell** Alg
63C2 **Cheremkhovo** Russian Fed
60E2 **Cherepovets** Russian Fed
60D4 **Cherkassy** Ukraine
61F5 **Cherkessk** Russian Fed
60D3 **Chernigov** Ukraine
60D2 **Chernobyl** Ukraine
60C4 **Chernovtsy** Ukraine
61J2 **Chernushka** Russian Fed

60B3 **Chernyakhovsk** Russian Fed
61G4 **Chernyye Zemli** Region, Russian Fed
18A2 **Cherokees,L o'the** USA
34A3 **Cherquenco** Chile
86C1 **Cherrapunji** India
60C3 **Cherven'** Belorussia
59C2 **Chervonograd** Ukraine
10C3 **Chesapeake** B USA
42C3 **Cheshire** County, Eng
16C1 **Cheshire** USA
64F3 **Chëshskaya Guba** B Russian Fed
21A1 **Chester** California, USA
42C3 **Chester** Eng
18C2 **Chester** Illinois, USA
16C1 **Chester** Massachusets, USA
15C3 **Chester** Pennsylvania, USA
17B1 **Chester** S Carolina, USA
16A3 **Chester** R USA
42D3 **Chesterfield** Eng
6A3 **Chesterfield Inlet** Can
16A3 **Chestertown** USA
25D3 **Chetumal** Mexico
13C1 **Chetwynd** Can
12A2 **Chevak** USA
111B2 **Cheviot** NZ
40C2 **Cheviots** Hills Eng/ Scot
13D3 **Chewelah** USA
8C2 **Cheyenne** USA
86A1 **Chhapra** India
86C1 **Chhatak** Bang
85D4 **Chhatarpur** India
85D4 **Chhindwära** India
86B1 **Chhuka** Bhutan
73E5 **Chia'i** Taiwan
100A2 **Chiange** Angola
76C2 **Chiang Kham** Thai
76B2 **Chiang Mai** Thai
47C1 **Chiavenna** Italy
74E3 **Chiba** Japan
86B2 **Chibāsa** India
100A2 **Chibia** Angola
7C4 **Chibougamou** Can
75A1 **Chiburi-jima** I Japan
101C3 **Chibuto** Mozam
10B2 **Chicago** USA
14A2 **Chicago Heights** USA
12G3 **Chichagof I** USA
43D4 **Chichester** Eng
75B1 **Chichibu** Japan
69G4 **Chichi-jima** I Japan
11B3 **Chickamauga L** USA
19C3 **Chickasawhay** R USA
9D3 **Chickasha** USA
12F2 **Chicken** USA
32A5 **Chiclayo** Peru
8A3 **Chico** USA
29C4 **Chico** R Arg
101C2 **Chicoa** Mozam
15D2 **Chicopee** USA
7C5 **Chicoutimi** Can
101C3 **Chicualacuala** Mozam
87B2 **Chidambaram** India
6D3 **Chidley,C** Can
17B2 **Chiefland** USA
99C3 **Chiengi** Zambia
47B2 **Chieri** Italy
46C2 **Chiers** R France
47C1 **Chiesa** Italy
47D2 **Chiese** R Italy
52B2 **Chieti** Italy
72D1 **Chifeng** China
12C3 **Chiginigak,Mt** USA
4C3 **Chigmit Mts** USA
23B2 **Chignahuapán** Mexico
12C3 **Chignik** USA
24B2 **Chihuahua** Mexico
87B2 **Chik Ballāpur** India
87B2 **Chikmagalūr** India
12C2 **Chikuminuk L** USA

101C2 **Chikwawa** Malawi
76A1 **Chi-kyaw** Burma
87C1 **Chilakalūrupet** India
23B2 **Chilapa** Mexico
87B3 **Chilaw** Sri Lanka
28B6 **Chile** Republic
34B2 **Chilecito** Mendoza, Arg
100B2 **Chililabombwe** Zambia
86B2 **Chilka** L India
13C2 **Chilko** R Can
5F4 **Chilko L** Can
13C2 **Chilkotin** R Can
34A3 **Chillán** Chile
34D3 **Chillar** Arg
18B2 **Chillicothe** Missouri, USA
14B3 **Chillicothe** Ohio, USA
13C3 **Chilliwack** Can
86B1 **Chilmari** India
101C2 **Chilongozi** Zambia
20B2 **Chiloquin** USA
24C3 **Chilpancingo** Mexico
43D4 **Chiltern Hills** Upland Eng
14A2 **Chilton** USA
101C2 **Chilumba** Malawi
69E4 **Chi-lung** Taiwan
101C2 **Chilwa** L Malawi
100C2 **Chimanimani** Zim
46C1 **Chimay** Belg
65G5 **Chimbay** Uzbekistan
32B4 **Chimborazo** Mt Ecuador
32B5 **Chimbote** Peru
65H5 **Chimkent** Kazakhstan
101C2 **Chimoio** Mozam
67E3 **China** Republic, Asia
China National Republic = Taiwan
25D3 **Chinandega** Nic
32B6 **Chincha Alta** Peru
109D1 **Chinchilla** Aust
101C2 **Chinde** Mozam
86C2 **Chindwin** R Burma
100B2 **Chingola** Zambia
100A2 **Chinguar** Angola
96A2 **Chinguetti** Maur
74B3 **Chinhae** S Korea
100C2 **Chinhoyi** Zim
12D3 **Chiniak,C** USA
84C2 **Chiniot** Pak
74B3 **Chinju** S Korea
98C2 **Chinko** R CAR
75B1 **Chino** Japan
101C2 **Chinsali** Zambia
52B1 **Chioggia** Italy
101C2 **Chipata** Zambia
101C3 **Chipinge** Zim
87A1 **Chiplūn** India
43C4 **Chippenham** Eng
10A2 **Chippewa Falls** USA
32A4 **Chira** R Peru
87C1 **Chīrāla** India
101C3 **Chiredzi** Zim
96A2 **Chirfa** Niger
32A2 **Chiriqui** Mt Panama
54C2 **Chirpan** Bulg
32A2 **Chirrípo Grande** Mt Costa Rica
100B2 **Chirundu** Zim
100B2 **Chisamba** Zambia
7C4 **Chisasibi** Can
73B4 **Chishui He** R China
Chişinău = Kishinev
47B2 **Chisone** R Italy
61H2 **Chistopol** Russian Fed
68D1 **Chita** Russian Fed
100A2 **Chitado** Angola
100A2 **Chitembo** Angola
12F2 **Chitina** USA
12F2 **Chitina** R USA
87B2 **Chitradurga** India
84C1 **Chitral** Pak
32A2 **Chitré** Panama
86C2 **Chittagong** Bang
85C4 **Chittaurgarh** India
87B2 **Chittoor** India
100B2 **Chiume** Angola
47D1 **Chiusa** Italy

47B2 **Chivasso** Italy
100C2 **Chivhu** Zim
29D2 **Chivilcoy** Arg
100C2 **Chivu** Zim
75A1 **Chizu** Japan
29C3 **Choele Choel** Arg
34C3 **Choique** Arg
24B2 **Choix** Mexico
58B2 **Chojnice** Pol
99D1 **Choke** Mts Eth
48B2 **Cholet** France
23B2 **Cholula** Mexico
100B2 **Choma** Zambia
86B1 **Chomo Yummo** Mt China/India
57C2 **Chomutov** Czech Republic
63C1 **Chona** R Russian Fed
74B3 **Ch'ŏnan** S Korea
76C3 **Chon Buri** Thai
32A4 **Chone** Ecuador
74B2 **Ch'ŏngjin** N Korea
74B3 **Chongju** N Korea
74B3 **Ch'ŏngju** S Korea
100A2 **Chongoroi** Angola
73B4 **Chongqing** China
74B3 **Chŏngŭp** S Korea
74B3 **Chŏnju** S Korea
86B1 **Chooyu** Mt China/Nepal
59D3 **Chortkov** Ukraine
74B3 **Ch'ŏrwŏn** N Korea
59B2 **Chorzow** Pol
74E3 **Choshi** Japan
34A3 **Chos-Malal** Arg
58B2 **Choszczno** Pol
86A2 **Chotanāgpur** Region, India
96C1 **Chott Melrhir** Alg
22B2 **Chowchilla** USA
63D3 **Choybalsan** Mongolia
6A3 **Chrantrey Inlet** B Can
111B2 **Christchurch** NZ
101G1 **Christiana** S Africa
6D2 **Christian,C** Can
12H3 **Christian Sd** USA
6E3 **Christianshab** Greenland
104D4 **Christmas I** Indian O
65J5 **Chu** Kazakhstan
65J5 **Chu** R Kazakhstan
29C4 **Chubut** State, Arg
29C4 **Chubut** R Arg
60D2 **Chudovo** Russian Fed
Chudskoye Ozero = Peipus, Lake
4D3 **Chugach Mts** USA
12E2 **Chugiak** USA
75A1 **Chūgoku-sanchi** Mts Japan
29F2 **Chui** Brazil
29B3 **Chuillán** Chile
77C5 **Chukai** Malay
76D2 **Chu Lai** Viet
21B3 **Chula Vista** USA
12E2 **Chulitna** USA
63E2 **Chulman** Russian Fed
32A5 **Chulucanas** Peru
30C2 **Chulumani** Bol
65K4 **Chulym** Russian Fed
63A2 **Chulym** R Russian Fed
63B2 **Chuma** R Russian Fed
84D2 **Chumar** India
63F2 **Chumikan** Russian Fed
77B3 **Chumphon** Thai
74B3 **Ch'unch'ŏn** S Korea
86B2 **Chunchura** India
74B3 **Ch'ungju** S Korea
Chungking = Chongqing
99D3 **Chunya** Tanz
63C1 **Chunya** R Russian Fed
27L1 **Chupara Pt** Trinidad
30C3 **Chuquicamata** Chile
52A1 **Chur** Switz

19C3 **Columbia** Mississippi, USA
10A3 **Columbia** Missouri, USA
15C2 **Columbia** Pennsylvania, USA
11B3 **Columbia** S Carolina, USA
11B3 **Columbia** Tennessee, USA
13D2 **Columbia** *R* Can
8A2 **Columbia** *R* USA
5G4 **Columbia,Mt** Can
20C1 **Columbia Plat** USA
11B3 **Columbus** Georgia, USA
14A3 **Columbus** Indiana, USA
11B3 **Columbus** Mississippi, USA
8D2 **Columbus** Nebraska, USA
10B2 **Columbus** Ohio, USA
19A4 **Columbus** Texas, USA
20C1 **Colville** USA
4C3 **Colville** *R* USA
110C1 **Colville,C** NZ
4F3 **Colville L** Can
42C3 **Colwyn Bay** Wales
47E2 **Comacchio** Italy
22B1 **Comanche Res** USA
112C2 **Comandante Ferraz** *Base* Ant
25D3 **Comayagua** Honduras
34A2 **Combarbalá** Chile
45C2 **Comeragh** *Mts* Irish Rep
86C2 **Comilla** Bang
25C3 **Comitán** Mexico
46C2 **Commercy** France
6B3 **Committees B** Can
52A1 **Como** Italy
29C5 **Comodoro Rivadavia** Arg
23A1 **Comonfort** Mexico
87B3 **Comorin,C** India
101D2 **Comoros** *Is* Indian O
49C2 **Compiègne** France
23A1 **Compostela** Mexico
34B2 **Comte Salas** Arg
86C1 **Cona** China
97A4 **Conakry** Guinea
34B2 **Conarán** Arg
48B2 **Concarneau** France
35D1 **Conceiçao da Barra** Brazil
31B3 **Conceição do Araguaia** Brazil
35C1 **Conceiçao do Mato Dentro** Brazil
29B3 **Concepción** Chile
30E3 **Concepción** Par
29E2 **Concepción** *R* Arg
24B2 **Concepcion del Oro** Mexico
34D2 **Concepcion del Uruguay** Arg
9A3 **Conception,Pt** USA
35B2 **Conchas** Brazil
9C4 **Conchos** *R* Mexico
21A2 **Concord** California, USA
10C2 **Concord** New Hampshire, USA
29E2 **Concordia** Arg
8D3 **Concordia** USA
20B1 **Concrete** USA
109D1 **Condamine** Aust
107D4 **Condobolin** Aust
20B1 **Condon** USA
46C1 **Condroz** *Mts* Belg
17A1 **Conecuh** *R* USA
47E2 **Conegliano** Italy
89F8 **Congo** Republic, Africa
89F8 **Congo** *R* Congo
Congo,R = Zaïre
14B1 **Coniston** Can
45B2 **Connaught** Region, Irish Rep
14B2 **Conneaut** USA
10C2 **Connecticut** State, USA
15D2 **Connecticut** *R* USA
15C2 **Connellsville** USA
45B2 **Connemara,Mts of** Irish Rep
14A3 **Connersville** USA
108B2 **Conoble** Aust
19A3 **Conroe** USA
35C2 **Conselheiro Lafaiete** Brazil
77D4 **Con Son** *Is* Viet
Constance,L = Bodensee
60C5 **Constanta** Rom
96C1 **Constantine** Alg
12C3 **Constantine,C** USA
29B3 **Constitución** Chile
13F3 **Consul** Can
47E2 **Contarina** Italy
31C4 **Contas** *R* Brazil
23B2 **Contreras** Mexico
4H3 **Contuoyto L** Can
11A3 **Conway** Arkansas, USA
15D2 **Conway** New Hampshire, USA
17C1 **Conway** South Carolina, USA
108A1 **Conway,L** Aust
42C3 **Conwy** Wales
106C3 **Coober Pedy** Aust
110B2 **Cook** *Str* NZ
13B2 **Cook,C** Can
4C3 **Cook Inlet** *B* USA
105H4 **Cook Is** Pacific O
111B2 **Cook,Mt** NZ
107D2 **Cooktown** Aust
109C2 **Coolabah** Aust
108C1 **Cooladdi** Aust
109C2 **Coolah** Aust
109C2 **Coolamon** Aust
106B4 **Coolgardie** Aust
109C3 **Cooma** Aust
109C2 **Coonabarabran** Aust
109C2 **Coonambie** Aust
108B2 **Coonbah** Aust
108A2 **Coondambo** Aust
108C1 **Coongoola** Aust
87B2 **Coonoor** India
108B1 **Cooper Basin** Aust
106C3 **Cooper Creek** Aust
108B1 **Cooper Creek** *R* Aust
108A3 **Coorong,The** Aust
109D1 **Cooroy** Aust
20B2 **Coos B** USA
20B2 **Coos Bay** USA
107D4 **Cootamundra** Aust
45C1 **Cootehill** Irish Rep
23B2 **Copala** Mexico
23B2 **Copalillo** Mexico
Copenhagen = København
30B4 **Copiapó** Chile
47D2 **Copparo** Italy
12F2 **Copper** *R* USA
4D3 **Copper Centre** USA
14B1 **Copper Cliff** Can
Coppermine = Qurlurtuuk
4G3 **Coppermine** *R* Can
Coquilhatville = Mbandaka
30B4 **Coquimbo** Chile
54B2 **Corabia** Rom
17B2 **Coral Gables** USA
6B3 **Coral Harbour** Can
107D2 **Coral S** Aust/PNG
104F4 **Coral Sea Basin** Pacific O
107E2 **Coral Sea Island Territories** Aust
108B3 **Corangamite,L** Aust
33F3 **Corantijn** *R* Surinam/ Guyana
46B2 **Corbeil-Essonnes** France
50A1 **Corcubión** Spain
11B3 **Cordele** USA
50A1 **Cordillera Cantabrica** *Mts* Spain
26C3 **Cordillera Central** *Mts* Dom Rep
79B2 **Cordillera Central** *Mts* Phil
34B2 **Cordillera de Ansita** *Mts* Arg
32B5 **Cordillera de los Andes** *Mts* Peru
30C4 **Cordillera del Toro** *Mt* Arg
32C2 **Cordillera de Mérida** Ven
34A3 **Cordillera de Viento** *Mts* Arg
25D3 **Cordillera Isabelia** *Mts* Nic
32B3 **Cordillera Occidental** *Mts* Colombia
32B3 **Cordillera Oriental** *Mts* Colombia
108B1 **Cordillo Downs** Aust
29D2 **Córdoba** Arg
24C3 **Córdoba** Mexico
50B2 **Córdoba** Spain
29D2 **Córdoba** State, Arg
4D3 **Cordova** USA
Corfu = Kérkira
109D2 **Coricudgy,Mt** Aust
53C3 **Corigliano Calabro** Italy
11B3 **Corinth** Mississippi, USA
31C5 **Corinto** Brazil
45B2 **Cork** County, Irish Rep
41B3 **Cork** Irish Rep
92A1 **Çorlu** Turk
31C5 **Cornel Fabriciano** Brazil
35A2 **Cornelio Procópio** Brazil
7E5 **Corner Brook** Can
109C3 **Corner Inlet** *B* Aust
15C2 **Corning** USA
7C5 **Cornwall** Can
43B4 **Cornwall** County, Eng
43B4 **Cornwall,C** Eng
4H2 **Cornwall I** Can
6A2 **Cornwallis I** Can
32D1 **Coro** Ven
31C2 **Coroatá** Brazil
30C2 **Coroico** Bol
35B1 **Coromandel** Brazil
87C2 **Coromandel Coast** India
110C1 **Coromandel Pen** NZ
110C1 **Coromandel Range** *Mts* NZ
22D4 **Corona** California, USA
13E2 **Coronation** Can
4G3 **Coronation G** Can
34C2 **Coronda** Arg
29B3 **Coronel** Chile
34D3 **Coronel Brandsen** Arg
34C3 **Coronel Dorrego** Arg
35C1 **Coronel Fabriciano** Brazil
30E4 **Coronel Oviedo** Par
29D3 **Coronel Pringles** Arg
34C3 **Coronel Suárez** Arg
34D3 **Coronel Vidal** Arg
30B2 **Coropuna** *Mt* Peru
109C3 **Corowa** Aust
49D3 **Corps** France
9D4 **Corpus Christi** USA
9D4 **Corpus Christi,L** USA
79B3 **Corregidor** *I* Phil
35A1 **Corrente** *R* Mato Grosso, Brazil
30E4 **Corrientes** Arg
30E4 **Corrientes** State, Arg
19B3 **Corrigan** USA
106A4 **Corrigin** Aust
107E2 **Corringe Is** Aust
109C3 **Corryong** Aust
52A2 **Corse** *I* Medit S
42B2 **Corsewall** *Pt* Scot
Corsica = Corse
9D3 **Corsicana** USA
52A2 **Corte** Corse
9C3 **Cortez** USA
52B1 **Cortina d'Ampezzo** Italy
15C2 **Cortland** USA
23A2 **Coruca de Catalan** Mexico
93D1 **Çoruh** *R* Turk
60E5 **Çorum** Turk
30E2 **Corumbá** Brazil
35B1 **Corumba** *R* Brazil
35B1 **Corumbaiba** Brazil
20B2 **Corvallis** USA
96A1 **Corvo** *I* Açores
43C3 **Corwen** Wales
23B2 **Coscomatopec** Mexico
53C3 **Cosenza** Italy
101D1 **Cosmoledo** *Is* Seychelles
34C2 **Cosquín** Arg
51B2 **Costa Blanca** Region, Spain
51C1 **Costa Brava** Region, Spain
50B2 **Costa de la Luz** Region, Spain
50B2 **Costa del Sol** Region, Spain
22D4 **Costa Mesa** USA
25D3 **Costa Rica** Republic, Cent America
79B4 **Cotabato** Phil
30C3 **Cotagaita** Bol
49D3 **Côte d'Azur** Region, France
46C2 **Côtes de Meuse** *Mts* France
97C4 **Cotonou** Benin
32B4 **Cotopaxi** *Mt* Ecuador
43C4 **Cotswold Hills** *Upland* Eng
20B2 **Cottage Grove** USA
56C2 **Cottbus** Germany
108A3 **Couedic,C du** Aust
20C1 **Couer d'Alene L** USA
46B2 **Coulommiers** France
15C1 **Coulonge** *R* Can
22B2 **Coulterville** USA
4B3 **Council** USA
8D2 **Council Bluffs** USA
58C1 **Courland Lagoon** *Lg* Lithuania/Russian Fed
47B2 **Courmayeur** Italy
13B3 **Courtenay** Can
Courtrai = Kortrijk
48B2 **Coutances** France
43D3 **Coventry** Eng
50A1 **Covilhã** Spain
17B1 **Covington** Georgia, USA
19B3 **Covington** Louisiana, USA
109C2 **Cowal,L** Aust
108B3 **Cowangie** Aust
15D1 **Cowansville** Can
108A1 **Coward Springs** Aust
108A2 **Cowell** Aust
108C3 **Cowes** Aust
20B1 **Cowichan L** Can
20B1 **Cowiltz** *R* USA
109C2 **Cowra** Aust
30F2 **Coxim** Brazil
16C1 **Coxsackie** USA
86C2 **Cox's Bazar** Bang
22B2 **Coyote** USA
23A2 **Coyuca de Benitez** Mexico
59B2 **Cracow** Pol
100B4 **Cradock** S Africa
8C2 **Craig** USA
57C3 **Crailsheim** Germany
54B2 **Craiova** Rom
15D2 **Cranberry L** USA
5G5 **Cranbrook** Can
20C2 **Crane** Oregon, USA
16D2 **Cranston** USA
20B2 **Crater L** USA
20B2 **Crater Lake Nat Pk** USA
31C3 **Crateus** Brazil
31D3 **Crato** Brazil
14A2 **Crawfordsville** USA
17B1 **Crawfordville** USA
43D4 **Crawley** Eng
5H4 **Cree L** Can
46B2 **Creil** France

Crema

103J7 **Discovery Tablemount** Atlantic O
47C1 **Disentis Muster** Switz
6E3 **Disko** Greenland
6E3 **Disko Bugt** B Greenland
6E3 **Diskorjord** Greenland
58D1 **Disna** R Belorussia
35B1 **Distrito Federal** Federal District, Brazil
85C4 **Diu** India
79C4 **Diuat Mts** Phil
31C6 **Divinópolis** Brazil
61F4 **Divnoye** Russian Fed
93C2 **Divriği** Turk
22B1 **Dixon** California, USA
5E4 **Dixon Entrance** Sd Can/USA
13D1 **Dixonville** Can
93E3 **Diyālā** R Iraq
65F6 **Diyarbakir** Turk
90A3 **Diz** R Iran
98B2 **Dja** R Cam
96C1 **Djadi** R Alg
95A2 **Djado,Plat du** Niger
98B3 **Djambala** Congo
96C2 **Djanet** Alg
50A2 **Djebel Bouhalla** Mt Mor
96C1 **Djelfa** Alg
98C2 **Djéma** CAR
97B3 **Djenné** Mali
97B3 **Djibo** Burkina
99E1 **Djibouti** Djibouti
99E1 **Djibouti** Republic, E Africa
98C2 **Djolu** Zaïre
97C4 **Djougou** Benin
99D2 **Djugu** Zaïre
38C2 **Djúpivogur** Iceland
51C2 **Djurdjura** Mts Alg
60E2 **Dmitrov** Russian Fed
Dnepr = Dnieper
60D4 **Dneprodzerzhinsk** Ukraine
60E4 **Dnepropetrovsk** Ukraine
60C3 **Dneprovskaya Nizmennost'** Region, Belorussia
Dnestr = Dniester
60D4 **Dnieper** R Ukraine
60B4 **Dniester** R Ukraine
60D2 **Dno** Russian Fed
98B2 **Doba** Chad
58C1 **Dobele** Latvia
34C3 **Doblas** Arg
71E4 **Dobo** Indon
54A2 **Doboj** Bosnia-Herzegovina
54B2 **Dobreta-Turnu-Severin** Rom
54C2 **Dobrich** Bulg
60D3 **Dobrush** Belorussia
31C5 **Doce** R Brazil
30D3 **Doctor R P Peña** Arg
87B2 **Dod** India
87B2 **Doda Betta** Mt India
Dodecanese = Sporádhes
9C3 **Dodge City** USA
99D3 **Dodoma** Tanz
75A1 **Dōgo** I Japan
97C3 **Dogondoutchi** Niger
93D2 **Doğubayazit** Turk
91B4 **Doha** Qatar
7C5 **Dolbeau** Can
49D2 **Dôle** France
43C3 **Dolgellau** Wales
47D1 **Dolomitche** Mts Italy
99E2 **Dolo Odo** Eth
29E3 **Dolores** Arg
34D2 **Dolores** Urug
23A1 **Dolores Hidalgo** Mexico
4G3 **Dolphin and Union Str** Can
29E6 **Dolphin,C** Falkland Is
71E4 **Dom** Mt Indon
65G4 **Dombarovskiy** Russian Fed

38F6 **Dombas** Nor
46D2 **Dombasle-sur-Meurthe** France
54A1 **Dombóvár** Hung
48B2 **Domfront** France
27E3 **Dominica** I Caribbean S
27C3 **Dominican Republic** Caribbean S
6C3 **Dominion,C** Can
7E4 **Domino** Can
68D1 **Domna** Russian Fed
52A1 **Domodossola** Italy
78D4 **Dompu** Indon
29B3 **Domuyo** Mt Arg
109D1 **Domville,Mt** Aust
44C3 **Don** R Scot
61F4 **Don** R Russian Fed
45C1 **Donaghadee** N Ire
57C3 **Donau** R Germany
57C3 **Donauwörth** Germany
50A2 **Don Benito** Spain
42D3 **Doncaster** Eng
98B3 **Dondo** Angola
101C2 **Dondo** Mozam
87C3 **Dondra Head** C Sri Lanka
45B1 **Donegal** County, Irish Rep
40B3 **Donegal** Irish Rep
40B3 **Donegal** B Irish Rep
45B1 **Donegal** Mts Irish Rep
60E4 **Donetsk** Ukraine
73C4 **Dong'an** China
106A3 **Dongara** Aust
73A4 **Dongchuan** China
76D2 **Dongfang** China
74B2 **Dongfeng** China
70C4 **Donggala** Indon
68B3 **Donggi Cona** L China
74A3 **Donggou** China
73C5 **Donghai Dao** I China
72A1 **Dong He** R China
76D2 **Dong Hoi** Viet
73C5 **Dong Jiang** R China
95C3 **Dongola** Sudan
73D5 **Dongshan** China
68D4 **Dongsha Qundao** I China
72C2 **Dongsheng** China
72E3 **Dongtai** China
73C4 **Dongting Hu** L China
73B5 **Dongxing** China
73D3 **Dongzhi** China
18B2 **Doniphan** USA
52C2 **Donji Vakuf** Bosnia-Herzegovina
38G5 **Dönna** I Nor
21A2 **Donner** P USA
46D2 **Donnersberg** Mt Germany
101G1 **Donnybrook** S Africa
Donostia = San Sebastian
22B2 **Don Pedro Res** USA
12D1 **Doonerak,Mt** USA
79B4 **Dopolong** Phil
73A3 **Do Qu** R China
47B2 **Dora Baltea** R Italy
49D2 **Dorbirn** Austria
43C4 **Dorchester** Eng
6C3 **Dorchester,C** Can
48C2 **Dordogne** R France
56A2 **Dordrecht** Neth
13F2 **Dore** L Can
13F2 **Dore Lake** Can
93B3 **Dori** Burkina
46B2 **Dormans** France
57B3 **Dornbirn** Austria
44B3 **Dornoch** Scot
44B3 **Dornoch Firth** Estuary Scot
38H6 **Dorotea** Sweden
109D2 **Dorrigo** Aust
20B2 **Dorris** USA
43C4 **Dorset** County, Eng
46D1 **Dorsten** Germany
56B2 **Dortmund** Germany
98C2 **Doruma** Zaïre
63D2 **Dosatuy** Russian Fed
84B1 **Doshi** Afghan

22B2 **Dos Palos** USA
97C3 **Dosso** Niger
65G5 **Dossor** Kazakhstan
11B3 **Dothan** USA
49C1 **Douai** France
98A2 **Douala** Cam
109D1 **Double Island Pt** Aust
49D2 **Doubs** R France
111A3 **Doubtful Sd** NZ
97B3 **Douentza** Mali
9C3 **Douglas** Arizona, USA
42B2 **Douglas** Eng
17B1 **Douglas** Georgia, USA
8C2 **Douglas** Wyoming, USA
12A1 **Douglas,C** USA
13B2 **Douglas Chan** Can
12D3 **Douglas,Mt** USA
46B1 **Doullens** France
45C1 **Doun** County, N Ire
30F3 **Dourados** Brazil
50A1 **Douro** R Port
15C3 **Dover** Delaware, USA
43E4 **Dover** Eng
15D2 **Dover** New Hampshire, USA
16B2 **Dover** New Jersey, USA
14B2 **Dover** Ohio, USA
43D3 **Dover** R Eng
41D3 **Dover,Str of** UK/France
16B3 **Downington** USA
42B2 **Downpatrick** N Ire
13C2 **Downton,Mt** USA
16B2 **Doylestown** USA
75A1 **Dōzen** I Japan
96A2 **Dr'aa** R Mor
35A2 **Dracena** Brazil
16D1 **Dracut** USA
49D3 **Draguignan** France
101C3 **Drakensberg** Mts S Africa
101G1 **Drakensberg** Mt S Africa
103E7 **Drake Pass** Pacific/Atlantic O
55B2 **Dráma** Greece
39G7 **Drammen** Nor
38A1 **Drangajökull** Iceland
52C1 **Drava** R Slovenia
13D2 **Drayton Valley** Can
49C2 **Dreaux** France
57C2 **Dresden** Germany
48C2 **Dreux** France
20C2 **Drewsey** USA
54B2 **Drin** R Alb
54A2 **Drina** R Bosnia-Herzegovina/Serbia
58D1 **Drissa** R Belorussia
45C2 **Drogheda** Irish Rep
59C3 **Drogobych** Ukraine
112B12 **Dronning Maud Land** Region, Ant
30D3 **Dr P.P. Pená** Par
5G4 **Drumheller** Can
14B1 **Drummond I** USA
15D1 **Drummondville** Can
58C2 **Druskininksi** Lithuania
12G3 **Dry B** USA
7A5 **Dryden** Can
27H1 **Dry Harbour Mts** Jamaica
76B3 **Duang** I Burma
91C4 **Dubai** UAE
5H3 **Dubawnt** R Can
4H3 **Dubawnt L** Can
107D4 **Dubbo** Aust
45C2 **Dublin** County, Irish Rep
45C2 **Dublin** Irish Rep
17B1 **Dublin** USA
60E2 **Dubna** Russian Fed
60C3 **Dubno** Ukraine
15C2 **Du Bois** USA
13B2 **Dubose,Mt** Can
58D2 **Dubrovica** Ukraine
54A2 **Dubrovnik** Croatia
10A2 **Dubuque** USA

46D2 **Dudelange** Lux
1C10 **Dudinka** Russian Fed
43C3 **Dudley** Eng
97B4 **Duekoué** Ivory Coast
50B1 **Duero** R Spain
44C3 **Dufftown** Scot
52B2 **Dugi Otok** I Croatia
56B2 **Duisburg** Germany
93E3 **Dūkan** Iraq
99D2 **Duk Faiwil** Sudan
91B4 **Dukhān** Qatar
73A4 **Dukou** China
68B3 **Dulan** China
34C2 **Dulce** R Arg
78C2 **Dulit Range** Mts Malay
86C2 **Dullabchara** India
10A2 **Duluth** USA
94C2 **Dūmā** Syria
78A2 **Dumai** Indon
79A3 **Dumaran** I Phil
9C3 **Dumas** USA
94C2 **Dumayr** Syria
42B2 **Dumbarton** Scot
42C2 **Dumfries** Scot
42B2 **Dumfries and Galloway** Region, Scot
86B2 **Dumka** India
15C1 **Dumoine,L** Can
112C8 **Dumont d'Urville** Base Ant
95C1 **Dumyat** Egypt
54C2 **Dunărea** R Rom
45C2 **Dunary Head** Pt Irish Rep
54B2 **Dunav** R Bulg
59D3 **Dunayevtsy** Ukraine
13C3 **Duncan** Can
16A2 **Duncannon** USA
44C2 **Duncansby Head** Pt Scot
45C1 **Dundalk** Irish Rep
16A3 **Dundalk** USA
45C2 **Dundalk B** Irish Rep
6D2 **Dundas** Greenland
4G2 **Dundas Pen** Can
71E5 **Dundas Str** Aust
101H1 **Dundee** S Africa
44C3 **Dundee** Scot
108B1 **Dundoo** Aust
42B2 **Dundrum** B N Ire
111B3 **Dunedin** NZ
17B2 **Dunedin** USA
109C2 **Dunedoo** Aust
44C3 **Dunfermline** Scot
85C4 **Dungarpur** India
45C2 **Dungarvan** Irish Rep
43E4 **Dungeness** Eng
109D2 **Dungog** Aust
99C2 **Dungu** Zaïre
95C2 **Dungunab** Sudan
68B2 **Dunhuang** China
46B1 **Dunkerque** France
10C2 **Dunkirk** USA
99D1 **Dunkur** Eth
97B4 **Dunkwa** Ghana
41B3 **Dun Laoghaire** Irish Rep
45B3 **Dunmanway** Irish Rep
26B1 **Dunmore Town** The Bahamas
44C2 **Dunnet Head** Pt Scot
42C2 **Duns** Scot
20B2 **Dunsmuir** USA
111A2 **Dunstan Mts** NZ
46C2 **Dun-sur-Meuse** France
72D1 **Duolun** China
18C2 **Du Quoin** USA
94B3 **Dura** Israel
49D3 **Durance** R France
24B2 **Durango** Mexico
50B1 **Durango** Spain
9C3 **Durango** USA
29E2 **Durano** Urug
9D3 **Durant** USA
94C1 **Duraykīsh** Syria
101H1 **Durban** S Africa
46D1 **Duren** Germany
86A2 **Durg** India
86B2 **Durgapur** India
42D2 **Durham** County, Eng

Elsterwerde

14B3 **Fairmont** W Virginia, USA
13D1 **Fairview** Can
4E4 **Fairweather,Mt** USA
71F3 **Fais** *I* Pacific O
84C2 **Faisalabad** Pak
8C2 **Faith** USA
44E1 **Faither,The** *Pen* Scot
86A1 **Faizābād** India
43E3 **Fakenham** Eng
39G7 **Faköping** Sweden
86C2 **Falam** Burma
24C2 **Falcon Res** Mexico/USA
97A3 **Falémé** *R* Mali/Sen
39G7 **Falkenberg** Sweden
42C2 **Falkirk** Scot
29D6 **Falkland Is** Dependency, S Atlantic
29E6 **Falkland Sd** Falkland Is
22D4 **Fallbrook** USA
8B3 **Fallon** USA
15D2 **Fall River** USA
18A1 **Falls City** USA
43B4 **Falmouth** Eng
27H1 **Falmouth** Jamaica
16D2 **Falmouth** Massachusetts, USA
100A4 **False B** S Africa
24A2 **Falso,C** Mexico
56C2 **Falster** *I* Den
54C1 **Fälticeni** Rom
39H6 **Falun** Sweden
92B2 **Famagusta** Cyprus
46C1 **Famenne** Region, Belg
76B2 **Fang** Thai
99D2 **Fangak** Sudan
73E5 **Fang liao** Taiwan
52B2 **Fano** Italy
112C3 **Faraday** *Base* Ant
99C2 **Faradje** Zaïre
101D3 **Farafangana** Madag
95B2 **Farafra Oasis** Egypt
80E2 **Farah** Afghan
71F2 **Farallon de Medinilla** *I* Pacific O
97A3 **Faranah** Guinea
71F3 **Faraulep** *I* Pacific O
43D4 **Fareham** Eng
Farewell,C = Kap Farvel
107G5 **Farewell,C** NZ
110B2 **Farewell Spit** *Pt* NZ
8D2 **Fargo** USA
94B2 **Fari'a** *R* Israel
10A2 **Faribault** USA
86B2 **Faridpur** Bang
90C2 **Farīmān** Iran
18B2 **Farmington** Missouri, USA
9C3 **Farmington** New Mexico, USA
22B2 **Farmington Res** USA
42D2 **Farne Deep** N Sea
13D2 **Farnham,Mt** Can
12H2 **Faro** Can
50A2 **Faro** Port
39H7 **Fåro** *I* Sweden
89K9 **Farquhar** *Is* Indian O
44B3 **Farrar** *R* Scot
14B2 **Farrell** USA
55B3 **Fársala** Greece
91B4 **Fasā** Iran
45B3 **Fastnet Rock** Irish Rep
60C3 **Fastov** Ukraine
86A1 **Fatehpur** India
13D1 **Father** Can
30F2 **Fatima du Sul** Brazil
101G1 **Fauresmith** S Africa
47B2 **Faverges** France
7B4 **Fawn** *R* Can
38H6 **Fax** *R* Sweden
38A2 **Faxaflói** *B* Iceland
95A3 **Faya** Chad
11A3 **Fayetteville** Arkansas, USA
11C3 **Fayetteville** N Carolina, USA
93E4 **Faylakah** *I* Kuwait
84C2 **Fāzilka** India
96A2 **Fdérik** Maur
11C3 **Fear,C** USA
21A2 **Feather Middle Fork** *R* USA
48C2 **Fécamp** France
34D2 **Federación** Arg
34D2 **Federal** Arg
71F3 **Federated States of Micronesia** *Is* Pacific O
56C2 **Fehmarn** *I* Germany
32C5 **Feijó** Brazil
73C5 **Feilai Xai Bei Jiang** *R* China
110C2 **Feilding** NZ
100C2 **Feira** Zambia
31D4 **Feira de Santan** Brazil
92C2 **Feke** Turk
57B3 **Feldkirch** Austria
34D2 **Feliciano** *R* Arg
41D3 **Felixstowe** Eng
47D1 **Feltre** Italy
38G6 **Femund** *L* Nor
74A2 **Fengcheng** China
73B4 **Fengdu** China
72D1 **Fenging** China
73B3 **Fengjie** China
72B3 **Feng Xian** China
72C1 **Fengzhen** China
72C2 **Fen He** *R* China
101D2 **Fenoarivo Atsinanana** Madag
60E5 **Feodosiya** Ukraine
90C3 **Ferdow** Iran
46B2 **Fère-Champenoise** France
82B2 **Fergana** Uzbekistan
45C1 **Fermanagh** County, N Ire
45B2 **Fermoy** Irish Rep
47D1 **Fern** *Mt* Austria
32J7 **Fernandina** *I* Ecuador
17B1 **Fernandina Beach** USA
103G5 **Fernando de Noronha** *I* Atlantic O
35A2 **Fernandópolis** Brazil
20B1 **Ferndale** USA
21B2 **Fernley** USA
52B2 **Ferrara** Italy
32B5 **Ferreñafe** Peru
19B3 **Ferriday** USA
96B1 **Fès** Mor
18B2 **Festus** USA
54C2 **Feteşti** Rom
92A2 **Fethiye** Turk
61H5 **Fetisovo** Kazakhstan
44E1 **Fetlar** *I* Scot
84C1 **Feyzabad** Afghan
101D3 **Fianarantsoa** Madag
99D2 **Fichē** Eth
101G1 **Ficksburg** S Africa
47D2 **Fidenza** Italy
55A2 **Fier** Alb
47D1 **Fiera Di Primeiro** Italy
44C3 **Fife** Region, Scot
44C3 **Fife Ness** *Pen* Scot
48C3 **Figeac** France
50A1 **Figueira da Foz** Port
51C1 **Figueras** Spain
Figueres = Figueras
96B1 **Figuig** Mor
105G4 **Fiji** *Is* Pacific O
30D3 **Filadelfia** Par
54B2 **Filiaşi** Rom
55B3 **Filiatrá** Greece
53B3 **Filicudi** *I* Italy
21B3 **Fillmore** California, USA
44B3 **Findhorn** *R* Scot
10B2 **Findlay** USA
13D2 **Findlay,Mt** Can
15C2 **Finger Lakes** USA
101C2 **Fingoè** Mozam
92B2 **Finike** Turk
106C3 **Finke** *R* Aust
108A1 **Finke Flood Flats** Aust
64D3 **Finland** Republic, N Europe
39J7 **Finland,G of** N Europe
5F4 **Finlay** *R* Can
5F4 **Finlay Forks** Can
108C3 **Finley** Aust
38H5 **Finnsnes** Nor
71F4 **Finschhafen** PNG
47C1 **Finsteraarhorn** *Mt* Switz
56C2 **Finsterwalde** Germany
45C1 **Fintona** N Ire
111A3 **Fiordland Nat Pk** NZ
94B2 **Fiq** Syria
93C2 **Firat** *R* Turk
22B2 **Firebaugh** USA
52B2 **Firenze** Italy
34C2 **Firmat** Arg
85D3 **Firozābād** India
84C2 **Firozpur** India
39H7 **Firspång** Sweden
42B2 **Firth of Clyde** *Estuary* Scot
44C3 **Firth of Forth** *Estuary* Scot
44A3 **Firth of Lorn** *Estuary* Scot
40C2 **Firth of Tay** *Estuary* Scot
91B4 **Firūzābād** Iran
100A3 **Fish** *R* Namibia
22C2 **Fish Camp** USA
16C2 **Fishers I** USA
6B3 **Fisher Str** Can
43B4 **Fishguard** Wales
6E3 **Fiskenaesset** Greenland
46B2 **Fismes** France
15D2 **Fitchburg** USA
44E2 **Fitful Head** *Pt* Scot
17B1 **Fitzgerald** USA
106B2 **Fitzroy** *R* Aust
106B2 **Fitzroy Crossing** Aust
14B1 **Fitzwilliam I** Can
Fiume = Rijeka
99C3 **Fizi** Zaïre
9B3 **Flagstaff** USA
42D2 **Flamborough Head** *C* Eng
8C2 **Flaming Gorge Res** USA
44A2 **Flannan Isles** *Is* Scot
12J2 **Flat** *R* Can
13E3 **Flathead** *R* USA
8B2 **Flathead L** USA
18B2 **Flat River** USA
8A2 **Flattery,C** USA
42C3 **Fleetwood** Eng
39F7 **Flekkefjord** Nor
69G4 **Fleming Deep** Pacific O
16B2 **Flemington** USA
56B2 **Flensburg** Germany
47B1 **Fleurier** Switz
106C4 **Flinders** *I* Aust
107D4 **Flinders** *I* Aust
107D2 **Flinders** *R* Aust
106C4 **Flinders Range** *Mts* Aust
5H4 **Flin Flon** Can
10B2 **Flint** USA
42C3 **Flint** Wales
11B3 **Flint** *R* USA
46B1 **Flixecourt** France
17A1 **Florala** USA
Florence = Firenze
11B3 **Florence** Alabama, USA
18A2 **Florence** Kansas, USA
20B2 **Florence** Oregon, USA
11C3 **Florence** S Carolina, USA
32B3 **Florencia** Colombia
46C2 **Florenville** Belg
25D3 **Flores** Guatemala
96A1 **Flores** *I* Açores
106B1 **Flores** *I* Indon
34D3 **Flores** *R* Arg
70C4 **Flores S** Indon
31C3 **Floriano** Brazil
30G4 **Florianópolis** Brazil
25D2 **Florida** State, USA
29E2 **Florida** Urug
17B2 **Florida B** USA
17B2 **Florida City** USA
107E1 **Florida Is** Solomon Is
11B4 **Florida Keys** *Is* USA
11B4 **Florida,Strs of** USA
55B2 **Flórina** Greece
38F6 **Florø** Nor
47D1 **Fluchthorn** *Mt* Austria
54C1 **Focsani** Rom
53C2 **Foggia** Italy
97A4 **Fogo** *I* Cape Verde
48C3 **Foix** France
6C3 **Foley I** Can
52B2 **Foligno** Italy
43E4 **Folkestone** Eng
17B1 **Folkston** USA
52B2 **Follonica** Italy
22B1 **Folsom** USA
22B1 **Folsom L** *L* USA
5H4 **Fond-du-Lac** Can
10B2 **Fond du Lac** USA
48C2 **Fontainebleau** France
18B2 **Fontenac** USA
48B2 **Fontenay-le-Comte** France
52C1 **Fonyód** Hung
Foochow = Fuzhou
12D2 **Foraker,Mt** USA
46D2 **Forbach** France
109C2 **Forbes** Aust
97C4 **Forcados** Nig
38F6 **Forde** Nor
108C1 **Fords Bridge** Aust
19B3 **Fordyce** USA
97A4 **Forécariah** Guinea
6G3 **Forel,Mt** Greenland
14B2 **Forest** Can
17B1 **Forest Park** USA
22A1 **Forestville** USA
44C3 **Forfar** Scot
46A2 **Forges-les-Eaux** France
20B1 **Forks** USA
52B2 **Forlì** Italy
51C2 **Formentera** *I* Spain
53B2 **Formia** Italy
96A1 **Formigas** *I* Açores
Formosa = Taiwan
30E4 **Formosa** Arg
31B5 **Formosa** Brazil
30D3 **Formosa** State, Arg
73D5 **Formosa Str** Taiwan/China
47D2 **Fornovo di Taro** Italy
38D3 **Føroyar** *Is* N Atlantic O
44C3 **Forres** Scot
106B4 **Forrest** Aust
11A3 **Forrest City** USA
107D2 **Forsayth** Aust
39J6 **Forssa** Fin
109D2 **Forster** Aust
18B2 **Forsyth** Missouri, USA
84C3 **Fort Abbas** Pak
7B4 **Fort Albany** Can
31D2 **Fortaleza** Brazil
44B3 **Fort Augustus** Scot
100B4 **Fort Beaufort** S Africa
21A2 **Fort Bragg** USA
8C2 **Fort Collins** USA
15C1 **Fort Coulogne** Can
27E4 **Fort de France** Martinique
17A1 **Fort Deposit** USA
10A2 **Fort Dodge** USA
106A3 **Fortescue** *R* Aust
7A5 **Fort Frances** Can
4F3 **Fort Franklin** Can
4F3 **Fort Good Hope** Can
108B1 **Fort Grey** Aust
44B3 **Forth** *R* Scot
7B4 **Fort Hope** Can
34B3 **Fortin Uno** Arg
4F3 **Fort Laird** Can
96C1 **Fort Lallemand** Alg
Fort Lamy = Ndjamena
11B4 **Fort Lauderdale** USA
4F3 **Fort Liard** Can

Fort Mackay

5G4	Fort Mackay Can
5G5	Fort Macleod Can
5G4	Fort McMurray Can
4E3	Fort McPherson Can
18B2	Fort Madison USA
8C2	Fort Morgan USA
11B4	Fort Myers USA
5F4	Fort Nelson Can
4F3	Fort Norman Can
17A1	Fort Payne USA
8C2	Fort Peck Res USA
11B4	Fort Pierce USA
4G3	Fort Providence Can
5G3	Fort Resolution Can
98B3	Fort Rousset Congo
5F4	Fort St James Can
13C1	Fort St John Can
13E2	Fort Saskatchewan Can
18B2	Fort Scott USA
4E3	Fort Selkirk Can
7B4	Fort Severn Can
61H5	Fort Shevchenko Kazakhstan
4F3	Fort Simpson Can
5G3	Fort Smith Can
4G3	Fort Smith Region, Can
11A3	Fort Smith USA
9C3	Fort Stockton USA
20B2	Fortuna California, USA
5G4	Fort Vermillion Can
17A1	Fort Walton Beach USA
10B2	Fort Wayne USA
44B3	Fort William Scot
9D3	Fort Worth USA
12F2	Fortymile R USA
12E1	Fort Yukon USA
73C5	Foshan China
47B2	Fossano Italy
12G3	Foster,Mt USA
98B3	Fougamou Gabon
48B2	Fougères France
44D1	Foula I Scot
43E4	Foulness I Eng
111B2	Foulwind,C NZ
98B2	Foumban Cam
49C1	Fourmies France
55C3	Foúrnoi I Greece
97A3	Fouta Djallon Mts Guinea
111B3	Foveaux Str NZ
43B4	Fowey Eng
13D2	Fox Creek Can
6B3	Foxe Basin G Can
6B3	Foxe Chan Can
6C3	Foxe Pen Can
110C2	Foxton NZ
13F2	Fox Valley Can
45B2	Foynes Irish Rep
100A2	Foz do Cuene Angola
30F4	Foz do Iquaçu Brazil
16A2	Frackville USA
34B2	Fraga Arg
16D1	Framingham USA
31B6	Franca Brazil
49C2	France Republic, Europe
10A2	Frances Can
12J2	Frances R Can
49D2	Franche Comté Region, France
100B3	Francistown Botswana
13B2	Francois L Can
14A2	Frankfort Indiana, USA
11B3	Frankfort Kentucky, USA
101G1	Frankfort S Africa
57B2	Frankfurt Germany
46E1	Frankfurt am Main Germany
56C2	Frankfurt-an-der-Oder Germany
57C3	Fränkischer Alb Upland Germany
14A3	Franklin Indiana, USA
19B4	Franklin Louisiana, USA
16D1	Franklin Massachusetts, USA
16B2	Franklin New Jersey, USA
14C2	Franklin Pennsylvania, USA
4F2	Franklin B Can
20C1	Franklin D Roosevelt L USA
4F3	Franklin Mts Can
4J2	Franklin Str Can
111B2	Franz Josef Glacier NZ
	Franz-Joseph-Land = Zemlya Frantsa Iosifa
5F5	Fraser R Can
44C3	Fraserburgh Scot
107E3	Fraser I Aust
13B2	Fraser L Can
47B1	Frasne France
47C1	Frauenfield Switz
34D2	Fray Bentos Urug
40C2	Frazerburgh Scot
16B3	Frederica USA
56B1	Fredericia Den
15C3	Frederick Maryland, USA
15C3	Fredericksburg Virginia, USA
12H3	Frederick Sd USA
18B2	Fredericktown USA
7D5	Fredericton Can
6E3	Frederikshab Greenland
39G7	Frederikshavn Den
15C2	Fredonia USA
39G7	Fredrikstad Nor
16B2	Freehold USA
26B1	Freeport The Bahamas
19A4	Freeport Texas, USA
97A4	Freetown Sierra Leone
57B3	Freiburg Germany
57C3	Freistadt Austria
106A4	Fremantle Aust
22B2	Fremont California, USA
18A1	Fremont Nebraska, USA
14B2	Fremont Ohio, USA
33G3	French Guiana Dependency, S America
109C4	Frenchmans Cap Mt Aust
105J4	French Polynesia Is Pacific O
24B2	Fresnillo Mexico
8B3	Fresno USA
22C2	Fresno R USA
47A1	Fretigney France
46B1	Frévent France
109C4	Freycinet Pen Aust
97A3	Fria Guinea
22C2	Friant USA
22C2	Friant Dam USA
52A1	Fribourg Switz
57B3	Friedrichshafen Germany
6D3	Frobisher B Can
6D3	Frobisher Bay Can
5H4	Frobisher L Can
61F4	Frolovo Russian Fed
43C4	Frome Eng
108A1	Frome R Aust
43C4	Frome R Eng
106C4	Frome,L Aust
25C3	Frontera Mexico
15C3	Front Royal USA
53B2	Frosinone Italy
73C5	Fuchuan China
73E4	Fuding China
24B2	Fuerte R Mexico
30E3	Fuerte Olimpo Par
96A2	Fuerteventura I Canary Is
72C2	Fugu China
68A2	Fuhai China
91C4	Fujairah UAE
75B1	Fuji Japan
73D4	Fujian Province, China
69F2	Fujin China
75B1	Fujinomiya Japan
74D3	Fuji-san Mt Japan
75B1	Fujisawa Japan
75B1	Fuji-Yoshida Japan
63A3	Fukang China
74C3	Fukuchiyima Japan
74D3	Fukui Japan
74C4	Fukuoka Japan
74E3	Fukushima Japan
74C4	Fukuyama Japan
57B2	Fulda Germany
57B2	Fulda R Germany
73B4	Fuling China
27L1	Fullarton Trinidad
22D4	Fullerton USA
18C2	Fulton Kentucky, USA
15C2	Fulton New York, USA
46C1	Fumay France
75C1	Funabashi Japan
96A1	Funchal Medeira
35C1	Fundão Brazil
7D5	Fundy,B of Can
101C3	Funhalouro Mozam
72D3	Funing China
73B5	Funing China
97C3	Funtua Nig
73D4	Fuqing China
101C2	Furancungo Mozam
91C4	Fürg Iran
47C1	Furka P Switz
107D5	Furneaux Group Is Aust
56C2	Fürstenwalde Germany
57C3	Fürth Germany
74D3	Furukawa Japan
6B3	Fury and Hecla St Can
74A2	Fushun Liaoning, China
73A4	Fushun Sichuan, China
74B2	Fusong China
57C3	Füssen Germany
72E2	Fu Xian China
72E1	Fuxin China
72D3	Fuyang China
72E1	Fuyuan Liaoning, China
73A4	Fuyuan Yunnan, China
68A2	Fuyun China
73D4	Fuzhou China
56C1	Fyn I Den

G

99E2	Gaalkacyo Somalia
21B2	Gabbs USA
100A2	Gabela Angola
96D1	Gabe's Tunisia
22B2	Gabilan Range Mts USA
98B3	Gabon Republic, Africa
100B3	Gaborone Botswana
54C2	Gabrovo Bulg
91B3	Gach Sārān Iran
17A1	Gadsden Alabama, USA
10A1	Gads L Can
53B2	Gaeta Italy
71F3	Gaferut I Pacific O
96C1	Gafsa Tunisia
60D2	Gagarin Russian Fed
97B4	Gagnoa Ivory Coast
7D4	Gagnon Can
61F5	Gagra Georgia
86B1	Gaibanda India
29C4	Gaimán Arg
17B2	Gainesville Florida, USA
17B1	Gainesville Georgia, USA
19A3	Gainesville Texas, USA
42D3	Gainsborough Eng
108A2	Gairdner,L Aust
44B3	Gairloch Scot
16A3	Gaithersburg USA
87B1	Gajendragarh India
73D4	Ga Jiang R China
99D3	Galana R Kenya
103D5	Galapagos Is Pacific O
42C2	Galashiels Scot
54C1	Galaţi Rom
4C3	Galena Alaska, USA
18B2	Galena Kansas, USA
27L1	Galeota Pt Trinidad
27L1	Galera Pt Trinidad
10A2	Galesburg USA
15C2	Galeton USA
61F2	Galich Russian Fed
50A1	Galicia Region, Spain
	Galilee,S of = Tiberias,L
27J1	Galina Pt Jamaica
99D1	Gallabat Sudan
47C2	Gallarate Italy
87C3	Galle Sri Lanka
51B1	Gállego R Spain
	Gallipoli = Gelibolu
55A2	Gallipoli Italy
38J5	Gällivare Sweden
42B2	Galloway District
42B2	Galloway,Mull of C Scot
8C3	Gallup USA
22B1	Galt USA
96A2	Galtat Zemmour Mor
25C2	Galveston USA
11A4	Galveston B USA
34C2	Galvez Arg
49D3	Galvi Corse
45B2	Galway County, Irish Rep
41B3	Galway Irish Rep
41B3	Galway B Irish Rep
86B1	Gamba China
97B3	Gambaga Ghana
4A3	Gambell USA
97A3	Gambia R The Gambia/Sen
97A3	Gambia,The Republic, Africa
98B3	Gamboma Congo
100A2	Gambos Angola
87C3	Gampola Sri Lanka
99E2	Ganale Dorya R Eth
15C2	Gananoque Can
	Gand = Gent
100A2	Ganda Angola
98C3	Gandajika Zaïre
84B3	Gandava Pak
7E5	Gander Can
85C4	Gāndhīdhām India
85C4	Gāndhīnagar India
85D4	Gāndhi Sāgar L India
51B2	Gandia Spain
86B2	Ganga R India
85C3	Ganganar India
86C2	Gangaw Burma
72A2	Gangca China
82C2	Gangdise Shan Mts China
	Ganges = Ganga
86B1	Gangtok India
72B3	Gangu China
8C2	Gannett Peak Mt USA
72B2	Ganquan China
108A3	Gantheaume C Aust
39K8	Gantsevichi Belorussia
73D4	Ganzhou China
97C3	Gao Mali
72A2	Gaolan China
72C2	Gaoping China
97B3	Gaoua Burkina
97A3	Gaoual Guinea
72D3	Gaoyou Hu L China
73C5	Gaozhou China
49D3	Gap France
79B2	Gapan Phil
84D2	Gar China
109C1	Garah Aust
31D3	Garanhuns Brazil
21A1	Garberville USA
35B2	Garça Brazil
35A2	Garcias Brazil
47D2	Garda Italy
9C3	Garden City USA
14A1	Garden Pen USA
34D3	Gardey Arg
84B2	Gardez Afghan

16C2 **Gardiners I** USA
16D1 **Gardner** USA
47D2 **Gardone** Italy
47D2 **Gargano** Italy
85D4 **Garhākota** India
61K2 **Gari** Russian Fed
100A4 **Garies** S Africa
99D3 **Garissa** Kenya
19A3 **Garland** USA
57C3 **Garmisch-Partenkirchen** Germany
90B2 **Garmsar** Iran
18A2 **Garnett** USA
8B2 **Garnett Peak** *Mt* USA
48C3 **Garonne** *R* France
44B3 **Garry** *R* Scot
78B4 **Garut** Indon
86A2 **Garwa** India
14A2 **Gary** USA
82C2 **Garyarsa** China
4H3 **Gary L** Can
19A3 **Garza-Little Elm** *Res* USA
90B2 **Gasan Kuli** Turkmenistan
48B3 **Gascogne** Region, France
18B2 **Gasconade** *R* USA
106A3 **Gascoyne** *R* Aust
98B2 **Gashaka** Nig
97D3 **Gashua** Nig
10D2 **Gaspé** Can
10D2 **Gaspé,C. de** Can
94A1 **Gata,C** Cyprus
60C2 **Gatchina** Russian Fed
42D2 **Gateshead** Eng
19A3 **Gatesville** USA
15C1 **Gatineau** Can
15C1 **Gatineau** *R* Can
109D1 **Gatton** Aust
86C1 **Gauháti** India
58C1 **Gauja** *R* Latvia
86A1 **Gauri Phanta** India
22B3 **Gaviota** USA
39H6 **Gävle** Sweden
108A2 **Gawler Ranges** *Mts* Aust
72A1 **Gaxun Nur** *L* China
86A2 **Gaya** India
97C3 **Gaya** Niger
14B1 **Gaylord** USA
109D1 **Gayndah** Aust
61H1 **Gayny** Russian Fed
60C4 **Gaysin** Ukraine
92B3 **Gaza** Israel
92C2 **Gaziantep** Turk
97D4 **Gbaringa** Lib
58B2 **Gdańsk** Pol
58B2 **Gdańsk,G of** Pol
39K7 **Gdov** Russian Fed
58B2 **Gdynia** Pol
94A3 **Gebel Halál** *Mt* Egypt
95C2 **Gebel Hamata** *Mt* Egypt
92D4 **Gebel Katherina** *Mt* Egypt
94A3 **Gebel Libni** *Mt* Egypt
94A3 **Gebel Maghâra** *Mt* Egypt
99D1 **Gedaref** Sudan
55C3 **Gediz** *R* Turk
56C2 **Gedser** Den
46C1 **Geel** Belg
108B3 **Geelong** Aust
109C4 **Geeveston** Aust
97D3 **Geidam** Nig
46D1 **Geilenkirchen** Germany
99D3 **Geita** Tanz
73A5 **Gejiu** China
53B3 **Gela** Italy
99E2 **Geladī** Eth
46D1 **Geldern** Germany
55C2 **Gelibolu** Turk
92B2 **Gelidonya Burun** Turk
46D1 **Gelsenkirchen** Germany
39F8 **Gelting** Germany

77C5 **Gemas** Malay
46C1 **Gembloux** Belg
98B2 **Gemena** Zaïre
92C2 **Gemerek** Turk
92A1 **Gemlik** Turk
52B1 **Gemona** Italy
100B3 **Gemsbok** *Nat Pk* Botswana
98C1 **Geneina** Sudan
34C3 **General Acha** Arg
34C3 **General Alvear** Buenos Aires, Arg
34B2 **General Alvear** Mendoza, Arg
34C2 **General Arenales** Arg
34D3 **General Belgrano** Arg
112B2 **General Belgrano** *Base* Ant
112C2 **General Bernardo O'Higgins** *Base* Ant
34D3 **General Conesa** Buenos Aires, Arg
30D3 **General Eugenio A Garay** Par
34D3 **General Guido** Arg
34C3 **General La Madrid** Arg
34C2 **General Levalle** Arg
30C4 **General Manuel Belgrano** *Mt* Arg
34D3 **General Paz** Buenos Aires, Arg
34C3 **General Pico** Arg
34C2 **General Pinto** Arg
34D3 **General Pirán** Arg
29C3 **General Roca** Arg
112C3 **General San Martin** *Base* Ant
79C4 **General Santos** Phil
34C3 **General Viamonte** Arg
34C3 **General Villegas** Arg
15C2 **Genesee** *R* USA
15C2 **Geneseo** USA
Geneva = Genève
18A1 **Geneva** Nebraska, USA
15C2 **Geneva** New York, USA
Geneva,L of = LacLéman
52A1 **Genève** Switz
50B2 **Genil** *R* Spain
Genoa = Genova
109C3 **Genoa** Aust
52A2 **Genova** Italy
32J7 **Genovesa** *I* Ecuador
46B1 **Gent** Belg
78B4 **Genteng** Indon
56C2 **Genthin** Germany
93E1 **Geokchay** Azerbaijan
100B4 **George** S Africa
7D4 **George** *R* Can
109C2 **George,L** Aust
17B2 **George,L** Florida, USA
15D2 **George,L** New York, USA
111A2 **George Sd** NZ
109C4 **George Town** Aust
15C3 **Georgetown** Delaware, USA
33F2 **Georgetown** Guyana
14B3 **Georgetown** Kentucky, USA
77C4 **George Town** Malay
27N2 **Georgetown** St Vincent and the Grenadines
17C1 **Georgetown** S Carolina, USA
19A3 **Georgetown** Texas, USA
97A3 **Georgetown** The Gambia
112C8 **George V Land** Region, Ant
65F5 **Georgia** Republic, Europe
112C12 **Georg Forster** *Base* Ant
17B1 **Georgia** State, USA

14B1 **Georgian B** Can
13C3 **Georgia,Str of** Can
106C3 **Georgina** *R* Aust
61F5 **Georgiyevsk** Russian Fed
57C2 **Gera** Germany
46B1 **Geraardsbergen** Belg
111B2 **Geraldine** NZ
106A3 **Geraldton** Aust
10B2 **Geraldton** Can
94B3 **Gerar** *R* Israel
4C3 **Gerdine,Mt** USA
12E2 **Gerdova Peak** *Mt* USA
77C4 **Gerik** Malay
60B4 **Gerlachovsky** *Mt* Pol
13C1 **Germanson Lodge** Can
56C2 **Germany** Republic, Europe
101G1 **Germiston** S Africa
46D1 **Gerolstein** Germany
51C1 **Gerona** Spain
46E1 **Geseke** Germany
99E2 **Gestro** *R* Eth
50B1 **Getafe** Spain
16A3 **Gettysburg** Pennsylvania, USA
93D2 **Gevaş** Turk
55B2 **Gevgelija** Macedonia
47B1 **Gex** France
94C2 **Ghabāghib** Syria
96C1 **Ghadamis** Libya
90B2 **Ghaem Shahr** Iran
86A1 **Ghāghara** *R* India
97B4 **Ghana** Republic, Africa
100B3 **Ghanzi** Botswana
96C1 **Ghardaïa** Alg
95A1 **Gharyan** Libya
95A2 **Ghat** Libya
84D3 **Ghāziābād** India
84C3 **Ghazi Khan** Pak
84B2 **Ghazni** Afghan
54C1 **Gheorgheni** Rom
88E4 **Ghudamis** Alg
90D3 **Ghurian** Afghan
95B2 **Gialo** Libya
99E2 **Giamame** Somalia
53C3 **Giarre** Italy
100A3 **Gibeon** Namibia
50A2 **Gibraltar** Colony, SW Europe
50A2 **Gibraltar,Str of** Spain/Africa
106B3 **Gibson Desert** Aust
20B1 **Gibsons** Can
87B1 **Giddalūr** India
99D2 **Gīdolē** Eth
67B2 **Giessen** Germany
17B2 **Gifford** USA
74D3 **Gifu** Japan
42B2 **Gigha** *I* Scot
52B2 **Giglio** *I* Italy
50A1 **Gijón** Spain
107D2 **Gilbert** *R* Aust
13C2 **Gilbert,Mt** Can
101C2 **Gilé** Mozam
94B2 **Gilead** Region, Jordan
95B2 **Gilf Kebir Plat** Egypt
109C2 **Gilgandra** Aust
84C1 **Gilgit** Pak
84C1 **Gilgit** *R* Pak
108C2 **Gilgunnia** Aust
7A4 **Gillam** Can
108A2 **Gilles** L Aust
13B2 **Gill I** Can
14A1 **Gills Rock** USA
14A2 **Gilman** USA
22B2 **Gilroy** USA
8D1 **Gimli** Can
101H1 **Gingindlovu** S Africa
79C4 **Gingoog** Phil
99E2 **Ginir** Eth
55B3 **Gióna** *Mt* Greece
109C3 **Gippsland** *Mts* Aust
14B2 **Girard** USA
32C3 **Girardot** Colombia
44C3 **Girdle Ness** *Pen* Scot
93C1 **Giresun** Turk
85C4 **Gir Hills** India
98B2 **Giri** *R* Zaïre

86B2 **Girīdīh** India
Girona = Gerona
48B2 **Gironde** *R* France
42B2 **Girvan** Scot
111C2 **Gisborne** NZ
46A2 **Gisors** France
99C3 **Gitega** Burundi
Giuba,R = Juba,R
54C2 **Giurgiu** Rom
46C1 **Givet** Belg
58C2 **Gizycko** Pol
55B2 **Gjirokastër** Alb
4J3 **Gjoatlaven** Can
39G6 **Gjøvik** Nor
7D5 **Glace Bay** Can
12G3 **Glacier Bay Nat Mon** USA
13E3 **Glacier Nat Pk** USA/Can
20B1 **Glacier Peak** *Mt* USA
6B2 **Glacier Str** Can
107E3 **Gladstone** Queensland, Aust
108A2 **Gladstone** S Aust, Aust
109C4 **Gladstone** Tasmania, Aust
14A1 **Gladstone** USA
38A1 **Glama** *Mt* Iceland
39G6 **Glåma** *R* Nor
46D2 **Glan** *R* Germany
47C1 **Glarner** *Mts* Switz
47C1 **Glarus** Switz
18A2 **Glasco** USA
8C2 **Glasgow** Montana, USA
42B2 **Glasgow** Scot
16B3 **Glassboro** USA
43C4 **Glastonbury** Eng
61H2 **Glazov** Russian Fed
59B3 **Gleisdorf** Austria
110C1 **Glen Afton** NZ
16A3 **Glen Burnie** USA
101H1 **Glencoe** S Africa
9B3 **Glendale** Arizona, USA
22C3 **Glendale** California, USA
12E2 **Glenhallen** USA
109D1 **Glen Innes** Aust
109C1 **Glenmorgan** Aust
109D2 **Glenreagh** Aust
16A3 **Glen Rock** USA
19A3 **Glen Rose** USA
44C3 **Glenrothes** UK
15D2 **Glens Falls** USA
45B1 **Glenties** Irish Rep
19B3 **Glenwood** Arkansas, USA
8C3 **Glenwood Springs** USA
39F6 **Glittertind** *Mt* Nor
59B2 **Gliwice** Pol
9B3 **Globe** USA
58B2 **Głogów** Pol
38G5 **Glomfjord** Nor
109D2 **Gloucester** Aust
43C4 **Gloucester** Eng
16D1 **Gloucester** USA
58D1 **Glubokoye** Belorussia
60D3 **Glukhov** Russian Fed
59B3 **Gmünd** Austria
57C3 **Gmunden** Austria
58B2 **Gniezno** Pol
100A3 **Goabeg** Namibia
87A1 **Goa, Daman and Diu** Union Territory, India
86C1 **Goālpāra** India
99D2 **Goba** Eth
100A3 **Gobabis** Namibia
34C2 **Gobernador Crespo** Arg
34B3 **Gobernador Duval** Arg
72B1 **Gobi** *Desert* China/Mongolia
75B2 **Gobo** Japan
87B1 **Godag** India
87C1 **Godāvari** *R* India
14B2 **Goderich** Can
6E3 **Godhavn** Greenland
85C4 **Godhra** India
34B2 **Godoy Cruz** Arg

7A4 **Gods L** Can
6E3 **Godthab** Greenland
Godwin Austen = K2
35B1 **Goiandira** Brazil
35B1 **Goianésia** Brazil
35B1 **Goiânia** Brazil
35A1 **Goiás** Brazil
31B4 **Goiás** State, Brazil
35A2 **Goio-Erê** Brazil
99D2 **Gojab** *R* Eth
55C2 **Gökçeada** *I* Turk
55C3 **Gökova Körfezi** *B* Turk
92C2 **Göksun** Turk
63C3 **Gol** *R* Mongolia
86C1 **Golāghāt** India
93C2 **Gölbaşi** Turk
20C2 **Golconda** USA
20B2 **Gold Beach** USA
109D1 **Gold Coast** Aust
13D2 **Golden** Can
110B2 **Golden B** NZ
20B1 **Goldendale** USA
22A2 **Golden Gate** *Chan* USA
19B4 **Golden Meadow** USA
21B2 **Goldfield** USA
13B3 **Gold River** Can
56C2 **Goleniów** Pol
22C3 **Goleta** USA
52A2 **Golfe d'Ajaccio** *G* Corse
96D1 **Golfe de Gabes** *G* Tunisia
Golfe de Gascogne = Biscay,Bay of
52A2 **Golfe de St Florent** *G* Corse
48B2 **Golfe de St-Malo** *B* France
49C3 **Golfe du Lion** *G* France
29B4 **Golfo Corcovado** *G* Chile
50B2 **Golfo de Almeira** *G* Spain
29B4 **Golfo de Ancud** *G* Chile
25D2 **Golfo de Batabano** *G* Cuba
50A2 **Golfo de Cadiz** *G* Spain
53A3 **Golfo de Cagliari** *G* Sardegna
24A1 **Golfo de California** *G* Mexico
25D4 **Golfo de Chiriqui** *G* Panama
25D3 **Golfo de Fonseca** Honduras
26B2 **Golfo de Guacanayabo** *G* Cuba
32A4 **Golfo de Guayaquil** *G* Ecuador
26B5 **Golfo del Darien** *G* Colombia/Panama
32A2 **Golfo de los Mosquitos** *G* Panama
25D3 **Golfo del Papagaya** *G* Nic
51B2 **Golfo de Mazarrón** *G* Spain
25D4 **Golfo de Nicoya** *G* Costa Rica
53A3 **Golfo de Oristano** *G* Sardegna
25E4 **Golfo de Panamá** *G* Panama
25D3 **Golfo de Papagayo** *G* Costa Rica
27E4 **Golfo de Paria** *G* Ven
29B5 **Golfo de Penas** *G* Chile
49D3 **Golfo de St Florent** Corse
51C1 **Golfo de San Jorge** *G* Spain
24C3 **Golfo de Tehuantepec** *G* Mexico
32B3 **Golfo de Torugas** *G* Colombia
32B2 **Golfo de Uraba** *G* Colombia
51C2 **Golfo de Valencia** *G* Spain
27C4 **Golfo de Venezuela** *G* Ven
52A2 **Golfo di Genova** *G* Italy
53C3 **Golfo di Policastro** *G* Italy
53C3 **Golfo di Squillace** *G* Italy
53C2 **Golfo di Taranto** *G* Italy
52B1 **Golfo di Venezia** *G* Italy
25D4 **Golfo Dulce** *G* Costa Rica
29C5 **Golfo San Jorge** *G* Arg
29D4 **Golfo San Matías** *G* Arg
68B3 **Golmud** China
99E2 **Golocha** Eth
12B2 **Golovin B** USA
74F2 **Golovnino** Russian Fed
99C3 **Goma** Zaïre
97D3 **Gombe** Nig
60D3 **Gomel** Belorussia
96A2 **Gomera** *I* Canary Is
24B2 **Gómez Palacio** Mexico
63E2 **Gonam** *R* Russian Fed
90C2 **Gonbad-e Kāvūs** Iran
86A1 **Gonda** India
85C4 **Gondal** India
99D1 **Gonder** Eth
92A1 **Gönen** Turk
55C3 **Gonen** *R* Turk
73A4 **Gongga Shan** *Mt* China
72A2 **Gonghe** China
97D3 **Gongola** *R* Nig
22B2 **Gonzales** California, USA
19A4 **Gonzales** Texas, USA
34C3 **Gonzalez Chaves** Arg
13C2 **Good Hope Mt** Can
8C2 **Goodland** USA
12B3 **Goodnews Bay** USA
109C1 **Goodooga** *R* Aust
42D3 **Goole** Eng
108C2 **Goolgowi** Aust
108A3 **Goolwa** Aust
106A4 **Goomalling** Aust
108C2 **Goombalie** Aust
109D1 **Goomer** Aust
109D1 **Goomeri** Aust
109D1 **Goondiwindi** Aust
7E4 **Goose Bay** Can
17C1 **Goose Creek** USA
20B2 **Goose L** USA
87B1 **Gooty** India
63C2 **Gora Munku Sardyk** *Mt* Mongolia/ Russian Fed
64H3 **Gora Narodnaya** *Mt* Russian Fed
64G3 **Gora Tel'pos-iz** Russian Fed
54A2 **Goražde** Bosnia-Herzegovina
4D3 **Gordon** USA
13E1 **Gordon L** Can
15C3 **Gordonsville** USA
98B2 **Goré** Chad
99D2 **Gorē** Eth
111A3 **Gore** NZ
63F2 **Gore Topko** *Mt* Russian Fed
45C2 **Gorey** Irish Rep
90B2 **Gorgān** Iran
93E2 **Goris** Armenia
52B1 **Gorizia** Italy
Gor'kiy = Nizniy Novgorod
61F2 **Gor'kovskoye Vodokhranilishche** *Res* Russian Fed
57C2 **Gorlitz** Germany
60E4 **Gorlovka** Ukraine
22C3 **Gorman** USA
54C2 **Gorna Orjahovica** Bulg
68A1 **Gorno-Altaysk** Russian Fed
69G2 **Gornozavodsk** Russian Fed
61F2 **Gorodets** Russian Fed
59C3 **Gorodok** Ukraine
59D3 **Gorodok** Ukraine
71F4 **Goroka** PNG
86A1 **Gorokhpur** India
101C2 **Gorongosa** Mozam
71D3 **Gorontalo** Indon
61K2 **Goro Yurma** *Mt* Russian Fed
45B2 **Gort** Irish Rep
63C2 **Goryachinsk** Russian Fed
59D3 **Goryn'** *R* Ukraine
59C2 **Góry Świetokrzyskie** *Upland* Pol
64G3 **Gory Tel'pos-iz'** *Mt* Russian Fed
39H8 **Gorzów Wielkopolski** Pol
74E2 **Goshogawara** Japan
52C2 **Gospić** Croatia
54B2 **Gostivar** Macedonia
58B2 **Gostynin** Pol
39G7 **Göteborg** Sweden
98B2 **Gotel** *Mts* Nig
39H7 **Gotland** *I* Sweden
74B4 **Gotō-retto** *I* Japan
39H7 **Gotska Sandön** *I* Sweden
74C3 **Gōtsu** Japan
98B1 **Goudoumaria** Niger
103H7 **Gough I** Atlantic O
109C2 **Goulburn** Aust
97B3 **Goumbou** Mali
97B3 **Goundam** Mali
98B1 **Gouré** Niger
97B3 **Gourma Rharous** Mali
46A2 **Gournay-en-Bray** France
95A3 **Gouro** Chad
71E5 **Gove Pen** Aust
60B4 **Goverla** *Mt* Ukraine
35C1 **Governador Valadares** Brazil
86A2 **Govind Ballabh Paht Sāgar** *L* India
15C2 **Gowanda** USA
84B3 **Gowārān** Afghan
30E4 **Goya** Arg
98C1 **Goz-Beída** Chad
53B3 **Gozo** *I* Medit S
95C3 **Goz Regeb** Sudan
100B4 **Graaff-Reinet** S Africa
15C1 **Gracefield** Can
109D1 **Grafton** Aust
8D2 **Grafton** N Dakota, USA
14B3 **Grafton** W Virginia, USA
5E4 **Graham** *I* Can
13C1 **Graham** *R* Can
13E1 **Graham L** Can
100B4 **Grahamstown** S Africa
31B3 **Grajaú** Brazil
58C2 **Grajewo** Pol
55B2 **Grámmos** *Mt* Greece/Alb
44C3 **Grampian** Region, Scot
44B3 **Grampian** *Mts* Scot
32C3 **Granada** Colombia
25D3 **Granada** Nic
50B2 **Granada** Spain
15D1 **Granby** Can
96A2 **Gran Canaria** *I* Canary Is
30D4 **Gran Chaco** *Region* Arg
14A2 **Grand** *R* Michigan, USA
18B1 **Grand** *R* Missouri, USA
27Q2 **Grand B** Dominica
11C4 **Grand Bahama** *I* The Bahamas
7E5 **Grand Bank** Can
102F2 **Grand Banks** Atlantic O
97B4 **Grand Bassam** Ivory Coast
9B3 **Grand Canyon** USA
26A3 **Grand Cayman** *I* Caribbean S
13E2 **Grand Centre** Can
20C1 **Grand Coulee** USA
34B3 **Grande** *R* Arg
31C4 **Grande** *R* Bahia, Brazil
35B1 **Grande** *R* Minas Gerais/São Paulo, Brazil
13D2 **Grande Cache** Can
47A2 **Grande Chartreuse** Region, France
101D2 **Grande Comore** *I* Comoros
13D1 **Grande Prairie** Can
19A3 **Grande Prairie** USA
95A3 **Grand Erg de Bilma** *Desert* Niger
96B2 **Grand erg Occidental** *Mts* Alg
96C2 **Grand erg Oriental** *Mts* Alg
7C4 **Grande Rivière de la Baleine** *R* Can
20C1 **Grande Ronde** *R* USA
7D5 **Grand Falls** New Brunswick, Can
7E5 **Grand Falls** Newfoundland, Can
20C1 **Grand Forks** Can
8D2 **Grand Forks** USA
16B1 **Grand Gorge** USA
14A2 **Grand Haven** USA
19C3 **Grand Isle** USA
19B4 **Grand L** USA
15D1 **Grand Mère** Can
50A2 **Grândola** Port
5J4 **Grand Rapids** Can
14A2 **Grand Rapids** Michigan, USA
10A2 **Grand Rapids** Minnesota, USA
47B2 **Grand St Bernard** *P* Italy/Switz
8B2 **Grand Teton** *Mt* USA
8B2 **Grand Teton Nat Pk** USA
46A2 **Grandvilliers** France
25D1 **Grangeburg** USA
51C1 **Granollérs** Spain
52A1 **Gran Paradiso** *Mt* Italy
47D1 **Gran Pilastro** *Mt* Austria/Italy
43D3 **Grantham** Eng
21B2 **Grant,Mt** USA
44C3 **Grantown-on-Spey** Scot
9C3 **Grants** USA
20B2 **Grants Pass** USA
48B2 **Granville** France
5H4 **Granville L** Can
35C1 **Grão Mogol** Brazil
49D3 **Grasse** France
21A2 **Grass Valley** USA
5H5 **Gravelbourg** Can
46B1 **Gravelines** France
100C3 **Gravelotte** S Africa
15C2 **Gravenhurst** Can
109D1 **Gravesend** Aust
12H3 **Gravina I** USA
12B2 **Grayling** USA
20B1 **Grays Harbor** *B* USA
14B3 **Grayson** USA
18C2 **Grayville** USA
59B3 **Graz** Austria
27H1 **Great** *R* Jamaica
11C4 **Great Abaco** *I* The Bahamas

106B4	**Great Australian Bight** *G* Aust
16B3	**Great B** New Jersey, USA
25E2	**Great Bahama Bank** The Bahamas
110C1	**Great Barrier I** NZ
107D2	**Great Barrier Reef** *Is* Aust
16C1	**Great Barrington** USA
4F3	**Great Bear L** Can
9D2	**Great Bend** USA
107D3	**Great Dividing Range** *Mts* Aust
42D2	**Great Driffield** Eng
16B3	**Great Egg Harbor** *B* USA
112B10	**Greater Antarctic** Region, Ant
26B2	**Greater Antilles** *Is* Caribbean S
43D4	**Greater London** Metropolitan County, Eng
43C3	**Greater Manchester** County, Eng
25E2	**Great Exuma** *I* The Bahamas
8B2	**Great Falls** USA
44B3	**Great Glen** *V* Scot
86B1	**Great Himalayan Range** *Mts* Asia
11C4	**Great Inagua** *I* The Bahamas
100B4	**Great Karroo** *Mts* S Africa
109C4	**Great L** Aust
100A3	**Great Namaland** Region, Namibia
42C3	**Great Ormes Head** *C* Wales
11C4	**Great Ragged** *I* The Bahamas
99D3	**Great Ruaha** *R* Tanz
15D2	**Great Sacandaga L** USA
0D2	**Great Salt L** USA
95B2	**Great Sand Sea** Libya/Egypt
106B3	**Great Sandy Desert** Aust
8A2	**Great Sandy Desert** USA
	Great Sandy I = Fraser I
4G3	**Great Slave L** Can
16C2	**Great South B** USA
106B3	**Great Victoria Desert** Aust
112C2	**Great Wall** *Base* Ant
72B2	**Great Wall** China
43E3	**Great Yarmouth** Eng
94B1	**Greco,C** Cyprus
55B3	**Greece** Republic, Europe
15C2	**Greece** USA
8C2	**Greeley** USA
6B1	**Greely Fjord** Can
14A1	**Green B** USA
14A2	**Green Bay** USA
14A3	**Greencastle** Indiana, USA
16C1	**Greenfield** Massachusetts, USA
14A2	**Greenfield** Wisconsin, USA
13F2	**Green Lake** Can
6F2	**Greenland** Dependency, N Atlantic O
102H1	**Greenland Basin** Greenland S
1B1	**Greenland S** Greenland
42B2	**Greenock** Scot
16C2	**Greenport** USA
16B3	**Greensboro** Maryland, USA
11C3	**Greensboro N** Carolina, USA
15C2	**Greensburg** Pennsylvania, USA
44B3	**Greenstone** *Pt* Scot

18C2	**Greenup** USA
17A1	**Greenville** Alabama, USA
97B4	**Greenville** Lib
19B3	**Greenville** Mississippi, USA
16D1	**Greenville** N Hampshire, USA
14B2	**Greenville** Ohio, USA
17B1	**Greenville** S Carolina, USA
19A3	**Greenville** Texas, USA
43E4	**Greenwich** Eng
16C2	**Greenwich** USA
16B3	**Greenwood** Delaware, USA
19B3	**Greenwood** Mississippi, USA
17B1	**Greenwood S** Carolina, USA
18B2	**Greers Ferry L** USA
108A1	**Gregory,L** Aust
107D2	**Gregory Range** *Mts* Aust
56C2	**Greifswald** Germany
64F3	**Gremikha** Russian Fed
56C1	**Grenå** Den
19C3	**Grenada** USA
27E4	**Grenada** *I* Caribbean S
109C2	**Grenfell** Aust
49D2	**Grenoble** France
27M2	**Grenville** Grenada
107D2	**Grenville,C** Aust
20B1	**Gresham** USA
78C4	**Gresik** Jawa, Indon
78A3	**Gresik** Sumatera, Indon
19B4	**Gretna** USA
111B2	**Grey** *R* NZ
12G2	**Grey Hunter Pk** *Mt* Can
7E4	**Grey Is** Can
16C1	**Greylock,Mt** USA
111B2	**Greymouth** NZ
107D3	**Grey Range** *Mts* Aust
45C2	**Greystones** Irish Rep
101H1	**Greytown** S Africa
101F1	**Griekwastad** S Africa
17B1	**Griffin** USA
108C2	**Griffith** Aust
107D5	**Grim,C** Aust
15C2	**Grimsby** Can
42D3	**Grimsby** Eng
38B1	**Grimsey** *I* Iceland
13D1	**Grimshaw** Can
39F7	**Grimstad** Nor
47C1	**Grindelwald** Switz
6A2	**Grinnell Pen** Can
6B2	**Grise Fjord** Can
61H1	**Griva** Russian Fed
39J7	**Grobina** Latvia
58C2	**Grodno** Belorussia
86A1	**Gromati** *R* India
56B2	**Groningen** Neth
106C2	**Groote Eylandt** *I* Aust
100A2	**Grootfontein** Namibia
100B3	**Grootvloer** *Salt L* S Africa
27P2	**Gros Islet** St Lucia
46F1	**Grosser Feldberg** *Mt* Germany
52B2	**Grosseto** Italy
46E2	**Gross-Gerau** Germany
57C3	**Grossglockner** *Mt* Austria
47E1	**Gross Venediger** *Mt* Austria
12C3	**Grosvenor,L** USA
22B2	**Groveland** USA
21A2	**Grover City** USA
15D2	**Groveton** USA
61G5	**Groznyy** Russian Fed
58B2	**Grudziądz** Pol
100A3	**Grünau** Namibia
44E2	**Grutness** Scot
61F3	**Gryazi** Russian Fed

61E2	**Gryazovets** Russian Fed
29G8	**Grytviken** South Georgia
45A2	**Gt Blasket** *I* Irish Rep
35C2	**Guaçuí** Brazil
23A1	**Guadalajara** Mexico
50B1	**Guadalajara** Spain
107E1	**Guadalcanal** *I* Solomon Is
50B2	**Guadalimar** *R* Spain
51B1	**Guadalope** *R* Spain
50B2	**Guadalqivir** *R* Spain
24B2	**Guadalupe** Mexico
3G6	**Guadalupe** *I* Mexico
27E3	**Guadeloupe** *I* Caribbean S
50B2	**Guadian** *R* Spain
50A2	**Guadiana** *R* Port
50B2	**Guadix** Spain
32D6	**Guajará Mirim** Brazil
32C1	**Guajira,Pen de** Colombia
32B4	**Gualaceo** Ecuador
34D2	**Gualeguay** Arg
34D2	**Gualeguaychú** Arg
71F2	**Guam** *I* Pacific O
34C3	**Guamini** Arg
77C5	**Gua Musang** Malay
23A1	**Guanajuato** Mexico
23A1	**Guanajuato** State, Mexico
32D2	**Guanare** Ven
25D2	**Guane** Cuba
73C5	**Guangdong** Province, China
73A3	**Guanghan** China
72C3	**Guanghua** China
73A4	**Guangmao Shan** *Mt* China
73B5	**Guangnan** China
72D3	**Guangyuan** China
73D4	**Guangze** China
67F3	**Guangzhou** China
35C1	**Guanhães** Brazil
32D3	**Guania** *R* Colombia
27E5	**Guanipa** *R* Ven
26B2	**Guantánamo** Cuba
72D1	**Guanting Shuiku** *Res* China
73B5	**Guanxi** Province, China
73A3	**Guan Xian** China
32B2	**Guapa** Colombia
33E6	**Guaporé** *R* Brazil/Bol
30C2	**Guaqui** Bol
32B4	**Guaranda** Ecuador
30F4	**Guarapuava** Brazil
35D2	**Guaratinguetá** Brazil
50A1	**Guarda** Port
35B1	**Guarda Mor** Brazil
9C4	**Guasave** Mexico
47D2	**Guastalla** Italy
25C3	**Guatemala** Guatemala
25C3	**Guatemala** Republic, Cent America
34C3	**Guatraché** Arg
32C3	**Guavrare** *R* Colombia
35B2	**Guaxupé** Brazil
27L1	**Guayaguayare** Trinidad
32A4	**Guayaquil** Ecuador
24A2	**Guaymas** Mexico
34D2	**Guayquiraro** *R* Arg
100B2	**Guba** Zaïre
99E2	**Guban** *Region* Somalia
79B3	**Gubat** Phil
56C2	**Gubin** Pol
87B2	**Güdür** India
14B2	**Guelpho** Can
26A2	**Guenabacoa** Cuba
98C1	**Guéréda** Chad
48C2	**Guéret** France
48B2	**Guernsey** *I* UK
23A2	**Guerrero** State, Mexico
99D2	**Gughe** *Mt* Eth
63E2	**Gugigu** China
71F2	**Guguan** *I* Pacific O
109C2	**Guiargambone** Aust

73C4	**Guidong** China
97B4	**Guiglo** Ivory Coast
73C5	**Gui Jiang** *R* China
43D4	**Guildford** Eng
73C4	**Guilin** China
47B2	**Guillestre** France
72A2	**Guinan** China
97A3	**Guinea** Republic, Africa
102H4	**Guinea Basin** Atlantic O
97A3	**Guinea-Bissau** Republic, Africa
97C4	**Guinea,G of** W Africa
26A2	**Güines** Cuba
97B3	**Guir** *Well* Mali
84C2	**Guiranwala** Pak
33E1	**Güiria** Ven
46B2	**Guise** France
79C3	**Guiuan** Phil
73B5	**Gui Xian** China
73B4	**Guiyang** China
73B4	**Guizhou** Province, China
85C4	**Gujarāt** State, India
84C2	**Gujrat** Pak
87B1	**Gulbarga** India
58D1	**Gulbene** Latvia
87B1	**Guledagudda** India
80D3	**Gulf,The** S W Asia
109C2	**Gulgong** Aust
73B4	**Gulin** China
12E2	**Gulkana** USA
12E2	**Gulkana** *R* USA
13E2	**Gull L** Can
13F2	**Gull Lake** Can
55C3	**Güllük Körfezi** *B* Turk
99D2	**Gulu** Uganda
109C1	**Guluguba** Aust
97C3	**Gumel** Nig
46D1	**Gummersbach** Germany
86A2	**Gumpla** India
93C1	**Gümüşhane** Turk
85D4	**Guna** India
99D1	**Guna** *Mt* Eth
109C3	**Gundagai** Aust
98B3	**Gungu** Zaïre
6H3	**Gunnbjørn Fjeld** *Mt* Greenland
109D2	**Gunnedah** Aust
87B1	**Guntakal** India
17A1	**Guntersville** USA
17A1	**Guntersville L** USA
87C1	**Guntür** India
77C5	**Gunung Batu Putch** *Mt* Malay
78D3	**Gunung Besar** *Mt* Indon
78D2	**Gunung Bulu** *Mt* Indon
78A3	**Gunung Gedang** *Mt* Indon
78C2	**Gunung Lawit** *Mt* Malay
78C4	**Gunung Lawu** *Mt* Indon
78D2	**Gunung Menyapa** *Mt* Indon
78D2	**Gunung Niapa** *Mt* Indon
78A3	**Gunung Patah** *Mt* Indon
78C4	**Gunung Raung** *Mt* Indon
78A3	**Gunung Resag** *Mt* Indon
78D3	**Gunung Sarempaka** *Mt* Indon
78C4	**Gunung Sumbing** *Mt* Indon
77C5	**Gunung Tahan** *Mt* Malay
78A2	**Gunung Talakmau** *Mt* Indon
100A2	**Gunza** Angola
72D3	**Guoyang** China
84D2	**Gurdāspur** India
84D3	**Gurgaon** India
86A1	**Gurkha** Nepal
92C2	**Gürün** Turk
31B2	**Gurupi** *R* Brazil

Guruve

100C2 **Guruve** Zim
72A1 **Gurvan Sayhan Uul**
 Upland Mongolia
61H4 **Gur'yev** Kazakhstan
97C3 **Gusau** Nig
58C2 **Gusev** Russian Fed
74A3 **Gushan** China
61F2 **Gus'khrustalnyy**
 Russian Fed
12G3 **Gustavus** USA
22B2 **Gustine** USA
11B3 **Guston** USA
56B2 **Gütersloh** Germany
18C2 **Guthrie** Kentucky,
 USA
18A2 **Guthrie** Oklahoma,
 USA
23B1 **Gutiérrez Zamora**
 Mexico
33F3 **Guyana** Republic,
 S America
102F4 **Guyana Basin**
 Atlantic O
72C1 **Guyang** China
48B3 **Guyenne** Region,
 France
9C3 **Guymon** USA
109D2 **Guyra** Aust
72B2 **Guyuan** China
109C2 **Gwabegar** Aust
85D3 **Gwalior** India
100B3 **Gwanda** Zim
98C2 **Gwane** Zaire
82A3 **Gwardar** Pak
45B1 **Gweebarra B**
 Irish Rep
89G9 **Gwelo** Zim
43C4 **Gwent** County,
 Wales
100B2 **Gweru** Zim
109C1 **Gwydir** *R* Aust
43C3 **Gwynedd** Wales
65F5 **Gyandzha**
 Azerbaijan
86B1 **Gyangzê** China
68B3 **Gyaring Hu** *L* China
64J2 **Gydanskiy Poluostrov**
 Pen Russian Fed
86B1 **Gyirong** China
6F3 **Gyldenløues**
 Greenland
109D1 **Gympie** Aust
59B3 **Gyöngyös** Hung
59B3 **Györ** Hung

H

38K6 **Haapajärvi** Fin
60B2 **Haapsalu** Estonia
56A2 **Haarlem** Neth
46D1 **Haarstrang** Region,
 Germany
25D2 **Habana** Cuba
86C2 **Habiganj** Bang
74D4 **Hachijō-jima** *I* Japan
75B1 **Hachiman** Japan
74E2 **Hachinohe** Japan
75B1 **Hachioji** Japan
16B2 **Hackettstown** USA
108A2 **Hack,Mt** *Mt* Aust
42C2 **Haddington** Scot
108B1 **Haddon Corner** Aust
108B1 **Haddon Downs** Aust
97D3 **Hadejia** Nig
97C3 **Hadejia** *R* Nig
94B2 **Hadera** Israel
56B1 **Haderslev** Den
81D4 **Hadiboh** Socotra
4H2 **Hadley B** Can
73B5 **Hadong** Vietnam
81C4 **Hadramawt** Region,
 Yemen
56C1 **Hadsund** Den
74B3 **Haeju** N Korea
91A4 **Hafar al Bātin**
 S Arabia
6D2 **Haffners Bjerg** *Mt*
 Greenland
84C2 **Hafizabad** Pak
86C1 **Häflong** India
38A2 **Hafnafjörður** Iceland
12B3 **Hagemeister** *I* USA
56B2 **Hagen** Germany
15C3 **Hagerstown** USA
75A2 **Hagi** Japan

73A5 **Ha Giang** Vietnam
46D2 **Hagondange** France
45B2 **Hags Hd** *C* Irish Rep
46D2 **Haguenan** France
96A2 **Hagunia** *Well* Mor
69G4 **Haha-jima** *I* Japan
68B3 **Hah Xil Hu** *L* China
74A2 **Haicheng** China
76D1 **Hai Duong** Viet
94B2 **Haifa** Israel
94B2 **Haifa,B of** Israel
72D2 **Hai He** *R* China
73C5 **Haikang** China
76E1 **Haikou** China
80C3 **Ha'īl** S Arabia
86C2 **Hailākāndi** India
63D3 **Hailar** China
74B2 **Hailong** China
69E2 **Hailun** China
38J5 **Hailuoto** *I* Fin
76D2 **Hainan** *I* China
12G3 **Haines** USA
12G2 **Haines Junction**
 Can
59B3 **Hainfeld** Austria
73B5 **Haiphong** Vietnam
26C3 **Haiti** Republic,
 Caribbean S
95C3 **Haiya** Sudan
72A2 **Haiyan** China
72B2 **Haiyuan** China
72D3 **Haizhou Wan** *B*
 China
59C3 **Hajdúböszörmény**
 Hung
75B1 **Hajiki-saki** *Pt* Japan
86C2 **Haka** Burma
21C4 **Hakalau** Hawaiian Is
93D2 **Hakkâri** Turk
74E2 **Hakodate** Japan
 Hakwa = Haka
75B1 **Hakui** Japan
75B1 **Haku-san** *Mt* Japan
92C2 **Halab** Syria
93E3 **Halabja** Iraq
95C2 **Halaib** Sudan
94C1 **Halba** Leb
68B2 **Halban** Mongolia
56C2 **Halberstadt**
 Germany
79B3 **Halcon,Mt** Phil
39G7 **Halden** Nor
86B2 **Haldia** India
84D3 **Haldwāni** India
13C1 **Halfway** *R* Can
7D5 **Halifax** Can
42D3 **Halifax** Eng
6D1 **Hall Basin** *Sd* Can
6B3 **Hall Beach** Can
46C1 **Halle** Belg
56C2 **Halle** Germany
112B1 **Halley** *Base* Ant
39F6 **Hallingdal** *R* Nor
6D3 **Hall Pen** Can
106B2 **Hall's Creek** Aust
71D3 **Halmahera** *I* Indon
39G7 **Halmstad** Sweden
56B2 **Haltern** Germany
38J5 **Halti** *Mt* Nor
42C2 **Haltwhistle** Eng
91B4 **Halul** *I* Qatar
94B3 **Haluza** *Hist Site*
 Israel
75A2 **Hamada** Japan
96C2 **Hamada de Tinrhert**
 Desert Region Alg
96B2 **Hamada du Dra**
 Upland Alg
90A3 **Hamadān** Iran
96B2 **Hamada Tounassine**
 Region, Alg
92C2 **Hamāh** Syria
75B2 **Hamamatsu** Japan
39G6 **Hamar** Nor
87C3 **Hambantota**
 Sri Lanka
19B3 **Hamburg** Arkansas,
 USA
18A1 **Hamburg** Iowa, USA
16B2 **Hamburg**
 Pennsylvania, USA
56B2 **Hamburg** Germany
16C2 **Hamden** USA
39J6 **Hämeeninna** Fin

106A3 **Hamersley Range**
 Mts Aust
74B2 **Hamgyong Sanmaek**
 Mts N Korea
74B2 **Hamhŭng** N Korea
68B2 **Hami** China
94B1 **Hamīdīyah** Syria
108B3 **Hamilton** Aust
14C2 **Hamilton** Can
110C1 **Hamilton** NZ
14B3 **Hamilton** Ohio, USA
42B2 **Hamilton** Scot
22B2 **Hamilton,Mt** USA
38K6 **Hamina** Fin
86A1 **Hamirpur** India
56B2 **Hamm** Germany
95A2 **Hammādāh al Hamra**
 Upland Libya
38H6 **Hammerdal** Sweden
38J4 **Hammerfest** Nor
14A2 **Hammond** Illinois,
 USA
19B3 **Hammond** Louisiana,
 USA
16B3 **Hammonton** USA
111B3 **Hampden** NZ
43D4 **Hampshire** County,
 Eng
19B3 **Hampton** Arkansas,
 USA
91C4 **Hāmūn-e Jaz Mūrīan**
 L Iran
84B3 **Hamun-i-Lora** *Salt L*
 Pak
21C4 **Hana** Hawaiian Is
21C4 **Hanalei** Hawaiian Is
74E3 **Hanamaki** Japan
72C2 **Hancheng** China
73C3 **Hanchuan** China
15C3 **Hancock** Maryland,
 USA
10B2 **Hancock** Michigan,
 USA
75B2 **Handa** Japan
72C2 **Handan** China
99D3 **Handeni** Tanz
72B2 **Hanggin Qi** China
39J7 **Hangö** Fin
73E3 **Hangzhou** China
73E3 **Hangzhou Wan** *B*
 China
111B2 **Hanmer Springs** NZ
13E2 **Hanna** Can
18B2 **Hannibal** USA
56B2 **Hannover** Germany
39G7 **Hanöbukten** *B*
 Sweden
76D1 **Hanoi** Viet
16A3 **Hanover** USA
29B6 **Hanover** *I* Chile
72B3 **Han Shui** China
73C3 **Han Shui** *R* China
85D3 **Hänsi** India
68C2 **Hantay** Mongolia
72B3 **Hanzhong** China
86B2 **Hāora** India
38J5 **Haparanda** Sweden
86C1 **Hāpoli** India
92C4 **Haql** S Arabia
91A5 **Haradh** S Arabia
99E2 **Hara Fanna** Eth
75C1 **Haramachi** Japan
101C2 **Harare** Zim
98C1 **Harazé** Chad
14B2 **Harbor Beach** USA
85D4 **Harda** India
39F6 **Hardangerfjord** *Inlet*
 Nor
46D2 **Hardt** Region,
 Germany
18B2 **Hardy** USA
99E2 **Harēr** Eth
99E2 **Hargeysa** Somalia
94B3 **Har Hakippa** *Mt*
 Israel
68B3 **Harhu** *L* China
78A3 **Hari** *R* Indon
75A2 **Harima-nada** *B*
 Japan
56B2 **Harlingen** Neth
9D4 **Harlingen** USA
43E4 **Harlow** Eng
94B2 **Har Meron** *Mt* Israel

20C2 **Harney Basin** USA
20C2 **Harney L** USA
38H6 **Härnösand** Sweden
63B3 **Har Nuur** *L* Mongolia
97B4 **Harper** Lib
12F2 **Harper,Mt** USA
15C3 **Harpers Ferry** USA
94B3 **Har Ramon** *Mt*
 Israel
7C4 **Harricanaw** *R* Can
16B3 **Harrington** USA
7E4 **Harrington Harbour**
 Can
44A3 **Harris** *District* Scot
18C2 **Harrisburg** Illinois,
 USA
16A2 **Harrisburg**
 Pennsylvania, USA
101G1 **Harrismith** S Africa
18B2 **Harrison** USA
15C3 **Harrisonburg** USA
7E4 **Harrison,C** Can
13C3 **Harrison L** Can
18B2 **Harrisonville** USA
44A3 **Harris,Sound of** *Chan*
 Scot
14B2 **Harrisville** USA
42D3 **Harrogate** Eng
94B3 **Har Saggi** *Mt* Israel
38H5 **Harstad** Nor
12G2 **Hart** *R* Can
39F6 **Hårteigen** *Mt* Nor
16C2 **Hartford** Connecticut,
 USA
14A2 **Hartford** Michigan,
 USA
38G6 **Hartkjølen** *Mt* Nor
108A2 **Hart,L** Aust
43B4 **Hartland Pt** Eng
42D2 **Hartlepool** Eng
19A3 **Hartshorne** USA
17B1 **Hartwell Res** USA
101F1 **Hartz** *R* S Africa
68B2 **Har Us Nuur** *L*
 Mongolia
43E4 **Harwich** Eng
84D3 **Haryana** State, India
94B3 **Hāsā** Jordan
94B2 **Hāsbaiya** Leb
43D4 **Haselmere** Eng
75B2 **Hashimoto** Japan
90A2 **Hashtpar** Iran
90A2 **Hashtrūd** Iran
87B2 **Hassan** India
56B2 **Hasselt** Belg
96C2 **Hassi Inifel** Alg
96B2 **Hassi Mdakane** *Well*
 Alg
96C1 **Hassi Messaoud** Alg
108C3 **Hastings** Aust
43E4 **Hastings** Eng
8D2 **Hastings** Nebraska,
 USA
110C1 **Hastings** NZ
108B2 **Hatfield** Aust
12B1 **Hatham Inlet** USA
85D3 **Hāthras** India
76D2 **Ha Tinh** Viet
108B2 **Hattah** Aust
11C3 **Hatteras,C** USA
19C3 **Hattiesburg** USA
59B3 **Hatvan** Hung
76D3 **Hau Bon** Viet
99E2 **Haud** Region, Eth
39F7 **Haugesund** Nor
110C1 **Hauhungaroa Range**
 Mts NZ
13F1 **Haultain** *R* Can
110B1 **Hauraki G** NZ
111A3 **Hauroko,L** NZ
47C1 **Hausstock** *Mt* Switz
96B1 **Haut Atlas** *Mts* Mor
98C2 **Haute Kotto** Region,
 CAR
46C1 **Hautes Fagnes** *Mts*
 Belg
46B1 **Hautmont** Belg
96B1 **Hauts Plateaux** *Mts*
 Alg
90D3 **Hauzdar** Iran
18B1 **Havana** USA
 Havana = Habana
87B3 **Havankulam**
 Sri Lanka

110C1 **Havelock North** NZ
43B4 **Haverfordwest** Wales
16D1 **Haverhill** USA
87B2 **Hāveri** India
16C2 **Haverstraw** USA
59B3 **Havlíčkův Brod** Czech Republic
8C2 **Havre** USA
16A3 **Havre de Grace** USA
7D4 **Havre-St-Pierre** Can
54C2 **Havsa** Turk
21C4 **Hawaii** *I* Hawaiian Is
21C4 **Hawaii Volcanoes Nat Pk** Hawaiian Is
111A2 **Hawea,L** NZ
110B1 **Hawera** NZ
42C2 **Hawick** Scot
111A2 **Hawkdun Range** *Mts* NZ
110C1 **Hawke B** NZ
109D2 **Hawke,C** Aust
108A2 **Hawker** Aust
76B1 **Hawng Luk** Burma
93D3 **Hawr al Habbaniyah** *L* Iraq
93E3 **Hawr al Hammár** *L* Iraq
21B2 **Hawthorne** USA
108B2 **Hay** Aust
5G3 **Hay** *R* Can
46D2 **Hayange** France
4B3 **Haycock** USA
7A4 **Hayes** *R* Can
6D2 **Hayes Halvø** *Region* Greenland
12E2 **Hayes,Mt** USA
5G3 **Hay River** Can
18A2 **Haysville** USA
22A2 **Hayward** California, USA
86B2 **Hazārībāg** India
46B1 **Hazebrouck** France
19B3 **Hazelhurst** USA
4G2 **Hazel Str** Can
5F4 **Hazelton** Can
13B1 **Hazelton Mts** Can
6C1 **Hazen L** Can
94B3 **Hazeva** Israel
16B2 **Hazleton** USA
22A1 **Healdsburg** USA
108C3 **Healesville** Aust
12E2 **Healy** USA
104B6 **Heard I** Indian O
19A3 **Hearne** USA
10B2 **Hearst** Can
72D2 **Hebei** Province, China
109C1 **Hebel** Aust
72C2 **Hebi** China
72C2 **Hebian** China
7D4 **Hebron** Can
94B3 **Hebron** Israel
18A1 **Hebron** Nebraska, USA
5E4 **Hecate** *Str* Can
12H3 **Heceta I** USA
73B5 **Hechi** China
4G2 **Hecla and Griper B** Can
111C2 **Hector,Mt** NZ
38G6 **Hede** Sweden
39H6 **Hedemora** Sweden
20C1 **He Devil Mt** USA
56B2 **Heerenveen** Neth
46C1 **Heerlen** Neth
Hefa = Haifa
73D3 **Hefei** China
73B4 **Hefeng** China
69F2 **Hegang** China
75B1 **Hegura-jima** *I* Japan
94B3 **Heidan** *R* Jordan
56B2 **Heide** Germany
101G1 **Heidelberg** Transvaal, S Africa
57B3 **Heidelberg** Germany
63E2 **Heihe** China
101G1 **Heilbron** S Africa
57B3 **Heilbronn** Germany
56C2 **Heiligenstadt** Germany
38K6 **Heinola** Fin
73B4 **Hejiang** China
6J3 **Hekla** *Mt* Iceland
76C1 **Hekou** Viet
73A5 **Hekou Yaozou Zizhixian** China
72B2 **Helan** China
72B2 **Helan Shan** *Mt* China
19B3 **Helena** Arkansas, USA
8B2 **Helena** Montana, USA
22D3 **Helendale** USA
71E3 **Helen Reef** *I* Pacific O
44B3 **Helensburgh** Scot
91B4 **Helleh** *R* Iran
51B2 **Hellin** Spain
20C1 **Hells Canyon** *R* USA
46D1 **Hellweg** Region, Germany
22B2 **Helm** USA
80E2 **Helmand** *R* Afghan
100A3 **Helmeringhausen** Namibia
46C1 **Helmond** Neth
44C2 **Helmsdale** Scot
74B2 **Helong** China
39G7 **Helsingborg** Sweden
Helsingfors = Helsinki
56C1 **Helsingør** Den
38J6 **Helsinki** Fin
43B4 **Helston** Eng
92B4 **Helwân** Egypt
19A3 **Hempstead** USA
39H7 **Hemse** Sweden
72A3 **Henan** China
72C3 **Henan** Province, China
110B1 **Hen and Chicken Is** NZ
14A3 **Henderson** Kentucky, USA
9B3 **Henderson** Nevada, USA
19B3 **Henderson** Texas, USA
73E5 **Heng-ch'un** Taiwan
68B4 **Hengduan Shan** *Mts* China
56B2 **Hengelo** Neth
72B2 **Hengshan** China
72D2 **Hengshui** China
76D1 **Heng Xian** China
73C4 **Hengyang** China
77A4 **Henhoaha** Nicobar Is
43D4 **Henley-on-Thames** Eng
16B3 **Henlopen,C** USA
7B4 **Henrietta Maria,C** Can
18A2 **Henryetta** USA
112C2 **Henryk Arctowski** *Base* Ant
6D3 **Henry Kater Pen** Can
68C2 **Hentiyn Nuruu** *Mts* Mongolia
76B2 **Henzada** Burma
73B5 **Hepu** China
80E2 **Herat** Afghan
5H4 **Herbert** Can
110C2 **Herbertville** NZ
46E1 **Herborn** Germany
26A4 **Heredia** Costa Rica
43C3 **Hereford** Eng
43C3 **Hereford & Worcester** County, Eng
46C1 **Herentals** Belg
47B1 **Héricourt** France
18A2 **Herington** USA
111A3 **Heriot** NZ
47C1 **Herisau** Switz
15D2 **Herkimer** USA
44E1 **Herma Ness** *Pen* Scot
109C2 **Hermidale** Aust
111B2 **Hermitage** NZ
Hermon,Mt = Jebel ash Shaykh
24A2 **Hermosillo** Mexico
16A2 **Herndon** Pennsylvania, USA
22C2 **Herndon** California, USA
46D1 **Herne** Germany
56B1 **Herning** Den
90A2 **Herowābad** Iran
50A2 **Herrera del Duque** Spain
16A2 **Hershey** USA
43D4 **Hertford** County, Eng
94B2 **Herzliyya** Israel
46C1 **Hesbaye** Region, Belg
46B1 **Hesdin** France
72B2 **Heshui** China
22D3 **Hesperia** USA
12H2 **Hess** *R* Can
57B2 **Hessen** State, Germany
22C2 **Hetch Hetchy Res** USA
42C2 **Hexham** Eng
73C5 **He Xian** China
73C5 **Heyuan** China
108B3 **Heywood** Aust
72D2 **Heze** China
17B2 **Hialeah** USA
10A2 **Hibbing** USA
110C1 **Hicks Bay** NZ
109C3 **Hicks,Pt** Aust
23B1 **Hidalgo** State, Mexico
24B2 **Hidalgo del Parral** Mexico
35B1 **Hidrolândia** Brazil
96A2 **Hierro** *I* Canary Is
75C1 **Higashine** Japan
74B4 **Higashi-suidō** *Str* Japan
20B2 **High Desert** USA
19B4 **High Island** USA
44B3 **Highland** Region, Scot
22D3 **Highland** USA
22C1 **Highland Peak** *Mt* USA
16B2 **Highlands Falls** USA
11B3 **High Point** USA
13D1 **High Prairie** Can
5G4 **High River** Can
17B2 **High Springs** USA
16B2 **Hightstown** USA
43D4 **High Wycombe** Eng
39J7 **Hiiumaa** *I* Estonia
80B3 **Hijaz** Region, S Arabia
75B2 **Hikigawa** Japan
75B1 **Hikone** Japan
110B1 **Hikurangi** NZ
9C4 **Hildago** Mexico
9C4 **Hildago del Parral** Mexico
56B2 **Hildesheim** Germany
27R3 **Hillaby,Mt** Barbados
56C1 **Hillerød** Den
14B3 **Hillsboro** Ohio, USA
20B1 **Hillsboro** Oregon, USA
19A3 **Hillsboro** Texas, USA
108C2 **Hillston** Aust
44E1 **Hillswick** Scot
21C4 **Hilo** Hawaiian Is
93C2 **Hilvan** Turk
56B2 **Hilversum** Neth
84D2 **Himachal Pradesh** State, India
82B3 **Himalaya** *Mts* Asia
85C4 **Himatnagar** India
74C4 **Himeji** Japan
74D3 **Himi** Japan
92C3 **Himş** Syria
12E2 **Hinchinbrook Entrance** USA
12E2 **Hinchinbrook I** USA
85D3 **Hindaun** India
84B1 **Hindu Kush** *Mts* Afghan
87B2 **Hindupur** India
13D1 **Hines Creek** Can
85D4 **Hinganghāt** India
69E2 **Hinggan Ling** *Upland* China
85B3 **Hingol** *R* Pak
85D5 **Hingoli** India
38H5 **Hinnøya** *I* Nor
16C1 **Hinsdale** USA
13D2 **Hinton** Can
34B2 **Hipolito Itrogoyen** Arg
86A2 **Hirakud Res** India
92B2 **Hirfanli Baraji** *Res* Turk
87B2 **Hirihar** India
74E2 **Hirosaki** Japan
74C4 **Hiroshima** Japan
46C2 **Hirson** France
54C2 **Hîrşova** Rom
56B1 **Hirtshals** Den
84D3 **Hisār** India
26C3 **Hispaniola** *I* Caribbean S
94C1 **Hisyah** Syria
93D3 **Hīt** Iraq
74E3 **Hitachi** Japan
75C1 **Hitachi-Ota** Japan
43D4 **Hitchin** Eng
38F6 **Hitra** *I* Nor
75A2 **Hiuchi-nada** *B* Japan
75A2 **Hiwasa** Japan
56B1 **Hjørring** Den
76B1 **Hka** *R* Burma
97C4 **Ho** Ghana
76D1 **Hoa Binh** Viet
76D3 **Hoa Da** Viet
109C4 **Hobart** Aust
9C3 **Hobbs** USA
56B1 **Hobro** Den
13C2 **Hobson L** Can
99E2 **Hobyo** Somalia
76D3 **Ho Chi Minh** Viet
57C3 **Hochkonig** *Mt* Austria
54B1 **Hódmezó'hely** Hung
59B3 **Hodonin** Czech Republic
74B2 **Hoeryong** N Korea
57C2 **Hof** Germany
38B2 **Hofsjökull** *Mts* Iceland
74C4 **Hōfu** Japan
96C2 **Hoggar** *Upland* Alg
46D1 **Hohe Acht** *Mt* Germany
72C1 **Hohhot** China
6J3 **Höhn** Iceland
68B3 **Hoh Sai Hu** *L* China
82C2 **Hoh Xil Shan** *Mts* China
99D2 **Holma** Uganda
86C1 **Hojāi** India
75A2 **Hojo** Japan
110B1 **Hokianga Harbour** *B* NZ
111B2 **Hokitika** NZ
74E2 **Hokkaidō** Japan
90C2 **Hokmābād** Iran
109C3 **Holbrook** Aust
9B3 **Holbrook** USA
19A2 **Holdenville** USA
87B2 **Hole Narsipur** India
27R3 **Holetown** Barbados
26B2 **Holguín** Cuba
111B2 **Holitika** NZ
12C2 **Holitna** *R* USA
59B3 **Hollabrunn** Austria
14A2 **Holland** USA
22B2 **Hollister** USA
19C3 **Holly Springs** USA
22C3 **Hollywood** California, USA
17B2 **Hollywood** Florida, USA
4G2 **Holman Island** Can
38J6 **Holmsund** Sweden
94B2 **Holon** Israel
56B1 **Holstebro** Den
6E3 **Holsteinborg** Greenland
14B2 **Holt** USA
18A2 **Holton** USA
12C2 **Holy Cross** USA
42B3 **Holyhead** Wales
42D2 **Holy I** Eng
43B3 **Holy I** Wales
16C1 **Holyoke** Massachusetts, USA
86C2 **Homalin** Burma
6D3 **Home B** Can
12D3 **Homer** Alaska, USA
19B3 **Homer** Louisiana, USA
111A2 **Homer Tunnel** NZ
17B1 **Homerville** USA

17B2 **Homestead** USA
17A1 **Homewood** USA
87B1 **Homnābād** India
101C3 **Homoine** Mozam
25D3 **Hondo** *R* Mexico
25D3 **Honduras** Republic, Cent America
25D3 **Honduras,G of** Honduras
39G6 **Hønefoss** Nor
15C2 **Honesdale** USA
21A1 **Honey L** USA
76C1 **Hong** *R* Viet
76D1 **Hon Gai** Viet
73A4 **Hongguo** China
73C4 **Hong Hu** *L* China
72B2 **Honghui** China
73C4 **Hongjiang** China
73C5 **Hong Kong** Colony, S E Asia
68D2 **Hongor** Mongolia
73B5 **Hongshui He** *R* China
72A3 **Hongyuan** China
72D3 **Hongze Hu** *L* China
107E1 **Honiara** Solomon Is
77C4 **Hon Khoai** *I* Camb
76D3 **Hon Lan** *I* Viet
38K4 **Honnigsvåg** Nor
21C4 **Honolulu** Hawaiian Is
77C4 **Hon Panjang** *I* Viet
74D3 **Honshu** *I* Japan
20B1 **Hood,Mt** USA
20B1 **Hood River** USA
45C2 **Hook Head** *C* Irish Rep
12G3 **Hoonah** USA
12A2 **Hooper Bay** USA
101G1 **Hoopstad** S Africa
56A2 **Hoorn** Neth
9B3 **Hoover Dam** USA
12E2 **Hope** Alaska, USA
19B3 **Hope** Arkansas, USA
13C3 **Hope** Can
7D4 **Hopedale** Can
64D2 **Hopen** *I* Barents S
6D3 **Hopes Advance,C** Can
108B3 **Hopetoun** Aust
100B3 **Hopetown** S Africa
18C2 **Hopkinsville** USA
20B1 **Hoquiam** USA
93D1 **Horasan** Turk
99F1 **Hordiyo** Somalia
47C1 **Horgen** Switz
105H5 **Horizon Depth** Pacific O
91C4 **Hormuz,Str of** Oman/Iran
59B3 **Horn** Austria
6H3 **Horn** *C* Iceland
38H5 **Hornavan** *L* Sweden
19B3 **Hornbeck** USA
20B2 **Hornbrook** USA
111B2 **Hornby** NZ
7B5 **Hornepayne** Can
4F3 **Horn Mts** Can
42D3 **Hornsea** Eng
72B1 **Horn Uul** *Mt* Mongolia
30E3 **Horqueta** Par
15C2 **Horseheads** USA
56C1 **Horsens** Den
20B1 **Horseshoe Bay** Can
108B3 **Horsham** Aust
43D4 **Horsham** Eng
39G7 **Horten** Nor
4F3 **Horton** *R* Can
78C2 **Hose Mts** Malay
85D4 **Hoshangābād** India
84D2 **Hoshiārpur** India
87B1 **Hospet** India
29C7 **Hoste** *I* Chile
82B2 **Hotan** China
19B3 **Hot Springs** Arkansas, USA
8C2 **Hot Springs** S. Dakota, USA
4G3 **Hottah** Can
46A2 **Houdan** France
72C2 **Houma** China
19B4 **Houma** USA
16C2 **Housatonic** *R* USA
13B2 **Houston** Can
19C3 **Houston** Mississippi, USA
19A4 **Houston** Texas, USA
106A3 **Houtman** *Is* Aust
68B2 **Hovd** Mongolia
68C1 **Hövsgol Nuur** *L* Mongolia
14A2 **Howard City** USA
12C1 **Howard P** USA
109C3 **Howe,C** Aust
101H1 **Howick** S Africa
44C2 **Hoy** *I* Scot
39F6 **Høyanger** Nor
59B2 **Hradeç-Králové** Czech Republic
59B3 **Hranice** Czech Republic
59B3 **Hron** *R* Slovakia
73E5 **Hsin-chu** Taiwan
73E5 **Hsüeh Shan** *Mt* Taiwan
72B2 **Huachi** China
32B6 **Huacho** Peru
72C1 **Huade** China
72D3 **Huaibei** China
72D3 **Huaibin** China
72D3 **Huai He** *R* China
73C4 **Huaihua** China
73C5 **Huaiji** China
72D3 **Huainan** China
69E4 **Hua-lien** Taiwan
32B5 **Huallaga** *R* Peru
32B5 **Huallanca** Peru
32B5 **Huamachuco** Peru
100A2 **Huambo** Angola
30C2 **Huanay** Bol
32B5 **Huancabamba** Peru
32B6 **Huancavelica** Peru
32B6 **Huancayo** Peru
73D3 **Huangchuan** China
Huang Hai = Yellow S
72D2 **Huang He** *R* China
72B2 **Huangling** China
76D2 **Huangliu** China
73C3 **Huangpi** China
73D4 **Huangshan** China
73D3 **Huangshi** China
34C3 **Huanguelén** Arg
73E4 **Huangyan** China
74B2 **Huanren** China
32B5 **Huānuco** Peru
30C2 **Huanuni** Bol
72B2 **Huan Xian** China
32B5 **Huaráz** Peru
32B6 **Huarmey** Peru
32B5 **Huascarán** *Mt* Peru
30B4 **Huasco** Chile
23B2 **Huatusco** Mexico
23B1 **Huauchinango** Mexico
23B2 **Huautla** Mexico
72C2 **Hua Xian** China
24B2 **Huayapan** *R* Mexico
73C3 **Hubei** Province, China
87B1 **Hubli** India
34C3 **Hucal** Arg
74B2 **Huch'ang** N Korea
42D3 **Huddersfield** Eng
39H6 **Hudiksvall** Sweden
17B2 **Hudson** Florida, USA
14B2 **Hudson** Michigan, USA
16C1 **Hudson** New York, USA
16C1 **Hudson** *R* USA
7B4 **Hudson B** Can
5H4 **Hudson Bay** Can
13C1 **Hudson's Hope** Can
6C3 **Hudson Str** Can
76D2 **Hue** Viet
23B1 **Huejutla** Mexico
50A2 **Huelva** Spain
23A2 **Hueramo** Mexico
51B2 **Húercal Overa** Spain
51B1 **Huesca** Spain
23B2 **Huexotla** *Hist Site* Mexico
107D3 **Hughenden** Aust
12D1 **Hughes** USA
86B2 **Hugli** *R* India
19A3 **Hugo** USA
73D4 **Hui'an** China
110C1 **Huiarau Range** *Mts* NZ
74B2 **Huich'ŏn** N Korea
74B2 **Huifa He** *R* China
32B3 **Huila** *Mt* Colombia
73D5 **Huilai** China
73A4 **Huili** China
74B2 **Huinan** China
34C2 **Huinca Renancó** Arg
25C3 **Huixtla** Mexico
73A4 **Huize** China
73C5 **Huizhou** China
23B2 **Hujuápan de Léon** Mexico
69F2 **Hulin** China
15C1 **Hull** Can
42D3 **Hull** Eng
58B1 **Hultsfred** Sweden
63D3 **Hulun Nur** *L* China
69E1 **Huma** China
33E5 **Humaita** Brazil
100B4 **Humansdorp** S Africa
42D3 **Humber** *R* Eng
42D3 **Humberside** County, Eng
5H4 **Humboldt** Can
20C2 **Humboldt** *R* USA
20B2 **Humboldt B** USA
6D2 **Humboldt Gletscher** *Gl* Greenland
21B2 **Humboldt L** USA
108C1 **Humeburn** Aust
109C3 **Hume,L** Aust
100A2 **Humpata** Angola
22C2 **Humphreys** USA
38A1 **Húnaflóri** *B* Iceland
73C4 **Hunan** Province, China
74C2 **Hunchun** China
13C2 **Hundred Mile House** Can
54B1 **Hunedoara** Rom
59B3 **Hungary** Republic, Europe
108B1 **Hungerford** Aust
74B3 **Hŭngnam** N Korea
74B2 **Hunjiang** China
46D2 **Hunsrück** Mts, Germany
109D2 **Hunter** *R* Aust
13B2 **Hunter I** Can
109C4 **Hunter Is** Aust
12D2 **Hunter,Mt** USA
14A3 **Huntingburg** USA
43D3 **Huntingdon** Eng
14A2 **Huntingdon** Indiana, USA
14B3 **Huntington** W Virginia, USA
22C4 **Huntington Beach** USA
22C2 **Huntington L** USA
110C1 **Huntly** NZ
44C3 **Huntly** Scot
12J2 **Hunt,Mt** Can
108A1 **Hunt Pen** Aust
17A1 **Huntsville** Alabama, USA
15C1 **Huntsville** Can
19A3 **Huntsville** Texas, USA
76D2 **Huong Khe** Viet
71F4 **Huon Peninsula** *Pen* PNG
109C4 **Huonville** Anst
14B1 **Hurd,C** Can
80B3 **Hurghada** Egypt
8D2 **Huron** S. Dakota, USA
14B1 **Huron,L** Can/USA
34A2 **Hurtado** Chile
111B2 **Hurunui** *R* NZ
38B1 **Husavik** Iceland
54C1 **Huși** Rom
39G7 **Huskvarna** Sweden
12C1 **Huslia** USA
94B2 **Husn** Jordan
56B2 **Husum** Germany
109C1 **Hutton,Mt** Aust
72D2 **Hutuo He** *R* China
46C1 **Huy** Belg
72A2 **Huzhu** China
52C2 **Hvar** *I* Croatia
100B2 **Hwange** Zim
100B2 **Hwange Nat Pk** Zim
15D2 **Hyannis** USA
68B2 **Hyaryas Nuur** *L* Mongolia
5E4 **Hydaburg** Can
16C2 **Hyde Park** USA
87B1 **Hyderābād** India
85B3 **Hyderabad** Pak
49D3 **Hyères** France
12J2 **Hyland** *R* Can
8B2 **Hyndman Peak** *Mt* USA
38K6 **Hyrynsalmi** Fin
13D1 **Hythe** Can
74C4 **Hyūga** Japan
39J6 **Hyvikää** Fin

I

31C4 **Iaçu** Brazil
54C2 **Ialomița** *R* Rom
54C1 **Iași** Rom
97C4 **Ibadan** Nig
32B3 **Ibagué** Colombia
54B2 **Ibar** *R* Montenegro/Serbia, Yugos
32B3 **Ibarra** Ecuador
35B1 **Ibiá** Brazil
30E4 **Ibicui** *R* Brazil
34D2 **Ibicuy** Arg
51C2 **Ibiza** Spain
51C2 **Ibiza** *I* Spain
101D2 **Ibo** Mozam
31C4 **Ibotirama** Brazil
91C5 **'Ibrī** Oman
32B6 **Ica** Peru
32D4 **Içá** *R* Brazil
32D3 **Içana** Brazil
38A1 **Iceland** Republic, N Atlantic O
13C2 **Ice Mt** Can
87A1 **Ichalkaranji** India
74E3 **Ichihara** Japan
75B1 **Ichinomiya** Japan
74E3 **Ichinoseki** Japan
12F3 **Icy B** USA
4B2 **Icy C** USA
19B3 **Idabell** USA
8B2 **Idaho Falls** USA
20B2 **Idanha** USA
46D2 **Idar Oberstein** Germany
95A2 **Idehan Marzūg** *Desert* Libya
95A2 **Idehan Ubari** *Desert* Libya
96C2 **Idelés** Alg
68B2 **Iderlym Gol** *R* Mongolia
95C2 **Idfu** Egypt
55B3 **Ídhi Óros** *Mt* Greece
55B3 **Ídhra** *I* Greece
98B3 **Idiofa** Zaïre
12C2 **Iditarod** *R* USA
92C2 **Idlib** Syria
39K7 **Idritsa** Russian Fed
100B4 **Idutywa** S Africa
55C3 **Ierápetra** Greece
46B1 **Ieper** Belg
63D2 **Iet Oktyobr'ya** Russian Fed
99D3 **Ifakara** Tanz
71F3 **Ifalik** *I* Pacific O
101D3 **Ifanadiana** Madag
97C4 **Ife** Nig
97C3 **Iférouane** Niger
78C2 **Igan** Malay
35B2 **Igaranava** Brazil
93E2 **Igdir** Iran
39H6 **Iggesund** Sweden
34B2 **Iglesia** Arg
53A3 **Iglesias** Sardegna
6B3 **Igloolik** Can
10A2 **Ignace** Can
55B3 **Igoumenítsa** Greece
61H2 **Igra** Russian Fed
23B2 **Iguala** Mexico
35B2 **Iguape** Brazil
35B2 **Iguatama** Brazil
31D3 **Iguatu** Brazil
98A3 **Iguéla** Gabon
101D3 **Ihosy** Madag
74D3 **Iida** Japan
75B1 **Iide-san** *Mt* Japan
38K6 **Iisalmi** Fin

75A2 **Iizuka** Japan
97C4 **Ijebu Ode** Nig
56B2 **Ijsselmeer** *S* Neth
55C3 **Ikaría** *I* Greece
74E2 **Ikeda** Japan
98C3 **Ikela** Zaïre
54B2 **Ikhtiman** Bulg
12D3 **Ikolik,C** USA
101D2 **Ikopa** *R* Madag
79B2 **Ilagan** Phil
90A3 **Ilām** Iran
47C1 **Ilanz** Switz
13F1 **Île à la Crosse** Can
13F1 **Île à la Crosse,L** Can
89G8 **Ilebo** Zaïre
96D1 **Île de Jerba** *I* Tunisia
48B2 **Ile de Noirmoutier** *I* France
48B2 **Ile de Ré** *I* France
107F3 **Île des Pins** *I* Nouvelle Calédonie
48A2 **Ile d'Ouessant** *I* France
48B2 **Ile d'Yeu** *I* France
61J3 **Ilek** *R* Russian Fed
107F2 **Îles Bélèp** Nouvelle Calédonie
107E2 **Îles Chesterfield** Nouvelle Calédonie
49D3 **Iles d'Hyères** *Is* France
43B4 **Ilfracombe** Eng
92B1 **Ilgaz Dağları** *Mts* Turk
101C3 **Ilha Bazaruto** *I* Mozam
33G3 **Ilha De Maracá** *I* Brazil
33G4 **Ilha de Marajó** *I* Brazil
35B2 **Ilha de São Sebastiao** *I* Brazil
33G6 **Ilha do Bananal** *Region* Brazil
35C2 **Ilha Grande** *I* Brazil
35B2 **Ilha Santo Amaro** *I* Brazil
96A1 **Ilhas Selvegens** *I* Atlantic O
35A2 **Ilha Solteira Dam** Brazil
31D4 **Ilhéus** Brazil
12C3 **Iliamna L** USA
12D2 **Iliamna V** USA
79B4 **Iligan** Phil
63C2 **Ilim** *R* Russian Fed
63C2 **Ilim** Russian Fed
63C3 **Il'inskiy** Russian Fed
55B3 **Iliodhrómia** *I* Greece
79B4 **Illana B** Phil
34A2 **Illapel** Chile
34A2 **Illapel** *R* Chile
97C3 **Illéla** Niger
47D1 **Iller** *R* Germany
4C4 **Illiamna L** USA
10A2 **Illinois** State, USA
10B2 **Illinois** *R* USA
96C2 **Illizi** Alg
30B2 **Ilo** Peru
79B3 **Iloilo** Phil
38L6 **Ilomantsi** Fin
97C4 **Ilorin** Nig
75A2 **Imabari** Japan
75B1 **Imalchi** Japan
60C1 **Imatra** Fin
30G4 **Imbituba** Brazil
99E2 **Imi** Eth
20C2 **Imlay** USA
47D1 **Immenstadt** Germany
52B2 **Imola** Italy
31B3 **Imperatriz** Brazil
52A2 **Imperia** Italy
98B2 **Impfondo** Congo
86C2 **Imphāl** India
47D1 **Imst** Austria
12B1 **Imuruk L** USA
75B1 **Ina** Japan
96C2 **In Afahleleh** *Well* Alg
75B2 **Inamba-jima** *I* Japan
96C2 **In Amenas** Alg
38K5 **Inari** Fin
38K5 **Inarijärvi** *L* Fin
75C1 **Inawashiro-ko** *L* Japan
96C2 **In Belbel** Alg
60E5 **Ince Burun** *Pt* Turk
92B2 **Incekum Burun** *Pt* Turk
74B3 **Inch'ŏn** S Korea
96B2 **In Dagouber** *Well* Mali
35B1 **Indaia** *R* Brazil
38H6 **Indals** *R* Sweden
21B2 **Independence** California, USA
18A2 **Independence** Kansas, USA
18B2 **Independence** Missouri, USA
78A3 **Inderagiri** *R* Indon
61H4 **Inderborskly** Kazakhstan
83B3 **India** Federal Republic, Asia
14A2 **Indiana** State, USA
15C2 **Indiana** USA
104C6 **Indian-Antarctic Ridge** Indian O
14A3 **Indianapolis** USA
Indian Desert = Thar Desert
7E4 **Indian Harbour** Can
104B4 **Indian O**
18B1 **Indianola** Iowa, USA
19B3 **Indianola** Mississippi, USA
35B1 **Indianópolis** Brazil
76D2 **Indo China** Region, S E Asia
70C4 **Indonesia** Republic, S E Asia
85D4 **Indore** India
78B4 **Indramayu** Indon
48C2 **Indre** *R* France
85B3 **Indus** *R* Pak
60D5 **Inebdu** Turk
96C2 **In Ebeggi** *Well* Alg
96C2 **In Ecker** Alg
92A1 **Inegöl** Turk
96D2 **In Ezzane** Alg
97C3 **Ingal** Niger
14B2 **Ingersoll** Can
107D2 **Ingham** Aust
6D2 **Inglefield Land** *Region* Can
110B1 **Inglewood** NZ
109D1 **Inglewood** Queensland, Aust
22C4 **Inglewood** USA
108B3 **Inglewood** Victoria, Aust
38B2 **Ingólfshöfði** *I* Iceland
57C3 **Ingolstadt** Germany
86B2 **Ingrāj Bāzār** India
96C3 **In-Guezzam** *Well* Alg
101C3 **Inhambane** Mozam
101C3 **Inharrime** Mozam
35B1 **Inhumas** Brazil
32D3 **Inirida** *R* Colombia
45A2 **Inishbofin** *I* Irish Rep
45A1 **Inishkea** *I* Irish Rep
45B2 **Inishmaan** *I* Irish Rep
45B2 **Inishmore** *I* Irish Rep
45B1 **Inishmurray** *I* Irish Rep
45C1 **Inishowen** District, Irish Rep
45A2 **Inishshark** *I* Irish Rep
45A2 **Inishturk** *I* Irish Rep
109C1 **Injune** Aust
12H3 **Inklin** Can
12H3 **Inklin** *R* Can
12C1 **Inland L** USA
47D1 **Inn** *R* Austria
108B1 **Innamincka** Aust
68C2 **Inner Mongolia** Autonomous Region, China
107D2 **Innisfail** Aust
12C2 **Innoko** *R* USA
57C3 **Innsbruck** Austria
98B3 **Inongo** Zaïre
58B2 **Inowrocław** Pol
96C2 **In Salah** Alg
47B1 **Interlaken** Switz
24C3 **Intexpec** Mexico
47C2 **Intra** Italy
78D3 **Intu** Indon
75C1 **Inubo-saki** *C* Japan
7C4 **Inukjuak** Can
4E3 **Inuvik** Can
4F3 **Inuvik** *Region* Can
44B3 **Inveraray** Scot
111A3 **Invercargill** NZ
109D1 **Inverell** Aust
13D2 **Invermere** Can
44B3 **Inverness** Scot
44C3 **Inverurie** Scot
108A3 **Investigator Str** Aust
68A1 **Inya** Russian Fed
21B2 **Inyokern** USA
98B3 **Inzia** *R* Zaïre
55B3 **Ioánnina** Greece
18A2 **Iola** USA
44A3 **Iona** *I* Scot
100A2 **Iôna Nat Pk** Angola
20C1 **Ione** USA
Ionian Is = Ioníoi Nísoi
55A3 **Ionian S** Italy/Greece
55B3 **Ioníoi Nísoi** *Is* Greece
55C3 **Íos** *I* Greece
10A2 **Iowa** *R* USA
10A2 **Iowa City** USA
35B1 **Ipameri** Brazil
35C1 **Ipanema** Brazil
61F4 **Ipatovo** Russian Fed
32B3 **Ipiales** Colombia
77C5 **Ipoh** Malay
30F2 **Iporá** Brazil
55C2 **Ipsala** Turk
109D1 **Ipswich** Aust
43E3 **Ipswich** Eng
16D1 **Ipswich** USA
30B3 **Iquique** Chile
32C4 **Iquitos** Peru
55C3 **Iráklion** Greece
80D2 **Iran** Republic, S W Asia
91D4 **Irānshahr** Iran
23A1 **Irapuato** Mexico
93D3 **Iraq** Republic, S W Asia
95A2 **Irā Wan** *Watercourse* Libya
94B2 **Irbid** Jordan
61K2 **Irbit** Russian Fed
36C3 **Ireland** Republic NW Europe
33F3 **Ireng** *R* Guyana
74B3 **Iri** S Korea
71E4 **Irian Jaya** Province, Indon
95B3 **Iriba** Chad
79B3 **Iriga** Phil
99D3 **Iringa** Tanz
69E4 **Iriomote** *I* Japan
33G5 **Iriri** *R* Brazil
42B3 **Irish S** Eng/Irish Rep
12D1 **Irkillik** *R* USA
63C2 **Irkutsk** Russian Fed
65J4 **Irlysh** *R* Kazakhstan
108A2 **Iron Knob** Aust
14A1 **Iron Mountain** USA
107D2 **Iron Range** Aust
14A1 **Iron River** USA
14B3 **Irontown** USA
10A2 **Ironwood** USA
10B2 **Iroquois Falls** Can
75B2 **Iro-zaki** *C* Japan
76A2 **Irrawaddy,Mouths of the** Burma
65H4 **Irtysh** *R* Russian Fed
51B1 **Irun** Spain
42B2 **Irvine** Scot
19A3 **Irving** USA
79B4 **Isabela** Phil
32J7 **Isabela** *I* Ecuador
4H2 **Isachsen** Can
4H2 **Isachsen,C** Can
6H3 **Ísafjörður** Iceland
74C4 **Isahaya** Japan
98C2 **Isangi** Zaïre
47D1 **Isar** *R* Germany
47D1 **Isarco** *R* Italy
44E1 **Isbister** Scot
47D1 **Ischgl** Austria
53B2 **Ischia** *I* Italy
75B2 **Ise** Japan
47D2 **Iseo** Italy
46D1 **Iserlohn** Germany
53B2 **Isernia** Italy
75B2 **Ise-wan** *B* Japan
69E4 **Ishigaki** *I* Japan
74E2 **Ishikari** *R* Japan
74E2 **Ishikari-wan** *B* Japan
65H4 **Ishim** Russian Fed
65H4 **Ishim** *R* Kazakhstan
74E3 **Ishinomaki** Japan
75C1 **Ishioka** Japan
84C1 **Ishkashim** Afghan
14A1 **Ishpeming** USA
65J4 **Isil'kul** Russian Fed
99D2 **Isiolo** Kenya
98C2 **Isiro** Zaïre
92C2 **Iskenderun** Turk
92C2 **Iskenferun Körfezi** *B* Turk
92B1 **İskilip** Turk
65K4 **Iskitim** Russian Fed
54B2 **Iskur** *R* Bulg
12H3 **Iskut** *R* Can/USA
23B2 **Isla** Mexico
34C3 **Isla Bermejo** *I* Arg
27E4 **Isla Blanquilla** Ven
32A2 **Isla Coiba** *I* Panama
9B4 **Isla de Cedros** *I* Mexico
29B4 **Isla de Chiloé** *I* Chile
25D2 **Isla de Cozumel** *I* Mexico
26C3 **Isla de la Gonâve** Cuba
26A2 **Isla de la Juventud** *I* Cuba
34D2 **Isla de las Lechiguanas** *I* Arg
3K8 **Isla del Coco** *I* Costa Rica
25D3 **Isla del Maiz** *I* Caribbean S
23B1 **Isla de Lobos** *I* Mexico
29D6 **Isla de los Estados** *I* Arg
28E2 **Isla de Marajó** *I* Brazil
105L5 **Isla de Pascua** *I* Pacific O
26A4 **Isla de Providencia** *I* Caribbean S
26A4 **Isla de San Andres** *I* Caribbean S
30G4 **Isla de Santa Catarina** *I* Brazil
33G2 **Isla du Diable** *I* French Guiana
31E2 **Isla Fernando de Noronha** *I* Brazil
29C6 **Isla Grande de Tierra del Fuego** *I* Arg/Chile
27D4 **Isla la Tortuga** *I* Ven
84C2 **Islamabad** Pak
24A2 **Isla Magdalena** *I* Mexico
27E4 **Isla Margarita** Ven
34A3 **Isla Mocha** Chile
17B2 **Islamorada** USA
10A1 **Island L** Can
108A2 **Island Lg** Aust
110B1 **Islands,B of** NZ
32A4 **Isla Puná** *I* Ecuador
103D6 **Isla San Ambrosia** *I* Pacific O
103D6 **Isla San Felix** *I* Pacific O
24A2 **Isla Santa Margarita** *I* Mexico
34A3 **Isla Santa Maria** *I* Chile
51C2 **Islas Baleares** *Is* Spain
96A2 **Islas Canarias** *Is* Atlantic O
51C2 **Islas Columbretes** *Is* Spain
25D3 **Islas de la Bahia** *Is* Honduras
26A4 **Islas del Maíz** *Is* Caribbean S
33E1 **Islas de Margarita** *Is* Ven

Islas Diego Ramírez

29C7 **Islas Diego Ramírez** *Is* Chile
32J7 **Islas Galapagos** *Is* Pacific O
30H6 **Islas Juan Fernández** Chile
32D1 **Islas los Roques** *Is* Ven
Islas Malvinas = Falkland Is
105L3 **Islas Revilla Gigedo** *Is* Pacific O
29C7 **Islas Wollaston** *Is* Chile
97A3 **Isla Tidra** *I* Maur
29B5 **Isla Wellington** *I* Chile
48C2 **Isle** *R* France
104B5 **Isle Amsterdam** *I* Indian O
43D4 **Isle of Wight** *I* Eng
10B2 **Isle Royale** *I* USA
104B5 **Isle St Paul** *I* Indian O
104A6 **Isles Crozet** *I* Indian O
105J4 **Isles de la Société** Pacific O
105K5 **Isles Gambier** *Is* Pacific O
101D2 **Isles Glorieuses** *Is* Madag
104B6 **Isles Kerguelen** *Is* Indian O
105K4 **Isles Marquises** *Is* Pacific O
105J4 **Isles Tuamotu** *Is* Pacific O
105J5 **Isles Tubai** *Is* Pacific O
22B1 **Isleton** USA
92B3 **Ismâ'îlîya** Egypt
101D3 **Isoanala** Madag
101C2 **Isoka** Zambia
53B3 **Isola Egadi** *I* Italy
52B2 **Isola Ponziane** *I* Italy
53B3 **Isole Lipari** *Is* Italy
52C2 **Isoles Tremiti** *Is* Italy
75B1 **Isosaki** Japan
92B2 **Isparta** Turk
94B2 **Israel** Republic, S W Asia
51C2 **Isser** *R* Alg
48C2 **Issoire** France
49C2 **Issoudun** France
92A1 **Istanbul** Turk
55B3 **Istiáia** Greece
25C3 **Istmo de Tehuantepec** *Isthmus* Mexico
17B2 **Istokpoga,L** USA
52B1 **Istra** *Pen* Croatia
35B1 **Itaberai** Brazil
35C1 **Itabira** Brazil
35C2 **Itabirito** Brazil
31D4 **Itabuna** Brazil
33F4 **Itacoatiara** Brazil
32B2 **Itagui** Colombia
33F4 **Itaituba** Brazil
30G4 **Itajaí** Brazil
35B2 **Itajuba** Brazil
52B2 **Italy** Repubic, Europe
35D1 **Itamaraju** Brazil
35C1 **Itamarandiba** Brazil
35C1 **Itambacuri** Brazil
35C1 **Itambé** *Mt* Brazil
86C1 **Itānagar** India
35B2 **Itanhaém** Brazil
35C1 **Itanhém** Brazil
35C1 **Itanhém** *R* Brazil
35C1 **Itaobím** Brazil
35B2 **Itapecerica** Brazil
35C2 **Itaperuna** Brazil
31C5 **Itapetinga** Brazil
35B2 **Itapetininga** Brazil
35B2 **Itapeva** Brazil
31D2 **Itapipoca** Brazil
35B1 **Itapuranga** Brazil
30E4 **Itaqui** Brazil
35C1 **Itarantim** Brazil
35B2 **Itararé** Brazil
35B2 **Itararé** *R* Brazil
35C2 **Itaúna** Brazil
33E6 **Iténez** *R* Brazil/Bol

15C2 **Ithaca** USA
98C2 **Itimbiri** *R* Zaïre
35C1 **Itinga** Brazil
6E3 **Itivdleg** Greenland
75B2 **Ito** Japan
74D3 **Itoigawa** Japan
33E6 **Itonomas** *R* Bol
35B2 **Itu** Brazil
35B1 **Itumbiara** Brazil
35A1 **Iturama** Brazil
30C3 **Iturbe** Arg
35B1 **Iturutaba** Brazil
56B2 **Itzehoe** Germany
58D2 **Ivacevichi** Belorussia
35A2 **Ivai** *R* Brazil
38K5 **Ivalo** Fin
54A2 **Ivangrad** Montenegro, Yugos
108B2 **Ivanhoe** Aust
59C3 **Ivano-Frankovsk** Ukraine
61F2 **Ivanovo** Russian Fed
65H3 **Ivdel'** Russian Fed
98B2 **Ivindo** *R* Gabon
101D3 **Ivohibe** Madag
101D2 **Ivongo Soanierana** Madag
97B4 **Ivory Coast** Republic, Africa
52A1 **Ivrea** Italy
6C3 **Ivujivik** Can
74E3 **Iwaki** Japan
74C4 **Iwakuni** Japan
74E2 **Iwanai** Japan
97C4 **Iwo** Nig
69G4 **Iwo Jima** *I* Japan
23B1 **Ixmiquilpa** Mexico
23A2 **Ixtapa** Mexico
23A1 **Ixtlán** Mexico
75A2 **Iyo** Japan
75A2 **Iyo-nada** *B* Japan
65G4 **Izhevsk** Russian Fed
64G3 **Izhma** Russian Fed
91C5 **Izki** Oman
60C4 **Izmail** Ukraine
92A2 **Izmir** Turk
55C3 **Izmir Körfezi** *B* Turk
92A1 **Iznik** Turk
92A1 **Iznik** Turk
55C2 **Iznik Golü** *L* Turk
94C2 **Izra'** Syria
23B2 **Izúcar de Matamoros** Mexico
75B2 **Izumi-sano** Japan
75A1 **Izumo** Japan
74D4 **Izu-shotō** *Is* Japan

J

95B1 **Jabal al Akhdar** *Mts* Libya
94C2 **Jabal al 'Arab** Syria
95A2 **Jabal as Sawdā** *Mts* Libya
91B5 **Jabal az Zannah** UAE
94C1 **Jabal Halimah** *Mt* Leb/Syria
83B3 **Jabalpur** India
59B2 **Jablonec nad Nisou** Czech Republic
31D3 **Jaboatão** Brazil
35B2 **Jaboticabal** Brazil
51B1 **Jaca** Spain
23B1 **Jacala** Mexico
33F5 **Jacareacanga** Brazil
35B2 **Jacarei** Brazil
30F3 **Jacarezinho** Brazil
29C2 **Jáchal** Arg
35C1 **Jacinto** Brazil
13F2 **Jackfish L** Can
109C1 **Jackson** Aust
22B1 **Jackson** California, USA
14B2 **Jackson** Michigan, USA
19B3 **Jackson** Mississippi, USA
18C2 **Jackson** Missouri, USA
14B3 **Jackson** Ohio, USA
11B3 **Jackson** Tennessee, USA
111B2 **Jackson,C** NZ
111A2 **Jackson Head** *Pt* NZ

19B3 **Jacksonville** Arkansas, USA
17B1 **Jacksonville** Florida, USA
18B2 **Jacksonville** Illinois, USA
17C1 **Jacksonville** N Carolina, USA
19A3 **Jacksonville** Texas, USA
17B1 **Jacksonville Beach** USA
26C3 **Jacmel** Haiti
84B3 **Jacobabad** Pak
31C4 **Jacobina** Brazil
23A2 **Jacona** Mexico
Jadotville = Likasi
32B5 **Jaén** Peru
50B2 **Jaén** Spain
Jaffa = Tel Aviv Yafo
108A3 **Jaffa,C** Aust
87B3 **Jaffna** Sri Lanka
86B2 **Jagannathganj Ghat** Bang
87C1 **Jagdalpur** India
91C4 **Jagin** *R* Iran
87B1 **Jagtial** India
29F2 **Jaguarão** *R* Brazil
35B2 **Jaguarialva** Brazil
91B4 **Jahrom** Iran
85D5 **Jāina** India
72A2 **Jainca** China
85D3 **Jaipur** India
85C3 **Jaisalmer** India
90C2 **Jajarm** Iran
52C2 **Jajce** Bosnia-Herzegovina
78B4 **Jakarta** Indon
6E3 **Jakobshavn** Greenland
38J6 **Jakobstad** Fin
23B2 **Jalaca** Mexico
84B2 **Jalai-Kut** Afghan
84D2 **Jalandhar** India
23B2 **Jalapa** Mexico
35A2 **Jales** Brazil
86B1 **Jaleswar** Nepal
85D4 **Jalgaon** India
97D4 **Jalingo** Nig
51B1 **Jalón** *R* Spain
85C3 **Jālor** India
23A1 **Jalostotitlan** Mexico
86B1 **Jalpāiguri** India
23B1 **Jalpan** Mexico
95B2 **Jālū Oasis** Libya
32A4 **Jama** Ecuador
26B3 **Jamaica** *I* Caribbean S
26B3 **Jamaica Chan** Caribbean S
86B2 **Jamalpur** Bang
78A3 **Jambi** Indon
85C4 **Jambussar** India
7B4 **James B** Can
5J5 **Jameston** USA
108A2 **Jamestown** Aust
8D2 **Jamestown** N. Dakota, USA
15C2 **Jamestown** New York, USA
16D2 **Jamestown** Rhode Island, USA
23B2 **Jamiltepec** Mexico
87B1 **Jamkhandi** India
84C2 **Jammu** India
84D2 **Jammu and Kashmir** State, India
85B4 **Jamnagar** India
84C3 **Jampur** Pak
38K6 **Jämsä** Fin
86B2 **Jamshedpur** India
86B1 **Janakpur** Nepal
35C1 **Janaúba** Brazil
90B3 **Jandaq** Iran
109D1 **Jandowae** Aust
1B1 **Jan Mayen** *I* Norwegian S
35C1 **Januária** Brazil
85D4 **Jaora** India
51 **Japan** Empire, E Asia
74C3 **Japan,S of** S E Asia
104F2 **Japan Trench** Pacific O

32D4 **Japurá** *R* Brazil
93C2 **Jarābulus** Syria
35B1 **Jaraguá** Brazil
50B1 **Jarama** *R* Spain
94B2 **Jarash** Jordan
30E3 **Jardim** Brazil
51B2 **Jardin** *R* Spain
26B2 **Jardines de la Reina** *Is* Cuba
Jargalant = Hovd
33G3 **Jari** *R* Brazil
86C1 **Jaria Jhānjail** Bang
46C2 **Jarny** France
58B2 **Jarocin** Pol
59C2 **Jaroslaw** Pol
38G6 **Järpen** Sweden
72B2 **Jartai** China
85C4 **Jasdan** India
97C4 **Jasikan** Ghana
91C4 **Jāsk** Iran
59C3 **Jaslo** Pol
29D6 **Jason Is** Falkland Is
18B2 **Jasper** Arkansas, USA
13D2 **Jasper** Can
17B1 **Jasper** Florida, USA
14A3 **Jasper** Indiana, USA
19B3 **Jasper** Texas, USA
13D2 **Jasper Nat Pk** Can
58B2 **Jastrowie** Pol
35A1 **Jataí** Brazil
51B2 **Játiva** Spain
35B2 **Jau** Brazil
32B6 **Jauja** Peru
86A1 **Jaunpur** India
Java = Jawa
87B2 **Javadi Hills** India
Javari = Yavari
70B4 **Java S** Indon
106A2 **Java Trench** Indon
78B4 **Jawa** *I* Indon
71F4 **Jayapura** Indon
94C2 **Jayrūd** Syria
96B2 **Jbel Ouarkziz** *Mts* Mor
96B1 **Jbel Sarhro** *Mt* Mor
19B4 **Jeanerette** USA
97C4 **Jebba** Nig
93D2 **Jebel 'Abd al 'Azīz** *Mt* Syria
95B3 **Jebel Abyad** Sudan
91C5 **Jebel Akhdar** *Mt* Oman
92C4 **Jebel al Lawz** *Mt* S Arabia
94B2 **Jebel ash Shaykh** *Mt* Syria
95C2 **Jebel Asoteriba** *Mt* Sudan
94B3 **Jebel Ed Dabab** *Mt* Jordan
94B3 **Jebel el Ata'ita** *Mt* Jordan
92C3 **Jebel esh Sharqi** *Mts* Leb/Syria
94C3 **Jebel Ithrīyat** *Mt* Jordan
91C5 **Jebel Ja'lan** *Mt* Oman
94B2 **Jebel Liban** *Mts* Leb
94C2 **Jebel Ma'lūlā** *Mt* Syria
98C1 **Jebel Marra** *Mt* Sudan
94C3 **Jebel Mudeisisat** *Mt* Jordan
95C2 **Jebel Oda** *Mt* Sudan
94B3 **Jebel Qasr ed Deir** *Mt* Jordan
94B2 **Jebel Um ed Daraj** *Mt* Jordan
95B2 **Jebel Uweinat** *Mt* Sudan
42C2 **Jedburgh** Scot
Jedda = Jiddah
59C2 **Jedrzejów** Pol
19B3 **Jefferson** Texas, USA
11A3 **Jefferson City** USA
8B3 **Jefferson,Mt** USA
14A3 **Jeffersonville** USA
60C2 **Jekabpils** Latvia
59B2 **Jelena Gora** Pol
60B2 **Jelgava** Latvia

78C4 **Jember** Indon
57C2 **Jena** Germany
78B2 **Jenaja** *I* Indon
47D1 **Jenbach** Austria
94B2 **Jenin** Israel
19B3 **Jennings** USA
59B2 **Jeseníky** *Upland* Czech Republic
6F3 **Jensen Nunatakker** *Mt* Greenland
6B3 **Jens Munk** *I* Can
108B3 **Jeparit** Aust
31D4 **Jequié** Brazil
35C1 **Jequital** *R* Brazil
35C1 **Jequitinhonha** Brazil
31C5 **Jequitinhonha** *R* Brazil
50A2 **Jerez de la Frontera** Spain
50A2 **Jerez de los Caballeros** Spain
94B3 **Jericho** Israel
108C3 **Jerilderie** Aust
48B2 **Jersey** *I* UK
10C2 **Jersey City** USA
15C2 **Jersey Shore** USA
18B2 **Jerseyville** USA
92C3 **Jerusalem** Israel
109D3 **Jervis B** Aust
13C2 **Jervis Inlet** *Sd* Can
52B1 **Jesenice** Slovenia
86B2 **Jessore** Bang
11B3 **Jesup** USA
34C2 **Jesus Maria** Arg
16D2 **Jewett City** USA
54A2 **Jezerce** *Mt* Alb
58C2 **Jezioro Mamry** *L* Pol
58C2 **Jezioro Śniardwy** *L* Pol
94B2 **Jezzine** Leb
85C4 **Jhābua** India
85D4 **Jhālāwār** India
84C2 **Jhang Maghiana** Pak
85D3 **Jhānsi** India
86A2 **Jhārsuguda** India
84C2 **Jhelum** Pak
84C2 **Jhelum** *R* Pak
11C3 **J H Kerr L** USA
84D3 **Jhunjhunūn** India
69F2 **Jiamusi** China
73C4 **Ji'an** Jiangxi, China
74B2 **Ji'an** Jilin, China
73D4 **Jiande** China
73B4 **Jiang'an** China
73D4 **Jiangbiancun** China
73A5 **Jiangcheng** China
73B3 **Jiang Jiang** *R* China
73C5 **Jiangmen** China
72D3 **Jiangsu** Province, China
73C4 **Jiangxi** Province, China
73A3 **Jiangyou** China
72D1 **Jianping** China
73A5 **Jianshui** China
73D4 **Jian Xi** *R* China
73D4 **Jianyang** China
72E2 **Jiaonan** China
72E2 **Jiao Xian** China
72E2 **Jiaozhou Wan** *B* China
72C2 **Jiaozuo** China
73E3 **Jiaxiang** China
68B3 **Jiayuguan** China
81B3 **Jiddah** S Arabia
72D3 **Jieshou** China
72C2 **Jiexiu** China
72A3 **Jigzhi** China
59B3 **Jihlava** Czech Republic
99E2 **Jilib** Somalia
69E2 **Jilin** China
51B1 **Jiloca** *R* Spain
99D2 **Jima** Eth
9C4 **Jiménez** Coahuila, Mexico
72D2 **Jinan** China
84D3 **Jind** India
72B2 **Jingbian** China
73D4 **Jingdezhen** China
76C1 **Jinghong** China
73C3 **Jingmen** China
72B2 **Jingning** China
73B4 **Jing Xiang** China
73D4 **Jinhua** China
72C1 **Jining** Nei Monggol, China
72D2 **Jining** Shandong, China
99D2 **Jinja** Uganda
76C1 **Jinping** China
73A4 **Jinsha Jiang** *R* China
73C4 **Jinshi** China
72E1 **Jinxi** China
72E2 **Jin Xian** China
72E1 **Jinzhou** China
33E5 **Jiparaná** *R* Brazil
32A4 **Jipijapa** Ecuador
23A2 **Jiquilpan** Mexico
91C4 **Jīroft** Iran
99E2 **Jirriban** Somalia
73B4 **Jishou** China
92C2 **Jisr ash Shughūr** Syria
54B2 **Jiu** *R* Rom
73D4 **Jiujiang** China
73A4 **Jiulong** China
73D4 **Jiulong Jiang** *R* China
69F2 **Jixi** China
94B3 **Jiza** Jordan
81C4 **Jīzan** S Arabia
97A3 **Joal** Sen
35C1 **João Monlevade** Brazil
31E3 **João Pessoa** Brazil
35B1 **João Pirheiro** Brazil
34B2 **Jocoli** Arg
85C3 **Jodhpur** India
38K6 **Joensuu** Fin
46C2 **Joeuf** France
13D2 **Joffre,Mt** Can
86B1 **Jogbani** India
87A2 **Jog Falls** India
101G1 **Johannesburg** S Africa
21B2 **Johannesburg** USA
6C2 **Johan Pen** Can
12D1 **John** *R* USA
20C2 **John Day** USA
20B1 **John Day** *R* USA
44C2 **John O'Groats** Scot
18A2 **John Redmond Res** USA
11B3 **Johnson City** Tennessee, USA
17B1 **Johnston** USA
27N2 **Johnston Pt** St Vincent and the Grenadines
15C2 **Johnstown** Pennsylvania, USA
77C5 **Johor Bharu** Malay
49C2 **Joigny** France
30G4 **Joinville** Brazil
61H3 **Jok** *R* Russian Fed
38H5 **Jokkmokk** Sweden
93E2 **Jolfa** Iran
10B2 **Joliet** USA
7C5 **Joliette** Can
79B4 **Jolo** Phil
79B4 **Jolo** *I* Phil
82D2 **Joma** *Mt* China
58C1 **Jonava** Lithuania
72A3 **Jonê** China
11A3 **Jonesboro** Arkansas, USA
19B3 **Jonesboro** Louisiana, USA
6B2 **Jones Sd** Can
58C1 **Joniśkis** Lithuania
39G7 **Jönköping** Sweden
11A3 **Joplin** USA
92C3 **Jordan** Kingdom, S W Asia
94B2 **Jordan** *R* Israel
20C2 **Jordan Valley** USA
86C1 **Jorhāt** India
38J5 **Jörn** Sweden
78C3 **Jorong** Indon
39F7 **Jørpeland** Nor
79B3 **Jose Pañganiban** Phil
106B2 **Joseph Bonaparte G** Aust
64B3 **Jotunheimen** *Mt* Nor
94B2 **Jouai'ya** Leb
94B2 **Jounié** Leb
86C1 **Jowal** India
99E2 **Jowhar** Somalia
12H2 **Joy,Mt** Can
5F5 **Juan de Fuca,Str of** Can/USA
101D2 **Juan de Nova** *I* Mozam Chan
34D3 **Juárez** Arg
31C3 **Juàzeiro** Brazil
31D3 **Juazeiro do Norte** Brazil
99D2 **Juba** Sudan
99E2 **Juba** *R* Somalia
94B1 **Jubail** Leb
93D3 **Jubbah** S Arabia
96A2 **Juby,C** Mor
51B2 **Jucar** *R* Spain
23B2 **Juchatengo** Mexico
23A1 **Juchipila** *R* Mexico
23A1 **Juchitlan** Mexico
57C3 **Judenburg** Austria
30B2 **Juilaca** Peru
73C4 **Juiling Shan** *Hills* China
31C6 **Juiz de Fora** Brazil
30C3 **Jujuy** State, Arg
30C2 **Juli** Peru
33F3 **Julianatop** *Mt* Surinam
6F3 **Julianehab** Greenland
46D1 **Jülich** Germany
86A1 **Jumla** Nepal
94B3 **Jum Suwwāna** *Mt* Jordan
85C4 **Jūnāgadh** India
72D2 **Junan** China
9D3 **Junction City** USA
31B6 **Jundiaí** Brazil
4E4 **Juneau** USA
107D4 **Junee** Aust
22C2 **June Lake** USA
52A1 **Jungfrau** *Mt* Switz
16A2 **Juniata** *R* USA
29D2 **Junín** Arg
73A4 **Junlian** China
31B6 **Juquiá** Brazil
99C2 **Jur** *R* Sudan
42B2 **Jura** *I* Scot
49D2 **Jura** *Mts* France
44B3 **Jura,Sound of** *Chan* Scot
94B3 **Jurf ed Darāwīsh** Jordan
65K4 **Jurga** Russian Fed
60B2 **Jurmala** Latvia
32D4 **Juruá** *R* Brazil
33F6 **Juruena** *R* Brazil
94C1 **Jūsīyah** Syria
34B2 **Justo Daract** Arg
32D4 **Jutai** *R* Brazil
25D3 **Juticalpa** Honduras
Jutland = Jylland
90C3 **Jūymand** Iran
56B1 **Jylland** *Pen* Den
38K6 **Jyväskyla** Fin

K

82B2 **K2** *Mt* China/India
90C2 **Kaakhka** Turkmenistan
101H1 **Kaapmuiden** S Africa
71D4 **Kabaena** *I* Indon
97A4 **Kabala** Sierra Leone
99D3 **Kabale** Rwanda
98C3 **Kabalo** Zaïre
98C3 **Kabambaro** Zaïre
99D2 **Kabarole** Uganda
98C3 **Kabinda** Zaïre
90A3 **Kabir Kuh** *Mts* Iran
100B2 **Kabompo** Zambia
100B2 **Kabompo** *R* Zambia
98C3 **Kabongo** Zaïre
84B2 **Kabul** Afghan
85B4 **Kachchh,G of** India
61J2 **Kachkanar** Russian Fed
63C2 **Kachug** Russian Fed
76B3 **Kadan** Burma
78D3 **Kadapongan** *I* Indon
85C4 **Kadi** India
108A2 **Kadina** Aust
92B2 **Kadinhanı** Turk
87B2 **Kadiri** India
60E4 **Kadiyevka** Ukraine
100B2 **Kadoma** Zim
99C1 **Kadugli** Sudan
97C3 **Kaduna** Nig
97C3 **Kaduna** *R* Nig
87B2 **Kadūr** India
97A3 **Kaédi** Maur
21C4 **Kaena Pt** Hawaiian Is
74B3 **Kaesŏng** N Korea
97C4 **Kafanchan** Nig
97A3 **Kaffrine** Sen
94C1 **Kafrūn Bashūr** Syria
100B2 **Kafue** Zambia
100B2 **Kafue** *R* Zambia
100B2 **Kafue Nat Pk** Zambia
74D3 **Kaga** Japan
65H6 **Kagan** Kazakhstan
93D1 **Kağizman** Turk
74C4 **Kagoshima** Japan
90C2 **Kāhak** Iran
99D3 **Kahama** Tanz
84B3 **Kahan** Pak
78C3 **Kahayan** *R* Indon
98B3 **Kahemba** Zaïre
46E1 **Kahler Asten** *Mt* Germany
91C4 **Kahnūj** Iran
18B1 **Kahoka** USA
21C4 **Kahoolawe** *I* Hawaiian Is
92C2 **Kahramanmaraş** Turk
21C4 **Kahuku Pt** Hawaiian Is
111B2 **Kaiapoi** NZ
33F2 **Kaieteur Fall** Guyana
72C3 **Kaifeng** China
110B1 **Kaikohe** NZ
111B2 **Kaikoura** NZ
111B2 **Kaikoura Pen** NZ
111B2 **Kaikoura Range** *Mts* NZ
73B4 **Kaili** China
21C4 **Kailua** Hawaiian Is
71E4 **Kaimana** Indon
75B2 **Kainan** Japan
97C3 **Kainji Res** Nig
110D1 **Kaipara Harbour** *B* NZ
73C5 **Kaiping** China
96D1 **Kairouan** Tunisia
22C2 **Kaiser Peak** *Mt* USA
57B3 **Kaiserslautern** Germany
74B2 **Kaishantun** China
58D2 **Kaisiadorys** Lithuania
110B1 **Kaitaia** NZ
111A3 **Kaitangata** NZ
84D3 **Kaithal** India
21C4 **Kaiwi Chan** Hawaiian Is
73B3 **Kai Xian** China
73A5 **Kaiyuan** Liaoning, China
74A2 **Kaiyuan** Yunnan, China
12C2 **Kaiyuh Mts** USA
38K6 **Kajaani** Fin
84B2 **Kajaki** Afghan
99D3 **Kajiado** Kenya
84B2 **Kajrān** Afghan
99D1 **Kaka** Sudan
99D2 **Kakamega** Kenya
75A2 **Kake** Japan
12H3 **Kake** USA
12D3 **Kakhonak** USA
65E5 **Kakhovskoye Vodokhranilishche** *Res* Ukraine
91B4 **Kākī** Iran
87C1 **Kākināda** India
75A2 **Kakogawa** Japan
4D2 **Kaktovik** USA
75C1 **Kakuda** Japan
Kalaallit Nunaat = Greenland
55B3 **Kalabáka** Greece
78D1 **Kalabakan** Malay
100B2 **Kalabo** Zambia
61F3 **Kalach** Russian Fed
61F4 **Kalach-na-Donu** Russian Fed
86C2 **Kaladan** *R* Burma
21C4 **Ka Lae** *C* Hawaiian Is

Kalahari Desert

100B3	**Kalahari Desert** Botswana
38J6	**Kalajoki** Fin
63D2	**Kalakan** Russian Fed
70A3	**Kalakepen** Indon
84C1	**Kalam** Pak
55B3	**Kalámai** Greece
10B2	**Kalamazoo** USA
84B3	**Kalat** Pak
92B1	**Kalecik** Turk
78D3	**Kalembau** *I* Indon
99C3	**Kalémié** Zaïre
38L5	**Kalevala** Russian Fed
86C2	**Kalewa** Burma
12D2	**Kalgin I** USA
106B4	**Kalgoorlie** Aust
78B4	**Kalianda** Indon
79B3	**Kalibo** Phil
98C3	**Kalima** Zaïre
78C3	**Kalimantan** Province, Indon
55C3	**Kálimnos** *I* Greece
86B1	**Kälimpang** India
60B3	**Kaliningrad** Russian Fed
60C3	**Kalinkovichi** Belorussia
8B2	**Kalispell** USA
58B2	**Kalisz** Pol
99D3	**Kaliua** Tanz
38J5	**Kalix** *R* Sweden
100A3	**Kalkfeld** Namibia
100A3	**Kalkrand** Namibia
108A1	**Kallakoopah** *R* Aust
38K6	**Kallávesi** *L* Fin
55C3	**Kallonis Kólpos** *B* Greece
39H7	**Kalmar** Sweden
61G4	**Kalmytskaya Respublika,** Russian Fed
100B2	**Kalomo** Zambia
18B1	**Kalona** USA
13B2	**Kalone Peak** *Mt* Can
87A2	**Kalpeni** *I* India
85D3	**Kālpi** India
53A3	**Kalsat Khasba** Tunisia
12B2	**Kalskag** USA
12C2	**Kaltag** USA
60E3	**Kaluga** Russian Fed
39G7	**Kalundborg** Den
59C3	**Kalush** Ukraine
87B2	**Kalyandurg** India
60E2	**Kalyazin** Russian Fed
61H1	**Kama** *R* Russian Fed
74E3	**Kamaishi** Japan
84C2	**Kamalia** Pak
110C1	**Kamanawa Mts** NZ
100A2	**Kamanjab** Namibia
84D2	**Kamat** *Mt* India
87B3	**Kamban** India
61H2	**Kambarka** Russian Fed
97A4	**Kambia** Sierra Leone
59D3	**Kamenets Podolskiy** Ukraine
61F3	**Kamenka** Russian Fed
65K4	**Kamen-na-Obi** Russian Fed
61K2	**Kamensk-Ural'skiy** Russian Fed
5H3	**Kamilukuak L** Can
98C3	**Kamina** Zaïre
7A3	**Kaminak L** Can
75C1	**Kaminoyama** Japan
5F4	**Kamloops** Can
93E1	**Kamo** Armenia
75C1	**Kamogawa** Japan
99D2	**Kampala** Uganda
77C5	**Kampar** Malay
78A2	**Kampar** *R* Indon
56B2	**Kampen** Neth
76B2	**Kamphaeng Phet** Thai
77C3	**Kampot** Camb
91D4	**Kamsaptar** Iran
61J2	**Kamskoye Vodokhranilishche** *Res* Russian Fed
85D4	**Kāmthi** India
61G3	**Kamyshin** Russian Fed
61K2	**Kamyshlov** Russian Fed
7C4	**Kanaaupscow** *R* Can
98C3	**Kananga** Zaïre
61G2	**Kanash** Russian Fed
75B1	**Kanayama** Japan
74D3	**Kanazawa** Japan
4C3	**Kanbisha** USA
87B2	**Kānchipuram** India
84B2	**Kandahar** Afghan
64E3	**Kandalaksha** Russian Fed
38L5	**Kandalakshskaya Guba** *B* Russian Fed
97C3	**Kandi** Benin
109C2	**Kandos** Aust
87C3	**Kandy** Sri Lanka
15C2	**Kane** USA
6C1	**Kane Basin** *B* Can
98B1	**Kanem** *Desert Region* Chad
97B3	**Kangaba** Mali
92C2	**Kangal** Turk
6E3	**Kangâmiut** Greenland
91B4	**Kangān** Iran
77C4	**Kangar** Malay
106C4	**Kangaroo I** Aust
6E3	**Kangâtsiaq** Greenland
90A3	**Kangavar** Iran
72C1	**Kangbao** China
82C3	**Kangchenjunga** *Mt* Nepal
73A4	**Kangding** China
6G3	**Kangerdlugssuaq** *B* Greenland
6G3	**Kangerdlugssvatsaiq** *B* Greenland
99D2	**Kangetet** Kenya
74B2	**Kanggye** N Korea
7D4	**Kangiqsualujjuaq** Can
6C3	**Kangiqsujuaq** Can
7C3	**Kangirsuk** Can
74B3	**Kangnŭng** S Korea
98B2	**Kango** Gabon
68B4	**Kangto** *Mt* China
72B3	**Kang Xian** China
77D4	**Kanh Hung** Viet
98C3	**Kaniama** Zaïre
87B1	**Kani Giri** India
39J6	**Kankaanpää** Fin
14A2	**Kankakee** USA
14A2	**Kankakee** *R* USA
97B3	**Kankan** Guinea
86A2	**Kānker** India
87B3	**Kanniyākuman** India
97C3	**Kano** Nig
74C4	**Kanoya** Japan
86A1	**Kānpur** India
9D3	**Kansas** State, USA
18A2	**Kansas** *R* USA
10A3	**Kansas City** USA
73D5	**Kanshi** China
63B2	**Kansk** Russian Fed
97C3	**Kantchari** Burkina
86B2	**Kanthi** India
12D2	**Kantishna** USA
12D2	**Kantishna** *R* USA
100B3	**Kanye** Botswana
68D4	**Kao-hsiung** Taiwan
100A2	**Kaoka Veld** *Plain* Namibia
97A3	**Kaolack** Sen
100B2	**Kaoma** Zambia
21C4	**Kapaau** Hawaiian Is
98C3	**Kapanga** Zaïre
6F3	**Kap Cort Adelaer** *C* Greenland
6H3	**Kap Dalton** *C* Greenland
39H7	**Kapellskär** Sweden
6F3	**Kap Farvel** *C* Greenland
6G3	**Kap Gustav Holm** *C* Greenland
100B2	**Kapiri** Zambia
78C2	**Kapit** Malay
19B3	**Kaplan** USA
57C3	**Kaplice** Czech Republic
77B4	**Kapoe** Thai
99C3	**Kapona** Zaïre
52C1	**Kaposvár** Hung
6C2	**Kap Parry** *C* Can
6H3	**Kap Ravn** *C* Greenland
78B3	**Kapuas** *R* Indon
108A2	**Kapunda** Aust
84D2	**Kapurthala** India
7B5	**Kapuskasing** Can
109D2	**Kaputar** *Mt* Aust
93E2	**Kapydzhik** *Mt* Armenia
6D2	**Kap York** *C* Greenland
92B1	**Karabük** Turk
55C2	**Karacabey** Turk
85B4	**Karachi** Pak
87A1	**Karād** India
60E5	**Kara Daglari** *Mt* Turk
54C5	**Karadeniz Boğazi** *Sd* Turk
68D1	**Karaftit** Russian Fed
65J5	**Karaganda** Kazakhstan
65J5	**Karagayly** Kazakhstan
87B2	**Kāraikāl** India
90B2	**Karaj** Iran
92C3	**Karak** Jordan
65G5	**Kara Kalpakskaya Respublika,** Uzbekistan
84D1	**Karakax He** *R* China
71D3	**Karakelong** *I* Indon
84D1	**Karakoram Mts** India
84D1	**Karakoram** *P* India/China
97A3	**Karakoro** *R* Maur/Sen
65G6	**Karakumy** *Desert* Russian Fed
94B3	**Karama** Jordan
92B2	**Karaman** Turk
65K5	**Karamay** China
111B2	**Karamea** NZ
111B2	**Karamea Bight** *B* NZ
85D4	**Kāranja** India
92B2	**Karapınar** Turk
64H2	**Kara S** Russian Fed
100A3	**Karasburg** Namibia
38K5	**Karasjok** Nor
65J4	**Karasuk** Russian Fed
92C2	**Karataş** Turk
65H5	**Kara Tau** *Mts* Kazakhstan
76B3	**Karathuri** Burma
74B4	**Karatsu** Japan
91B4	**Karāz** Iran
93D3	**Karbalā'** Iraq
59C3	**Karcag** Hung
55B3	**Kardhitsa** Greece
64E3	**Karel'skaya Respublika,** Russian Fed
38J5	**Karesvando** Sweden
96B2	**Karet** *Desert Region* Maur
65K4	**Kargasok** Russian Fed
97D3	**Kari** Nig
100B2	**Kariba** Zim
100B2	**Kariba** *L* Zim/Zambia
100B2	**Kariba Dam** Zim/Zambia
95C3	**Karima** Sudan
78B3	**Karimata** *I* Indon
86C2	**Karimganj** Bang
87B1	**Karimnagar** India
99E1	**Karin** Somalia
39J6	**Karis** Fin
99C3	**Karishimbe** *Mt* Zaïre
55B3	**Káristos** Greece
87A2	**Kārkal** India
71F4	**Karkar** *I* PNG
90A3	**Karkheh** *R* Iran
60D4	**Karkinitskiy Zaliv** *B* Ukraine
63B3	**Karlik Shan** *Mt* China
52B2	**Karlino** Pol
52C2	**Karlobag** Croatia
52C1	**Karlovac** Croatia
54B2	**Karlovo** Bulg
57C2	**Karlovy Vary** Czech Republic
39G7	**Karlshamn** Sweden
39G7	**Karlskoga** Sweden
39H7	**Karlskrona** Sweden
57B3	**Karlsruhe** Germany
39G7	**Karlstad** Sweden
12D3	**Karluk** USA
86C2	**Karnafuli Res** Bang
84D3	**Karnal** India
87A1	**Karnataka** State, India
54C2	**Karnobat** Bulg
100B2	**Karoi** Zim
99D3	**Karonga** Malawi
95C3	**Karora** Sudan
78D3	**Karossa** Indon
55C3	**Kárpathos** *I* Greece
6E2	**Karrats Fjord** Greenland
93D1	**Kars** Turk
65H4	**Karsakpay** Kazakhstan
58D1	**Kärsava** Latvia
80E2	**Karshi** Uzbekistan
38J6	**Karstula** Fin
94B1	**Kartaba** Leb
54C2	**Kartal** Turk
61K3	**Kartaly** Russian Fed
90A3	**Kārūn** *R* Iran
86A1	**Karwa** India
87A2	**Kārwār** India
68D1	**Karymskoye** Russian Fed
98B3	**Kasai** *R* Zaïre
100B2	**Kasaji** Zaïre
101C2	**Kasama** Zambia
99D3	**Kasanga** Tanz
87A2	**Kāsaragod** India
5H3	**Kasba L** Can
100B2	**Kasempa** Zambia
100B2	**Kasenga** Zaïre
99D2	**Kasese** Uganda
90B3	**Kāshān** Iran
12C2	**Kashegelok** USA
82B2	**Kashi** China
84D3	**Kashipur** India
74D3	**Kashiwazaki** Japan
90C2	**Kashmar** Iran
66D3	**Kashmir** State, India
61F3	**Kasimov** Russian Fed
18C2	**Kaskaskia** *R* USA
38J6	**Kaskinen** Fin
61K2	**Kasli** Russian Fed
5G5	**Kaslo** Can
98C3	**Kasongo** Zaïre
98B3	**Kasongo-Lunda** Zaïre
55C3	**Kásos** *I* Greece
	Kaspiyskiy = Lagan'
95C3	**Kassala** Sudan
56B2	**Kassel** Germany
96C1	**Kasserine** Tunisia
100A2	**Kassinga** Angola
92B1	**Kastamonou** Turk
55B3	**Kastélli** Greece
92A2	**Kastellorizon** *I* Greece
55B2	**Kastoría** Greece
55C3	**Kástron** Greece
74D3	**Kasugai** Japan
75A1	**Kasumi** Japan
101C2	**Kasungu** Malawi
84C2	**Kasur** Pak
100B2	**Kataba** Zambia
98C3	**Katako-kombe** Zaïre
4D3	**Katalla** USA
63G2	**Katangli** Russian Fed
106A4	**Katanning** Aust
55B2	**Katerini** Greece
5E4	**Kates Needle** *Mt* Can/USA
82D3	**Katha** Burma
106C2	**Katherine** Aust
85C4	**Kāthiāwār** *Pen* India
86B1	**Kathmandu** Nepal
84D1	**Kathua** India
86B1	**Katihār** India
100B2	**Katima Mulilo** Namibia
4C4	**Katmai,Mt** USA
12D3	**Katmai Nat Mon** USA
86A2	**Katni** India
109D2	**Katoomba** Aust
59B2	**Katowice** Pol
39H7	**Katrineholm** Sweden

Kiambi

75A2 **Komatsushima** Japan
64G3 **Komi Respublika,** Russian Fed
70C4 **Komodo** *I* Indon
71E4 **Komoran** *I* Indon
75B1 **Komoro** Japan
55C2 **Komotiní** Greece
76D3 **Kompong Cham** Camb
76C3 **Kompong Chhnang** *Mts* Camb
77C3 **Kompong Som** Camb
76C3 **Kompong Thom** Camb
76D3 **Kompong Trabek** Camb
63F2 **Komsomol'sk na Amure** Russian Fed
65H4 **Konda** *R* Russian Fed
99D3 **Kondoa** Tanz
87B1 **Kondukūr** India
6G3 **Kong Christian IX Land** *Region* Greenland
6F3 **Kong Frederik VI Kyst** *Mts* Greenland
64C2 **Kong Karls Land** *Is* Barents S
78D2 **Kongkemul** *Mt* Indon
98C3 **Kongolo** Zaïre
39F7 **Kongsberg** Den
39G6 **Kongsvinger** Nor
Königsberg = Kaliningrad
58B2 **Konin** Pol
54A2 **Konjic** Bosnia-Herzegovina
61F1 **Konosha** Russian Fed
75B1 **Konosu** Japan
60D3 **Konotop** Ukraine
59C2 **Końskie** Pol
49D2 **Konstanz** Germany
97C3 **Kontagora** Nig
76D3 **Kontum** Viet
92B2 **Konya** Turk
13D3 **Kootenay** *R* Can
85C5 **Kopargaon** India
6J3 **Kópasker** Iceland
38A2 **Kópavogur** Iceland
52B1 **Koper** Slovenia
80D2 **Kopet Dag** *Mts* Iran/Turkmenistan
61K2 **Kopeysk** Russian Fed
77C4 **Ko Phangan** *I* Thai
77B4 **Ko Phuket** *I* Thai
39H7 **Köping** Sweden
87B1 **Koppal** India
52C1 **Koprivnica** Croatia
85B4 **Korangi** Pak
87C1 **Koraput** India
86A2 **Korba** India
57B2 **Korbach** Germany
4B3 **Korbuk** *R* USA
55B2 **Korçe** Alb
52C2 **Korčula** *I* Croatia
72E2 **Korea B** China/Korea
74B4 **Korea Str** S Korea/Japan
59D2 **Korec** Ukraine
92B1 **Körğlu Tepesi** *Mt* Turk
97D4 **Korhogo** Ivory Coast
85B4 **Kori Creek** India
55B3 **Korinthiakós Kólpos** *G* Greece
55B3 **Kórinthos** Greece
74E3 **Kōriyama** Japan
61K3 **Korkino** Russian Fed
92B2 **Korkuteli** Turk
82C1 **Korla** China
52C2 **Kornat** *I* Croatia
60D5 **Köroğlu Tepesi** *Mt* Turk
99D3 **Korogwe** Tanz
108B3 **Koroit** Aust
71E3 **Koror** Palau Is, Pacific O
59C3 **Körös** *R* Hung
60C3 **Korosten** Ukraine
95A3 **Koro Toro** Chad
12B3 **Korovin** *I* USA
69G2 **Korsakov** Russian Fed
39G7 **Korsør** Den
46B1 **Kortrijk** Belg
55C3 **Kós** *I* Greece
77C4 **Ko Samui** *I* Thai
58B2 **Koscierzyna** Pol
107D4 **Kosciusko** *Mt* Aust
12H3 **Kosciusko I** USA
74B4 **Koshikijima-retto** *I* Japan
59C3 **Košice** Slovakia
74B3 **Kosong** N Korea
54B2 **Kosovo** Aut Republic, Serbia, Yugos
97B4 **Kossou** *L* Ivory Coast
101G1 **Koster** S Africa
99D1 **Kosti** Sudan
59D2 **Kostopol'** Ukraine
61F2 **Kostroma** Russian Fed
56C2 **Kostrzyn** Pol
39H8 **Koszalin** Pol
85D3 **Kota** India
78A4 **Kotaagung** Indon
78C3 **Kotabaharu** Indon
78D3 **Kotabaru** Indon
77C4 **Kota Bharu** Malay
78A3 **Kotabum** Indon
84C2 **Kot Addu** Pak
78D1 **Kota Kinabulu** Malay
87C1 **Kotapad** India
61G2 **Kotel'nich** Russian Fed
61F4 **Kotel'nikovo** Russian Fed
39K6 **Kotka** Fin
64F3 **Kotlas** Russian Fed
12B2 **Kotlik** USA
54A2 **Kotor** Montenegro, Yugos
60C4 **Kotovsk** Ukraine
85B3 **Kotri** Pak
87C1 **Kottagūdem** India
87B3 **Kottayam** India
98C2 **Kotto** *R* CAR
87B2 **Kottūru** India
12B1 **Kotzebue** USA
4B3 **Kotzebue Sd** USA
97C3 **Kouande** Benin
98C2 **Kouango** CAR
97B3 **Koudougou** Burkina
98B3 **Koulamoutou** Gabon
97B3 **Koulikoro** Mali
97B3 **Koupéla** Burkina
33G2 **Kourou** French Guiana
97B3 **Kouroussa** Guinea
98B1 **Kousséri** Cam
39K6 **Kouvola** Fin
38L5 **Kovdor** Russian Fed
60B3 **Kovel'** Ukraine
Kovno = Kaunas
61F2 **Kovrov** Russian Fed
61F3 **Kovylkino** Russian Fed
60E1 **Kovzha** *R* Russian Fed
77C4 **Ko Way** *I* Thai
73C5 **Kowloon** Hong Kong
84B2 **Kowt-e-Ashrow** Afghan
92A2 **Köyceğğiz** Turk
38L5 **Koydor** Russian Fed
87A1 **Koyna Res** India
12B2 **Koyuk** USA
12B1 **Koyuk** *R* USA
12C2 **Koyukuk** USA
12C1 **Koyukuk** *R* USA
92C2 **Kozan** Turk
55B2 **Kozańi** Greece
Kozhikode = Calicut
61G2 **Koz'modemyansk** Russian Fed
75B2 **Kōzu-shima** *I* Japan
39F7 **Kragerø** Nor
54B2 **Kragujevac** Serbia, Yugos
77B3 **Kra,Isthmus of** Burma/Malay
Krakatau = Rakata
94C1 **Krak des Chevaliers** *Hist Site* Syria
Kraków = Cracow
54B2 **Kraljevo** Serbia, Yugos
60E4 **Kramatorsk** Ukraine
38H6 **Kramfors** Sweden
52B1 **Kranj** Slovenia
61G1 **Krasavino** Russian Fed
64G2 **Krasino** Russian Fed
59C2 **Kraśnik** Pol
61G3 **Krasnoarmeysk** Russian Fed
60E5 **Krasnodar** Russian Fed
61J2 **Krasnokamsk** Russian Fed
61K2 **Krasnotur'insk** Russian Fed
61J2 **Krasnoufimsk** Russian Fed
61J3 **Krasnousol'-skiy** Russian Fed
65G3 **Krasnovishersk** Russian Fed
65G5 **Krasnovodsk** Turkmenistan
63B2 **Krasnoyarsk** Russian Fed
59C2 **Krasnystaw** Pol
61G3 **Krasnyy Kut** Russian Fed
60E4 **Krasnyy Luch** Ukraine
61G4 **Krasnyy Yar** Russian Fed
76D3 **Kratie** Camb
6E2 **Kraulshavn** Greenland
56B2 **Krefeld** Germany
60D4 **Kremenchug** Ukraine
60D4 **Kremenchugskoye Vodokhranilische** *Res* Ukraine
59D2 **Kremenets** Ukraine
98A2 **Kribi** Cam
60D3 **Krichev** Belorussia
47C1 **Krimml** Austria
87B1 **Krishna** *R* India
87B2 **Krishnagiri** India
86B2 **Krishnangar** India
39F7 **Kristiansand** Nor
39G7 **Kristianstad** Sweden
64B3 **Kristiansund** Nor
39G7 **Kristinehamn** Sweden
38J6 **Kristiinankaupunki** Fin
55B3 **Kríti** *I* Greece
60D4 **Krivoy Rog** Ukraine
52B1 **Krk** *I* Croatia
6G3 **Kronpris Frederik Bjerge** *Mts* Greenland
39K7 **Kronshtadt** Russian Fed
101G1 **Kroonstad** S Africa
65F5 **Kropotkin** Russian Fed
101G1 **Krugersdorp** S Africa
78A4 **Krui** Indon
55A2 **Kruje** Alb
58D2 **Krupki** Belorussia
12B1 **Krusenstern,C** USA
54B2 **Kruševac** Serbia, Yugos
39K7 **Krustpils** Latvia
12G3 **Kruzof I** USA
65E5 **Krym** *Pen* Ukraine
60E5 **Krymsk** Russian Fed
58B2 **Krzyz** Pol
96C1 **Ksar El Boukhari** Alg
96B1 **Ksar el Kebir** Mor
70A3 **Kuala** Indon
77C5 **Kuala Dungun** Malay
77C4 **Kuala Kerai** Malay
77C5 **Kuala Kubu Baharu** Malay
77C5 **Kuala Lipis** Malay
77C5 **Kuala Lumpur** Malay
77C4 **Kuala Trengganu** Malay
78D1 **Kuamut** Malay
74A2 **Kuandian** China
77C5 **Kuantan** Malay
93E1 **Kuba** Azerbaijan
71F4 **Kubar** PNG
78C2 **Kuching** Malay
70C3 **Kudat** Malay
78C4 **Kudus** Indon
61H2 **Kudymkar** Russian Fed
57C3 **Kufstein** Austria
90C3 **Kuh Duren** *Upland* Iran
91C4 **Kūh e Bazmān** *Mt* Iran
90B3 **Kūh-e Dinar** *Mt* Iran
90C2 **Kūh-e-Hazār Masjed** *Mts* Iran
91C4 **Kūh-e Jebāl Barez** *Mts* Iran
90B3 **Kūh-e Karkas** *Mts* Iran
91C4 **Kuh-e Laleh Zar** *Mt* Iran
90A2 **Kūh-e Sahand** *Mt* Iran
91D4 **Kuh e Taftān** *Mt* Iran
90A2 **Kūhhaye Sabalan** *Mts* Iran
90A3 **Kūhhā-ye Zāgros** *Mts* Iran
38K6 **Kuhmo** Fin
90B3 **Kūhpāyeh** Iran
90C3 **Kūhpāyeh** *Mt* Iran
91C4 **Kūh ye Bashākerd** *Mts* Iran
90A2 **Kūh ye Sabalan** *Mt* Iran
100A3 **Kuibis** Namibia
4B4 **Kuigillingok** USA
100A2 **Kuito** Angola
12H3 **Kuiu I** USA
74E2 **Kuji** Japan
75A2 **Kuju-san** *Mt* Japan
12C3 **Kukaklek L** USA
54B2 **Kukës** Alb
77C5 **Kukup** Malay
91C4 **Kūl** *R* Iran
55C3 **Kula** Turk
61J4 **Kulakshi** Kazakhstan
99D2 **Kulal,Mt** Kenya
55B2 **Kulata** Bulg
60B2 **Kuldīga** Latvia
61H4 **Kul'sary** Kazakhstan
84D2 **Kulu** India
92B2 **Kulu** Turk
65J4 **Kulunda** Russian Fed
108B2 **Kulwin** Aust
61G5 **Kuma** *R* Russian Fed
75B1 **Kumagaya** Japan
78C3 **Kumai** Indon
74C4 **Kumamoto** Japan
75B2 **Kumano** Japan
54B2 **Kumanovo** Macedonia
63E2 **Kumara** China
97B4 **Kumasi** Ghana
65F5 **Kumayri** Armenia
98A2 **Kumba** Cam
87B2 **Kumbakonam** India
61J3 **Kumertau** Russian Fed
74B3 **Kūmhwa** S Korea
39H7 **Kumla** Sweden
87A2 **Kumta** India
82C1 **Kümüx** China
84C2 **Kunar** *R* Afghan
39K7 **Kunda** Estonia
87A2 **Kundāpura** India
85C4 **Kundla** India
84B1 **Kunduz** Afghan
89F9 **Kunene** *R* Angola
39G7 **Kungsbacka** Sweden
61J2 **Kungur** Russian Fed
76B1 **Kunhing** Burma
82B2 **Kunlun Shan** *Mts* China
73A4 **Kunming** China
74B3 **Kunsan** S Korea
38K6 **Kuopio** Fin
52C1 **Kupa** *R* Croatia/Bosnia-Herzegovina
106B2 **Kupang** Indon
107D2 **Kupiano** PNG
12H3 **Kupreanof I** USA

Leine

56B2 Leine *R* Germany
45C2 Leinster Region, Irish Rep
57C2 Leipzig Germany
50A2 Leiria Port
39F7 Leirvik Nor
45B1 Leitrim County, Irish Rep
73C4 Leiyang China
73B5 Leizhou Bandao *Pen* China
73C5 Leizhou Wan *B* China
56A2 Lek *R* Neth
96C1 Le Kef Tunisia
19B3 Leland USA
54A2 Lelija *Mt* Bosnia-Herzegovina
47B1 Le Locle France
48C2 Le Mans France
6D3 Lemicux Is Can
8C2 Lemmon USA
21B2 Lemoore USA
49C2 Lempdes France
86C2 Lemro *R* Burma
52C2 Le Murge Region, Italy
63C2 Lena *R* Russian Fed
38L6 Lendery Russian Fed
73C4 Lengshujiang China
Leningrad = Sankt-Peterburg
112B7 Leningradskaya *Base* Ant
61H3 Leninogorsk Tatarskaya Respublika, Russian Fed
68A1 Leninogorsk Kazakhstan
65K4 Leninsk-Kuznetskiy Russian Fed
69F2 Leninskoye Russian Fed
65F6 Lenkoran' Azerbaijan
46E1 Lenne *R* Germany
16C1 Lenox USA
46B1 Lens France
63D1 Lensk Russian Fed
53B3 Lentini Italy
76B3 Lenya *R* Burma
52B1 Leoben Austria
43C3 Leominster Eng
16D1 Leominster USA
24B2 Leon Mexico
25D3 León Nic
50A1 Leon Region, Spain
50A1 León Spain
100A3 Leonardville Namibia
106B3 Leonora Aust
35C2 Leopoldina Brazil
Léopoldville = Kinshasa
60C3 Lepel Belorussia
73D4 Leping China
49C2 Le Puy-en-Velay France
98B2 Léré Chad
101G1 Leribe Lesotho
47C2 Lerici Italy
51C1 Lérida Spain
23A1 Lerma *R* Mexico
47D1 Lermoos Austria
55C3 Léros *I* Greece
44E1 Lerwick Scot
46A2 Les Andelys France
26C3 Les Cayes Haiti
47B2 Les Ecrins *Mt* France
73A4 Leshan China
54B2 Leskovac Serbia, Yugos
48B3 Les Landes Region, France
101G1 Leslie S Africa
61H2 Lesnoy Russian Fed
63B2 Lesosibirsk Russian Fed
101G1 Lesotho Kingdom, S Africa
69F2 Lesozavodsk Russian Fed
48B2 Les Sables-d'Olonne France

112A Lesser Antarctica Region, Ant
27D4 Lesser Antilles *Is* Caribbean S
65F5 Lesser Caucasus *Mts* Azerbaijan/Georgia
13E1 Lesser Slave L Can
55C3 Lésvos *I* Greece
58B2 Leszno Pol
86C2 Letha Range *Mts* Burma
5G5 Lethbridge Can
33F3 Lethem Guyana
59D3 Letichev Ukraine
63D2 Let Oktyobr'ya Russian Fed
78B2 Letong Indon
46A1 Le Touquet-Paris-Plage France
76B2 Letpadan Burma
48C1 Le Tréport France
47B1 Leuk Switz
57A2 Leuven Belg
55B3 Levádhia Greece
38G6 Levanger Nor
47B2 Levanna *Mt* Italy
71D5 Lévèque,C Aust
46D1 Leverkusen Germany
59B3 Levice Slovakia
47D1 Levico Italy
110C2 Levin NZ
7C5 Lévis Can
15D2 Levittown USA
55B3 Lévka -ri *Mt* Greece
55B3 Levkás Greece
55B3 Levkás *I* Greece
106B2 Lévèque,C Aust
54C2 Levski Bulg
43E4 Lewes Eng
40B2 Lewis *I* Scot
16A2 Lewisburg USA
111B2 Lewis P NZ
8B2 Lewis Range *Mts* USA
8B2 Lewiston Idaho, USA
10C2 Lewiston Maine, USA
8C2 Lewistown Montana, USA
15C2 Lewistown Pennsylvania, USA
19B3 Lewisville USA
11B3 Lexington Kentucky, USA
18B2 Lexington Missouri, USA
15C3 Lexington Park USA
79C3 Leyte G Phil
54A2 Lezhe Alb
82D3 Lhasa China
86B1 Lhazê China
70A3 Lhokseumawe Indon
86C1 Lhozhag China
68B4 Lhunze China
Liancourt Rocks = Tok-do
79C4 Lianga Phil
72B3 Liangdang China
73C5 Lianjiang China
73C5 Lianping China
73C5 Lian Xian China
72D3 Lianyungang China
72E1 Liaoding Bandao *Pen* China
72E1 Liaodong Wan *B* China
72E1 Liao He *R* China
72E1 Liaoning Province, China
72E1 Liaoyang China
72E1 Liaoyuan China
74B2 Liaoyuang China
4F3 Liard *R* Can
4F4 Liard River Can
46C2 Liart France
98B2 Libenge Zaïre
9C3 Liberal USA
57C2 Liberec Czech Republic
97A4 Liberia Republic, Africa
18B2 Liberty Missouri, USA

15D2 Liberty New York, USA
19B3 Liberty Texas, USA
48B3 Libourne France
23B2 Libres Mexico
98A2 Libreville Gabon
95A2 Libya Republic, Africa
95B2 Libyan Desert Libya
95B1 Libyan Plat Egypt
53B3 Licata Italy
43D3 Lichfield Eng
101C2 Lichinga Mozam
101G1 Lichtenburg S Africa
14B3 Licking *R* USA
22B2 Lick Observatory USA
60C3 Lida Belorussia
39G7 Lidköping Sweden
53B2 Lido di Ostia Italy
52A1 Liechtenstein Principality, Europe
57B2 Liège Belg
58C1 Lielupe *R* Latvia
98C2 Lienart Zaïre
57C3 Lienz Austria
60B2 Liepäja Latvia
46C1 Lier Belg
47B1 Liestal Switz
15C1 Liévre *R* Can
57C3 Liezen Austria
45C2 Liffey *R* Irish Rep
45C1 Lifford Irish Rep
107F3 Lifu *I* Nouvelle Calédonie
109C1 Lightning Ridge Aust
46C2 Ligny-en-Barrois France
101C2 Ligonha *R* Mozam
47C2 Liguria Region, Italy
52A2 Ligurian *S* Italy
21C4 Lihue Hawaiian Is
100B2 Likasi Zaïre
49C1 Lille France
39G6 Lillehammer Nor
46B1 Lillers France
39G7 Lillestøm Nor
13C2 Lillooet Can
13C2 Lillooet *R* Can
101C2 Lilongwe Malawi
79B4 Liloy Phil
54A2 Lim *R* Montenegro/Serbia, Yugos
32B6 Lima Peru
50A1 Lima Spain
10B2 Lima USA
92B3 Limassol Cyprus
45C1 Limavady N Ire
34B3 Limay *R* Arg
34B3 Limay Mahuida Arg
98A2 Limbe Cam
101C2 Limbe Malawi
57B2 Limburg W Gem
31B6 Limeira Brazil
45B2 Limerick County, Irish Rep
41B3 Limerick Irish Rep
56B1 Limfjorden *L* Den
106C2 Limmen Bight *B* Aust
55C3 Límnos *I* Greece
31D3 Limoeiro Brazil
48C2 Limoges France
25D4 Limón Costa Rica
8C3 Limon USA
48C2 Limousin Region, France
79A3 Linapacan Str Phil
29B3 Linares Chile
9D4 Linares Mexico
50B2 Linares Spain
68B4 Lincang China
29D2 Lincoln Arg
18A1 Lincoln California, USA
42D3 Lincoln County, Eng
42D3 Lincoln Eng
18C1 Lincoln Illinois, USA
8D2 Lincoln Nebraska, USA
15D2 Lincoln New Hampshire, USA
111B2 Lincoln NZ
80A Lincoln *S* Greenland

20B2 Lincoln City USA
14B2 Lincoln Park USA
52A2 L'Incudina *Mt* Corse
57B3 Lindau Germany
33F2 Linden Guyana
39F7 Lindesnes *C* Nor
99D3 Lindi Tanz
98C2 Lindi *R* Zaïre
101G1 Lindley S Africa
55C3 Lindos Greece
15C2 Lindsay Can
105J3 Line Is Pacific O
72C2 Linfen China
76D2 Lingao China
79B2 Lingayen Phil
56B2 Lingen Germany
73C4 Lingling China
73B5 Lingshan China
72C2 Lingshi China
97A3 Linguère Sen
73E4 Linhai Rhejiang, China
31D5 Linhares Brazil
72B1 Linhe China
74B2 Linjiang China
39H7 Linköping Sweden
72D2 Linqing China
35B2 Lins Brazil
72A2 Lintao China
47C1 Linthal Switz
68D2 Linxi China
72A2 Linxia China
57C3 Linz Austria
79B3 Lipa Phil
53B3 Lipari *I* Italy
61E3 Lipetsk Russian Fed
54B1 Lipova Rom
56B2 Lippe *R* Germany
46E1 Lippstadt Germany
99D2 Lira Uganda
98B3 Liranga Congo
98C2 Lisala Zaïre
50A2 Lisboa Port
Lisbon = Lisboa
45C1 Lisburn N Ire
45B2 Liscannor B Irish Rep
73D4 Lishui China
73C4 Li Shui *R* China
60E4 Lisichansk Ukraine
48C2 Lisieux France
60E3 Liski Russian Fed
46B2 L'Isle-Adam France
47B1 L'Isle-sur-le-Doubs France
107E3 Lismore Aust
45B2 Listowel Irish Rep
73B5 Litang China
94B2 Litani *R* Leb
33G3 Litani *R* Surinam
18C2 Litchfield USA
107E4 Lithgow Aust
60B2 Lithuania Republic, Europe
16A2 Lititz USA
69F2 Litovko Russian Fed
19A3 Little *R* USA
11C4 Little Abaco *I* The Bahamas
110C1 Little Barrier I NZ
13E2 Little Bow *R* Can
25D3 Little Cayman *I* Caribbean S
16B3 Little Egg Harbor *B* USA
26C2 Little Inagua *I* Caribbean S
77A4 Little Nicobar *I* Nicobar Is
11A3 Little Rock USA
22D3 Littlerock USA
13D2 Little Smoky Can
13D2 Little Smoky *R* Can
16A3 Littlestown USA
15D2 Littleton New Hampshire, USA
74B2 Liuhe China
73B5 Liuzhou China
55B3 Livanátais Greece
58D1 Līvāni Latvia
12E1 Livengood USA
17B1 Live Oak USA
21A2 Livermore USA
7D5 Liverpool Can
42C3 Liverpool Eng

Lubudi

4E2 **Liverpool B** Can
42C3 **Liverpool B** Eng
6C2 **Liverpool,C** Can
109D2 **Liverpool Range** *Mts* Aust
8B2 **Livingston** Montana, USA
19B3 **Livingston** Texas, USA
44C4 **Livingston** UK
Livingstone = Maramba
19A3 **Livingston,L** USA
52C2 **Livno** Bosnia-Herzegovina
60E3 **Livny** Russian Fed
14B2 **Livonia** USA
52B2 **Livorno** Italy
99D3 **Liwale** Tanz
52B1 **Ljubljana** Slovenia
38G6 **Ljungan** *R* Sweden
39G7 **Ljungby** Sweden
39H6 **Ljusdal** Sweden
38H6 **Ljusnan** *R* Sweden
43C4 **Llandeilo** Wales
43C4 **Llandovery** Wales
43C3 **Llandrindod Wells** Wales
42C3 **Llandudno** Wales
43B4 **Llanelli** Wales
43C3 **Llangollen** Wales
9C3 **Llano Estacado** *Plat* USA
32C2 **Llanos** Region, Colombia/Ven
30D2 **Llanos de Chiquitos** Region, Bol
Lleida = Lérida
50A2 **Llerena** Spain
43B3 **Lleyn** *Pen* Wales
89E7 **Llorin** Nig
5H4 **Lloydminster** Can
30C3 **Llullaillaco** *Mt* Arg/Chile
30C3 **Loa** *R* Chile
49C2 **Loan** France
98B3 **Loange** *R* Zaïre
100B3 **Lobatse** Botswana
98B2 **Lobaye** *R* CAR
34D3 **Loberia** Arg
100A2 **Lobito** Angola
34D3 **Lobos** Arg
47B2 **Locano** Italy
47C1 **Locarno** Switz
44B3 **Loch Awe** *L* Scot
44A3 **Lochboisdale** Scot
44A3 **Loch Bracadale** *Inlet* Scot
44B3 **Loch Broom** *Estuary* Scot
42B2 **Loch Doon** *L* Scot
44B3 **Loch Earn** *L* Scot
44B2 **Loch Eriboll** *Inlet* Scot
44B3 **Loch Ericht** *L* Scot
48C2 **Loches** France
44B3 **Loch Etive** *Inlet* Scot
44B3 **Loch Ewe** *Inlet* Scot
44B3 **Loch Fyne** *Inlet* Scot
44B3 **Loch Hourn** *Inlet* Scot
44B2 **Lochinver** Scot
44B3 **Loch Katrine** *L* Scot
44C3 **Loch Leven** *L* Scot
44B3 **Loch Linnhe** *Inlet* Scot
44B3 **Loch Lochy** *L* Scot
44B3 **Loch Lomond** *L* Scot
44B3 **Loch Long** *Inlet* Scot
44A3 **Lochmaddy** Scot
44B3 **Loch Maree** *L* Scot
44B3 **Loch Morar** *L* Scot
44C3 **Lochnagar** *Mt* Scot
44B3 **Loch Ness** *L* Scot
44B3 **Loch Rannoch** *L* Scot
44A2 **Loch Roag** *Inlet* Scot
44B3 **Loch Sheil** *L* Scot
44B2 **Loch Shin** *L* Scot
44A3 **Loch Snizort** *Inlet* Scot
44B3 **Loch Sunart** *Inlet* Scot
44B3 **Loch Tay** *L* Scot

44B3 **Loch Torridon** *Inlet* Scot
108A2 **Lock** Aust
42C2 **Lockerbie** Scot
15C2 **Lock Haven** USA
15C2 **Lockport** USA
76D3 **Loc Ninh** Viet
53C3 **Locri** Italy
94B3 **Lod** Israel
108B3 **Loddon** *R* Aust
60D1 **Lodeynoye Pole** Russian Fed
84C3 **Lodhran** Pak
52A1 **Lodi** Italy
21A2 **Lodi** USA
98C3 **Lodja** Zaïre
47B1 **Lods** France
99D2 **Lodwar** Kenya
58B2 **Łódź** Pol
38G5 **Lofoten** *Is* Nor
8B2 **Logan** Utah, USA
4D3 **Logan,Mt** Can
14A2 **Logansport** Indiana, USA
19B3 **Logansport** Louisiana, USA
50B1 **Logroño** Spain
86A2 **Lohärdaga** India
39J6 **Lohja** Fin
76B2 **Loikaw** Burma
39J6 **Loimaa** Fin
48C2 **Loir** *R* France
49C2 **Loire** *R* France
32B4 **Loja** Ecuador
50B2 **Loja** Spain
38K5 **Lokan Tekojärvi** *Res* Fin
46B1 **Lokeren** Belg
99D2 **Lokitaung** Kenya
58D1 **Loknya** Russian Fed
98C3 **Lokolo** *R* Zaïre
98C3 **Lokoro** *R* Zaïre
6D3 **Loks Land** *I* Can
56C2 **Lolland** *I* Den
54B2 **Lom** Bulg
98C3 **Lomami** *R* Zaïre
97A4 **Loma Mts** Sierra Leone/Guinea
47C2 **Lombardia** Region, Italy
71D4 **Lomblen** *I* Indon
78D4 **Lombok** *I* Indon
97C4 **Lomé** Togo
98C3 **Lomela** Zaïre
98C3 **Lomela** *R* Zaïre
60C2 **Lomonosov** Russian Fed
47B1 **Lomont** Region, France
21A3 **Lompoc** USA
58C2 **Łomza** Pol
87A1 **Lonävale** India
29B3 **Loncoche** Chile
7B6 **London** Can
43D4 **London** Eng
45C1 **Londonderry** County, N Ire
45C1 **Londonderry** N Ire
29B7 **Londonderry** *I* Chile
106B2 **Londonderry,C** Aust
30C4 **Londres** Arg
30F3 **Londrina** Brazil
21B2 **Lone Pine** USA
11C4 **Long** *I* The Bahamas
71F4 **Long** *I* PNG
78C2 **Long Akah** Malay
47E1 **Longarone** Italy
34A3 **Longavi** *Mt* Chile
27H2 **Long B** Jamaica
17C1 **Long B** USA
9B3 **Long Beach** California, USA
15D2 **Long Beach** New York, USA
15D2 **Long Branch** USA
73D5 **Longchuan** China
20C2 **Long Creek** USA
109C4 **Longford** Aust
45C2 **Longford** County, Irish Rep
45C2 **Longford** Irish Rep
44D3 **Long Forties** *Region* N Sea
72D1 **Longhua** China

7C4 **Long I** Can
10C2 **Long I** USA
16C2 **Long Island Sd** USA
7B4 **Longlac** Can
73B5 **Longlin** China
8C2 **Longmont** USA
78D2 **Longnawan** Indon
29B3 **Longquimay** Chile
107D3 **Longreach** Aust
72A2 **Longshou Shan** Upland China
42C2 **Longtown** Eng
15D1 **Longueuil** Can
34A3 **Longuimay** Chile
46C2 **Longuyon** France
11A3 **Longview** Texas, USA
8A2 **Longview** Washington, USA
46C2 **Longwy** France
72A3 **Longxi** China
77D3 **Long Xuyen** Viet
73D4 **Longyan** China
73B5 **Longzhou** China
47D2 **Lonigo** Italy
49D2 **Lons-le-Saunier** France
11C3 **Lookout,C** USA
99D3 **Loolmalasin** *Mt* Tanz
13D1 **Loon** *R* Can
45B2 **Loop Hd** *C* Irish Rep
76C3 **Lop Buri** Thai
98A3 **Lopez** *C* Gabon
68B2 **Lop Nur** *L* China
50A2 **Lora del Rio** Spain
10D2 **Lorain** USA
84B2 **Loralai** Pak
90B3 **Lordegān** Iran
107F4 **Lord Howe** *I* Aust
105G5 **Lord Howe Rise** Pacific O
6A3 **Lord Mayor B** Can
9C3 **Lordsburg** USA
35B2 **Lorena** Brazil
47E2 **Loreo** Italy
23A1 **Loreto** Mexico
40D2 **Lorient** France
108B3 **Lorne** Aust
57B3 **Lörrach** Germany
49D2 **Lorraine** Region, France
9C3 **Los Alamos** USA
34A2 **Los Andes** Chile
29B3 **Los Angeles** Chile
9B3 **Los Angeles** USA
21A2 **Los Banos** USA
34B2 **Los Cerrillos** Arg
21A2 **Los Gatos** USA
52B2 **Lošinj** *I* Croatia
29B3 **Los Lagos** Chile
24B2 **Los Mochis** Mexico
22B3 **Los Olivos** USA
34A3 **Los Sauces** Chile
44C3 **Lossiemouth** Scot
27E4 **Los Testigos** *Is* Ven
29B2 **Los Vilos** Chile
48C3 **Lot** *R* France
34A3 **Lota** Chile
42C2 **Lothian** Region, Scot
99D2 **Lotikipi Plain** Sudan/Kenya
98C3 **Loto** Zaïre
47B1 **Lötschberg Tunnel** Switz
38K5 **Lotta** *R* Fin/Russian Fed
48B2 **Loudéac** France
97A3 **Louga** Sen
41B3 **Lough Allen** *L* Irish Rep
45C2 **Lough Boderg** *L* Irish Rep
43D3 **Loughborough** Eng
45C2 **Lough Bowna** *L* Irish Rep
45C1 **Lough Carlingford** *L* N Ire
41B3 **Lough Conn** *L* Irish Rep
41B3 **Lough Corrib** *L* Irish Rep
41B3 **Lough Derg** *L* Irish Rep

45C2 **Lough Derravaragh** *L* Irish Rep
4H2 **Loughead I** Can
45C2 **Lough Ennell** *L* Irish Rep
41B3 **Lough Erne** *L* N Ire
40B2 **Lough Foyle** *Estuary* N Ire/Irish Rep
40B3 **Lough Neagh** *L* N Ire
45C1 **Lough Oughter** *L* Irish Rep
45B2 **Loughrea** Irish Rep
45C2 **Lough Ree** *L* Irish Rep
45C2 **Lough Sheelin** *L* Irish Rep
42B2 **Lough Strangford** *L* Irish Rep
45C1 **Lough Swilly** *Estuary* Irish Rep
14B3 **Louisa** USA
70C3 **Louisa Reef** *I* S E Asia
12E2 **Louise,L** USA
107E2 **Louisiade Arch** Solomon Is
11A3 **Louisiana** State, USA
17B1 **Louisville** Georgia, USA
11B3 **Louisville** Kentucky, USA
38L5 **Loukhi** Russian Fed
48B3 **Lourdes** France
108C2 **Louth** Aust
45C2 **Louth** County, Irish Rep
42D3 **Louth** Eng
Louvain = Leuven
48C2 **Louviers** France
60D2 **Lovat** *R* Russian Fed
54B2 **Lovech** Bulg
21B1 **Lovelock** USA
52B1 **Lóvere** Italy
9C3 **Lovington** USA
38L5 **Lovozero** Russian Fed
6B3 **Low,C** Can
10C2 **Lowell** Massachusetts, USA
20B2 **Lowell** Oregon, USA
16D1 **Lowell** USA
111B2 **Lower Hutt** NZ
43E3 **Lowestoft** Eng
58B2 **Łowicz** Pol
108B2 **Loxton** Aust
5F4 **Loyd George,Mt** Can
54A2 **Loznica** Serbia, Yugos
23A2 **Loz Reyes** Mexico
65H3 **Lozva** *R* Russian Fed
100B2 **Luacano** Angola
98C3 **Luachimo** Angola
98C3 **Lualaba** *R* Zaïre
100B2 **Luampa** Zambia
100B2 **Luân** Angola
73D3 **Lu'an** China
98B3 **Luanda** Angola
100A2 **Luando** *R* Angola
100B2 **Luanginga** *R* Angola
76C1 **Luang Namtha** Laos
76C2 **Luang Prabang** Laos
98B3 **Luangue** *R* Angola
100C2 **Luangwa** *R* Zambia
72D1 **Luan He** *R* China
72D1 **Luanping** China
100B2 **Luanshya** Zambia
100B2 **Luapula** *R* Zaïre
50A1 **Luarca** Spain
98B3 **Lubalo** Angola
58B2 **L'uban** Belorussia
79B3 **Lubang Is** Phil
100A2 **Lubango** Angola
9C3 **Lubbock** USA
56C2 **Lübeck** Germany
98C3 **Lubefu** Zaïre
98C3 **Lubefu** *R* Zaïre
99C3 **Lubero** Zaïre
98C3 **Lubilash** *R* Zaïre
59C2 **Lublin** Pol
60D3 **Lubny** Ukraine
78C2 **Lubok Antu** Malay
98C3 **Lubudi** Zaïre
98C3 **Lubudi** *R* Zaïre

Lubuklinggau

15D1	**Magog** Can
23B1	**Magosal** Mexico
13E2	**Magrath** Can
7A3	**Maguse River** Can
76B1	**Magwe** Burma
90A2	**Mahābād** Iran
86B1	**Mahabharat Range** *Mts* Nepal
87A1	**Mahād** India
85D4	**Mahadeo Hills** India
101D2	**Mahajanga** Madag
100B3	**Mahalapye** Botswana
86A2	**Mahānadi** *R* India
101D2	**Mahanoro** Madag
16A2	**Mahanoy City** USA
87A1	**Maharashtra** State, India
86A2	**Māhāsamund** India
76C2	**Maha Sarakham** Thai
101D2	**Mahavavy** *R* Madag
87B1	**Mahbūbnagar** India
96D1	**Mahdia** Tunisia
87B2	**Mahe** India
85D4	**Mahekar** India
101D2	**Mahéli** *I* Comoros
86A2	**Mahendragarh** India
99D3	**Mahenge** Tanz
85C4	**Mahesāna** India
110C1	**Mahia Pen** NZ
85D3	**Mahoba** India
51C2	**Mahón** Spain
12J1	**Mahony L** Can
96D1	**Mahrés** Tunisia
85C4	**Mahuva** India
32C1	**Maicao** Colombia
47B1	**Maiche** France
43E4	**Maidstone** Eng
98B1	**Maiduguri** Nig
06A2	**Maihar** India
86C2	**Maijdi** Bang
70D3	**Mail Kyun** *I* Burma
84A1	**Maimana** Afghan
14B1	**Main Chan** Can
98B3	**Mai-Ndombe** *L* Zaïre
10D2	**Maine** State, USA
48B2	**Maine** *Region* France
44C2	**Mainland** *I* Scot
85D3	**Mainpuri** India
46A2	**Maintenon** France
101D2	**Maintirano** Madag
57B2	**Mainz** Germany
97A4	**Maio** *I* Cape Verde
29C2	**Maipó** *Mt* Arg/Chile
34D3	**Maipú** Arg
32D1	**Maiquetia** Ven
47B2	**Maira** *R* Italy
86C1	**Mairābāri** India
86C2	**Maiskhal I** Bang
107E4	**Maitland** New South Wales, Aust
108A2	**Maitland** S Australia, Aust
112C12	**Maitri** *Base* Ant
74D3	**Maizuru** Japan
70C4	**Majene** Indon
30B2	**Majes** *R* Peru
99D2	**Maji** Eth
72D2	**Majia He** *R* China
	Majunga = **Mahajanga**
70C4	**Makale** Indon
86B1	**Makalu** *Mt* China/Nepal
98B2	**Makanza** Zaïre
52C2	**Makarska** Croatia
61F2	**Makaryev** Russian Fed
	Makassar = **Ujung Pandang**
78D3	**Makassar Str** Indon
61H4	**Makat** Kazakhstan
97A4	**Makeni** Sierra Leone
60E4	**Makeyevka** Ukraine
100B3	**Makgadikgadi** *Salt Pan* Botswana
61G5	**Makhachkala** Russian Fed
99D3	**Makindu** Kenya
88H5	**Makkah** S Arabia
7E4	**Makkovik** Can
59C3	**Makó** Hung
98B2	**Makokou** Gabon
110C1	**Makorako,Mt** NZ

98B2	**Makoua** Congo
85C3	**Makrāna** India
85A3	**Makran Coast Range** *Mts* Pak
96C1	**Makthar** Tunisia
93D2	**Mākū** Iran
98C3	**Makumbi** Zaïre
74C4	**Makurazaki** Japan
97C4	**Makurdi** Nig
79B4	**Malabang** Phil
87A2	**Malabar Coast** India
89E7	**Malabo** Bioko
77C5	**Malacca,Str of** S E Asia
32C2	**Málaga** Colombia
50B2	**Malaga** Spain
101D3	**Malaimbandy** Madag
107F1	**Malaita** *I* Solomon Is
99D2	**Malakal** Sudan
84C2	**Malakand** Pak
78C4	**Malang** Indon
98B3	**Malange** Angola
97C3	**Malanville** Benin
39H7	**Mälaren** *L* Sweden
34B3	**Malargüe** Arg
12F3	**Malaspina GI** USA
93C2	**Malatya** Turk
101C2	**Malawi** Republic, Africa
	Malawi,L = Nyasa,L
79C4	**Malaybalay** Phil
90A3	**Malāyer** Iran
70B3	**Malaysia** Federation, S E Asia
93D2	**Malazgirt** Turk
58B2	**Malbork** Pol
56C2	**Malchin** Germany
18C2	**Malden** USA
83B5	**Maldives Is** Indian O
104B4	**Maldives Ridge** Indian O
29F2	**Maldonado** Urug
47D1	**Male** Italy
85C4	**Malegaon** India
69B3	**Malé Karpaty** *Upland* Slovakia
101C2	**Malema** Mozam
84B2	**Mālestān** Afghan
38H5	**Malgomaj** *L* Sweden
95B3	**Malha** *Well* Sudan
20C2	**Malheur L** USA
97B3	**Mali** Republic, Africa
78D1	**Malinau** Indon
99F3	**Malindi** Kenya
	Malines = Mechelen
40B2	**Malin Head** *Pt* Irish Rep
86A2	**Malkala Range** *Mts* India
85D4	**Malkāpur** India
55C2	**Malkara** Turk
54C2	**Malko Tŭrnovo** Bulg
44B3	**Mallaig** Scot
95C2	**Mallawi** Egypt
47D1	**Málles Venosta** Italy
51C2	**Mallorca** *I* Spain
45B2	**Mallow** Irish Rep
38G6	**Malm** Nor
38J5	**Malmberget** Sweden
46D1	**Malmédy** Germany
43C4	**Malmesbury** Eng
100A4	**Malmesbury** S Africa
39G7	**Malmö** Sweden
61G2	**Malmyzh** Russian Fed
79B3	**Malolos** Phil
15D2	**Malone** USA
101G1	**Maloti Mts** Lesotho
38F6	**Måløy** Nor
28A2	**Malpelo** *I* Colombia
34A2	**Malpo** *R* Chile
85D3	**Mālpura** India
8C2	**Malta** Montana, USA
53B3	**Malta** *Chan* Malta/Italy
53B3	**Malta** *I* Medit S
100A3	**Maltahöhe** Namibia
42D2	**Malton** Eng
39G6	**Malung** Sweden
87A1	**Mālvan** India
19B3	**Malvern** USA
85D4	**Malwa Plat** India

61G4	**Malyy Uzen'** *R* Kazakhstan
63D2	**Mama** Russian Fed
61H2	**Mamadysh** Russian Fed
99C2	**Mambasa** Zaïre
71E4	**Mamberamo** *R* Indon
98B2	**Mambéré** *R* CAR
98A2	**Mamfé** Cam
33D6	**Mamoré** *R* Bol
97A3	**Mamou** Guinea
101D2	**Mampikony** Madag
97B4	**Mampong** Ghana
94B3	**Mamshit** *Hist Site* Israel
100B3	**Mamuno** Botswana
97B4	**Man** Ivory Coast
21C4	**Mana** Hawaiian Is
101D3	**Manabo** Madag
33E4	**Manacapuru** Brazil
51C2	**Manacor** Spain
71D3	**Manado** Indon
25D3	**Managua** Nic
101D3	**Manakara** Madag
101D2	**Mananara** Madag
101D3	**Mananjary** Madag
111A3	**Manapouri** NZ
111A3	**Manapouri,L** NZ
86C1	**Manas** Bhutan
82C1	**Manas** China
65K5	**Manas Hu** *L* China
86A1	**Manaslu** *Mt* Nepal
16B2	**Manasquan** USA
33F4	**Manaus** Brazil
92B2	**Manavgat** Turk
93C2	**Manbij** Syria
42B2	**Man,Calf of** *I* Eng
87B1	**Mancheral** India
15D2	**Manchester** Connecticut, USA
42C3	**Manchester** Eng
10C2	**Manchester** New Hampshire, USA
16A2	**Manchester** Pennsylvania, USA
69E2	**Manchuria** *Hist Region*, China
91D4	**Mand** *R* Iran
101C2	**Manda** Tanz
35A2	**Mandaguari** Brazil
39F7	**Mandal** Nor
76B1	**Mandalay** Burma
00C2	**Mandalgovi** Mongolia
8C2	**Mandan** USA
14A2	**Mandelona** USA
99E2	**Mandera** Eth
26B3	**Mandeville** Jamaica
101C2	**Mandimba** Mozam
86A2	**Mandla** India
101D2	**Mandritsara** Madag
85D4	**Mandsaur** India
53C2	**Manduria** Italy
85B4	**Māndvi** India
87B2	**Mandya** India
58D2	**Manevichi** Ukraine
42D3	**Manfield** Eng
53C2	**Manfredonia** Italy
98B1	**Manga** *Desert Region* Niger
110C1	**Mangakino** NZ
54C2	**Mangalia** Rom
98B1	**Mangalmé** Chad
87A2	**Mangalore** India
78B3	**Manggar** Indon
68B3	**Mangnia** China
101C2	**Mangoche** Malawi
101D3	**Mangoky** *R* Madag
71D4	**Mangole** *I* Indon
85B4	**Māngral** India
63E2	**Mangui** China
8D3	**Manhattan** USA
31C6	**Manhuacu** Brazil
101D2	**Mania** *R* Madag
101C2	**Manica** Mozam
7D5	**Manicouagan** *R* Can
91A4	**Manifah** S Arabia
79B3	**Manila** Phil
109D2	**Manilla** Aust
97B3	**Maninian** Ivory Coast
86C2	**Manipur** State, India
86C2	**Manipur** *R* Burma
92A2	**Manisa** Turk

41C3	**Man,Isle of** Irish S
14A2	**Manistee** USA
14A2	**Manistee** *R* USA
14A1	**Manistique** USA
5H4	**Manitoba** Province, Can
5J4	**Manitoba,L** Can
13F2	**Manito L** Can
14A1	**Manitou Is** USA
7B5	**Manitoulin** *I* Can
14A2	**Manitowoc** USA
15C1	**Maniwaki** Can
32B2	**Manizales** Colombia
101D3	**Manja** Madag
106A4	**Manjimup** Aust
87B1	**Mānjra** *R* India
10A2	**Mankato** USA
97B4	**Mankono** Ivory Coast
12D2	**Manley Hot Springs** USA
110B1	**Manly** NZ
85C4	**Manmād** India
78A3	**Manna** Indon
108A2	**Mannahill** Aust
87B3	**Mannar** Sri Lanka
87B3	**Mannār,G of** India
87B2	**Mannārgudi** India
57B3	**Mannheim** Germany
13D1	**Manning** Can
17B1	**Manning** USA
108A2	**Mannum** Aust
97A4	**Mano** Sierra Leone
71E4	**Manokwari** Indon
98C3	**Manono** Zaïre
76B3	**Manoron** Burma
75B1	**Mano-wan** *B* Japan
74B2	**Manp'o** N Korea
84D3	**Mānsa** India
100B2	**Mansa** Zambia
6B3	**Mansel I** Can
19B2	**Mansfield** Arkansas, USA
108C3	**Mansfield** Aust
19B3	**Mansfield** Louisiana, USA
16D1	**Mansfield** Massachusetts, USA
10B2	**Mansfield** Ohio, USA
15C2	**Mansfield** Pennsylvania, USA
71E2	**Mansyu Deep** Pacific O
32A4	**Manta** Ecuador
79A4	**Mantalingajan,Mt** Phil
32B6	**Mantaro** *R* Peru
22B2	**Manteca** USA
48C2	**Mantes** France
52B1	**Mantova** Italy
38J0	**Mantta** Fin
61F2	**Manturovo** Russian Fed
35A2	**Manuel Ribas** Brazil
79B4	**Manukan** Phil
110B1	**Manukau** NZ
71F4	**Manus** *I* Pacific O
50B2	**Manzanares** Spain
25E2	**Manzanillo** Cuba
24B3	**Manzanillo** Mexico
63D3	**Manzhouli** China
94C3	**Manzil** Jordan
101C3	**Manzini** Swaziland
98B1	**Mao** Chad
72A2	**Maomao Shan** *Mt* China
73C5	**Maoming** China
101C3	**Mapai** Mozam
71E3	**Mapia** *Is* Pacific O
79A4	**Mapin** *I* Phil
5H5	**Maple Creek** Can
101H1	**Maputo** Mozam
101H1	**Maputo** *R* Mozam
	Ma Qu = Huange He
72A3	**Maqu** China
86B1	**Maquan He** *R* China
98B3	**Maquela do Zombo** Angola
29C4	**Maquinchao** Arg
31B3	**Marabá** Brazil
32C1	**Maracaibo** Ven
32D1	**Maracay** Ven
95A2	**Marādah** Libya
97C3	**Maradi** Niger
90A2	**Marāgheh** Iran

Mount Holly

50A1 **Monforte de Lemos** Spain
98C2 **Monga** Zaïre
98C2 **Mongala** *R* Zaïre
99D2 **Mongalla** Sudan
76D1 **Mong Cai** Viet
98B1 **Mongo** Chad
68B2 **Mongolia** Republic, Asia
100B2 **Mongu** Zambia
21B2 **Monitor Range** *Mts* USA
98C3 **Monkoto** Zaïre
43C4 **Monmouth** Eng
18B1 **Monmouth** USA
13C2 **Monmouth,Mt** Can
97C4 **Mono** *R* Togo
21B2 **Mono L** USA
53C2 **Monopoli** Italy
51B1 **Monreal del Campo** Spain
19B3 **Monroe** Louisiana, USA
14B2 **Monroe** Michigan, USA
20B1 **Monroe** Washington, USA
18B2 **Monroe City** USA
97A4 **Monrovia** Lib
20D3 **Monrovia** USA
56A2 **Mons** Belg
47D2 **Monselice** Italy
16C1 **Monson** USA
58B1 **Mönsterås** Sweden
101D? **Montagne d'Ambre** *Mt* Madag
96C1 **Montagnes des Ouled Nail** *Mts* Alg
12E3 **Montague I** USA
49C3 **Mont Aigoual** *Mt* France
48B2 **Montaigu** France
53C3 **Montallo** *Mt* Italy
8B2 **Montana** State, USA
50A1 **Montañas de León** *Mts* Spain
49C2 **Montargis** France
48C3 **Montauban** France
15D2 **Montauk** USA
15D2 **Montauk Pt** USA
49D2 **Montbéliard** France
52A1 **Mont Blanc** *Mt* France/Italy
49C2 **Montceau les Mines** France
51C1 **Montceny** *Mt* Spain
49D3 **Mont Cinto** *Mt* Corse
46C2 **Montcornet** France
48B3 **Mont-de-Marsan** France
48C2 **Montdidier** France
30D2 **Monteagudo** Bol
33G4 **Monte Alegre** Brazil
52B2 **Monte Amiata** *Mt* Italy
47D2 **Monte Baldo** *Mt* Italy
15C1 **Montebello** Can
106A3 **Monte Bello Is** Aust
47E2 **Montebelluna** Italy
49D3 **Monte Carlo** Monaco
35B1 **Monte Carmelo** Brazil
34D2 **Monte Caseros** Arg
52B2 **Monte Cimone** *Mt* Italy
52A2 **Monte Cinto** *Mt* Corse
34B2 **Monte Coman** Arg
52B2 **Monte Corno** *Mt* Italy
27C3 **Montecristi** Dom Rep
52B2 **Montecristo I** Italy
23A1 **Monte Escobedo** Mexico
53C2 **Monte Gargano** *Mt* Italy
26B3 **Montego Bay** Jamaica
47D2 **Monte Grappa** *Mt* Italy
47C2 **Monte Lesima** *Mt* Italy

49C3 **Montélimar** France
53B2 **Monte Miletto** *Mt* Italy
50A2 **Montemo-o-Novo** Port
24C2 **Montemorelos** Mexico
26B5 **Montená** Colombia
54A2 **Montenegro** Republic, Yugos
35D1 **Monte Pascoal** *Mt* Brazil
34A2 **Monte Patria** Chile
53C3 **Monte Pollino** *Mt* Italy
101C2 **Montepuez** Mozam
8A3 **Monterey** California, USA
15C3 **Monterey** Virginia, USA
8A3 **Monterey B** USA
32B2 **Monteria** Colombia
30D2 **Montero** Bol
47B2 **Monte Rosa** *Mt* Italy/Switz
24B2 **Monterrey** Mexico
31C5 **Montes Claros** Brazil
50B2 **Montes de Toledo** *Mts* Spain
29E2 **Montevideo** Urug
52A2 **Monte Viso** *Mt* Italy
27P2 **Mont Gimie** *Mt* St Lucia
11B3 **Montgomery** Alabama, USA
96C2 **Mont Gréboun** Niger
46C2 **Montherme** France
47B1 **Monthey** Switz
19B3 **Monticello** Arkansas, USA
16B2 **Monticello** New York, USA
9C3 **Monticello** Utah, USA
53A2 **Monti del Gennargentu** *Mt* Sardegna
47D2 **Monti Lessini** *Mts* Italy
53B3 **Monti Nebrodi** *Mts* Italy
7C5 **Mont-Laurier** Can
48C2 **Montluçon** France
7C5 **Montmagny** Can
46C2 **Montmédy** France
49C3 **Mont Mézenc** *Mt* France
46B2 **Montmirail** France
50B2 **Montoro** Spain
49D3 **Mont Pelat** *Mt* France
14B2 **Montpelier** Ohio, USA
10C2 **Montpelier** Vermont, USA
49C3 **Montpellier** France
7C5 **Montréal** Can
48C1 **Montreuil** France
52A1 **Montreux** Switz
47B1 **Mont Risoux** *Mt* France
8C3 **Montrose** Colorado, USA
40C2 **Montrose** Scot
48B2 **Mont-St-Michel** France
96B1 **Monts des Ksour** *Mts* Alg
51C3 **Monts des Ouled Neil** *Mts* Alg
51C2 **Monts du Hodna** *Mts* Alg
27E3 **Montserrat I** Caribbean S
10C1 **Monts Otish** *Mts* Can
12B1 **Monument Mt** USA
9B3 **Monument V** USA
98C2 **Monveda** Zaïre
76B1 **Monywa** Burma
52A1 **Monza** Italy
100B2 **Monze** Zambia
101H1 **Mooi** *R* S Africa
101G1 **Mooi River** S Africa

108B1 **Moomba** Aust
109D2 **Moonbi Range** *Mts* Aust
108B1 **Moonda L** Aust
109D1 **Moonie** Aust
109C1 **Moonie** *R* Aust
108A2 **Moonta** Aust
106A4 **Moora** Aust
106A3 **Moore,L** Aust
42C2 **Moorfoot Hills** Scot
8D2 **Moorhead** USA
22C3 **Moorpark** USA
7B4 **Moose** *R* Can
5H4 **Moose Jaw** Can
5H4 **Moosomin** Can
7B4 **Moosonee** Can
16D2 **Moosup** USA
101C2 **Mopeia** Mozam
97B3 **Mopti** Mali
30B2 **Moquegua** Peru
39G6 **Mora** Sweden
31D3 **Morada** Brazil
84D3 **Morādābād** India
35B1 **Morada Nova de Minas** *L* Brazil
101D2 **Morafenobe** Madag
101D2 **Moramanga** Madag
27J2 **Morant Bay** Jamaica
27J2 **Morant Pt** Jamaica
87B3 **Moratuwa** Sri Lanka
59B3 **Morava** *R* Austria/Slovakia
54B2 **Morava** *R* Serbia, Yugos
90C2 **Moraveh Tappeh** Iran
40C2 **Moray Firth** *Estuary* Scot
47C1 **Morbegno** Italy
85C4 **Morbi** India
93D2 **Mor Dağ** *Mt* Turk
5J5 **Morden** Can
61F3 **Mordovskaya Respublika,** Russian Fed
42C2 **Morecambe** Eng
42C2 **Morecambe B** Eng
107D3 **Moree** Aust
14B3 **Morehead** USA
47C1 **Mörel** Switz
24B3 **Morelia** Mexico
23B2 **Morelos** State, Mexico
85D3 **Morena** India
5E4 **Moresby I** Can
109D1 **Moreton I** Aust
46B2 **Moreuil** France
47B1 **Morez** France
19B4 **Morgan City** USA
22B2 **Morgan Hill** USA
14C3 **Morgantown** USA
101G1 **Morgenzon** S Africa
47B1 **Morges** Switz
46D2 **Morhange** France
74E2 **Mori** Japan
27K1 **Moriatio** Tobago
13B2 **Morice L** Can
13E2 **Morinville** Can
74E3 **Morioka** Japan
109D2 **Morisset** Aust
63D1 **Morkoka** *R* Russian Fed
48B2 **Morlaix** France
27Q2 **Morne Diablotin** *Mt* Dominica
106C2 **Mornington I** Aust
85B3 **Moro** Pak
96B2 **Morocco** Kingdom, Africa
79B4 **Moro G** Phil
99D3 **Morogoro** Tanz
23A1 **Moroleon** Mexico
101D3 **Morombe** Madag
26B2 **Morón** Cuba
101D3 **Morondava** Madag
50A2 **Moron de la Frontera** Spain
101D2 **Moroni** Comoros
71D3 **Morotai I** Indon
99D2 **Moroto** Uganda
61F4 **Morozovsk** Russian Fed
42D2 **Morpeth** Eng
19B2 **Morrilton** USA
35B1 **Morrinhos** Brazil

110C1 **Morrinsville** NZ
16B2 **Morristown** New Jersey, USA
15C2 **Morristown** New York, USA
16B2 **Morrisville** Pennsylvania, USA
21A2 **Morro Bay** USA
23A2 **Morro de Papanoa** Mexico
23A2 **Morro de Petatlán** Mexico
101C2 **Morrumbala** Mozam
101C3 **Morrumbene** Mozam
61F3 **Morshansk** Russian Fed
47C2 **Mortara** Italy
34C2 **Morteros** Arg
33G6 **Mortes** *R* Mato Grosso, Brazil
35C2 **Mortes** *R* Minas Gerais, Brazil
108B3 **Mortlake** Aust
27L1 **Moruga** Trinidad
109D3 **Moruya** Aust
109C1 **Morven** Aust
44B3 **Morvern** *Pen* Scot
109C3 **Morwell** Aust
76B3 **Moscos Is** Burma
Moscow = Moskva
20C1 **Moscow** Idaho, USA
56B2 **Mosel** *R* Germany
46D2 **Moselle** Department, France
46D2 **Moselle** *R* France
20C1 **Moses Lake** USA
111B3 **Mosgiel** NZ
99D3 **Moshi** Tanz
38G5 **Mosjøen** Nor
63G? **Moskal'vo** Russian Fed
64E4 **Moskva** Russian Fed
35C1 **Mosquito** *R* Brazil
39G7 **Moss** Nor
98B3 **Mossaka** Congo
100B4 **Mossel Bay** S Africa
98B3 **Mossendjo** Congo
108B2 **Mossgiel** Aust
31D3 **Mossoró** Brazil
57C2 **Most** Czech Republic
96C1 **Mostaganem** Alg
54A2 **Mostar** Bosnia-Herzegovina
58C? **Mosty** Belorussia
Mosul = Al Mawşil
39H7 **Motala** Sweden
42C2 **Motherwell** Scot
86A1 **Motihāri** India
51B2 **Motilla del Palancar** Spain
50B2 **Motril** Spain
111B2 **Motueka** NZ
111B2 **Motueka** *R* NZ
47B1 **Moudon** Switz
98B3 **Mouila** Gabon
108B2 **Moulamein** Aust
4G2 **Mould Bay** Can
49C2 **Moulins** France
76B2 **Moulmein** Burma
96B1 **Moulouya** *R* Mor
17B1 **Moultrie** USA
17C1 **Moultrie,L** USA
18C2 **Mound City** Illinois, USA
18A1 **Mound City** Missouri, USA
98B2 **Moundou** Chad
14B3 **Moundsville** USA
12J1 **Mountain** *R* Can
17A1 **Mountain Brook** USA
18B2 **Mountain Grove** USA
18B2 **Mountain Home** Arkansas, USA
22A2 **Mountain View** USA
12B2 **Mountain Village** USA
16A3 **Mount Airy** Maryland, USA
16A2 **Mount Carmel** USA
108A1 **Mount Dutton** Aust
108A2 **Mount Eba** Aust
108B3 **Mount Gambier** Aust
16B3 **Mount Holly** USA

19B3 **Nacogdoches** USA
76A3 **Nacondam** /, Indian O
24B1 **Nacozari** Mexico
85C4 **Nadiād** India
50B2 **Nador** Mor
90B3 **Nadūshan** Iran
59C3 **Nadvornaya** Ukraine
56C1 **Naestved** Den
95B2 **Nāfūrah** Libya
75A2 **Nagahama** Japan
82D3 **Naga Hills** Burma
75B1 **Nagai** Japan
86C1 **Nāgāland** State, India
74D3 **Nagano** Japan
74D3 **Nagaoka** Japan
86C1 **Nagaon** India
87B2 **Nāgappattinam** India
85C4 **Nagar Parkar** Pak
74B4 **Nagasaki** Japan
75B2 **Nagashima** Japan
75A2 **Nagato** Japan
85C3 **Nāgaur** India
87B3 **Nāgercoil** India
85B3 **Nagha Kalat** Pak
84D3 **Nagīna** India
74D3 **Nagoya** Japan
85D4 **Nāgpur** India
82D2 **Nagqu** China
59B3 **Nagykanizsa** Hung
59B3 **Nagykörös** Hung
69E4 **Naha** Japan
8A2 **Nahaimo** Can
84D2 **Nāhan** India
4F3 **Nahanni Butte** Can
94B2 **Nahariya** Israel
90A3 **Nahāvand** Iran
46D2 **Nahe** R Germany
72D2 **Nahpu** China
72E1 **Naimen Qi** China
7D4 **Nain** Can
90B3 **Nā'īn** Iran
84D3 **Naini Tal** India
44C3 **Nairn** Scot
99D3 **Nairobi** Kenya
90D3 **Najafābād** Iran
74C2 **Najin** N Korea
75A2 **Nakama** Japan
74E3 **Nakaminato** Japan
75A2 **Nakamura** Japan
75B1 **Nakano** Japan
75A1 **Nakano-shima** /, Japan
74C4 **Nakatsu** Japan
75B1 **Nakatsu-gawa** Japan
95C3 **Nak'fa** Eritrea
93E2 **Nakhichevan** Azerbaijan
92B4 **Nakhl** Egypt
74C2 **Nakhodka** Russian Fed
76C3 **Nakhon Pathom** Thai
76C3 **Nakhon Ratchasima** Thai
77C4 **Nakhon Si Thammarat** Thai
12H3 **Nakina** Can
7B4 **Nakina** Ontario, Can
12C3 **Naknek** USA
12C3 **Naknek L** USA
4C4 **Nakrek** USA
39G8 **Nakskov** Den
99D3 **Nakuru** Kenya
13D2 **Nakusp** Can
61F5 **Nal'chik** Russian Fed
87B1 **Nalgonda** India
87B1 **Nallamala Range** Mts India
95A1 **Nālūt** Libya
101H1 **Namaacha** Mozam
65G6 **Namak** L Iran
90C3 **Namakzar-e Shadad** Salt Flat Iran
65J5 **Namangan** Uzbekistan
101C2 **Namapa** Mozam
100A4 **Namaqualand** Region, S Africa
109D1 **Nambour** Aust
109D2 **Nambucca Heads** Aust
77C4 **Nam Can** Viet
82D2 **Nam Co** L China

76D1 **Nam Dinh** Viet
101C2 **Nametil** Mozam
74B4 **Namhae-do** / S Korea
100A2 **Namib Desert** Namibia
100A2 **Namibe** Angola
100A3 **Namibia** Republic, Africa
82D3 **Namjagbarwa Feng** Mt China
71D4 **Namlea** Indon
109C2 **Namoi** R Aust
13D1 **Nampa** Can
20C2 **Nampa** USA
97B3 **Nampala** Mali
76C2 **Nam Phong** Thai
74B3 **Namp'o** N Korea
101C2 **Nampula** Mozam
38G6 **Namsos** Nor
76B1 **Namton** Burma
86D2 **Namtu** Burma
13B2 **Namu** Can
101C2 **Namuno** Mozam
46C1 **Namur** Belg
100A2 **Namutoni** Namibia
74B3 **Namwŏn** S Korea
13C3 **Nanaimo** Can
74B2 **Nanam** N Korea
109D1 **Nanango** Aust
74D3 **Nanao** Japan
75B1 **Nanatsu-jima** /, Japan
73B3 **Nanbu** China
73D4 **Nanchang** China
73B3 **Nanchong** China
49D2 **Nancy** France
87B1 **Nanded** India
109D2 **Nandewar Range** Mts Aust
85C4 **Nandurbar** India
87B1 **Nandyāl** India
98B2 **Nanga Eboko** Cam
84C1 **Nanga Parbat** Mt Pak
78C3 **Nangapinoh** Indon
78C3 **Nangatayap** Indon
74B2 **Nangnim Sanmaek** Mts N Korea
86C1 **Nang Xian** China
67F3 **Nangzhou** China
87B2 **Nanjangud** India
72D3 **Nanjing** China
Nanking = Nanjing
75A2 **Nankoku** Japan
73C4 **Nan Ling** Region, China
76D1 **Nanliu** R China
73B5 **Nanning** China
6F3 **Nanortalik** Greenland
73A5 **Nanpan Jiang** R China
86A1 **Nānpāra** India
73D4 **Nanping** China
6A1 **Nansen Sd** Can
99D3 **Nansio** Tanz
48B2 **Nantes** France
13E2 **Nanton** Can
72E3 **Nantong** China
10C2 **Nantucket** / USA
35C1 **Nanuque** Brazil
72C3 **Nanyang** China
72D2 **Nanyang Hu** L China
99D2 **Nanyuki** Kenya
74D3 **Naoetsu** Japan
85B4 **Naokot** Pak
22A1 **Napa** USA
12D2 **Napaiskak** USA
15C2 **Napanee** Can
65K4 **Napas** Russian Fed
6E3 **Napassoq** Greenland
76D2 **Nape** Laos
110C1 **Napier** NZ
Naples = Napoli
17B2 **Naples** Florida, USA
19B3 **Naples** Texas, USA
73B5 **Napo** China
32C4 **Napo** R Peru/Ecuador
53B2 **Napoli** Italy
90A2 **Naqadeh** Iran
92C4 **Naqb Ishtar** Jordan
75B2 **Nara** Japan

97B3 **Nara** Mali
107D4 **Naracoorte** Aust
23B1 **Naranjos** Mexico
87C1 **Narasarāopet** India
77C4 **Narathiwat** Thai
86C2 **Narayanganj** Bang
87B1 **Nārāyenpet** India
49C3 **Narbonne** France
84D2 **Narendranagar** India
6C2 **Nares Str** Can
58C2 **Narew** R Pol
75C1 **Narita** Japan
85C4 **Narmada** R India
84D3 **Narnaul** India
60E2 **Naro Fominsk** Russian Fed
99D3 **Narok** Kenya
84C2 **Narowal** Pak
107D4 **Narrabri** Aust
109C1 **Narran** L Aust
109C1 **Narran** R Aust
109C2 **Narrandera** Aust
106A4 **Narrogin** Aust
109C2 **Narromine** Aust
85D4 **Narsimhapur** India
87C1 **Narsīpatnam** India
6F3 **Narssalik** Greenland
6F3 **Narssaq** Greenland
6F3 **Narssarssuaq** Greenland
75C1 **Narugo** Japan
75A2 **Naruto** Japan
60C2 **Narva** Russian Fed
38H5 **Narvik** Nor
84D3 **Narwāna** India
64G3 **Nar'yan Mar** Russian Fed
108B1 **Narylico** Aust
65J5 **Naryn** Kirghizia
97C4 **Nasarawa** Nig
103D5 **Nasca Ridge** Pacific O
16D1 **Nashua** USA
19B3 **Nashville** Arkansas, USA
11B3 **Nashville** Tennessee, USA
54A1 **Našice** Croatia
85D4 **Nāsik** India
99D2 **Nasir** Sudan
13B1 **Nass** R Can
26B1 **Nassau** The Bahamas
16C1 **Nassau** USA
95C2 **Nasser,L** Egypt
39G7 **Nässjö** Sweden
7C4 **Nastapoka Is** Can
100B3 **Nata** Botswana
31D3 **Natal** Brazil
70A3 **Natal** Indon
101H1 **Natal** Province, S Africa
90B3 **Natanz** Iran
7D4 **Natashquan** Can
7D4 **Natashquan** R Can
19B3 **Natchez** USA
19B3 **Natchitoches** USA
100C3 **Nathalia** Aust
6H2 **Nathorsts Land** Region Greenland
13C1 **Nation** R Can
21B3 **National City** USA
75C1 **Natori** Japan
99D3 **Natron** L Tanz
106A4 **Naturaliste,C** Aust
47D1 **Nauders** Austria
56C2 **Nauen** Germany
16C2 **Naugatuck** USA
57C2 **Naumburg** Germany
94B3 **Naur** Jordan
105G4 **Nauru** / Pacific O
63C2 **Naushki** Russian Fed
23B1 **Nautla** Mexico
9C3 **Navajo Res** USA
50A2 **Navalmoral de la Mata** Spain
29C7 **Navarino** / Chile
51B1 **Navarra** Province, Spain
34D3 **Navarro** Arg
19A3 **Navasota** USA
19A3 **Navasota** R USA
50A1 **Navia** R Spain
34A2 **Navidad** Chile

85C4 **Navlakhi** India
60D3 **Navlya** Russian Fed
24B2 **Navojoa** Mexico
55B3 **Návpaktos** Greece
55B3 **Návplion** Greece
85C4 **Navsāri** India
94C2 **Nawá** Syria
86B2 **Nawāda** India
84B2 **Nawah** Afghan
85B3 **Nawrabshah** Pak
73B4 **Naxi** China
55C3 **Náxos** / Greece
23A1 **Nayar** Mexico
90C3 **Nay Band** Iran
91B4 **Nay Band** Iran
74E2 **Nayoro** Japan
94B2 **Nazareth** Israel
48B2 **Nazay** France
32C6 **Nazca** Peru
92A2 **Nazilli** Turk
63B2 **Nazimovo** Russian Fed
13C2 **Nazko** R Can
99D2 **Nazret** Eth
91C5 **Nazwa** Oman
65J4 **Nazyvayevsk** Russian Fed
98B3 **Ndalatando** Angola
98C2 **Ndélé** CAR
98B3 **Ndendé** Gabon
98B1 **Ndjamena** Chad
98B3 **Ndjolé** Gabon
100B2 **Ndola** Zambia
109C1 **Neabul** Aust
108A1 **Neales** R Aust
55B3 **Neápolis** Greece
43C4 **Neath** Wales
109C1 **Nebine** R Aust
65G6 **Nebit Dag** Turkmenistan
8C2 **Nebraska** State, USA
10A1 **Nebraska City** USA
13C2 **Nechako** R Can
19A3 **Neches** R USA
34D3 **Necochea** Arg
86C1 **Nêdong** China
9B3 **Needles** USA
14A2 **Neenah** USA
5J4 **Neepawa** Can
46C1 **Neerpelt** Belg
63C2 **Neftelensk** Russian Fed
99D2 **Negelē** Eth
94B3 **Negev** Desert Israel
60B4 **Negolu** Mt Rom
87B3 **Negombo** Sri Lanka
76A2 **Negrais,C** Burma
32A4 **Negritos** Peru
33E4 **Negro** R Amazonas, Brazil
29C4 **Negro** R Arg
34D2 **Negro** R Urug
79B4 **Negros** / Phil
54C2 **Negru Voda** Rom
90D3 **Nehbāndan** Iran
73B4 **Neijiang** China
72B1 **Nei Monggol** Autonomous Region, China
32B3 **Neiva** Colombia
99D2 **Nejo** Eth
99D2 **Nek'emtē** Eth
60D2 **Nelidovo** Russian Fed
87B2 **Nellore** India
69F2 **Nel'ma** Russian Fed
13D3 **Nelson** Can
111B2 **Nelson** NZ
7A4 **Nelson** R Can
108B3 **Nelson,C** Aust
12B2 **Nelson I** USA
97B3 **Néma** Maur
72A1 **Nemagt Uul** Mt Mongolia
58C1 **Neman** R Lithuania
54C1 **Nemira** Mt Rom
74F2 **Nemuro** Japan
63E3 **Nen** R China
41B3 **Nenagh** Irish Rep
12E2 **Nenana** USA
12E2 **Nenana** R USA
43D3 **Nene** R Eng
69E2 **Nenjiang** China
18A2 **Neodesha** USA

Neosho

18B2 **Neosho** USA
63C2 **Nepa** Russian Fed
82C3 **Nepal** Kingdom, Asia
86A1 **Nepalganj** Nepal
45B1 **Nephin** *Mt* Irish Rep
94B3 **Neqarot** *R* Israel
34A3 **Nequén** State, Arg
68D1 **Nerchinsk**
Russian Fed
52C2 **Neretva** *R* Bosnia-
Herzegovina/Croatia
71F2 **Nero Deep** Pacific O
38C1 **Neskaupstaður**
Iceland
46B2 **Nesle** France
7E5 **Nesleyville** Can
55B2 **Néstos** *R* Greece
94B2 **Netanya** Israel
16B2 **Netcong** USA
56B2 **Netherlands**
Kingdom, Europe
3M7 **Netherlands Antilles**
Is Caribbean S
86C2 **Netrakona** Bang
6C3 **Nettilling L** Can
56C2 **Neubrandenburg**
Germany
47B1 **Neuchâtel** Switz
46C2 **Neufchâteau** Belg
48C2 **Neufchâtel** France
46A2 **Neufchâtel-en-Bray**
France
56B2 **Neumünster**
Germany
52C1 **Neunkirchen** Austria
46D2 **Neunkirchen**
Germany
34B3 **Neuquén** Arg
29B4 **Neuquén** State, Arg
34B3 **Neuquén** *R* Arg
56C2 **Neuruppin** Germany
46D1 **Neuss** Germany
46E2 **Neustadt** Germany
56C2 **Neustadt** Germany
56C2 **Neustrelitz** Germany
46D1 **Neuwied** Germany
8B3 **Nevada** State, USA
18B2 **Nevada** USA
34A3 **Nevada de Chillán**
Mts Arg/Chile
23A2 **Nevada de Collima**
Mexico
23B2 **Nevada de Toluca** *Mt*
Mexico
94B3 **Nevatim** Israel
60C2 **Nevel'** Russian Fed
49C2 **Nevers** France
109C2 **Nevertire** Aust
27E3 **Nevis** *I* Caribbean S
58D2 **Nevis** *R* Belorussia/
Lithuania
92B2 **Nevşehir** Turk
61K2 **Nev'yansk**
Russian Fed
101C2 **Newala** Tanz
14A3 **New Albany** Indiana,
USA
19C3 **New Albany**
Mississippi, USA
33F2 **New Amsterdam**
Guyana
109C1 **New Angledool** Aust
15C3 **Newark** Delaware,
USA
10C2 **Newark** New Jersey,
USA
14B2 **Newark** Ohio, USA
43D3 **Newark-upon-Trent**
Eng
15D2 **New Bedford** USA
13B2 **New Bella Bella** Can
20B1 **Newberg** USA
11C3 **New Bern** USA
17B1 **Newberry** USA
26B2 **New Bight**
The Bahamas
14B3 **New Boston** USA
9D4 **New Braunfels** USA
16C2 **New Britain** USA
7D5 **New Brunswick**
Province, Can
16B2 **New Brunswick** USA
16B2 **Newburgh** USA
43D4 **Newbury** Eng

16D1 **Newburyport** USA
16C2 **New Canaan** USA
109D2 **Newcastle** Aust
14A3 **New Castle** Indiana,
USA
42B2 **Newcastle** N Ire
14B2 **New Castle**
Pennsylvania, USA
101G1 **Newcastle** S Africa
8C2 **Newcastle** Wyoming,
USA
42D2 **Newcastle upon Tyne**
Eng
106C2 **Newcastle Waters**
Aust
45B2 **Newcastle West**
Irish Rep
84D3 **New Delhi** India
109D2 **New England Range**
Mts Aust
12B3 **Newenham,C** USA
43D4 **New Forest,The** Eng
7D4 **Newfoundland**
Province, Can
7E5 **Newfoundland** *I*
Can
102F2 **Newfoundland Basin**
Atlantic O
18B2 **New Franklin** USA
42B2 **New Galloway** Scot
107E1 **New Georgia** *I*
Solomon Is
7D5 **New Glasgow** Can
71F4 **New Guinea** SE Asia
12D3 **Newhalen** USA
22C3 **Newhall** USA
10C2 **New Hampshire**
State, USA
101H1 **New Hanover**
S Africa
43E4 **Newhaven** Eng
15D2 **New Haven** USA
13B1 **New Hazelton** Can
19B3 **New Iberia** USA
10C2 **New Jersey** State,
USA
7C5 **New Liskeard** Can
16C2 **New London** USA
106A3 **Newman** Aust
22B2 **Newman** USA
43E3 **Newmarket** Eng
45B2 **Newmarket** Irish Rep
15C3 **New Market** USA
9C3 **New Mexico** State,
USA
16C2 **New Milford**
Connecticut, USA
17B1 **Newnan** USA
109C4 **New Norfolk** Aust
11A3 **New Orleans** USA
16B2 **New Paltz** USA
14B2 **New Philadelphia**
USA
110B1 **New Plymouth** NZ
18B2 **Newport** Arkansas,
USA
43D4 **Newport** Eng
14B3 **Newport** Kentucky,
USA
20B2 **Newport** Oregon,
USA
16A2 **Newport**
Pennsylvania, USA
15D2 **Newport** Rhode
Island, USA
15D2 **Newport** Vermont,
USA
43C4 **Newport** Wales
20C1 **Newport**
Washington, USA
22D4 **Newport Beach** USA
11C3 **Newport News** USA
26B1 **New Providence** *I*
Caribbean S
43B4 **Newquay** Eng
6C3 **New Quebec Crater**
Can
45C2 **New Ross** Irish Rep
45C1 **Newry** N Ire
**New Siberian Is =
Novosibirskye
Ostrova**
17B2 **New Smyrna Beach**
USA

107D4 **New South Wales**
State, Aust
12C3 **New Stuyahok** USA
18A2 **Newton** Kansas,
USA
16D1 **Newton**
Massachusetts, USA
19C3 **Newton** Mississippi,
USA
16B2 **Newton** New York,
USA
43C4 **Newton Abbot** Eng
45C1 **Newton Stewart**
N Ire
42B2 **Newton Stewart**
Scot
43C3 **Newtown** Wales
42B2 **Newtownards** N Ire
16A2 **Newville** USA
5F5 **New Westminster**
Can
10C2 **New York** State, USA
10C2 **New York** USA
110 **New Zealand**
Dominion, SW
Pacific O
105G6 **New Zealand Plat**
Pacific O
61F2 **Neya** Russian Fed
91B4 **Neyriz** Iran
90C2 **Neyshābūr** Iran
60D3 **Nezhin** Russian Fed
98B3 **Ngabé** Congo
100B3 **Ngami** *L* Botswana
110C1 **Ngaruawahia** NZ
110C1 **Ngaruroro** *R* NZ
110C1 **Ngauruhoe,Mt** NZ
98B3 **Ngo** Congo
76D2 **Ngoc Linh** *Mt* Viet
98B2 **Ngoko** *R* Cam
68B3 **Ngoring Hu** *L* China
99D3 **Ngorongoro Crater**
Tanz
98B3 **N'Gounié** *R* Gabon
98B1 **Nguigmi** Niger
71E3 **Ngulu** *I* Pacific O
97D3 **Nguru** Nig
76D3 **Nha Trang** Viet
108B3 **Nhill** Aust
101H1 **Nhlangano**
Swaziland
76D2 **Nhommarath** Laos
106C2 **Nhulunbuy** Aust
97B3 **Niafounké** Mali
14A1 **Niagara** USA
15C2 **Niagara Falls** Can
15C2 **Niagara Falls** USA
70C3 **Niah** Malay
97B4 **Niakaramandougou**
Ivory Coast
97C3 **Niamey** Niger
99C2 **Niangara** Zaïre
98C2 **Nia Nia** Zaïre
70A3 **Nias** *I* Indon
25D3 **Nicaragua** Republic,
Cent America
53C3 **Nicastro** Italy
49D3 **Nice** France
26B1 **Nicholl's Town**
The Bahamas
83D5 **Nicobar Is** Indian O
92B2 **Nicosia** Cyprus
25D3 **Nicoya,Pen de**
Costa Rica
58C2 **Nidzica** Pol
46D2 **Niederbronn** France
56B2 **Niedersachsen** State,
Germany
99C3 **Niemba** Zaïre
56B2 **Nienburg** Germany
46D1 **Niers** *R* Germany
97B4 **Niete,Mt** Lib
33F2 **Nieuw Amsterdam**
Surinam
33F2 **Nieuw Nickerie**
Surinam
46B1 **Nieuwpoort** Belg
92B2 **Niğde** Turk
97C3 **Niger** Republic,
Africa
97C4 **Niger** *R* Nig
97C4 **Nigeria** Federal
Republic, Africa
55B2 **Nigríta** Greece

75C1 **Nihommatsu** Japan
74D3 **Niigata** Japan
74C4 **Niihama** Japan
75B2 **Nii-jima** *I* Japan
75A2 **Niimi** Japan
74D3 **Niitsu** Japan
94B3 **Nijil** Jordan
56B2 **Nijmegen** Neth
64E3 **Nikel'** Russian Fed
97C3 **Nikki** Benin
74D3 **Nikko** Japan
60D4 **Nikolayev** Ukraine
61G4 **Nikolayevsk**
Russian Fed
63G2 **Nikolayevsk-na-**
Amure Russian Fed
61G2 **Nikol'sk** Russian Fed
61G3 **Nikol'sk** Russian Fed
60D4 **Nikopol** Ukraine
92C1 **Niksar** Turk
91D4 **Nīkshahr** Iran
54A2 **Nikšić** Montenegro,
Yugos
71D4 **Nila** *I* Indon
80B3 **Nile** *R* N E Africa
14A2 **Niles** USA
87B2 **Nilgiri Hills** India
85C4 **Nimach** India
49C3 **Nimes** France
109C3 **Nimmitabel** Aust
99D2 **Nimule** Sudan
83B5 **Nine Degree Chan**
Indian O
104C4 **Ninety-East Ridge**
Indian O
109C3 **Ninety Mile Beach**
Aust
73D4 **Ningde** China
73D4 **Ningdu** China
68B3 **Ningjing Shan** *Mts*
China
76D1 **Ningming** China
73A4 **Ningnan** China
72B2 **Ningxia** Province,
China
72B2 **Ning Xian** China
73B5 **Ninh Binh** Vietnam
107D1 **Ninigo Is** PNG
12D2 **Ninilchik** USA
8D2 **Niobrara** *R* USA
98B3 **Nioki** Zaïre
97B3 **Nioro du Sahel** Mali
48B2 **Niort** France
5H4 **Nipawin** Can
7B5 **Nipigon** Can
7B5 **Nipigon,L** Can
7B5 **Nipissing** *R* Can
14B1 **Nipissing,L** Can
87B1 **Nirmal** India
86B1 **Nirmāli** India
54B2 **Niš** Serbia, Yugos
81C4 **Nisāb** Yemen
69F4 **Nishino-shima** *I*
Japan
75A1 **Nishino-shima** *I*
Japan
75A2 **Nishiwaki** Japan
12G2 **Nisling** *R* Can
12H2 **Nisutlin** *R* Can
7C4 **Nitchequon** Can
31C6 **Niterói** Brazil
42C2 **Nith** *R* Scot
59B3 **Nitra** Slovakia
14B3 **Nitro** USA
78C2 **Niut** *Mt* Malay
46C1 **Nivelles** Belg
49C2 **Nivernais** Region,
France
38L5 **Nivskiy** Russian Fed
87B1 **Nizāmābād** India
94B3 **Nizana** *Hist Site*
Israel
61J2 **Nizhniye Sergi**
Russian Fed
65F4 **Nizhniy Novgorod**
Russian Fed
61F3 **Nizhniy Lomov**
Russian Fed
65G4 **Nizhniy Tagil**
Russian Fed
63B1 **Nizhnyaya Tunguska**
R Russian Fed
93C2 **Nizip** Turk
100B2 **Njoko** *R* Zambia

99D3 **Njombe** Tanz
98B2 **Nkambé** Cam
101C2 **Nkhata Bay** Malawi
98B2 **Nkongsamba** Cam
97C3 **N'Konni** Niger
86C2 **Noakhali** Bang
12B1 **Noatak** USA
12C1 **Noatak** *R* USA
74C4 **Nobeoka** Japan
47D1 **Noce** *R* Italy
23A1 **Nochistlán** Mexico
23B2 **Nochixtlán** Mexico
19A3 **Nocona** USA
24A1 **Nogales** Sonora, Mexico
9B3 **Nogales** USA
23B2 **Nogales** Veracruz, Mexico
47D2 **Nogara** Italy
75A2 **Nogata** Japan
60E2 **Noginsk** Russian Fed
34D2 **Nogoyá** Arg
34D2 **Nogoyá** *R* Arg
84C3 **Nohar** India
75B2 **Nojima-zaki** *C* Japan
98B2 **Nola** CAR
61G2 **Nolinsk** Russian Fed
16D2 **Nomans Land** *I* USA
12A2 **Nome** USA
46D2 **Nomeny** France
72B1 **Nomgon** Mongolia
5H3 **Nonachol L** Can
76C2 **Nong Khai** Thai
101H1 **Nongoma** S Africa
12B1 **Noorvik** USA
13B3 **Nootka Sd** Can
98B3 **Noqui** Angola
7C5 **Noranda** Can
46B1 **Nord** Department, France
64D2 **Nordaustlandet** *I* Barents S
13D2 **Nordegg** Can
38F6 **Nordfjord** *Inlet* Nor
39F8 **Nordfriesische** *Is* Germany
56C2 **Nordhausen** Germany
56B2 **Nordhrein Westfalen** State, Germany
38J4 **Nordkapp** *C* Nor
6E3 **Nordre** Greenland
38H5 **Nord Stronfjället** *Mt* Sweden
1B9 **Nordvik** Russian Fed
45C2 **Nore** *R* Irish Rep
43E3 **Norfolk** County, Eng
8D2 **Norfolk** Nebraska, USA
11C3 **Norfolk** Virginia, USA
107F3 **Norfolk I** Aust
18B2 **Norfolk L** USA
105G5 **Norfolk Ridge** Pacific O
1C10 **Noril'sk** Russian Fed
18C1 **Normal** USA
19A2 **Norman** USA
48B2 **Normandie** Region, France
107D2 **Normanton** Aust
12J1 **Norman Wells** Can
4B3 **Norne** USA
15C2 **Norristown** USA
39H7 **Norrköping** Sweden
39H6 **Norrsundet** Sweden
39H7 **Norrtälje** Sweden
106B4 **Norseman** Aust
63F2 **Norsk** Russian Fed
102J2 **North** *S* N W Europe
42D2 **Northallerton** Eng
106A4 **Northam** Aust
102E3 **North American Basin** Atlantic O
106A3 **Northampton** Aust
43D3 **Northampton** County, Eng
43D3 **Northampton** Eng
15D2 **Northampton** USA
4G3 **North Arm** *B* Can
17B1 **North Augusta** USA
6D4 **North Aulatsvik** *I* Can
13F2 **North Battleford** Can
7C5 **North Bay** Can
20B2 **North Bend** USA
44C3 **North Berwick** Scot
7D5 **North,C** Can
7G4 **North C** NZ
11B3 **North Carolina** State, USA
20B1 **North Cascade Nat Pk** USA
14B1 **North Chan** Can
42B2 **North Chan** Ire/Scot
8C2 **North Dakota** State, USA
43E4 **North Downs** Eng
14C2 **North East** USA
102H2 **North East Atlantic Basin** Atlantic O
4B3 **Northeast C** USA
40B3 **Northern Ireland** UK
27L1 **Northern Range** *Mts* Trinidad
106C2 **Northern Territory** Aust
44C3 **North Esk** *R* Scot
16C1 **Northfield** Massachusetts, USA
12D2 **North Fork** *R* USA
110B1 **North I** NZ
74B3 **North Korea** Republic, S E Asia
North Land = Severnaya Zemlya
19B3 **North Little Rock** USA
1B4 **North Magnetic Pole** Can
17B2 **North Miami** USA
17B2 **North Miami Beach** USA
8C2 **North Platte** USA
8C2 **North Platte** *R* USA
27R3 **North Pt** Barbados
14B1 **North Pt** USA
40B2 **North Rona** *I* Scot
44C2 **North Ronaldsay** *I* Scot
13F2 **North Saskatchewan** *R* Can
40D2 **North Sea** N W Europe
4D3 **North Slope** *Region* USA
100D1 **North Stradbroke** *I* Aust
110B1 **North Taranaki Bight** *B* NZ
9C3 **North Truchas Peak** *Mt* USA
44A3 **North Uist** *I* Scot
42C2 **Northumberland** County, Eng
107E3 **Northumberland Is** Aust
7D5 **Northumberland Str** Can
20B1 **North Vancouver** Can
43E3 **North Walsham** Eng
12F2 **Northway** USA
106A3 **North West C** Aust
84C2 **North West Frontier** Province, Pak
7D4 **North West River** Can
4F3 **North West Territories** Can
42D2 **North York Moors Nat Pk** Eng
12B2 **Norton B** USA
12B2 **Norton Sd** USA
112B1 **Norvegia,C** Ant
16C2 **Norwalk** Connecticut, USA
14B2 **Norwalk** Ohio, USA
39F6 **Norway** Kingdom, Europe
5J4 **Norway House** Can
6A2 **Norwegian B** Can
102H1 **Norwegian Basin** Norewegian S
64A3 **Norwegian S** N W Europe
16C2 **Norwich** Connecticut, USA
43E3 **Norwich** Eng
16D1 **Norwood** Massachusetts, USA
14B3 **Norwood** Ohio, USA
54C2 **Nos Emine** *C* Bulg
74D2 **Noshiro** Japan
54C2 **Nos Kaliakra** *C* Bulg
44E1 **Noss** *I* Scot
91D4 **Nostrābād** Iran
101D2 **Nosy Barren** *I* Madag
101D2 **Nosy Bé** *I* Madag
101E2 **Nosy Boraha** *I* Madag
101D3 **Nosy Varika** Madag
58B2 **Notéc** *R* Pol
5G4 **Notikeuin** Can
53C3 **Noto** Italy
39F7 **Notodden** Nor
75B1 **Noto-hantō** *Pen* Japan
7E5 **Notre Dams B** Can
43D3 **Nottingham** County, Eng
43D3 **Nottingham** Eng
6C3 **Nottingham** *I* Can
6C3 **Nottingham Island** Can
96A2 **Nouadhibou** Maur
97A3 **Nouakchott** Maur
107F3 **Nouméa** Nouvelle Calédonie
97B3 **Nouna** Burkina
107F3 **Nouvelle Calédonie** *I* S W Pacific O
98B3 **Nova Caipemba** Angola
35A2 **Nova Esparança** Brazil
35C2 **Nova Friburgo** Brazil
100A2 **Nova Gaia** Angola
35B2 **Nova Granada** Brazil
35B2 **Nova Horizonte** Brazil
35C1 **Nova Lima** Brazil
Nova Lisboa = Huambo
35A2 **Nova Londrina** Brazil
101C3 **Nova Mambone** Mozam
47C2 **Novara** Italy
7D5 **Nova Scotia** Province, Can
22A1 **Novato** USA
35C1 **Nova Venécia** Brazil
60D4 **Novaya Kakhovka** Ukraine
64G2 **Novaya Zemlya** *I* Barents S
54C2 **Nova Zagora** Bulg
31C2 **Nove Russas** Brazil
54A1 **Nové Zámky** Slovakia
60D2 **Novgorod** Russian Fed
47C2 **Novi Ligure** Italy
54C2 **Novi Pazar** Bulg
54B2 **Novi Pazar** Serbia, Yugos
54A1 **Novi Sad** Serbia, Yugos
61J3 **Novoalekseyevka** Kazakhstan
61F3 **Novoanninskiy** Russian Fed
61E4 **Novocherkassk** Russian Fed
60C3 **Novograd Volynskiy** Ukraine
58D2 **Novogrudok** Russian Fed
30F4 **Novo Hamburgo** Brazil
65H5 **Novokazalinsk** Kazakhstan
65K4 **Novokuznetsk** Russian Fed
112B12 **Novolazarevskaya** *Base* Ant
52C1 **Novo Mesto** Slovenia
60E3 **Novomoskovsk** Russian Fed
60E5 **Novorossiysk** Russian Fed
65K4 **Novosibirsk** Russian Fed
1B8 **Novosibirskiye Ostrova** *I* Russian Fed
61J3 **Novotroitsk** Russian Fed
61G3 **Novo Uzensk** Russian Fed
59C2 **Novovolynsk** Ukraine
61G2 **Novo Vyatsk** Russian Fed
60D3 **Novozybkov** Russian Fed
58C2 **Novy Dwór Mazowiecki** Pol
61K2 **Novyy Lyalya** Russian Fed
61H5 **Novyy Port** Russian Fed
61H5 **Novyy Uzen** Kazakhstan
58B2 **Nowa Sól** Pol
18A2 **Nowata** USA
Nowgong = Nagaon
12D2 **Nowitna** *R* USA
109D2 **Nowra** Aust
90B2 **Now Shahr** Iran
84C2 **Nowshera** Pak
59C3 **Nowy Sącz** Pol
12H3 **Noyes I** USA
46B2 **Noyon** France
97B4 **Nsawam** Ghana
99D1 **Nuba** *Mts* Sudan
81B3 **Nubian Desert** Sudan
34A3 **Nuble** *R* Chile
9D4 **Nueces** *R* USA
5J3 **Nueltin L** Can
26A2 **Nueva Gerona** Cuba
34A3 **Nueva Imperial** Chile
9C4 **Nueva Laredo** Mexico
34D2 **Nueva Palmira** Urug
24B2 **Nueva Rosita** Mexico
26B2 **Nuevitas** Cuba
24B1 **Nuevo Casas Grandes** Mexico
24C2 **Nuevo Laredo** Mexico
99E2 **Nugaal** Region, Somalia
6E2 **Nûgâtsiaq** Greenland
6E2 **Nugssuag** *Pen* Greenland
6E2 **Nûgussaq** *I* Greenland
108A2 **Nukey Bluff** *Mt* Aust
93D3 **Nukhayb** Iraq
65G5 **Nukus** Uzbekistan
12C2 **Nulato** USA
106B4 **Nullarbor Plain** Aust
97D4 **Numan** Nig
75B1 **Numata** Japan
98C2 **Numatinna** *R* Sudan
74D3 **Numazu** Japan
71E4 **Numfoor** *I* Indon
108C3 **Numurkah** Aust
12B2 **Nunapitchuk** USA
84D2 **Nunkun** *Mt* India
53A2 **Nuoro** Sardegna
91B3 **Nurābād** Iran
47C2 **Nure** *R* Italy
108A2 **Nuriootpa** Aust
84C1 **Nuristan** *Upland* Afghan
61H3 **Nurlat** Russian Fed
38K6 **Nurmes** Fin
57C3 **Nürnberg** Germany
108C2 **Nurri,Mt** Aust
93D2 **Nusaybin** Turk
12C3 **Nushagak** *R* USA
12C3 **Nushagak B** USA
12C3 **Nushagak Pen** USA
84B3 **Nushki** Pak
7D4 **Nutak** Can
12F2 **Nutzotin Mts** USA
Nuuk = Godthåb
86A1 **Nuwakot** Nepal
87C3 **Nuwara-Eliya** Sri Lanka
6C3 **Nuyukjuak** Can

Nyack

16C2 **Nyack** USA
99D2 **Nyahururu** Kenya
108B3 **Nyah West** Aust
4C3 **Nyai** USA
68B3 **Nyainqentanglha Shan** Mts China
99D3 **Nyakabindi** Tanz
98C1 **Nyala** Sudan
86B1 **Nyalam** China
98C2 **Nyamlell** Sudan
64F3 **Nyandoma** Russian Fed
100C2 **Nyanga** Zim
98B3 **Nyanga** R Gabon
101C2 **Nyasa L** Malawi/Mozam
76B2 **Nyaunglebin** Burma
61J2 **Nyazepetrovsk** Russian Fed
39G7 **Nyborg** Den
39H7 **Nybro** Sweden
64J3 **Nyda** Russian Fed
6D1 **Nyeboes Land** Region Can
99D3 **Nyeri** Kenya
101C2 **Nyimba** Zambia
82D3 **Nyingchi** China
59C3 **Nyíregyháza** Hung
99D2 **Nyiru,Mt** Kenya
38J6 **Nykarleby** Fin
39F7 **Nykøbing** Den
39G8 **Nykøbing** Den
39H7 **Nyköping** Sweden
100B3 **Nylstroom** S Africa
109C2 **Nymagee** Aust
39H7 **Nynäshamn** Sweden
109C2 **Nyngan** Aust
47B1 **Nyon** Switz
98B2 **Nyong** R Cam
49D3 **Nyons** France
59B2 **Nysa** Pol
20C2 **Nyssa** USA
63D1 **Nyurba** Russian Fed
99D3 **Nzega** Tanz
97B4 **Nzérékore** Guinea
98B3 **N'zeto** Angola

O

6F3 **Oaggsimiut** Greenland
8C2 **Oahe Res** USA
21C4 **Oahu** I Hawaiian Is
108B2 **Oakbank** Aust
22B2 **Oakdale** USA
109D1 **Oakey** Aust
21A2 **Oakland** California, USA
20B2 **Oakland** Oregon, USA
14A3 **Oakland City** USA
14A2 **Oak Lawn** USA
22B2 **Oakley** California, USA
20B2 **Oakridge** USA
14C2 **Oakville** Can
111B3 **Oamaru** NZ
112B7 **Oates Land** Region, Ant
109C4 **Oatlands** Aust
23B2 **Oaxaca** Mexico
23B2 **Oaxaca** State, Mexico
65J3 **Ob'** R Russian Fed
75B1 **Obama** Japan
111A3 **Oban** NZ
44B3 **Oban** Scot
75C1 **Obanazawa** Japan
47D1 **Oberammergau** Germany
46D1 **Oberhausen** Germany
47D1 **Oberstdorf** Germany
71D4 **Obi** I Indon
33F4 **Obidos** Brazil
74E2 **Obihiro** Japan
98C2 **Obo** CAR
99E1 **Obock** Djibouti
58B2 **Oborniki** Pol
60E3 **Oboyan** Russian Fed
20B2 **O'Brien** USA
61H3 **Obshchiy Syrt** Mts Russian Fed
64J3 **Obskava Guba** B Russian Fed

97B4 **Obuasi** Ghana
17B2 **Ocala** USA
32C2 **Ocana** Colombia
50B2 **Ocaño** Spain
12G3 **Ocean C** USA
15C3 **Ocean City** Maryland, USA
16B3 **Ocean City** New Jersey, USA
5F4 **Ocean Falls** Can
22D4 **Oceanside** USA
19C3 **Ocean Springs** USA
61H2 **Ocher** Russian Fed
44C3 **Ochil Hills** Scot
17B1 **Ochlockonee** R USA
27H1 **Ocho Rios** Jamaica
17B1 **Ocmulgee** R USA
17B1 **Oconee** R USA
14A2 **Oconto** USA
23A1 **Ocotlán** Jalisco, Mexico
23B2 **Ocotlán** Oaxaca, Mexico
97B4 **Oda** Ghana
75A1 **Oda** Japan
38B2 **Ódáðahraun** Region, Iceland
74E2 **Odate** Japan
74D3 **Odawara** Japan
39F6 **Odda** Nor
50A2 **Odemira** Port
55C3 **Ödemiş** Turk
101G1 **Odendaalsrus** S Africa
39G7 **Odense** Den
56C2 **Oder** R Pol/Germany
9C3 **Odessa** Texas, USA
60D4 **Odessa** Ukraine
20C1 **Odessa** Washington, USA
97B4 **Odienné** Ivory Coast
59B2 **Odra** R Pol
31C3 **Oeiras** Brazil
53C2 **Ofanto** R Italy
94B3 **Ofaqim** Israel
45C2 **Offaly** County, Irish Rep
49D1 **Offenbach** Germany
49D2 **Offenburg** Germany
74D3 **Ogaki** Japan
99E2 **Ogaden** Region, Eth
74D3 **Ogaki** Japan
8C2 **Ogallala** USA
69G4 **Ogasawara Gunto** Is Japan
97C4 **Ogbomosho** Nig
8B2 **Ogden** Utah, USA
15C2 **Ogdensburg** USA
17B1 **Ogeechee** R USA
12G1 **Ogilvie** Can
4E3 **Ogilvie Mts** Can
17B1 **Oglethorpe,Mt** USA
47D2 **Oglio** R Italy
47B1 **Ognon** R France
97C4 **Ogoja** Nig
98A3 **Ogooué** R Gabon
58C1 **Ogre** Latvia
96B2 **Oguilet Khenachich** Well Mali
52C1 **Ogulin** Croatia
111A3 **Ohai** NZ
110C1 **Ohakune** NZ
96C2 **Ohanet** Alg
111A2 **Ohau,L** NZ
10B2 **Ohio** State, USA
14A3 **Ohio** R USA
100A2 **Ohopoho** Namibia
57C2 **Ohre** R Czech Republic
55B2 **Ohrid** Macedonia
55B2 **Ohridsko Jezero** L Macedonia/Alb
110B1 **Ohura** NZ
33G3 **Oiapoque** French Guiana
68B2 **Oijiaojing** China
14C2 **Oil City** USA
21B2 **Oildale** USA
46B2 **Oise** Department, France
49C2 **Oise** R France
74C4 **Oita** Japan
22C3 **Ojai** USA
24B2 **Ojinaga** Mexico

23B2 **Ojitlán** Mexico
75B1 **Ojiya** Japan
30C4 **Ojos del Salado** Mt Arg
23A1 **Ojueloz** Mexico
60E3 **Oka** R Russian Fed
100A3 **Okahandja** Namibia
20C1 **Okanagan Falls** Can
13D2 **Okanagan L** Can
20C1 **Okanogan** USA
20C1 **Okanogan** R USA
20B1 **Okanogan Range** Mts Can/USA
84C2 **Okara** Pak
100A2 **Okavango** R Angola/Namibia
100B2 **Okavango Delta** Marsh Botswana
74D3 **Okaya** Japan
74C4 **Okayama** Japan
75B2 **Okazaki** Japan
17B2 **Okeechobee** USA
17B2 **Okeechobee,L** USA
17B1 **Okefenokee Swamp** USA
97C4 **Okene** Nig
85B4 **Okha** India
69G1 **Okha** Russian Fed
86B1 **Okhaldunga** Nepal
62J3 **Okhotsk,S of** Russian Fed
29D3 **Okinawa** I Japan
69E4 **Okinawa** I Japan
69E4 **Okinawa gunto** Arch Japan
74C3 **Oki-shoto** Is Japan
9D3 **Oklahoma** State, USA
18A2 **Oklahoma City** USA
18A2 **Okmulgee** USA
98B3 **Okondja** Gabon
98B3 **Okoyo** Congo
97C4 **Okpara** R Nig
61J4 **Oktyabr'sk** Kazakhstan
61H3 **Oktyabr'skiy** Russian Fed
74D2 **Okushiri-tō** I Japan
38A2 **Ólafsvik** Iceland
39H7 **Öland** I Sweden
108B2 **Olary** Aust
18B2 **Olathe** USA
29D3 **Olavarría** Arg
53A2 **Olbia** Sardegna
12G1 **Old Crow** Can
56B2 **Oldenburg** Niedersachsen, Germany
56C2 **Oldenburg** Schleswig-Holstein, Germany
15C2 **Old Forge** USA
42C3 **Oldham** Eng
12D3 **Old Harbor** USA
41B3 **Old Head of Kinsale** C Scot
16C2 **Old Lyme** USA
13E2 **Olds** Can
72B1 **Öldziyt** Mongolia
15C2 **Olean** USA
63E2 **Olekma** R Russian Fed
63D1 **Olekminsk** Russian Fed
38L5 **Olenegorsk** Russian Fed
58D2 **Olevsk** Ukraine
69F2 **Ol'ga** Russian Fed
100A3 **Olifants** R Namibia
55B2 **Ólimbos** Mt Greece
35B2 **Olímpia** Brazil
23B2 **Olinala** Mexico
31E3 **Olinda** Brazil
34C2 **Oliva** Arg
29C2 **Olivares** Mt Arg
35C2 **Oliveira** Brazil
13D3 **Oliver** Can
30C3 **Ollague** Chile
30C3 **Ollagüe** Mt Bol
18C2 **Olney** USA
68E1 **Olochi** Russian Fed
39G7 **Olofstrom** Sweden
98B3 **Olombo** Congo
59B3 **Olomouc** Czech Republic

60D1 **Olonets** Russian Fed
79B3 **Olongapa** Phil
48B3 **Oloron Ste Marie** France
68D1 **Olovyannaya** Russian Fed
46D1 **Olpe** Germany
58C2 **Olsztyn** Pol
54B2 **Olt** R Rom
47B1 **Olten** Switz
20B1 **Olympia** USA
20B1 **Olympic Nat Pk** USA
Olympus = Ólimbos
20B1 **Olympus,Mt** USA
65J4 **Om'** R Russian Fed
75B1 **Omachi** Japan
75B2 **Omae-zaki** C Japan
45C1 **Omagh** N Ire
18A1 **Omaha** USA
20C1 **Omak** USA
91C5 **Oman** Sultanate, Arabian Pen
91C4 **Oman,G of** UAE
98A3 **Omboué** Gabon
99D1 **Omdurman** Sudan
23B2 **Ometepec** Mexico
99D1 **Om Häjer** Eritrea
13B1 **Omineca** R Can
13B1 **Omineca Mts** Can
75B1 **Omiya** Japan
12H3 **Ommaney,C** USA
4H2 **Ommanney B** Can
99D2 **Omo** R Eth
65J4 **Omsk** Russian Fed
74B4 **Omura** Japan
74C4 **Omuta** Japan
61H2 **Omutninsk** Russian Fed
78D3 **Onang** Indon
14B1 **Onaping L** Can
100A2 **Oncócua** Angola
100A2 **Ondangua** Namibia
59C3 **Ondava** R Slovakia
68D2 **Öndörhaan** Molgolia
83B5 **One and Half Degree Chan** Indian O
64E3 **Onega** Russian Fed
64E3 **Onega** R Russian Fed
15C2 **Oneida L** USA
8D2 **O'Neill** USA
69H2 **Onekotan** I Russian Fed
98C3 **Onema** Zaire
15D2 **Oneonta** USA
54C1 **Oneşti** Rom
64E3 **Onezhskoye Ozero** L Russian Fed
100A2 **Ongiva** Angola
74B3 **Ongjin** N Korea
72D1 **Ongniud Qi** China
87C1 **Ongole** India
15C2 **Onieda L** USA
101D3 **Onilahy** R Madag
97C4 **Onitsha** Nig
68C2 **Onjüül** Mongolia
75B1 **Ono** Japan
75B2 **Onohara-jima** I Japan
74C4 **Onomichi** Japan
106A3 **Onslow** Aust
17C1 **Onslow B** USA
75B1 **Ontake-san** Mt Japan
22D3 **Ontario** California, USA
20C2 **Ontario** Oregon, USA
7A4 **Ontario** Province, Can
15C2 **Ontario,L** Can/USA
51B2 **Onteniente** Spain
106C3 **Oodnadatta** Aust
106C4 **Ooldea** Aust
18A2 **Oologah L** USA
46B1 **Oostende** Belg
46B1 **Oosterschelde** Estuary Neth
87B2 **Ootacamund** India
13B2 **Ootsa L** Can
69H1 **Opala** Russian Fed
98C3 **Opala** Zaire
87C3 **Opanake** Sri Lanka
61G2 **Oparino** Russian Fed

59B3 **Opava** Czech Republic
17A1 **Opelika** USA
19B3 **Opelousas** USA
12C2 **Ophir** USA
58D1 **Opochka** Russian Fed
59B2 **Opole** Pol
Oporto = Porto
110C1 **Opotiki** NZ
17A1 **Opp** USA
38F6 **Oppdal** Nor
110B1 **Opunake** NZ
54B1 **Oradea** Rom
38B2 **Oraefajökull** *Mts* Iceland
85D3 **Orai** India
96B1 **Oran** Alg
30D3 **Orán** Arg
109C2 **Orange** Aust
22D4 **Orange** California, USA
49C3 **Orange** France
19B3 **Orange** Texas, USA
100A3 **Orange** *R* S Africa
17B1 **Orangeburg** USA
101G1 **Orange Free State** Province, S Africa
17B1 **Orange Park** USA
14B2 **Orangeville** Can
56C2 **Oranienburg** Germany
79C3 **Oras** Phil
54B1 **Orăstie** Rom
54B1 **Oraviţa** Rom
52B2 **Orbetello** Italy
109C3 **Orbost** Aust
46B1 **Orchies** France
47B2 **Orco** *R* Italy
106B2 **Ord** *R* Aust
106B2 **Ord,Mt** Aust
93C1 **Ordu** Turk
39H7 **Örebro** Sweden
8A2 **Oregon** State, USA
14B2 **Oregon** USA
20B1 **Oregon City** USA
39H6 **Oregrund** Sweden
60E2 **Orekhovo Zuyevo** Russian Fed
60E3 **Orel** Russian Fed
61H3 **Orenburg** Russian Fed
34D3 **Orense** Arg
50A1 **Orense** Spain
56C1 **Oresund** *Str* Den/ Sweden
111A3 **Oreti** *R* NZ
55C3 **Orhaneli** *R* Turk
68C2 **Orhon Gol** *R* Mongolia
23B2 **Oriental** Mexico
108B1 **Orientos** Aust
51B2 **Orihuela** Spain
15C2 **Orillia** Can
33E2 **Orinoco** *R* Ven
86A2 **Orissa** State, India
53A3 **Oristano** Sardegna
38K6 **Orivesi** *L* Fin
33F4 **Oriximina** Brazil
23B2 **Orizaba** Mexico
35B1 **Orizona** Brazil
44C2 **Orkney** *I* Scot
35B2 **Orlândia** Brazil
17B2 **Orlando** USA
48C2 **Orléanais** *Region* France
48C2 **Orléans** France
63B2 **Orlik** Russian Fed
82A3 **Ormara** Pak
79B3 **Ormoc** Phil
17B2 **Ormond Beach** USA
46C2 **Ornain** *R* France
47B1 **Ornans** France
48B2 **Orne** *R* France
38H6 **Örnsköldsvik** Sweden
32C3 **Orocué** Colombia
94B3 **Oron** Israel
Orontes = 'Āṣī
79B4 **Oroquieta** Phil
59C3 **Orosháza** Hung
21A2 **Oroville** California, USA
20C1 **Oroville** Washington, USA
47B1 **Orsières** Switz
65G4 **Orsk** Russian Fed
38F6 **Ørsta** Nor
48B3 **Orthez** France
50A1 **Ortigueira** Spain
47D1 **Ortles** *Mts* Italy
27L1 **Ortoire** *R* Trinidad
93E2 **Orūmīyeh** Iran
30C2 **Oruro** Bol
61J2 **Osa** Russian Fed
18B2 **Osage** *R* USA
75B1 **Osaka** Japan
25D4 **Osa,Pen de** Costa Rica
18C2 **Osceola** Arkansas, USA
18B1 **Osceola** Iowa, USA
20C2 **Osgood Mts** USA
15C2 **Oshawa** Can
75B2 **O-shima** *I* Japan
10B2 **Oshkosh** USA
97C4 **Oshogbo** Nig
7B5 **Oshosh** USA
98B3 **Oshwe** Zaïre
54A1 **Osijek** Croatia
65K5 **Osinniki** Russian Fed
58D2 **Osipovichi** Belorussia
18B1 **Oskaloosa** USA
60A2 **Oskarshamn** Sweden
39G7 **Oslo** Nor
92C2 **Osmaniye** Turk
56B2 **Osnabrück** Germany
30F4 **Osório** Brazil
29B4 **Osorno** Chile
50B1 **Osorno** Spain
20C1 **Osoyoos** Can
13C1 **Ospika** *R* Can
107D5 **Ossa,Mt** Aust
16C2 **Ossining** USA
60D2 **Ostashkov** Russian Fed
Ostend = Oostende
38G6 **Østerdalen** *V* Nor
38G6 **Östersund** Sweden
56B2 **Ostfriesische Inseln** *Is* Germany
39H6 **Östhammär** Sweden
53B2 **Ostia** Italy
47D2 **Ostiglia** Italy
59B3 **Ostrava** Czech Republic
58B2 **Ostróda** Pol
58B2 **Ostroleka** Pol
60C2 **Ostrov** Russian Fed
64J2 **Ostrov Belyy** *I* Russian Fed
64H1 **Ostrov Greem Bell** *I* Barents S
64F3 **Ostrov Kolguyev** *I* Russian Fed
74F2 **Ostrov Kunashir** *I* Russian Fed
64F2 **Ostrov Mechdusharskiy** *I* Barents S
90D2 **Ostrov Ogurchinskiy** *I* Turkmenistan
64G1 **Ostrov Rudol'fa** *I* Barents S
64G2 **Ostrov Vaygach** *I* Russian Fed
1B7 **Ostrov Vrangelya** *I* Russian Fed
58B2 **Ostrów Wlkp.** Pol
59C2 **Ostrowiec** Pol
58C2 **Ostrów Mazowiecka** Pol
50A2 **Osuna** Spain
15C2 **Osweg** USA
15C2 **Oswego** USA
43C3 **Oswestry** Eng
59B2 **Oświęcim** Pol
75B1 **Ota** Japan
111B3 **Otago Pen** NZ
110C2 **Otaki** NZ
74E2 **Otaru** Japan
32B3 **Otavalo** Ecuador
100A2 **Otavi** Namibia
75C1 **Otawara** Japan
20C1 **Othello** USA
55B3 **Óthris** *Mt* Greece
16C1 **Otis** Massachusetts, USA
16B2 **Otisville** USA
100A3 **Otjiwarongo** Namibia
72B2 **Otog Qi** China
110C1 **Otorohanga** NZ
55A2 **Otranto** Italy
55A2 **Otranto,Str of** *Chan* Italy/Alb
14A2 **Otsego** USA
75B1 **Otsu** Japan
39F6 **Otta** Nor
39F7 **Otta** *R* Nor
15C1 **Ottawa** Can
18A2 **Ottawa** Kansas, USA
15C1 **Ottawa** *R* Can
7B4 **Ottawa Is** Can
7B4 **Otter Rapids** Can
6B1 **Otto Fjord** Can
101G1 **Ottosdal** S Africa
18B1 **Ottumwa** USA
46D2 **Ottweiler** Germany
97C4 **Oturkpo** Nig
32B5 **Otusco** Peru
108B3 **Otway,C** Aust
58C2 **Otwock** Pol
47D1 **Ötz** Austria
47D1 **Ötztal** *Mts* Austria
76C1 **Ou** *R* Laos
19B3 **Ouachita** *R* USA
19B3 **Ouachita,L** USA
19B3 **Ouachita Mts** USA
96A2 **Ouadane** Maur
98C2 **Ouadda** CAR
98C1 **Ouaddai** *Desert Region* Chad
97B3 **Ouagadougou** Burkina
97B3 **Ouahigouya** Burkina
98C2 **Ouaka** CAR
97C3 **Oualam** Niger
96C2 **Ouallen** Alg
98C2 **Ouanda Djallé** CAR
96A2 **Ouarane** Region, Maur
96C1 **Ouargla** Alg
98C2 **Ouarra** *R* CAR
96B1 **Ouarzazate** Mor
51C2 **Ouassel** *R* Alg
98B2 **Oubangui** *R* Congo
46B1 **Oudenaarde** Belg
100B4 **Oudtshoorn** S Africa
51B2 **Oued Tlělat** Alg
96B1 **Oued Zem** Mor
98B2 **Ouesso** Congo
96B1 **Ouezzane** Mor
98B2 **Ouham** *R* Chad
97C4 **Ouidah** Benin
96B1 **Oujda** Mor
38J6 **Oulainen** Fin
38K5 **Oulu** Fin
38K6 **Oulu** *R* Fin
38K6 **Oulujärvi** *L* Fin
95B3 **Oum Chalouba** Chad
98B1 **Oum Hadjer** Chad
95B3 **Oum Haouach** *Watercourse* Chad
38K5 **Ounas** *R* Fin
95B3 **Ounianga Kébir** Chad
46D1 **Our** *R* Germany
46B2 **Ourcq** *R* France
Ourense = Orense
31C3 **Ouricurí** Brazil
35B2 **Ourinhos** Brazil
35C2 **Ouro Prêto** Brazil
46C1 **Ourthe** *R* Belg
42D2 **Ouse** *R* Eng
43E3 **Ouse** *R* Eng
40B2 **Outer Hebrides** *Is* Scot
22C4 **Outer Santa Barbara** *Chan* USA
100A3 **Outjo** Namibia
38K6 **Outokumpu** Fin
108B3 **Ouyen** Aust
47C2 **Ovada** Italy
34A2 **Ovalle** Chile
100A2 **Ovamboland** Region, Namibia
61H5 **Ova Tyuleni** *Is* Kazakhstan
38J5 **Övertorneå** Sweden
50A1 **Oviedo** Spain
60C3 **Ovruch** Ukraine
63E2 **Ovsyanka** Russian Fed
111A3 **Owaka** NZ
75B2 **Owase** Japan
11B3 **Owensboro** USA
21B2 **Owens L** USA
14B2 **Owen Sound** Can
107D1 **Owen Stanley Range** *Mts* PNG
97C4 **Owerri** Nig
97C4 **Owo** Nig
14B2 **Owosso** USA
20C2 **Owyhee** *R* USA
20C2 **Owyhee Mts** USA
32B6 **Oxapampa** Peru
39H7 **Oxelösund** Sweden
43D4 **Oxford** County, Eng
43D4 **Oxford** Eng
16D1 **Oxford** Massachusetts, USA
19C3 **Oxford** Mississippi, USA
45B1 **Ox Mts** Irish Rep
22C3 **Oxnard** USA
74D3 **Oyama** Japan
13E2 **Oyen** Can
98B2 **Oyem** Gabon
44B3 **Oykel** *R* Scot
39F6 **Øyre** Nor
109C4 **Oyster B** Aust
79B4 **Ozamiz** Phil
17A1 **Ozark** USA
18B2 **Ozark Plat** USA
18B2 **Ozarks,L of the** USA
59C3 **Ózd** Hung
65K5 **Ozero Alakol** *L* Kazakhstan/ Russian Fed
65J5 **Ozero Balkhash** *L* Kazakhstan
63C2 **Ozero Baykal** *L* Kazakhstan
65J4 **Ozero Chany** *L* Russian Fed
69F1 **Ozero Chukchagirskoye** Russian Fed
69F1 **Ozero Evoron** Russian Fed
Ozero Chudskoye = Peipus,L
60D2 **Ozero Il'men** *L* Russian Fed
38L5 **Ozero Imandra** *L* Russian Fed
82B1 **Ozero Issyk Kul'** *L* Kirghizia
69F2 **Ozero Khanka** *L* China/Russian Fed
38L5 **Ozero Kovdozero** *L* Russian Fed
38L5 **Ozero Kuyto** *L* Russian Fed
38L5 **Ozero Pyaozero** *L* Russian Fed
65H4 **Ozero Tengiz** *L* Kazakhstan
38L5 **Ozero Topozero** *L* Russian Fed
65K5 **Ozero Zaysan** Kazakhstan
23B1 **Ozuluama** Mexico

P

100A4 **Paarl** S Africa
44A3 **Pabbay** *I* Scot
58B2 **Pabianice** Pol
86B2 **Pabna** Bang
58D2 **Pabrade** Lithuania
32B5 **Pacasmayo** Peru
23B1 **Pachuca** Mexico
105K6 **Pacific-Antarctic Ridge** Pacific O
22B2 **Pacific Grove** USA
78C4 **Pacitan** Indon
35C1 **Pacuí** *R* Brazil
70B4 **Padang** Indon
56B2 **Paderborn** Germany
5J3 **Padlei** Can
86C2 **Padma** *R* Bang
47D2 **Padova** Italy
9D4 **Padre I** USA

61F2 **Pavlovo** Russian Fed
61F3 **Pavlovsk** Russian Fed
78C3 **Pawan** *R* Indon
18A2 **Pawhuska** USA
16D2 **Pawtucket** USA
47B1 **Payerne** Switz
20C2 **Payette** USA
7C4 **Payne,L** Can
34D2 **Paysandu** Urug
46A2 **Pays-de-Bray** Region, France
54B2 **Pazardzhik** Bulg
13D1 **Peace** *R* Can
17B2 **Peace** *R* USA
13D1 **Peace River** Can
43D3 **Peak District Nat Pk** Eng
108A1 **Peake** *R* Aust
109C2 **Peak Hill** Aust
71E4 **Peak Mandala** *Mt* Indon
42D3 **Peak,The** *Mt* Eng
19B3 **Pearl** *R* USA
21C4 **Pearl City** Hawaiian Is
21C4 **Pearl Harbor** Hawaiian Is
4H2 **Peary Chan** Can
101C2 **Pebane** Mozam
54B2 **Peć** Serbia, Yugos
35C1 **Peçanha** Brazil
19B4 **Pecan Island** USA
38L5 **Pechenga** Russian Fed
64F3 **Pechora** *R* Russian Fed
64G3 **Pechorskoye More** *S* Russian Fed
53C3 **Pecoraro** *Mt* Italy
9C3 **Pecos** USA
9C3 **Pecos** *R* USA
59B3 **Pécs** Hung
108A1 **Pedirka** Aust
35C1 **Pedra Azul** Brazil
35B2 **Pedregulho** Brazil
26B3 **Pedro Cays** *Is* Caribbean S
30C3 **Pedro de Valdivia** Chile
30E3 **Pedro Juan Caballero** Par
34C3 **Pedro Luro** Arg
23B1 **Pedro Mentova** Mexico
87C3 **Pedro,Pt** Sri Lanka
108B2 **Peebinga** Aust
42C2 **Peebles** Scot
17C1 **Pee Dee** *R* USA
16C2 **Peekskill** USA
42B2 **Peel** Eng
12H1 **Peel** *R* Can
4J2 **Peel Sd** Can
108A1 **Peera Peera Poolanna** *L* Aust
13E1 **Peerless L** Can
71E4 **Peg Arfak** *Mt* Indon
111D2 **Pegasus B** NZ
83D4 **Pegu** Burma
78A3 **Pegunungan Barisan** *Mts* Indon
78C2 **Pegunungan Iran** *Mts* Malay/Indon
71E4 **Pegunungan Maoke** *Mts* Indon
78D3 **Pegunungan Meratus** *Mts* Indon
78C2 **Pegunungan Muller** *Mts* Indon
78C3 **Pegunungan Schwanet** *Mts* Indon
78A3 **Pegunungan Tigapuluh** *Mts* Indon
76B2 **Pegu Yoma** *Mts* Burma
34C3 **Pehuajó** Arg
Péipsi Järve = Peipus,L
39K7 **Peipus, Lake** Estonia/ Russian Fed
35A2 **Peixe** *R* Sao Paulo, Brazil
72D3 **Pei Xian** China
78B4 **Pekalongan** Indon
77C5 **Pekan** Malay
78A2 **Pekanbaru** Indon
18C1 **Pekin** USA
Peking = Beijing
77C5 **Pelabohan Kelang** Malay
78D4 **Pelau Pelau Kangean** *Is* Indon
78C4 **Pelau Pelau Karimunjawa** *Arch* Indon
78D4 **Pelau Pelau Postilyon** *Is* Indon
54B1 **Peleaga** *Mt* Rom
63D2 **Peleduy** Russian Fed
14B2 **Pelee I** Can
71D4 **Peleng** *I* Indon
12G3 **Pelican** USA
69F1 **Peliny Osipenko** Russian Fed
34C3 **Pellegrini** Arg
38J5 **Pello** Fin
12H2 **Pelly** *R* Can
6A3 **Pelly Bay** Can
12G2 **Pelly Crossing** Can
12H2 **Pelly Mts** Can
30F5 **Pelotas** Brazil
30F4 **Pelotas** *R* Brazil
47B2 **Pelvoux** Region, France
78B4 **Pemalang** Indon
78A3 **Pematang** Indon
101D2 **Pemba** Mozam
99D3 **Pemba** *I* Tanz
13C2 **Pemberton** Can
13D2 **Pembina** *R* Can
15C1 **Pembroke** Can
17B1 **Pembroke** USA
43B4 **Pembroke** Wales
34A3 **Pemuco** Chile
78D2 **Penambo Range** *Mts* Malay
35A2 **Penápolis** Brazil
50A2 **Peñarroya** Spain
51B1 **Penarroya** *Mt* Spain
50A1 **Peña Trevina** *Mt* Spain
98B2 **Pende** *R* Chad
12J3 **Pendelton,Mt** Can
20C1 **Pendleton** USA
20C1 **Pend Oreille** *R* USA
31D4 **Penedo** Brazil
85D5 **Penganga** *R* India
73D5 **P'eng hu Lieh-tao** *Is* Taiwan
72E2 **Penglai** China
73B4 **Pengshui** China
71E4 **Pengunungan Maoke** *Mts* Indon
26C4 **Península de la Guajiri** *Pen* Colombia
27E4 **Península de Paria** *Pen* Ven
77C5 **Peninsular Malaysia** Malay
10D2 **Peninsule de Gaspé** *Pen* Can
23A1 **Penjamo** Mexico
87B2 **Penner** *R* India
42C2 **Pennine Chain** *Mts* Eng
16B3 **Penns Grove** USA
10C2 **Pennsylvania** State, USA
6D3 **Penny Highlands** *Mts* Can
108B3 **Penola** Aust
106C4 **Penong** Aust
42C2 **Penrith** Eng
11B3 **Pensacola** USA
112A **Pensacola Mts** Ant
78D1 **Pensiangan** Malay
13D3 **Penticton** Can
44C2 **Pentland Firth** *Chan* Scot
42C2 **Pentland Hills** Scot
61G3 **Penza** Russian Fed
43B4 **Penzance** Eng
10B2 **Peoria** USA
78A3 **Perabumulih** Indon
77C5 **Perak** *R* Malay
78A2 **Perawang** Indon
32B3 **Pereira** Colombia
35A2 **Pereira Barreto** Brazil
61F4 **Perelazovskiy** Russian Fed
12D3 **Perenosa B** USA
34C2 **Pergamino** Arg
7C4 **Peribonca** *R* Can
48C2 **Périqueux** France
25E4 **Perlas Arch de** *Is* Panama
61J2 **Perm'** Russian Fed
Pernambuco = Recife
31D3 **Pernambuco** State, Brazil
108A2 **Pernatty Lg** Aust
54B2 **Pernik** Bulg
46B2 **Péronne** France
23B2 **Perote** Mexico
49C3 **Perpignan** France
22D4 **Perris** USA
17B1 **Perry** Florida, USA
17B1 **Perry** Georgia, USA
18A2 **Perry** Oklahoma, USA
4H3 **Perry River** Can
14B2 **Perrysburg** USA
12C3 **Perryville** Alaska, USA
18C2 **Perryville** Missouri, USA
106A4 **Perth** Aust
15C2 **Perth** Can
44C3 **Perth** Scot
16B2 **Perth Amboy** USA
32C6 **Peru** Republic, S America
18C1 **Peru** USA
103E5 **Peru-Chile Trench** Pacific O
52B2 **Perugia** Italy
52C2 **Perušic** Croatia
93D2 **Pervari** Turk
61F3 **Pervomaysk** Russian Fed
60D4 **Pervomaysk** Ukraine
61J2 **Pervoural'sk** Russian Fed
52B2 **Pesaro** Italy
22A2 **Pescadero** USA
Pescadores = P'eng-hu Lieh-tao
52B2 **Pescara** Italy
47D2 **Peschiera** Italy
84C2 **Peshawar** Pak
54B2 **Peshkopi** Alb
14A1 **Peshtigo** USA
60E2 **Pestovo** Russian Fed
94B2 **Petah Tiqwa** Israel
21A2 **Petaluma** USA
46C2 **Pétange** Lux
23A2 **Petatlán** Mexico
101C2 **Petauke** Zambia
108A2 **Peterborough** Aust
15C2 **Peterborough** Can
43D3 **Peterborough** Eng
44D3 **Peterhead** Scot
6D1 **Petermann Gletscher** *Gl* Greenland
106B3 **Petermann Range** *Mts* Aust
29B3 **Peteroa** *Mt* Arg/Chile
13F1 **Peter Pond L** Can
12H3 **Petersburg** Alaska, USA
85C4 **Petlād** India
23B2 **Petlalcingo** Mexico
25D2 **Peto** Mexico
63D2 **Petomskoye Nagor'ye** *Upland* Russian Fed
34A2 **Petorca** Chile
14B1 **Petoskey** USA
31C3 **Petrolina** Brazil
65H4 **Petropavlovsk** Kazakhstan
35C2 **Petrópolis** Brazil
61G3 **Petrovsk** Russian Fed
68C1 **Petrovsk Zabaykal'skiy** Russian Fed
64E3 **Petrozavodsk** Russian Fed
101G1 **Petrus** S Africa
101G1 **Petrusburg** S Africa
1B7 **Pevek** Russian Fed
46D2 **Pfälzer Wald** Region, Germany
57B3 **Pforzheim** Germany
84D2 **Phagwara** India
85C3 **Phalodi** India
46D2 **Phalsbourg** France
87A1 **Phaltan** India
77B4 **Phangnga** Thai
76C3 **Phanom Dang** *Mts* Camb
76D3 **Phan Rang** Viet
76D3 **Phan Thiet** Viet
17A1 **Phenix City** USA
76B3 **Phet Buri** Thai
76D3 **Phiafay** Laos
19C3 **Philadelphia** Mississippi, USA
16B2 **Philadelphia** Pennsylvania, USA
Philippeville = Skikda
46C1 **Philippeville** Belg
71D2 **Philippine S** Pacific O
71D2 **Philippines** Republic, S E Asia
104E3 **Philippine Trench** Pacific O
15C2 **Philipsburg** Pennsylvania, USA
12E1 **Philip Smith Mts** USA
79B2 **Phillipine S** Phil
6B1 **Phillips B** Can
16B2 **Phillipsburg** New Jersey, USA
6B2 **Philpots Pen** Can
76C3 **Phnom Penh** Camb
9B3 **Phoenix** Arizona, USA
16B2 **Phoenixville** USA
76C1 **Phong Saly** Laos
Phra Nakhon = Bangkok
76C2 **Phu Bia** *Mt* Laos
76D3 **Phu Cuong** Viet
77B4 **Phuket** Thai
86A2 **Phulbāni** India
76C2 **Phu Miang** *Mt* Thai
76D2 **Phu Set** *Mt* Laos
76D1 **Phu Tho** Viet
77D4 **Phu Vinh** Viet
47C2 **Piacenza** Italy
109C2 **Pian** *R* Aust
52B2 **Pianosa** *I* Italy
52C2 **Pianosa** *I* Italy
58C2 **Piaseczno** Pol
54C1 **Piatra-Neamţ** Rom
31C3 **Piauí** State, Brazil
47E2 **Piave** *R* Italy
99D2 **Pibor** *R* Sudan
99D2 **Pibor Post** Sudan
46B1 **Picardie** Region, France
19C3 **Picayune** USA
47B2 **Pic de Rochebrune** *Mt* France
34A2 **Pichilemu** Chile
34C3 **Pichi Mahuida** Arg
42D2 **Pickering** Eng
7A4 **Pickle Lake** Can
96A1 **Pico** *I* Açores
47C1 **Pico Bernina** *Mt* Switz
51C1 **Pico de Anito** *Mt* Spain
24B3 **Pico del Infiernillo** *Mt* Mexico
27C3 **Pico Duarte** *Mt* Dom Rep
31C3 **Picos** Brazil
50B1 **Picos de Europa** *Mt* Spain
109D2 **Picton** Aust
111B2 **Picton** NZ
95A2 **Pic Toussidé** *Mt* Chad
35B2 **Piedade** Brazil
22C2 **Piedra** USA
24B2 **Piedras Negras** Mexico
38K6 **Pieksämäki** Fin
38K6 **Pielinen** *L* Fin
47B2 **Piemonte** Region, Italy

Pierre

Provo

Provost

13E2 **Provost** Can
4D2 **Prudhoe Bay** USA
6D2 **Prudhoe Land** Greenland
58C2 **Pruszkow** Pol
60C4 **Prut** *R* Romania/ Moldavia
60C4 **Prutul** *R* Romania
58C2 **Pruzhany** Belorussia
18A2 **Pryor** USA
59C3 **Przemys'l** Pol
55C3 **Psará** *I* Greece
60C2 **Pskov** Russian Fed
58D2 **Ptich** *R* Belorussia
55B2 **Ptolemaïs** Greece
32C5 **Pucallpa** Peru
73D4 **Pucheng** China
34A3 **Pucón** Chile
38K5 **Pudasjärvi** Fin
87B2 **Pudukkottai** India
23B2 **Puebla** Mexico
23B2 **Puebla** State, Mexico
50A1 **Puebla de Sanabria** Spain
50A1 **Puebla de Trives** Spain
9C2 **Pueblo** USA
34B3 **Puelches** Arg
34B3 **Puelén** Arg
23A2 **Puenta Ixbapa** Mexico
34B2 **Puente del Inca** Arg
32A5 **Puerta Aguja** Peru
30B2 **Puerta Coles** Peru
34B2 **Puerta de los Llanos** Arg
31D3 **Puerta do Calcanhar** *Pt* Brazil
32C1 **Puerta Gallinas** Colombia
23B2 **Puerta Maldonado** *Pt* Mexico
32A2 **Puerta Mariato** Panama
29C5 **Puerta Médanosa** *Pt* Arg
23A2 **Puerta Mongrove** Mexico
25E4 **Puerta San Blas** *Pt* Panama
23A2 **Puerta San Telmo** Mexico
29B5 **Puerto Aisén** Chile
25D4 **Puerto Armuelles** Panama
33F6 **Puerto Artur** Brazil
32B3 **Puerto Asis** Colombia
32D2 **Puerto Ayacucho** Ven
25D3 **Puerto Barrios** Guatemala
32C2 **Puerto Berrio** Colombia
32D1 **Puerto Cabello** Ven
25D3 **Puerto Cabezas** Nic
32D2 **Puerto Carreño** Colombia
25D4 **Puerto Cortes** Costa Rica
25D3 **Puerto Cortés** Honduras
96A2 **Puerto del Rosario** Canary Is
30F3 **Puerto E Cunha** Brazil
32C1 **Puerto Fijo** Ven
31B3 **Puerto Franco** Brazil
32D6 **Puerto Heath** Bol
25D2 **Puerto Juarez** Mexico
33E1 **Puerto la Cruz** Ven
50B2 **Puertollano** Spain
27C4 **Puerto Lopez** Colombia
29D4 **Puerto Madryn** Arg
32D6 **Puerto Maldonado** Peru
23B2 **Puerto Marquéz** Mexico
29B4 **Puerto Montt** Chile
30E3 **Puerto Murtinho** Brazil
29B6 **Puerto Natales** Chile

24A1 **Puerto Peñasco** Mexico
29D4 **Puerto Pirámides** Arg
27C3 **Puerto Plata** Dom Rep
79A4 **Puerto Princesa** Phil
32B3 **Puerto Rico** Colombia
27D3 **Puerto Rico** *I* Caribbean S
27D3 **Puerto Rico Trench** Caribbean S
23A2 **Puerto San Juan de Lima** Mexico
33G4 **Puerto Santanga** Brazil
30E2 **Puerto Suárez** Bol
24B2 **Puerto Vallarta** Mexico
29B4 **Puerto Varas** Chile
30D2 **Puerto Villarroel** Bol
61G3 **Pugachev** Russian Fed
84C3 **Pugal** India
51C1 **Puigcerdá** Spain
111B2 **Pukaki,L** *L* NZ
74B2 **Pukch'ông** N Korea
110B1 **Pukekobe** NZ
111B2 **Puketeraki Range** *Mts* NZ
52B2 **Pula** Croatia
15C2 **Pulaski** New York, USA
71E4 **Pulau Kolepom** *I* Indon
70A4 **Pulau Pulau Batu** *Is* Indon
58C2 **Pulawy** Pol
87C2 **Pulicat,L** India
84B1 **Pul-i-Khumri** Afghan
87B3 **Puliyangudi** India
20C1 **Pullman** USA
71E3 **Pulo Anna Merir** *I* Pacific O
79B2 **Pulog,Mt** Phil
38L5 **Pulozero** Russian Fed
58C2 **Pultusk** Pol
30C4 **Puna de Atacama** Arg
86B1 **Punakha** Bhutan
84C2 **Punch** Pak
87A1 **Pune** India
23A2 **Punéper** Mexico
98C3 **Punia** Zaire
34A2 **Punitaquí** Chile
84C2 **Punjab** Province, Pak
84D2 **Punjab** State, India
30B2 **Puno** Peru
24A2 **Punta Abreojos** *Pt* Mexico
53C3 **Punta Alice** *Pt* Italy
34C3 **Punta Alta** Arg
29B6 **Punta Arenas** Chile
24A2 **Punta Baja** *Pt* Mexico
34A2 **Punta Curaumilla** *Pt* Chile
100A2 **Punta da Marca** *Pt* Angola
101C3 **Punta de Barra Falsa** *Pt* Mozam
29F2 **Punta del Este** Urug
24A2 **Punta Eugenia** *Pt* Mexico
25D3 **Punta Gorda** Belize
17B2 **Punta Gorda** USA
34A3 **Punta Lavapié** *Pt* Chile
34A2 **Punta Lengua de Vaca** *Pt* Chile
53B2 **Punta Licosa** *Pt* Italy
34A1 **Punta Poroto** *Pt* Chile
9B4 **Punta San Antonia** *Pt* Mexico
34A2 **Punta Topocalma** Chile
73C4 **Puqi** China
64J3 **Pur** *R* Russian Fed
19A2 **Purcell** USA
12C1 **Purcell Mt** USA
13D2 **Purcell Mts** Can
34A3 **Purén** Chile

86B2 **Puri** India
87B1 **Pūrna** India
86B1 **Pūrnia** India
76C3 **Pursat** Camb
23A1 **Puruandro** Mexico
33E4 **Purus** *R* Brazil
19C3 **Purvis** USA
78B4 **Purwokerto** Indon
78C4 **Purworejo** Indon
85D5 **Pusad** India
74B3 **Pusan** S Korea
60D2 **Pushkin** Russian Fed
58D1 **Pustoshka** Russian Fed
82D3 **Puta** Burma
34A2 **Putaendo** Chile
110C1 **Putaruru** NZ
73D4 **Putian** China
16D2 **Putnam** USA
87B3 **Puttalam** Sri Lanka
56C2 **Puttgarden** Germany
32B4 **Putumayo** *R* Ecuador
78C2 **Putussibau** Indon
38K6 **Puulavesl** *L* Fin
20B1 **Puyallup** USA
49C2 **Puy de Sancy** *Mt* France
111A3 **Puysegur Pt** NZ
99C3 **Pweto** Zaïre
43B3 **Pwllheli** Wales
76B2 **Pyapon** Burma
61F5 **Pyatigorsk** Russian Fed
Pyè = Prome
74B3 **P'yŏngyang** N Korea
108B3 **Pyramid Hill** Aust
21B1 **Pyramid L** USA
111A2 **Pyramid,Mt** NZ
48B3 **Pyrénées** *Mts* France
58D1 **Pytalovo** Russian Fed
76B2 **Pyu** Burma

Q

94B2 **Qabatiya** Israel
94C3 **Qa'el Hafira** *Mud Flats* Jordan
94C3 **Qa'el Jinz** *Mud Flats* Jordan
68B3 **Qaidam Pendi** *Salt Flat* China
94C2 **Qa Khanna** *Salt Marsh* Jordan
99D1 **Qala'en Nahl** Sudan
84B2 **Qalat** Afghan
94C1 **Qal'at al Hisn** Syria
81C3 **Qal'at Bishah** S Arabia
93E3 **Qal'at Sālih** Iraq
68B3 **Qamdo** China
99E1 **Qandala** Somalia
99E2 **Qardho** Somalia
95B2 **Qara** Egypt
90A3 **Qare Shirin** Iran
91A4 **Qaryat al Ulyā** S Arabia
94C3 **Qasr el Kharana** Jordan
91D4 **Qasr-e-Qand** Iran
95B2 **Qasr Farafra** Egypt
94C2 **Qatana** Syria
91B4 **Qatar** Emirate, Arabian Pen
94C3 **Qatrāna** Jordan
95B2 **Qattâra Depression** Egypt
90C3 **Qãyen** Iran
90A2 **Qazvin** Iran
95C2 **Qena** Egypt
90A2 **Qeydār** Iran
91B4 **Qeys** *I* Iran
94B3 **Qeziot** Israel
73B5 **Qian Jiang** *R* China
72E1 **Qian Shan** *Upland* China
72E3 **Qidong** China
73B4 **Qijiang** China
84B2 **Qila Saifullah** Pak
72A2 **Qilian** China
68B3 **Qilian Shan** China
72B3 **Qin'an** China
72E2 **Qingdao** China
72A2 **Qinghai** Province, China

68B3 **Qinghai Hu** *L* China
72D3 **Qingjiang** Jiangsu, China
73D4 **Qingjiang** Jiangxi, China
72B3 **Qing Jiang** *R* China
72C2 **Qingshuihe** China
72B2 **Qingshui He** *R* China
72B2 **Qingtonxia** China
72B2 **Qingyang** China
74B2 **Qingyuan** Liaoning, China
73D4 **Qingyuan** Zhejiang, China
82C2 **Qing Zang** *Upland* China
72D2 **Qinhuangdao** China
72B3 **Qin Ling** *Mts* China
73B5 **Qinzhou** China
76E2 **Qionghai** China
73A3 **Qionglai Shan** *Upland* China
76D1 **Qiongzhou Haixia** *Str* China
69E2 **Qiqihar** China
94B2 **Qiryat Ata** Israel
94B3 **Qiryat Gat** Israel
94B2 **Qiryat Shemona** Israel
94B2 **Qiryat Yam** Israel
94B2 **Qishon** *R* Israel
63A3 **Qitai** China
73C4 **Qiyang** China
72B1 **Qog Qi** China
90B2 **Qolleh-ye Damavand** *Mt* Iran
90B3 **Qom** Iran
90B3 **Qomisheh** Iran
Qomolangma Feng = Everest,Mt
94C1 **Qornet es Saouda** *Mt* Leb
6E3 **Qôrnoq** Greenland
90A2 **Qorveh** Iran
91C4 **Qotābad** Iran
16C1 **Quabbin Res** USA
16B2 **Quackertown** USA
77C3 **Quam Phu Quoc** *I* Viet
76D2 **Quang Ngai** Viet
76D2 **Quang Tri** Viet
77D4 **Quan Long** Viet
73D5 **Quanzhou** Fujian, China
73C4 **Quanzhou** Guangxi, China
5H4 **Qu' Appelle** *R* Can
91C5 **Quarayyāt** Oman
13B2 **Quatsino Sd** Can
90C2 **Quchan** Iran
109C3 **Queanbeyan** Aust
15D1 **Québec** Can
7C4 **Quebec** Province, Can
35B1 **Quebra-Anzol** *R* Brazil
34D2 **Quebracho** Urug
30F4 **Quedas do Iguaçu** Brazil/Arg
16A3 **Queen Anne** USA
13B2 **Queen Bess,Mt** Can
5E4 **Queen Charlotte Is** Can
13B2 **Queen Charlotte Sd** Can
13B2 **Queen Charlotte Str** Can
4H1 **Queen Elizabeth Is** Can
112B9 **Queen Mary Land** Region, Ant
4H3 **Queen Maud G** Can
112A **Queen Maud Mts** Ant
16C2 **Queens** Borough, New York, USA
108B3 **Queenscliff** Aust
107D3 **Queensland** State, Aust
109C4 **Queenstown** Aust
111A3 **Queenstown** NZ
100B4 **Queenstown** S Africa
16A3 **Queenstown** USA
98B3 **Quela** Angola
101C2 **Quelimane** Mozam

Remeshk

84D3 **Roorkee** India	
46C1 **Roosendaal** Neth	
112B6 **Roosevelt I** Ant	
106C2 **Roper** R Aust	
33E3 **Roraima** State, Brazil	
33E2 **Roraime** Mt Ven	
38G6 **Røros** Nor	
47C1 **Rorschach** Switz	
38G6 **Rørvik** Nor	
27Q2 **Rosalie** Dominica	
22C3 **Rosamond L** USA	
34C2 **Rosario** Arg	
31C2 **Rosário** Brazil	
34D2 **Rosario del Tala** Arg	
48B2 **Roscoff** France	
45B2 **Roscommon** County, Irish Rep	
41B3 **Roscommon** Irish Rep	
45C2 **Roscrea** Irish Rep	
27E3 **Roseau** Dominica	
109C4 **Rosebery** Aust	
20B2 **Roseburg** USA	
19A4 **Rosenberg** USA	
57C3 **Rosenheim** Germany	
13F2 **Rosetown** Can	
54B2 **Roşiori de Vede** Rom	
39G7 **Roskilde** Den	
60D3 **Roslavl'** Russian Fed	
61E2 **Roslyatino** Russian Fed	
111B2 **Ross** NZ	
12H2 **Ross** R Can	
40B3 **Rossan** Pt Irish Rep	
53C3 **Rossano** Italy	
19C3 **Ross Barnet Res** USA	
15C1 **Rosseau L** L Can	
107E2 **Rossel** I Solomon Is	
112A **Ross Ice Shelf** Ant	
20B1 **Ross L** USA	
13D3 **Rossland** Can	
45C2 **Rosslare** Irish Rep	
111C2 **Ross,Mt** NZ	
97A3 **Rosso** Maur	
43C4 **Ross-on-Wye** Eng	
60E4 **Rossosh** Russian Fed	
4E3 **Ross River** Can	
112B6 **Ross S** Ant	
91D4 **Rostāq** Iran	
56C2 **Rostock** Germany	
Rostov = Rostov-na-Donu	
61E4 **Rostov-na-Donu** Russian Fed	
17B1 **Roswell** Georgia, USA	
9C3 **Roswell** New Mexico, USA	
71F2 **Rota** Pacific O	
56B2 **Rotenburg** Niedersachsen, Germany	
46E1 **Rothaar-Geb** Region Germany	
112C3 **Rothera** Base Ant	
42D3 **Rotherham** Eng	
42B2 **Rothesay** Scot	
71D5 **Roti** I Indon	
108C2 **Roto** Aust	
111B2 **Rotoiti,L** NZ	
111B2 **Rotoroa,L** NZ	
110C1 **Rotorua** NZ	
110C1 **Rotorua,L** NZ	
56A2 **Rotterdam** Neth	
46B1 **Roubaix** France	
48C2 **Rouen** France	
42E3 **Rough** Oilfield N Sea	
Roulers = Roeselare	
101E3 **Round I** Mauritius	
109D2 **Round Mt** Aust	
8C2 **Roundup** USA	
44C2 **Rousay** I Scot	
48C3 **Roussillon** Region, France	
10C2 **Rouyn** Can	
38K5 **Rovaniemi** Fin	
47D2 **Rovereto** Italy	
47D2 **Rovigo** Italy	
52B1 **Rovinj** Croatia	
59D2 **Rovno** Ukraine	
90A2 **Row'ān** Iran	
109C1 **Rowena** Aust	
6C3 **Rowley I** Can	
106A2 **Rowley Shoals** Aust	
79A3 **Roxas** Palawan, Phil	
79B3 **Roxas** Panay, Phil	
111A3 **Roxburgh** NZ	
45C2 **Royal Canal** Irish Rep	
43D3 **Royal Leamington Spa** Eng	
14B2 **Royal Oak** USA	
43E4 **Royal Tunbridge Wells** Eng	
48B2 **Royan** France	
46B2 **Roye** France	
43D3 **Royston** Eng	
59C3 **Rožňava** Slovakia	
46B2 **Rozoy** France	
61F3 **Rtishchevo** Russian Fed	
99D3 **Ruaha Nat Pk** Tanz	
110C1 **Ruahine Range** Mts NZ	
110C1 **Ruapehu,Mt** NZ	
65D3 **Rub al Khālī** Desert S Arabia	
44A3 **Rubha Hunish** Scot	
35A2 **Rubinéia** Brazil	
65K4 **Rubtsovsk** Russian Fed	
12C2 **Ruby** USA	
91C4 **Rudan** Iran	
90A2 **Rūdbār** Iran	
69F2 **Rudnaya Pristan'** Russian Fed	
54B2 **Rudoka Planina** Mt Macedonia	
72E3 **Rudong** China	
14B1 **Rudyard** USA	
46A1 **Rue** France	
48C2 **Ruffec** France	
99D3 **Rufiji** R Tanz	
34C2 **Rufino** Arg	
97A3 **Rufisque** Sen	
100B2 **Rufunsa** Zambia	
43D3 **Rugby** Eng	
39G8 **Rügen** I Germany	
56B2 **Ruhr** R Germany	
73D4 **Ruijin** China	
54B2 **Rujen** Mt Bulg/ Macedonia	
99D3 **Rukwa** L Tanz	
44A3 **Rum** I Scot	
54A1 **Ruma** Serbia, Yugos	
91A4 **Rumāh** S Arabia	
98C2 **Rumbek** Sudan	
26C2 **Rum Cay** I Caribbean S	
47A2 **Rumilly** France	
106C2 **Rum Jungle** Aust	
101C2 **Rumphi** Malawi	
111B2 **Runanga** NZ	
110C1 **Runaway,C** NZ	
100C3 **Rundi** R Zim	
100A2 **Rundu** Namibia	
99D3 **Rungwa** Tanz	
99D3 **Rungwa** R Tanz	
99D3 **Rungwe** Mt Tanz	
82C2 **Ruoqiang** China	
68C2 **Ruo Shui** R China	
54C1 **Rupea** Rom	
7C4 **Rupert** R Can	
46D1 **Rur** R Germany	
32D6 **Rurrenabaque** Bol	
101C2 **Rusape** Zim	
54C2 **Ruse** Bulg	
18B1 **Rushville** Illinois, USA	
108B3 **Rushworth** Aust	
19A3 **Rusk** USA	
17B2 **Ruskin** USA	
110B1 **Russell** NZ	
18B2 **Russellville** Arkansas, USA	
18C2 **Russellville** Kentucky, USA	
21A2 **Russian** R USA	
62C3 **Russian Fed** Asia/ Europe	
93E1 **Rustavi** Georgia	
101G1 **Rustenburg** S Africa	
19B3 **Ruston** USA	
99C3 **Rutana** Burundi	
46E1 **Rüthen** Germany	
23B2 **Rutla** Mexico	
15D2 **Rutland** USA	
84D2 **Rutog** China	
Ruvu = Pangani	
101D2 **Ruvuma** R Tanz/ Mozam	
99D2 **Ruwenzori Range** Mts Uganda/Zaïre	
101C2 **Ruya** R Zim	
59B3 **Ružomberok** Slovakia	
99C3 **Rwanda** Republic, Africa	
60E3 **Ryazan'** Russian Fed	
61F3 **Ryazhsk** Russian Fed	
60E2 **Rybinsk** Russian Fed	
60E2 **Rybinskoye Vodokhranilishche** Res Russian Fed	
13D1 **Rycroft** Can	
43D4 **Rye** Eng	
43E4 **Rye** Eng	
20C2 **Rye Patch Res** USA	
60D3 **Ryl'sk** Russian Fed	
61G4 **Ryn Peski** Desert Kazakhstan	
74D3 **Ryōtsu** Japan	
59D3 **Ryskany** Moldavia	
69E4 **Ryūkyū Retto** Arch Japan	
59C2 **Rzeszów** Pol	
60D2 **Rzhev** Russian Fed	

S

91B3 **Sa'ādatābād** Iran	
56C2 **Saale** R Germany	
47B1 **Saanen** Switz	
46D2 **Saar** R Germany	
46D2 **Saarbrücken** Germany	
46D2 **Saarburg** Germany	
39J7 **Saaremaa** I Estonia	
46D2 **Saarland** State, Germany	
46D2 **Saarlouis** Germany	
34C3 **Saavedra** Arg	
54A2 **Šabac** Serbia, Yugos	
51C1 **Sabadell** Spain	
75B1 **Sabae** Japan	
78D1 **Sabah** State, Malay	
26C4 **Sabanalarga** Colombia	
70A3 **Sabang** Indon	
87C1 **Sabari** R India	
94B2 **Sabastiya** Israel	
30C2 **Sabaya** Bol	
93C3 **Sab'Bi'ār** Syria	
94C2 **Sabhā** Jordan	
95A2 **Sabhā** Libya	
24B2 **Sabinas** Mexico	
24B2 **Sabinas Hidalgo** Mexico	
19A3 **Sabine** R USA	
19B4 **Sabine L** USA	
91B5 **Sabkhat Maṭṭi** Salt Marsh UAE	
94A3 **Sabkhet El Bardawil** Lg Egypt	
79B3 **Sablayan** Phil	
7D5 **Sable,C** Can	
17B2 **Sable,C** USA	
7D5 **Sable I** Can	
90C2 **Sabzevār** Iran	
20C1 **Sacajawea Peak** USA	
10A1 **Sachigo** R Can	
57C2 **Sachsen** State, Germany	
56C2 **Sachsen-Anhalt** State, Germany	
4F2 **Sachs Harbour** Can	
47B1 **Säckingen** Germany	
22B1 **Sacramento** USA	
22B1 **Sacramento** R USA	
21A1 **Sacramento** V USA	
9C3 **Sacramento Mts** USA	
81C4 **Sa'dah** Yemen	
54B2 **Sadanski** Bulg	
82D3 **Sadiya** India	
50A2 **Sado** R Port	
74D3 **Sado-shima** I Japan	
85C3 **Sādri** India	
Safad = Zefat	
84A2 **Safed Koh** Mts Afghan	
39G7 **Säffle** Sweden	
92C3 **Safi** Jordan	
96B1 **Safi** Mor	
90D3 **Safīdabeh** Iran	
94C1 **Şāfītā** Syria	
93E3 **Şafwān** Iraq	
75A2 **Saga** Japan	
76B1 **Sagaing** Burma	
75B2 **Sagami-nada** B Japan	
85D4 **Sāgar** India	
16C2 **Sag Harbor** USA	
14B2 **Saginaw** USA	
14B2 **Saginaw B** USA	
26B2 **Sagua de Tánamo** Cuba	
26B2 **Sagua la Grande** Cuba	
7C5 **Saguenay** R Can	
51B2 **Sagunto** Spain	
94C3 **Sahāb** Jordan	
50A1 **Sahagún** Spain	
96C2 **Sahara** Desert N Africa	
84D3 **Saharanpur** India	
84C2 **Sahiwal** Pak	
93D3 **Sahrā al Hijārah** Desert Region Iraq	
23A1 **Sahuayo** Mexico	
107D1 **Saibai I** Aust	
96C1 **Saïda** Alg	
94B2 **Säida** Leb	
91C4 **Sa'īdabad** Iran	
51B2 **Saidia** Mor	
86B1 **Saidpur** India	
84C2 **Saidu** Pak	
75A1 **Saigō** Japan	
Saigon = Ho Chi Minh	
86C2 **Saiha** India	
68D2 **Saihan Tal** China	
75A2 **Saijo** Japan	
74C4 **Saiki** Japan	
42C2 **St Abb's Head** Pt Scot	
43D4 **St Albans** Eng	
15D2 **St Albans** Vermont, USA	
14B3 **St Albans** West Virginia, USA	
43C4 **St Albans Head** C Eng	
13E2 **St Albert** Can	
46B1 **St Amand-les-Eaux** France	
48C2 **St Amand-Mont Rond** France	
17A2 **St Andrew B** USA	
44C3 **St Andrews** Scot	
17B1 **St Andrew Sd** USA	
27H1 **St Ann's Bay** Jamaica	
7E4 **St Anthony** Can	
100B3 **St Arnaud** Aust	
17B2 **St Augustine** USA	
43B4 **St Austell** Eng	
46D2 **St-Avold** France	
42C2 **St Bees Head** Pt Eng	
47B2 **St-Bonnet** France	
43B4 **St Brides B** Wales	
48B2 **St-Brieuc** France	
15C2 **St Catharines** Can	
27M2 **St Catherine,Mt** Grenada	
17B1 **St Catherines I** USA	
43D4 **St Catherines Pt** Eng	
49C2 **St Chamond** France	
18B2 **St Charles** Missouri, USA	
14B2 **St Clair** USA	
14B2 **St Clair,L** Can/USA	
14B2 **St Clair Shores** USA	
49D2 **St Claud** France	
10A2 **St Cloud** USA	
47B1 **Ste Croix** Switz	
27E3 **St Croix** I Caribbean S	
43B4 **St Davids Head** Pt Wales	
46B2 **St Denis** France	
101E3 **St Denis** Réunion	
46C2 **St Dizier** France	
12F2 **St Elias,Mt** USA	
12G2 **St Elias Mts** Can	
48B2 **Saintes** France	
49C2 **St Étienne** France	
18B2 **St Francis** R USA	
100B4 **St Francis,C** S Africa	

29B4 **San Carlos de Bariloche** Arg
69E4 **San-chung** Taiwan
61G2 **Sanchursk** Russian Fed
34A3 **San Clemente** Chile
22D4 **San Clemente** USA
21B3 **San Clemente I** USA
34C2 **San Cristóbal** Arg
25C3 **San Cristóbal** Mexico
32C2 **San Cristóbal** Ven
32J7 **San Cristóbal** I Ecuador
107F2 **San Cristobal** I Solomon Is
25E2 **Sancti Spíritus** Cuba
78C3 **Sandai** Indon
70C3 **Sandakan** Malay
44C2 **Sanday** I Scot
9C3 **Sanderson** USA
13F1 **Sandfly L** Can
21B3 **San Diego** USA
92B2 **Sandikli** Turk
86A1 **Sandila** India
39F7 **Sandnes** Nor
38G5 **Sandnessjøen** Nor
98C3 **Sandoa** Zaïre
59C2 **Sandomierz** Pol
38D3 **Sandoy** Føroyar
20C1 **Sandpoint** USA
49D2 **Sandrio** Italy
18A2 **Sand Springs** USA
106A3 **Sandstone** Aust
73C4 **Sandu** China
14B2 **Sandusky** USA
39H6 **Sandviken** Sweden
7A4 **Sandy L** Can
34C2 **San Elcano** Arg
9B3 **San Felipe** Baja Cal, Mexico
34A2 **San Felipe** Chile
23A1 **San Felipe** Guanajuato, Mexico
27D4 **San Felipe** Ven
51C1 **San Feliu de Guixols** Spain
28A5 **San Felix** I Pacific O
34A2 **San Fernando** Chile
79B2 **San Fernando** Phil
79B2 **San Fernando** Phil
50A2 **San Fernando** Spain
27E4 **San Fernando** Trinidad
22C3 **San Fernando** USA
32D2 **San Fernando** Ven
1/B2 **Sanford** Florida, USA
12F2 **Sanford,Mt** USA
34C2 **San Francisco** Arg
27C3 **San Francisco** Dom Rep
22A2 **San Francisco** USA
22A2 **San Francisco B** USA
24B2 **San Francisco del Oro** Mexico
23A1 **San Francisco del Rincon** Mexico
22D3 **San Gabriel Mts** USA
85C5 **Sangamner** India
18C2 **Sangamon** R USA
71F2 **Sangan** I Pacific O
87B1 **Sangareddi** India
78D4 **Sangeang** I Indon
22C2 **Sanger** USA
72C2 **Sanggan He** R China
78C2 **Sanggau** Indon
98B2 **Sangha** R Congo
85B3 **Sanghar** Pak
76B2 **Sangkhla Buri** Thai
78D2 **Sangkulirang** Indon
87A1 **Sāngli** India
98B2 **Sangmélima** Cam
9B3 **San Gorgonio Mt** USA
9C3 **Sangre de Cristo** Mts USA
34C2 **San Gregorio** Arg
22A2 **San Gregorio** USA
84D2 **Sangrür** India
30E4 **San Ignacio** Arg
79B3 **San Isidro** Phil
32B2 **San Jacinto** Colombia
21B3 **San Jacinto Peak** Mt USA

34A3 **San Javier** Chile
34D2 **San Javier** Sante Fe, Arg
74D3 **Sanjō** I Japan
31C6 **San João del Rei** Brazil
22B2 **San Joaquin** R USA
22B2 **San Joaquin Valley** USA
32A1 **San José** Costa Rica
25C3 **San José** Guatemala
79B2 **San Jose** Luzon, Phil
79B3 **San Jose** Mindoro, Phil
22B2 **San Jose** USA
9B4 **San José** I Mexico
30D2 **San José de Chiquitos** Bol
34D2 **San José de Feliciano** Arg
34B2 **San José de Jachal** Arg
34C2 **San José de la Dormida** Arg
31B6 **San José do Rio Prêto** Brazil
24B2 **San José del Cabo** Mexico
34B2 **San Juan** Arg
27D3 **San Juan** Puerto Rico
34B2 **San Juan** State, Arg
27L1 **San Juan** Trinidad
32D2 **San Juan** Ven
26B2 **San Juan** Mt Cuba
8C3 **San Juan** Mts USA
34B2 **San Juan** R Arg
34B2 **San Juan** R Mexico
25D3 **San Juan** R Nic/ Costa Rica
23B2 **San Juan Bautista** Mexico
30E4 **San Juan Bautista** Par
22B2 **San Juan Bautista** USA
26D3 **San Juan del Norte** Nic
27D4 **San Juan de los Cayos** Ven
23A1 **San Juan de loz Lagoz** Mexico
23A1 **San Juan del Rio** Mexico
25D3 **San Juan del Sur** Nic
20B1 **San Juan Is** USA
23B2 **San Juan Tepozcolula** Mexico
29C5 **San Julián** Arg
34C2 **San Justo** Arg
60D2 **Sankt-Peterburg** Russian Fed
98C3 **Sankuru** R Zaïre
22A2 **San Leandro** USA
93C2 **Şanlıurfa** Turk
32B3 **San Lorenzo** Ecuador
34C2 **San Lorenzo** Arg
22D2 **San Lucas** USA
34B2 **San Luis** Arg
34B2 **San Luis** State, Arg
23A1 **San Luis de la Paz** Mexico
21A2 **San Luis Obispo** USA
23A1 **San Luis Potosi** Mexico
22B2 **San Luis Res** USA
53A3 **Sanluri** Sardegna
33D2 **San Maigualida** Mts Ven
34D3 **San Manuel** Arg
34A2 **San Marcos** Chile
23B2 **San Marcos** Mexico
52B2 **San Marino** Republic, Europe
34B2 **San Martin** Mendoza, Arg
112C3 **San Martin** Base Ant
47D1 **San Martino di Castroza** Italy
23B2 **San Martin Tuxmelucan** Mexico
22A2 **San Mateo** USA
30E2 **San Matias** Bol
72C3 **Sanmenxia** China

25D3 **San Miguel** El Salvador
22B3 **San Miguel** I USA
23A1 **San Miguel del Allende** Mexico
34D3 **San Miguel del Monte** Arg
30C4 **San Miguel de Tucumán** Arg
73D4 **Sanming** China
9B3 **San Nicolas** I USA
34C2 **San Nicolás de los Arroyos** Arg
101G1 **Sannieshof** S Africa
97B4 **Sanniquellie** Lib
59C3 **Sanok** Pol
26B5 **San Onofore** Colombia
22D4 **San Onofre** USA
79B3 **San Pablo** Phil
22A1 **San Pablo B** USA
34D2 **San Pedro** Buenos Aires, Arg
97B4 **San Pédro** Ivory Coast
30D3 **San Pedro** Jujuy, Arg
30E3 **San Pedro** Par
22C4 **San Pedro Chan** USA
9C4 **San Pedro de los Colonias** Mexico
25D3 **San Pedro Sula** Honduras
53A3 **San Pietro** I Medit S
24A1 **San Quintin** Mexico
34B2 **San Rafael** Arg
22A2 **San Rafael** USA
22C3 **San Rafael Mts** USA
49D3 **San Remo** Italy
34D2 **San Salvador** Arg
26C2 **San Salvador** I Caribbean S
32J7 **San Salvador** I Ecuador
30C3 **San Salvador de Jujuy** Arg
51B1 **San Sebastian** Spain
53C2 **San Severo** Italy
30C2 **Santa Ana** Bol
25C3 **Santa Ana** Guatemala
22D4 **Santa Ana** USA
22D4 **Santa Ana Mts** USA
34A3 **Santa Bárbara** Chile
24B2 **Santa Barbara** Mexico
22C3 **Santa Barbara** USA
22C4 **Santa Barbara** I USA
22B3 **Santa Barbara Chan** USA
22C3 **Santa Barbara Res** USA
22C4 **Santa Catalina** I USA
22C4 **Santa Catalina,G of** USA
30F4 **Santa Catarina** State, Brazil
26B2 **Santa Clara** Cuba
22B2 **Santa Clara** USA
22C3 **Santa Clara** R USA
29C6 **Santa Cruz** Arg
30D2 **Santa Cruz** Bol
34A2 **Santa Cruz** Chile
79B3 **Santa Cruz** Phil
29B5 **Santa Cruz** State, Arg
22A2 **Santa Cruz** USA
22C4 **Santa Cruz** I USA
35D1 **Santa Cruz Cabrália** Brazil
22C3 **Santa Cruz Chan** USA
96A2 **Santa Cruz de la Palma** Canary Is
26B2 **Santa Cruz del Sur** Cuba
96A2 **Santa Cruz de Tenerife** Canary Is
100B2 **Santa Cruz do Cuando** Angola
35B2 **Santa Cruz do Rio Pardo** Brazil
22A2 **Santa Cruz Mts** USA
34D2 **Santa Elena** Arg

33E3 **Santa Elena** Ven
34C2 **Santa Fe** Arg
34C2 **Santa Fe** State, Arg
9C3 **Santa Fe** USA
35A1 **Santa Helena de Goiás** Brazil
73B3 **Santai** China
29B6 **Santa Inés** I Chile
34B3 **Santa Isabel** La Pampa, Arg
34C2 **Santa Isabel** Sante Fe, Arg
107E1 **Santa Isabel** I Solomon Is
21A2 **Santa Lucia** Ra USA
21A2 **Santa Lucia Range** Mts USA
97A4 **Santa Luzia** I Cape Verde
9B4 **Santa Margarita** I Mexico
22D4 **Santa Margarita** R USA
30F4 **Santa Maria** Brazil
26C4 **Santa Maria** Colombia
21A3 **Santa Maria** USA
96A1 **Santa Maria** I Açores
23B1 **Santa Maria** R Queretaro, Mexico
23A1 **Santa Maria del Rio** Mexico
32C1 **Santa Marta** Colombia
22C3 **Santa Monica** USA
22C4 **Santa Monica B** USA
29E2 **Santana do Livramento** Brazil
32B3 **Santander** Colombia
50B1 **Santander** Spain
51C2 **Santañy** Spain
22C3 **Santa Paula** USA
31C2 **Santa Quitéria** Brazil
33G4 **Santarém** Brazil
50A2 **Santarém** Port
22A1 **Santa Rosa** California, USA
25D3 **Santa Rosa** Honduras
34C3 **Santa Rosa** La Pampa, Arg
34B2 **Santa Rosa** Mendoza, Arg
34B2 **Santa Rosa** San Luis, Arg
22B3 **Santa Rosa** I USA
24A2 **Santa Rosalía** Mexico
20C2 **Santa Rosa Range** Mts USA
31D3 **Santa Talhada** Brazil
35C1 **Santa Teresa** Brazil
53A2 **Santa Teresa di Gallura** Sardogna
22B3 **Santa Ynez** R USA
22B3 **Santa Ynez Mts** USA
17C1 **Santee** R USA
47C2 **Santhia** Italy
34A2 **Santiago** Chile
27C3 **Santiago** Dom Rep
32A2 **Santiago** Panama
79B2 **Santiago** Phil
32B4 **Santiago** R Peru
50A1 **Santiago de Compostela** Spain
26B2 **Santiago de Cuba** Cuba
30D4 **Santiago del Estero** Arg
30D4 **Santiago del Estero** State, Arg
22D4 **Santiago Peak** Mt USA
31C5 **Santo** State, Brazil
35A2 **Santo Anastatácio** Brazil
30F4 **Santo Angelo** Brazil
97A4 **Santo Antão** I Cape Verde
35A2 **Santo Antonio da Platina** Brazil
27D3 **Santo Domingo** Dom Rep

13D2 **Selkirk Mts** Can
22C2 **Selma** California, USA
50B2 **Selouane** Mor
12H2 **Selous,Mt** Can
78B3 **Selta Karimata** *Str* Indon
32C5 **Selvas** Region, Brazil
107D3 **Selwyn** Aust
4E3 **Selwyn Mts** Can
78C4 **Semarang** Indon
61E2 **Semenov** Russian Fed
12C3 **Semidi Is** USA
60E3 **Semiluki** Russian Fed
19A2 **Seminole** Oklahoma, USA
17B1 **Seminole,L** USA
65K4 **Semipalatinsk** Kazakhstan
79B3 **Semirara Is** Phil
90B3 **Semirom** Iran
78C2 **Semitau** Indon
90B2 **Semnān** Iran
46C2 **Semois** *R* Belg
23B2 **Sempoala** Hist Site, Mexico
32D5 **Sena Madureira** Brazil
100B2 **Senanga** Zambia
19C3 **Senatobia** USA
74E3 **Sendai** Honshū, Japan
74C4 **Sendai** Kyūshū, Japan
85D4 **Sendwha** India
15C2 **Seneca Falls** USA
97A3 **Senegal** Republic, Africa
97A3 **Sénégal** *R* Maur Sen
101G1 **Senekal** S Africa
31D4 **Senhor do Bonfim** Brazil
52B2 **Senigallia** Italy
52C2 **Senj** Croatia
69E4 **Senkaku Gunto** *Is* Japan
46B2 **Senlis** France
99D1 **Sennar** Sudan
7C5 **Senneterre** Can
49C2 **Sens** France
54A1 **Senta** Serbia, Yugos
98C3 **Sentery** Zaïre
13C2 **Sentinel Peak** *Mt* Can
85D4 **Seoni** India
Seoul = Soul
110B2 **Separation Pt** NZ
70D2 **Sepone** Laos
7D4 **Sept-Iles** Can
95A2 **Séquédine** Niger
21B2 **Sequoia** Nat Pk, USA
71D4 **Seram** *I* Indon
78B4 **Serang** Indon
78B2 **Serasan** *I* Indon
54A2 **Serbia** Republic, Yugos
61F3 **Serdobsk** Russian Fed
77C5 **Seremban** Malay
99D3 **Serengeti Nat Pk** Tanz
100C2 **Serenje** Zambia
59D3 **Seret** *R* Ukraine
61G2 **Sergach** Russian Fed
65H3 **Sergino** Russian Fed
31D4 **Sergipe** State, Brazil
60E2 **Segiyev Posad** Russian Fed
78C2 **Seria** Brunei
78C2 **Serian** Malay
55B3 **Sérifos** *I* Greece
47C2 **Serio** *R* Italy
95B2 **Serir Calanscio** *Desert* Libya
46C2 **Sermaize-les-Bains** France
71D4 **Sermata** *I* Indon
61H3 **Sernovodsk** Russian Fed
65H4 **Serov** Russian Fed
100B3 **Serowe** Botswana
50A2 **Serpa** Port
60E3 **Serpukhov** Russian Fed
35B2 **Serra da Canastra** *Mts* Brazil
50A1 **Serra da Estrela** *Mts* Port
35B2 **Serra da Mantiqueira** *Mts* Brazil
35A1 **Serra da Mombuca** Brazil
35C1 **Serra do Cabral** *Mt* Brazil
33F5 **Serra do Cachimbo** *Mts* Brazil
35A1 **Serra do Caiapó** *Mts* Brazil
35A2 **Serra do Cantu** *Mts* Brazil
35C2 **Serra do Caparaó** *Mts* Brazil
31C5 **Serra do Chifre** Brazil
35C1 **Serra do Espinhaço** *Mts* Brazil
35B2 **Serra do Mar** *Mts* Brazil
35A2 **Serra do Mirante** *Mts* Brazil
33G3 **Serra do Navio** Brazil
35B2 **Serra do Paranapiacaba** *Mts* Brazil
33F6 **Serra dos Caiabis** *Mts* Brazil
35A2 **Serra dos Dourados** *Mts* Brazil
33E6 **Serra dos Parecis** *Mts* Brazil
35B1 **Serra dos Pilões** *Mts* Brazil
35A1 **Serra Dourada** *Mts* Brazil
33F6 **Serra Formosa** *Mts* Brazil
55B2 **Sérrai** Greece
25D3 **Serrana Bank** *Is* Caribbean S
51B1 **Serrana de Cuenca** *Mts* Spain
35A1 **Serranópolis** Brazil
33E3 **Serra Pacaraima** *Mts* Brazil/Ven
33E3 **Serra Parima** *Mts* Brazil
33G3 **Serra Tumucumaque** Brazil
46B2 **Serre** *R* France
34B2 **Serrezuela** Arg
31D4 **Serrinha** Brazil
6G3 **Serrmilik** Greenland
35C1 **Serro** Brazil
35A2 **Sertanópolis** Brazil
72A3 **Sêrtar** China
78C3 **Seruyan** *R* Indon
100A2 **Sesfontein** Namibia
100B2 **Sesheke** Zambia
47B2 **Sestriere** Italy
74D2 **Setana** Japan
49C3 **Sète** France
35C1 **Sete Lagoas** Brazil
96C1 **Sétif** Alg
75B1 **Seto** Japan
75A2 **Seto Naikai** *S* Japan
96B1 **Settat** Mor
42C2 **Settle** Eng
5G4 **Settler** Can
50A2 **Sêtúbal** Port
93E1 **Sevan,Oz** *L* Armenia
60D5 **Sevastopol'** Ukraine
7B4 **Severn** *R* Can
43C3 **Severn** *R* Eng
1B9 **Severnaya Zemlya** *I* Russian Fed
63C2 **Severo-Baykalskoye Nagorye** *Mts* Russian Fed
60E4 **Severo Donets** Ukraine
64E3 **Severodvinsk** Russian Fed
64H3 **Severo Sos'va** *R* Russian Fed
8B3 **Sevier** *R* USA
8B3 **Sevier L** USA
50A2 **Sevilla** Spain
Seville = Sevilla
54C2 **Sevlievo** Bulg
97A4 **Sewa** *R* Sierra Leone
12E2 **Seward** Alaska, USA
18A1 **Seward** Nebraska, USA
12A1 **Seward Pen** USA
13D1 **Sexsmith** Can
89K8 **Seychelles** *Is* Indian O
38C1 **Seyðisfjörður** Iceland
92C2 **Seyhan** Turk
60E3 **Seym** *R* Russian Fed
108C3 **Seymour** Aust
16C2 **Seymour** Connecticut, USA
14A3 **Seymour** Indiana, USA
46B2 **Sézanne** France
96D1 **Sfax** Tunisia
54C1 **Sfînto Gheorghe** Rom
56A2 **'s-Gravenhage** Neth
72B3 **Shaanxi** Province, China
98C3 **Shabunda** Zaïre
82B2 **Shache** China
112C9 **Shackleton Ice Shelf** Ant
85B3 **Shadadkot** Pak
91B3 **Shādhām** *R* Iran
43C4 **Shaftesbury** Eng
29G8 **Shag Rocks** *Is* South Georgia
90A3 **Shāhabād** Iran
94C2 **Shahbā** Syria
91C3 **Shahdap** Iran
86A2 **Shahdol** India
90A2 **Shāhīn Dezh** Iran
90C3 **Shāh Kūh** Iran
91C3 **Shahr-e Bābak** Iran
Shahresa = Qomisheh
90B3 **Shahr Kord** Iran
87B1 **Shājābād** India
84D3 **Shājahānpur** India
85D4 **Shājāpur** India
61F4 **Shakhty** Russian Fed
61G2 **Shakhun'ya** Russian Fed
97C4 **Shaki** Nig
12B2 **Shaktoolik** USA
61J2 **Shamary** Russian Fed
99D2 **Shambe** Sudan
16A2 **Shamokin** USA
16B1 **Shandaken** USA
72D2 **Shandong** Province, China
73C5 **Shangchuan Dao** *I* China
72C1 **Shangdu** China
73E3 **Shanghai** China
72C3 **Shangnan** China
100B2 **Shangombo** Zambia
73D4 **Shangra** China
73B5 **Shangsi** China
72C3 **Shang Xian** China
41B3 **Shannon** *R* Irish Rep
72D3 **Shanqiu** China
74B2 **Shansonggang** China
63F2 **Shantarskiye Ostrova** *I* Russian Fed
73D5 **Shantou** China
72C2 **Shanxi** Province, China
72D3 **Shan Xian** China
73C5 **Shaoguan** China
73E4 **Shaoxing** China
73C4 **Shaoyang** China
44C2 **Shapinsay** *I* Scot
94C2 **Shaqqā** Syria
72A1 **Sharhulsan** Mongolia
90C2 **Sharifābād** Iran
91C4 **Sharjah** UAE
106A3 **Shark B** Aust
90C2 **Sharlauk** Turkmenistan
94B2 **Sharon,Plain of** Israel
61G2 **Sharya** Russian Fed
99D2 **Shashemenē** Eth
73C3 **Shashi** China
20B2 **Shasta L** USA
20B2 **Shasta,Mt** USA
93E3 **Shaṭṭ al Gharrat** *R* Iraq
94B3 **Shaubak** Jordan
13F3 **Shaunavon** Can
22C2 **Shaver L** USA
16B2 **Shawangunk Mt** USA
15D1 **Shawinigan** Can
19A2 **Shawnee** Oklahoma, USA
73D4 **Sha Xian** China
106B3 **Shay Gap** Aust
94C2 **Shaykh Miskīn** Syria
99E1 **Shaykh 'Uthmān** Yemen
60E3 **Shchekino** Russian Fed
60E3 **Shchigry** Russian Fed
60D3 **Shchors** Ukraine
65J4 **Shchuchinsk** Kazakhstan
99E2 **Shebele** *R* Eth
14A2 **Sheboygan** USA
98B2 **Shebshi** *Mts* Nig
12F1 **Sheenjek** *R* USA
45C1 **Sheep Haven** *Estuary* Irish Rep
43E4 **Sheerness** Eng
94B2 **Shefar'am** Israel
42D3 **Sheffield** Eng
84C2 **Shekhupura** Pak
13B1 **Shelagyote Peak** *Mt* Can
16C1 **Shelburne Falls** USA
14A2 **Shelby** Michigan, USA
8B2 **Shelby** Montana, USA
14A3 **Shelbyville** Indiana, USA
12H2 **Sheldon,Mt** Can
12D3 **Shelikof Str** USA
109D2 **Shellharbour** Aust
111A3 **Shelter Pt** NZ
20B1 **Shelton** USA
93E1 **Shemakha** Azerbaijan
18A1 **Shenandoah** USA
15C3 **Shenandoah** *R* USA
15C3 **Shenandoah Nat Pk** USA
97C4 **Shendam** Nig
95C2 **Shendi** Sudan
72C2 **Shenmu** China
72E1 **Shenyang** China
73C5 **Shenzhen** China
85D3 **Sheopur** India
59D2 **Shepetovka** Ukraine
108C3 **Shepparton** Aust
6B2 **Sherard,C** Can
43C4 **Sherborne** Eng
97A4 **Sherbro I** Sierra Leone
15D1 **Sherbrooke** Can
85C3 **Shergarh** India
19B3 **Sheridan** Arkansas, USA
8C2 **Sheridan** Wyoming, USA
19A3 **Sherman** USA
56B2 **s-Hertogenbosh** Neth
12H3 **Sheslay** Can
40C1 **Shetland** *Is* Scot
Shevchenko = Aktau
91B4 **Sheyk Sho'eyb** *I* Iran
69H2 **Shiashkotan** *I* Russian Fed
84B1 **Shibarghan** Afghan
74D3 **Shibata** Japan
95C1 **Shibin el Kom** Egypt
75B1 **Shibukawa** Japan
72C2 **Shijiazhuang** China
84B3 **Shikarpur** Pak
67G3 **Shikoku** *I* Japan
75A2 **Shikoku-sanchi** *Mts* Japan
86B1 **Shiliguri** India
68D1 **Shilka** Russian Fed
68D1 **Shilka** *R* Russian Fed
16B2 **Shillington** USA
86C1 **Shillong** India
61F3 **Shilovo** Russian Fed
75A2 **Shimabara** Japan

75B2	**Shimada** Japan
69E1	**Shimanovsk** Russian Fed
74D3	**Shimizu** Japan
84D2	**Shimla** India
75B2	**Shimoda** Japan
87B2	**Shimoga** India
74C4	**Shimonoseki** Japan
75B1	**Shinano** *R* Japan
91C5	**Shināṣ** Oman
74D4	**Shingū** Japan
75C1	**Shinjō** Japan
74D3	**Shinminato** Japan
94C1	**Shinshār** Syria
99D3	**Shinyanga** Tanz
74E3	**Shiogama** Japan
75B2	**Shiono-misaki** *C* Japan
73A5	**Shiping** China
16A2	**Shippensburg** USA
72B3	**Shiquan** China
75C1	**Shirakawa** Japan
75B1	**Shirane-san** *Mt* Japan
75B1	**Shirani-san** *Mt* Japan
91B4	**Shīrāz** Iran
90B3	**Shīr Kūh** Iran
75B1	**Shirotori** Japan
90C2	**Shirvān** Iran
12A1	**Shishmaref** USA
12A1	**Shishmaref Inlet** USA
4B3	**Shishmaret** USA
72B2	**Shitanjing** China
14A3	**Shively** USA
85D3	**Shivpuri** India
94B3	**Shivta** *Hist Site* Israel
101C2	**Shiwa Ngandu** Zambia
72C3	**Shiyan** China
72B2	**Shizuishan** China
75B1	**Shizuoka** Japan
54A2	**Shkodër** Alb
109D2	**Shoalhaven** *R* Aust
75A2	**Shobara** Japan
87B2	**Shoranūr** India
87B1	**Shorāpur** India
21B2	**Shoshone Mts** USA
60D3	**Shostka** Ukraine
19B3	**Shreveport** USA
43C3	**Shrewsbury** Eng
43C3	**Shropshire** County, Eng
72E1	**Shuanglia** China
69F2	**Shuangyashan** China
61J4	**Shubar-Kuduk** Kazakhstan
72D2	**Shu He** *R* China
73A4	**Shuicheng** China
84C3	**Shujaabad** Pak
85D4	**Shujālpur** India
68B2	**Shule He** China
54C2	**Shumen** Bulg
61G2	**Shumerlya** Russian Fed
73D4	**Shuncheng** China
12C1	**Shungnak** USA
72C2	**Shuo Xian** China
91C4	**Shūr Gaz** Iran
100B2	**Shurugwi** Zim
13D2	**Shuswap L** Can
61F2	**Shuya** Russian Fed
12D3	**Shuyak I** USA
82D3	**Shwebo** Burma
76B2	**Shwegyin** Burma
84A2	**Siah Koh** *Mts* Afghan
84C2	**Sialkot** Pak
	Sian = Xi'an
79C4	**Siarao** *I* Phil
79B4	**Siaton** Phil
58C1	**Šiauliai** Lithuania
65G4	**Sibay** Russian Fed
101H1	**Şibayi L** S Africa
52C2	**Šibenik** Croatia
70A4	**Siberut** *I* Indon
84B3	**Sibi** Pak
68C1	**Sibirskoye** Russian Fed
98B3	**Sibiti** Congo
99D3	**Sibiti** *R* Tanz
54B1	**Sibiu** Rom
70A3	**Sibolga** Indon
86C1	**Sibsāgār** India
78C2	**Sibu** Malay
79B4	**Sibuguay B** Phil
98B2	**Sibut** CAR
79B3	**Sibuyan** *I* Phil
79B3	**Sibuyan S** Phil
73A3	**Sichuan** Province, China
53B3	**Sicilia** *I* Medit S
53B3	**Sicilian** *Chan* Italy/ Tunisia
	Sicily = Sicilia
32C6	**Sicuani** Peru
85C4	**Siddhapur** India
87B1	**Siddipet** India
86A2	**Sidhi** India
95B1	**Sidi Barrani** Egypt
96B1	**Sidi Bel Abbès** Alg
96B1	**Sidi Kacem** Mor
44C3	**Sidlaw Hills** Scot
112B5	**Sidley,Mt** Ant
20B1	**Sidney** Can
8C2	**Sidney** Nebraska, USA
15C2	**Sidney** New York, USA
14B2	**Sidney** Ohio, USA
17B1	**Sidney Lanier,L** USA
	Sidon = Säida
58C2	**Siedlce** Pol
46D1	**Sieg** *R* Germany
46D1	**Siegburg** Germany
46D1	**Siegen** Germany
76C3	**Siem Reap** Camb
52B2	**Siena** Italy
58B2	**Sierpc** Pol
23B2	**Sierra Andrés Tuxtla** Mexico
34B3	**Sierra Auca Mahuida** *Mts* Arg
9C3	**Sierra Blanca** USA
51B1	**Sierra de Albarracin** *Mts* Spain
50B2	**Sierra de Alcaraz** *Mts* Spain
34B2	**Sierra de Cordoba** *Mts* Arg
50A1	**Sierra de Gredos** *Mts* Spain
50A2	**Sierra de Guadalupe** *Mts* Spain
50B1	**Sierra de Guadarrama** *Mts* Spain
51B1	**Sierra de Guara** *Mts* Spain
51B1	**Sierra de Gudar** *Mts* Spain
23B2	**Sierra de Juárez** Mexico
34C3	**Sierra de la Ventana** *Mts* Arg
51C1	**Sierra del Codi** *Mts* Spain
34B2	**Sierra del Morro** *Mt* Arg
34B3	**Sierra del Nevado** *Mts* Arg
24B2	**Sierra de los Alamitos** *Mts* Mexico
50B2	**Sierra de los Filabres** Spain
23A1	**Sierra de los Huicholes** Mexico
23B2	**Sierra de Miahuatlán** Mexico
23A1	**Sierra de Morones** *Mts* Mexico
50A2	**Sierra de Ronda** *Mts* Spain
34B2	**Sierra de San Luis** *Mts* Arg
50B2	**Sierra de Segura** *Mts* Spain
50B1	**Sierra de Urbion** *Mts* Spain
34B2	**Sierra de Uspallata** *Mts* Arg
34B2	**Sierra de Valle Fértil** *Mts* Arg
23B2	**Sierra de Zongolica** Mexico
34C2	**Sierra Grande** *Mts* Arg
97A4	**Sierra Leone** Republic, Africa
97A4	**Sierra Leone,C** Sierra Leone
79B2	**Sierra Madre** *Mts* Phil
23A2	**Sierra Madre del Sur** *Mts* Mexico
24B2	**Sierra Madre Occidental** *Mts* Mexico
24C2	**Sierra Madre Oriental** *Mts* Mexico
34B2	**Sierra Malanzan** *Mts* Arg
9C4	**Sierra Mojada** Mexico
50A2	**Sierra Morena** *Mts* Spain
50B2	**Sierra Nevada** *Mts* Spain
21A2	**Sierra Nevada** *Mts* USA
32C1	**Sierra Nevada de Santa Marta** *Mts* Colombia
34B2	**Sierra Pié de Palo** *Mts* Arg
47B1	**Sierre** Switz
55B3	**Sifnos** *I* Greece
59C3	**Sighetu Marmaţiei** Rom
54B1	**Sighişoara** Rom
38B1	**Siglufjörður** Iceland
50B1	**Sigüenza** Spain
97B3	**Siguiri** Guinea
	Sihanoukville = Kompong Som
85E4	**Sihora** India
93D2	**Siirt** Turk
68B3	**Sikai Hu** *L* China
85D3	**Sikar** India
84B2	**Sikaram** *Mt* Afghan
97B3	**Sikasso** Mali
18C2	**Sikeston** USA
55C3	**Sikinos** *I* Greece
55B3	**Sikionía** Greece
86B1	**Sikkim** State, India
50A1	**Sil** *R* Spain
47D1	**Silandro** Italy
23A1	**Silao** Mexico
79B3	**Silay** Phil
86C2	**Silchar** India
96C2	**Silet** Alg
86A1	**Silgarhi** Nepal
92B2	**Silifke** Turk
82C2	**Siling Co** *L* China
54C2	**Silistra** Bulg
39F7	**Silkeborg** Den
47E1	**Sillian** Austria
18B2	**Siloam Springs** USA
19B3	**Silsbee** USA
95A3	**Siltou** *Well* Chad
58C1	**Šilute** Lithuania
93D2	**Silvan** Turk
35B1	**Silvania** Brazil
85C4	**Silvassa** India
21B2	**Silver City** Nevada, USA
9C3	**Silver City** New Mexico, USA
20B2	**Silver Lake** USA
16A3	**Silver Spring** USA
13B2	**Silverthrone Mt** Can
108B2	**Silverton** Aust
47C1	**Silvretta** *Mts* Austria/Switz
78C2	**Simanggang** Malay
76C1	**Simao** China
90A3	**Simareh** *R* Iran
55C3	**Simav** Turk
55C3	**Simav** *R* Turk
61G3	**Simbirsk** Russian Fed
15C2	**Simcoe,L** Can
70A3	**Simeulue** *I* Indon
60D5	**Simferopol'** Ukraine
55C3	**Sími** *I* Greece
46D1	**Simmern** Germany
13B2	**Simoon Sound** Can
49D2	**Simplon** *Mt* Switz
47C1	**Simplon** *P* Switz
4C2	**Simpson,C** USA
106C3	**Simpson Desert** Aust
6B3	**Simpson Pen** Can
39G7	**Simrishamn** Sweden
69H2	**Simushir** *I* Russian Fed
99E2	**Sina Dhaqa** Somalia
92B4	**Sinai** *Pen* Egypt
32B2	**Sincelejo** Colombia
17B1	**Sinclair,L** USA
85D3	**Sind** *R* India
85B3	**Sindh** Region, Pak
55C3	**Sindirği** Turk
86B2	**Sindri** India
50A2	**Sines** Port
99D1	**Singa** Sudan
77C5	**Singapore** Republic, S E Asia
77C5	**Singapore,Str of** S E Asia
78D4	**Singaraja** Indon
99D3	**Singida** Tanz
78B2	**Singkawang** Indon
109D2	**Singleton** Aust
78A3	**Singtep** *I* Indon
76B1	**Singu** Burma
53A2	**Siniscola** Sardgena
93D2	**Sinjār** Iraq
84B2	**Sinkai Hills** *Mts* Afghan
95C3	**Sinkat** Sudan
82C1	**Sinkiang** Autonomous Region, China
33G2	**Sinnamary** French Guiana
92C1	**Sinop** Turk
54B1	**Sîntana** Rom
78C2	**Sintang** Indon
50A2	**Sintra** Port
32B2	**Sinú** *R* Colombia
74A2	**Sinǔiju** N Korea
59B3	**Siofok** Hung
47B1	**Sion** Switz
8D2	**Sioux City** USA
8D2	**Sioux Falls** USA
10A2	**Sioux Lookout** Can
79B4	**Sipalay** Phil
27L1	**Siparia** Trinidad
69E2	**Siping** China
112B3	**Siple** *Base* Ant
112B5	**Siple I** Ant
79B3	**Sipocot** Phil
70A4	**Sipora** Indon
79B4	**Siquijor** *I* Phil
87B2	**Sira** India
53C3	**Siracusa** Italy
86B2	**Sirajganj** Bang
13C2	**Sir Alexander,Mt** Can
91B5	**Sir Banī Yās** *I* UAE
106C2	**Sir Edward Pellew Group** *Is* Aust
54C1	**Siret** *R* Rom
12J2	**Sir James McBrien,Mt** Can
87B2	**Sir Kālahasti** India
13D2	**Sir Laurier,Mt** Can
93D2	**Şirnak** Turk
85C4	**Sirohi** India
87B1	**Sironcha** India
85D4	**Sironj** India
55B3	**Síros** *I* Greece
91B4	**Sirri** *I* Iran
84D3	**Sirsa** India
13D2	**Sir Sandford,Mt** Can
87A2	**Sirsi** India
95A1	**Sirte Desert** Libya
95A1	**Sirte,G of** Libya
52C1	**Sisak** Croatia
76C2	**Sisaket** Thai
76C3	**Sisophon** Camb
46B2	**Sissonne** France
90D3	**Sistan** Region, Iran/Afghan
49D3	**Sisteron** France
63B2	**Sistig Khem** Russian Fed
86A1	**Sītapur** India
55C3	**Sitia** Greece
4E4	**Sitka** USA
12D3	**Sitkalidak I** USA
12D3	**Sitkinak I** USA

4F3 **South Nahanni** *R* Can
26G1 **South Negril Pt** Jamaica
103F8 **South Orkney** *Is* Atlantic O
8C2 **South Platte** *R* USA
80E **South Pole** Ant
42C3 **Southport** Eng
27R3 **South Pt** Barbados
16B2 **South River** USA
44C2 **South Ronaldsay** *I* Scot
103G7 **South Sandwich Trench** Atlantic O
22A2 **South San Francisco** USA
5H4 **South Saskatchewan** *R* Can
42D2 **South Shields** Eng
110B1 **South Taranaki Bight** *B* NZ
44A3 **South Uist** *I* Scot
South West Africa = Namibia
107D5 **South West C** Aust
105J5 **South West Pacific Basin** Pacific O
103D5 **South West Peru Ridge** Pacific O
43D3 **South Yorkshire** County, Eng
58C1 **Sovetsk** Russian Fed
61G2 **Sovetsk** Russian Fed
101G1 **Soweto** S Africa
98B3 **Soyo Congo** Angola
60D3 **Sozh** *R* Belorussia
46C1 **Spa** Belg
50A1 **Spain** Kingdom
Spalato = Split
43D3 **Spalding** Eng
14B1 **Spanish** *R* Can
26B3 **Spanish Town** Jamaica
21B2 **Sparks** USA
11B3 **Spartanburg** USA
55B3 **Spartí** Greece
69F2 **Spassk Dal'niy** Russian Fed
27R3 **Speightstown** Barbados
12E2 **Spenard** USA
14A3 **Spencer** Indiana, USA
8D2 **Spencer** Iowa, USA
6A3 **Spencer Bay** Can
108A3 **Spencer,C** Aust
108A2 **Spencer G** Aust
6C3 **Spencer I** Can
111B2 **Spenser Mts** NZ
45C1 **Sperrin** *Mts* N Ire
44C3 **Spey** *R* Scot
57B3 **Speyer** Germany
27K1 **Speyside** Tobago
47B1 **Spiez** Switz
12F1 **Spike Mt** USA
20C1 **Spirit Lake** USA
5G4 **Spirit River** Can
Spitsbergen = Svalbard
64C2 **Spitsbergen** *I* Barents S
57C3 **Spittal** Austria
38F6 **Spjelkavik** Nor
52C2 **Split** Croatia
47C1 **Splügen** Switz
20C1 **Spokane** USA
55C3 **Sporádhes** *Is* Greece
20C2 **Spray** USA
56C2 **Spree** *R* Germany
100A3 **Springbok** S Africa
18B2 **Springdale** USA
10B3 **Springfield** Illinois, USA
10C2 **Springfield** Massachusetts, USA
18B2 **Springfield** Missouri, USA
14B3 **Springfield** Ohio, USA
20B2 **Springfield** Oregon, USA
15D2 **Springfield** Vermont, USA
100B4 **Springfontein** S Africa
101G1 **Springs** S Africa
41D3 **Spurn Head** *Pt* Eng
13C3 **Squamish** Can
60E3 **Sredne-Russkaya Vozvyshennost** *Upland* Russian Fed
63B1 **Sredne Sibirskoye Ploskogorve** *Tableland* Russian Fed
61J2 **Sredniy Ural** *Mts* Russian Fed
76D3 **Srepok** *R* Camb
68D1 **Sretensk** Russian Fed
76C3 **Sre Umbell** Camb
83C5 **Sri Lanka** Republic, S Asia
84C2 **Srīnagar** Pak
87A1 **Şrīvardhan** India
58B2 **Środa Wlk.** Pol
30H6 **Sta Clara** *I* Chile
32J7 **Sta Cruz** *I* Ecuador
56B2 **Stade** Germany
44A3 **Staffa** *I* Scot
43C3 **Stafford** County, Eng
43C3 **Stafford** Eng
16C2 **Stafford Springs** USA
Stalingrad = Volgograd
6A1 **Stallworthy,C** Can
59C2 **Stalowa Wola** Pol
32J7 **Sta Maria** *I* Ecuador
16C2 **Stamford** Connecticut, USA
16B1 **Stamford** New York, USA
100A3 **Stampriet** Namibia
101G1 **Standerton** S Africa
14B2 **Standish** USA
101H1 **Stanger** S Africa
22B2 **Stanislaus** *R* USA
54B2 **Stanke Dimitrov** Bulg
109C4 **Stanley** Aust
29E6 **Stanley** Falkland Is
87B2 **Stanley Res** India
Stanleyville = Kisangani
25D3 **Stann Creek** Belize
63E2 **Stanovoy Khrebet** *Mts* Russian Fed
47C1 **Stans** Switz
109D1 **Stanthorpe** Aust
59C2 **Starachowice** Pol
54B2 **Stara Planiná** *Mts* Bulg
60D2 **Staraya Russa** Russian Fed
54C2 **Stara Zagora** Bulg
58B2 **Stargard Szczecinski** Pol
19C3 **Starkville** USA
57C3 **Starnberg** Germany
58B2 **Starogard Gdanski** Pol
59D3 **Starokonstantinov** Ukraine
43C4 **Start Pt** Eng
60E3 **Staryy Oskol** Russian Fed
15C2 **State College** USA
16B2 **Staten I** USA
17B1 **Statesboro** USA
15C3 **Staunton** USA
39F7 **Stavanger** Nor
46C1 **Stavelot** Belg
61F4 **Stavropol'** Russian Fed
108B3 **Stawell** Aust
58B2 **Stawno** Pol
20B2 **Stayton** USA
12B2 **Stebbins** USA
12F2 **Steele,Mt** Can
16A2 **Steelton** USA
20C2 **Steens Mt** USA
6E2 **Steenstrups Gletscher** *Gl* Greenland
4H2 **Stefansson I** Can
101H1 **Stegi** Swaziland
47D1 **Steinach** Austria
8D2 **Steinback** Can
38G6 **Steinkjer** Nor
13C2 **Stein Mt** Can
23B2 **Stemaco** Mexico
46C2 **Stenay** France
56C2 **Stendal** Germany
110B2 **Stephens,C** NZ
108B2 **Stephens Creek** Aust
14A1 **Stephenson** USA
12H3 **Stephens Pass** USA
7E5 **Stephenville** Can
100B4 **Sterkstroom** S Africa
8C2 **Sterling** Colorado, USA
14B2 **Sterling Heights** USA
61J3 **Sterlitamak** Russian Fed
13E2 **Stettler** Can
14B2 **Steubenville** USA
4D3 **Stevens Village** USA
13B1 **Stewart** Can
21B2 **Stewart** USA
12G2 **Stewart** *R* Can
12G2 **Stewart Crossing** Can
111A3 **Stewart I** NZ
107F1 **Stewart Is** Solomon Is
4E3 **Stewart River** Can
16A3 **Stewartstown** USA
101G1 **Steyn** S Africa
57C3 **Steyr** Austria
12G3 **Stika** USA
12H3 **Stikine** *R* Can
12H3 **Stikine Ranges** *Mts* Can
18A2 **Stillwater** Oklahoma, USA
21B2 **Stillwater Range** *Mts* USA
108A2 **Stirling** Aust
44C3 **Stirling** Scot
16C1 **Stockbridge** USA
59B3 **Stockerau** Austria
39H7 **Stockholm** Sweden
42C3 **Stockport** Eng
22B2 **Stockton** California, USA
42D2 **Stockton** Eng
18B2 **Stockton L** USA
43C3 **Stoke-on-Trent** Eng
38A2 **Stokkseyri** Iceland
38G5 **Stokmarknes** Nor
39K8 **Stolbtsy** Belorussia
58D2 **Stolin** Belorussia
16B3 **Stone Harbor** USA
44C3 **Stonehaven** Scot
19A3 **Stonewall** USA
12D2 **Stony** *R* USA
38H5 **Storavan** *L* Sweden
38G6 **Støren** Nor
109C4 **Storm B** Aust
44A2 **Stornoway** Scot
59D3 **Storozhinets** Ukraine
16C2 **Storrs** USA
38G6 **Stors168jon** *L* Sweden
38H5 **Storuman** Sweden
16D1 **Stoughton** USA
43E3 **Stowmarket** Eng
45C1 **Strablane** N Ire
109C4 **Strahan** Aust
56C2 **Stralsund** Germany
38F6 **Stranda** Nor
39H7 **Strängnäs** Sweden
42B2 **Stranraer** Scot
49D2 **Strasbourg** France
15C3 **Strasburg** USA
14B2 **Stratford** Can
16C2 **Stratford** Connecticut, USA
110B1 **Stratford** NZ
43D3 **Stratford-on-Avon** Eng
108A3 **Strathalbyn** Aust
42B2 **Strathclyde** Region, Scot
13E2 **Strathmore** Can
18C1 **Streator** USA
47C2 **Stresa** Italy
53C3 **Stretto de Messina** *Str* Italy/Sicily
38D3 **Streymoy** Føroyar
53C3 **Stroboli** *I* Italy
6E3 **Strømfjord** Greenland
44C2 **Stromness** Scot
18A1 **Stromsburg** USA
38H6 **Stromsund** Sweden
38G6 **Ströms Vattudal** *L* Sweden
44C2 **Stronsay** *I* Scot
43C4 **Stroud** Eng
16B2 **Stroudsburg** USA
54B2 **Struma** *R* Bulg
43B3 **Strumble Head** *Pt* Wales
55B2 **Strumica** Macedonia
59C3 **Stryy** Ukraine
59C3 **Stryy** *R* Ukraine
108B1 **Strzelecki Creek** *R* Aust
17B2 **Stuart** Florida, USA
13C2 **Stuart** *R* Can
12B2 **Stuart I** USA
13C2 **Stuart L** Can
47D1 **Stubaier Alpen** *Mts* Austria
76D3 **Stung Sen** Camb
76D3 **Stung Treng** Camb
52A2 **Stura** *R* Italy
112C7 **Sturge I** Ant
14A2 **Sturgeon Bay** USA
14C1 **Sturgeon Falls** Can
18C2 **Sturgis** Kentucky, USA
14A2 **Sturgis** Michigan, USA
106B2 **Sturt Creek** *R* Aust
108B1 **Sturt Desert** Aust
100B4 **Stuttemeim** S Africa
19B3 **Stuttgart** USA
57B3 **Stuttgart** Germany
38A1 **Stykkishólmur** Iceland
59D2 **Styr'** *R* Ukraine
35C1 **Suaçuí Grande** *R* Brazil
81B4 **Suakin** Sudan
73E5 **Su-ao** Taiwan
34C2 **Suardi** Arg
78B2 **Subi** *I* Indon
54A1 **Subotica** Serbia, Yugos
60C4 **Suceava** Rom
45B2 **Suck** *R* Irish Rep
30C2 **Sucre** Bol
35A1 **Sucuriú** *R* Brazil
98C1 **Sudan** Republic, Africa
14B1 **Sudbury** Can
43E3 **Sudbury** Eng
99C2 **Sudd** *Swamp* Sudan
33F2 **Suddie** Guyana
98C2 **Sue** *R* Sudan
4H2 **Suerdrup Is** Can
92B4 **Suez** Egypt
92B3 **Suez Canal** Egypt
92B4 **Suez,G of** Egypt
16B2 **Suffern** USA
43E3 **Suffolk** County, Eng
109D2 **Sugarloaf Pt** Aust
91C5 **Suhār** Oman
68C1 **Sühbaatar** Mongolia
84B3 **Sui** Pak
72C2 **Suide** China
69E2 **Suihua** China
73B3 **Suining** China
46C2 **Suippes** France
41B3 **Suir** *R* Irish Rep
73C3 **Sui Xian** China
72E1 **Suizhong** China
85C3 **Sujāngarth** India
78B4 **Sukabumi** Indon
78C3 **Sukadana** Borneo, Indon
78B4 **Sukadana** Sumatra, Indon
74E3 **Sukagawa** Japan
78C3 **Sukaraya** Indon
60E3 **Sukhinichi** Russian Fed
61F2 **Sukhona** *R* Russian Fed
61F5 **Sukhumi** Georgia
6E3 **Sukkertoppen** Greenland

6E3	**Sukkertoppen** *L* Greenland
38L6	**Sukkozero** Russian Fed
85B3	**Sukkur** Pak
87C1	**Sukma** India
95A2	**Süknah** Libya
100A3	**Sukses** Namibia
75A2	**Sukumo** Japan
13C1	**Sukunka** *R* Can
60E3	**Sula** *R* Russian Fed
84B3	**Sulaiman Range** *Mts* Pak
70C4	**Sulawesi** *I* Indon
54C1	**Sulina** Rom
38H5	**Sulitjelma** Nor
32A4	**Sullana** Peru
18B2	**Sullivan** USA
13B2	**Sullivan Bay** Can
13E2	**Sullivan L** Can
52B2	**Sulmona** Italy
19B3	**Sulphur** Louisiana, USA
19A3	**Sulphur** Oklahoma, USA
19A3	**Sulphur Springs** USA
86A1	**Sultānpur** India
79B4	**Sulu Arch** Phil
70C3	**Sulu S** Philip
30D4	**Sumampa** Arg
70B4	**Sumatera** *I* Indon
70C4	**Sumba** *I* Indon
78D4	**Sumbawa** *I* Indon
78D4	**Sumbawa Besar** Indon
99D3	**Sumbawanga** Tanz
100A2	**Sumbe** Angola
44E2	**Sumburgh Head** *Pt* Scot
78C4	**Sumenep** Indon
69G3	**Sumisu** *I* Japan
13D3	**Summerland** Can
5F4	**Summit Lake** Can
21B2	**Summit Mt** USA
111B2	**Sumner,L** NZ
75A2	**Sumoto** Japan
17B1	**Sumter** USA
60D3	**Sumy** Ukraine
16A2	**Sunbury** USA
34C2	**Sunchales** Arg
74B3	**Sunch'ŏn** N Korea
74B4	**Sunch'ŏn** S Korea
86A2	**Sundargarh** India
86B2	**Sunderbans** *Swamp* India
42D2	**Sunderland** Eng
13E2	**Sundre** Can
15C1	**Sundridge** Can
38H6	**Sundsvall** Sweden
38D3	**Suduroy** Føroyar
78D3	**Sungaianyar** Indon
78A3	**Sungaisalak** Indon
20C1	**Sunnyside** USA
21A2	**Sunnyvale** USA
63D1	**Suntar** Russian Fed
97B4	**Sunyani** Ghana
75A2	**Suō-nada** *B* Japan
38K6	**Suonejoki** Fin
86B1	**Supaul** India
18A1	**Superior** Nebraska, USA
10A2	**Superior** Wisconsin, USA
10B2	**Superior,L** Can/USA
76C3	**Suphan Buri** Thai
93D2	**Süphan Dağ** Turk
71E4	**Supiori** *I* Indon
93E3	**Suq ash Suyukh** Iraq
72D3	**Suqian** China
	Suqutra = Socotra
91C5	**Sūr** Oman
61G3	**Sura** *R* Russian Fed
78C4	**Surabaya** Indon
75B2	**Suraga-wan** *B* Japan
78C4	**Surakarta** Indon
109C1	**Surat** Aust
85C4	**Sürat** India
84C3	**Süratgarh** India
77B4	**Surat Thani** Thai
85C4	**Surendranagar** India
16B3	**Surf City** USA
64J3	**Surgut** Russian Fed
87B1	**Suriāpet** India
49D2	**Sürich** Switz
79C4	**Surigao** Phil
76C3	**Surin** Thai
33F3	**Surinam** Republic, S America
43D4	**Surrey** County, Eng
47C1	**Sursee** Switz
95A1	**Surt** Libya
38A2	**Surtsey** *I* Iceland
78A3	**Surulangan** Indon
47B2	**Susa** Italy
75A2	**Susa** Japan
21A1	**Susanville** USA
47D1	**Süsch** Switz
12E2	**Susitna** *R* USA
16A3	**Susquehanna** *R* USA
16B2	**Sussex** USA
43D4	**Sussex West** Eng
13B1	**Sustut Peak** *Mt* Can
100B4	**Sutherland** S Africa
84C2	**Sutlej** *R* Pak
21A2	**Sutter Creek** USA
14B3	**Sutton** USA
12C3	**Sutwik I** USA
74D3	**Suwa** Japan
58C2	**Suwałki** Pol
17B2	**Suwannee** *R* USA
94B2	**Suweilih** Jordan
74B3	**Suwŏn** S Korea
72D3	**Su Xian** China
75B1	**Suzaka** Japan
73E3	**Suzhou** China
74D3	**Suzu** Japan
75B2	**Suzuka** Japan
75B1	**Suzu-misaki** *C* Japan
64C2	**Svalbard** *Is* Barents S
59C3	**Svalyava** Ukraine
38G5	**Svartisen** *Mt* Nor
76D3	**Svay Rieng** Camb
38G6	**Sveg** Sweden
39G7	**Svendborg** Den
	Sverdlovsk = Yekaterinburg
6A1	**Sverdrup Chan** Can
69F2	**Svetlaya** Russian Fed
58C2	**Svetlogorsk** Russian Fed
39K6	**Svetogorsk** Russian Fed
54B2	**Svetozarevo** Serbia, Yugos
54C2	**Svilengrad** Bulg
50D2	**Svir'** Belorussia
59B3	**Svitavy** Czech Republic
69E1	**Svobodnyy** Russian Fed
38G5	**Svolvaer** Nor
107E3	**Swain Reefs** Aust
17B1	**Swainsboro** USA
100A3	**Swakopmund** Namibia
42D2	**Swale** *R* Eng
70C3	**Swallow Reef** *I* S E Asia
87B2	**Swāmihalli** India
25D3	**Swan I** Honduras
43D4	**Swanage** Eng
108B3	**Swan Hill** Aust
13D2	**Swan Hills** Can
13D2	**Swan Hills** *Mts* Can
26A3	**Swan I** Caribbean S
5H4	**Swan River** Can
43C4	**Swansea** Wales
43C4	**Swansea B** Wales
101G1	**Swartruggens** S Africa
	Swatow = Shantou
101H1	**Swaziland** Kingdom, S Africa
39G7	**Sweden** Kingdom, N Europe
20B2	**Sweet Home** USA
9C3	**Sweetwater** USA
100B4	**Swellendam** S Africa
59B2	**Świdnica** Pol
58B2	**Świdwin** Pol
58B2	**Świebodzin** Pol
58B2	**Świecie** Pol
5H4	**Swift Current** Can
43D4	**Swindon** Eng
45B2	**Swinford** Irish Rep
56C2	**Świnoujście** Pol
49D2	**Switzerland** Federal Republic, Europe
45C2	**Swords** Irish Rep
109D2	**Sydney** Aust
7D5	**Sydney** Can
64G3	**Syktyvkar** Russian Fed
17A1	**Sylacauga** USA
38G6	**Sylarna** *Mt* Sweden
86C2	**Sylhet** Bang
56B1	**Sylt** *I* Germany
14B2	**Sylvania** USA
112C11	**Syowa** *Base* Ant
	Syracuse = Siracusa
15C2	**Syracuse** USA
65H5	**Syr Darya** *R* Kazakhstan
93C2	**Syria** Republic, S W Asia
61J2	**Sysert'** Russian Fed
61G3	**Syzran'** Russian Fed
56C2	**Szczecin** Pol
58B2	**Szczecinek** Pol
58C2	**Szczytno** Pol
59C3	**Szeged** Hung
59B3	**Székesfehérvár** Hung
59B3	**Szekszard** Hung
59B3	**Szolnok** Hung
59B3	**Szombathely** Hung
58B2	**Szprotawa** Pol

T

90C3	**Tabas** Iran
23A1	**Tabasco** Mexico
32D4	**Tabatinga** Brazil
96B2	**Tabelbala** Alg
76C3	**Tabeng** Camb
13E2	**Taber** Can
79B3	**Tablas** *I* Phil
100A4	**Table Mt** S Africa
12F1	**Table Mt** USA
18D2	**Table Rock Res** USA
78B3	**Taboali** Indon
57C3	**Tábor** Czech Republic
99D3	**Tabora** Tanz
97B4	**Tabou** Ivory Coast
90A2	**Tabrīz** Iran
92C4	**Tabūk** S Arabia
23A2	**Tacámbaro** Mexico
82C1	**Tacheng** China
79C3	**Tacloban** Phil
30B2	**Tacna** Peru
8A2	**Tacoma** USA
99E1	**Tadjoura** Djibouti
87B2	**Tādpatri** India
74B3	**Taebaek Sanmaek** *Mts* S Korea
74B3	**Taegu** S Korea
74B4	**Taehüksan** *I* S Korea
74B3	**Taejŏn** S Korea
51B1	**Tafalla** Spain
96C2	**Tafasaset** *Watercourse* Alg
43C4	**Taff** *R* Wales
94B3	**Tafila** Jordan
60E4	**Taganrog** Ukraine
97A3	**Tagant** Region, Maur
79B4	**Tagbilaran** Phil
96B2	**Taguenout Hagguerete** *Well* Maur
107E2	**Tagula** *I* Solomon Is
79C4	**Tagum** Phil
	Tagus = Tejo
96C2	**Tahat** *Mt* Alg
105J4	**Tahiti** *I* Pacific O
18A2	**Tahlequah** USA
21A2	**Tahoe City** USA
21A2	**Tahoe,L** USA
97C3	**Tahoua** Niger
71D3	**Tahuna** Indon
72D2	**Tai'an** China
72B3	**Taibai Shan** *Mt* China
72D1	**Taibus Qi** China
73E5	**T'ai-chung** Taiwan
111B3	**Taieri** *R* NZ
72C2	**Taihang Shan** China
110C1	**Taihape** NZ
72E3	**Tai Hu** *L* China
108A3	**Tailem Bend** Aust
44B3	**Tain** Scot
73E5	**T'ai-nan** Taiwan
35C1	**Taiobeiras** Brazil
73E5	**T'ai pei** Taiwan
77C5	**Taiping** Malay
75C1	**Taira** Japan
78A3	**Tais** Indon
75A1	**Taisha** Japan
29B5	**Taitao,Pen de** Chile
73E5	**T'ai-tung** Taiwan
38K5	**Taivelkoski** Fin
69E4	**Taiwan** Republic, China
	Taiwan Haixia = Formosa Str
72C2	**Taiyuan** China
72D3	**Taizhou** China
81C4	**Ta'izz** Yemen
82A2	**Tajikistan** Republic, Asia
50B1	**Tajo** *R* Spain
76B2	**Tak** Thai
74D3	**Takada** Japan
75A2	**Takahashi** Japan
110B2	**Takaka** NZ
74C4	**Takamatsu** Japan
74D3	**Takaoka** Japan
110B1	**Takapuna** NZ
74D3	**Takasaki** Japan
75B1	**Takayama** Japan
74D3	**Takefu** Japan
70A3	**Takengon** Indon
76C3	**Takeo** Camb
75A2	**Takeo** Japan
	Take-shima = Tok-do
90A2	**Takestān** Iran
75A2	**Taketa** Japan
4G3	**Takjvak L** Can
99D1	**Takkaze** *R* Eritrea/Eth
13B1	**Takla L** Can
13B1	**Takla Landing** Can
12B2	**Taklesluk L** USA
12H2	**Taku Arm** *R* Can
23A1	**Tala** Mexico
59B3	**Talabanya** Hung
84C2	**Talagang** Pak
34A2	**Talagante** Chile
87B3	**Talaimannar** Sri Lanka
97C3	**Talak** *Desert* Region, Niger
78A3	**Talangbetutu** Indon
32A4	**Talara** Peru
50B2	**Talavera de la Reina** Spain
34A3	**Talca** Chile
34A3	**Talcahuano** Chile
86B2	**Tālcher** India
82B1	**Taldy Kurgan** Kazakhstan
71D4	**Taliabu** Indon
84B1	**Taligan** Afghan
99D2	**Tali Post** Sudan
78D4	**Taliwang** Indon
12D2	**Talkeetna** USA
12F2	**Talkeetna Mts** USA
17A1	**Talladega** USA
93D2	**Tall 'Afar** Iraq
17B1	**Tallahassee** USA
94C1	**Tall Bīsah** Syria
60B2	**Tallinn** Estonia
92C3	**Tall Kalakh** Syria
19B3	**Tallulah** USA
60D4	**Tal'noye** Ukraine
58C2	**Talpaki** Russian Fed
30B4	**Taltal** Chile
109C1	**Talwood** Aust
78D1	**Tamabo Range** *Mts* Malay
97B4	**Tamale** Ghana
96C2	**Tamanrasset** Alg
96C2	**Tamanrasset** *Watercourse* Alg
16B2	**Tamaqua** USA
	Tamatave = Toamasina
23A2	**Tamazula** Jalisco, Mexico
23B2	**Tamazulapán** Mexico
23B1	**Tamazunchale** Mexico
97A3	**Tambacounda** Sen
61F3	**Tambov** Russian Fed
50A1	**Tambre** *R* Spain
98C2	**Tambura** Sudan

Tamchaket

97A3	**Tamchaket** Maur
50A1	**Tamega** *R* Port
23B1	**Tamiahua** Mexico
87B2	**Tamil Nādu** State, India
76D2	**Tam Ky** Viet
17B2	**Tampa** USA
17B2	**Tampa B** USA
39J6	**Tampere** Fin
23B1	**Tampico** Mexico
68D2	**Tamsagbulag** Mongolia
86C2	**Tamu** Burma
23B1	**Tamuis** Mexico
109D2	**Tamworth** Aust
43D3	**Tamworth** Eng
38K4	**Tana** Nor
99D1	**Tana** *L* Eth
99E3	**Tana** *R* Kenya
38K5	**Tana** *R* Nor/Fin
75B2	**Tanabe** Japan
38K4	**Tanafjord** *Inlet* Nor
78D3	**Tanahgrogot** Indon
71E4	**Tanahmerah** Indon
12D1	**Tanana** USA
12E2	**Tanana** *R* USA
	Tananarive = Antananarivo
47C2	**Tanaro** *R* Italy
74B2	**Tanch'ŏn** N Korea
34D3	**Tandil** Arg
78B2	**Tandjong Datu** *Pt* Indon
71E4	**Tandjung d'Urville** *C* Indon
78D3	**Tandjung Layar** *C* Indon
78B3	**Tandjung Lumut** *C* Indon
78D2	**Tandjung Mangkalihet** *C* Indon
78C3	**Tandjung Sambar** *C* Indon
78C2	**Tandjung Sirik** *C* Malay
71E4	**Tandjung Vals** *C* Indon
85B3	**Tando Adam** Pak
85B3	**Tando Muhammad Khan** Pak
108B2	**Tandou L** Aust
87B1	**Tāndūr** India
110C1	**Taneatua** NZ
76B2	**Tanen Range** *Mts* Burma/Thai
96B2	**Tanezrouft** *Desert Region* Alg
91C4	**Tang** Iran
99D3	**Tanga** Tanz
60E4	**Tanganrog** Russian Fed
99C3	**Tanganyika,L** Tanz/Zaïre
96B1	**Tanger** Mor
82C2	**Tanggula Shan** *Mts* China
	Tangier = Tanger
78A2	**Tangjungpinang** Indon
82C2	**Tangra Yumco** *L* China
72D2	**Tangshan** China
79B4	**Tangub** Phil
63C2	**Tanguy** Russian Fed
	Tanintharyi = Tenasserim
79B4	**Tanjay** Phil
101D3	**Tanjona Ankaboa** *C* Madag
101D2	**Tanjona Babaomby** *C* Madag
101D2	**Tanjona Vilanandro** *C* Madag
101D3	**Tanjona Vohimena** *C* Madag
78C4	**Tanjong Bugel** *C* Indon
78B4	**Tanjong Cangkuang** *C* Indon
78C3	**Tanjong Puting** *C* Indon
78C3	**Tanjong Selatan** *C* Indon
78D3	**Tanjung** Indon
70A3	**Tanjungbalai** Indon
78A3	**Tanjung Jabung** *Pt* Indon
78B3	**Tanjungpandan** Indon
78B4	**Tanjung Priok** Indon
78D2	**Tanjungredeb** Indon
78D2	**Tanjungselor** Indon
84C2	**Tank** Pak
68B1	**Tannu Ola** *Mts* Russian Fed
97B4	**Tano** *R* Ghana
97C3	**Tanout** Niger
23B1	**Tanquián** Mexico
73E4	**Tan-shui** Taiwan
86A1	**Tansing** Nepal
95C1	**Tanta** Egypt
96A2	**Tan-Tan** Mor
4B3	**Tanunak** USA
99D3	**Tanzania** Republic, Africa
72A3	**Tao He** *R* China
72B2	**Taole** China
96B1	**Taourirt** Mor
60C2	**Tapa** Estonia
25C3	**Tapachula** Mexico
33F4	**Tapajós** *R* Brazil
34C3	**Tapalquén** Arg
70B4	**Tapan** Indon
111A3	**Tapanui** NZ
32D5	**Tapauá** *R* Brazil
85D4	**Tapi** *R* India
86B1	**Taplejung** Nepal
111B2	**Tapuaeniku** *Mt* NZ
35B2	**Tapuaritinga** Brazil
79B4	**Tapul Group** *Is* Phil
33E4	**Tapurucuara** Brazil
109D1	**Tara** Aust
65J4	**Tara** Russian Fed
65J4	**Tara** *R* Russian Fed
54A2	**Tara** *R* Bosnia-Herzegovina/Montenegro, Yugos
97D4	**Taraba** *R* Nig
30D2	**Tarabuco** Bol
	Tarābulus = Tripoli
50B1	**Taracón** Spain
110C1	**Taradale** NZ
78D2	**Tarakan** Indon
44A3	**Taransay** *I* Scot
53C2	**Taranto** Italy
32B5	**Tarapoto** Peru
49C2	**Tarare** France
110C2	**Tararua Range** *Mts* NZ
96C2	**Tarat** Alg
110C1	**Tarawera** NZ
51B1	**Tarazona** Spain
44C3	**Tarbat Ness** *Pen* Scot
84C2	**Tarbela Res** Pak
42B2	**Tarbert** Strathclyde, Scot
44A3	**Tarbert** Western Isles, Scot
48C3	**Tarbes** France
106C4	**Tarcoola** Aust
109C2	**Tarcoon** Aust
109D2	**Taree** Aust
96A2	**Tarfaya** Mor
95A1	**Tarhūnah** Libya
91B5	**Tarif** UAE
30D3	**Tarija** Bol
87B2	**Tarikere** India
81C4	**Tarim** Yemen
99D3	**Tarime** Tanz
82C1	**Tarim He** *R* China
82C2	**Tarim Pendi** *Basin* China
84B2	**Tarin Kut** Afghan
18A1	**Tarkio** USA
79B2	**Tarlac** Phil
32B6	**Tarma** Peru
49C3	**Tarn** *R* France
59C2	**Tarnobrzeg** Pol
59C3	**Tarnów** Pol
107D3	**Taroom** Aust
51C1	**Tarragona** Spain
109C4	**Tarraleah** Aust
51C1	**Tarrasa** Spain
16C2	**Tarrytown** USA
92B2	**Tarsus** Turk
44D2	**Tartan** *Oilfield* N Sea
47D2	**Tartaro** *R* Italy
60C2	**Tartu** Estonia
92C3	**Tartūs** Syria
35C1	**Tarumirim** Brazil
70A3	**Tarutung** Indon
52B1	**Tarvisio** Italy
80D1	**Tashauz** Turkmenistan
86C1	**Tashigang** Bhutan
82A1	**Tashkent** Uzbekistan
65K4	**Tashtagol** Russian Fed
63A2	**Tashtyp** Russian Fed
78B4	**Tasikmalaya** Indon
94B2	**Tasīl** Syria
6E2	**Tasiussaq** Greenland
95A3	**Tasker** *Well* Niger
110B2	**Tasman B** NZ
107D5	**Tasmania** *I* Aust
111B2	**Tasman Mts** NZ
109C4	**Tasman Pen** Aust
107E4	**Tasman S** NZ Aust
92C1	**Taşova** Turk
96C2	**Tassili du Hoggar** *Desert* Region, Alg
96C2	**Tassili N'jjer** *Desert* Region, Alg
96B2	**Tata** Mor
96D1	**Tataouine** Tunisia
65J4	**Tatarsk** Russian Fed
69G2	**Tatarskiy Proliv** *Str* Russian Fed
61G2	**Tatarstan** Russian Fed
75B1	**Tateyama** Japan
5G3	**Tathlina L** Can
12E2	**Tatitlek** USA
13C2	**Tatla Lake** Can
59B3	**Tatry** *Mts* Pol/Slovakia
75A2	**Tatsuno** Japan
85B4	**Tatta** Pak
35B2	**Tatuí** Brazil
93D2	**Tatvan** Turk
31C3	**Tauá** Brazil
35B2	**Taubaté** Brazil
110C1	**Taumarunui** NZ
101F1	**Taung** S Africa
76B2	**Taungdwingyi** Burma
76B1	**Taung-gyi** Burma
76A2	**Taungup** Burma
84C2	**Taunsa** Pak
43C4	**Taunton** Eng
16D2	**Taunton** USA
46E1	**Taunus** Region, Germany
110C1	**Taupo** NZ
110C1	**Taupo,L** NZ
58C1	**Taurage** Lithuania
110C1	**Tauranga** NZ
110C1	**Tauranga Harbour** *B* NZ
110B1	**Tauroa Pt** NZ
7A3	**Tavani** Can
7A3	**Tavani** Can
65H4	**Tavda** *R* Russian Fed
43B4	**Tavistock** Eng
76B3	**Tavoy** Burma
76B3	**Tavoy Pt** Burma
92A2	**Tavsanli** Turk
111B2	**Tawa** NZ
19A3	**Tawakoni,L** USA
14B2	**Tawas City** USA
70C3	**Tawau** Malay
98C1	**Taweisha** Sudan
79B4	**Tawitawi** *I* Phil
79B4	**Tawitawi Group** *Is* Phil
23B2	**Taxco** Mexico
23B2	**Taxcoco** Mexico
44C3	**Tay** *R* Scot
78C3	**Tayan** Indon
12B1	**Taylor** Alaska, USA
13C1	**Taylor** Can
14B2	**Taylor** Michigan, USA
19A3	**Taylor** Texas, USA
18C2	**Taylorville** USA
80B3	**Tayma'** S Arabia
63B1	**Taymura** *R* Russian Fed
76D3	**Tay Ninh** Viet
63B2	**Tayshet** Russian Fed
68B2	**Tayshir** Mongolia
44C3	**Tayside** Region, Scot
79A3	**Taytay** Phil
90D3	**Tayyebāt** Iran
96B1	**Taza** Mor
95B2	**Tazirbu** Libya
12E2	**Tazlina L** USA
64J3	**Tazovskiy** Russian Fed
65F5	**Tbilisi** Georgia
98B3	**Tchibanga** Gabon
95A2	**Tchigai,Plat du** Niger
97C3	**Tchin Tabaradene** Niger
98B2	**Tcholliré** Cam
58B2	**Tczew** Pol
111A3	**Te Anau** NZ
111A3	**Te Anau,L** NZ
110C1	**Te Aroha** NZ
110C1	**Te Awamutu** NZ
96C1	**Tébessa** Alg
23A2	**Teboman** Mexico
23A2	**Tecailtlän** Mexico
21B3	**Tecate** Mexico
61K2	**Techa** *R* Russian Fed
23A1	**Tecolotlán** Mexico
23A2	**Tecpan** Mexico
54C1	**Tecuci** Rom
18A1	**Tecumseh** USA
80E2	**Tedzhen** Turkmenistan
65H6	**Tedzhen** *R* Turkmenistan
42D2	**Tees** *R* Eng
33E4	**Tefé** Brazil
78B4	**Tegal** Indon
78B4	**Tegineneng** Indon
25D3	**Tegucigalpa** Honduras
21B3	**Tehachapi Mts** USA
21B2	**Tehachapi P** USA
4J3	**Tehek L** Can
90B2	**Tehrān** Iran
23B2	**Tehuacán** Mexico
23B2	**Tehuantepec** Mexico
23B2	**Tehuitzingo** Mexico
43B3	**Teifi** *R* Wales
50A2	**Tejo** *R* Port
23A2	**Tejupilco** Mexico
111B2	**Tekapo,L** NZ
82B1	**Tekeli** Kazakhstan
92A1	**Tekirdağ** Turk
55C2	**Tekir Dağlari** *Mts* Turk
86C2	**Teknaf** Bang
110C1	**Te Kuiti** NZ
25D3	**Tela** Honduras
94B2	**Tel Aviv Yafo** Israel
34B3	**Telén** Arg
21B2	**Telescope Peak** *Mt* USA
33F5	**Teles Pires** *R* Brazil
47D1	**Telfs** Austria
63A2	**Teli** Russian Fed
94B3	**Tell el Meise** *Mt* Jordan
12A1	**Teller** USA
87B2	**Tellicherry** India
77C5	**Telok Anson** Malay
78D2	**Telok Darvel** Malay
71E4	**Tělok Flamingo** Indon
78C3	**Tělok Kumai** *B* Indon
78B4	**Tělok Pelabuanratu** *B* Indon
78D4	**Tělok Saleh** *B* Indon
78C3	**Tělok Sampit** *B* Indon
78B3	**Tělok Sukadona** *B* Indon
23B2	**Teloloapán** Mexico
64G3	**Tel'pos-iz** *Mt* Russian Fed
58C1	**Telsiai** Lithuania
78C3	**Telukbatang** Indon
71E4	**Teluk Berau** *B* Indon
78B4	**Telukbetung** Indom
70D4	**Teluk Bone** *B* Indon
71E4	**Teluk Cendrawasih** *B* Indon
78D3	**Teluk Mandar** *B* Indon
71D4	**Teluk Tolo** *B* Indon

Tisīyah

94C2	**Tisīyah** Syria
59C3	**Tisza** *R* Hung
86A2	**Titlagarh** India
54B2	**Titov Veles** Macedonia
98C2	**Titule** Zaïre
17B2	**Titusville** USA
43C4	**Tiverton** Eng
52B2	**Tivoli** Italy
23B2	**Tixtla** Mexico
99E2	**Tiyeglow** Somalia
23B2	**Tizayuca** Mexico
25D2	**Tizimin** Mexico
96C1	**Tizi Ouzou** Alg
96B2	**Tiznit** Mor
23A1	**Tizpan el Alto** Mexico
23B2	**Tlacolula** Mexico
23B2	**Tlacotalpan** Mexico
23A2	**Tlalchana** Mexico
23B2	**Tlalnepantla** Mexico
23B2	**Tlalpan** Mexico
23A1	**Tlaltenango** Mexico
23B2	**Tlancualpicán** Mexico
23B2	**Tlapa** Mexico
23B2	**Tlapacoyan** Mexico
23A1	**Tlaquepaque** Mexico
23B2	**Tlaxcala** Mexico
23B2	**Tlaxcala** State, Mexico
23B2	**Tlaxiaco** Mexico
96B1	**Tlemcem** Alg
101D2	**Toamasina** Madag
34C3	**Toay** Arg
75B2	**Toba** Japan
84B2	**Toba and Kakar Ranges** *Mts* Pak
27E4	**Tobago** *I* Caribbean S
13C2	**Toba Inlet** *Sd* Can
71D3	**Tobelo** Indon
14B1	**Tobermory** Can
44A3	**Tobermory** Scot
71E3	**Tobi** *I* Pacific O
21B1	**Tobin,Mt** USA
65H4	**Tobol** *R* Kazakhstan
70D4	**Toboli** Indon
65H4	**Tobol'sk** Russian Fed
	Tobruk = Tubruq
31B2	**Tocantins** *R* Brazil
31B3	**Tocantins** State, Brazil
17B1	**Toccoa** USA
47C1	**Toce** *R* Italy
30B3	**Tocopilla** Chile
30C3	**Tocorpuri** *Mt* Chile
32D1	**Tocuyo** *R* Ven
85D3	**Toda** India
47C1	**Tödi** *Mt* Switz
75A1	**Todong** S Korea
9B4	**Todos Santos** Mexico
13E2	**Tofield** Can
13B3	**Tofino** Can
12B3	**Togiak** USA
12B3	**Togiak B** USA
97C4	**Togo** Republic, Africa
72C1	**Togtoh** China
12F2	**Tok** USA
74E2	**Tokachi** *R* Japan
75B1	**Tokamachi** Japan
95C3	**Tokar** Sudan
69E4	**Tokara Retto** *Arch* Japan
92C1	**Tokat** Turk
74B3	**Tŏkchŏk-kundo** *Arch* S Korea
75A1	**Tok-do** *I* S Korea
82B1	**Tokmak** Kirghizia
110C1	**Tokomaru Bay** NZ
12H3	**Toku** *R* Can/USA
78C3	**Tokung** Indon
69E4	**Tokuno** *I* Japan
74C4	**Tokushima** Japan
75A2	**Tokuyama** Japan
74D3	**Tōkyō** Japan
110C1	**Tolaga Bay** NZ
101D3	**Tôlañaro** Madag
30F3	**Toledo** Brazil
50B2	**Toledo** Spain
14B2	**Toledo** USA
19B3	**Toledo Bend Res** USA

101D3	**Toliara** Madag
23B1	**Toliman** Mexico
32B3	**Tolina** *Mt* Colombia
51B1	**Tolosa** Spain
29B3	**Toltén** Chile
23B2	**Toluca** Mexico
61G3	**Tol'yatti** Russian Fed
74E2	**Tomakomai** Japan
78D1	**Tomani** Malay
58C2	**Tomaszów Mazowiecka** Pol
11B3	**Tombigbee** *R* USA
98B3	**Tomboco** Angola
35C2	**Tombos** Brazil
97B3	**Tombouctou** Mali
100A2	**Tombua** Angola
34A3	**Tomé** Chile
50B2	**Tomelloso** Spain
50A2	**Tomer** Port
106B3	**Tomkinson Range** *Mts* Aust
63E2	**Tommot** Russian Fed
55B2	**Tomorrit** *Mt* Alb
65K4	**Tomsk** Russian Fed
16B3	**Toms River** USA
25C3	**Tonalá** Mexico
20C1	**Tonasket** USA
15C2	**Tonawanda** USA
105H4	**Tonga** *Is* Pacific O
101H1	**Tongaat** S Africa
73D3	**Tongcheng** China
72B2	**Tongchuan** China
72A2	**Tongde** China
46C1	**Tongeren** Belg
76E2	**Tonggu Jiao** *I* China
73A5	**Tonghai** China
74B2	**Tonghua** China
74B3	**Tongjosŏn-man** N Korea
76D1	**Tongkin,G of** China/Viet
72E1	**Tonglia** China
73D3	**Tongling** China
108B2	**Tongo** Aust
34A2	**Tongoy** Chile
73B4	**Tongren** Guizhou, China
72A2	**Tongren** Qinghai, China
86C1	**Tongsa** Bhutan
76B1	**Tongta** Burma
68B3	**Tongtian He** *R* China
44B2	**Tongue** Scot
72D2	**Tong Xian** China
72B2	**Tongxin** China
73B4	**Tongzi** China
9C4	**Tonich** Mexico
99C2	**Tonj** Sudan
85D3	**Tonk** India
18A2	**Tonkawa** USA
76C3	**Tonle Sap** *L* Camb
21B2	**Tonopah** USA
12E2	**Tonsina** USA
8B2	**Tooele** USA
109D1	**Toogoolawah** Aust
108B1	**Toompine** Aust
109D1	**Toowoomba** Aust
22C1	**Topaz L** USA
18A2	**Topeka** USA
9C4	**Topolobampo** Mexico
20B1	**Toppenish** USA
99D2	**Tor** Eth
55C3	**Torbali** Turk
90C2	**Torbat-e-Heydarīyeh** Iran
90D2	**Torbat-e Jām** Iran
12D2	**Torbert,Mt** USA
50A1	**Tordesillas** Spain
56C2	**Torgau** Germany
46B1	**Torhout** Belg
69G3	**Tori** *I* Japan
47B2	**Torino** Italy
99D2	**Torit** Sudan
35A1	**Torixoreu** Brazil
50A1	**Tormes** *R* Spain
13E2	**Tornado Mt** Can
38J5	**Torne** *L* Sweden
38H5	**Torneträsk** Sweden
7D4	**Torngat** *Mts* Can
38J5	**Tornio** Fin
34C3	**Tornquist** Arg
15C2	**Toronto** Can

60D2	**Toropets** Russian Fed
99D2	**Tororo** Uganda
92B2	**Toros Dağlari** *Mts* Turk
43C4	**Torquay** Eng
22C4	**Torrance** USA
50A2	**Torrão** Port
51C1	**Torreblanca** Spain
53B2	**Torre del Greco** Italy
50B1	**Torrelavega** Spain
50B2	**Torremolinos** Spain
108A2	**Torrens,L** Aust
24B2	**Torreón** Mexico
47B2	**Torre Pellice** Italy
107D2	**Torres Str** Aust
50A2	**Torres Vedras** Port
16C2	**Torrington** Connecticut, USA
8C2	**Torrington** Wyoming, USA
9C4	**Torrón** Mexico
38D3	**Tórshavn** Føroyar
47C2	**Tortona** Italy
51C1	**Tortosa** Spain
90C2	**Torūd** Iran
58B2	**Toruń** Pol
40B2	**Tory** *I* Irish Rep
60D2	**Torzhok** Russian Fed
75A2	**Tosa** Japan
74C4	**Tosa-shimizu** Japan
74C4	**Tosa-wan** *B* Japan
75B2	**To-shima** *I* Japan
	Toshkent = Tashkent
60D2	**Tosno** Russian Fed
75A2	**Tosu** Japan
92B1	**Tosya** Turk
61F1	**Tot'ma** Russian Fed
43C4	**Totnes** Eng
33F2	**Totness** Surinam
23B2	**Totolapan** Mexico
51B2	**Totona** Spain
109C2	**Tottenham** Aust
74C3	**Tottori** Japan
97B4	**Touba** Ivory Coast
97A3	**Touba** Sen
96B1	**Toubkal** *Mt* Mor
97B3	**Tougan** Burkina
96C1	**Touggourt** Alg
97A3	**Tougué** Guinea
46C2	**Toul** France
49D3	**Toulon** France
48C3	**Toulouse** France
97B4	**Toumodi** Ivory Coast
76B2	**Toungoo** Burma
46B1	**Tourcoing** France
96A2	**Tourine** Maur
46B1	**Tournai** Belg
48C2	**Tours** France
74E2	**Towada** Japan
74E2	**Towada-ko** *L* Japan
15C2	**Towanda** USA
107D2	**Townsville** Aust
16A3	**Towson** USA
43C4	**Towy** *R* Wales
74D3	**Toyama** Japan
75B1	**Toyama-wan** *B* Japan
75B2	**Toyohashi** Japan
75B2	**Toyonaka** Japan
75A1	**Toyooka** Japan
74D3	**Toyota** Japan
96C1	**Tozeur** Tunisia
46D2	**Traben-Trarbach** Germany
93C1	**Trabzon** Turk
22B2	**Tracy** California, USA
34A3	**Traiguén** Chile
13D3	**Trail** Can
41B3	**Tralee** Irish Rep
45B2	**Tralee B** Irish Rep
45C2	**Tramore** Irish Rep
39G7	**Tranås** Sweden
77B4	**Trang** Thai
71E4	**Trangan** *I* Indon
109C2	**Trangie** Aust
12E2	**Transalaskan Pipeline** USA
100B3	**Transvaal** Province, S Africa
	Transylvanian Alps = Muntii Carpatii Meridionali
53B3	**Trapani** Italy

109C3	**Traralgon** Aust
97A3	**Trarza** Region, Maur
76C3	**Trat** Thai
108B2	**Traveller's** *L* Aust
56C2	**Travemünde** Germany
14A2	**Traverse City** USA
12C1	**Traverse Peak** *Mt* USA
111B2	**Travers,Mt** NZ
47C2	**Trebbia** *R* Italy
59B3	**Třebíč** Czech Republic
54A2	**Trebinje** Bosnia-Herzegovina
57C3	**Trebon** Czech Republic
29F2	**Treinta y Tres** Urug
29C4	**Trelew** Arg
39G7	**Trelleborg** Sweden
43B3	**Tremadog B** Wales
15D1	**Tremblant,Mt** Can
13C2	**Trembleur L** Can
16A2	**Tremont** USA
59B3	**Trenčin** Slovakia
34C3	**Trenque Lauquén** Arg
43D3	**Trent** *R* Eng
47D1	**Trentino** Region, Italy
47D1	**Trento** Italy
15C2	**Trenton** Can
18B1	**Trenton** Missouri, USA
16B2	**Trenton** New Jersey, USA
7E5	**Trepassey** Can
34C3	**Tres Arroyos** Arg
35B2	**Tres Corações** Brazil
30F3	**Três Lagoas** Brazil
34C3	**Tres Lomas** Arg
22B2	**Tres Pinos** USA
35C2	**Três Rios** Brazil
47C2	**Treviglio** Italy
47E2	**Treviso** Italy
47C2	**Trezzo** Italy
87B2	**Trichūr** India
108C2	**Trida** Aust
46D2	**Trier** Germany
52B1	**Trieste** Italy
45C2	**Trim** Irish Rep
87C3	**Trincomalee** Sri Lanka
33E6	**Trinidad** Bol
29E2	**Trinidad** Urug
9C3	**Trinidad** USA
34C3	**Trinidad** *I* Arg
27E4	**Trinidad** *I* Caribbean S
103G6	**Trindade** *I* Atlantic O
27E4	**Trinidad & Tobago** Republic Caribbean S
19A3	**Trinity** USA
9D3	**Trinity** *R* USA
7E5	**Trinity B** Can
12D3	**Trinity Is** USA
17A1	**Trion** USA
94B1	**Tripoli** Leb
95A1	**Tripoli** Libya
55B3	**Trípolis** Greece
86C2	**Tripura** State, India
103H6	**Tristan da Cunha** *Is* Atlantic O
87B3	**Trivandrum** India
59B3	**Trnava** Slovakia
107E1	**Trobriand Is** PNG
15D1	**Trois-Riviéres** Can
65H4	**Troitsk** Russian Fed
39G7	**Trollhättan** Sweden
38F6	**Trollheimen** *Mt* Nor
89K9	**Tromelin** *I* Indian O
38H5	**Tromsø** Nor
38G6	**Trondheim** Nor
38G6	**Trondheimfjord** *Inlet* Nor
42B2	**Troon** Scot
102J3	**Tropic of Cancer**
103J6	**Tropic of Capricorn**
96B2	**Troudenni** Mali
7A4	**Trout L** Ontario, Can
17A1	**Troy** Alabama, USA
16C1	**Troy** New York, USA
14B2	**Troy** Ohio, USA
54B2	**Troyan** Bulg
49C2	**Troyes** France

Umm al Qaiwain

91C5	**Umm as Samīm** *Salt Marsh* Oman
99C1	**Umm Bell** Sudan
98C1	**Umm Keddada** Sudan
99D1	**Umm Ruwaba** Sudan
91B5	**Umm Sa'id** Qatar
20B2	**Umpqua** *R* USA
85D4	**Umred** India
100B4	**Umtata** S Africa
35A2	**Umuarama** Brazil
52C1	**Una** *R* Bosnia-Herzegovina/Croatia
35B1	**Unaí** Brazil
12B2	**Unalakleet** USA
80C3	**Unayzah** S Arabia
16C2	**Uncasville** USA
101G1	**Underberg** S Africa
60D3	**Unecha** Russian Fed
94B3	**Uneisa** Jordan
7D4	**Ungava B** Can
30F4	**União de Vitória** Brazil
34B3	**Unión** Arg
18B2	**Union** Missouri, USA
17B1	**Union** S Carolina, USA
14C2	**Union City** Pennsylvania, USA
17A1	**Union Springs** USA
15C3	**Uniontown** USA
91B5	**United Arab Emirates** Arabian Pen
36C3	**United Kingdom** Kingdom, W Europe
2H4	**United States of America**
6B1	**United States Range** *Mts* Can
13F2	**Unity** Can
20C2	**Unity** USA
46D1	**Unna** Germany
86A1	**Unnão** India
44E1	**Unst** *I* Scot
13A1	**Unuk** *R* USA
92C1	**Unye** Turk
61F2	**Unzha** *R* Russian Fed
33E2	**Upata** Ven
98C3	**Upemba Nat Pk** Zaïre
6E2	**Upernavik** Greenland
22D3	**Upland** USA
100B3	**Uplington** S Africa
14B2	**Upper Arlington** USA
13D2	**Upper Arrow L** Can
111C2	**Upper Hutt** NZ
20B2	**Upper Klamath L** USA
20B2	**Upper L** USA
45C1	**Upper Lough Erne** *L* N Ire
27L1	**Upper Manzanilla** Trinidad
39H7	**Uppsala** Sweden
72B1	**Urad Qianqi** China
91A4	**Urairah** S Arabia
61H3	**Ural** *R* Kazakhstan
109D2	**Uralla** Aust
61H3	**Ural'sk** Kazakhstan
65G4	**Uralskiy Khrebet** *Mts* Russian Fed
5H4	**Uranium City** Can
75B1	**Urawa** Japan
18C1	**Urbana** Illinois, USA
14B2	**Urbana** Ohio, USA
52B2	**Urbino** Italy
42C2	**Ure** *R* Eng
61G2	**Uren'** Russian Fed
80E1	**Urgench** Uzbekistan
84B2	**Urgun** Afghan
55C3	**Urla** Turk
54B2	**Uroševac** Serbia, Yugos
31B4	**Uruaçu** Brazil
23A2	**Uruapan** Mexico
35B1	**Urucuia** *R* Brazil
30E4	**Uruguaiana** Brazil
29E2	**Uruguay** Republic, S America
29E2	**Uruguay** *R* Urug
82C1	**Urümqi** China
69H2	**Urup** *I* Russian Fed
84B2	**Uruzgan** Afghan

61F3	**Uryupinsk** Russian Fed
61H2	**Urzhum** Russian Fed
54C2	**Urziceni** Rom
82C1	**Usa** China
75A2	**Usa** Japan
64G3	**Usa** *R* Russian Fed
92A2	**Uşak** Turk
100A3	**Usakos** Namibia
99D3	**Ushashi** Tanz
65J5	**Ush Tobe** Kazakhstan
29C6	**Ushuaia** Arg
63E2	**Ushumun** Russian Fed
43C4	**Usk** *R* Wales
92A1	**Usküdar** Turk
63C2	**Usolye Sibirskoye** Russian Fed
34B2	**Uspallata** Arg
69F2	**Ussuriysk** Russian Fed
47C1	**Uster** Switz
53B3	**Ustica** *I* Italy
57C2	**Ústi nad Labem** Czech Republic
65J4	**Ust'Ishim** Russian Fed
58B2	**Ustka** Pol
65K5	**Ust'-Kamenogorsk** Kazakhstan
63B2	**Ust Karabula** Russian Fed
61J2	**Ust'Katav** Russian Fed
63C2	**Ust'-Kut** Russian Fed
61E4	**Ust Labinsk** Russian Fed
63F1	**Ust'Maya** Russian Fed
1C8	**Ust'Nera** Russian Fed
63E2	**Ust'Nyukzha** Russian Fed
63C2	**Ust'Ordynskiy** Russian Fed
64G3	**Ust'Tsil'ma** Russian Fed
63F2	**Ust'Umal'ta** Russian Fed
75A2	**Usuki** Japan
25C3	**Usumacinta** *R* Guatemala/Mexico
101H1	**Usutu** *R* Swaziland
8B3	**Utah** State, USA
8B2	**Utah L** USA
58D1	**Utena** Russian Fed
85B3	**Uthal** Pak
10C2	**Utica** USA
51B2	**Utiel** Spain
13D1	**Utikuma L** Can
56B2	**Utrecht** Neth
101H1	**Utrecht** S Africa
50A2	**Utrera** Spain
38K5	**Utsjoki** Fin
74D3	**Utsunomiya** Japan
76C2	**Uttaradit** Thai
86A1	**Uttar Pradesh** State, India
65H4	**Uval** Russian Fed
107F3	**Uvéa** *I* Nouvelle Calédonie
99D3	**Uvinza** Tanz
99C3	**Uvira** Zaïre
6E2	**Uvkusigssat** Greenland
39J6	**Uvsikaupunki** Fin
68B1	**Uvs Nuur** *L* China
74C4	**Uwajima** Japan
72B2	**Uxin Qi** China
30C3	**Uyuni** Bol
80E1	**Uzbekistan** Republic, Asia
48C2	**Uzerche** France
59C3	**Uzhgorod** Ukraine
54A2	**Užice** Serbia, Yugos
60E3	**Uzlovaya** Russian Fed
92A1	**Uzunköprü** Turk

V

101F1	**Vaal** *R* S Africa
101G1	**Vaal Dam** *Res* S Africa

100B3	**Vaalwater** S Africa
38J6	**Vaasa** Fin
59B3	**Vác** Hung
30F4	**Vacaria** Brazil
35C1	**Vacaria** *R* Minas Gerais, Brazil
21A2	**Vacaville** USA
85C4	**Vadodara** India
38K4	**Vadsø** Nor
47C1	**Vaduz** Leichtenstein
38D3	**Vágar** Føroyar
29E3	**Va Gesell** Arg
59B3	**Váh** *R* Slovakia
87B2	**Vaigai** *R* India
65K3	**Vakh** *R* Russian Fed
60B4	**Vâlcea** Rom
29C4	**Valcheta** Arg
47D2	**Valdagno** Italy
60D2	**Valday** Russian Fed
60D2	**Valdayskaya Vozvyshennost'** *Upland* Russian Fed
32D2	**Val de la Pascua** Ven
50B2	**Valdepeñas** Spain
12E2	**Valdez** USA
29B3	**Valdivia** Chile
46B2	**Val d'Oise** Department France
17B1	**Valdosta** USA
20C2	**Vale** USA
13D2	**Valemount** Can
31D4	**Valença** Bahia, Brazil
35C2	**Valença** Rio de Janeiro, Brazil
49C3	**Valence** France
51B2	**Valencia** Region, Spain
51B2	**Valencia** Spain
32D1	**Valencia** Ven
45A3	**Valencia** *I* Irish Rep
50A2	**Valencia de Alcantara** Spain
46B1	**Valenciennes** France
47C2	**Valenza** Italy
32C2	**Valera** Ven
39K7	**Valga** Estonia
54A2	**Valjevo** Serbia, Yugos
	Valka = Valga
39J6	**Valkeakoski** Fin
25D2	**Valladolid** Mexico
50B1	**Valladolid** Spain
47B2	**Valle d'Aosta** Region, Italy
27D5	**Valle de la Pascua** Ven
23A1	**Valle de Santiago** Mexico
47B2	**Valle d'Isére** France
32C1	**Valledupar** Colombia
97C3	**Vallée de l'Azaouak** V Niger
97C3	**Vallée Tilemis** *V* Mali
30D2	**Valle Grande** Bol
22A1	**Vallejo** USA
30B4	**Vallenar** Chile
53B3	**Valletta** Malta
8D2	**Valley City** USA
20B2	**Valley Falls** USA
15D1	**Valleyfield** Can
13D1	**Valleyview** Can
47E2	**Valli di Comacchio** *Lg* Italy
51C1	**Valls** Spain
58D1	**Valmiera** Latvia
35A2	**Valparaíso** Brazil
34A2	**Valparaiso** Chile
23A1	**Valparaiso** Mexico
17A1	**Valparaiso** USA
101G1	**Vals** *R* S Africa
85C4	**Valsād** India
60E3	**Valuyki** Russian Fed
50A2	**Valverde del Camino** Spain
38J6	**Vammala** Fin
93D2	**Van** Turk
63C1	**Vanavara** Russian Fed
18B2	**Van Buren** Arkansas, USA
13C3	**Vancouver** Can
20B1	**Vancouver** USA
5F5	**Vancouver I** Can
12G2	**Vancouver,Mt** Can

18C2	**Vandalia** Illinois, USA
14B3	**Vandalia** Ohio, USA
13C2	**Vanderhoof** Can
106C2	**Van Diemen G** *Gulf* Aust
39G7	**Vänern** *L* Sweden
39G7	**Vänersborg** Sweden
101D3	**Vangaindrano** Madag
93D2	**Van Gölü** *Salt L* Turk
76C2	**Vang Vieng** Laos
9C3	**Van Horn** USA
15C1	**Vanier** Can
1C6	**Vankarem** Russian Fed
38H6	**Vännäs** Sweden
48B2	**Vannes** France
47B2	**Vanoise** *Mts* France
100A4	**Vanrhynsdorp** S Africa
6B3	**Vansittart I** Can
105G4	**Vanuatu** *Is* Pacific O
14B2	**Van Wert** USA
47C2	**Varallo** Italy
90B2	**Varāmīn** Iran
86A1	**Vārānasi** India
38K4	**Varangerfjord** *Inlet* Nor
38K4	**Varangerhalvøya** *Pen* Nor
52C1	**Varazdin** Croatia
39G7	**Varberg** Sweden
39F7	**Varde** Den
38L4	**Vardø** Nor
58C2	**Varéna** Lithuania
47C2	**Varenna** Italy
47C2	**Varese** Italy
35B2	**Varginha** Brazil
38K6	**Varkaus** Fin
54C2	**Varna** Bulg
39G7	**Värnamo** Sweden
17B1	**Varnville** USA
35C1	**Várzea da Palma** Brazil
47C2	**Varzi** Italy
50B1	**Vascongadas** Region, Spain
60D3	**Vasil'kov** Ukraine
14B2	**Vassar** USA
39H7	**Västerås** Sweden
39H7	**Västervik** Sweden
52B2	**Vasto** Italy
65J4	**Vasyugan** *R* Russian Fed
38B2	**Vatnajökull** *Mts* Iceland
38A1	**Vatneyri** Iceland
54C1	**Vatra Dornei** Rom
39G7	**Vättern** *L* Sweden
9C3	**Vaughn** USA
32C3	**Vaupés** *R* Colombia
13E2	**Vauxhall** Can
87C3	**Vavunija** Sri Lanka
39G7	**Växjö** Sweden
64G2	**Vaygach, Ostrov** *I* Russian Fed
34C2	**Vedia** Arg
38G5	**Vega** *I* Nor
13E2	**Vegreville** Can
50A2	**Vejer de la Frontera** Spain
39F7	**Vejle** Den
52C2	**Velebit** *Mts* Croatia
52C1	**Velenje** Slovenia
35C1	**Velhas** *R* Brazil
39K7	**Velikaya** *R* Russian Fed
60D2	**Velikiye Luki** Russian Fed
61G1	**Velikiy Ustyug** Russian Fed
54C2	**Veliko Türnovo** Bulg
97A3	**Vélingara** Sen
87B2	**Vellore** India
61F1	**Vel'sk** Russian Fed
87B3	**Vembanad L** India
34C2	**Venado Tuerto** Arg
35B2	**Vençeslau Braz** Brazil
49C2	**Vendôme** France
12E1	**Venetie** USA
47D2	**Veneto** Region, Italy
47E2	**Venezia** Italy

Volgodonsk

32D2	**Venezuela** Republic, S America
87A1	**Vengurla** India
12C3	**Veniaminof V** USA
	Venice = Venezia
87B2	**Venkatagiri** India
56B2	**Venlo** Neth
58C1	**Venta** *R* Latvia
101G1	**Ventersburg** S Africa
58C1	**Ventspils** Latvia
32D3	**Ventuari** *R* Ven
22C3	**Ventura** USA
60D1	**Vepsovskaya Vozvyshennost'** *Upland* Russian Fed
30D4	**Vera** Arg
51B2	**Vera** Spain
23B2	**Veracruz** Mexico
23B1	**Veracruz** State, Mexico
85C4	**Veräval** India
47C2	**Verbania** Italy
47C2	**Vercelli** Italy
35A1	**Verde** *R* Goias, Brazil
23A1	**Verde** *R* Jalisco, Mexico
35A1	**Verde** *R* Mato Grosso do Sul, Brazil
23B2	**Verde** *R* Oaxaca, Mexico
	Verde,C = Cap Vert
35C1	**Verde Grande** *R* Brazil
34C3	**Verde,Pen** Arg
49D3	**Verdon** *R* France
46C2	**Verdun** France
101G1	**Vereeniging** S Africa
61H2	**Vereshchagino** Russian Fed
97A3	**Verga,C** Guinea
34D3	**Vergara** Arg
50A1	**Verin** Spain
63D2	**Verkh Angara** *R* Russian Fed
61J3	**Verkhneural'sk** Russian Fed
63E1	**Verkhnevilyuysk** Russian Fed
1C8	**Verkhoyansk** Russian Fed
35A1	**Vermelho** *R* Brazil
13E2	**Vermilion** Can
10C2	**Vermont** State, USA
22B2	**Vernalis** USA
13D2	**Vernon** Can
46A2	**Vernon** France
9D3	**Vernon** USA
17B2	**Vero Beach** USA
54B2	**Veroia** Greece
47D2	**Verolanuova** Italy
47D2	**Verona** Italy
46B2	**Versailles** France
101H1	**Verulam** S Africa
40C1	**Verviers** Belg
46B2	**Vervins** France
46C2	**Vesle** *R* France
49D2	**Vesoul** France
38G5	**Vesterålen** *Is* Nor
38G5	**Vestfjorden** *Inlet* Nor
38A2	**Vestmannaeyjar** Iceland
53B2	**Vesuvio** *Mt* Italy
59B3	**Veszprém** Hung
39H7	**Vetlanda** Sweden
61F2	**Vetluga** *R* Russian Fed
46B1	**Veurne** Belg
47B1	**Vevey** Switz
46A2	**Vexin** Region, France
47A2	**Veynes** France
50A1	**Viana do Castelo** Port
	Viangchan = Vientiane
49E3	**Viareggio** Italy
39F7	**Viborg** Den
53C3	**Vibo Valentia** Italy
	Vic = Vich
112C2	**Vicecomodoro Marambio** *Base* Ant
52B1	**Vicenza** Italy
51C1	**Vich** Spain
32D3	**Vichada** *R* Colombia
61F2	**Vichuga** Russian Fed
49C2	**Vichy** France
19B3	**Vicksburg** USA
35C2	**Vicosa** Brazil
106C4	**Victor Harbour** Aust
34C2	**Victoria** Arg
13C3	**Victoria** Can
34A3	**Victoria** Chile
78D1	**Victoria** Malay
108B3	**Victoria** State, Aust
9D4	**Victoria** USA
106C2	**Victoria** *R* Aust
26B2	**Victoria de las Tunas** Cuba
100B2	**Victoria Falls** Zambia/Zim
4G2	**Victoria I** Can
108B2	**Victoria,L** Aust
99D3	**Victoria,L** C Africa
112B7	**Victoria Land** Region, Ant
86C2	**Victoria,Mt** Burma
99D2	**Victoria Nile** *R* Uganda
111B2	**Victoria Range** *Mts* NZ
106C2	**Victoria River Downs** Aust
4H3	**Victoria Str** Can
15D1	**Victoriaville** Can
100B4	**Victoria West** S Africa
34B3	**Victorica** Arg
21B3	**Victorville** USA
34A2	**Vicuña** Chile
34C2	**Vicuña Mackenna** Arg
17B1	**Vidalia** USA
54C2	**Videle** Rom
54B2	**Vidin** Bulg
85D4	**Vidisha** India
58D1	**Vidzy** Belorussia
29D4	**Viedma** Arg
26A4	**Viejo** Costa Rica
	Vielha = Viella
51C1	**Viella** Spain
	Vienna = Wien
18C2	**Vienna** Illinois, USA
14B3	**Vienna** W Virginia, USA
49C2	**Vienne** France
48C2	**Vienne** *R* France
76C2	**Vientiane** Laos
47C1	**Vierwaldstätter See** *l* Switz
48C2	**Vierzon** France
53C2	**Vieste** Italy
70B2	**Vietnam** Republic, S E Asia
76D1	**Vietri** Viet
27P2	**Vieux Fort** St Lucia
79B2	**Vigan** Phil
47C2	**Vigevano** Italy
48B3	**Vignemale** *Mt* France
50A1	**Vigo** Spain
87C1	**Vijayawāda** India
55A2	**Vijosë** *R* Alb
38B2	**Vik** Iceland
54B2	**Vikhren** *Mt* Bulg
13E2	**Viking** Can
38G6	**Vikna** *I* Nor
101C2	**Vila da Maganja** Mozam
101C2	**Vila Machado** Mozam
101C3	**Vilanculos** Mozam
	Vilanova i la Geltrú = Villanueva-y-Geltrú
50A1	**Vila Real** Port
101C2	**Vila Vasco da Gama** Mozam
35C2	**Vila Velha** Brazil
58D2	**Vileyka** Belorussia
38H6	**Vilhelmina** Sweden
33E6	**Vilhena** Brazil
60C2	**Viljandi** Estonia
101G1	**Viljoenskroon** S Africa
9C3	**Villa Ahumada** Mexico
34B2	**Villa Atuel** Arg
50A1	**Villaba** Spain
23A2	**Villa Carranza** Mexico
52B1	**Villach** Austria
34B2	**Villa Colon** Arg
34C2	**Villa Constitución** Arg
34C1	**Villa de Maria** Arg
23A1	**Villa de Reyes** Mexico
34B2	**Villa Dolores** Arg
47D2	**Villafranca di Verona** Italy
34C2	**Villa General Mitre** Arg
34B2	**Villa General Roca** Arg
34D2	**Villaguay** Arg
25C3	**Villahermosa** Mexico
23A1	**Villa Hidalgo** Mexico
34C2	**Villa Huidobro** Arg
34C3	**Villa Iris** Arg
34C2	**Villa Maria** Arg
30D3	**Villa Montes** Bol
23A1	**Villanueva** Mexico
50A1	**Villa Nova de Gaia** Port
50A2	**Villanueva de la Serena** Spain
51C1	**Villanueva-y-Geltrú** Spain
34B3	**Villa Regina** Arg
51B2	**Villarreal** Spain
29B3	**Villarrica** Chile
30E4	**Villarrica** Par
50B2	**Villarrobledo** Spain
34D2	**Villa San José** Arg
34C2	**Villa Valeria** Arg
32C3	**Villavicencio** Colombia
49C2	**Villefranche** France
7C5	**Ville-Marie** Can
51B2	**Villena** Spain
46B2	**Villeneuve-St-Georges** France
48C3	**Villeneuve-sur-Lot** France
19B3	**Ville Platte** USA
46B2	**Villers-Cotterêts** France
49C2	**Villeurbanne** France
101G1	**Villiers** S Africa
87B2	**Villupuram** India
58D2	**Vilnius** Lithuania
63D1	**Vilyuy** *R* Russian Fed
63E1	**Vilyuysk** Russian Fed
34A2	**Viña del Mar** Chile
51C1	**Vinaroz** Spain
14A3	**Vincennes** USA
38H5	**Vindel** *R* Sweden
85D4	**Vindhya Range** *Mts* India
16B3	**Vineland** USA
16D2	**Vineyard Haven** USA
76D2	**Vinh** Viet
76D3	**Vinh Cam Ranh** *B* Viet
77D4	**Vinh Loi** Viet
77D3	**Vinh Long** Viet
18A2	**Vinita** USA
54A1	**Vinkovci** Croatia
60C4	**Vinnitsa** Ukraine
112B3	**Vinson Massif** *Upland* Ant
100A3	**Vioolsdrift** S Africa
47D1	**Vipiteno** Italy
79B3	**Virac** Phil
87B2	**Virddhāchalam** India
100A2	**Virei** Angola
35C1	**Virgem da Lapa** Brazil
101G1	**Virginia** S Africa
10C3	**Virginia** State, USA
10A2	**Virginia** USA
21B2	**Virginia City** USA
27E3	**Virgin Is** Caribbean S
52C1	**Virovitica** Croatia
46C2	**Virton** Belg
87B3	**Virudunagar** India
52C2	**Vis** *I* Croatia
21B2	**Visalia** USA
79B3	**Visayan S** Phil
39H7	**Visby** Sweden
4H2	**Viscount Melville Sd** Can
54A2	**Višegrad** Bosnia-Herzegovina
50A1	**Viseu** Port
83C4	**Vishākhapatnam** India
47B1	**Visp** Switz
49C1	**Vissingen** Neth
21B3	**Vista** USA
	Vistula = Wisla
57C3	**Vitavia** *R* Czech Republic
87A1	**Vite** India
60D2	**Vitebsk** Belorussia
52B2	**Viterbo** Italy
50A1	**Vitigudino** Spain
63D2	**Vitim** *R* Russian Fed
50B1	**Vitora** Spain
31C6	**Vitória** Brazil
31C4	**Vitória da Conquista** Brazil
48B2	**Vitré** France
46C2	**Vitry-le-Francois** France
38J5	**Vittangi** Sweden
53B3	**Vittoria** Italy
47E2	**Vittorio Veneto** Italy
69H2	**Vityaz Depth** Pacific O
50A1	**Vivero** Spain
63B1	**Vivi** *R* Russian Fed
34D3	**Vivorata** Arg
63C2	**Vizhne-Angarsk** Russian Fed
83C4	**Vizianagaram** India
54B1	**Vlădeasa** *Mt* Rom
61F5	**Vladikavkaz** Russian Fed
65F4	**Vladimir** Russian Fed
59C2	**Vladimir Volynskiy** Ukraine
74C2	**Vladivostok** Russian Fed
56A2	**Vlieland** *I* Neth
46B1	**Vlissingen** Neth
55A2	**Vlorë** Alb
57C3	**Vöcklabruck** Austria
76D3	**Voeune Sai** Camb
47C2	**Voghera** Italy
101D2	**Vohibinany** Madag
101E2	**Vohimarina** Madag
99D3	**Voi** Kenya
97B4	**Voinjama** Lib
40D2	**Voiron** France
54A1	**Vojvodina** *Aut Republic* Serbia, Yugos
26A5	**Volcán Baru** *Mt* Panama
23B2	**Volcán Citlaltepetl** *Mt* Mexico
30C3	**Volcán Lullaillaco** *Mt* Chile
34A3	**Volcáno Copahue** *Mt* Chile
34A3	**Volcáno Domuyo** *Mt* Arg
	Volcano Is = Kazan Retto
29B3	**Volcáno Lanin** *Mt* Arg
30C3	**Volcáno Ollagüe** *Mt* Chile
34A3	**Volcáno Llaima** *Mt* Chile
34B2	**Volcáno Maipo** *Mt* Arg
34A3	**Volcáno Peteroa** *Mt* Chile
34B3	**Volcáno Tromen** *V* Arg
23A2	**Volcán Paracutin** *Mt* Mexico
32B3	**Volcán Puraće** *Mt* Colombia
34A2	**Volcán Tinguiririca** *Mt* Arg/Chile
61J2	**Volchansk** Russian Fed
61G4	**Volga** *R* Russian Fed
61F4	**Volgodonsk** Russian Fed

Volgograd

34C3 **Winifreda** Arg
7B4 **Winisk** *R* Can
7B4 **Winisk L** Can
76B2 **Winkana** Burma
20B1 **Winlock** USA
97B4 **Winneba** Ghana
14A2 **Winnebago,L** USA
20C2 **Winnemucca** USA
19B3 **Winnfield** USA
5J4 **Winnipeg** Can
5J4 **Winnipeg,L** Can
5J4 **Winnipegosis** Can
4J4 **Winnipegosis,L** Can
15D2 **Winnipesaukee,L** USA
10A2 **Winona** Minnesota, USA
19C3 **Winona** Mississippi, USA
15D2 **Winooski** USA
9B3 **Winslow** USA
16C2 **Winsted** USA
11B3 **Winston-Salem** USA
46E1 **Winterberg** Germany
17B2 **Winter Garden** USA
17B2 **Winter Park** USA
22B1 **Winters** USA
47C1 **Winterthur** Switz
107D3 **Winton** Aust
111A3 **Winton** NZ
43E3 **Wisbech** Eng
10B2 **Wisconsin** State, USA
7B5 **Wisconsin Rapids** USA
12D1 **Wiseman** USA
58B2 **Wisla** *R* Pol
56C2 **Wismar** Germany
33F2 **Witagron** Surinam
101G1 **Witbank** S Africa
9D3 **Witchita Falls** USA
43D3 **Witham** *R* Eng
42E3 **Withernsea** Eng
43D4 **Witney** Eng
46D1 **Witten** Germany
56C2 **Wittenberg** Germany
106A3 **Wittenoom** Aust
46D1 **Wittlich** Germany
58B2 **Wladyslawowo** Pol
58B2 **Włoclawek** Pol
58C2 **Włodawa** Pol
109C3 **Wodonga** Aust
47C1 **Wohlen** Switz
71E4 **Wokam** Indon
43D4 **Woking** Eng
71F3 **Woleai** *I* Pacific O
20B2 **Wolf Creek** USA
8C2 **Wolf Point** USA
57C3 **Wolfsberg** Austria
56C2 **Wolfsburg** Germany
5H4 **Wollaston L** Can
5H4 **Wollaston Lake** Can
4G3 **Wollaston Pen** Can
109D2 **Wollongong** Aust
101G1 **Wolmaransstad** S Africa
59B2 **Wolow** Pol
108B3 **Wolseley** Aust
43C3 **Wolverhampton** Eng
16A2 **Womelsdorf** USA
109D1 **Wondai** Aust
74B3 **Wŏnju** S Korea
108B2 **Wonominta** *R* Aust
13C1 **Wonowon** Can
74B3 **Wŏnsan** N Korea
108C3 **Wonthaggi** Aust
108A2 **Woocalla** Aust
16B3 **Woodbine** USA
15C3 **Woodbridge** USA
5G4 **Wood Buffalo Nat Pk** Can
109D1 **Woodburn** Aust
20B1 **Woodburn** USA
16B3 **Woodbury** USA
12F1 **Woodchopper** USA
21A2 **Woodland** California, USA
20B1 **Woodland** Washington, USA
107E1 **Woodlark** *I* PNG
106C4 **Woodmera** Aust
106C3 **Woodroffe,Mt** Aust
14B2 **Woodstock** Ontario, Can
16B3 **Woodstown** USA
110C2 **Woodville** NZ
19B3 **Woodville** USA
108A2 **Woomera** Aust
15D2 **Woonsocket** USA
14B2 **Wooster** USA
43C3 **Worcester** Eng
100A4 **Worcester** S Africa
16D1 **Worcester** USA
47E1 **Wörgl** Austria
42C2 **Workington** Eng
8C2 **Worland** USA
46E2 **Worms** Germany
43B4 **Worms Head** *Pt* Wales
43D4 **Worthing** Eng
8D2 **Worthington** USA
71D4 **Wowoni** *I* Indon
12H3 **Wrangell** USA
12H3 **Wrangell I** USA
12F2 **Wrangell Mts** USA
40B2 **Wrath,C** Scot
43C3 **Wrexham** Wales
17B1 **Wrightsville** USA
22D3 **Wrightwood** USA
4F3 **Wrigley** Can
59B2 **Wrocław** Pol
58B2 **Września** Pol
69E2 **Wuchang** China
76E1 **Wuchuan** China
72E2 **Wuda** China
72C2 **Wuding He** *R* China
72A3 **Wudu** China
73C4 **Wugang** China
72B2 **Wuhai** China
73C3 **Wuhan** China
73D3 **Wuhu** China
73D5 **Wuhua** China
84D2 **Wūjang** China
72B1 **Wujia He** *R* China
73B4 **Wu Jiang** *R* China
97C4 **Wukari** Nig
73B4 **Wuling Shan** *Mts* China
97D4 **Wum** Cam
73A4 **Wumeng Shan** *Upland* China
46D1 **Wuppertal** Germany
72B2 **Wuqi** China
72D2 **Wuqing** China
57B3 **Würzburg** Germany
57C2 **Wurzen** Germany
72C2 **Wutai Shan** *Mt* China
71F4 **Wuvulu** *I* Pacific O
72A2 **Wuwei** China
73E3 **Wuxi** China
73E3 **Wuxing** China
72C2 **Wuyang** China
73D4 **Wuyi Shan** *Mts* China
72B1 **Wuyuan** China
76D2 **Wuzhi Shan** *Mts* China
72B2 **Wuzhong** China
73C5 **Wuzhou** China
14B2 **Wyandotte** USA
109C1 **Wyandra** Aust
43C4 **Wye** *R* Eng
43C4 **Wylye** *R* Eng
43E3 **Wymondham** Eng
106B2 **Wyndham** Aust
18B2 **Wynne** USA
4G2 **Wynniatt B** Can
109C4 **Wynyard** Aust
8C2 **Wyoming** State, USA
14A2 **Wyoming** USA
109D2 **Wyong** Aust

X

84D1 **Xaidulla** China
72D1 **Xai Moron He** *R* China
101C3 **Xai Xai** Mozam
23B2 **Xaltinguis** Mexico
100A2 **Xangongo** Angola
46D1 **Xanten** Germany
55B2 **Xánthi** Greece
100B3 **Xau,L** Botswana
14B3 **Xenia** USA
72A2 **Xiahe** China
73D5 **Xiamen** China
72B3 **Xi'an** China
73B4 **Xianfeng** China
73C3 **Xiangfan** China
73C4 **Xiang Jiang** *R* China
73C4 **Xiangtan** Province, China
73C4 **Xianning** China
72B3 **Xianyang** China
73C4 **Xiao Shui** *R* China
73D4 **Xiapu** China
73A4 **Xichang** China
23B1 **Xicotepec** Mexico
76C2 **Xieng Khouang** Laos
73B4 **Xifeng** China
86B1 **Xigazê** China
72A1 **Xi He** *R* China
72B2 **Xiji** China
73C5 **Xi Jiang** *R* China
72E1 **Xiliao He** *R* China
73B5 **Xilin** China
23B1 **Xilitla** Mexico
73D4 **Xinfeng** China
72C1 **Xinghe** China
73D5 **Xingning** China
73B4 **Xingren** China
72C2 **Xingtai** China
33G4 **Xingu** *R* Brazil
68B2 **Xingxingxia** China
73A4 **Xingyi** China
72A2 **Xining** China
72E2 **Xinjin** Liaoning, China
73A3 **Xinjin** Sichuan, China
72D2 **Xinwen** China
72C2 **Xin Xian** China
72C2 **Xinxiang** China
73C3 **Xinyang** China
73C5 **Xinyi** Guangdong, China
72D3 **Xinyi** Jiangsu, China
72D1 **Xi Ujimqin Qi** China
74A2 **Xiuyan** China
23B2 **Xochimilco** Mexico
73D3 **Xuancheng** China
73B3 **Xuanhan** China
72D1 **Xuanhua** China
73A4 **Xuanwei** China
72C3 **Xuchang** China
99E2 **Xuddur** Somalia
72A2 **Xunhua** China
73C5 **Xun Jiang** *R* China
69E2 **Xunke** China
73D5 **Xunwu** China
73C4 **Xupu** China
76E1 **Xuwen** China
73B4 **Xuyong** China
72D3 **Xuzhou** China

Y

73A4 **Ya'an** China
108B3 **Yaapeet** Aust
98B2 **Yabassi** Cam
68C1 **Yablonovyy Khrebet** *Mts* Russian Fed
94C2 **Yabrūd** Syria
20B2 **Yachats** USA
30D3 **Yacuiba** Bol
87B1 **Yādgīr** India
95A1 **Yafran** Libya
23A1 **Yahualica** Mexico
98C2 **Yahuma** Zaïre
75B1 **Yaita** Japan
75B2 **Yaizu** Japan
73A4 **Yajiang** China
20B1 **Yakima** USA
20B1 **Yakima** *R* USA
97B3 **Yako** Burkina
98C2 **Yakoma** Zaïre
74E2 **Yakumo** Japan
12G3 **Yakutat** USA
12G3 **Yakutat B** USA
63E1 **Yakutsk** Russian Fed
77C4 **Yala** Thai
23B2 **Yalalag** Mexico
98C2 **Yalinga** CAR
109C3 **Yallourn** Aust
68B3 **Yalong** *R* China
73A4 **Yalong Jiang** *R* China
54C2 **Yalova** Turk
60D5 **Yalta** Ukraine
74B2 **Yalu Jiang** *R* China
74D3 **Yamagata** Japan
74C4 **Yamaguchi** Japan
68D1 **Yamarovka** Russian Fed
109D1 **Yamba** New S Wales, Aust
108B2 **Yamba** S Australia, Aust
99C2 **Yambio** Sudan
54C2 **Yambol** Bulg
71E4 **Yamdena** *I* Indon
Yam Kinneret = Tiberias,L
108B1 **Yamma Yamma,L** Aust
97B4 **Yamoussoukro** Ivory Coast
85D3 **Yamuna** *R* India
86C1 **Yamzho Yumco** *L* China
63F1 **Yana** *R* Russian Fed
108B3 **Yanac** Aust
75A2 **Yanagawa** Japan
87C1 **Yanam** India
72B2 **Yan'an** China
80B3 **Yanbu'al Bahr** S Arabia
108B2 **Yancannia** Aust
72E3 **Yancheng** China
72B2 **Yanchi** China
108B1 **Yandama** *R* Aust
98C2 **Yangambi** Zaïre
72C1 **Yang He** *R* China
73C5 **Yangjiang** China
76B2 **Yangon** Burma
72C2 **Yangquan** China
73C5 **Yangshan** China
73C3 **Yangtze Gorges** China
72E3 **Yangtze,Mouths of the** China
72D3 **Yangzhou** China
73B4 **Yanhe** China
74B2 **Yanji** China
108C3 **Yanko** *R* Aust
8D2 **Yankton** USA
68A2 **Yanqqi** China
72D1 **Yan Shan** *Hills*
108B1 **Yantabulla** Aust
72E2 **Yantai** China
72D2 **Yanzhou** China
98B2 **Yaoundé** Cam
71E4 **Yapen** *I* Indon
71E3 **Yap Is** Pacific O
24B2 **Yaqui** *R* Mexico
61G2 **Yaransk** Russian Fed
32C3 **Yari** *R* Colombia
74D3 **Yariga-dake** *Mt* Japan
82B2 **Yarkant He** *R* China
86C1 **Yarlung Zangbo Jiang** *R* China
7D5 **Yarmouth** Can
94B2 **Yarmūk** *R* Syria/Jordan
61E2 **Yaroslavl'** Russian Fed
94B2 **Yarqon** *R* Israel
109C3 **Yarram** Aust
109D1 **Yarraman** Aust
109C3 **Yarrawonga** Aust
60D2 **Yartsevo** Russian Fed
63B1 **Yartsevo** Russian Fed
32B2 **Yarumal** Colombia
97C3 **Yashi** Nig
97C4 **Yashikera** Nig
61F4 **Yashkul'** Russian Fed
84C1 **Yasin** Pak
59C3 **Yasinya** Ukraine
109C2 **Yass** Aust
109C2 **Yass** *R* Aust
75A1 **Yasugi** Japan
18A2 **Yates Center** USA
98C2 **Yatolema** Zaïre
74C4 **Yatsushiro** Japan
94B3 **Yatta** Israel
32C4 **Yavari** Peru
85D4 **Yavatmāl** India
74C4 **Yawatahama** Japan
76D2 **Ya Xian** China
90B3 **Yazd** Iran
90B3 **Yazd-e Khvāst** Iran
19B3 **Yazoo** *R* USA

Zhengou

72C3 **Zhengzhou** China
72D3 **Zhenjiang** China
73A4 **Zhenxiong** China
73B4 **Zhenyuan** China
61F3 **Zherdevka**
    Russian Fed
73C3 **Zhicheng** China
68C1 **Zhigalovo**
    Russian Fed
73B4 **Zhijin** China
58D2 **Zhitkovichi**
    Belorussia
60C3 **Zhitomir** Ukraine
60D3 **Zhlobin** Belorussia
60C4 **Zhmerinka** Ukraine
84B2 **Zhob** Pak
58D2 **Zhodino** Latvia
72B2 **Zhongning** China
112C10 **Zhongshan** *Base* Ant
73C5 **Zhongshan** China
72B2 **Zhongwei** China
68B4 **Zhougdian** China
73E3 **Zhoushan Quandao**
    Arch China
72E2 **Zhuanghe** China
72A3 **Zhugqu** China
73C3 **Zhushan** China

73C4 **Zhuzhou** China
72D2 **Zibo** China
106C3 **Ziel,Mt** Aust
58B2 **Zielona Góra** Pol
76A1 **Zigaing** Burma
73A4 **Zigong** China
97A3 **Ziguinchor** Sen
23A2 **Zihuatanejo** Mexico
94B2 **Zikhron Ya'aqov**
    Israel
59B3 **Žilina** Slovakia
95A2 **Zillah** Libya
47D1 **Ziller** *R* Austria
47D1 **Zillertaler Alpen** *Mts*
    Austria
58D1 **Zilupe** Russian Fed
63C2 **Zima** Russian Fed
23B1 **Zimapan** Mexico
23B2 **Zimatlan** Mexico
100B2 **Zimbabwe** Republic,
    Africa
94B3 **Zin** *R* Israel
23B2 **Zinacatepec** Mexico
23A2 **Zinapécuaro** Mexico
97C3 **Zinder** Niger
73C4 **Zi Shui** China
23A2 **Zitácuaro** Mexico

57C2 **Zittau** Germany
72D2 **Ziya He** *R* China
72A3 **Ziyang** China
61J2 **Zlatoust**
    Russian Fed
59B3 **Zlin** Czech Republic
65K4 **Zmeinogorsk**
    Russian Fed
58B2 **Znin** Pol
59B3 **Znoimo**
    Czech Republic
100B3 **Zoekmekaar**
    S Africa
47B1 **Zofinger** Switz
72A3 **Zoigê** China
59D3 **Zolochev** Ukraine
101C2 **Zomba** Malawi
98B2 **Zongo** Zaïre
92B1 **Zonguldak** Turk
97B4 **Zorzor** Lib
96A2 **Zouerate** Maur
54B1 **Zrenjanin** Serbia,
    Yugos
47C1 **Zug** Switz
47D1 **Zugspitze** *Mt*
    Germany
50A2 **Zújar** *R* Spain

100C2 **Zumbo** Mozam
23B2 **Zumpango** Mexico
97C4 **Zungeru** Nig
73B4 **Zunyi** China
76D1 **Zuo** *R* China
73B5 **Zuo Jiang** *R* China
47C1 **Zürich** Switz
47C1 **Zürichsee** *L* Switz
95A1 **Zuwärah** Libya
95A2 **Zuwaylah** Libya
61H2 **Zuyevka**
    Russian Fed
100B4 **Zvishavane** Zim
59B3 **Zvolen** Slovakia
54A2 **Zvornik** Bosnia-
    Herzegovina
97B4 **Zwedru** Lib
46D2 **Zweibrücken**
    Germany
47B1 **Zweisimmen** Switz
57C2 **Zwickau** Germany
56B2 **Zwolle** Neth
58C2 **Zyrardów** Pol
65K5 **Zyryanovsk**
    Kazakhstan
59B3 **Żywiec** Pol
94A1 **Zyyi** Cyprus